P9-EMF-111

DISORDERS OF LEARNING IN CHILDHOOD

WILEY SERIES IN CHILD AND ADOLESCENT MENTAL HEALTH

Joseph D. Noshpitz, Editor

DISORDERS OF LEARNING IN CHILDHOOD

ARCHIE A. SILVER, M.D.
Professor of Psychiatry
Director, Child and Adolescent Psychiatry
University of South Florida
College of Medicine

Adjunct Professor of Clinical Psychiatry
Department of Psychiatry
New York University
College of Medicine

ROSA A. HAGIN, Ph.D.
Professor of Psychology
Director, School Consultation Center
School of Education
Fordham University

Research Professor of Psychology
Department of Psychiatry
New York University
College of Medicine

A Wiley-Interscience Publication
JOHN WILEY & SONS
New York   Chichester   Brisbane   Toronto   Singapore

Library of Congress Cataloging-in-Publication Data
Silver, Archie A.
    Disorders of learning in childhood/Archie A. Silver, Rosa A.
Hagin.
    p.   cm.—(Wiley series in child and adolescent mental
health)
    Includes bibliographical references.
    ISBN 0-471-50828-4
    1. Learning disabilities—United States.   2. Learning disabled
       children—Education—United States.   3. Learning disabilities—
       Treatment—United States.   I. Hagin, Rosa A.   II. Title.
III. Series.
LC4705.S59   1990
371.92—dc20   89–28492

Printed and bound by Quinn - Woodbine, Inc..

Series Preface

This series is intended to serve a number of functions. It includes works on child development; it presents material on child advocacy; it publishes contributions to child psychiatry; and it gives expression to cogent views on child rearing and child management. The mental health of parents and their interaction with their children is a major theme of the series, and emphasis is placed on the child as individual, as family member, and as a part of the larger social surround.

Child development is regarded as the basic science of child mental health, and within that framework research works are included in this series. The many ethical and legal dimensions of the way society relates to its children are the central theme of the child advocacy publications, as well as a primarily demographic approach that highlights the role and status of children within society. The child psychiatry publications span studies that concern the diagnosis, description, therapeutics, rehabilitation, and prevention of the emotional disorders of childhood. And the views of thoughtful and creative contributors to the handling of children under many different circumstances (retardation, acute and chronic illness, hospitalization, handicap, disturbed social conditions, etc.) find expression within the framework of child rearing and child management.

Family studies with a central child mental health perspective are included in the series, and explorations into the nature of parenthood and the parenting process are emphasized. This includes books about divorce, the single parent, the absent parent, parents with physical and emotional illnesses, and other conditions that significantly affect the parent-child relationship.

Finally, the series examines the impact of larger social forces, such as war, famine, migration, and economic failure, on the adaptation of children and families. In the largest sense, the series is devoted to books that illuminate the special needs, status, and history of children and their families, within all perspectives that bear on their collective mental health.

JOSEPH D. NOSHPITZ

Children's Hospital Medical Center and
The George Washington University
Washington, D.C.

Preface

This book presents a point of view: that children with a learning disorder are best served by a comprehensive understanding of their problems. This understanding encompasses data from biological, psychological, educational, and social perspectives and forms the basis for treatment decisions appropriate to the child's needs. We have become increasingly concerned that in clinics and classrooms the heterogeneity of children with a learning disorder is being obscured by the inclusive term "learning disability"; we feel that such children are being treated with little consideration for the many interacting factors that may lead to academic failure, including the idiosyncratic ways in which a child processes, stores, and retrieves information and the psychological reactions to failure within the child, family, and teachers. Accordingly, this book presents a clinically based classification of learning disorders; offers general principles of diagnosis and management from biological, psychological, educational, and social perspectives; and describes the categories of children with learning disorders most frequently seen in clinics and classrooms. Finally it offers specific recommendations for management of the various disorders.

This book thus naturally divides itself into three major sections. Part One is a general view of learning disorders including the problems of definition, of clinical classification and its relationship to Public Law 94-142, of typing based on neuropsychological subgroup studies, and of estimates of prevalence. Part Two describes general principles of management, including educational, psychological, psychiatric, and neurological diagnosis; considers educational remediation, use of drugs to influence learning and memory, and psychological therapies; and concludes with an important chapter on prevention. Part Three details clinical patterns found in children with learning disorders: specific language disability (pure dyslexia); the effects of poverty and inappropriate language stimulation in the first few years of life; attention deficit hyperactivity disorder (ADHD), organic defects of the central nervous system; Gilles de la Tourette's syndrome; and autism. Intervention procedures for each are derived from the clinical description and natural history. The chapter on poverty, usually omitted in books on learning disorders, is included here because children of the poor are still overrepresented in academic failure and school drop-out. Tourette's syndrome and learning is a problem virtually every school is beginning to face, and children with autistic behavior present unique, long-term, expensive demands on all professionals who work with them. Major emphasis, however, is placed on consideration of the child with the specific language disability, ADHD, and the child with a structural defect of the central nervous system. In each chapter, pertinent literature is reviewed and integrated, and opinions other than our own are presented.

Part Four in this book, "Future Directions for Service and Research," attempts to look ahead into trends in the neurosciences that have implications for learning disorders and at the impact of economic and social influences that will shape research and practices. This part also looks at promising innovations in education, science, and technology and discusses gaps in our current knowledge.

Our approach to the problems of children with learning disorders is an interdisciplinary one, stemming from the early 1950s when Dr. Rosa A. Hagin, a psychologist, joined with Dr. Archie A Silver, a psychiatrist trained in neurology and psychoanalysis, for a "Neurological and Perceptual Survey of Children with Learning Disabilities." This study, supported by the Field Foundation and done at New York University Medical School, initiated a long-term working relationship between Drs. Hagin and Silver that has persisted to this day. Over the years their interest in learning in childhood developed into a unit for the Study of Learning Disorders at New York University Medical School in which an interdisciplinary group was concerned with diagnosis, classification, management, and finally prevention of learning disorders. Data from the group's work were included in over 100 publications. Very early, the usefulness of the work was stressed, not only in clinics and private practices of psychiatry and psychology, but also in schools. Teams from our unit spent most of their days working in school-based programs, testing findings in natural settings. In the past 10 years, although Dr. Silver has been director of Child and Adolescent Psychiatry at the University of South Florida Medical School and Dr. Hagin has been professor of psychology and director of the School Consultation Center at Fordham University, their working relationship has continued, tied together by the many patients they have shared and their many discussions of research and clinical findings. The programs developed at New York University have continued to thrive in new sites; the Prevention Program has expanded into new schools throughout the United States; school-based programs for children considered emotionally or behaviorally disturbed have been developed; and literacy programs for adults with learning disorders have been established.

Throughout the years, we have been fortunate, in having our work supported by many agencies and foundations. Since our initial study supported by the Field Foundation in the early 1950s, specific research projects of the Learning Disorders Unit have been funded by the New York Community Trust, the Ritter Foundation, the Carnegie Corporation of New York, the Ford Foundation, the Oak Foundation, and private donors. In addition, we have received long-term and generous funding from the New York City Department of Health and Mental Retardation Services and from the U.S. Department of Education. Successive chairmen of the Department of Psychiatry at New York University Medical School, Drs. Bernard Wortis, Morris Herman, and Robert Cancro, have made it possible for us to use these grants effectively. At the University of South Florida, the chairman of the Department of Psychiatry, Dr. Anthony Reading, continues to be supportive, and at Fordham University, Dean Max Weiner gave the Learning Disorders Unit a new home and a new role at the Graduate School of Education at Fordham University, Lincoln Center.

In this book we have attempted to bring together theory and practice, experiment and experience, with data from relevant fields—the neurosciences, clinical psychiatry, psychology, and education. Each issue in this book is discussed with the detail that we would discuss among ourselves. We hope that psychiatrists, psychologists and educators will find this book helpful as they evaluate and treat children with learning disorders.

Archie A. Silver, M.D.
Rosa A. Hagin, Ph.D.

Acknowledgments

Writing a book is only the beginning of a process that requires many hands and many minds to transform the typed manuscript into a volume typographically clean, syntactically correct, pleasant to hold and to read. Herbert Reich, senior editor of John Wiley & Sons, initiated our efforts, encouraging our thoughts when we had only an outline of a book to show him. Lester Kaplan of The Book Studio, Inc., who was assigned by John Wiley to shepherd this book through the publication processes—designing the text, copyediting the manuscript, arranging for type setting and proofreading— calmly directed each of these activities, making our mountain of questions into easily overcome molehills. The copyediting of the manuscript was done by Cynthia Garver. This statement does not begin to describe the heroic job Ms. Garver did in going over our work word by word, line by line, page by page. That this book says what we mean it to say, is largely due to her pains-taking work. The manuscript itself was typed into readable form by Wendy Merlin, secretary at the Division of Child and Adolescent Psychiatry at the University of South Florida. Ms. Merlin's unfailing pleasantness, infinite patience, and technical ability with computer and word processor made the many changes we made with each rereading flow from the laser printer with apparent ease, each page somehow in its proper place. Finally Marilyn Wilson, librarian at the Department of Psychiatry at the University of South Florida, found obscure references when we could not and kept us up to date with bibliographic searches. To all of these people we acknowledge their contributions and hope each will accept our gratitude.

Earlier versions of portions of this book have appeared in print before. Portions of Chapter 10 (Prevention of Disorders of Learning) were in a position paper prepared for the Academy of Child and Adolescent Psychiatry Project Prevention and in modified form printed in the Office for Substance Abuse Prevention Monograph—2, *Prevention of mental disorders, alcohol and other drug use in children and adolescents* (1989). The section of Chapter 15 (Tourette's syndrome) dealing with the intrapsychic process in Tourette's syndrome appears in part in A. A. Silver (1983), Intrapsychic processes and adjustment in Tourette's syndrome, pp. 197–206, in D. J. Cohen, R. D. Bruun, & J. F. Leckman (Eds.) *Tourette's Syndrome and Tic Disorders,* published by John Wiley & Sons. Tables 4 and 5 in Chapter 6 (Principles of Interdisciplinary Diagnosis: Psychiatric and Neurological) are reprinted with permission of Williams & Wilkins from A. A. Silver (1984), Children in classes for the severely emotionally handicapped, *Journal of Developmental and Behavioral Pediatrics, 5,* 49–54. Table 2 of Chapter 16 (Autism) is reprinted with permission of John Wiley & Sons from D. J. Cohen, R. Paul, and F. R. Volkmar, (1987) Issues in Classification, in D. J. Cohen and A. M. Donnellan (Eds.), *Handbook of Autism and Pervasive Developmental Disorders,* p. 30. Table 1 of Chapter 13 (Attention Deficit Hyperactivity Disorder), and Table 1 of Chapter 16 (Autism) are reprinted with permission from the American Psychiatric Association: *Diagnostic and Statistical Manual of Mental Disorders. Third Edition, Revised* (Washington, D.C., American Psychiatric Association, 1987). Figures 4 and 6 of Chapter 14 (The Organic States) are reproduced with permission of the University of Chicago Press from A. A. Silver and R. A. Hagin (1985), Outcomes of Learning Disabilities in Adolescence, in S. G. Feinstein (Ed.), *Adolescent Psychiatry: Developmental and Clinical Studies, 12,* 197–213.

With all these helpful hands and minds, the final product, however, with its errors of commission and omission, is our own.

A.A.S.
R.A.H.

Contents

PART TWO: PRINCIPLES OF MANAGEMENT

**PART THREE: CLINICAL PATTERNS IN
                 DISORDERS OF LEARNING**

PART ONE

A GENERAL VIEW OF DISORDERS OF LEARNING

CHAPTER ONE

The Problem of Definition

Although the problem of the intelligent child, born of intelligent parents, who is unable to read despite appropriate educational opportunity has been known for nearly a century (Morgan, 1896), it is only recently that attempts have been made to define with any precision what is meant when a child is described as having a learning disability. This chapter will place some of these definitions within a historical context, point out their theoretical, clinical, political, legal, and practical implications, and establish some operational concepts to guide contemporary work with children with learning disorders.

CLINICAL IMPLICATIONS OF DEFINITIONS

While general definitions of learning disabilities are not difficult to frame, their applications in specific cases are not quite so simple. The following cases illustrate this point.

CASE STUDY: JOHNNY

Johnny was a handsome boy, physically small for his 12 years. He was in the fifth grade of a public school in a large city in the southeastern part of the United States, receiving 2 hours of tutoring each day in a resource room for emotionally handicapped children. His teachers reported that he did not listen to directions, talked out often, and threw books about the classroom. His behavior disrupted lessons because he had a low tolerance for frustration.

Psychological testing (Wechsler Intelligence Scale for Children-Revised, Wisc-R) at age 11 years, 6 months yielded a full scale IQ of 81 with a verbal IQ of 77 and a performance IQ of 90. Academically his word attack skills and his arithmetic computation were at the second-grade level, while spelling was at the beginning second-grade level.

His mother was an unmarried 16-year-old when he was born. The physical events of his birth were normal, but during the first year of life he was cared for by a variety of female relatives, with little consistency in management. By his fifth year he had been in three foster homes, and not until he was 6 were his mother's living conditions stable enough for him to join her household.

Classical neurological examination was within normal limits, but he had difficulties with many perceptual tasks. He could not match or recall simple asymmetric visual figures. His visual-motor control was primitive, and his body image was markedly impaired. Immediate auditory recall was at the 7-year level. On psychiatric interview he was depressed, frustrated, and concerned about the safety of his grandmother, mother, and father. He was troubled by dreams that his mother had been poisoned and that his father might be hit by a bus.

Johnny is a child whose academic achievement is 3 years below his grade placement and 1 year below expectancy as calculated from his WISC-R scores.

This vignette is not a chimera composed of the most pathological bits of many children. Johnny is real. He illustrates a most difficult problem faced by our public school system: the education of children reared in a culture of poverty with inconsistent affective support. Because of his socioeconomic heritage and his disruptive behavior he does not meet the school's criteria for a learning disability. The advantage of remedial education was not offered to him.

But is Johnny learning disabled? This is not a simple or an unimportant question. Any definition used has practical significance both to school programs as a whole and to the individual children served. For the schools, the definition will determine how many children will be considered learning disabled, which, in turn, determines how much money school districts will expend to provide personnel, physical space, and teaching materials—all the resources the school district must mobilize to serve these children. Definitions will also determine what federal funding will be available to states and, in turn, what funding will be available to school districts. The definition of learning disability is also important to any individual child because it outlines the criteria that a given child must meet to qualify for the services that are available. Indeed, the educational future of children may hinge upon the definition of learning disability. As for Johnny, professional debate on precise definitions and classification cannot hide the fact that he has severe learning problems and needs special educational provisions for them.

David illustrates the problems faced by a bright child with specific language defects who, with difficulty, is managing average academic work. Yet he too is considered ineligible for special education.

CASE STUDY: DAVID

David is just 7 years old, a pleasant, cooperative child in the first grade of a public school whose pupils, for the most part, come from upper middle-class, high-achievement, professional families. David's parents are concerned that he "cannot remember sight words, alphabet sounds, or numbers. He has difficulty completing his school work." David was adopted by his present concerned family in the first week of his life. Examination of his birth record revealed no prenatal or perinatal problems other than the fact that his mother, a college student, was unmarried. Development, except for repeated middle ear infections that required insertion of tubes at age 2, was normal. Auditory acuity as tested by audiometry at age 7, however, was normal. On psychological examination at age 7, David earned a full scale IQ on the WISC-R of 112 (verbal IQ of 98, performance IQ of 132). On the verbal scale, his strengths were in similarities, arithmetic, and comprehension, each with a scaled score of 12; however, information (scaled score 5) and vocabulary (scaled score 4) were weak. It was noted that he had difficulty defining words and verbally expressing his ideas. On neurological examination, the language problems were grossly evident. His speech was fragmented with incomplete, laconic, single-word responses. He had difficulty expressing thoughts and finding words. He needed to have ideas presented to him simply and repetitiously, otherwise verbal comprehension suffered. In addition to his language difficulty, there was poor fine motor coordination and markedly immature praxic ability.

David is aware that he has problems and becomes increasingly frustrated as increased demands are made in school. He is restless when he does not fully understand what his teacher tells him, and he has difficulty finishing written work. He is developing fears of the dark, of noises, and even of footsteps of people in his house.

David's school, however, cannot place him in a class where he can receive help in language. His work is average and so he cannot be classified as learning disabled and cannot receive special remedial help. How should David be classified? Is he learning disabled? Must we wait until he fails to offer him needed support and remediation? David, like Johnny, needs special educational help. Having him meet the definitional criteria for failure before he may receive that help only increases the probability of his failure, together with his frustration, and makes subsequent remediation more difficult, more prolonged, and more costly. Here again the educational future of David may hinge upon the definition of learning disability.

RESEARCH IMPLICATIONS OF DEFINITIONS

A clear definition, moreover, is essential to research. To understand children with learning problems, samples under study must be clearly defined. To some extent, the conflicts in research findings may result from differences in the definitions of learning disability. For instance, what may be true for the sample in one study may not be true for the sample in another study because "learning disability" was defined differently. One cannot assume that the characteristics associated with learning failure in one child are the same as those in any other child who fails to learn. In reality, within the group of children with learning problems, there are marked individual differences in functioning and in assets and deficits. The significance of these variations is that in any study of large numbers of children, these differences may cancel each other out. The balancing effect may cause an investigator to dismiss as unimportant some variables that may be crucial to some children in the sample. Variations in definition among studies has resulted in confusion, frustration, and failure of replication in research on learning failure. Meaningful research requires clear, specific definitions.

HISTORICAL REVIEW OF DEFINITIONS OF LEARNING DISABILITIES

Definitions of learning disabilities have been confusing, reflecting our lack of knowledge of the learning process, the factors that may interfere with it, and the particular bias of the observers. The lack of precision in our currently used definitions of learning disability may be understood from a brief historical review of the conceptual streams leading to them. Table 1-1 gives a list of terminology used in this field.

The Concept of Brain Damage

The neurological identification of learning disabilities had its origins in early studies on aphasia (Broca, 1861). Broca's studies, and those of the neurologists of his era, stemmed from observations of adults with acquired brain

Table 1-1   Historical Definitions of Learning Disorders

Year	Definition
1887	Dyslexia (Berlin)
1895–1917	Congenital Word Blindness (Hinshelwood; Kerr; Morgan)
1922–1925	Post-Influenzal Behavioral Syndrome (Ebaugh; Hohman; Stryker)
1928	Strephosymbolia (Orton)
1929	Congenital Auditory Imperception (Worcester-Drought & Allen)
1934	Organic Driveness (Kahn & Cohen)
1941	Developmental Lag (L. A. Bender & Yarnell)
1943–1947	Brain-Injured or -Damaged Child (Strauss & Lehtinen; Strauss & Werner)
1947	Minimally Brain-Damaged Child (Gesell & Amatruda)
1960	Psychoneurological Learning Disorders (Mykelbust & Boshes)
1962	Learning Disabilities (Kirk)
1962–1963	Minimal Brain Dysfunction (MBD) (Bax & MacKeith)
1964	Developmental Dyslexia (Critchley)
1967–1968	Specific Learning Disabilities (National Advisory Committee on Handicapped Children, USOE)
1969	Specific Learning Disabilities (P. L. 91-230)
1971	Psycholinguistic Learning Disabilities (Kirk & Kirk)
1977	Learning Disabilities (P. L. 94-142)
1980	Specific Developmental Disorders (*Diagnostic and Statistical Manual of Mental Disorders,* Third Edition)
1987	Specific Developmental Disorders (*Diagnostic and Statistical Manual of Mental Disorders,* Third Edition-revised)

damage. For patients with aphasia and a loss of the ability to read, Kussmaul (1877) proposed the term *word blindness*. According to Critchley (1964) the term *dyslexia* first appeared in 1887 in a monograph, *Eine besondere Art der Wortblindheit (Dyslexia)* (Berlin, 1887), in which was described two groups of dyslexics classified according to whether or not the ability to write was retained.

The emphasis on acquired brain pathology continued when, following the influenza epidemic of 1918 with its sequel of encephalitis, children were observed with a disorder characterized by antisocial behavior, irritability, impulsiveness, emotional lability, hyperactivity, and learning problems (E. D. Bond & Appel, 1931; E. D. Bond & Smith, 1935; Ebaugh, 1923; L. B. Hohman, 1922; Neal, 1942; Stryker, 1925). These symptoms were considered postencephalitic. The presence of the discrete anatomic pathology, perivascular infiltration, found in postinfluenzal encephalitis, related behavior to specific structural defects involving specific areas of the central nervous system. By a process of reasoning by analogy, the diagnosis of structural brain damage was subsequently attached to all children who displayed behavioral and learning symptoms similar to those found in postinfluenzal encephalitis.

This diagnosis by analogy was reinforced by reports of hyperactivity, short attention span, irritability, and learning problems in children apparently recovered from head injury (Blau, 1936; Bowman & Blau, 1943; Strecker & Ebaugh, 1924); obstetrical casualty; and prematurity (Shirley, 1939) (see Chapter14, "The Organic Group"). In 1934, E. Kahn and Cohen described a hyperkinetic behavior disorder in children, which they, too, related to brain stem pathology and which they labeled *organic driveness*. This paper had great influence in reinforcing an organic stamp upon behavior disorders. The thinking in those years is summarized by L. A. Bender (1956), who, in reviewing the history of the Child Psychiatry Service at Bellevue Hospital in New York City, noted that "In the 1930s it was assumed that most of the children in residence at Bellevue Psychiatric Hospital were disturbed because of some form of brain damage" (p. 114).

The use of the term *brain-injured* or *brain-damaged child* became generally accepted after Strauss and Lehtinen (1947) published their classic volume *The Psychopathology and Education of the Brain-Injured Child*. Strauss, a neuropsychiatrist trained in Heidelberg, first served at the Wayne County Training School in Northville, Michigan, and then founded the Cove School in Racine, Wisconsin. Both schools attained recognition for their pioneering work in special education.

Strauss, working with Werner, a developmental psychologist, first explored the perceptual world of retarded children and described perceptual differences between children whose history suggested a pre-, peri-, or postnatal brain injury, and those who, although retarded, did not have such histories. These studies stressed the importance of perceptual functioning in the diagnosis of brain-injured children, particularly in figure–ground perception in both the visual and the auditory fields, in grouping ability on the basis of unusual or insignificant detail, and in the tendency toward perseveration and rigidity. Strauss felt that diagnosis of brain damage could be based on the presence of neuropsychological disturbance in perception and in conceptual thinking (Strauss & Werner, 1943). In a second volume, published in 1955, Strauss joined with Kephart to study the "brain-injured" child with normal intelligence and emphasized again the perceptual, integrative, and motor problems with which the "brain-injured" child struggled.

L. A. Bender (1956) considered the hyperkinesis of the "brain-injured" child as secondary to the perceptual problems of these children, their inability to get gratification from perceptions, from contact with the world of reality, or from their drive to experience reality in perceptual experiences of the world, their own bodies, their body images, and their self-images. Thus, she conceptualized hyperactivity as resulting from poorly patterned motor-perceptual experiences and impulses.

Clinical observations of these investigators added the perceptual dimension to the behavioral symptoms described by E. Kahn and Cohen in 1934 and the disorder became known as the *Werner-Strauss syndrome.* The perceptual dimension broadened the concept of organicity to include children whose basic symptomatology was neuropsychological even though no other evidence of damage to the brain was elicited by either history or clinical examination.

The attribution of brain injury to children with learning and behavior problems was further reinforced by a series of investigations in which Pasamanick and his colleagues identified a *continuum of reproductive casualty,* which extended from spontaneous abortion, stillbirth, mental deficiency, and epilepsy at one end to learning disabilities and behavior disorders at the other (Kawi & Pasamanick, 1959; Knobloch & Pasamanick, 1966; K. B. Nelson, 1968; Pasamanick, Rogers, & Lilienfeld, 1956; Rogers, Lilienfeld, & Pasamanick, 1955). This retrospective study demonstrated that the frequency of complications of pregnancy and of abnormalities of the prenatal and perinatal periods involving either the mother or the child was significantly greater among children with a reading disability than it was with control groups with no reading problems. More recent studies implicated cerebral hypoxia during the first hours of life as being a critical determinant for the development of later cognitive disorders (Sarnoff, Mednick, & Baert, 1981; Skov, Lou, & Pederson, 1984). Sequential follow-up studies also implicated low birth weight (M. A. Stewart, 1980, 1983), low protein diet during pregnancy, and even dietary deficiency during the nursing period (Cravioto & Arrieta, 1983).

There was sufficient evidence that organic factors were implicated in *some* behavior and learning problems in children. However, the term brain-injured began to appear in the literature as a designation for *all* children with learning and behavior disorders even though in many of these children classical neurological examination and laboratory studies were entirely within normal limits. Conversely, children with known and independently verified brain damage were described who did not exhibit the patterns of behavior presumably characteristic of "brain damage," such as difficulty with academic learning, hyperactivity, attentional deficit, perceptual anomalies, impulsivity, abnormal rigidity, and perseveration. In 1964, Birch pointed out that there was a difference between the *fact of brain damage* as referring to any anatomic or physiologic alteration of the central nervous system and the *concept of brain-damaged child* to designate a pattern or set of patterns of behavioral disturbance.

Two related trends appeared to modify the terms *brain injury* and *brain damage;* one was the description of "soft" neurological signs, the other the concept of developmental lag. *Soft neurological signs* have been described in two ways: first, as a designation of equivocal or minimal classical neurological findings, particularly the inability of a child to perform adequately on tasks requiring coordination and synergy; second, as evidence of neurophysiological immaturity, involving such functions as posture, equilibrium, and postural reflexes; the development of laterality, praxis, finger-gnosis, and right–left orientation; and immaturity in the perceptual apparatus, particularly in visual-motor function and auditory sequencing. Viewed as an indication of central nervous system immaturity, soft signs are findings that are developmentally normal at one age but abnormal if found at a later age. A standard battery of soft signs, evaluated by standardized procedures in children selected by the same criteria, is lacking at the present time. Standardization for some of these signs is found in the review by Denckla (1985), and in the papers edited by Tupper (1987). These will be discussed in Chapter 6 ("Psychiatric and Neurological Diagnosis") of this book.

The presence of soft signs as indications of neurological immaturity led to the concept of *developmental* or *maturational lag*. As Kinsbourne (1973) stated, a soft sign represents the persistence of a primitive form of response; as such, it represents a developmental delay or lag in the differentiation of a sensory or motor system. The concept of a lag in development was originally postulated by Gesell and Thompson (1934). Discussing the question of early growth, these researchers asked, "Does the infant present specific lags and accelerations among components of his behavior equipment?" L. A. Bender and Yarnell (1941) were the first to apply the term *developmental lag* or *maturational lag* to children with reading disability in whom classical neurological examination was normal. In a subsequent paper, L. A. Bender (1956) stated that some of our problem preschool children, whose hyperkinesis and infantile associal behavior had no other explanation, have since proved to have reading disabilities.

One interpretation of the relationship between preschool hyperkinesis and later reading disability is that both conditions are part of a syndrome of a developmental lag. There is no structural defect of the brain, only a physiological immaturity in development that has the potential for maturation. As early as 1949, L. A. Bender and A. Silver emphasized that the perceptual and behavioral findings in many of the children called, at that time, organic or brain-damaged or brain-injured were better understood as developmental lags rather than as structural defects of the central nervous system. They stated that maturational lag does not signify that the deficit is local, structural, specific, or fixed. (It is of interest that in 1891 Freud noted that "there were cases of aphasia in which no localized lesion need be assumed and the symptoms could be attributed to an alteration of a physiological constant in the special apparatus.") On the other hand, if untreated, there is no guarantee that a developmental lag will undergo spontaneous maturation. L. A. Bender pointed out (1958) that for those parts of the neopallium that serve the functions associated with hemisphere specialization, particularly for language, there is a wide range of maturational age.

The presence of soft signs and the concept of developmental lag led to some qualification of the terms brain-damaged and brain-injured so that the more restrictive term *minimally brain-damaged child* came into use (Gesell & Amatruda, 1947). But this modification was subjected to criticism. Bax and MacKeith (1963) stated: "The word minimal is bad because there is no constant correlation between the symptoms and signs and the extent of brain lesions. The term suggests that either the symptoms or signs are minimal and that the brain lesion is too. This is frequently not the case." With much reservation on the part of these and other clinicians, however, the concept of the brain-damaged or brain-injured child did give way to the concept of the minimally brain-damaged child.

The Concept of Minimal Brain Dysfunction

In 1962, the International Study Group in Child Neurology suggested that the term *damage* should be discarded because to lay people it represented the deleterious results of injury, and that the term *dysfunction* should be used instead (Bax & MacKeith, 1963; MacKeith 1963, 1968). This recommendation produced the term *minimal brain dysfunction*, which, aided by the Ciba Pharmaceutical Company's promotion of the acronym MBD, caught on and became widely used—so much so that it was adopted in 1966 by a task force on terminology and identification that was cosponsored by the National Society for Crippled Children and Adults and the National Institute of Neurological Diseases and Blindness. In the resulting monograph, the concept of minimal brain dysfunction was described in detail.

The term "minimal brain dysfunction syndrome" refers in this paper to children of near average, average, and above average intelligence with certain learning or behavioral disabilities ranging from mild to severe, which are associated with devi-

ations of function of the central nervous system. These deviations may manifest them-selves by various combinations of impairment of perception, conceptualization, lan-guage, memory, and control of attention, impulse, or motor function.

Similar symptoms may or may not complicate the problems of children with cerebral palsy, epilepsy, mental retardation, blindness or deafness.

These aberrations may arise from genetic variations, biochemical irregularities, prenatal brain insults or other illnesses or injuries sustained during the years which are critical for the development and maturation of the central nervous system, or for unknown causes.

The definition also allows for the possibility that early sensory deprivation could result in central nervous system alteration which may be permanent.

During the school years a variety of learning disabilities is the most prominent manifestation of the condition which can be designated by this term. (Clements, 1966, pp. 9–10)

This definition does not use the term dysfunction to imply etiology. Rather, the term was selected to avoid the implication that all individuals with the comprehensive group of symptoms described necessarily have suf-fered damage to the brain and that the symptoms may stem from a consti-tutional deviation in the development of the central processing system. However, it did recognize the importance of biological factors in behavior.

Despite its rapid acceptance, the term MBD did little to solve problems of definition. The term encompasses such a heterogeneous group of symp-toms with such diverse etiology that, in effect, it hindered the search for conceptual clarity. It also did not meet the needs of educators who were faced with the problem of teaching children with learning disorders who were so conveniently placed in the MBD category. This is especially crucial, because education represents a major source of services for learning dis-abled children and because, inevitably, definitions of learning disorders influence the field of education.

The Narrowing of Definition to the Concept of Specific Language Disability

In 1896 W. Pringle Morgan reported on a case of reading difficulty that he called *congenital word blindness*.

Percy F., age 14 . . . the eldest son of intelligent parents . . . was a bright and intel-ligent boy, quick at games and in no way inferior to others his age. His inability [to read] is so remarkable and so pronounced that I have no doubt it is due to some congenital defect. . . . In spite of . . . laborious and persistent training, he can only with difficulty spell words of one syllable. (Morgan, 1896, p. 1378)

Morgan's case report was prompted by a note on word blindness, written by James Hinshelwood, a Glasgow eye surgeon, which appeared in *Lancet* in

1895. In 1887 James Kerr, Medical Officer of Health to the city of Bradford, also reported on a boy with agraphia who "can do arithmetic well so long as it involves Arabic numerals only, but writes gibberish in a neat hand to dictation exercises" (quoted by Critchley, 1964, p. 7). Four additional cases occurring in a single family were reported by Hinshelwood in 1907.

In 1900 Hinshelwood published a first monograph on *Letter, Word, and Mind Blindness* and in 1917 a second monograph on *Congenital Word-Blindness.* He defined congenital word blindness as a "congenital defect occurring in children with otherwise normal and undamaged brains, characterized by a disability in learning to read" (p. 1229). Hinshelwood felt this was presumably due to an agenesis of the dominant angular gyrus. It is remarkable that recent anatomical studies suggest that Hinshelwood was not far from wrong (see Chapter 11, "Specific Language Disability").

That the symptoms involved aspects of language other than reading was indicated by Samuel Orton, whose conclusions from a study of almost 1,000 cases were summarized in the 1936 Salmon Memorial Lecture (Orton, 1937/1989) at the New York City Academy of Medicine. Orton stressed the wide variation in symptoms, all relating to disorder in the acquisition of language. He described five major symptom complexes: developmental alexia, writing disability, developmental word deafness, motor speech delay, and developmental apraxia. He felt these syndromes reflected a delay or difficulty in establishing cerebral dominance for language functions, probably on a hereditary basis. As a result, Orton reasoned, information was received equally by both hemispheres and the nondominant images were not normally suppressed in awareness so that symbols were confused and visual symbols were "twisted." Reading disability was thus termed *strephosymbolia.*

Like Orton, many investigators have attempted to minimize the concept of organicity or brain damage. Myklebust and Boshes (1960) referred to *psychoneurological learning disorders;* Myklebust (1967) and Kirk, McCarthy, and Kirk (1968) to *psycholinguistic learning disorders;* Rabinovitch (Rabinovitch, Drew, De Jong, Ingram, & Withey, 1954; Rabinovitch, 1968) recognized the broad spectrum of problems implicated in reading retardation when he proposed the classifications of *primary reading retardation* to reflect psychoneurological dysfunction in the absence of history or signs of brain injury and of *secondary reading retardation* to reflect a reaction to other pathology or problems. Critchley (1964) defined developmental dyslexia as a primary constitutional reading disability. More recently the American Psychiatric Association in its *Diagnostic and Statistical Manual of Mental Disorders,* (DSM-III, 1980 and DSM-III-R, 1987) has used the term *specific developmental disorders* as the overall designation "for disorders that are characterized by inadequate development of specific academic, language, speech and motor skills that are not due to demonstrable physical or neurologic disorders, a pervasive developmental disorder, mental retardation or deficient educational opportunities" (DSM-III-R, p. 39–40). Unlike the term MBD, which was widely accepted by the psychological and medical communities, the clinical concept did not achieve general acceptance in the educational community and did little to solve the practical problems of definition and educational management.

The Learning Disability Movement

The term *learning disability* was proposed by Kirk in 1962 as a substitute for such labels as brain injured, perceptually handicapped, or minimal brain dysfunction.

> *A learning disability refers to a retardation, disorder, or delayed development in one or more of the processes of speech, language, reading, spelling, writing or arithmetic resulting from possible cerebral dysfunction and/or emotional or behavioral disturbance and not from mental retardation, sensory deprivation, or cultural or instructional factors. (Kirk, 1962, p. 261)*

This early definition contributed substantially to the definition presented to Congress by the National Advisory Committee on Handicapped Children in 1967.

> *The term "children with specific learning disabilities" means those children who have a disorder in one or more of the basic psychological processes involved in understanding or in using language, spoken or written, which disorder may manifest itself in imperfect ability to listen, think, speak, read, write, spell, or do mathematical calculations. Such disorders include such conditions as perceptual handicaps, brain injury, minimal brain dysfunction, dyslexia, and developmental aphasia. Such term does not include learning problems which are primarily the result of visual, hearing, or motor handicaps, of mental retardation, of emotional disturbance, or of environmental, cultural, or economic disadvantage. (National Advisory Committee on Handicapped Children, 1967)*

This definition served as the basis for early learning disabilities legislation in 1969. In 1975 it was incorporated into P. L. 94-142, the federal law mandating education for all handicapped children. It is interesting that Kirk's original definition included emotional and behavioral disturbance as a possible causative factor in "learning disability." Although the 1969 definition and the definition in P. L. 94-142 eliminated emotional and behavioral factors in the description of "learning disabilities," they did include "such conditions as perceptual handicaps, brain injury, minimal brain dysfunction, dyslexia, and developmental aphasia." The term thus encompasses such a heterogeneous group of symptoms with such diverse etiology that definitional problems continue.

The P. L. 94-142 definition, however, remains as government policy, although the many attempts at redefinition suggest some dissatisfaction with it. In 1981 representatives of six professional organizations concerned with learning disabilities (American Speech and Hearing Association, Association for Children and Adults with Learning Disabilities, Council for Learning Disabilities, the Division for Children with Communication Disorders, the International Reading Association, and the Orton Dyslexia Society) agreed on the following definition.

> *Learning Disabilities is a generic term that refers to a heterogeneous group of disorders manifested by significant difficulties in the acquisition and use of listening, speaking, reading, writing, reasoning, or mathematical abilities. These disorders are intrinsic to the individual and presumed to be due to central nervous system dysfunction. Even though a learning disability may occur concomitantly with other handicapping conditions (i.e., sensory impairment, mental retardation), social and emotional disturbances or environmental influences (i.e., cultural differences, insufficient/inappropriate instruction, psychogenic factors), it is not the direct result of those conditions or influences. (Hammill, Leigh, McNutt, & Larson, 1981, 1987, p. 109)*

This revised definition by the National Joint Committee on Learning Disabilities is well regarded among professional and lay groups because it clarifies some aspects of the earlier definitions. It emphasized the heterogeneity of learning disabilities. By the use of the term "individual" rather than "children," it recognized the fact that one may continue to experience the problems associated with learning disabilities in adulthood. Finally, it recognized the complexities of clinical diagnosis by stating that a learning disability can occur concomitantly with other handicapping conditions.

The Interagency Committee on Learning Disabilities, mandated as part of the Health Research Extension Act of 1985 (P. L. 99-158), also looked favorably upon the National Joint Committee's definition. However, the report of the interagency committee highlighted still another definitional problem, that of the relationship of social skills deficits to learning disability. This report states, perhaps prematurely, "In recent years, there has developed a consensus that social skills deficit also represents a specific learning disability" (Interagency Committee on Learning Disabilities, 1987, p. 221). On the basis of this assumption, the report recommended that social skills deficit should be added to the definition of learning disabilities so that the first sentence would read as follows.

> *Learning disabilities is a generic term that refers to a heterogeneous group of disorders manifested by significant difficulties in the acquisition and use of listening, speaking, reading, writing, reasoning, or mathematical abilities,* or of social skills. . . . *(Interagency Committee on Learning Disabilities, 1987, p. 222)* [italics added]

However, consensus was lacking on this modification. A footnote in the interagency report states that the Department of Education could not endorse the addition of social skills deficits to the definition of learning disabilities for two basic reasons: legal and economic. This addition, according to the footnote, would necessitate a change in existing legislation, the Education for All Handicapped Children Act, and would result in "increased confusion in the criteria to determine who is eligible for special education services and who is not eligible" (p. 222). Furthermore, in view of the Department of Education's efforts to avoid overidentification of children as learning disabled when their educational needs can be met appropriately in the regular classroom, the Department of Education took the position that the inclusion of "social skills deficiencies" would be expected to increase rather than decrease the number of children who would be classified as learning disabled, thus adding to the currently escalating costs of special education services.

Recent developments in the field have not solved the problems of definition (Kavanaugh, 1988). It is difficult to draft a definition statement that fulfills the purposes for which administrators, researchers, clinicians, and educators need to apply it. The frustrations of definition-making have caused the field to look for mathematical solutions to the problem of definition.

PROBLEMS INHERENT IN CURRENT DEFINITIONS

The definitions of learning disabilities in government documents have both inclusionary and exclusionary features (summarized in Table 1-2) and each poses a most difficult task with questions and problems as one attempts practical application in the cases of individual children. For example, while it may be reasonable to differentiate a child who has problems with learning stemming from sensory defects, mental retardation, emotional disturbance, and social disadvantage, the application of these exclusionary criteria in individual cases is not easy. The problems of real children are complex and multidetermined. Does learning disability occur independently of other handicapping conditions? Does poverty produce a different kind of learning problem from affluence? Can we separate emotional reactions to learning failure from the learning disability itself? Is it not possible that the organizational and retrieval problems associated with learning disabilities will result in intelligence test scores that underestimate a child's potential abilities? These exclusionary criteria, rather than simplifying the problem of definition, make it more complex. Eisenberg (1978) stated that "the categories of exclusion will deny service to a significant number of children with learning disabilities, particularly those who suffer from socio-cultural disadvantages and emotional disturbances" (p. 41).

Table 1-2   Definition of Learning Disability

A disorder in one or more basic psychological processes in understanding or using language, spoken or written.

Inclusionary Criteria	Exclusionary Criteria
Perceptual handicaps	Sensory or motor handicaps
Brain injury	Mental retardation
Minimal brain dysfunction	Emotional disturbance
Dyslexia	Environmental disadvantage

Note. Abstracted from "The Education for All Handicapped Children Act (Public Law 94-142)," 1977, *Federal Register, 42,* pp. 42496–42497.

The inclusionary criteria of the federal definition create additional problems, not the least of which are the measurement issues. For example, how can one determine that a child has "a disorder" or "significant difficulty" in the skills areas? Is this to be determined on the basis of achievement testing, and, if so, what level of performance constitutes learning disability? The Federal Register (1977) proposed that this decision be made on the basis of achievement 50% below expectancy level as measured by the formula not essentially different from one originally offered by Harris (1970).

The Harris formula derives a Reading Expectancy Age from mental age and chronological age:

$$\text{Reading Expectancy Age} \atop \text{(RExpA)} = \frac{2 \text{ Mental Age (MA)} + \text{Chronological Age (CA)}}{3}$$

where MA and CA are expressed in months, giving RExpA also in months. "This formula gives essentially the same result as using a simple regression equation for predicting reading age from mental age alone, assuming an average correlation of .67 between MA and RA" (Harris, 1970, p. 212). To compare actual reading level with RExpA, the attained reading age is divided by reading expectancy age:

$$\text{Reading Expectancy Quotient} \atop \text{(RExpQ)} = \frac{2 \text{ Reading Age (RA)} \times 100}{\text{RExpA}}$$

the difference between reading performance and expectancy is considered within normal limits when the RExpQ is between 90 and 110. The lower the RExpQ (below 90), the more severe the disability. A reading quotient is obtained by dividing the actual reading age by the chronological age:

$$\text{Reading Quotient} \atop \text{(RQ)} = \frac{2 \text{ RA} \times 100}{\text{CA}}$$

This will identify the child who although reading sufficiently well for grade placement is at a level below his or her expectancy.

The Federal Register formula, provided in order to offer some restraint on the number of children labeled as learning disabled, was not universally accepted in the implementation of P. L. 94-142 at the state level because of (a) criticism of its statistical assumptions and (b) dissatisfaction with existing measures of intelligence and achievement. Regression effects and errors in validity in the test scores have also been pointed out (Rutter, 1978b). Moreover, the use of a simple achievement ratio between test age and mental age is misleading since it is based on the assumption that IQ and reading achievement have a perfect correlation. Use of this ratio will overestimate the number of high-IQ children classified as learning disabled and underestimate the number of low-IQ children so designated. It is worthy of note that by 1977 the Federal Register deleted the 50% discrepancy formula. Discrepancy between educational achievement and intellectual level remains, however, a major part of any definition of learning disability.

Measurement of intellectual level itself poses a problem. What test should be used? Even with individual clinical tests there are questions of validity. The cumulative effects of difficulties in attention, visual-motor skills, reading comprehension, and many aspects of language may constitute threats to the validity of test results with learning disabled youngsters.

In evaluating educational experience, it is frequently assumed that by being enrolled in school the child has had adequate educational experience. For a variety of reasons, including inadequate or inappropriate teaching, instability in educational administration of some schools, changes in teaching personnel, children's limited English language proficiency, effects of chronic illness, truancy, or family mobility, and emotional disturbance such as school phobia, this may be an unwarranted assumption.

The problem of distinguishing the "primary influence" of sensory or motor handicaps or of emotional disturbance is not an all-or-none proposition. Each of these areas must be evaluated in a child who is not learning. Objective measurement is also difficult when one attempts to evaluate social and cultural disadvantage. If one concludes that the child comes from an economically deprived home, or from a culture different from the majority, does this mean that such a child cannot have a learning disability? Such an assumption is contrary to any experience in inner city schools, in which the incidence of reading retardation is highest in children of the poor (Eisenberg, 1966; Rutter, 1978b; Chapter 12 of this book, "Effects of Poverty, Cultural Differences, and Inappropriate Stimulation").

Efforts to formulate a workable definition of learning disability continue to the present time. Mindful of the legal and fiscal implications of definitions of learning disabilities and concerned about what has been termed the "overidentification" of such children, the United States Department of Education convened a Working Group in September 1983 to suggest "best practice–state-of-the-art" measurement solutions that would be independent of costs, numbers of children to be served, or difficulties in implementation.

The Working Group's final report (C. R. Reynolds, 1983) characterized the federal definition as "vague and subjective." Its implementation at the state and local levels was found to have resulted in procedures that represent improper application of the concept of severe discrepancy and failure to develop appropriate mathematical models. Recognizing that establishing a severe discrepancy between aptitude and achievement was a critical component of the definition, the report addressed the definition of a severe discrepancy by surveying a number of measurement models.

The report criticized the use of constant grade-equivalent discrepancies (i.e., at least one standard deviation difference between aptitude and achievement when both tests are expressed on a common scale) as lacking statistical sophistication. The standard deviation of a distribution created by subtracting the scores of one univariate distribution (for example, intelligence test scores) from another (for example, achievement test scores) could not be expected to be the same as the standard deviations for the two original distributions.

Grade-level discrepancies were also rejected because such models may preclude services to children in the higher IQ ranges and overidentify children in the lower IQ groups. Standard score comparison models were rejected for the opposite reason—i. e., they do not take into account the regression of an IQ score on achievement scores and may result in overidentification of children from higher IQ groups.

The report concluded that severe discrepancy required definition from a statistical perspective. Consensus favored a regression model that dealt with reliable differences that were relatively infrequent in the normal population and used standard scores rather than age or grade equivalents. Four models were reviewed, with only one considered by the Working Group to be appropriate. According to this approach, the discrepancy between predicted achievement (y) and obtained score (Yi) is considered severe when it equals or exceeds the value of the standard deviation of the distribution of differences between y and Yi, when both measures are expressed in a common metric, z-scores.

The Working Group chose this formula because it properly addresses the regression between IQ and achievement and assesses the magnitude or severity of this discrepancy by comparing it with the base rate in the population from which the correlation of the two measures was derived. It addresses the question of what is a severe discrepancy between the obtained achievement score of a given child and the average achievement scores of all other children with the same IQ. This answer requires the determination of a value for the point in a normal distribution at which a severe discrepancy occurs, a difficult matter in that, according to the Working Group's report, no strictly empirical criteria or research methods exist for this purpose. In the absence of such methods, the Working Group recommended the use of "rational, statistical, and traditional criteria: infrequent occurrence as exemplified by a value of two standard deviations from the mean of the distribution under consideration." A further caveat is represented in the recommendation that this value be corrected for unreliability through the computation of the standard error of the relevant difference score.

The report points out that the formula does not diagnose learning disability. It would merely indicate the children who are *eligible* for a diagnosis of learning disability. It further notes that not all children who have a severe discrepancy will ultimately be diagnosed as learning disabled, because severe discrepancies may exist for other reasons, such as economic, environmental, and cultural disadvantage.

In addition to the formidable computational requirements of this method for defining severe discrepancies in learning, the Working Group also recommended stringent requirements for input data for application of the formula. Adding to the customary provisions for reliable, valid, nonbiased measures, implementation of this approach to identification would require normative data from a large, nationally stratified, random sample of children extending across the entire age range of schoolchildren in the United States. Measurement of aptitude should be based on individually administered tests of general ability, with age-based standard scores corrected at 2- to 5-month intervals. Most important of all, co-normed aptitude and achievement tests for the *same* children in the *same* time period are essential for the implementation of the Working Group's recommendations.

Apart from the enormity of the psychometric and statistical tasks required by this approach, both practical and theoretical issues would seem to question its adoption. First of all there are practical issues centered around the organization and data collection this formula involves. Even more crucial is the understanding of the statistical procedures required for implementation and interpretation of the process in local school districts in order to provide services for individual children. Finally, there are theoretical questions relating to a number of assumptions on which this procedure is based:

- that a single global aptitude score is representative of a child's abilities
- that achievement could somehow be reduced to a single score for purposes of comparison with aptitude
- that regression-based predictions made at the national or state level would be appropriate for crucial decision making for individual children at the local level

- that the heterogeneous condition we call learning disability is normally distributed in the population and can be regarded as a unified trait for purposes of statistical analysis

It would seem that this Working Group still has considerable work to do.

SURVEY OF CURRENT DEFINITION PRACTICES

Theoretical considerations aside, state and local education agencies are faced with application of legally constituted definitions in the provision of special education services. Concerns in these quarters about definition have recently centered around the rapid increase in the number of children identified as learning disabled. Since the enactment of P. L. 94-142, the number of learning disabled children receiving special education services has increased from 797,213 in 1977 to more than 1,914,000 in 1987 (U.S. Department of Education, 1987), an increase of more than 1 million children in a 10-year period. Some investigators have attributed this increase to confusions over definitions (Epps, Ysseldyke, & McQue, 1984).

Frankenberger and Harper (1987) solicited all state departments of education for copies of the states' requirements and procedures in 1981/82 and again in 1985/86 and received replies from 49 states. These data were the subject of an analysis of existing definitions to determine their (1) consistency with the Federal Register definition (1977) and (2) use of criteria to quantify a severe discrepancy between ability and achievement. Based on a comparison of the state guidelines over the 5-year period, these authors concluded that the states were responding to the apparent overidentification of children as learning disabled by adopting achievement and discrepancy criteria and by reducing reliance on the unrestricted judgment of the multidisciplinary teams.

Although the original definition of learning disability as it appeared in the Federal Register (1977) stated that there must be a severe discrepancy between ability and achievement, it did not include specific diagnostic procedures. Thus, it placed the responsibility for implementing the definition on the individual state plans. This implementation was highly variable. In 1986, 57% of the state plans contained specific methods for quantifying the discrepancy (Frankenberger & Harper, 1987).

It was with respect to the quantification of the discrepancy between ability and achievement, rather than in the alteration of definitions or in the inclusion of IQ limitations, that the most visible changes in state guidelines appeared over the 5-year period studied (Frankenberger & Harper, 1987). These changes are shown in Table 1–3.

As can be seen from the data in Table 1-3, there was increased use of discrepancy criteria over the 5-year period with only 33% of the state plans

Table 1-3   *Achievement Discrepancy Methods Used by States to*
Identify Learning Disabled Children

	Number of States Using Method			
	Grade Deviation	Expectancy Formula	Standard Score	Regression Analysis
1981/82	4	2	10	1
1985/86	4	13	11	6

Adapted from Frankenberger and Harper, 1987; organized according to Cone and Wilson's (1981) categorization.
Note: Because multiple methods of identification are in use in some states, numbers in this table differ from several percentages cited in the text.

specifying such criteria in 1981/82, but 57% doing so in 1985/86. Furthermore, this period saw an increase in the use of the more statistically sophisticated methods, such as expectancy formulas and regression analyses. However, variation continues to characterize the state of art of definition, both within and between states. In 1981/82, the one state that used regression analysis acknowledged that it might not be possible to implement in all school districts and permitted the use of other methods as well. Even greater variation was found in the 1985/86 survey, in which the number of states permitting the use of more than one method had increased to four and a fifth state required the use of two methods (Frankenberger & Harper, 1987).

Thus, while it seems that the general trend is toward more specific and more sophisticated methods for defining who is and who is not learning disabled, the situation continues to be highly variable. Although more than half of the 50 states use some quantitative criterion for determining a discrepancy, 21 states (43% of the respondents) do not. As Frankenberger and Harper (1987) pointed out, children identified as eligible for special education services for a learning disability in one state might not be so identified or eligible if they moved to a different state.

THE DILEMMA

Both statistical and clinical investigators have thus encountered difficulties in devising a simple and clear definition of learning disability. These complications have led some individuals to despair of the task and to comment that the term is incapable of "precise and persistent definition" (Rutter, 1978b).

The cases of Johnny and David presented at the beginning of this chapter illustrate some of the difficulties in definition that are faced by clinicians and educators. Johnny's academic achievement is far below his age and grade placement. He certainly has problems in learning. However, there are a number of complicating factors: (a) his early years were characterized by inconsistent mothering, possibly even deprivation, with all this implies for his early cognitive development, (b) he demonstrates emotional and behavioral problems. By strict definition of P. L. 94-142 (see the exclusionary criteria in Table 1-2) Johnny does not have a learning disability. Each of these factors would exclude his being classified as learning disabled, thus precluding the provision of the special education services he needs. It is ironic that his academic difficulties may have been exacerbated by the very factors that result in his exclusion from special education services for the learning disabled. Yet there is no doubt that he is not learning well and needs educational assistance for his learning problems. In accordance with prevailing criteria, however, he is not considered learning disabled and does not qualify for the remedial services of learning disability programs. In fact, he was placed in a class for emotionally disturbed children, where the primary concern was control over behavior. How should Johnny (and other children like him enrolled in schools) be classified? Should he be given a convenient label so that he can have the benefits of special education? If so, which one? Or should he be sent back to the regular classroom to struggle with the conventional curriculum because he is not severely disabled enough to merit such help?

David, by contrast, has had the benefit of caring parents with a stimulating environment. His specific word storage and word finding difficulty is already creating problems in learning in the first grade. Yet with his high overall cognitive abilities, he is managing to obtain average achievement scores. Because of this he is not considered learning disabled and is not eligible for remedial help. Do our criteria for learning disability put a premium on failure?

SUMMARY

The definition of disorders of learning in children is important. It determines the number of children who need special educational provisions and the resources schools must mobilize to educate them; it guides the decisions to provide services to every individual child, and it is essential for selection of samples for research. There is, however, little evidence of consensus among professionals in the field, either in terms of terminology or of methods of identification.

Definitions arose from neurological, psychological, and educational perspectives. Historically, neurological definitions, stressing the analogy between children with learning disorders and those with the behavioral and cognitive sequelae of epidemic encephalitis, considered these children *brain damaged.* In most children with learning problems, however, there was no firm evidence for structural damage to the central nervous system. To describe them, the term *minimal brain dysfunction* was introduced. This term encompassed such a heterogeneous group of children and created such definitional confusion that it yielded to the term *learning disability,* as defined by the National Advisory Committee on Handicapped Children to include children who "have a disorder in one or more of the basic psychological processes in understanding and using language, spoken or written" but where this disorder "is not primarily the result of visual, hearing or motor handicaps, mild retardation, emotional disturbance or cultural or economic disadvantage." This definition was included in Public Law 94-142, which serves as the basis for government policy. The definition thus has both inclusionary and exclusionary factors. It is essentially based upon a discrepancy between academic achievement and academic expectancy. This definition, however, just like MBD, comprises a heterogeneous group of children and poses problems in measurement of discrepancy that have not yet been solved.

CHAPTER TWO

Clinical Classification of Disorders of Learning

Our approach to the problem of definition of learning disability is essentially clinical and educational. We view learning as a necessary component of the developing personality and as the end result of a wide variety of psychological and physiological processes, accomplished by the interaction of numerous internal and environmental factors. Learning failure is thus a symptom, a final common pathway stemming from a multitude of factors that influence a child's development. These factors may be at a biological level (genetic, developmental, or pathological), a psychological level (cognitive, motivational, or attentional) or any other level—social, economic, cultural, and educational. Most often these factors operate in combination. The prevailing definition of learning disabilities, however, specifically excludes many of these factors.

We pointed out in Chapter 1 that while it may be reasonable to attempt to differentiate "learning disability" from the effects of social disadvantage, cognitive limitations, emotional disturbance, poor educational experience, neurological dysfunction, and sensory deficits, applying these exclusionary criteria to cases of individual children is not easy. The problems of real children are often complex and multidetermined. Many questions may be raised. Does a learning disability always occur independently of other handicapping conditions? Does poverty produce a different kind of learning failure than affluence does? Can the emotional reactions to learning failure be separated from the learning disability itself? Can the organizational and retrieval problems associated with a learning disability result in a lower score on intelligence tests? The exclusionary criteria seem to be based on the assumption that one kind of problem precludes any other.

Definitions of learning disability on the basis of discrepancy between scores on intelligence and achievement tests (Bond & Tinker, 1967; Harris, 1970) have also been criticized. Regression effects and errors of measurement of the test scores themselves have been pointed out (Rutter, 1978b). The use of predicted values based on regression equations between aptitude and achievement tests has been proposed as mathematically, psychometrically, and logically more justifiable. As we saw in Chapter 1, however, the clinical utility of such an approach is questionable.

Here are our guiding principles for classification of learning disabilities. Classification should:

1. be based on multidimensional, multidisciplinary data
2. provide for variations within individual subjects and for ages of subjects and sources of samples
3. provide for variations in measurement used by different investigators
4. provide a taxonomy clinically useful in guiding management and theoretically valuable in defining samples for research

With these considerations in mind, we propose a classification that would encompass all children who fail in learning. In this classification, the term *learning disordered* would apply to *all children whose academic achievement is below that expected from their age and intelligence.*

This broad category of learning disorders is obviously a most heterogeneous group, including within it some children who would *not* qualify for remedial education under P. L. 94-142. Our definition is specifically designed to include children from socially deprived environments, those with emotional problems and conduct disorders, those whose early educational experiences were inadequate and/or inappropriate, those with structural or known physiological defects of the central nervous system, and those with attention deficit hyperactivity disorders (ADHD). In this taxonomy, children with structural or known physiological defects of the central nervous system and those with attention deficit hyperactivity disorder are considered discrete from the child with a "specific learning disability," and children with learning problems related to their early social, cultural, and educational experiences are brought into the domain of educational responsibility for learning disorders. As described later in this chapter, each of these groups differs not only in possible etiology but also in the clinical picture each presents and in the educational support each needs. The broad definition of a learning disordered child as one whose academic achievement is below that expected from his age and intelligence emphasizes the responsibility of clinician and educator to identify needs and to provide appropriate educational and clinical management for all children who fail to learn.

To say a child is learning disordered, however, only begins to define the problems. It highlights a broad, nonspecific symptom for which we must find the cause. If learning disorders in all children came from the same cause, had the same cluster of dysfunction, required the same management, and had the same outcome, there would be no need for further classification. Such obviously is not the case. There are unique combinations of factors in each child that contribute to his or her learning disorder. How can these factors be classified?

CLINICAL CLASSIFICATION OF POSSIBLE CAUSES

Clinically the unique combinations of disorders of learning may be classified into (a) the possible causes of the learning disorder and (b) the patterns of central nervous system dysfunction characteristic of each child. This chapter focuses on classification based on possible causes of the disorder; the following chapter describes the patterns of central nervous system dysfunction found in children with learning disorders.

Table 2-1   Disorders of Learning: Clinical Classification Based on Possible Causative Factors

Group I: Extrinsic Factors	Group II: Intrinsic Factors	Group III: Combinations
a. Social and economic deprivation b. Language differences c. Inappropriate or inadequate prior education d. Emotional barriers to learning	a. Maturational lags 　1. Specific language disabilities 　2. Attention deficit hyperactivity disorder b. Organic defect of the central nervous system c. Tourette's syndrome d. Autism e. Generalized cognitive immaturity, cause unknown	Categories in Group I and Group II

A clinical classification of possible causative factors in disorders of learning is seen in Table 2-1. Two major groups are indicated: learning disorders that result from extrinsic factors and those that result from intrinsic factors. Although these factors may be discrete, they are not mutually exclusive; frequently combinations of these factors may exist in any one child. For example, a child may have had impoverished cultural opportunities and suffer from perinatal hypoxia, or he may have mild birth trauma superimposed upon a specific language disability.

Learning Disorders that Result from Extrinsic Factors

Extrinsic factors act *on* the child, particularly those factors related to socioeconomic disadvantage, such as the culture of poverty that offers inappropriate or inadequate stimulation in the early years of life. (The effect of such environmental conditions on learning is discussed in Chapter 12 (Effects of Poverty and Inappropriate Stimulation), where, as we will see, this factor is important not only in terms of the sheer number of children who suffer from such disorders, but also in terms of the high percentage of these children who do not complete high school.) Also included in the extrinsic group are children whose learning disorder results from inappropriate or inadequate educational experiences or from language differences; the latter primarily occurs in children whose dominant language at home differs from the language in which they are taught at school.

Emotional barriers to learning are included in this extrinsic group. Emotional barriers include problems in motivation; inhibition to learning resulting from anxiety, depression, or obsession or from psychogenically induced behaviors, such as regressions and phase-inappropriate behaviors; and resistance to learning because of conduct disorders, aggression, truancy, or drug or alcohol abuse. While current psychiatric thought implicates biological differences in the organism to account for many of these symptoms, they are included here among the extrinsically induced learning disorders largely because of the importance of experience in their genesis, because these children do not necessarily have the neuropsychological dysfunction of the intrinsic group, and because their management and prognosis requires other disciplines in addition to education.

Learning Disorders That Result From Intrinsic Factors

Intrinsic factors lie within the biological makeup of the child and are expressed in dysfunction of the central nervous system. Diverse biological factors may be identified. In some children an organic defect of the central nervous system—for example, that resulting from prematurity and/or hypoxia or from any of the hundreds of reasons for structural or physiological defect in the central nervous system—may be found (see Chapter 14, "The Organic Group"). In others, the dysfunction may result from an unevenness in maturation in which the neuropsychological functions related to language in any of its dimensions—in the perception, association, retention, and retrieval of symbols or in the metalinguistic functions of understanding, thought, and conceptualization—do not develop in an age-appropriate fashion. The cause of such maturational lags may not be known with certainty. The entity known as specific language disability is the prime example of this group of disorders. The term specific language disability includes the group of children that Denckla (1985) referred to as "dyslexia pure", and Hinshelwood (1907) called "congenitally word-blind"; Orton (1928) called their disability "strephosymbolia," and Critchley (1964) called it "developmental dyslexia, a primary constitutional reading disability." It is the equivalent of the primary reading disability of Rabinovitch (1968) and of the specific reading retardation of Rutter (1978b).

This group of disorders constitutes the most prevalent group of learning disorders found in classrooms. Unfortunately, the term learning disabilities, or dyslexia, has also been used to include children with "brain damage," "minimal brain dysfunction," and "attention deficit hyperactivity disorder" (see Table 1-1). Its use has been virtually synonymous with our term *learning disorders*. As such, it is difficult, at times, to understand just what group of children an investigator has included in his sample or even what an educator means when she says a child has a learning disability. We prefer to restrict the term *specific language disability* to a group of learning disorders for which no etiological agent has as yet been found and in whom there is a constellation of psychoneurological dysfunction that subsumes the use of language as we have broadly defined it. We use the term "specific," both in its medical sense (meaning cause unknown) and in its descriptive sense (focusing on one area of function, namely language). In elementary-school children, it may manifest itself educationally in problems with achievement in any of the language arts—reading, spelling, speaking, writing—or in arithmetic; in secondary-school children, it may affect metalinguistic function. Specific language disability itself, however, may be a heterogeneous entity not only in etiology but also in the pattern of neuropsychological defects. Even where homogeneous clusters of neuropsychological defect may be found, as we will see in Chapter 3 ("Patterns of Neuropsychological Dysfunction"), these clusters themselves may be a manifestation of heterogeneous causes. The management and prognosis for this group is different from that for the other etiological groups inTable 2-1.

Within the group of developmentally determined disorders is also included the child with an attention deficit hyperactivity disorder. There may be questions as to why, in this classification, attention deficit hyperactivity disorder is included among the "maturational dysfunctions." Just as the term learning disability, as used in the literature, encompasses an etiologically heterogeneous group of children, so does the term attention deficit hyperactivity disorder include a heterogeneous group. Attention deficit and hyperactivity are symptoms that may have many causes, just as the symptom of learning failure has many causes. Some of these possible causes are listed in Table 13-2 (Chapter 13, "Attention Deficit Hyperactivity Disorder"). Moreover, one group of children has the symptoms of ADHD, but no causative factor for them may be found. Again, just as in the specific learning disability, there appears to be a familial incidence in the emergence of the symptom. We presume that in these children there is a developmental lag in the maturation of the pathways in the central nervous system that modulate attention and impulsivity. This group, as a parallel with specific language disability (SLD), might be called *specific attention deficit hyperactivity disorder*. This is the group included as a maturational lag in this classification. Learning problems of these children may result from the attention-impulse-control immaturity itself, without the neuropsychological deficits found in SLD. On the other hand, the combination of SLD and ADHD may be found in some; in that event, both factors are considered in diagnoses and treatment.

There is a group of children whose academic achievement in their early elementary years is consistent with their grade placement, but as they go on to the higher grades, they fall behind, and only then are recognized as having a learning disorder. These are children who score in the bright normal–

superior range on intelligence tests. They do have a learning disorder, but their intelligence manages to carry them through the early grades. Where higher level tasks of organization and conceptualization are demanded, they do not achieve as well as their IQs indicate. They are frequently called "underachievers." They may suffer from any of the etiological factors in Table 2-1.

Within the intrinsic group, too, are included disorders of the biological function such as autism and Tourette's syndrome. Each of these entities will be discussed in Part Three of this book.

RELATIONSHIP TO P. L. 94-142

How does this scheme relate to the prevailing definitions of learning disability? We have pointed out that P. L. 94-142 specifically excludes environmental disadvantage, emotional disturbances, and inappropriate educational experience. Yet the learning problems of these children need to be recognized so that adequate provision can be made for their educational and clinical management. Environmental disadvantage does not rule out the neuropsychological dysfunctions that may underlie learning failure. As a matter of fact, environmental disadvantage, through lack of stimuli needed to develop skills, may actually contribute to the neuropsychological dysfunction, particularly as it relates to language. Although social background, by P. L. 94-142 definition, may be an excuse for not offering the specific remedial help that these children so sorely need, children who are victims of experiences that do not equip them for learning are the most likely to drop out of school and never to fulfill their social, vocational, and financial potential.

In its definition of learning disabilities, P. L. 94-142 includes children with perceptual handicaps, children with organic insult to the central nervous system, and children suffering from specific developmental learning disability. Our classification, however, recognizes the differences among these groups. The child with a structural defect of the central nervous system, the so-called "organic" child, has more than perceptual deficits. She has a lowered threshold for anxiety, impulsivity, rigidity of psychological defenses, and possible difficulty with long-term memory—all of which must be considered in management. The child with an attention deficit hyperactivity disorder may or may not have perceptual deficits, but in all cases his impulsivity and his possible need for medication must be considered. The unique learning problems of Tourette's syndrome are just beginning to be recognized. Further, the prognosis for children with a structural defect of the central nervous system and those with attention deficit hyperactivity disorder is less optimistic than that for children with a specific language disability and may be less amenable to preventive intervention.

In one way our classification does parallel P. L. 94-142. We retain the term *specific learning (language) disability* to designate the large number of children with a learning disorder for which no etiological factor can be found, that appears to have a strong familial pattern, that is marked with neuropsychological dysfunction, albeit in a variety of patterns, and for which remedial education is most important in management. We have pointed out that the qualifying term "specific" has been used in two senses: (a) in the medical usage, "specific" implies that we do not know the cause; (b) in the behavioral sense, it implies circumscribed areas of dysfunction. The distinctions made in Table 2-1 are important in that each group requires different tactics in management. The groups differ in prognosis and in preventive approaches. The variations within and among each group of learning disorders form a major section, Part Three, of this book.

The utility of this classification in an educational setting may be seen from a study of 650 children born in 1971 and at the time of the study in the first grade of seven elementary schools on the Lower East Side of Manhattan (Hagin, Beecher, & Silver, 1982). There were slightly more boys (52%) than girls (48%); 11.5% of the children were black, 18.5% caucasian, 34% hispanic, and 36% oriental. Of the 650 children, 13 did not have sufficient English for valid testing and were dropped from this sample. Each child was first examined with a scanning test (called *Search*, A. A. Silver & Hagin, 1981), which, in a previous study of 168 children, correctly predicted the children who by third grade would fail in reading. There was one false positive and nine false negatives. *Search* (as will be discussed in Chapter 10) is an individual test consisting of ten components (three in visual perception dealing with spatial orientation and visual motor function, two in auditory perception relating to discrimination and sequencing, two intermodal skills, and three in spatial orientation of the body image). It is designed to be used with children 5 and 6 years old. A total *Search* score delineates vulnerability to learning failure; an individual score yields a profile of assets and deficits.

Of the 650 children tested in 1978, 192, or 29%, of the group were found to be vulnerable to learning failure. By the end of first grade, family mobility reduced the total number of children to 494 and the number of children for whom learning failure was predicted to 138, or 28% of the total first-grade population, 60% boys, 40% girls. The IQ scores (Wechsler Preschool and Primary Scale of Intelligence, WPPSI) for these children ranged from 61 to 124 with a mean of 93.39 ± 12.43. These 124 children were then subjected to a multidisciplinary, individual, clinical study consisting of neuropsychiatric, psychological, social and educational evaluations. Developmental history was obtained from parents and from school and hospital (birth) records. Details of these examinations, including ratings for the neurological and psychiatric examination and diagnostic use of the WPPSI, are described in Hagin, Silver, and Corwin, 1972; and A. A. Silver and Hagin, 1972b.

This diagnostic, clinical study identified a number of subgroups within the sample of vulnerable children.

1. Children with specific language disabilities (17% of the total 494 children). These children demonstrated basic problems in spatial orientation and temporal organization, immaturity in body image including finger-gnosis and right–left discrimination, and difficulty with associative learning tasks such as association of sounds with their written symbols and with the Animal-House subtest of the WPPSI. There was no evidence for structural defects of the central nervous system or of the peripheral sensory apparatus; there was adequate experiential background for school learning. The percentage of boys (58%) and of girls (42%) was not significantly different in this group. Function on the WPPSI was within average range.

2. Children with neurological deviations (8.5% of the total sample) were of two types:
   a. Those with diffuse neurological findings that did not point to focal defects and in whom causal factors could rarely be found in their histories (6.2% of the total population). These children had problems in spatial orientation and/or in temporal orientation but in addition had deviations in one or more areas of the neurological examination including evaluation of muscle tone, power and synergy, gross and fine motor coordination, cranial nerves, posture and equilibrium, and deep, superficial, and pathological reflexes. Immaturities in praxis, right–left discrimination and finger-gnosis were found.
   b. Those with focal neurological signs (2.3% of the total, boys:girls = 5:1) such as mild cerebral or cerebellar palsies, dyskinesias, fetal alcohol syndrome, vasomotor and pupillary abnormalities, and extinction of tactile stimuli. These children were variable in function, depending on the extent, location, and age of onset of their pathology and the environmental support they had received.

3. Children with attention deficit hyperactivity disorder (1.2% of the total). These children were restless and driven, their movements quick and impulsive. Subtest scores on the WPPSI in any individual child varied from a scaled score low of 4 to a high of 14. These children had to be repeatedly instructed to attend to the task.

4. Children with a generalized immaturity (0.6% of the total). These children had nonspecific learning problems but had a history of slow development in reaching normal developmental landmarks. They appeared to be younger than their chronological age. Their WPPSI scores were in the borderline range.

5. Children with emotional problems (1.2% of the total). Some of these were reacting to pathological conditions within the family; others presented severe neurotic and behavior problems reflected in every aspect of their lives including school. Neurological examination was within normal limits. Perceptual examination did not reveal specific areas of deficit.

6. Other children identified as vulnerable:

   a. Those with hearing loss, which needed further evaluation (two children).

   b. Those with cultural differences (two children newly arrived in the United States); although they could speak and understand English, their cultural difference made some of the testing inappropriate.

   c. Those identified as false positives; four children identified as vulnerable through *Search* proved to be normal learners (1% false positive).

Thus, even at this early age of first grade, children who will develop academic problems are not a homogeneous group. The diagnostic clusters found in this study correspond well with the classification presented in Table 2-1. The essential point is that to call all children who fail in reading "dyslexic" or "learning disabled" obscures the heterogeneity that exists in this population and blurs the etiological factors that lead to the final common symptom of learning failure.

This book is not alone in attempting to classify learning disorders on the basis of causative factors. Rabinovitch (1968; Rabinovitch et al., 1954) proposed classifying learning disorders as either "primary" (those for which we do not know the cause) or "secondary" (those that appear to result from a known disturbance such as structural damage to the central nervous system). Quadfasel and Goodglass (1968) also thought of learning disorders as "symptomatic" (resulting from early brain damage), "primary" (without evidence of brain damage but possibly genetic), and "secondary" (resulting from environmental, emotional, or health factors). Bannatyne (1971) classified the universe of "all language and reading disabilities" into six major groupings: low IQ, "dyslexia," emotional, aphasia, autism, and other. The "dyslexia" group, in turn, was divided into four groups of factors: genetic, social or environmental deprivation, minor neurological dysfunction, and primarily emotional. The characteristics of "genetic" dyslexia were considered to be language delays and deficits; the minor neurological group was thought to encompass a series of disorders in each perceptual avenue. Thus, the classification presented in this book is not unique. It has attempted to classify the population of learning disordered children as they are seen in the classroom and not as preselected from neurological, neuropsychological, and psychiatric clinics.

Both cross-sectional and longitudinal clinical studies of children with learning disorders also support the classification described here. Tables 2-2, 2-3, 2-4, and 2-5 contrast children with specific language disability, with structural defects of the central nervous system, with attention deficit hyperactivity disorder, and with an overall cognitive function in the borderline range in various academic, social, and emotional parameters as the children grow from preschool age into adulthood.

In preschool the child who will develop a specific language disability frequently has delayed speech with articulation errors, generally good gross motor ability but immature fine motor skills, good mathematical ability except where sequencing is needed, and good conceptual organization, particularly in nonverbal concepts; socially and emotionally he is at this age normal. The organic child at preschool age may also be delayed in language ability; however, he may be dysarthric with oral inaccuracies. His gross and fine motor skills are poor, he may be hyper- or hypoactive, he has difficulty matching and counting in arithmetic, his conceptual organization may already be concrete and perseverative, and he may have difficulty in social adjustment. The ADHD child is already exhibiting hasty, impulsive behavior, with generally unfocused conceptual organization; she may already be self-centered and feel misunderstood. The cognitive borderline child is immature in all aspects of functioning.

By elementary school the SLD child will have decoding and encoding difficulty; he is not highly verbal, his body image problems are seen in right–left confusion, his mathematics suffers when verbal problems are introduced and multiplication and long division errors may be made, his conceptual abilities particularly nonverbal are generally good, but he is suffering emotionally from his academic difficulties and may feel that he is stupid. The organic child is more uneven in her academic skills; she may lack systematic decoding and encoding, her written work is difficult, she may be impulsive and clumsy; she may be sloppy, she may have difficulty organizing her daily activities and be rigid in her thinking. She is often lonely and anxious. The ADHD child has difficulty completing work although he can do it; he is driven, self-centered, and impulsive, and he has a superficial conceptual organization. The cognitively borderline child is generally weeks behind her peers in academic skills, although her written work may be legible and orderly and her thinking is generally concrete.

At the secondary school level the SLD child continues to have difficulty. She may still need to learn decoding skills or methods to avoid the specific deficits with which she suffers; she has trouble putting her thoughts together for compositions and reports, her fine motor coordination may have improved, and mathematics (particularly problems involving complex verbal mediation or requiring spatial skills or geometry) may be difficult but, on the other hand, she may be proficient with computers. Her school difficulties may be reflected in self-doubts and in social adjustment. The organic child continues to be disorganized and rigid; his achievement is uneven and his anxiety is still present; he may develop compulsive patterns and become

Table 2-2   *Etiological Subtypes of Learning Disorders: A Longitudinal View of Specific Language Disability*

	Reading and Language Arts	Motor Skills	Mathematics	Conceptual Organization	Social Development	Psychological Development
Preschool	Delayed speech Articulation errors	Gross motor—good Fine motor—immature	Good except sequences	Good—especially nonverbal	Within normal limits	Within normal limits
Elementary	Decoding and encoding difficulty Not highly verbal	Gross motor—good Left–right errors Fine motor—improving	Good if not too verbal Multiplication and long division errors	Good, nonverbal	Reactive to learning problems	Feels stupid
Secondary	Needs mastery of decoding or bypass methods Difficulty with compositions	Improved Often exceptional artwork	Trouble with algebra and geometry Loves computers	Depends upon language stimulation Compulsive approaches	Reactive to school success	Worries about competency
Adult	Not an eager reader	Enters visual/mechanical/quantitative/graphic fields	Loves computers Strength for vocations	Well organized	Reactive	May be depressed Over- or underassertive Noninvesting

Table 2-3 Etiological Subtypes of Learning Disorders: A Longitudinal View of Classical Organic Defects

	Reading and Language Arts	Motor Skills	Mathematics	Conceptual Organization	Social Development	Psychological Development
Preschool	May be delayed, accelerated, or dysarthric	Poor— hyperactive or hypoactive	Sequencing errors	Chaotic Concrete	Poor	Depends upon environmental support
Elementary	Uneven Lacks systematic decoding and encoding Written work difficult	Poor Impulsive Clumsy	Uneven Rapid Erratic	Rigid Difficulty integrating	Often lonely Sometimes clowning	Sees self as misunderstood Anxious May be ingratiating
Secondary	Uneven	Uneven	Homework problems Sloppy	Disorganized Verbal may be good Nonverbal poor	Not social	Defensive Suspicious Anxious Sometimes an "operator"
Adult	Uneven May take refuge in reading May be overly verbal	Clumsy	Uneven	Disorganized Depends upon others	Self-centered	Defensive Anxious Potential unrealized

Table 2-4 *Etiological Subtypes of Learning Disorders: A Longitudinal View of Attention Deficit and Hyperactivity Disorders*

	Reading and Language Arts	Motor Skills	Mathematics	Conceptual Organization	Social Development	Psychological Development
Preschool	Little opportunity to learn	Hasty Primitive	Sequencing difficulties	Poor	Poor	Driven Self-centered Impulsive Feels misunderstood
Elementary	Uneven Difficulty in completing work although often *can* do it	Sloppy Hasty	Mechanical approach	Superficial	Provocative	Driven Self-centered Impulsive Feels misunderstood
Secondary	Uneven Gaps in background Illogical	Sloppy Impatient	Gaps in background Weak logic	Superficial	Impatient Often unpopular	Feels misunderstood Weak defenses
Adult	Uneven Seeks verbal-type occupations Easily bored	Avoids motor tasks	Avoid details of this field	Superficial	"Own worst enemy"	Dissatisfied Restless Dependent on others Vulnerable to anxiety

Table 2-5   Etiological Subtypes of Learning Disorders: A Longitudinal View of Developmental Immaturity, Borderline Cognitive Function

	Reading and Language Arts	Motor Skills	Mathematics	Conceptual Organization	Social Development	Emotional Development
Preschool	Immature for age.					
Elementary	Out of sync with curriculum	Within normal limits	Concrete	Concrete	Immature for age	Within normal limits
Secondary	Difficulties with abstractions	Within normal limits	Difficulties with abstractions	Concrete	Within normal limits	Within normal limits
	School day retardates if schooling is not modified.					
Adult	Skills fairly good but does not read much	Within normal limits	Fair	"Popular" taste	Within normal limits Responsible about work done	Within normal limits

socially isolated; the physical coordination needed in writing is still not developed and written work is difficult, although his reading itself is good. The ADHD child is sloppy and impatient; his academic skills are uneven and his thinking is sometimes superficial and illogical. There are gaps in the knowledge he has acquired; socially he is often unpopular and he tends to project his problems to others. The borderline child now has obvious difficulty with understanding of abstractions; he may be considered "retarded" if the academic demands are not adjusted to his limitations.

As an adult, the SLD is not an avid reader, although she may have learned to be well-organized; she generally enters visual/mechanical, quantitative, or graphic fields; emotionally, however, she may be suffering from the self-doubts engendered by her disability. The organic adult may be a good reader and be overly verbal; his motor clumsiness remains, and his academic achievement is not in keeping with his potential; he may still be disorganized and may have developed compensatory mechanisms of rigidity; his anxiety is still present. The ADHD adult is also uneven in academic achievement; he avoids detailed work requiring sustained attention; he seeks verbal-type occupations and becomes easily bored; he may appear dissatisfied, restless, and dependent on others. The borderline adult may have skills consistent with her abilities and may be conscientious and responsible in routine work.

This cross-sectional and longitudinal observation of children with learning disorders provides additional justification for the separation of children with structural defects of the central nervous system, those with attention deficit hyperactivity disorder, and those with generalized cognitive immaturity from children with a specific language disability.

To classify children into the groups outlined in Table 2-1, however, is not yet enough. Within each of the categories in Table 2-1, patterns of neuropsychological functioning may be found. These functions form a second order of classification, and the findings of this second-order research are discussed in the next chapter of this book. In Chapter 3 we explore the differences in patterns of neuropsychological dysfunction in motor and in neurological signs for each of the groups in Table 2-1 and consider both intragroup and intergroup differences. The importance of subgroup patterns, regardless of cause, lies in the fact that with such second-order classification, our understanding of each child will be broadened, clues for prognosis and for prevention may be offered, and patterns for educational remedial techniques may be suggested.

DECISION TREE FOR CLASSIFICATION

In theory, to make the distinctions outlined in Table 2-1 for each child, a complex multiaxial evaluation may be needed. In practice, however, each child may not need all aspects of the evaluation. Resources are more pru-

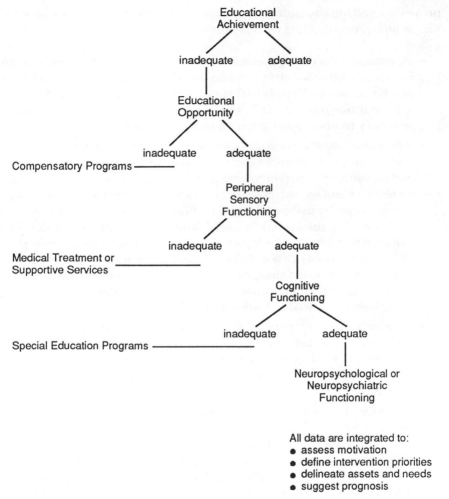

Figure 2-1   Decision Tree
Decision Making in the Diagnosis of Learning Disorders

dently used in a decision tree that prioritizes levels of definition. This decision tree (Figure 2-1) offers a systems approach in which each successive step provides a finer level of definition of the learning problem.

This decision tree indicates the decision points necessary for definition of the various disorders of learning: educational achievement, educational opportunity, peripheral sensory functioning, cognitive functioning, and neuropsychological and neuropsychiatric functioning. At each point, a decision of adequacy or inadequacy implies consideration of specific program provisions and/or the future diagnostic studies necessary for understanding, defining, and meeting each child's educational needs:

- *Educational achievement* is assessed both informally in the classroom and in the child's developmental history as well as formally through measures of educational achievement. This step represents the first definition level for a learning disorder. If it is found to be inadequate, further study is necessary to understand the reasons for the disorder.

- *Educational opportunity* is assessed through a reconstruction of formal and informal educational experiences the child has enjoyed. The quality and consistency of parenting and early stimulation, preschool education, elementary and secondary schooling, as well as language and cultural differences can be assessed from the child's history, school records, and work samples. Information secured from this second level of definition can then be related to the gaps suggested by the previous decision point. Where educational opportunity is found to be inadequate or inappropriate, programmatic changes to compensate for these inadequacies can be devised. Where educational opportunity is found to be adequate, other levels of assessment are required.

- *Peripheral sensory functioning,* the third level of definition, involves assessment of auditory and visual acuity. Where inadequate, recommendations for medical treatment and educational modifications can be devised. Where adequate, other levels of definition of the learning disorder are required.

- *Cognitive functioning,* the fourth definition level, involves assessment of children whose educational achievement has been found to be inadequate. It requires the administration and interpretation of an individual intelligence test in order to provide quantitative and qualitative data on the child's cognitive functioning and adaptive behavior. A decision of inadequacy at this level leads toward modification of educational requirements through provision of a special education program. A decision of adequacy leads to further diagnosis to tease out the nature of specific learning problems.

- *Neurological functioning,* the fifth and final level, is assessed to evaluate the integrity and the maturity of the child's central nervous system. The skills of neuropsychology and neuropsychiatry are used to examine brain–behavior relationships with emphasis on the sensory, motor, perceptual–integrative, associative, and language processes essential for learning. Where functioning is found to be unimpaired, further diagnosis can define the effect of motivational and emotional factors on learning. Results of these examinations define intervention priorities, delineate assets and needs, and suggest long-range outcomes.

This decision tree indicates the *minimal* amount of information needed for planning broad-based educational programs for children with learning disorders. A decision of inadequacy at any point does not imply that further assessment or diagnostic study is unnecessary for the appropriate education of the youngster. Rather, it seeks to focus diagnosis on those services that will provide information that is *relevant* to decision making about the needs of the child being served.

At the same time, this decision tree seeks to avoid the lengthy diagnostic studies that involve the administration of the same extensive battery to every child irrespective of the problems they represent. Territorial conflicts among the representatives of the multidisciplinary "teams" produce redundancy in the assessment process. Case reports and recommendations derived from these assessments are drafted more for the sake of legal compliance than for the clinical insights they provide. Thus, in recent years these ceremonial diagnostics have tended to become something of an end in themselves rather than an intermediary step to guide educational planning for intervention.

The decision tree offers a practical approach that is economical in the use of school services to define the learning problem for each child. By using this approach we can better understand the forces that created the problem, the unique pattern in which the problem is expressed in each child, and the appropriate educational and clinical services needed for remediation.

SUMMARY

This book uses the term *learning disorder* to describe the heterogeneous group of disorders characterized by the discrepancy between academic achievement and educational expectancy, which may result from a wide variety of biological, psychological, cognitive, environmental, and educational factors, acting singly or most often in combination. The strength of each of these factors in determining how the learning problem will manifest itself will vary with the life experiences and internal resources of each child. In this book, classification and definition are based on these variations in biological, psychological, cognitive, and environmental factors, as well as on the educational needs and strengths these children present. A decision tree with successive decision points serves as a framework for the evaluations necessary in the classification of learning disorders as they are experienced by individual children: educational achievement, educational opportunity, peripheral sensory functioning, cognitive functioning, and neuropsychological and neuropsychiatric functioning. Each level of the decision tree guides classification and practical management.

CHAPTER THREE

Subgroup Patterns of Neuropsychological Dysfunction

This chapter is concerned with subgroups of children who have central nervous system dysfunction and who have difficulty with academic achievement. What are the characteristic dysfunctions of the central nervous system that appear in this group? What characteristics other than inadequate academic achievement can separate the unsuccessful learner from the successful one? What homogeneous subgroups can be identified on the basis of the patterns of neuropsychological dysfunction that may be found? What is the maturational sequence of these patterns with treatment and without treatment?

To answer these questions is not a simple matter. In studying the nature of central nervous system dysfunction we are faced with the same problems encountered in studies of prevalence: namely problems of conflicting definition, disparate demographic characteristics of samples, and differences in research methodology. The demographic characteristics of children included in subgroup studies are varied as to source, age, sex, IQ, definitional boundaries, neurological signs, and socioeconomic status. The clinical diagnostic groupings as outlined in Table 2-1 are not clearly defined. Population samples have come from clinics with varying professional emphasis; from medical, neuropsychological, and educational settings, and from highly selected or from intact populations in the schools: Ages have varied from 5 to 18 years. The definitions of "adequate" intellectual functioning have differed. The tests used to decide whether a child is learning disabled may be limited to only one aspect of learning. The methodology has varied from clinical observation to statistical analysis. Statistical studies, in turn, have varied from univariate studies to multivariate investigations. The tests used to sample central nervous system functioning also have differed from study to study. Each investigator attempts to subsume his or her findings in a summary description—i. e., language, graphomotor, visual-spatial, or sequential disorder—the meanings of which may not be comparable across studies. The brain function underlying these tests may not be clear at all. The Metropolitan Readiness Test (Hildreth, Griffiths, & McGauvran, 1965), used by 36% of 93 school districts sampled by Maitland, Nadeau, and Nadeau (1974), is an example of the difficulty in describing the brain mechanism underlying a complex neuropsychological function. Section 1 of the Metropolitan Readiness Test is called "word meaning." In it the examiner names an object, which the child must select from a three-picture array and circle. Is this a test of word meaning, of picture recognition, of figure–ground perception, of attention, of praxis, or of audiovisual integration? What is measured is not necessarily what the label says it is. Finally, there is often no attempt to distinguish between tests that are causally related to the learning problems from those that, although representing areas of weakness, may be irrelevant to the tasks of learning. All these factors may present different pictures of central nervous system function, obscure the validity of subgroups in the sample studied, and prevent the generalization of the findings into other samples.

As an example of the importance of tests used, the classic work of Akelaites (1940, 1941, 1942) reported no neuropsychological abnormality in a
patient following surgical section of the corpus callosum. Twenty years later,
the use of specialized neuropsychological techniques in the study of similar
patients (Gazzaniga, Bogen, & Sperry, 1962; Sperry 1961, 1964) highlighted
the striking defects in interhemispheric transfer of information and uncovered the syndrome of hemisphere dissociation. Goldstein and Joynt (1969)
tested one of the very patients whom Akelaites had examined years earlier.
Akelaites found this patient to be neuropsychologically normal; Goldstein
and Joynt, however, found lasting defects in interhemispheric transfer with
no evidence of reorganization of function. It did not appear that the patient
deteriorated in the 27 years, but that the Goldstein and Joynt examination
used new techniques of testing that revealed new insights.

This chapter reviews subgroup studies based on univariate analysis, clinical inferential data, educational criteria, and multivariate analysis. It then
suggests a concept to unify the heterogenous subgroups found and reviews
the prognostic implications of subgroup classifications.

SUBGROUPS ON THE BASIS OF UNIVARIATE ANALYSIS

Early studies attempted to relate reading failure to single variables or to
combinations of variables within a single modality. As far back as 1928, N.
B. Smith found that letter matching in the first week of first grade yielded
a correlation of .87 with the Detroit Word Recognition Test. Barrett
(1965b, 1965c) found that measures of prereading visual discrimination and
knowledge of letter names were of value as predictors of reading. In another
paper, Barrett (1965a) stressed the additional importance of auditory discrimination of beginning sounds as a predictor of later reading skills. In
contrast, Hammill and Larsen (1974) found that auditory discrimination,
auditory memory, blending, and audiovisual integration were not useful in
predicting reading ability. G. L. Bond and Dykstra (1967), in a review of the
Cooperative Research Program in First-Grade Reading Instruction, concluded that such pupil capabilities as auditory or visual discrimination, pre–
first grade familiarity with print, and intelligence are all substantially related
to success in learning to read. In that study, knowledge of letter names
accounted for 25 to 36% of the variance in reading ability found at the end
of first grade; this predictive relationship persisted at the end of the second
grade (Dykstra, 1968). Intermodal integration function, particularly auditory-visual and visual-auditory integration, was considered by Birch and Belmont (1964, 1965) to distinguish normal from inadequate readers.

It has been suggested that functioning on higher levels of integration differentiates the normal from the retarded reader. Blank and Bridger (1967)
found that symbolic mediation was a necessary condition to solve problems

involving temporally presented stimuli regardless of modality. The difficulty is not in cross-modality transfer, they said, but in applying relevant verbal labels to stimuli. The need for verbal mediation was also stressed by Vellutino (1978), who believed that "apparent perceptual problems in poor readers at both younger (7–8 years) and older (9–14 years) age levels are a secondary manifestation of verbal mediation deficiencies, possibly associated with basic language problems" (p. 107). Vellutino and Scanlon (1985) reviewed the decade of the work they and their associates did at the Child Study Center in Albany, New York. Their work is a systematic exploration of the reasons for the difficulties encountered by poor readers in learning to identify the printed word. Exploring first the hypotheses that deficiencies in visual perception, cross-modality transfer, and temporal order recall are basic problems for the poor reader, Vellutino and his associates concluded that specific reading disability in young children is not caused by these dysfunctions and that the hypotheses are untenable. The visual perception hypothesis as advanced by Orton (1937/1989) and Hermann (1959) was not compatible with Vellutino's finding that poor readers (grades 2 through 8) could copy tachistoscopically presented scrambled letters, words, numbers, and geometric designs as well as normal readers, but could not name them as well. This finding was reinforced by poor readers (grades 2 through 6) performing as well as normal readers on immediate visual recall of three-, four-, and five-letter Hebrew words. The intersensory integration problems, which Birch and Belmont (1964, 1965) inferred by the difficulty poor readers had in associating the auditory stimulus of Morse code with the visual representation of that stimulus, were not confirmed when the Vellutino group used paired associative learning tasks using nonverbal as well as verbal associations. They found no appreciable differences between readers and nonreaders on nonverbal tasks including visual associations, auditory associations, and visual-auditory associations; however, there were significant differences on visual–verbal learning tasks. The Albany group also criticized the temporal order recall dysfunction (Bakker, 1972), suggesting that inaccuracies in serial order may be a function of the specific content of the items themselves used in the testing and that one cannot dissociate serial-order recall from memory. Vellutino concluded that the differences between poor and normal readers on the variety of measures used in the visual perception, cross-modality, and temporal sequencing research are secondary manifestations of reader-group differences in verbal encoding ability.

A series of studies, systematically varying verbal and nonverbal stimuli on measures of short- and long-term memory, found that poor readers were consistently differentiated when verbal factors were introduced but not when the effects of verbal encoding were minimized. Poor readers in the second grade were found to have significant difficulty encoding the structural properties, especially phonological properties, of spoken and written words. By sixth grade, the reader-group differences were greater on verbal learning and verbal memory tasks that relied more heavily on encoding of word meaning than on encoding of word structures. Vellutino and Scanlon (1985) concluded that "difficulties in learning to read, as measured by deficiencies in word identification, may be caused primarily by limitations in coding the structural or purely linguistic attributes of spoken and printed words" (p. 210).

The Haskins Laboratories group also concluded that the problems of most beginners in acquiring literacy is basically linguistic in nature, due to the ineffective use of phonological strategies needed for lexical access and representation in short-term memory. The problem is "linguistic awareness," the awareness of the units of speech that are represented by the orthography. This research is summarized by Liberman, Rubin, Duques, and Carlisle (1985) and Mann and Liberman (1984).

Benton and Pearl (1978) concluded that the univariate studies have identified "positive association of modest degree between reading retardation and deviant performance on a variety of tests making demands upon perceptual, linguistic, sequencing and intersensory integrative abilities" (p. 468). A summary of such studies may be found in Benton (1975), Rourke (1978, 1985), and Vellutino (1978, 1987).

One of the problems inherent in these univariate studies is that they view the symptoms of reading disability as a unitary condition. The single-symptom paradigm was criticized "on the basis that no workable definition of dyslexia as a unitary disorder is possible" (Doehring, Hoshko, & Bryans, 1979). Even controlling for age, sex, intelligence, socioeconomic status, and educational experience, and even ensuring as best we can that the child is free of emotional disorder and is neurologically intact, these studies assumed that the central nervous system dysfunction associated in one child with reading failure is the same as that in any other child who fails in reading. In reality, there are marked individual differences in a wide range of neuropsychological function in children designated as learning disabled. These differences may appear in all aspects of perceptual, associative, and emissive language functioning (A. A. Silver & Hagin, 1972b). The importance of these variations is that in any survey of large numbers of children, not only may the causative factors vary, but also individual differences in distribution of function may well cancel each other out. Some variables that may be dismissed as insignificant for the group may have critical importance to individual children. The admonition of Applebee (1971) is frequently quoted: ". . . research in reading retardation has far too long been methodologically oriented towards the simplest models. This research has been successful only in showing that these simplest models do not fit the problem. . . . we must concentrate on new models which correspond more closely to the heterogeneity of the disorder" (p. 112).

Satz and Morris (1981), long advocates of multivariate approaches, echoed this point of view. In a review of subtype research, they stated that "at the present time there is increasing recognition that reading or learning disability is not a homogeneous diagnostic entity (Benton & Pearl, 1978; Rutter 1978a). In fact, such disabilities may take several forms in terms of achievement patterns and/or associated cognitive information processing abilities that may additionally vary as a function of etiology or age" (p. 109).

SUBGROUPS ON THE BASIS OF CLINICAL INFERENTIAL STUDIES

An example of the clinical inferential approach is that of Mattis, French, and Rapin (1975). Mattis (1978) stated that "reading . . . requires the successful integration of moderately complex input, output and mediating subprocesses . . . . A defect of obstruction of any single one of these necessary subprocesses will impair subsequent interpretations, resulting in atypical development of reading skill. The population of dyslexic children is composed of several smaller groups, each of which presents differing deficits or clusters of deficits in higher cortical functions" (p. 52). Mattis, et al. (1975) isolated three independent "dyslexic syndromes" that accounted for 90% of the sample of 82 children they studied. The sample of "dyslexic children" was selected from a larger group ($N = 252$) of children referred by pediatric neurologists to a neuropsychology clinic of a large metropolitan hospital that drew its patients from a low socioeconomic population. The sample of 82 children was divided by clinical examination into two groups; 29 considered "developmental dyslexic" and 53 "brain damaged dyslexics." A comparison group of 31 additional children, "brain damaged normal readers," was also studied. Age range was 8 through 18 years with a mean age of 11 years, 5 months. As a result of the children's performance on a wide variety of language, speech, motor, and perceptual tasks, three distinct syndromes were identified:

1. A language disorder (39%) consisting of anomia (20% or greater proportion of errors on a Naming Test) and one of the following:
   a. disorder of comprehension (Token Test one sigma below mean)
   b. disorder of imitative speech (Sentence Repetition Test)
   c. disorder of sound discrimination (10% or greater errors on discrimination of rhythmic letters)
2. Articulatory and graphomotor dyscoordination (37%) consisting of:
   a. poor performance on the Illinois Test of Psycholinguistic Ability (ITPA) Sound Blending Test

　　b.　poor performance on graphomotor tests

　　c.　acustosensory and receptive language process within normal limits

3.　Visuospatial Perceptual Disorder (16%):

　　a.　verbal IQ more than 10 points above performance

　　b.　Raven's Colored Progressive Matrices less than the equivalent performance IQ

　　c.　Benton's visual retention test at or below borderline level

A cross-validation study (Mattis, 1978) of 163 "dyslexic" children ages 8 through 14 drawn from a clinic serving a black and hispanic population with a Hollingshead Scale of IV (craftsman, foreman, and operatives) or V (service workers, public and private) found the same three syndromes previously described but in different proportion. Language disorder accounted for 63%, articulatory-graphomotor 10%, and visual-spatial 5%; overlapping (i. e., two syndromes) was found in 9%. An additional 10% were found to have a "sequencing disorder" in which children did not have stable concepts of "before" or "after," and some could not identify their own left and right hands. It is not clear whether the hispanic children were tested in Spanish.

The Mattis et al. (1975) report illustrates the problems of trying to understand the manner in which subjects are classified. In a strict interpretation of the P. L. 94-142 criteria for diagnosis of learning disabilities, none of their subjects can properly qualify as having "developmental dyslexia," since all have come from a low socioeconomic population. Also the inclusion of organically impaired children within this group of children with reading problems may result in findings that may not be applicable to the child with "dyslexia pure" or to the child with a specific reading disability. It is to set boundaries among sets of children with academic problems that we have designated the entire group as *learning disordered,* and then identified the etiologically different subgroups in Table 2-1.

Denckla (1972, 1977), studying 52 children (ages 7 through 14) referred to her as a pediatric neurologist, found 54% demonstrated a language disorder in which anomia was prominent, 12% an articulatory-graphomotor-dyscoordination syndrome, and 4% a visual-spatial-perceptual disorder together with an anomia. Denckla also reported "dysphonic sequencing difficulty" in 13% and a "verbal memorization disorder" in 10% who demonstrated poor sentence repetition and poor verbal paired-associate learning. In practice, however, Denckla found that most children studied had mixed deficits. Ingram (1970) reviewed 82 children referred to the Department of Child Life and Health in Edinburgh for "dyslexia," the majority of whom had been examined in the neurological and speech clinics of the Royal Hospital for Sick Children. He was able to identify a group of children with specific reading disabilities, "without evidence of brain disease, and with a positive family history of reading and writing difficulties," in whom were those whose errors were predominantly "visuospatial" and those whose errors were predominantly "audiophonic." A mixed visuospatial and audiophonic group was also found (p. 419).

Performance patterns on the Wechsler Intelligence Scale for children with reading disorders were reported by M. Smith (1970) and by Kinsbourne and Warrington (1966). Smith identified three WISC profiles in retarded readers: (a) verbal deficit with poor symbol manipulation and auditory sequencing difficulty, but with intact spatial ability; (b) deficient spatial-perceptual ability with intact symbol manipulation and auditory sequencing; and (c) mixed characteristics of groups 1 and 2. Although age differences in patterns were found, these differences may be an artifact of the tests given. Ceiling effects on spatial-perceptual tests may be the cause of decreased spatial-perceptual error with increasing age and, conversely, floor effects may have influenced the increasing errors with increasing age on verbal tests. Kinsbourne and Warrington (1966) found one group of learning disabled children with depressed verbal IQs, delayed speech, and delayed vocabulary development and another group with depressed performance IQs, poor arithmetic, and poor constructional ability. Other studies found that low scores on the Vocabulary subtest of the WISC were seen in retarded readers more frequently than in adequately achieving readers (Belmont & Birch, 1966; Lyle & Goyen, 1969, McLeod, 1965).

Differences in the WPPSI in *clinically* defined groups were emphasized by Hagin et al. (1972) who reviewed findings on the WPPSI in all 86 children enrolled in the first grade in a public school on the East Side of New York City. Seventy-nine percent of the children were white, 12% were black, and 7% were Asian. Twenty-one percent were in Hollingshead Group I (professional and technical) and 31% were in Groups VI and VII (laborers and welfare). Thirty of the 86 children were selected as being vulnerable to learning failure and were placed in a special program of educational intervention. It was found that the intervention group means were significantly lower than the normal progress group on full scale, verbal, and performance IQs. The intervention group appeared to be more variable in subtest scores, but no consistent subtest pattern was found to characterize the intervention group. However, when patterns of the intervention group were considered in relation to clinical diagnosis, identifiable subgroups on WPPSI were found: children diagnosed as having a specific language disability ($n = 11$) showed a significantly lower verbal IQ than performance IQ; children with abnormal findings on neurological examination ($n = 12$) had marked variability in WPPSI subtest scores; and children who were considered "developmentally immature" ($n = 7$) had an essentially flat distribution of subtest scores, with overall cognitive functioning in the borderline range. It will be noted, however, that children in the intervention group were not preselected on the basis of "pure dyslexia" but were drawn from an intact group of children whom the authors' predictive instrument identified as potentially having learning disorders. As such they represented a heterogeneous group from the point of view of possible causative factors and did not represent biases in referred groups.

SUBGROUPS ON THE BASIS OF EDUCATIONAL CRITERIA

Classification of the basis of performance on education achievement variables has been proposed by Boder (1970, 1971, 1973; Boder & Jarrico, 1982), and Ingram (1970). Using a strict definition of specific developmental dyslexia (World Federation definition) Boder selected 92 boys and 15 girls ranging in age from 8 through 15 years who were attending school but who were 2 or more years behind grade placement in reading and spelling. Based on a qualitative analysis of their performance in reading and spelling, three subtypes were described: (a) a dysphonetic group (67%) that lacked word analysis skill, and had difficulty with sounding out and blending component letters and syllables; (b) a dyseidetic group (10%) with selective impairment in remembering and discriminating visual gestalts; and (c) a mixed dysphonetic and dyseidetic group (23%).

Bakker and his associates (Bakker, 1979, 1986; Bakker, Leeuwen, & Spyer, 1987), on the basis of reading errors made by children with reading disabilities, distinguish between an L- and P-type of "dyslexia." The L-type reads relatively fast while making substantive errors such as omissions, additions, and other "word-mutilating mistakes"; the P-dyslexics tend to read slowly and to make time-consuming errors such as fragmentations and repetitions. Bakker hypothesized that initial reading primarily requires the visuoperceptual analysis of the printed word and is thus primarily dependent on right-hemispheric processing. Fluent reading, on the other hand, a characteristic of more advanced reading, requires semantic-syntactic processing of text, a function primarily mediated by the left hemisphere. At some point in the normal development of reading, the primary subservience of reading switches from the right to the left hemisphere. The P-style of slow readers fails to make the "hemisphere shift," whereas the L-type dyslexics skip the initial phase of reading, in which the visual-perceptual features are mastered. Thus, although, the L-type readers are rapid readers, they are prone to substantive errors. Bakker validated this dichotomous taxonomy by finding that when words to be read are flashed on the central visual field, they are processed differently by the two groups, as evidenced by hemispheric differences in the evoked potentials. Interestingly, Bakker found that hemisphere-specific stimulation (i.e., right-hemisphere stimulation in L-dyslexics, left-hemisphere stimulation in P-dyslexics) not only brings about relative changes in the electrophysiologic activity of the stimulated hemispheres but also improves aspects of reading and spelling (Bakker & Vinke, 1985, p. 523).

SUBGROUPS ON THE BASIS OF MULTIVARIATE ANALYSIS

The use of more sophisticated methods of statistical analysis, of course, does not diminish basic methodological problems in variations in (a) the target sample (source, age, IQ, sex, definitional boundaries, socioeconomic status, and presence or absence of neurological signs), (b) clustering variables and their reliability and validity, and (c) statistical methodology, all of which may produce variations in the number of identified subgroups as well as in the nature of the identified subgroup. A brief review of methodological problems in Q-factor analysis and in cluster analysis may be found in Fletcher and Satz (1985).

One of the earliest attempts at statistical clustering of children with the learning disability syndrome was that of Myklebust and Boshes (1969) and Myklebust, Boshes, Olson, and Cole, (1969). This study screened 2,767 third and fourth graders from four suburban Chicago, Illinois, school districts. After eliminating 63 children because of low IQ scores, the authors administered a screening battery (Science Research Associates Primary Mental Abilities Tests and selected portions of the Metropolitan Achievement Test, elementary form), which identified 410 children who earned a learning quotient of 89 or less on any one test in the battery. These children were considered underachievers; those who earned a learning quotient between 85 and 89 were called borderline; 84 and below, learning disabled. Ninety-eight children in the learning disability group, 116 in the borderline group, and 238 normally achieving children were selected for intensive study. All children selected had normal vision and hearing, earned an IQ of at least 90 on either verbal or performance sections of the WISC, were free of gross motor disturbance, and appeared to have emotional adjustment adequate for learning.

The psychoeducational test battery used in the intensive examination consisted of 49 variables, of which 21 were used as a basis for statistical comparison of groups. This battery included tests of mental ability (WISC, Detroit Test of Learning Aptitude) and educational achievement (Gates-McKillop Reading Diagnostic Tests, Wide Range Achievement Tests, WRAT, and Metropolitan Achievement Tests). WISC records on the experimental (learning disabled and borderline) groups tended to earn higher scores on performance subtests, while normal achieving children tended to score higher on verbal subtests. Discriminant function analysis revealed that on educational testing "the ability to syllabicate was a critical factor as far as successful learning was concerned" (p. 142). Neurological study of the groups revealed that "both experimental groups (borderline and learning disabled) were found to show more signs of neurological disturbance in comparison with normal" (p. 246). The borderline children exhibited more soft signs; the learning disability group, more hard signs; the borderlines showed a disturbance of graphesthesia on both right and left sides, whereas the learning disabilities were deficient in horizontal movement of the tongue. The meaning of this last finding is obscure.

Doehring (1968) used multivariate statistics to differentiate characteristics of normal and retarded readers. He matched, in age and performance IQ, groups of 39 boys and 39 girls designated as normal readers with 39 boys who were retarded readers. The retarded readers were between the ages of 10 and 14 with retardation of 2 or more years in oral reading ability. Their performance IQ on the WISC was 90 or above. Psychiatric status, educational opportunity, home environment, hearing, vision, general health, and motor function were all considered normal. The samples were drawn from reading clinics or from direct referrals to the Indiana University Neuropsychology Laboratory. Fifty-seven measures divided into seven subtests were selected for study. These measures included the following: verbal subtests of the WISC, oral subtests from the Minnesota Aphasic test, and tests in vision, visual-motor, complex discrimination, memory, and sequential stored information. Stepwise multiple regression analysis and discriminant function analysis demonstrated that reading disability was associated with impairment of a wide variety of nonreading skills. Disabled readers were differentiated from normal readers by a small set of tasks: oral word rhyming, oral vocabulary, discrimination of reversed figures, and speed of perception of visual forms. The reading impairment, however, appeared to be directly associated with deficiencies in tasks that required sequential processing, such as speed of visual perception of sequences of forms and naming of verbal sequences. Doehring stated that "the individual differences which did occur took the form of variations in the amount and type of nonreading impairment that accompanied the seemingly basic *impairment of sequential processing abilities*" [italics added] (Doehring, 1968, p. 167).

Doehring and Hoshko (1977) studied the "individual differences" in two additional samples of children by means of the Q-sort clustering technique. These samples included 34 children aged 8 years, 8 months, through 17 years, 4 months (IQ varying from 71 to 125) with reading problems (Group R) and 31 children aged 8 years, 2 months through 12 years, 5 months (IQ from 79 to 105) with a variety of problems including learning disorders, language disorders, and mental retardation (Group M). Three subtypes emerged for each group. In Group R they found the following: (a) ($n = 12$) a linguistic defect with poor oral reading of words and syllables but good performance on all visual matching and three auditory-visual integration tests; (b) ($n = 11$) a phonological defect with poor auditory and visual integration on oral reading tests, but good performance on the visual scanning test; and (c) ($n = 8$) intersensory-integration defect with poor auditory-visual integration of words and syllables. In Group M they found that subtypes 1 and 2 were similar to those of Group R but subtype 3 ($n = 7$) showed poor performance on visual-perceptual tests. This subgrouping was subsequently confirmed by cluster analysis (Doehring et al., 1979) and also in a study of an additional 88 reading subjects by Doehring, Trites, Patel, and Fiedorowicz (1981) tested with a variety of statistical techniques. However, the 1981 study did not find a correspondence between types of reading errors and the deficits determined from language and/or neuropsychological measures. It was found, however, "that children with oral reading problems tended to be least impaired; those with sound-letter association problems, most impaired; and those with letter sequence problems tended to perform poorly in Progressive Matrices and on a measure of finger agnosia" (Doehring, 1985, p. 136).

Petrauskas and Rourke (1979) also applied a *Q*-sort technique on data from 160 children aged 7 and 8 years, of whom 133 were retarded readers scoring in the lowest quartile on the WRAT and 27 were normal readers. All were drawn from the Neuropsychology Laboratory and the University of Windsor and the Windsor Western Hospital Center. All children in the study had to have an IQ greater than 80, come at least from middle socioeconomic families, and have intact vision and hearing. The sample of 160 children was divided into two subsamples of 80 children each, with a similar number of normal readers assigned to each subsample.

Each child was studied with a battery of tests that may be grouped into six categories: tactile-perceptual, sequencing, motor, visual-spatial, auditory-verbal, and abstract-conceptual. Taken together, these clusters resemble those tasks which previous studies had shown to be deficient in reading disability. The following subtypes were identified:

1. ($n = 40$) (males:females = 3:1)—most difficulty on tasks that were primarily verbal in nature (i. e., verbal fluency and sentence memory); low scores on WISC Digit Span; largest discrepancy between verbal and performance tests on the WISC (lower verbal)

2. ($n = 26$) (males:females = 12:1)—most difficulty on test for finger agnosia on both hands and on a measure involving immediate memory for visual sequences; small WISC verbal-performance discrepancy with a so-called ACID pattern (poor Arithmetic, Coding, Information, and Digit Span); auditory, verbal, and language-related problems less severe than subgroup 1

3. ($n = 13$) of whom 2 were normal readers—better performance on left than on right side of the body on a Tactile Performance Test and on finger recognition test, difficulty with conceptual flexibility, especially when linguistic coding was involved (verbal coding); some diffi-

culty in psychomotor skills; lower verbal IQ than performance IQ on the WISC with AID (poor Arithmetic, Information, and Digit Span) pattern

Group 4 (8 of whom were normal readers) and Group 5 (normal readers) were not fully described.

In a subsequent study, Joschko and Rourke (1985) found that there are at least two reliable subtypes of learning disabled children who have the ACID pattern on the WISC and that "children who exhibit the ACID pattern are a heterogeneous population with respect to their adaptive ability structures" (p. 81). One hundred and eighty-one "learning disabled" children with the ACID pattern were compared with 181 learning disabled children who did not have the ACID pattern, but matched on age, full scale WISC IQ, sex, and handedness. All children were treated with a battery of measures similar to those used by Petrauskas and Rourke (1979)—110 measures for children 5 to 8 years of age, 103 for those 9 to 15 years old. Five different cluster analysis procedures were used. In the younger group, two subtypes were identified; one with a prominent deficiency in the "revisualization" of symbols, reflected in poor performance in neuropsychological measures considered tactile-perceptual, visual-perceptual, auditory-perceptual and language related, and motor. Sequencing, however, was within the average range. The second subtype had poor performance in the tactile-perceptual tests and consistently poor scores on tests of auditory and motor sequencing ability. In older children one subtype had deficient performance on symbolic sequencing and visual scanning tests and on a measure of "kinetic steadiness"; the second subtype resembled the perceptual patterns of the "revisualization" defects of one subtype found in younger children. It is not known whether the types seen at ages 9 through 15 represent an older version of the younger ACID subtypes.

The neuropsychological profiles of right-handed compared with left-handed learning disabled children were also studied by the Windsor Hospital Group (Del Dotto & Rourke, 1985) in a study of 161 left-handers and a comparable group of right-handers. The subjects, 9 years to approximately 15 years of age, drawn from the same population pool, were tested with 42 measures thought to represent six neuropsychological adaptive skills as outlined by Reitan (1974) and used in the Petrauskas and Rourke (1979) study, the Joschko and Rourke study (1985), and the Fisk and Rourke study (1979). Right-handed learning disabled children exhibit very similar adaptive ability profiles. The classification analysis (Q-type factor analysis and cluster analysis) suggested at least three highly similar subtypes of learning disabled children within two age-equivalent, handedness-based samples: subtype I with a normal visual information processing system and good nonverbal problem-solving capabilities, but with mild auditory processing deficits and pronounced haptic deficiencies, especially tactile finger localization;

subtype II with a "clear" weakness to process auditory-verbal information and some deficiencies in verbal coding or verbal labeling (this group also had the largest low verbal–high performance discrepancy on the WISC); and subtype III with poor auditory-verbal and psycholinguistic skills, mild right-sided finger recognition deficits, and pronounced haptic deficiencies involving the detection of numbers written on the fingertips of the right hand. These subtypes are said to resemble other dextral subtypes reported: Subtype I is similar to the Fisk and Rourke subtype A and type 2 of the Petrauskas and Rourke study; subtype III is similar to the Fisk and Rourke subtype B, to type I of the Petrauskas and Rourke study, to the language disorder of Kinsbourne and Warrington (1963) and Mattis et al. (1975), and to the dysphonetic group of Boder (1973); and subtype II is similar to subtype C of Fisk and Rourke. The authors concluded that "handedness *per se* may not be an important consideration in the search for sub-types of learning-disabled children" (Del Dotto & Rourke, 1985, p. 123).

Satz and Morris (1981) used cluster analysis techniques to describe the subtypes within a sample consisting of 89 Caucasian boys with a mean age of 11 years. The children were tested at the end of fifth grade in Alachua County, Florida, and they were sufficiently depressed in academic achievement (2-year deficit) to be considered learning disabled by the investigators. Four neuropsychological tests, selected from a larger group of measures based on high-factor loadings on a language factor (WISC similarities, verbal fluency) and on a perceptual factor (Berry-Buktenica tests of visual-motor integration, visual recognition, and visual discrimination) were given to each child. The Verbal Fluency Test (Spreen & Benton, 1969) requires children to verbalize words beginning with different letters of the alphabet under timed conditions. The Recognition and Discrimination Test (Fletcher & Satz, 1984) is a geometric-figure matching test. On cluster analysis five distinct groups emerged:

1. (n = 27)—global language impairment (severely impaired on language measures on the Peabody Picture Vocabulary Test (PPVT); performance on nonlanguage perceptual tests was within normal limits;

2. (n = 14)—specific language naming (selective impairment only on verbal fluency test; performance on all other tests including PPVT was within normal limits)

3. (n = 10)—mixed type: global language and perceptual

4. (n = 23)—visual-perceptual-motor impaired type (selectivity impaired on only the non-language perceptual test)

5. (n = 12)—unexpected subtype, no impairment on any of the neuropsychological tests.

Subtypes 1 (global language), 3 (mixed), and 4 (visual-perceptual-motor) had significantly higher proportions of soft neurological signs than did subtypes

2 and 5, and subtypes 1 and 3 tended to come from a lower socioeconomic level than the remaining subtypes. The parents of children in the specific verbal group and in the "unexpected" group had higher reading scores than did the parents of children in the other three groups.

Satz and Morris's group 5, which they call "unexpected," should not be unexpected at all. Their sample was drawn from an unselected population of children with learning disorders. As we discussed in Chapters 1 and 2, "learning disorder" is a heterogeneous classification, with many possible causative factors. One group in the classification of learning disorders includes children with intelligence adequate for learning but who do *not* have central nervous system dysfunction. The learning disorder in these children may stem from a number of causes, including emotional and motivational factors, inadequate or inappropriate educational experience, social and cultural factors, chronic illness, and peripheral sensory defects. Any of these may account for the findings of "no impairment" on neuropsychological tests.

The problem of a group of children whose reading disorder appeared to have emotional origins was stressed by A. A. Silver and Hagin in 1960 in an early study of 150 children aged 8 years, 6 months to 12 years with IQs ranging from 81 to 123 (full scale WISC). One hundred of these children were referred to the Bellevue Hospital Mental Hygiene Clinic for emotional behavior problems, but they were also retarded in reading; the remaining 50 children were drawn from a private practice of psychiatry. A control group of 30 children drawn from the same Bellevue clinic population but who were normal readers were also studied. Each child underwent a complete neurological examination, including so-called soft signs, and a variety of perceptual tests of visual, auditory, tactile, and intermodal skills. While 92% of all children with a reading disorder demonstrated some defect on the test battery, 8% did not. This compares with the Satz (1984) finding of 11% of his sample free of the linguistic and perceptual measures he used. A. A. Silver and Hagin (1964) stated that "It may be that these children (i. e., the 8%) have matured so that their perceptual defects are no longer apparent with the tests used, or that they have defects undetected by these means. It is possible, however, that the reading problem in these children may have an etiology entirely different from the vast majority of children with reading disability (i. e., disorder). This *may be the emotional group*" [italics added] (p.100).

In reviewing their data, Satz and Morris (1981) could not account for this unexpected subtype as a statistical artifact; nor did their "unexpected" group reveal significant motivational or emotional problems as determined by the Children's Personality Questionnaire. They concluded that "although no adequate explanation has yet been advanced, a subgroup of LD children may exist whose problems in reading and spelling may not be associated with deficiencies in higher-order cognitive or language processes" (Satz, Morris, & Fletcher, 1985, p. 31). Other investigators have also identified a subset of their reading disabled children to be relatively free of cognitive or linguistic deficit (De Fries & Decker, 1982; Lyon, Reitta, Watson, & Porch, 1981; Lyon, Stewart, & Freedman, 1982).

A longitudinal retrospective study to determine the stability of subtypes over time is reported by Satz et al. (1985) on children in the fifth grade. Separate cluster analyses, using the same cognitive measures that they used in their 1981 study, were computed on the same 89 boys of the 1981 sub-sample study of the Satz and Morris Florida Longitudinal Reading Study using retrospective data from kindergarten and from grade 2. The analyses were thus computed on the same children at ages 5, 8, and 11. Three of the five subtypes originally described remained essentially unchanged (general verbal, global deficit, and visual-perceptual-motor), whereas two subtypes (specific verbal deficit and unexpected) revealed significant changes. Except for a persistent deficit in verbal fluency in the specific verbal subtype, the change was characterized by increasing improvement in cognitive perfor-mance. Satz et al. (1985) postulated that these changes in cognitive abilities may predict improvement in reading achievement as these children grow into adolescence.

The longitudinal study of the 89 children designated as learning disabled was complemented by a longitudinal study of the 236 boys from whom the original 89 were drawn (Fletcher & Satz, 1985). This also was a retrospective cluster analysis of data retrieved from a study of these children when they were in kindergarten, in grade 2, and in grade 5 (ages 5, 8, and 11). Eight variables, including the original four in the study of the 89 learning disabled children, were included in the analysis: verbal skills (verbal fluency, WISC similarities, PPVT, and Dichotic Listening) and nonverbal skills (Beery Test, Recognition-Discrimination, Embedded Figures, and Auditory-Visual Inte-gration). A seven-cluster solution appeared appropriate, including five sub-types ($n = 189$) and two small groups of outliners ($n = 11$). The five sub-types included three of "disabled learners" and two of "good learners." Type A ($n = 45$) were, at age 5, deficient in both verbal and visual spatial skills; by age 11 there was improvement in visual-spatial skills. This group is said to resemble the general verbal subtype reported in the 1981 study. Type B ($n = 41$) had average verbal skills but poor visual-spatial skills at age 5; by age 11, verbal skills were only slightly better than visual-spatial skills. This also is a learning disabled group, resembling the mixed subtype previ-ously reported. Type C ($n = 24$) was deficient in verbal and visual-spatial skills at all ages. These children had the lowest PPVT scores and came from the lower socioeconomic backgrounds; they may simply represent a slow learner group. It is to be noted that the Fletcher and Satz (1985) report encompassed the unselected group of "virtually all white boys" in the kin-dergartens of Alachua County Public Schools at the time of testing. It is unfortunate that the educational experiences of the children in longitudinal studies are not documented, since the pattern of deficits originally seen may have responded differently to remedial measures and to life experiences as the child lived through the years from 5 through 11.

Spreen, too, has been concerned with a comprehensive longitudinal study of "learning disabled children." His data base includes cluster analysis of two groups of children, 8 through 12 years of age, who were referred to the University of Victoria Neuropsychology Clinic because of learning problems (Sarazin & Spreen, 1986; Spreen 1978b, 1978c; Spreen & Haaf, 1986). The first group ($n = 63$), meeting criteria of verbal or performance IQ greater than 79, no acquired brain damage, and no evidence of primary emotional disorders, was matched with 52 average readers with respect to age, sex, and socioeconomic status. A second group ($n = 96$) was similar to the first except that the full scale IQ cutoff was raised to greater than 79. Variables on the analysis included Sentence Repetition Tests (Spreen & Benton, 1969); right–left orientation, reading, spelling, and arithmetic subtests of the WRAT; and scaled scores for Similarities, Vocabulary, Coding, Block Design, and Arithmetic subtests of the WISC-R. While the cluster solutions for the two groups were not identical, "the main pattern of subtypes is similar" (Spreen & Haaf, 1986, p. 176). Visuoperceptual, linguistic and articulo-graphomotor types were identified. In addition, minimally impaired and severely impaired groups were noted. The visuoperceptual cluster was low in Vocabulary, Block Design, and Coding; the linguistic cluster was low in Similarities, Vocabulary, and Coding; the articulo-graphomotor group was low in Sentence Repetition, Right–Left Discrimination, and Coding. These findings are in general similar to the previous studies discussed in the preceding pages of this chapter.

Stokes (1987) studied a sample of children, similar to that reported in the Florida Longitudinal Reading Study drawn from the first-grade classes of local public schools and consisting of children for whom reading failure was predicted. Stoke's children, however, had the benefit of comprehensive interdisciplinary evaluation, including neuropsychiatric, psychological, educational, and social examinations. He was therefore able to statistically develop a series of subgroups and then relate them to the results of clinical examinations.

Stokes used data from the New York University Learning Disorders Unit school-based projects in which 650 children, enrolled in first grade in seven elementary schools in Manhattan in 1978, were screened with the test battery called *Search,* which identified children in kindergarten and in early first grade for whom reading failure was predicted. Details of its content, administration, and statistical constraints are found in A. A. Silver and Hagin (1981) and in Chapter 10 of this book. Of the 650 children, 192 (29%) were found to meet the criteria that predicted learning failure. After children from bilingual homes and those not completing the full comprehensive clinical evaluations were excluded, 141 children (85 boys, 56 girls) between the ages of 5 years, 4 months and 6 years, 5 months were available for analysis.

The sample had a mean full scale IQ (WPPSI) of 97.22 (*SD* = 13.92) with a mean verbal IQ of 96.78 (*SD* = 15.39) and a mean performance IQ of 98.12 (*SD* = 14.85). This obviously was not intended to be a "dyslexia-pure" sample.

Scores on 20 variables (the subtests of WPPSI and of *Search*) were used to generate clusters of perceptual and cognitive functions for each of the 141 children. The final cluster solution classified 126 individuals into seven homogeneous subgroups (leaving 16% unclassified), which appeared to correspond to the results of previous clinical examinations. Subgroup 1 (encompassing 15% of the entire sample) appeared to correspond to the emotionally handicapped group; subgroup 2 (14%) had difficulties with associative learning, particulary with auditory sequencing, and corresponded to the specific language disabled group; subgroup 3 (10%) had borderline cognitive function; subgroup 4 (5%) with major deficiencies in measures of body image, visual-motor function and visual-spatial orientation, had the greatest number with neurological impairment; subgroup 5 (25%) was a mixed group with both language and perceptual deficits; subgroup 6 (6%) may be associated with an attention deficit disorder, and subgroup 7 (9%) had a global language deficit, which was consistent with the language of children who had experienced inappropriate or inadequate language stimulation at a critical age.

One important finding to emerge from the Stokes data is the utility of clinical diagnosis in understanding findings of subgroup studies: that, in general, subgroup patterns reflect the clinical diagnostic entities with patterns for SLD, neurological impairment, attention deficit, emotional problems, borderline intelligence, and inadequate or inappropriate early language experiences.

A UNIFYING CONCEPT FOR SUBGROUP STUDIES

It is interesting that the spectrum of neuropsychological dysfunction described in this chapter reflects what William James had described in 1890. James stated that "In some individuals the habitual 'thought stuff,' if one may call it, is visual; in others it is auditory, articulatory or motor; in most perhaps it is evenly mixed" (James, 1890/1950, vol. 2, p. 58). By motor, James referred to those who "make use in memory, reasoning and all their intellectual operations, of images derived from movement" (i. e.; kinesthetic) (p. 61).

So it is in the studies reported in this chapter. In spite of the diversity in samples of children studied—their source, their ages, and intelligence, and the presence of cultural or neurological complications—the diversity in tests to which these samples were subjected, the diversity of professional bias, and the diversity of methodology, there appears to be a general consensus in the heterogenous range of subgroup patterns. Many children with reading disorders appear to have difficulty in the "language" functions of the central nervous system, with lower verbal scores than performance scores on the WISC-R; poor performance on the PPVT; disorders of naming, auditory comprehension, imitative speech, and sound discrimination; difficulty in putting sounds together to make words; and problems with the sequential processing abilities. These language dysfunctions may be general or "global" or they may involve very specific functions such as "naming." This group, the language impaired, appears to represent the largest group in terms of numbers of children impaired. Some children with learning disorders, however, are deficient in visual-spatial-graphomotor skills and in the orientation of the body image in space, but they have intact auditory-sequential-perceptual areas. Many have mixed skills and defects, both in the "language" functions and in the visuospatial body image areas. Where intact samples, selected only for their symptom of poor reading achievement, are tested, additional subgroups—namely an "unexpected" group and one representing borderline cognitive abilities—are found. The unanimity of findings in subgroup studies is more apparent than their diversity. As Kavale and Forness (1987) stated, however, "statistical methods alone cannot deal with the subtle tasks and nuances of subtype research" (p. 379) and "it is quite possible that clinical-inferential classification might possess more heuristic value for particular outcomes [i. e., treatment] than numerical techniques" (p. 38).

Is it possible to generalize, to find some unifying characteristics that will tie the subgroup findings together? Simply by examining the neuropsychological tests used in subgroup studies, one is impressed that they appear to be related to sequencing in the auditory and visual areas, to spatial orientation in the visual field, and to orientation of the body in space. Spreen (1978a) stated that "Full sensory and motor integration is a *sine qua non* for reading and writing. Temporal sequencing is an essential component of such integration, not an independent ability, since, in its relationship to the reading and writing process, temporal discrimination and temporal as well as spatial sequences are demanded if intersensory integration operates well" (p. 188). Benton and Pearl (1978) called this the "parietal" theory of dyslexia. Some evidence of this unifying concept may be found, however. Bakker (1972) and Senf (1973) found that retarded readers had difficulty remembering the temporal sequence of digits or figures, Young and Rourke (1975) found that younger poor readers made more errors than younger good readers on auditory and visual sequencing tasks. A. A. Silver and Hagin (1981) using the hypothesis that in younger children 5, 6 and 7 years old, immaturity in the functions of spatial orientation and/or temporal organization characterized the child who will later have a learning disorder, developed a test that predicts the child who will later fail on reading, writing, spelling, or arithmetic. A. A. Silver and Hagin stated that the functions of spatial orientation and temporal organization are basic to academic learning and that such skills serve as a foundation to learning. This theory does not state that the *cause* of learning disorders is immaturity in spatial orientation or temporal organization, but that whatever *is* the cause—be it genetic, traumatic, hypoxic, "developmental," or environmental—is reflected in a deficit in these functions. Thus the etiological factor may act on the central nervous system subsuming those functions or may act on a more fundamental property, such as interference with hemisphere specialization, to evoke those functional deficits. Spatial orientation and temporal organization may be used as a target variable to identify potential learning problems.

Rourke (1978), however, criticized the concept of temporal sequencing. While he agreed that retarded readers as a group exhibit deficiencies in temporal sequencing and serial positioning, he said that there are marked individual differences among normal and retarded readers on those variables, "which renders the interpretation of those results rather tenuous"(p. 153). That there are individual differences, of course, is not surprising and does not, in our mind, negate the hypothesis.

The whole subgroup literature dramatizes the different neuropsychological patterns of individual children. All varieties of combinations of problems in spatial orientation and/or temporal orientation may be found. More important is the criticism that a number of processes other than temporal sequencing (i. e., short-term memory) interact in unspecified ways in experimental testing to make interpretation difficult. Proponents of the spatial-sequencing hypothesis, however, may reply that sequencing is necessary for short-term memory.

A unifying principal, however, not only offers clues to understanding the beginning reading process, but it may also be used to guide effective educational intervention. It may be used to detect children in their kindergarten year with immaturities in these functions, from that predict their future fate in academic achievement, and then modify that fate with appropriate intervention before failure occurs.

PROGNOSTIC IMPLICATIONS OF SUBGROUP CLASSIFICATIONS AND CLINICAL DIAGNOSIS

As we might imagine, for any individual child with a learning disorder, the outcome in terms of persistence of linguistic and perceptual deficits and in academic, social, vocational, and psychological adjustment will vary with many factors: the causes, extent, and severity of the learning disorder; the presence of complicating attentional deficits, hyperactivity, and neurological signs; the cognitive substrate with which the child comes into the world; the psychological defenses the child has established; and, most important, the adequacy and appropriateness of the environmental and educational support he or she has received. With this complex interplay of forces, it is not surprising that long-term reviews of outcomes of children with learning disorders are varied in results. Schonhaut and Satz (1983), reviewing the follow-up studies of children with "learning disabilities," describe 4 studies reporting favorable outcomes, 12 with unfavorable outcomes, and 2 with mixed outcomes. Many variables influence outcome, but few studies attempt to evaluate all these variables. For example, in one favorable report, Rawson (1968) studied only occupational and educational outcomes. Her sample, however, was drawn from a private school with high socioeconomic level, with a mean IQ (Stanford-Binet) of 130, and with every educational support given. Satz, Taylor, Friel, and Fletcher (1978), on the other hand, studied the entire white male populations ($N = 426$) of a public school system in rural Florida in which IQ scores were not specified and educational approaches were not mentioned. In their sample, they found that of 49 boys who were severely retarded readers at the end of second grade, only 6% were rated as average or above average readers by the end of fifth grade. Of 62 mildly retarded readers at the end of second grade, only 17% were rated as average or above average by the end of fifth grade. Thus with two different samples from different socioeconomic and IQ levels and presumably with different educational intervention, these studies come to completely different conclusions.

Spreen followed children from the neuropsychology clinic of the University of Victoria, for 10 and for 15 years (Sarazin & Spreen, 1986; Spreen & Haaf, 1986). In a 10-year follow-up Spreen (1988) found that "in most aspects of educational, occupational, social and psychological adjustment, the outcome of learning disabled children was worse than that of a control group." Moreover, children with neurological signs had a poorer prognosis than those without them. It was noted that, with few exceptions, children from public schools and from clinics tended to have poor academic achievement on follow-up, while children in the higher socioeconomic groups, who had the benefit of excellent educational support, tended to have greater occupational and academic success.

Spreen (1988) and Haaf and Spreen (1986) followed these children for approximately 15 years. The adult group, now with a mean age of 24 years, 1 month, consisted of 82% of the original children. In addition, 27 new children from the original referral pool were added for a total of 170 subjects. The new test battery was comprised of tests of word fluency, right–left orientation, shortened Halstead Category Test, a Paired Associative Learning Test, Purdue-Pegboard Scores, reading comprehension subtest of the Peabody Individual Achievement Test (PIAT), scores of reading, spelling and arithmetic subtests of the WRAT, and scaled scores for Similarities, Vocabulary, Digit Symbol, Block Design, and Arithmetic subtests of the Wechsler Adult Intelligence Scale-Revised (WAIS-R). Hierarchical grouping analysis revealed more discrete clusters, which tended to resemble some of the types found at age 8 through 12 except that a primary linguistic type of impairment appeared to be absent in the adult group. Haaf and Spreen (1986) concluded that tracing individual subjects from childhood to adult clusters seems to suggest that learning disabled children who display a visuo-spatial defect maintain the impairment over their age span and that reading and arithmetic problems persist into adulthood. Where linguistic impairment was found in adults, it appeared in overall low-performance clusters. In adults, too, the most impaired subgroup had no subjects without neurological impairment. It appeared that in adults a relationship is found between degree of neurological impairment and the severity of the clustering results. Spreen (1988) stated that "the group with neurological hard signs showed poorer outcomes than the group with soft signs, with the best outcomes shown by those without neurological signs. Neurological signs at referral age were still present at age 25 and in fact increased to some degree" (p. 840).

The results are in accord with previous longitudinal studies, tracing the stability of perceptual dysfunction into adult years. A. A. Silver and Hagin (1964), in a 12-year follow-up of children with "learning disability" originally seen at Bellevue Hospital's Mental Hygiene Clinic in 1950 at ages 8 through 12 and reexamined 12 years later at ages 20 through 24, found that, in spite of maturity in some areas (right–left orientation and visual-motor function), telltale evidence of visual motor defects, figure–background problems in both visual and tactile areas, and finger-gnosis difficulty persist into adulthood. When subjects with and without neurological signs in childhood are compared, their perceptual defects are not markedly different in childhood, but a change becomes apparent as they emerge into adulthood. The "neurological group" retains its perceptual defects, whereas those without neurological signs partially recover. Seventy-eight percent of inadequate readers in adulthood tend to come from the "neurological group." A. A. Silver and Hagin concluded that "reading disability is a long term problem in the life of the individual, the results of which may be seen even in adulthood" (p. 102). Dykman, Peters, and Ackerman (1973) and Kleinpeter and Goellnitz (1976) found that children with "brain-damage" have educational outcomes poorer than those of the general population of learning disabled. Ackerman, Dykman, and Peters (1977) followed 82 learning disabled boys and 34 normal achievers (controls) for approximately 4 years to age 14. The 62 learning disabled children from whom follow-up data could be obtained remained, "as a group, seriously retarded on the Gray Oral Reading Test and on the spelling and arithmetic subtest of the WRAT" (p. 296). Fifteen percent of the learning disabled boys did overcome previously documented "basic skills" deficits, and all made some progress, but controls continued at great advantage. All but nine of the learning disabled group had no formal extra help with basic skills: 10 boys had been in full-day remediation programs: 24 had been in a resource room; and 16 received intermittent tutoring. Gottesman, Belmont, and Kaminer (1975) reported that their sample was more retarded in reading at follow-up than at initial evaluation; their sample, however, came from a city hospital clinic with a predominance of poor, hispanic families.

A longitudinal component is included in the Colorado Family Reading Study. Seventy children with a reading disability (reading achievement level of at least one-half grade below expectancy, aged 7 years, 5 months to 12, IQ 90 or above, no known emotional or neurological problems, no uncorrected visual or auditory defects) were matched with 75 controls on the basis of age, gender, grade in school, and home environment and were tested on two occasions over an average interval of 4.2 years. A smaller sample (35 reading disabled, 22 controls) were tested on three occasions over 8 years, 6 months. While extensive psychometric data were obtained, the study so far (De Fries, 1985) has evaluated composite measures of reading performance and symbol processing speed on the follow-up testing. The measures of reading performance included the PIAT in reading recognition, reading comprehension, and spelling; the symbol processing measures included the WISC, Coding subtest Form B, and the Colorado Perceptual Speed Test, rotatable letters and numbers. The *rates* of change were the same in the reading disabled and the control groups over time, but the scores differed "substantially" in the follow-up testing—the reading disabled group was just as far behind after 8 years, 6 months as they were at initial testing. The difference in symbol-processing speed, however, widened, with the reading-disabled group falling farther behind in each test. De Fries and Baker (1983) concluded that "results of the present study clearly demonstrate the persistent nature of reading disability" (p. 161).

In contrast to samples drawn from a clinic population, A. A. Silver and Hagin (1985) reviewed the educational and occupational adjustment of 79 individuals with learning disorders studied and treated in a private practice of psychiatry and psychology. There were 18 girls and 61 boys, all from middle- and upper-income families, all subjected to interdisciplinary diagnosis, and all given the benefit of remedial education. The age of these people when first evaluated ranged from 7 to 17 years, with 46 (more than half) between the ages of 8 and 10. Fifty-six fit the criteria for specific language disability; 19 had "organic signs" and were considered to have a neurological defect; 2 had attention deficit disorders; 1 was cognitively retarded, cause unknown; and 1 was suffering from schizophrenia. The follow-up period ranged from 5 to 24 years, but the greatest number (77%) was reexamined after 10 to 24 years. Thirty-eight of the group completed college; nine went on to graduate school; nine were in college at the time of the follow-up study; six did not complete college. Vocationally, 21 (27%) are in professional or technical occupations (engineers, filmmakers, art historians, attorney, teacher, journalist, psychologist); 23 (29%) are in managerial, clerical, or sales positions; 5 are service workers; 19 are still in school or college and 1 was unemployed. (Two were hospitalized because of emotional problems, one was killed in a boating accident, and no data were obtained on seven.) The result is that 26% of those with organic diagnosis, contrasted with 7% of the SLD group, had poor or marginal outcomes, whereas 14% of the SLD group, in contrast to 5% of the organic group, achieved excellent outcomes.

Thus the generally pessimistic outlook for learning disorders must be tempered by diagnosis, severity, and intelligence and by environmental support, including remedial education and parental understanding. In spite of "adequate" adjustment, however, the neuropsychological problems are tenacious and may persist throughout adolescence and into adulthood. This is particularly true of children who on neurological examination are found to have complicating "organic factors."

In summary, longitudinal studies conclude that children with learning disorders tend to retain their perceptual and cognitive dysfunction into adult life and that children with "neurological signs" are most resistant to neuropsychological maturation and tend to remain inadequate readers as adults. One cannot, therefore, say that children will spontaneously "outgrow" their reading disorder. However, much can be done to intervene to mitigate the impact of the disorder on academic, social, and vocational adjustment.

SUMMARY

The search for subgroups of neuropsychological dysfunction in children with learning disorders has suffered from the perennial problem of disparate samples and from problems of definition, boundaries, and methodology. Univariate studies have identified a "modest association between deviant performance in learning and a wide variety of perceptual, linguistic, sequencing, and intersensory integrating abilities" (Benton, 1978). Multivariate studies have proliferated, with all finding variations on a basic theme of a language defect, graphomotor problems, and visual-spatial-perceptual subgroups. Doehring found that the concept basic to these subgroups is impairment in sequential processing abilities; Petrauskas and Rourke found one group with most difficulty in tests for finger-gnosis and in immediate memory for visual sequences. Satz and Morris described one group with no impairment in their neuropsychological test. A. A. Silver and Hagin found that a unifying concept basic to all subgroup differences is difficulty with spatial orientation and/or temporal organization. Immaturity in these functions may be found in all varieties and combinations of dysgnosas, dyspraxias, and dysphasias, all of which have been described. This concept has theoretical importance in understanding the process of learning to read and practical importance in both educational remediation and prevention of learning disorders. Subgroups obtained with cluster analysis reflect well the subgroups found clinically.

CHAPTER FOUR

Prevalence of Disorders of Learning

Learning disorders cover a multitude of problems and encompass all children who have difficulty in learning, regardless of the cause. With rare exceptions, writing in the field does not make clear distinctions among the types of disorders of learning. Unfortunately many investigators continue to use the simplistic and overworked term minimal brain dysfunction (Schmitt, 1975) as if it were synonymous with learning disability. Even when writers agree on a broader definition of learning disabilities, the decision as to the boundaries of the group may vary, so that estimates of its prevalence in the general population may differ widely. In the Collaborative Perinatal Project, for example, children who earned IQs less than 80 were eliminated (Broman, Nichols, & Kennedy, 1975); Mykelbust and Boshes (1969), however, discarded data from their study for children who earned WISC verbal or performance IQs of less than 90, and Rutter, Tizard, and Whitmore (1970) used an IQ score of 70 to define the upper limit of mental retardation.

Evaluation instruments and methodologies are also not comparable, varying from broad surveys of school policy (Silverman & Metz, 1973), through questionnaires to teachers or parents (R. G. Miller, Palkes, & Stewart, 1973; Wender, 1971), to examinations of individual children from "normal" population samples (Rutter, Graham, & Yule, 1970; A. A. Silver & Hagin, 1972b; Hagin, Beecher, & Silver, 1982). No wonder that prevalence estimates for learning disorders, learning disabilities, and specific language disabilities may range from 2 to 20% of the grade school population in the United States.

This chapter is divided into four sections: (a) incidence estimates by school administrators, (b) estimates based on examination of intact samples, (c) studies focusing on specific symptoms, and (d) reports since passage of P. L. 94-142.

STUDIES FROM EXPERIENCES OF SCHOOL ADMINISTRATORS

Estimates based on responses from principals of 2,000 schools, to a written questionnaire survey conducted by the U. S. Office of Education in 1970, indicate that 1.16 million or almost 2.6% of the 45.102 million pupils in their schools were suffering from a specific learning disability. Slightly more than half of these pupils, or 1.4% of the total school enrollment, were actually receiving "designated forms of specialized instruction." Elementary schools reported a higher incidence of learning disabilities than did secondary schools, and schools located in low-income areas of large cities had higher rates than did those in higher income areas. Rates for secondary schools in low-income areas were nearly three times higher than those in higher income areas and twice as high as estimated rates for all secondary schools (L. A. Silverman & Metz, 1973). The sample of 2,000 schools was representative of 31,000 schools in the United States enrolling 300 or more pupils, stratified according to school level, school location, and school enrollment. The principals were asked to include perceptual handicaps, brain injury, and minimal brain dysfunction in their estimates of specific learning disability but to exclude mental retardation and environmental disadvantage. By 1986/87, approximately 1.914 million children aged 3 to 21, more than 4.8% of the total public school enrollment of 39.837 million, were being served in special education programs for learning disabilities.

In contrast, the report of the Canadian Commission on Emotional and Learning Disorders (1970) placed the estimate of the number of children in Canada believed to need specific diagnostic and remedial help to be between 10 and 16% of the total school-age population, although less than 2% were in special classes. As Gaddes pointed out (1976), "service statistics, since they are largely determined by budgetary restrictions and educational policy, are a minimum estimate (of prevalence) and indicate nothing about the number of neglected needy" (p. 12). The Canadian study also estimated that in Great Britain 14% of school-age children had "special needs," in France 12–14%, and in the United States 10–15%.

A report of the Interdisciplinary Committee on Reading Problems (Hayes & Silver, 1970) included a survey of prevalence as reported by persons responsible for reading instruction in the various state departments of education. The chairman of the task force on prevalence, Sheldon (1970), stated that "comments from educators and the few statistics available, suggest that reading disability is of major concern throughout the United States." Sheldon first quotes Julia Haven, formerly an English and reading specialist, that as a tentative guess 12% of elementary pupils and 22% of secondary pupils have "reading problems" (quoted by Sheldon, 1970, TF4.4).

From replies to a written questionnaire the task force extracted the following summaries:

Iowa: 8% of elementary pupils and 10% of secondary students received special help in reading from Title I-ESEA programs alone

Kentucky: 25% of the children were identified as needing help with reading and language skills; 790 teachers were employed to give remedial or corrective help to 147,899 children

Maryland: 20% disabled readers in the fifth-grade population

Michigan: overall incidence of learning problems was 15% of the enrollment, with the estimate climbing to 20–35% in Detroit, Flint, and Grand Rapids

Minnesota: 7% of the total population in schools representing 39% of 478 school districts of the state (excluding St. Paul, Minneapolis, and Duluth) were considered handicapped; the

	special treatment of these pupils cost $4 million and required the use of 657 full-time and 193 part-time correctional instructors; the state reading consultant, however, estimated that 20–25% of the school population had "learning disabilities"
Montana:	10% of pupils in grades 4 through 6 need help in reading
Nebraska:	5% of the total school population (27,559 children) received special reading help with Title I projects; a full-time staff of 724 and a half-time staff of 393 were required
New York:	The State Board of Regents in New York reported that 30% of the enrollment were having learning problems.
Pennsylvania:	approximately 80% of the programs submitted for funding through Title I-ESEA are reading programs
Texas:	20% of pupils in grades 1 through 12 were in the remedial category; 25% of seventh-grade pupils scored two grades below the expected grade score in reading
Vermont:	13% of all elementary-school children received special care and reading help under Title I-ESEA projects
Washington:	4% (341 teachers assigned to remedial reading instruction in 353 schools)

Studies from the experience of school administrators confirm the importance of learning disorders in their schools, not only in terms of the numbers of children affected but also in terms of the cost in staff resources. Actual estimates of the number of children actually receiving remedial instruction beyond that in their regular classes vary from 1.4 to 20% of the total enrollment. It is clear that the number of children receiving remedial instruction is far less than the estimated prevalence of learning disorders in our schools.

STUDIES FROM SURVEYS OF SPECIFIC POPULATIONS

The Collaborative Perinatal Project (Nichols & Chen, 1981) proposed "to identify children with symptoms of learning difficulties, hyperkinesis and impulsive behavior and/or equivocal neurological signs in a large unselected population, to examine associations among symptoms, and to identify socioeconomic, prenatal, genetic and early developmental factors that are characteristic of affected children" (p. 1). The project was obviously concerned with more than estimates of prevalence. However, because of its broad scope, this project has important implications for questions about the prevalence of learning disorders.

The Collaborative Perinatal Project was a longitudinal study of the relationship between perinatal problems and neurological and cognitive deficits in infancy and early childhood. Data on 53,000 pregnancies were collected in 12 university medical centers. The study encompassed prenatal visits, labor and delivery, and multidisciplinary examinations at stated intervals until the subjects were 7 years of age. Prevalence data generated by this project were based on 29,889 children who were studied at age 7 in the first and second grades. Of the original subject pool, more than 6,000 were eliminated for such reasons as invalid educational tests results because of emotional, sensory, or language factors or because of major neurological abnormalities including mental retardation.

At age 7 the children were studied in four major areas: behavioral, cognitive, academic, and neurological. Behavioral items included assessment of activity levels, impulsivity, attention, emotional lability, withdrawal, and socioemotional immaturity. Cognitive tasks included scores on the Bender Visual Motor Gestalt Test, figure drawing, auditory-vocal association tests from the ITPA, and achievement on the WISC. Academic skills were assessed on the WRAT with expected scores based on regression of achievement on IQ. Neurological examination evaluated soft signs.

Cumulative frequency scores for each cluster studied were drawn and a cut-off point of the lowest 8% of the scores was selected to "define abnormal scores." As Nichols and Chen pointed out, the cut-off point to separate "normal" from "abnormal" is an arbitrary one and prevalence estimates will obviously depend upon the cut-off point used. Nevertheless, using the 8% cut-off point to indicate significant deviation from the population under study, Nichols and Chen found 6.5% of their total population as suffering from "learning disability only," 5.8% from hyperactivity impulsivity only, and 6.2% from neurological signs only. The overlap between clusters was very low, with the percentage of children with learning problems totaling 8.4%. It was also noted that the prevalence of "learning disability only" was twice as high in boys as in girls and one-third higher in black than in white children.

The Isle of Wight study (Rutter, Tizard, & Whitmore, 1970; Yule & Rutter, 1976) also reported prevalence figures based on an intact sample. These studies dealt with a series of surveys carried out in 1964 and 1965 into the education, health, and behavior of all 9- to 12-year-old children living on the Isle of Wight, a British Island in the North Sea. The 2,334 children, comprising all 9- and 10-year-olds in the sample, were screened on two successive days with a battery of group tests involving verbal and nonverbal intelligence, a sentence reading test, an arithmetic test, a form copying test, and a behavior rating scale. In a second stage of the survey, children whose scores fell more than two standard deviations below the mean score of all children of the same age group were examined individually with a short form of the WISC (Similarities and Vocabulary subtests for an estimate of verbal IQ; Block Design and Object Assembly for an estimate on nonverbal IQ) and the Neal Analysis of Reading Ability. The Neal is an oral reading test that measures reading rate, accuracy, and comprehension.

On the basis of group screening tests 318 children were selected as "poor" readers and compared with a group of 160 "normal" readers randomly selected from the 9- and 10-year-old groups. Rutter, Tizard, & Whitmore (1970) distinguished two categories of "poor" readers: children with reading retardation and children with reading backwardness.

Reading retardation was defined as a score on either reading accuracy or reading comprehension that was 28 months or more below the level predicted on the basis of each child's age and short WISC IQ estimate. The 28-month cut-off was arbitrarily selected by the investigators as a level representing considerable handicap in learning. The prediction of estimated reading level was calculated by regression equations derived from data for 147 children from the sample.

Reading backwardness was defined as an attainment in reading accuracy or comprehension on the Neal test that was 28 months or more below the child's chronological age (independent of the child's IQ). These criteria identified 85 (3.7%) of 9- and 10-year-olds as retarded readers and 154 (6.6%) as backward readers. However, 75 of the "backward readers" met the definition of retarded readers as well—i.e., they earned normal intelligence test estimates but were reading 28 months or more below chronological age and predicted reading age. Seventy-five of the 154 backward readers earned low IQ estimates and earned reading scores within the range expected from their IQ estimates.

Thus, in this study the two groups of retarded and backward readers overlapped to some extent. A total of 173 children (7.9%) marks the prevalence of severe educational retardation in the Isle of Wight study. Rutter et al. stated that it was likely that the rate of educational retardation provided a slight underestimate of the real size of the problem. It is unfortunate that these researchers did not validate their statistical findings against actual school performance.

Mykelbust and Boshes (1969) and Mykelbust et al. (1969) provided another prevalence estimate based on a study of an intact group of children in their study of four suburban Illinois school districts. Their estimate was based on a battery of psychoeducational tests given to 2,767 third- and fourth-graders. A learning quotient score of 90 on any part of the screening battery identified 410 children (15.2%) as underachievers. The investigators further divided this group into two parts: "borderline" (those with learning quotients falling in the 85–89 range) and "learning disability" (those with learning quotients of 84 or below).

Surveying the reading performance of 12,000 children in the sixth grade of a large metropolitan area, Eisenberg (1966) found 28% of the total sample to be reading two or more grades below expected grade level on the Stanford Achievement Test. Of the sample, 57% were reading 1 year below expected grade level. In contrast, 6% of the sixth grade of suburban schools were 2 years below and 19% were 1 year below expected grade level. In even more marked contrast, only 1% of children in an independent private school were 1 year below expectancy and no children were 2 years below grade expectancy. Eisenberg cites these statistics not only to indicate the enormity of the problem of reading retardation, but also to point out the excessive burden of reading retardation among inner city schoolchildren.

In a different age group of inner city children, A. A. Silver and Hagin (1980) and Hagin, Beecher, and Silver (1982) examined every child ($N =$ 650) early in the first grade of seven elementary schools on the Lower East Side of Manhattan, New York City. Of these 124 (25%) were found to have learning disorders.

STUDIES FOCUSING ON SPECIFIC SYMPTOMS

In a review of epidemiological studies of the minimal brain dysfunction syndrome, Belmont (1980) listed 12 studies that evaluated prevalence rates of learning disability and hyperactivity. Five of these studies focused on the symptom of hyperkinesis, three on choreoform movement, and four on reading retardation.

The hyperactivity prevalence data were derived essentially from questionnaires compiled by teachers and parents. These studies revealed a prevalence rate ranging from 5 to 10% of the elementary school population, although some (i. e., Satin, Winsberg, Monetti, Sverd, & Foss, 1985; Wender, 1971) suggested an even higher prevalence. Werner (1980) and her associates (Werner, Bierman, & French, 1971; Werner et al., 1968; Werner & Smith, 1977, 1982) provided data on hyperactivity from a prospective study of 750 children on the Island of Kauai in the State of Hawaii. Hyperkinetic symptoms were found in 5.9% of the group. R. G. Miller et al. (1973), using teacher identification and teacher questionnaires, classified 47 children, or 5.5% of 849 children as hyperactive in a sample of third-through sixth-grade children in four elementary schools in suburban St. Louis. Wender (1971) reported on a stratified sample of 20% of the elementary schoolchildren of Montgomery County, Maryland, studied by teacher ratings. Of this sample, 15% of the children in grades 1 through 6 were considered to have problems with restlessness and 22% with attention. Using questionnaires, Huessy and Cohen (1976) found hyperactivity in 10% of second-grade schoolchildren in Vermont. Lambert, Sandoval, and Sassone (1978) found the prevalence of hyperactivity to be 1.9% when parent, school, and physician ratings were in agreement but an additional 3.3% were designated by the school only, for a total of 5.2%. Hagin, Beecher, & Silver (1982) found a prevalence of only 1.2% of hyperactivity and attention deficit disorders based on neuropsychiatric examinations. Although the Satin et al., (1985) study was primarily directed at the usefulness of the Abbreviated

Conners Teacher Rating Scale in identifying hyperactivity, their sample of 92 boys, 6 to 9 years of age, found 22 of their subjects (24%) to be classified as "hyperactive." Thus it seems clear that the prevalence of hyperactivity depends upon the criteria used for its definition and upon the source of the description (i. e., parent, teacher, or physician). In reviewing over 210 studies on hyperactivity conducted over the previous 20 years, Barkley (1982) found that more than 64% of the studies employed no specific criteria for the diagnosis of hyperactivity, relying on the opinion of the authors (cited by Ostrom & Jensen, 1988).

Prechtl and Stemmer (1962) are frequently quoted as providing evidence of the prevalence of the choreoform movement syndrome in 20% of 876 elementary-school boys and approximately 8% of 671 elementary-school girls. These data were not the focus of Prechtl's 1962 paper but are mentioned as an additional study of Stemmer's and are included in a bar graph in the body of the paper, with no information about the demographic characteristics of the samples. The graph indicates that in a special school for learning disabilities 40% of 157 boys and 11% of 58 girls gave evidence of choreoform movements. However, Wolff and Hurwitz (1966) studied 463 boys and 409 girls aged 10 to 12 in 10 elementary schools in Newton, Massachusetts, and found 11.4% with "choreoform twitch." A similar percentage (11.7%) was found in 1,130 boys aged 12 to 15 in two junior high schools in Newton. There was an overall ratio of 3:1 of boys to girls. A similar prevalence (12.0 and 13.7%) was found in boys attending public schools in Japan, but symptoms were significantly more frequent among delinquents, among children with learning disabilities, and among children treated for severe emotional disturbance.

Estimates of the clumsy child syndrome (developmental apraxia and agnostic ataxia) were reported by Gubbay (1975) and Gubbay, Ellis, Walton, and Court (1965). The symptoms reflect the inability to carry out willed, voluntary movement despite intact sensory and motor pathways in the control of that movement and in the understanding that is intended. The primary defect is related to perception or agnosia. In short, even though normal cognitive ability, physical strength, sensation, and coordination are present, skilled purposive movement is impaired. Gubbay reported that developmental clumsiness was recognized by Ingram (1970), Ingram, Mann, and Blackburn, 1970, Orton (1937/1989), Rueben and Bakwin (1968), and Rutter, Tizzard, and Whitmore (1970), but that prevalence can only be estimated to be 5% of the grade-school population

REPORTS SINCE THE PASSAGE OF P. L. 94-142

P. L. 94-142, the Education for All Handicapped Children Act of 1975, might have been expected to bring some semblance of order to the array of estimates and definitions that had characterized the field. Because Congress was reluctant to make a commitment to support the education of children with a handicap for which no consensual definition existed, the Office of Education held extensive hearings on the proposed regulations for identifying learning disabled children. (Federal Register, 1977, p. 42496). Four major steps evolved for the process of operationalizing the definition:

1. Each public agency or school must organize a multidisciplinary team to evaluate the child and/or adolescent, with the team composition mandated to include regular classroom as well as clinical personnel.
2. The team must determine the specific learning disability based on a significant discrepancy between the child's ability and achievement in specific skills areas.
3. The team must observe the pupil in the regular classroom setting.
4. The team must make a group decision and specify evaluation results to justify the decision.

One might have thought that such procedures would have produced data for more realistic estimates of prevalence. This has not been the case. Few reports of incidence have appeared in the professional literature. For example, a review of *Psychscan,* the American Psychological Association's abstracts on learning and communication disorders and mental retardation from 1982 through 1985, did not locate a single paper addressing the question of prevalence. It may be that local school districts are reluctant to deal with such questions because of concerns expressed about the "overidentification" of learning disabled youngsters in the schools. These concerns are primarily financial in origin with government agencies at the federal and local levels expressing alarm at the escalating costs of special education programs organized to serve the growing number of pupils identified as learning disabled.

That the number of youngsters so defined is growing rapidly can be seen from data collected by the U.S. Department of Education's Office of Special Education that appear in the *Ninth Annual Report to Congress on the Implementation of Public Law 94-142.* Table 4-1 displays this information. The total number of learning disabled children served nationwide in educational programs for the handicapped rose from 796,000 to 1.914 million during the 11-year period between the school years 1976/77 and 1986/87, representing an increase of over 100% in the number of children served for this handicap (U.S. Department of Education, 1987).

When these data are examined in terms of the distribution of youngsters served by educational programs for the handicapped, we find that the percentage for learning disability has doubled, rising from 21.5% in 1976/77 to 40.9 in 1982/83 to 43.8% in 1986/87, the 10 years covered by the data.

Table 4-1   Persons 3 to 21 Years Old Served Annually in Educational Programs for the Handicapped by Type of Handicap: 1976/77 to 1986/87

Type of Handicap	Number Served (in Thousands)										
	1976/77	1977/78	1978/79	1979/80	1980/81	1981/82	1982/83	1983/84	1984/85	1985/86	1986/87
All conditions	3,692	3,751	3,889	4,005	4,142	4,198	4,255	4,298	4,315	4,317	4,374
Learning disabled	796	964	1,130	1,276	1,462	1,622	1,741	1,806	1,832	1,862	1,914
Speech impaired	1,302	1,223	1,214	1,186	1,168	1,135	1,131	1,128	1,126	1,125	1,136
Mentally retarded	959	933	901	869	829	786	757	727	694	660	643
Emotionally disturbed	283	288	300	329	346	339	352	361	372	375	383
Hard of hearing and deaf	87	85	85	80	79	75	73	72	69	66	65
Orthopedically handicapped	87	87	70	66	58	58	57	56	56	57	57
Other health impaired	141	135	105	106	98	79	50	53	68	57	52
Visually handicapped	38	35	32	31	31	29	28	29	28	27	26
Multihandicapped	*	*	50	60	68	71	63	65	69	86	97
Deaf-blind	*	*	2	2	3	2	2	2	2	2	2

*Not available

Note. From The Condition of Education (p. 57), by National Center for Education Statistics, 1987. Data calculated from U. S. Department of Education, Office of Special Education and Rehabilitative Services, Ninth Annual Report to Congress on Implementation of Public Law 94-142 and unpublished tabulations. Washington, D.C.: Government Printing Office.

Table 4-2   *Persons 3 to 21 Years Old Served Annually in Educational Programs for the Handicapped by Type of Handicap: 1976/77 to 1986/87*

Type of Handicap	Distribution of Children Served (%)										
	1976/77	1977/78	1978/79	1979/80	1980/81	1981/82	1982/83	1983/84	1984/85	1985/86	1986/87
All conditions	100.0	100.0	100.0	100.0	100.0	100.0	100.0	100.0	100.0	100.0	100.0
Learning disabled	21.6	25.7	29.1	31.9	35.3	38.6	40.9	42.0	42.4	43.1	43.8
Speech impaired	35.3	32.6	31.2	29.6	28.2	27.0	26.6	26.2	26.1	26.1	26.0
Mentally retarded	26.0	24.9	23.2	21.7	20.0	18.7	17.8	16.9	16.1	15.3	14.7
Emotionally disturbed	7.7	7.7	7.7	8.2	8.4	8.1	8.3	8.4	8.6	8.7	8.8
Hard of hearing and deaf	2.4	2.3	2.2	2.0	1.9	1.8	1.7	1.7	1.6	1.5	1.5
Orthopedically handicapped	2.4	2.3	1.8	1.6	1.4	1.4	1.3	1.3	1.3	1.3	1.3
Other health impaired	3.8	3.6	2.7	2.6	2.4	1.9	1.2	1.2	1.6	1.3	1.2
Visually handicapped	1.0	0.9	0.8	0.8	0.8	0.7	0.7	0.7	0.7	0.6	0.6
Multihandicapped	*	*	1.3	1.5	1.6	1.7	1.5	1.5	1.6	2.0	2.2
Deaf-blind	*	*	0.1	(2)	0.1	(2)	(2)	0.1	(2)	(2)	(2)

*Not available

Note. From *The Condition of Education* (p. 57), by National Center for Education Statistics, 1987. Data calculated from U. S. Department of Education, Office of Special Education and Rehabilitative Services, *Ninth Annual Report to Congress on Implementation of Public Law 94-142* and unpublished tabulations. Washington, D.C.: Government Printing Office.

Table 4-3 *Persons 3 to 21 Years Old Served Annually in Educational Programs for the Handicapped by Type of Handicap: 1976/77 to 1986/87*

Type of Handicap	Number Served as a Percentage of Total Enrollment										
	1976/77	1977/78	1978/79	1979/80	1980/81	1981/82	1982/83	1983/84	1984/85	1985/86	1986/87
All conditions	8.33	8.61	9.14	9.62	10.11	10.46	10.73	10.92	10.98	10.93	10.97
Learning disabled	1.80	2.21	2.66	3.06	3.57	4.04	4.39	4.59	4.66	4.71	4.80
Speech impaired	2.94	2.81	2.85	2.85	2.85	2.83	2.85	2.87	2.87	2.85	2.85
Mentally retarded	2.16	2.14	2.12	2.09	2.02	1.96	1.91	1.85	1.77	1.67	1.61
Emotionally disturbed	0.64	0.66	0.71	0.79	0.85	0.85	0.89	0.92	0.95	0.95	0.96
Hard of hearing and deaf	0.20	0.20	0.20	0.19	0.19	0.19	0.18	0.18	0.17	0.17	0.16
Orthopedically handicapped	0.20	0.20	0.16	0.16	0.14	0.14	0.14	0.14	0.14	0.14	0.14
Other health impaired	0.32	0.31	0.25	0.25	0.24	0.20	0.13	0.13	0.17	0.14	0.13
Visually handicapped	0.9	0.08	0.08	0.08	0.08	0.07	0.07	0.07	0.07	0.07	0.07
Multihandicapped	*	*	0.14	0.14	0.17	0.18	0.16	0.17	0.17	0.22	0.24
Deaf-blind	*	*	0.01	0.01	0.01	(4)	0.01	0.01	(4)	0.01	(4)

*Not available

Note. From *The Condition of Education* (p. 57), by National Center for Education Statistics, 1987. Data calculated from U. S. Department of Education, Office of Special Education and Rehabilitative Services, *Ninth Annual Report to Congress on Implementation of Public Law 94-142* and unpublished tabulations. Washington, D.C.: Government Printing Office.

In comparison, services for emotional disturbance rose 24% during the same period and services to children with all other handicapping conditions declined. Of the total enrollment in the schools during 1986/87, 4.8% of the students were receiving special education services for learning disabilities. Tables 4-2 and 4-3 show the yearly trends in services to the learning disabled in contrast to services provided to children with other handicapping conditions.

These data confuse and confound educators, parents, government officials, and tax payers—in short anyone interested in providing the best education possible for schoolchildren. Is this indeed evidence of "overidentification" resulting from the subjective decision-making process by the teams mandated by P. L. 94-142? Does it indicate a lack of consensus among the members of these teams, representing as they do, a variety of professional disciplines? Does it indicate a new and undefined field of service (although obviously one cannot say that the field of learning disabilities lacks definitions!)? Does it indicate, as some iconoclasts have implied, that there really is no such entity as learning disability and that it is just a by-product of poor teaching and lazy, maladjusted pupils? Or is the rapid growth in services the result of efforts to provide services to youngsters whose needs have been virtually neglected by special education programs until the passage of P. L. 94-142? Answers to these and other questions relating to the prevalence of learning disorders await resolution. Such resolution will be more likely to occur:

- if people in the field—educators, clinicians, and researchers—arrive at some consensus on simple, uncomplicated ways of defining learning disorders
- if well-designed epidemiological research is conducted with population samples to obtain clear data on prevalence, so that program planning for learning disorders can be based on the educational needs of the learners, rather than on the amount of money available from local, state, and federal governments
- if all people working in the field understand and appreciate the heterogeneity represented by this handicapping condition and provide for this variation in any program of assessment, intervention, or research for youngsters with learning disorders

SUMMARY

Prevalence estimates of learning disorders in the public schools of the United States range between 5 and 30% of the total elementary-school population; the majority of reports of school administrators estimate prevalence to range from 10 to 15%. The prevalence of "reading retardation" in specific samples also averages about 12%. The symptom of hyperactivity is variously reported as being found in from 1.2% of inner city first graders to 20% of the elementary-school children of Montgomery County, Maryland. The choreoform syndrome is reported to be 2% of the school-age population. Although it is clear that prevalence estimates depend upon the definition of the syndrome, its boundaries, the instruments used for evaluation, and the methodology of the study, it is also clear that the total number of children nationwide in programs for the learning disabled, rose from 796,000 in 1976/77, to 1.741 million in 1982/83, to 1.914 million in 1987 and that approximately 4.8% of all elementary-school children were receiving special education for "learning disabilities." Learning disorders thus are a problem of great magnitude and importance.

PART TWO

PRINCIPLES OF MANAGEMENT

CHAPTER FIVE

Principles of Educational and Psychological Diagnosis

Effective intervention is based on a clear understanding of the factors that contribute to a learning disorder. The process by which this understanding is obtained is sometimes described as **assessment** or **evaluation;** we have chosen to use the term **diagnosis** because it is more appropriate to the multiaxial character of our approach.

Diagnosis is necessary because the constellation of contributing factors may differ for individual children, not only in terms of the mix of the specific factors involved but also in terms of compensations and supports available. In short, we believe that each child is unique within the population of children with learning disorders and that effective provision for the remediation of these disorders is more likely to occur when intervention is based on careful definition of the child's strengths and needs. We also believe that the complex nature of learning disorders implies that diagnostic processes will be broad based, because no single discipline can provide all the skills necessary for comprehensive diagnosis.

Among the various disciplines concerned with children with learning disorders, the term diagnosis has come to have varied meanings. Among reading specialists, for example, diagnosis implies an analysis of the child's educational skills—i. e., the manner in which a child deals with written text, the errors children make in word attack, the comprehension of written symbols, and their understanding of language. For such a survey educators may use conventional achievement tests, individual diagnostic tests of educational achievement, informal reading inventories, and other curriculum-based approaches to assessment. They may observe the child at work in classroom group activities, teach trial lessons to assess responses to various interventions, and assemble information on educational history from school records and interviews with parents and teacher.

School psychologists assess cognitive functioning quantitatively and qualitatively, analyze the extent to which academic achievement is appropriate to estimates of cognitive functioning, and study motivation, learning style, and defensive operations. They may also collect data on children's development and current school achievement and adjustment through interviews with parents and teachers and through observation of the children themselves.

Neuropsychologists view diagnosis in terms of a series of tests designed to elucidate brain–behavior relationships. Such tests tap the peripheral manifestations of brain functioning, such as visual, auditory, tactile, and kinesthetic perception; motor and psychomotor control; and language and conceptual abilities. From the results of these measures, neuropsychologists make inferences about the intactness of brain processes and the localization of brain pathology.

Neuropsychiatrists use the classical neurological examination, as well as the soft signs of neurological dysfunction to assess the integrity and maturation of the central nervous system. They study intrapsychic signs and symptoms through interviews and observation of parent–child interactions. These findings are viewed within the total body of medical knowledge to determine whether the findings relate to known groups that make up disease entities or specific syndromes, to understand the idiosyncratic way in which the disorder emerges in the individual child, to determine treatment modalities that have been helpful for the specific condition, and to predict the outlook for the child under study.

While each of these disciplines attempts to "diagnose" learning disorders within its own frame of reference and through its own unique skills, comprehensive diagnosis depends on the integration of these findings to answer specific questions about a specific child. What questions, then, should diagnosis answer for the child with a learning disorder? To some extent this question can be answered by considering the purposes for which diagnosis is done.

We view the purposes of diagnosis of learning disorders as an attempt (a) to determine the cause or causes of the disorder in an individual child, (b) to delineate the specific abilities and disabilities of the child and his or her environment as they relate to learning, (c) to guide the intervention processes, (d) to provide some idea of the prognosis, and (e) to set time lines for reevaluation. In the final analysis, diagnostic formulations that cover these points will serve the child well.

While comprehensive diagnostic data, well integrated in terms of intervention planning, are considered essential, practical considerations raise the question whether all aspects of diagnostic study can or should be provided to every child who experiences learning problems. In the light of consequences of the assessment procedures that have been mandated as part of the implementation of P. L. 94-142 (Algozzine & Ysseldyke, 1986; Cruickshank, 1986; J. J. Gallagher, 1986) this question requires serious consideration. Furthermore, from a practical standpoint, all aspects of a multidisciplinary examination may not be available in all the settings to which children with learning problems come for services.

Given that all of the multidisciplinary services may not be either necessary or available in the cases of specific children, the question becomes one of defining the specific diagnostic services that are necessary for the appropriate education of these children. This does not imply support for the extreme position that would eliminate all diagnosis as unnecessary. For example, the applied behavior analysis approach regards diagnosis as irrelevant to treatment and operates as though all learning failure results from the lack of properly reinforced practice or from learning inappropriate responses to instructional stimuli (Koorland, 1986). Wholesale acceptance of this approach would impoverish the field of learning disorders. Information secured in diagnostic study is not only important in understanding, planning, and intervening with individual children but also, as part of an accumulating data base, it can enrich theoretical knowledge of the nature and variety of learning disorders.

Too little diagnostic information can also have unfortunate results for both individual children and for the overall intervention program. For example, the decision to ignore cognitive differences among children and to offer remedial services to all children whose educational achievement scores fall below a given level can result in disservice to children at both ends of the distribution. Bright children who are "getting by" with low or average achievement may fail to be recognized and served; children with limited academic potential may be deprived of appropraite curricular provisions and classified instead as "learning disabled."

The field of learning disorders is faced with a dilemma, that of preserving the benefits diagnostic data provide while at the same time avoiding cumbersome and redundant assessment processes. The enactment of P. L. 94-142, particularly the sections dealing with the individualized educational program (IEP) and with procedural safeguards, has had a strong influence on assessment procedures. Implementation of the law at the state and local levels must deal with the diagnostic dilemma with a variety of prereferral, referral, and service delivery regulations. The resulting organizational and management procedures are discussed in Chapter 7, "Principles of Educational Remediation." This chapter, with its emphasis on diagnosis of the individual with a learning disorder, focuses on the step-wise process we have proposed (see Figure 2-1), which secures only that diagnostic information necessary to answer a single question at each of the points in the decision making process. As seen in Figure 2-1, there are five steps in the decision making process: the evaluation of educational achievement, a determination of educational opportunity, the adequacy of sensory acuity, the level of cognitive function, and the neuropsychological-neuropsychiatric status. This chapter and the next show how each of the steps in this decision making model is implemented in the diagnosis of learning disorders of individual children.

ADEQUACY OF EDUCATIONAL ACHIEVEMENT

At the first decision point the question to be answered is whether a learning disorder is present. Answering this question calls into play two data sources: historical information and educational assessment.

Assuming that the usual referral sources of teachers and parents have drawn attention to the child's learning difficulties, much of the historical information would be elicited in interviews with the parents and teachers involved. The teacher would provide concrete information about the child's learning progress in the classroom, drawing upon work samples, classroom anecdotes, grades, results of unit evaluations, and possibly group achievement test scores.

Descriptions of special abilities demonstrated in both academic and non-academic areas would also be valuable, as would objective reports of characteristic behavior patterns, particularly in relation to motivation, attendance, reactions to stress, adjustment to school rules, and interpersonal relationships.

Parents are able to provide information about the child's language development and educational history, including opportunities for informal and formal educational experiences. They also can provide anecdotal information about the child's responses to classroom instruction and school assignments. Information about patterns of language development in the family can also be elicited in parent interviews. Vogler, De Fries, and Decker (1984) have confirmed in research what clinicians have suspected: The presence of a learning disorder in either parent increases the possibility of the existence of a learning disorder in their children (see also Chapter 11, "Specific Language Disability," for data on genetic factors).

The first decision point also requires data on current academic skills. A variety of formal and informal methods for collecting data on school achievement are available. The selection of specific techniques would depend largely upon the level of training and personal preferences of the educator administering the measures. For example, some educators prefer to use informal reading inventories, consisting of selections from the curricular materials actually in use in the child's classroom. These informal inventories have the advantage of drawing on the content close to that the child has encountered in schooling. However, the proximity of the assessment practices may be outweighed by questions about the representativeness of the content sampled, as well by the fact that the validity and reliability of the measures may be unknown (Klesius & Homan 1985; Lerner, 1988).

The psychometric characteristics of the formal measures of achievement are usually more readily available, either in the technical manuals of the tests or in such publications as the *Eighth Mental Measurements Yearbook* (Buros, 1978), *Ninth Mental Measurements Yearbook* (J. V. Mitchell, 1985), and publications of the Test Corporation of America (Keyser & Sweetland, 1985). Although there are a wide number of achievement batteries in print, the educator would do well to base selection of testing instruments on careful assessment of the psychometric characteristics as described in the technical manuals and critiques. The following guidelines should be considered in test selections:

1. How recently was this test standardized?
2. What is the underlying rationale for the instrument?

3. How closely does the test content relate to the curriculum of the child's classroom?

4. What methods were used to ensure the representativeness of test items in terms of the domain being assessed?

5. How adequate was the sample on which the test was standardized?

6. Is the standardization sample representative of the child to whom the test will be administered?

7. What evidences of homogeneity of test content are presented in the test manual or critiques?

8. What evidences of reliability—consistency of measurement—are presented?

9. What evidences of validity—construct-related, content-related, criterion-related, or predictive—are presented?

10. What units of measurement are used to express scores? Are these units of measurement defensible statistically and useful in practice?

Other considerations that may guide selection are the expertise required on the part of the examiner, the time requirements for administration, and the test format, (group versus individual administration). Table 5-1 presents summaries of the psychometric characteristics of the most commonly used individual achievement tests.

Irrespective of the educator's choice of assessment instruments, the significant aspect at this decision point is the interpretation of results to determine whether the child's educational achievement is adequate. This question cannot be answered by numerical test scores alone but requires a formulation of the process by which the child handles the specific educational task. There are three major areas of such assessment—reading, spelling and written language, and mathematics—which are discussed in the next sections.

Assessment of Reading Achievement

Reading is a complex process that must be analyzed according to component skills in order to understand learning difficulties. One way to analyze the reading process is through the Job Analysis of Reading (Table 5-2), which describes four main areas in which children must learn to function effectively if they are to read well: prereading skills, word attack, comprehension, and study skills.

- *Prereading Skills*—This area includes such visual perceptual skills as the discrimination of likenesses and differences of letters, the recognition of these symbols in their correct orientation in two-dimensional space, and the organization of these symbols into groups as syllables or words.

Table 5-1 Individual Tests of Reading

Test (Standardization Dates)	Adequacy of Manual	Standardization Samples	Skills Tested	Grades	Evidence of Reliability	Evidence of Validity				Particular Strengths
						Construct-Related	Content-Related	Criterion-Related	
Assessing Reading Difficulties: A Diagnostic and Remedial Approach (Bradley, L.)	Inadequate	400 5-year-olds	Auditory discrimination	Beginning readers	None	Descriptive information	None	None provided	Practice items
Basic Achievement Skills Individual Screener (BASIS) (1983) (Psychological Corporation)	Adequate	n = 3296 (grades 1 through post-high school) National sample based on 1970 census	Mathematics, reading, spelling, writing optional	1–12+	Test-retest: reading .80–.95 mathematics .74–.82	Point bi-serial correlations of test items with grade placements	Matched to textbooks in skill areas	Comparisons with Metropolitan Achievement, Wide Range, and Degrees of Reading Power tests	Sound technical quality; efforts to eliminate bias due to handicap, race, sex, language
Boder Test of Reading Spelling Patterns (1982) (Boder, E. & Jarrico, S.)	Adequate for experienced clinicians	Clinical sample of 30–54 subjects	Screening for subtypes (dysphonetic, dyseidetic, mixed) of reading disability	K–12	Test-retest reliability for reading level, phonetic equivalents, and subtype classification	"soft" clinical data	None	None	Qualitative analysis of reading/spelling and phonic analysis/sight word recognition
Brigance Diagnostic Inventory of Basic Skills (1976) (Brigance, A. H.)	Inadequate	Not described in manual	Readiness, reading, language arts, mathematics	K–6	None	None	"judgment of 66 teachers and other curriculum personnel"	None	Format is useful for informal assessments

(continued)

Table 5-1 *Individual Tests of Reading (continued)*

Test (Standardization Dates)	Adequacy of Manual	Standardization Samples	Skills Tested	Grades	Evidence of Reliability	Evidence of Validity			Particular Strengths
						Construct-Related	Content-Related	Criterion-Related	
Durrell Analysis of Reading Difficulty (1937, 1980) (Durrell, D. & Catterson, J. H.)	Adequate	200 children per grade in grades 1–6 in five geographic regions of U. S.	Oral and silent reading, listening comprehension and vocabulary, word analysis, phonic skills, spelling, visual memory, knowledge of letters	1–6	$KR_{21} = $ .63–.97	None except the test's longevity	Judgment of professors of reading; literature review	Correlations with Metropolitan Reading Tests	Comprehensive assessment of many aspects of reading process
Gates-McKillop-Horowitz (1962, 1981) Reading Diagnostic Test (Gates, A. I., McKillop, A. S., & Horowitz, E. C.)	Adequate	600 children in grades 1–6; ethnic and residential stratification	Oral reading analysis, word attack, letter naming, phonics skills, auditory blending and discrimination, spelling	1–6	Test-retest of oral reading r = .94 (n = 27)	Intercorrelations of subtests *not* given; none except test's longevity	None	Oral reading score with standardized group tests r = .68–.96	Comprehensive assessment of many aspects of reading process
Peabody Individual Achievement Test (1970) (Dunn, L. M. & Markwardt, F. C.)	Adequate	Stratified, random sample (N = 2,889); approximately 200 at each grade level.	Mathematics, reading recognition and comprehension, spelling, general information	K–12	Test-retest r = .89–.64	Intercorrelations of subtests are provided	Item pool based on current textbooks	Concurrent validity with PVr = .42–.69 with WRAT Arithmetic .58 Reading .95 Spelling .85	Well-developed, wide-scale screening measure of achievement

Test		Sample	Skills	Grade/Age	Reliability		Items	Validity	Comments
Prescriptive Reading Performance Test (1978) (Fundala, J. B.)	Adequate	Considered to be representative	Phonic word attack and sight word recognition of graded word lists	1–12 and adult	Sperman-Brown corrected Split half r = .98; test-retest = .97	None	Word lists developed from graded reading materials	Correlation with Slosson, WRAT, Spache 7 r = .65–.94	Analysis of sight/phonic skills help examiner to place level for testing comprehension
Roswell-Chall Diagnostic Reading Test of Word Analysis Skills (1956, 1978) (Roswell, F. G. & Chall, J. S.)	Adequate	First to fourth graders (n = 203), clinic sample (n = 46) grades 2–10	Word reading, decoding, letter naming, writing from dictation	1–4	Alternate form r = .95–.99 test-retest r = .79–.90	None	Words drawn from Harris-Jacobson list	Correlations with Metropolitan and Gray Oral Rading Test r = .66–.84	Assesses component skills for word attack
Wide Range Achievement Test (1940, 1984) (Jastak, J. & Jastak, S.)	Adequate	5,600 individuals, 200 in each of 28 age groups from 5 to 75 years, geographic, sex, ethnic, metro/nonmetro balance according to 1982 Rand McNally Commercial Atlas	Oral reading, spelling, arithmetic	Ages 5–75	test-retest r = .79–.97	Rasch model used to verify range of items; increasing raw scores with age	"Apparent" according to manual	r's with other achievement tests reported .60–.80	Attempts to measure the codes needed to learn basic skills, avoids the effects of comprehension

(continued)

Table 5-1 Individual Tests of Reading (continued)

Test (Standardization Dates)	Adequacy of Manual	Standardization Samples	Skills Tested	Grades	Evidence of Reliability	Construct-Related	Content-Related	Criterion-Related	Particular Strengths
						Evidence of Validity			
Woodcock-Johnson Psychoeducational Battery Achievement Tests (1977–78) (Woodcock, R. B. & Johnson, M. B.)	Adequate	Approximately 5,000 subjects balanced for sex, race, region, urbanization by 1970 census	Oral reading, word attack, reading comprehension, computation and applied problems; dictation, proofing	K–12	$r = .92–.96$ for achievement cluster scores	Cluster analyses	Items were developed in consultation with expert judges; "spiraling principles" used to sample subareas on a cyclical basis	Correlations with WRAT and PIAT r = .70–.90	Part of a comprehensive battery of technically strong tests
Woodcock Reading Mastery Test—Revised (1987) (Woodcock, R. B.)	Adequate	Stratified sample controlled for region, sex, race, educational level, and (for adults) occupational status as represented in the 1980 census: K–12 sample (n = 4,201), college sample (n = 1,023), adult sample (n = 865)	Readiness, word identification, word attack, vocabulary passage comprehension	K–16 and adult	both internal consistency estimates and split-half coefficients are reported	Intercorrelations of subtests and clusters are reported	Contributions from outside experts in early stages of item selection and Rasch model in later stages of item selection	Concurrent validity with Woodcock-Johnson r = .60–.91; with Iowa Test of Basic Skill r = .78–83 PIAT r = .78–87 WRAT r = .86+.92	Manual provides excellent guidance for scoring

Table 5-2   Job Analysis of Reading

Prereading Skills	Word Atack Skills	Comprehension Skills	Study Skills
Visual:			
Discriminating	Sight words	Oral vocabulary	Locating
Chunking	Language cues	Literal comprehension	Selecting
Perceiving relationships	Picture cues	Interpretation	Organizing
Auditory:			
Discriminating	Context cues	Apreciation	Retaining
Sequencing	Phonics		
Blending	Word structure		
Laterality:			
Orientating symbols			
Using left-to-right progression			

Reading also requires auditory skills such as the discrimination and matching of sounds, the blending of isolated sounds so that a recognizable word results, and the accurate temporal sequencing of sounds in words and words in sentences. To read English, children must also accept the arbitrary convention of left-to-right progression. They must learn to separate figure from background and to focus on the figure, attending to words or parts of words on a line and ignoring the surrounding words, and making an accurate return sweep to the succeeding line when the end of a line is reached.

- *Word Attack*—This area involves the versatile use of a number of processes to decode words. Some words may be recognized visually on the basis of signal cues, such as letter combinations, downstrokes, and tall letters. Other words may be identified by the use of context cues, such as guessing what makes sense in terms of the ideas in the content and the grammatical conventions of the language. Children will also begin to use phonic cues, either by drawing their own conclusions about the letter–sound correspondences or by applying rules that have been taught for phonics generalizations. As word attack skills develop, children learn to use word structure cues to unlock new words. In English, word attack principles must always be qualified by a number of exceptions, so that the child must use all of these skills with what Gibson (1969) has termed "a set for diversity."

- *Comprehension*—Basic to getting meanings in reading is the development of a rich oral vocabulary. Reading requires children to select from the range of multiple definitions the exact meaning implicit in the content they are reading. Understandings may range from literal comprehension of factual content to inferential reasoning and appreciation of the abstract aspects of the content.

- *Study Skills*—This is the area in which reading becomes a tool for acquiring information. These skills enable children to locate and retrieve elements within a sequence. They learn to select relevant content and to organize for retention and application that content which is appropriate to the purposes for reading.

Below is an example of how the Job Analysis of Reading can be used to integrate the results for Michael, a 17-year-old tenth-grader.

CASE STUDY: MICHAEL

Michael earned a score at grade 6.8 (21st percentile) on the Reading Cluster of the Woodcock-Johnson Psychoeducational Battery. His oral reading shows that he needs to be taught independent word attack skills. When he meets an unfamiliar word, he tends to guess on the basis of its visual configuration. This results in miscalling (*early* read as "really," *benign* read as "begin"), omission of syllables (*deteriorate* read as "detorate" or *humiliate* read as "humilate"), or reversal of the order of syllables (*abysmal* reas as "absymal"). He read correctly 15 of the 26 phonetically regular nonsense syllables on the Word Attack test.

Thus, although some sound-symbol relationships are familiar to him, some key associations are not known: soft *g*, the diphthongs *ai* and *au*, final *y*, *qu*, and *-igh*. Because these decoding skills are not automatic, Michael tends to read in a word-by-word fashion that interferes with higher level comprehension. With text containing fewer difficult words, he was able to handle both factual and interpretive questions accurately.

In addition to his difficulties in word attack, Michael's limited oral vocabulary also contributes to his difficulties with reading. He has a general idea of word meanings, but is not always able to deal with the multiple meanings of words and select that meaning relevant to a given context. For example, he knew only one meaning for the word *till*, a place where cash is kept. The phrase, "tiller of the soil," used to describe a farmer, was completely incomprehensible to him. Because reading is not yet developed to the point that it is a tool for Michael, assessment of his progress with study skills must await the acquisition of more automatic word attack skills and more fluent comprehension.

The Job Analysis of Reading can be used to structure diffuse information about the way a youngster handles various aspects of the reading process. By highlighting *how* the youngster reads, it provides richer data than numerical estimates of reading levels for use in educational planning.

Assessment of Spelling and Written Language

Because of the interrelationships of reading and the language arts, it is essential that written language skills be evaluated as a part of the study of any youngster suspected of having a learning disorder. Formal and informal measures of written language make it possible to answer a number of diagnostic questions:

> What evidences are there of systematic teaching of written language skills?
>
> How fluently does this child communicate in writing?
>
> How accurately are commonly used words spelled? Have the irregular "sight words" been mastered?
>
> How familiar is this child with common spelling generalizations? What evidences are there of the application of phonics rules?
>
> How legibly and conveniently does this child write?

The examiner might begin this assessment with a review of the contents of the child's bookbag and samples of schoolwork. Examination of spelling papers and spelling books is particularly important so that one can understand how spelling is being taught at school. For example, it is important to ascertain whether the spelling approach has an interest-centered or linguistically centered focus.

Although most school administrators steadfastly maintain that the schools they manage teach phonics as part of the reading program, the application of linguistic principles in spelling instruction is less well supported administratively. Linguistics research has shown that, despite the apparent irregularities in English spelling, there are predictable spelling patterns and an underlying system of phonological and morphological regularity. For example, in an analysis of a corpus of 17,000 words, Hanna, Hodges, and Hanna (1971) reported that correct spelling patterns could be predicted for a phoneme 90% of the time when the main phonological facts of position in syllables, stress, and internal constraints in orthography are taken into account. Furthermore, organizing spelling lessons on the basis of phonic or structural generalizations (and their exceptions) would seem to be both logically and pedagogically sound. However, only a few spelling books use linguistic approaches. The word lists in most spelling books are selected and organized on the basis of interest themes (words such as *Halloween, costume, witches, ghost, trick, treat,* and *pumpkin* are listed in lessons that are expected to be taught in October or of frequency of use based on lists and word counts (generally those from Fitzgerald, 1951, and Rinsland, 1945) that fail to take into account recent developments in linguistic studies. Such lists often result in random placement of words, so that they must be learned by children as individual "sight" words, rather than in relation to phonological or morphological generalizations that would draw upon logical linguistic relationships rather than upon rote memory.

Examination of the spelling book the child is using at school can indicate whether the child has had an opportunity to learn spelling generalizations. Dictation of a few words from the recent spelling lessons can indicate the extent to which the child has retained the words "studied" for the weekly school spelling test.

A spontaneous writing sample is an essential part of this evaluation. However, most children need some structure to respond to a request for a writing sample. Some examiners solve this problem by following the request for a human figure drawing with instructions to "Draw a person doing something. I am going to ask you to write a few lines after you have finished the drawing. Please answer these three questions: Who is the person you drew? What is the person doing? What will happen next?" The writing sample can then be analyzed in terms of mechanics of written language, accuracy of spelling, verbal fluency, and syntactical maturity.

These structuring questions usually elicit at least minimal responses from children beyond the first grade. Sometimes they elicit considerable educational and clinical material, as is the case with the 8-year-old girl whose response to the questions appears in Figure 5-1.

From an educational point of view this third-grade youngster finds it easy to get her thoughts down on paper. She shows awareness of some written conventions and attempts to organize her thoughts in a numerical sequence. She has some idea of capitalization and punctuation (commas in a series, an apostrophe in one of the two contractions), but she has not learned to use periods to end sentences. Endings must be stated verbally and emphatically. She is learning cursive writing at school, but serious communication of ideas results in regression to print. With print, there are occasional doubts about letter orientation ("clud," plans) but most letters are oriented correctly. Although she has been taught reading and spelling primarily with a sight-word approach, sound-symbol associations are generally accurate. Her version of the word *capture* is a phonetically accurate transcription of the pronunciation of it, but it suggests the perils of transcribing unaccented syllables in English. The writing of thick as "thic" indicates that she has not mastered the redundancies of spelling. The most serious phonic error is the misspelling of *paper* as "papper." This error shows that she has not mastered the spelling generalization for open syllables. The general picture, however, (apart from the interpersonal relationships the essay suggests) is of a youngster who is making good progress in written communication.

A formal test of written spelling appropriate to the child's age and grade placement completes this section of the evaluation. Such a test represents a contrast with the spontaneous language sample in which children have the opportunity to select words they can spell and avoid those they can't. The formally dictated spelling test can provide both a normative estimate of

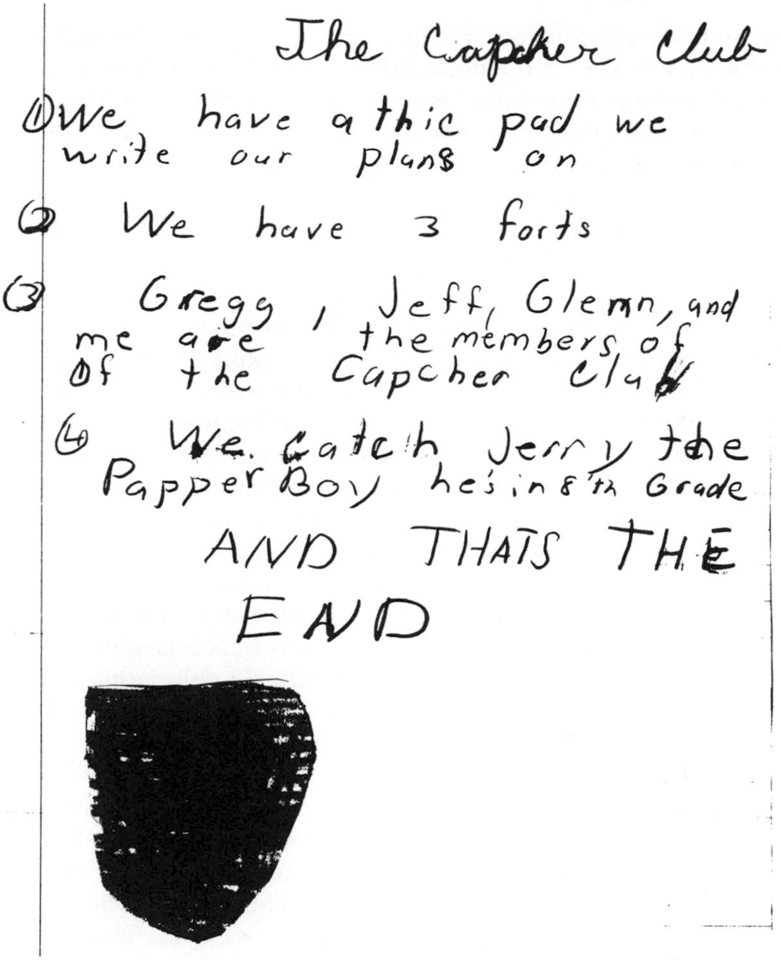
The Capcher Club

(1) We have a thic pad we write our plans on

(2) We have 3 forts

(3) Gregg, Jeff, Glenn, and me are the members of Of the Capcher Club

(4) We catch Jerry the Papper Boy he's in 8th Grade

AND THATS THE END

Figure 5-1 Spontaneous Writing Sample: The Capcher Club
Susan: Age 8 years, 3rd grade

spelling achievement and qualitative evidence of the extent to which rote spelling and encoding skills have been mastered.

Assessment of Mathematics Achievement

Assessing achievement in mathematics presents more difficulties than assessing progress in reading. One reason for this lies in basic differences in the way skills are acquired in the two areas. With reading, once children have mastered a rather limited set of basic word attack and comprehension skills, they can proceed more or less on their own. Mathematics achievement depends to a large extent on direct teaching. Only a very few gifted students are able to discover for themselves the skills and generalizations required in learning mathematics. Thus assessment in mathematics must take into account the content of the curriculum to which the child has been exposed through formal instruction.

To complicate matters further, there is less agreement about the curricular scope and sequences in mathematics than in reading and the language arts. Wide swings in educational philosophy have affected the field of mathematics education for the past 30 years, so that there is no generally accepted content domain on which assessment can be based. Moreover, the field of mathematics encompasses a broad range of skills, abilities, and understandings. For example, the National Council for Teachers of Mathematics (1980) has recommended 10 areas for inclusion in mathematics curricula: problem solving; applying mathematics in everyday situations; alertness to reasonableness of results; estimation and approximation; appropriate computation skills; geometry; measurement; understanding charts, tables, and graphs; using mathematics to predict; and computer literacy. In view of this breadth of content, it is not surprising that achievement tests may represent only minute samples of the curricular content in mathematics. Furthermore, different educational philosophies (and even different textbooks representing similar educational philosophies) may use different sequences of content, so that the times at which given skills are introduced in the classrooms may vary considerably.

Given the nature of the learning process in mathematics, the breadth of curricular content, and the variation in the scope and sequences in mathematics instruction, assessment of individual achievement must take into account the relationship between the content of the test and what this child has experienced at school. Accurate information from school personnel, parents, and the child's own schoolbooks is essential in the evaluation. Where formal tests are used, careful inquiry to determine *how* the problem was solved is as important as the accuracy of the child's response. Evaluation of both computational skills and applications in solving practical problems is essential. Answers to the following diagnostic questions would help to integrate the observations on both formal tests and informal measures in mathematics, all in relationship to previous instructional opportunities:

Has this child developed basic concepts of time, space, numeration, coin values, and measurement?

Has this child acquired functioning skills in the fundamental processes with whole numbers?

Does this child understand and apply mathematical symbols?

To what extent does this child comprehend the mathematical relationships presented in word problems and operationalize these relationships for accurate solution?

To what extent does this child use simple algebraic concepts?

To what extent are the concepts of geometry understood and applied?

Educational achievement in reading, language arts, and mathematics should be considered in terms of the child's age, ability, and current grade placement. At this point in the decision process, adequate achievement would indicate that further diagnosis is unnecessary, while inadequate achievement would require the second step on the decision model.

ADEQUACY OF EDUCATIONAL OPPORTUNITIES

At this point in the diagnostic process, a detailed educational history should be assembled from all available sources. This history should be relevant to the educational problems under consideration and, for this reason, may differ considerably from the usual family history that might be taken in a clinical setting. Clinical histories may often gloss over points essential to understanding the schooling a child has received and may focus on details of the parent's marital adjustment or aspects of gestation and delivery. In both cases this information may hamper rather than clarify diagnosis.

This is not to minimize the importance of historical data. However, it is not easy to define clear, one-to-one relationships between later outcomes in school learning and many individual events in gestation and early development. Obstetrical and pediatric data are best understood within the total context of the child's physical development. Taken by itself, a single early event may sound pessimistic, but it may have little relationship to the child's current functioning. There is danger of an interviewer's focusing on such an event, so that it becomes an unevaluated artifact, accepted by both parent and educator as unmodifiable. Such assumptions can produce a pessimistic attitude toward the youngster's learning problem. When educational interviewers approach these areas, parents are advised to take the Fifth Amendment.

By and large, children from stable, well-managed homes might be expected to achieve more easily at school than those from unstable homes. It might also be expected that good achievement would prevail in homes that were free from marital discord. Yet it is difficult to show a direct relationship between marital disharmony and learning disorders in children; conversely, one sees many children with learning disorders whose homes are tranquil and supportive. Interviews that focus too specifically on marital discord as it might, even by implication, be related to the child's learning problems may leave the parents guilt-ridden and defensive. The interviewer who expects to work cooperatively with these parents is advised to avoid such sensitive areas at this decision point.

What are the relevant data for assessing educational opportunity? First of all, the diagnostician is advised to make use of data that have already been accumulated in the first stage of the study. This would mean a careful rereading of notes of any conversations with teachers or parents taken during the referral process and the assessment of educational achievement. A second source of data on educational history would be gained in a thoughtful perusal of the school's permanent records. This should include objective information that has been recorded at regular intervals, such as attendance records, summaries of grades, results of group achievement tests, notes on health examinations and special health conditions, photographs, work samples, and communications between the school and the family. A few minutes spent in organizing the data chronologically will give the diagnostician clues for further exploration in face-to-face interviews. For example, records of excessive absences in the early grades or habitual tardiness may hold important clues on the continuity and intensity of educational opportunities available to the child.

The chronological record, starting with the nursery years and extending to the time of referral, should be expanded on the basis of information provided by parents and the children themselves. Comparing and contrasting data provided by adults with that provided by the referred child can be useful in obtaining a well-rounded picture of past developments and definition of the current problem. The focus should remain on the methods and content of the educational experiences. It is especially important to obtain information about the child's initial adjustment to nursery school and/or kindergarten and to get an impression of the prevailing school philosophy and organization (open education? individualized instruction? formal reading groups?). Such conversations usually evoke thumbnail sketches or the personal characteristics of teachers and tutors; these discussions should be kept on track by focusing on the methods and materials. It is especially important to elicit information about how beginning reading was taught and to secure concrete examples of any assistance that has been provided to the child. What may be described as "years and years of private tutoring" might, upon more careful questioning, turn out to have been once-a-week sessions with various high school students who helped the child with homework.

This decision point is also a useful time to obtain information about language development. This would include not only the usual information on age of talking, age when sentences were used, persistence of oral inaccuracies, or disfluencies in speech. It is also a time to ascertain the child's first language, the language background of the parents, and the nature of communication patterns in the household. The availability of educational opportunities for a youngster who heard little English before being enrolled in school is quite different from that of a child who heard only English throughout his life, even though both children may have attended school for the same number of years.

It is important at this point to determine the child's dominant language for use in other aspects of diagnosis. A cardinal principle of valid psychological testing is that it should be conducted in the child's major language; this principle has become a legal requirement since the enactment of P. L. 94-142. Of additional interest also is the fortunate situation of the child who may be truly bilingual, that is, fluent in more than one language. Recent research (Cummins, 1980) has shown that, far from impeding learning as the proverbial myth would have us believe, having more than one language enriches a child's language development.

To summarize, this step in the decision model obtains a record of the educational methods and content to which a child under study was exposed in order to assess whether she has had opportunities to learn. This record should be organized in a chronology, so that data from several sources (school records or interviews with children and parents) can be integrated to show the temporal sequence of the child's development. The final answer to the question raised by this step depends upon the judgment of the diagnostic team as they survey the information the chronology had accumulated. They must decide whether the youngster under study has indeed enjoyed formal and informal educational opportunities adequate for learning the skills and content children of his or her age and ability might be expected to have learned. Granted this is a subjective decision. At this point a major intervention decision is made: the choice between regular and special education. If educational opportunity is deemed adequate, further study should be directed according to the steps in the decision tree. If educational opportunity is deemed inadequate, the choice is for compensatory teaching within the framework of regular education. It should be emphasized that every child who is underachieving is not to be regarded as a candidate for special education. There can be a variety of reasons for the inadequate educational opportunity:

- chronic illness, such as rheumatic fever or asthma, that might interfere with both consistent attendance at school and active participation in the school program even when the child was attending school
- a mismatch between the child's developmental level and the demands of the school program; the misguided notion that parents "want" all 5-year-olds to be taught reading has resulted in the extension into kindergarten of much formal academic content; this trend may move some youngsters from home or informal nursery or day care programs to a formal classroom without the readiness activities they need as a basis for formal instruction in reading
- differences between the child's dominant language and that used in the classroom that are not provided for by bilingual or ELS (English as a second language) programs
- family disorganization and/or mobility that deprives children of educational "roots" and exposes them often to a conflicting sequence of instructional methods and content

- inadequate classroom instruction resulting from various conditions of school disorganization: lack of clearly defined instructional goals, curricular content, and educational philosophy; lack of supervision and training of beginning teachers; excessive mobility in the teaching and administrative staffs; and breakdowns in professional relationships between classroom and administrative and/or supervisory personnel.

Although these unfortunate educational circumstances are often cited as causes for the learning difficulties of inner city children, they can occur with children at any socioeconomic level or geographic location. The quality of educational opportunities that have been available to the child is a major consideration in planning appropriate intervention.

In a wider sense, the provision of appropriate educational opportunity is the responsibility of all people concerned with the welfare of children. This responsibility cannot be met by assigning children in need of better quality regular education to special education services. Teams may resort to such misclassification in the mistaken belief that it is "for the good of the child," but it represents an unacceptable response to the child's needs. His needs will be better met through effective teaching in the rich atmosphere of a regular classroom. Such misclassification will dissipate the resources of special education without providing constructive and appropriate services to the children thus classified. (The education of children with learning disorders of extrinsic origin is discussed at greater length in Chapter 12, "Effects of Poverty, Cultural Differences, and Inappropriate Stimulation.")

ADEQUACY OF SENSORY ACUITY FOR LEARNING

Except for gross clinical evaluation of vision and hearing, testing of these functions must be turned over to the specialists in these areas. This section draws on the work of J. B. Smith (1971) and Lobovits (1982) for recommendations on examinations of vision. Recommendations for auditory screening are based on the *Report of the Interdisciplinary Committee for Reading Problems* (Hayes & Silver, 1970).

Examinations of Vision

Ocular screening procedures that J. B. Smith (1971) recommended as part of regular health care for children include (a) vision testing appropriate for the age of the child (the :E: chart with preschoolers and the Snellen chart with school-age children), (b) inspection of the external appearance of the eyes and lids, (c) motility evaluation, (d) funduscopy to detect retinal pathology, and (e) the cover/uncover test to detect strabismus. The more sophisticated the examination is as part of regular health care by the pediatrician, the greater the opportunity for earlier detection of conditions that require the diagnostic and treatment services of an ophthalmologist.

The most frequent eye problems encountered among preschoolers are strabismus, infections of the conjunctiva and eyelids, refractive errors, and fundus abnormalities; with school-age children there is a shift, with refractive errors and strabismus appearing in greater frequency than retinal pathology and infections (J. B. Smith, 1971). The ophthalmologist's evaluation begins with a detailed history of family eye problems, the child's general health, previous eye conditions and treatment, and the symptoms requiring examination. The examination of preschool and school-age children uses both subjective and objective methods to determine visual acuity, motility, and the anterior structure of the globe. Smith stated that the use of eyedrops to dilate the pupil and relax lens accommodation is indicated in children if the initial evaluation discloses fundus abnormalities or the possibility of refractive error great enough to warrant glasses.

From an etiological point of view, visual defects (disorders of visual acuity, ocular motility, stereopsis, or fusion) are not usually found to be primary causes of learning disorders; they may contribute to learning problems by preventing children from obtaining and maintaining with ease a single clear visual image, by producing fatigue and resistance to reading, and by impairing concentration and making it difficult for them to respond to instruction.

Some unsophisticated concepts of learning disorders may attribute them to "something wrong with the child's eyes" and hold the expectation that an eye examination and glasses will resolve the problem. Thus the eye specialist may be the first person some parents consult in seeking help for their children. The eye specialist who understands the complexities of the diagnosis of learning disorders can guide the family in obtaining appropriate diagnostic and treatment services for the child.

Examinations of Hearing

In order to discriminate aurally among all the sounds of English uttered in isolation, a child should have good hearing in the frequency range from 100 to 6000 Hertz. While most audiologists recommend audiometric examination of all children with learning disorders, it is acknowledged that sufficient diagnostic facilities may not be available throughout the country for this. Practical considerations may require the use of screening methods to select those children most likely to require the service. First of all, the diagnostician should be alert for indications from history and behavior that might suggest the need for audiometric study. These indications might include a history of repeated middle ear infections particularly in the first 3 years of life, a history of allergies or repeated upper respiratory tract infections, the presence of articulatory defects (particularly with high frequency sounds), or frequent requests for repetition or misunderstanding of simple directions.

Some schools also use group audiometric procedures. The Western Electric 4A and 4C Fading Numbers test is administered by a phonograph record simultaneously feeding into 40 earphones. The content consists of pairs of digits spoken by a female voice. While this test offers a gross screening method, it has been criticized by audiologists because it fails to detect losses in hearing that affect the high-frequency portion of the range where most of the "intelligence" of the language is concentrated. Pure-tone audiometric techniques have also been adapted for use with groups by modification of the instrumentation. They are valuable in that they avoid the limitations of the fading numbers test, while permitting the screening of more than one person at a time.

The hearing examination of any child for whom sensory acuity is in doubt should include a threshold pure-tone audiogram. By itself this relatively simple test can provide the examiner with almost all the information required to determine the adequacy of the auditory system for normal language development. The test should be conducted in a sound-treated room with absolute minimum ambient noise. The room should be simply furnished so that no distracting influences interfere with the child's attention. Needless to say, the audiometric equipment must be precisely calibrated.

Use of whisper tests, ticking watches, and "calibrated" noisemakers is not recommended by audiologists because these techniques fail to adequately control the sound levels and frequencies and, in the case of whisper tests, variations in voice quality. Their use may result in invalid findings because the child may respond to the test situation itself or to random percussive elements rather than to the expected stimulus. In using such informal methods, the examiner might be misled into concluding that a major avenue of sensory input is adequate when, in fact, it is not.

Specialized methods, such as play audiometry using operant conditioning techniques, electrodermal audiometry, and evoked response audiometry using computer averaging of records may be utilized as an additional source of data. These methods will probably not be necessary with many school-age children.

All these examinations have but one purpose: to provide the examiner with a reasonably accurate estimate of the child's auditory thresholds to pure tones within the hearing range. Once this information has been obtained, further testing can be employed to add additional data about the child's hearing problem and its possible etiology. These other tests, however, must always be considered as adjuncts to, rather than replacements for, pure-tone audiometry. Speech reception threshold is an excellent indicator of the youngster's ability to hear simple samples of speech. The standardized auditory discrimination test using phonetically balanced word lists provides still more information about a child's ability to perceive speech once it has been made loud enough for her to hear comfortably.

It is also desirable to obtain bone conduction thresholds. By assessing hearing by means of bone conduction, it is possible to differentiate between pathologies affecting the conductive portion of the auditory mechanism and those defects of the sensorineural system. Conductive losses, as a rule, do not result in language pathology. That is, those hearing impairments caused by external or middle ear defects do not usually affect the development of language to a significant degree. One reason for this is that the child with a conductive hearing loss is able to hear his own voice normally and with adequate loudness and clarity. He can also hear the speech of others with normal clarity, although it may be a little soft for him. This categorical assertion, however, is questioned. The role of otitis media in language development is considered in this section.

Sensorineural losses, on the other hand, will almost always be accompanied by some retardation in language development. The child with a sensorineural loss may hear speech with adequate loudness, but may have poor auditory discrimination. Speech to him is loud enough, but often garbled and distorted. The child with a mild sensorineural loss has an especially subtle problem: She hears well enough so that deafness is not suspected, yet her hearing is deficient enough that some of the consonant sounds of English speech cannot be distinguished. Therefore, language development may be affected and learning problems will eventually result.

Traditionally, it has been assumed that a loss of less than 30 db in the middle-speech frequencies (500 to 2000 Hz) is not handicapping. When one considers all areas of language function, however, this is not true. Hearing may be good in the middle-frequency range and yet poor for frequencies above 2000 Hz. This will lead to a distortion in the hearing of high-frequency consonant sounds that will inevitably affect language development. Any deviation from normal, therefore, must be considered significant and taken into account in planning educational programs.

Otitis Media and Learning

In the summary of a 1983 workshop on the effects of otitis media on children, Bluestone et al. (1983) concluded that "little doubt exists that at least temporary developmental impairment results from hearing loss of moderate or severe degree that is long standing and unremitting, but no convincing evidence exists at present to relate developmental impairments to single or multiple episodes of short term hearing loss or to mild hearing loss irrespective of duration" (p. 651). A number of workshop participants were more emphatic in stating that "no causal link has been established between early recurrent middle ear effusion and any behavioral phenomena of interest—i. e., language delay, learning problems and the like" (Ventry, 1983, p. 644). In reviewing the literature on otitis media and later impairment of intellectual, speech, language, and psychological development, Paradise (1983) noted that "no such association has been established; should they be established serious problems remain in demonstrating causality; any developmental changes that did result from early conductive loss would probably be reversible if normal hearing were restored" (p. 640). The effect of early otitis media on the development of articulation was also minimized. McWilliams (1983) stated that "most of the articulatory disorders that may be related to otitis media are mild and tend to disappear with age" (p. 646).

Significant questions have not been answered, however (Gray, 1983). Are there sensitive periods of development, for example between 6 and 18 months, when fluctuating and occasional hearing loss may have especially important consequences for development? Where defects are found, do they indicate delay or permanent damage? If cognitive defects are found, are they direct effects of the hearing loss or are they mediated by changes in the child's motivation and in his perception of others? By and large research studies have not dealt with these and other methodological issues—the time of occurrence of otitis media, its duration, the severity and duration of hearing loss, and the success and frequency of treatment. Retrospective studies have difficulty documenting these parameters. For such data, prospective studies appear more reliable.

A series of such prospective reports came from the Frank Porter Graham Child Developmental Center. The relationship between otitis media in the first 3 years of life and subsequent speech development and cognitive, academic, and classroom performance during the third year of elementary school was evaluated (Roberts et al., 1989; Roberts, Burchinal, Koch, Footo, & Henderson, 1988; Roberts et al., 1986). The subjects were children in a day care program for socioeconomic and culturally disadvantaged people, entering the nursery between 6 weeks and 3 months of age and remaining until entrance into public school. Repeated examinations, in sickness and in health, resulted in a median number of 87 ear examinations for each child over the first 3 years of life. The duration of each episode of unilateral and of bilateral otitis media with effusion was documented. At 8 years of age, in their third year of public school, measures of cognitive ability (WISC-R verbal scale) academic achievement (Woodcock-Johnson Psychoeducational Battery), and classroom behavior (Schaeffer, Aaronson, & Edgerton, 1977) were administered. Between the ages of 2½ and 8, standardized tests of speech were given. Of the 44 children who completed the data for the cognitive-academic-behavioral study, no significant relationship was found between otitis media in early childhood and academic achievement and verbal intelligence in the third year of public school. The number of days of otitis media before 3 years of age, however, was significantly correlated with teachers' ratings of attentional behavior in the classroom. Of the 55 children whose language was evaluated, no significant relationship was found between otitis media and number of common phonological processes or consonants in error used during the preschool years. No consistent patterns for individual phonological processes were observed.

A long-term prospective follow-up of children, who at age 5 were evaluated for serial acoustic impedance at approximately monthly intervals for their entire first school year, is reported by Brooks (1986). Academic attainment levels for 64 of these subjects, 17 years after their initial hearing evaluations, found no correlation between middle ear dysfunction occurring in the early years of schooling and later academic achievement.

On the other hand Schlieper, Kisilevsky, Mattingly, and York (1985) found highly significant differences in tests for language (Auditory Comprehension, Northwest Syntax Screening Test, Developmental Sentence Scoring) between 13 children aged 3 to 5 with mild conductive hearing loss and matched, audiologically normal controls. The authors concluded that "the results support the hypothesis that children who experience recurrent middle-ear problems are at risk for persistent language delay."

Needleman (1977) also found that there were significant differences in production of phonemes in words and in connected speech, as well as in use of combinations of phonemes in word endings in varying morphological contexts when children 3 to 8 years of age, who had a documented first episode of otitis media between birth and 18 months with episodes continuing for at least 2 years, were compared with matched control children, who had no history of recurrent ear infections. Needleman speculated that although the amount (decibels) of hearing loss is small and the impairment, intermittent, the changes in hearing level during the early months of life may confuse the child, "causing difficulties in forming strategies and rules for the categorization and learning of the acoustic properties of speech sounds, the syntax or any aspect of language" (p. 649).

There is some evidence that infants who have had otitis media in their first year of pediatric office visits have reduced auditory sensitivity as measured by auditory brain stem response and poorer expressive language when tested at age 1. Differences in receptive language were not detected (Wallace et al. 1988).

From a practical point of view, the evidence is against the etiological role of otitis media in the first 3 years of life in the development of later language disability. If an intermittent conductive hearing defect does indeed disrupt the normal process of auditory processing, this does not appear to persist. On the other hand, a persistent conductive hearing loss certainly may make learning more difficult for a normal child and particularly more difficult for the child who already has the *anlage* for specific language disability. It is only prudent to screen all children for hearing as well as for vision. If auditory acuity is in doubt, specialized audiological consultation should be made available.

Results of sensory examinations by specialists provide answers to the questions at this stage of the decision model. In cases where these examinations have uncovered previously unrecognized problems, medical treatment is indicated. Obviously, such treatment plans should involve the child's pediatrician; they should also include advice to the child's family and school personnel so that any needed provisions for accommodation can be made. While most of these children would be expected to continue in mainstream placement in school, provisions such as supplementary educational services, modifications in seating arrangements, and special instructional materials and aids should be provided when they are necessary. With children for whom sensory examinations have proved negative, the diagnostic focus should move to the next step.

FUNCTIONING ON COGNITIVE MEASURES

Effective assessment of cognitive factors in diagnosis has a number of hallmarks. It is, first of all, data-based. The quantitative foundation on which it rests is one of the unique contributions of the field of psychology. Over the course of nearly a century psychologists have employed theoretical, statistical, and clinical approaches to improve the quality of these assessment methods. While imperfections remain, the *Standards for Educational and Psychological Testing,* first published in 1954 and updated at regular intervals, are evidence of the efforts to maintain high standards of technical quality for assessment methods (American Psychological Association, 1985).

Effective assessment of cognitive function requires the judgment of trained personnel. An integral part of training curricula in psychology is theoretical and supervised clinical instruction in test administration. This training goes beyond routine test giving to develop professional judgment in selection of appropriate instruments, critical understanding of their rationale and psychometric characteristics, and ethical use and interpretation of test results.

Effective cognitive assessment is parsimonious. Given the quality of the instruments and the professional training of the psychologists who administer them, effective diagnosis does not need to call upon a large number of measures to supply data for answering the diagnostic questions that have been raised. In the final analysis, these answers come from the conceptual integration of the data elicited from well-chosen clinical measures.

In a child with a learning disorder, assessment of cognitive functioning involves the use of one of the individual tests of intelligence, such as the WPPSI, the WISC-R, the Stanford-Binet Intelligence Scale, the K-ABC, or the McCarthy Scales of Children's Abilities. Although there are group tests of cognitive abilities, their use is to be discouraged in the diagnosis of learning disorders. The obvious reason for this is that many group tests use reading or other skills, of which the acquisition has already been found difficult for children referred for the diagnosis of learning disorders. Furthermore, group testing does not permit the observation of qualitative aspects of children's behavior that are essential in understanding the nature of resources and problems in learning.

Defining Intelligence

J. M. Hunt (1961) has wisely observed that "it is in connection with intelligence and the tests that measure it, that some of the most violent polemics in psychology and all the behavior sciences have raged" (p. 3). Although some common themes can be found, definitions of intelligence are almost as varied as the psychologists who provide them. The methods of assessment reflect these variations in conceptualization as well as the times in which the definitions were framed. For example, the earliest theorists conceptualized intelligence in terms of innate hereditary factors (Galton, 1907) and sought to measure it by methods involving sensory discrimination, motor coordination, attention, and memory (J. M. Cattell, 1890). As studies of intelligence moved outside the laboratory to the solution of practical problems in such settings as schools, the definitions became broader in scope and assessment methods began to draw upon more complex mental processes (Binet and Simon, 1916; Terman, 1916). Dissatisfaction with age-scale formats (Yerkes, 1917) and with the content and standardization of existing scales for use with adult subjects led Wechsler (1944) to develop the first of his series of scales. The rapid adoption of these scales was part of the expansion of clinical services to adults after World War II.

As technical resources for statistical analyses became available, definitions of intelligence focused on multifactor theories (E. L. Thorndike, 1927) and hierarchical models of intelligence (R. B. Cattell, 1963b; Guilford, 1967; Thurstone, 1938; Vernon, 1979). More recently, the emphasis on computer technology is reflected in information-processing models that use such terms as *capacity, storage, control processes,* and *knowledge base* in the formulation of the model (Campione & Brown, 1978).

Weinberg (1989) emphasized the implicit theories of intelligence that constitute popular definitions. People, in general, view intelligence as it is represented in intelligent behavior: the ability to reason and to solve practical problems, the ability to express one's ideas verbally, and the ability to sense social cues. Weinberg noted further that researchers in the field of human intelligence are in strong agreement with these popular conceptions. Note, for example, Wechsler's (1944) definition: "Intelligence is the aggregate or global capacity of the individual to act purposefully, to think rationally and to deal effectively with his environment" (p. 3). Not all the explicit definitions agree that intelligence is a global capacity. Some theorists such as Guilford (1967) and Gardner (1983) emphasize the multiple nature of intelligence, composed of many separate mental abilities that are independent of each other.

Between these two positions is an intermediate one that may be more meaningful for clinicians. This view holds that intelligence is hierarchically organized with one or two general factors and other more specific skills. These theorists have drawn upon the psychometric tradition that seeks, through statistical models, to understand the structure of the intellect. Also relevant for clinicians is the contribution of Piaget (Piaget & Inhelder, 1958) who studied cognitive development qualitatively, by probing ways in which children perceive and understand the world around them.

Vernon (1969) described three different kinds of intelligence. According to his formulation, Intelligence A represents the innate capacity of the individual, the genetic equipment with which the individual enters the world. Obviously this cannot be measured directly, although there have been attempts (largely unsuccessful) to do so by using various physiological measures (F. Davis, 1971). Intelligence B, according to Vernon, involves more than the individuals' capacities because it includes the total schemata and mental plans built up through an individual's interaction with the environment. Intelligence B can be influenced by such things as constitutional handicaps, physical deprivation, lack of sensory stimulation, lack of language stimulation, environmental disorganization, or inappropriate demands made by teachers or caretakers. Intelligence A and Intelligence B interact. Vernon proposed that Intelligence C represents the results obtained from individual psychological testing. This formulation highlights a major limitation of intelligence tests: that they represent very limited samples of the behaviors that become the basis for the inferences psychologists make about Intelligences A and B when they interpret test results.

A caution was sounded early in the history of intelligence testing by Terman (1921) when he advised psychologists to guard against defining intelligence as the ability to pass tests. His warning that "no existing scale is capable of measuring the ability to deal with all possible kinds of material on all intelligence levels" (p. 130) is no less true today than when it was written. Current theories stress a hierarchical and multifactorial view of intelligence with a general factor entering into a large variety of cognitive operations and narrower group factors and specialized abilities forming the core of the hierarchy (Sattler, 1988). It is also generally accepted that both innate and developmental influences are reflected in assessments of cognitive functioning.

Values and Limitations of Intelligence Tests

There have been criticisms both of the uses of intelligence tests and of the tests themselves. Test users are obliged to be aware of these criticisms and to modify testing practices so that tests are used responsibly. It is important, for example, to be aware of the extrinsic factors that can influence test behavior. A child's unfamiliarity with the test situation and the requirements of responding to formal cognitive measures can influence test results. Mistrust of the examiner may also affect an individual's performance. Past experience with testing can have both positive and negative effects upon test outcomes. Difficulties in communication between examiner and examinee (ranging from language differences to a lack of real rapport with the subject, even though the two people may speak a common language) may also invalidate test results.

Wechsler (1975) also has reminded us of nonintellectual factors that must be considered in any assessment of cognitive functioning. Intelligent behavior may call upon a host of factors that are more connative than cognitive. They are not so much skills and know-how, but, rather, drives, attitudes, and sensitivities to social, moral, or esthetic values. They may also involve effort, persistence, impulse control, and goal-awareness. They are seen as the "enzymes of personality" that affect the capabilites of all individuals. In a larger sense, they may account for the uniqueness in cognitive functioning that can be discovered through individual intelligence tests. Awareness of these influences on test behavior can do much to avoid the unfair educational consequences of invalid or incomplete interpretation of test results.

Bias in Testing While the validity of test results may to some extent depend upon the skill and resourcefulness of the examiner, the tests themselves have been the subject of criticism. Kaufman (1979a, 1979b) feels that charges of test bias based on single test items or on studies that demonstrate unequal mean scores for various ethnic groups are an oversimplification of the problems related to test bias. Careful psychometric studies of the validity of major instruments do not support systematic or intentional biases in test construction; abuses are more apt to occur in interpretation and the *uses* to which test results are put. Efforts to counteract these abuses have used both ethical and legal measures. The Joint Committee on Testing Practices (1988), a cooperative effort of several professional organizations, has aimed to improve the quality of testing through a *Code of Fair Testing Practices in Education.* The code states the obligations to test takers of professionals who develop or use tests. These obligations are particularly in matters of admissions, educational assessment, educational diagnosis, and student placement. Four areas comprise the standards defined in the code: developing and selecting appropriate tests, interpreting scores, striving for fairness, and informing test takers. Details of these standards appear in Appendix A.

Legal Safeguards P. L. 94-142 (Federal Register, 1977) made definite stipulations for testing procedures, mandating that:

- Tests and other evaluation devices must be administered in the child's primary language.
- Testing and evaluation materials and procedures must be selected and administered so as not to be discriminatory on the basis of racial or cultural differences.
- Tests must be administered by trained personnel.

- No single procedure should be used as the sole criterion for determining an educational placement for a child.

- Evaluation is the responsibility of a multidisciplinary team or group, including at least one classroom teacher and a specialist in the area of the suspected disability.

- Periodic reevaluations must be made to assess progress.

Further legal guarantees for the children and their families are contained in procedural safeguards that mandate written parental consent before evaluation, parental opportunity to see all information used in decision making, confidentiality of all reports and records, and opportunity for an impartial hearing conducted by regional or state education authorities if parents disagree with placements planned by the school team.

Despite these guarantees, litigation on the overrepresentation of minority children in special education has influenced diagnostic procedures. In the 1979 *Larry P. v Riles* decision, the U. S. Federal District Court in California ruled that standardized intelligence tests are culturally biased and cannot be used in the assessment of black children for possible placement in classes for educably mentally retarded children. Since psychologists cannot predict the outcome of a test before giving it, this decision effectively ended the use of conventional individual measures of intelligence in California schools. The decision was upheld by a 2–1 margin in the Ninth Circuit Court of Appeals in 1984. However, Judge William B. Enright noted in a minority opinion that evidence had not been presented that intelligence tests had resulted in improper placements and that the court was striking down the only objective criterion for placement decisions (Sattler, 1988). In 1986 the California State Department of Education issued a directive forbidding the use of individual intelligence tests with any special education placement decisions. Weinberg (1989) has commented that it is ironic that tests are outlawed in California for the very purpose that Binet and Simon originally designed the first individual intelligence test.

More confusion has been added to the issue by a decision *(P.A.S.E. v Joseph P. Hannon)* in the U. S. Federal District Court in Illinois that, when used with other criteria in the assessment process, individual intelligence tests comply with federal guidelines established by P. L. 94-142. Judge John Grady's examination of the test items led him to rule that the WISC, WISC-R, and Stanford-Binet tests were not culturally biased. It may be that the courts are not the best setting for considering the professional use of tests.

Substantive Criticisms of Tests   Some substantive criticisms have come from professionals in the field of measurement. Kaufman (1979a) argued that test construction has failed to grow conceptually along with advances in psychology. Test materials have been improved and modernized and advances in psychometric theory have been applied to test construction, but the content of tests remains virtually unchanged over the years and fails to reflect advances in learning theory, educational methods, and neuropsychology.

Kaufman also criticized current test instruments for their failure to include direct measures of new learning. Actual measures of learning ability are infrequent on most instruments, even though one of the most frequent uses of intelligence test results is to predict learning ability. In response to this failure there has been a growth of interest in nontraditional techniques, such as Feuerstein's (1979) Learning Potential Assessment Device or Campione's (1989) assisted assessment, both of which use a test-teach-retest model to assess ability for new learning.

In defense of existing tests, however, there is agreement on their psychometric excellence. There are relatively small standard errors of measurement of IQs, and the tasks of the tests lend themselves to analyses in keeping with different theoretical approaches. In general, they have been found to predict educational outcomes effectively. McCall (1977), for example, found the IQs for a sample of children aged 3 to 18 were significant predictors of educational success and occupational status at age 26 or older. Coefficients of correlation remained fairly stable at about .50. Sattler (1988) enumerated the many educational applications of tests as measures of accountability, evaluation of program effectiveness, and criteria for admission to enrichment programs. He believes that tests are a standard for evaluating the extent to which children of all ethnic groups have learned the basic cognitive and academic skills necessary for survival in our culture, adding that few "reasonable alternatives" have been proposed by critics.

Major Intelligence Tests

Wechsler Intelligence Scale for Children   This scale, first published in 1949, was revised in terms of norms and content in 1974 as the Wechsler Intelligence Scale for Children-Revised (WISC-R) (Wechsler, 1974). Probably the most frequently used measure in the diagnosis of learning problems, it provides a global scale (full scale IQ) as well as verbal and performance scale IQs, for children aged 6 through 16. The standardization sample of 2,200 children (200 at each of the 11 age groups) was selected to represent the U. S. census for 1970 in terms of ethnicity and occupational group of the head of household.

The WISC-R continues the practice Wechsler employed in his earlier work, particularly the renunciation of the concept of mental age as the basic measure of intelligence in favor of the use of deviation IQs. Thus all of the IQs on the WISC-R are deviation quotients obtained by "comparing each subject's performance not with a composite age group, but exclusively with the scores earned by individuals in a single (that is, his or her own) age group" (Wechsler, 1974, p. 3). This method, new in tests for children at the time of its first use in the WISC, makes it easier for the examiner to assess variability in cognitive functioning. Because the mean and standard deviation are identical from age to age (mean = 100, *SD* ± 15), variations in IQ beyond the standard error of measurement do not occur unless the child's actual test performance, as compared with his peers, varies. According to Wechsler (1974), "apart from test unreliabilities, IQs obtained by successive retests with the WISC automatically give the subject's relative position in the age group to which he belongs at each time of testing. If any changes are observed they may be ascribed to changes in the subject and not in the structure of the test nor its standardization" (p. 3). This feature of the WISC-R is particularly important in the assessment of children with learning disorders because of the inevitable relationship between school achievement and cognitive functioning.

Most authorities agree that the WISC-R is technically sound (Sattler, 1988; Witt & Cavell, 1986). Reliability is demonstrated in internal consistency coefficients averaging .96 for the full scale IQ, .94 for the verbal IQ, and .90 for the performance IQ. For the subtests, average internal consistency coefficients range from .70 to .86. Standard errors of measurement (expressed in IQ points) average 3.19 for the full scale IQ, 3.60 for the verbal IQ, and 4.66 for the performance IQ. Test–retest studies of 303 children in three age groups after 1 month yielded stability coefficients ranging from .90 to .95. There have been a large number of studies of the concurrent validity of the WISC-R using both nonreferred samples and various subsamples based on clinical diagnoses and ethnicity. The WISC-R is the measure against which other childrens' tests are validated.

The WISC-R consists of 12 subtests, 10 on which the computation of the IQ is based and 2 supplementary tests. These subtests are set tasks that provide samples of behavior on which inferences can be made about the child's cognitive functioning. The emphasis of the scale is on the importance of probing in as many ways as possible in order to assess not only the global entity, as represented by the IQ, but also other aspects that comprise each child's pattern of abilities.

Wechsler has cautioned examiners that WISC-R subtests should be regarded as "assortative" rather than hierarchical. Although they should not all be regarded as equally effective measures of intelligence, each is considered necessary for the fuller appraisal of intelligence (Wechsler, 1974, p. 9). It has also been pointed out that, although the subtests may have names similar to subtests of other Wechsler scales, they should not be interpreted as assessing the same functions, either in all children regardless of age or in children and adults. For this reason, the names of the various subtests do not imply the measurement of any specific function but are factual descriptions of the tasks involved. Six subtests comprise the verbal scale: Information, Similarities, Arithmetic, Vocabulary, Comprehension, and Digit Span.

The performance scale consists of Picture Completion, Picture Arrangement, Block Design, Object Assembly, Coding, and an alternate subtest, Mazes.

The data from the WISC-R subtests lend themselves to factor analysis. Such studies have been numerous, not only of the standardization sample and other nonreferred samples, but also of various ethnic and clinical groups. These studies also have been valuable in shedding light on the psychometric and clinical properties of the scale. The most frequently cited work in this area is Kaufman's (1979b) factor analysis that identified three factors, with each of the subtests loading primarily on one factor only:

Verbal Comprehension	*Perceptual Organization*	*Freedom from Distractibility*
Information	Picture Completion	Arithmetic
Similarities	Picture Arrangement	Digit Span
Vocabulary	Block Design	Coding
Comprehension	Object Assembly	
	Mazes	

Kaufman found striking consistency in results with three methods of factor analysis; cross validation occurred when other investigations demonstrated similar findings with various ethnic and clinical samples. These results show Wechsler's hypothetical organization of the WISC-R into verbal and performance scales to be real and meaningful dimensions. The consideration of these dimensions is especially useful in interpreting the records of children with learning disorders. With these children, however, the third factor may be seen as representing "memory and sequencing" rather than the somewhat negative description of "freedom from distractability."

Viewing children's WISC-R records in terms of the factorial composition of the scale can be exceedingly useful in understanding the strengths and needs they present and in planning educational intervention. However, some cautions are necessary to prevent overgeneralization in the educational application of these findings. For example, one must be especially careful in interpreting verbal-performance differences as indicators of variations in left and right-hemisphere integrity and in recommending teaching approaches that purport to "draw on" one side of the brain. In the first place, both the subtests themselves and the educational activities are complex in nature and probably do not represent pure functions. Furthermore, assumptions based on findings with adults may not be applied appropriately to children in whom neurological organization may be quite different.

Nevertheless the search for WISC-R patterns for use in differential diagnosis and educational planning continues. In a survey of fundamental concerns confronting prominent people in the field of learning disabilities, Adelman and Taylor (1986) found that over half the respondents mentioned the necessity for developing valid procedures for differential diagnosis and subtyping. This finding is significant in view of the research interest that in the past has been focused on the use of cognitive tests, particularly the WISC-R, to discover diagnostic patterns. In 1974 Bannatyne proposed recategorization of WISC-R subtests as a means of locating children with specific learning disabilities. However, recategorization failed to differentiate learning disabled children from normal children (Mueller, Matheson, & Short, 1983) from slow learners (Cooley & Lamson, 1983) or from emotionally disturbed or mentally retarded children (Henry & Wittman, 1981) or other types of handicapped children (Clarizio & Bernard, 1981). State-of-the-art papers by Galvin (1981), Kaufman (1981), and Kavale and Forness (1984) reported that no recategorization of WISC-R scores, profiles, or factor clusters could be used successfully to locate unique cognitive characteristics attributable to learning disability. Rather than seeking elusive patterns to account for the heterogeneous group of children, the most effective use of test data in the diagnostic assessment of children with learning disorders would seem to be in developing working hypotheses in order to understand the strengths and needs of individual children and relating these hypotheses to data elicited in examinations in other disciplines.

Stanford-Binet Intelligence Scale: Fourth Edition   The fourth American edition based on Binet and Simon's original intelligence scale appeared in 1986; therefore, there has been relatively little published research available on its use. The authors of this edition, who are distinguished in the field of measurement, have generously provided information to us about the development of the revision (R. L. Thorndike, Hagen, & Sattler, 1986). The fourth edition uses a point scale, rather than the age-scale format of previous editions of the Binet scales. It introduces some entirely new subtests and represents a complete restandardization. The authors of the fourth edition have attempted to meet criticisms of the previous editions of the Stanford-Binet scale regarding its emphasis on verbal content and the unrepresentativeness of its standardization sample. The 15 subtests of the scale are:

1. Vocabulary
2. Bead Memory
3. Quantitative
4. Memory for Sentences
5. Pattern Analysis
6. Comprehension
7. Absurdities
8. Memory for Digits
9. Copying (blocks or geometric designs)
10. Memory for Objects
11. Matrices
12. Number Series
13. Paper Folding and Cutting
14. Verbal Relations
15. Equation Building

Users of previous editions of the scales will recognize such subtests as Vocabulary, Picture Absurdities, Paper Folding and Cutting, and Memory for Sentences, but Memory for Objects, Number Series, and Equation Building are entirely new items. The authors of the fourth edition of the Stanford-Binet postulate a hierarchical model with general intelligence at the highest level; crystallized, fluid, and short-term memory factors at the second level; and specific abilities at a third level (Sattler, 1988).

The scale was standardized on a sample of more than 5,000 subjects in 17 age groups from 2 through 23 years. The sample was stratified in terms of geographic regions, size of community, ethnicity, age, gender, and socio-economic background. Because of overrepresentation of high socioeconomic status groups, some weighting was necessary to ensure that the sample represented the 1980 census.

The Composite Score yielded by the Stanford-Binet fourth edition is actually a deviation IQ, although the authors seem to avoid use of that term. It is, however, not completely comparable to WISC-R IQs because, like the other Binet scales, it has a mean of 100 and a standard deviation of 16 while the WISC-R has a mean of 100 and a standard deviation of 15. The subtests are organized into four areas: Verbal Reasoning, Abstract/Visual Reasoning, Quantitative Reasoning, and Short-Term Memory. However, factor analysis has not supported these areas, so that it is inadvisable to use them for test interpretation. Because all subtests are not used with all age levels, subtests are not continuous throughout the scale.

Technical characteristics of the Stanford-Binet fourth edition are excellent. The reliability ranges between .95 and .99 for the Composite Score and between .73 and .94 for the subtests. Standard errors of measurement are small and stability coefficients are respectable. A median r of .80 for concurrent validity is reported for both normal and special samples with Form L-M of the Stanford-Binet Intelligence Scale, WISC-R, WPPSI, WAIS-R, K-ABC, and educational tests as criteria. Construct validity is demonstrated in that the scores increase as a function of age, in the substantial correlations of subtests with the Composite Score, and in the factor analyses.

Sattler (1988) reported a principal-components factor analysis that can be used to guide interpretation of scores for individuals. His analysis yielded three factors: verbal comprehension, nonverbal reasoning/visualization, and memory. It is these factor scores, rather than the area scores, that Sattler recommends for use in test interpretation. These factors are not unlike the factors reported in analyses of the WISC-R, although the relationship of subtests (and the computations required for their use in interpretation) seem less straightforward than on the WISC-R. Sattler provides tables of critical values for within- and between-factor comparisons. However, the test is still too new for much research on profile interpretation to have been reported. At this point in its use, examiners are advised to examine individual test results along the following lines: level and percentile rank of the Composite Score; comparisons of absolute levels among factor scores; variations of subtests within factors; and qualitative aspects of test performance.

In response to criticisms on the length of time required by the age-scale organization of previous editions of the Binet scales, the authors have devised a "routing test" (Vocabulary) to be used by the examiner to determine the beginning point for testing. This helps somewhat, but the problem of test length continues, especially at the upper age levels. Another problem is the lack of a comparable battery through all age ranges, since only six subtests run throughout the scale. This variation in organization across age levels would present problems to the psychologist in reevaluating individuals or in longitudinal research with learning disorders. Finally, the nonuniformity of Composite Scores, factors, and scaled scores requires sophisticated interpretative skills on the part of the examiner.

Kaufman Assessment Battery for Children   This test, known as the K-ABC, was developed in response to recent interest in neuropsychology and recent criticisms of the use of conventional measures with children of diverse ethnic and cultural backgrounds. Kaufman and Kaufman (1983) set out to minimize the role of language and verbal tasks and to include stimuli that were as fair as possible for children of diverse backgrounds. Planned for use with children 2½ through 12½ years of age, the K-ABC yields scores on four scales: Sequential Processing, Simultaneous Processing, Achievement, and Nonverbal. The Simultaneous and Sequential Processing scales together provide a Mental Processing Composite that is essentially a measure of intelligence.

The K-ABC has as its theoretical basis, the information-processing model of Luria (1966) and Das, Kirby, and Jarman (1975) that proposes two primary modes of cognitive processing: *simultaneous processing*, which deals with many stimuli at once through spatial or analogic organization, and *successive processing*, which emphasizes serial organization of stimuli. The Achievement Scale, planned to measure factual knowledge, is not a test of educational achievement in the usual sense. Like the two mental processing scales, acquired skills are assessed through novel, game-like subtests including expressive vocabulary in picture identification, recognition of "Faces and Places," solving riddles, decoding in reading, and reading understanding, in which the child demonstrates comprehension through gestures. The Nonverbal scale draws from the Mental Processing Scales those subtests that do not require words in the instructions or the responses. Not all subtests run throughout the age levels; only three (Hand Movements, Gestalt Closure, and Faces and Places) run through all age levels.

The technical quality of the K-ABC is good. The test was standardized on 2,000 children at nine age levels. The standardization sample was stratified to match the 1980 census in terms of age, sex, geographic region, socioeconomic status, ethnicity, and community size. Handicapped children were included in the sample. Coefficients of internal consistency for the Mental Processing Composite average .93 for preschoolers and .97 for school-age children. Odd-even reliability coefficients average .80 to .90 for global scores and .70 to .80 for subtests. Test-retest reliabilities average .77 to .97 for global scales and .59 to .98 for subtests. Evidence of construct validity is seen in the increase in subtest scores for successive age groups. Factor analysis supports the organization of the K-ABC into three scales. Factor loadings for subtests are higher with the scales they were assigned to than with other scales. Evidence of concurrent validity is demonstrated in moderate correlations of the K-ABC with the WISC-R, WPPSI, and Form L-M of the Stanford-Binet Scale.

The finding that black/white and hispanic/white group differences are smaller on the K-ABC than on the WISC-R is seen by the test authors as an indication of its appropriateness for use with children from cultural and linguistic minority groups. These data have resulted in criticism of the test content, however. Page (1985) found no new testing principles in the K-ABC that would account for the smaller minority group differences the data show. He concluded that the test:

has been designed to emphasize skills on which blacks have performed best on traditional tests, have [sic] weighted these highly in the chosen intelligence portion, have excluded from this portion all vocabulary and other verbal tests, and have diminished the influence of more complex nonverbal tests which together with the verbal have frequently been the (justified) core of intelligence testing. (p. 777)

Whether or not Page's reasoning is accurate on this matter, it is clear that the K-ABC lacks verbal comprehension and verbal reasoning items. Instead, the nature of some of the items of the Simultaneous Processing Scale draws so heavily on attention and short-term memory that it may underestimate the cognitive abilities of children whose learning disorders center around attentional or memory difficulties.

There have also been questions raised about the simultaneous/successive information-processing model, which has its basis in hypotheses on hemisphere specialization in adults. The preliminary state of knowlege about such constructs, particularly with children, precludes practical applications in educational remediation. As Page stated, "The question is not where the process is carried out, but how well" (p. 775). Certainly the constructs are ambiguous and the data show some degree of overlap. Many of the subtests contain elements of more than one processing style.

It is also to be recognized that mental processing and achievement are not mutually exclusive. Some subtests on the achievement scale may measure verbal ability rather than achievement. Achievement scores correlate higher with scores on the WISC-R verbal scale than with the Iowa Test of Basic Skills. Sattler (1988), in pointing out this and other measurement problems with the K-ABC, warns that the K-ABC should not be used as the primary instrument for measuring intelligence in clinical assessments of learning disabled children.

McCarthy Scales of Children's Abilities   The McCarthy Scales of Children's Abilities were developed for the clinical evaluation of young children. Although norms are available for ages 2½ through 8½, the range for these scales' effective use is between 3 and 6½ years. Based on Dorothea McCarthy's extensive clinical experience, the battery consists of 18 tests of mental and motor ability organized into six reliable scales. Three scales tap content (Verbal, Perceptual-Performance and Quantitative), and two tap processes (Memory and Motor). A sixth scale, the General Cognitive Index, is based upon reasoning, concept formation, memory, and manipulative items drawn from the other scales.

The test materials contain toys and pictures likely to be attractive to young children. Technically sound, this test manual provides evidence of satisfactory internal consistency, split-half and test-retest reliability, and construct validity. However, the limited ceiling for children older than 6 and the nature of some of the content may result in underestimation of IQs in children with learning disorders. The lack of items tapping social judgment and abstract problem solving has also been noted by some critics. Therefore, despite some strengths as a clinical instrument, the McCarthy Scales of Children's Abilities cannot be recommended as a method of assessing children with learning disorders.

Answering the Diagnostic Questions

Whichever measure or measures one chooses, assessment of cognitive functioning is the means by which the fourth diagnostic question of the decision model is answered. If this question is answered negatively—i. e., if the child demonstrates general limitations in cognitive functioning—the decision model would indicate that special educational provisions are needed. These provisions would be curricular modification in terms of goals and content and timing of instruction appropriate to the level of cognitive functioning as determined by psychological study.

If, on the other hand, psychological study establishes that the child's cognitive functioning is adequate and that the child in question did not learn well despite conventional educational opportunities, the focus should move toward understanding the reasons for the learning disorder. At this point, clinicians should begin to integrate the multidisciplinary data already generated and to define further questions to clarify etiology. The data already generated would describe current levels of cognitive functioning and estimates of educational expectancy. These data could then be used to determine the extent to which educational achievement was appropriate and to define special instructional needs. Results of the cognitive assessment would also be used to build a picture of how the child went about solving cognitive tasks. The examiner would use knowledge of the organization of the cognitive measure that had been administered to set hypotheses about the child's resources for learning and deficits that must be considered in instructional planning. The examiner would not at this point be led astray in search of "typical patterns" or pathognomonic signs of learning disorders, but rather would use the behavior samples collected thus far in the decision model to answer the questions, "Why isn't this child learning? and "What can we do about it?"

SUMMARY

Because each child is unique within the population of children with disorders of learning, systematic diagnosis is necessary to understand the constellation of contributing factors in each case. Furthermore, intervention is more likely to be effective when it is based on a systematic formulation of each child's strengths and needs. The complex nature of learning disorders implies that broad-based, multidisciplinary skills are necessary to provide comprehensive diagnosis.

In order to provide sufficient diagnostic data and yet avoid redundant assessment processes, a five-step decision-making process is recommended to evaluate (a) educational achievement (b) educational opportunity, (c) sensory acuity, (d) cognitive functioning, and (e) neuropsychiatric functioning. Integration of the diagnostic data at each of these decision points will provide clues for appropriate intervention strategies.

Assessing the adequacy of educational skills may use data from informal observations and well-standardized measures. However, information thus obtained must be formulated so that strengths and needs in the complex skills of reading, handwriting, spelling, written language, and mathematics are readily apparent. Adequacy of educational opportunity is best judged from a thorough history that emphasizes opportunities for informal and formal schooling. Examination of sensory acuity is best left to specialists in the fields; however, a careful observation of the child may provide much useful data. Use and interpretation of one of the well-standardized individual measures of intelligence by a well-trained school or child clinical psychologist can provide both quantitative and qualitative descriptions of the child's cognitive functioning. Rather than combing the data for elusive "typical patterns" or pathognomonic signs of learning disorders, however, the psychologist might better use the data generated to answer the two questions that have practical significance for intervention: "Why isn't this child learning?" and "What can we do about it?"

CHAPTER SIX

Principles of Psychiatric and Neurological Diagnosis

The previous chapter took the reader through the first four steps in evaluating a child believed to be learning disordered. If educational achievement is found to be significantly less than that expected from the child's educational opportunities and cognitive ability, and his/her sensory acuity does not impede learning, as described in Chapter 5, then a final step in the evaluation of children with learning disorders is neuropsychiatric evaluation. Our approach to this evaluation involves gathering data on a pentaxial scheme, as shown in Table 6-1. This scheme, developed and used in the

Table 6-1   *Pentaxial Scheme for Diagnosis in Child Psychiatry*

	DSM-III-R

I. Psychiatric
  A. Content
  B. Dynamic-conflict-defense
  C. Personality structure
  D. Genesis
  E. Developmental lines (Erikson, 1968; A. Freud, 1977; Greenspan, 1981; Piaget, 1954)
	I. Clinical Syndromes

II. Biological
  A. Genetic
  B. Structural integrity
  C. Developmental levels (Frankenburg, 1968; Gesell, 1947)
  D. Perceptual *(Search)* (Silver & Hagin, 1976)
	II. Personality
	Specific developmental disorders

III. Cognitive-Intellectual
  A. Functioning, intelligence (WPPSI, WISC-R, Stanford-Binet, Kaufman)
  B. Development (Piaget, 1954)
	III. Physical disorders

IV. Environmental-Social
  A. Patterns of mothering (Brody and Axelrad, 1970; Greenspan, 1981)
  B. Stimuli at critical ages (E. Hess, 1970)
  C. Reality events
	IV. Severity of Psychosocial Stressors

V. Educational
  A. Quality and quantity
  B. Levels of achievement
	V. Highest Level of Adaptive Functioning Past Year

Learning Disorders Unit at New York University Medical School, has proven useful for the study of individual children and for the acquisition of a data base for clinical and statistical research. The multiaxial approach of DSM-III and DSM-III-R parallels in many respects our pentaxial scheme. Unlike the pentaxial scheme, however, the multiaxial scheme of DMS-III-R was not specifically designed for use with children.

The five parameters of study included in the pentaxial scheme are the psychiatric, the biological, the cognitive-intellectual, the environmental-social, and the educational.

Psychiatric data reveals the content, dynamics, genesis, and structure of the child's thoughts, wishes, and conflicts; it considers the nature and quality of his reactions to frustration, failure, and success and to the stresses and supports of home, society, and school; it evaluates the development and structure of his personality, the strength of its various components, its age appropriateness, and the child's capacity to deal with anxiety.

Biological data investigates the integrity of the central nervous system, particularly the level of maturation and integration of the central nervous system; it examines the neurological system, including soft neurological signs; it considers the presence of complicating problems with attention and impulse control and provides evidence for diffuse or focal organic syndromes. Integration of the central nervous system also implies a neuropsychological study; a profile of perceptual assets and deficits; the capacity for sequential information storage and its access for comprehension and expression; the metalinguistic functions of organization, abstraction, analysis, and synthesis; and the capacity for adjustment in time and space. At times, laboratory studies such as electroencephalograms, computerized tomography, nuclear magnetic resonance scan, genetic, and metabolic study are indicated.

Cognitive-intellectual data looks at the level of a child's overall cognitive function and the patterns of cognitive abilities as determined by an individual test of intelligence (recognizing, of course, that the learning disorder itself influences the child's achievement on intelligence testing).

Environmental-social data involves an understanding of the family, the stresses and strengths both independent of and dependent on the learning disorder; an evaluation of the emotional, social, and economic life of the parents; and an evaluation of the relationship between the child and her parents, the child and her social group, and the child and her siblings. We are also interested in the educational experience of other members of the family, the presence of other family members with a learning disorder, language disorder, or left-handedness, and historical evidence for a possible genetic disorder. Details of the pregnancy and labor with this child are obtained—the possibility of intrauterine toxemia, trauma, or infection and the presence of perinatal problems. Details of the child's growth and development are included.

Educational data include the levels of academic achievement together with the quality and quantity of educational experience and remedial effort.

By the time the child reaches the child psychiatrist, cognitive, social, and educational data, as described in Chapter 5 will have been obtained. It is the task of the child psychiatrist to integrate these data with the neuropsychiatric findings for a comprehensive understanding of the child and his or her problems.

The integration of data from these pentaxial parameters may be seen in the following study of Charles, who was 10 years, 3 months of age when he was referred from a class for severely emotionally disturbed children because he was making no academic progress and because of his daily temper outbursts. Psychological testing revealed a full scale IQ of 90 on the WISC-R (verbal IQ of 94, performance IQ of 88). Academically, his oral reading (WRAT) was at mid-third grade and spelling was at early second grade. There is a history of previous diagnosis of hyperactivity and attention deficit disorder for which he received methylphenidate for 3 years, but which Charles said only made him "worse."

CASE STUDY: CHARLES

Neurological Examination

Neurological examination revealed a sturdy 10-year-old, who came willingly for the examination. There is a tic of both eyes, a press of speech with mild circumstantiality, and gross motor restlessness. At times he is definitely hyperkinetic, distracted by small items in the examining room. His gross motor coordination is poor; muscle tone appears decreased in the upper extremities, slightly increased in the lower; synkinesis is marked. There is nystagmus on lateral gaze and a mild esophoria. He has difficulty with finger-gnosis, where he cannot correctly perceive bilateral asymmetric stimuli. Extinction phenomena are easily elicited and praxis is definitely immature, particularly on the left side. On extension of the arms, there are marked adventitious movements. Although it is his right hand which is elevated in this right-handed boy, pencil grip is abnormal. The remainder of the classical neurological examination is within normal limits. The electroencephalogram is abnormal with high-voltage slow waves characteristic of "diffuse cerebral dysfunction."

Perceptual Examination

Visual discrimination is accurate by our measures. Visual recall of asymmetric stimuli, however, is no higher than at a 7-year level, and visual-motor function is primitive—no higher than at an 8-year level, with gross angulation difficulty and verticalization (Figure 6-1). His figure drawing is made with wild, impulsive, pencil strokes, the head enlarged to be the most prominent feature, the mouth dominant,

Figure 6-1   Bender Gestalt Drawing
Charles: Age 10 years, 3 months

the body contained in two squares each filled in with a penciled scrawl, the arms and legs, small and puny (Figure 6-2).

Auditory discrimination appeared accurate. Auditory rote sequencing, however, is dramatically immature with confusion of the sequences of before and after. To do any segment of sequencing, he had to run through the entire sequence in his mind.

Emotional Examination

Here Charles shows great difficulty. Extremely anxious, he is afraid to go to sleep, has to take a baseball bat to bed with him, has many "scary" events to the extent of illusions and hallucinations: illusions of his chair "looking like a lady without a head," a snake coming at him, the devil talking to him, telling him to do things. The devil tells him he will "burn forever." He has bizarre thoughts of a ghost coming out of the picture in his bathroom, slicing up his grandmother into bits, hanging the bits on the wall. He feels that he has done some bad things, like killing a puppy by

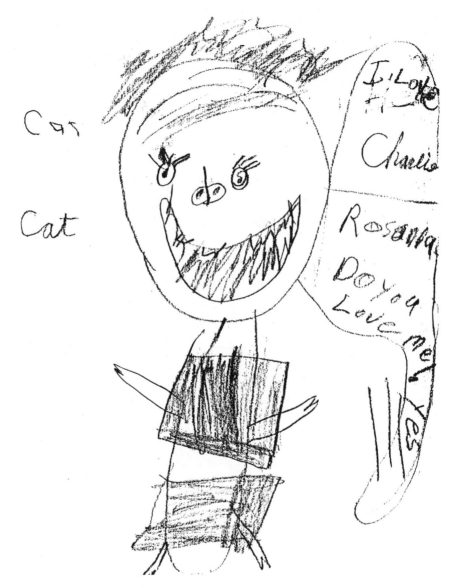

Figure 6-2   Goodenough Draw-a-Person
Charles: Age 10 years, 3 months

jumping on him by accident, and one time he "almost killed a newborn baby." He feels his classmates pick on him because they know he loses his temper quickly and then he hits himself. He fears to go into a dentist's office because he might "cut all my teeth out." He fears a robot dressed up as a real person and talking like a real person.

The relationship with his mother appears distant. A new sibling evokes ambivalent feelings, jealousy, sexual thoughts, affection, and aggression to the child. He had not had a male figure in his home with whom to identify.

As we review these data, we find that Charles has a neurological organization replete with soft neurological signs involving primarily motor impulse control, gross motor coordination, muscle tone, and perception in various modalities. The electroencephalogram is diffusely abnormal with excessive high-voltage slow waves. The cause of this defect is obscure, but the findings are consistent with the history of anoxia at birth, and indeed he remained in the newborn nursery for five days after his mother had returned home. In addition to his difficulty with motor impulse control, coordination, and perception, his biological defect makes him more vulnerable to anxiety. A major problem is emotional, characterized by marked anxiety and by the establishment of a masochistic personality structure. He is accordingly self-destructive, and his aggression to himself also may well be turned outward. Intrafamilial factors have contributed to his masochistic development. His father set the stage by beating his mother even to the extent, says Charles, of "tying her up" and burning Charles with a cigarette. His mother's remarriage has only this month produced a boy whose presence adds to Charles's emotional conflicts. In spite of all, this child is verbal and appealing, evoking sympathy and interest.

Data from each axis of the pentaxial scheme is essential for understanding and managing children such as Charles with academic difficulty and behavioral problems. Educationally Charles needs teaching to build the preacademic skills to form a foundation in reading and the language arts. His teacher, too, recognizing his low threshold for anxiety should try to protect him from anxiety-producing stimuli and to provide a verbal outlet for his aggression. When a task requires sustained attention, use of a quiet place where external stimuli are reduced, is helpful. In addition, however, medication (see Chapter 14, "The Organic Group") is indicated. Individual psychotherapeutic help for Charles to help him deal with his new family and with the sources of his anxiety is indicated. Support for his family will be helpful. This brief clinical vignette illustrates how the data from the multiaxial evaluation provide an understanding of the many facets of this child's academic difficulty—an understanding from which may be derived appropriate and adequate remedial measures.

PSYCHIATRIC EXAMINATION

The psychiatric examination explores the feelings and thoughts of the child, her goals and desires, her reactions to the stresses and supports of her life, and the abilities and the disabilities with which she confronts the world. It attempts to trace the origins and development of these reactions and views them within the framework of the events of the child's life as they unfold with time. To acquire the data to understand each of these parameters, and then to synthesize the data to make a coherent picture of the child in his world, is the task of the psychiatrist. *How* to acquire that data has been the subject of a vast body of literature, with each successive textbook on child psychiatry providing chapters on the assessment of children.

In the 1930s and 1940s, with the ascendancy of the child guidance movement, data about the child's behavior and development were obtained largely from the child's parents or caretakers. In the first edition (1935) of the classic Kanner text in child psychiatry, such a framework is emphasized, but the book also points the way to careful, individual examination of children. By 1947, M. B. Hall published one of the earliest texts on *Psychiatric Examination of the School Child,* and by 1957 the Group for the Advancement of Psychiatry (GAP), concerned with the rapidly developing field of child psychiatry, formulated *The Diagnostic Process in Child Psychiatry.* The GAP report, however, was concerned largely with statements of basic assumptions as they relate to the diagnostic process and described the actual diagnostic progress only in general terms. The authors state, for example, that "diagnosis involved primarily an investigation of the child's relative successes and failures in mastering, in orderly sequence, certain universal anxieties which confront all children as they move through the several stages of personality development. In general, the major task in this growth is directed toward the achievement of a biologically satisfying utilization of life energies (the libidinal or psychosexual and the aggressive drives) through constructive patterns which is socially and ethically satisfying." However weak on the *how* of psychiatric diagnosis, the 1957 GAP report did provide a standard for the child psychiatrist in examination of an individual child.

More recent and more specific descriptions of assessment procedures appear in *The Basic Handbook of Child Psychiatry* (R. L. Cohen, 1979), *Psychiatric Examination of Children* (Simmons, 1987), a section on clinical skills in *Beginning Child Psychiatry* (Adams & Fras, 1988), and *Handbook of Clinical Assessment of Children and Adolescents* (Kestenbaum & Williams, 1988). An assessment of young children within the Anna Freud-Hampstead model was presented by Flapan and Neubauer (1975), and an assessment of young children from a developmental structuralist concept was done by Greenspan (1981). Simmons' book, first published in 1969, has withstood the test of time for three editions and, as such, has been used by successive years of child psychiatry trainees. The practical details of the physical structure of the examining room, preparing the child for interview, and the observation of family interactions need not be reviewed here. More important, however, is the need to offer a template for the interview of the child, particularly in its relevance to learning disorders. The areas to be covered need to be spelled out specifically. Simmons, for example, includes in the mental status examination of a child, 11 areas for investigation: appearance, mood, orientation and perception, coping mechanisms, neuromuscular integration, thought processes and verbalization, fantasy (as seen in dreams, drawing, wishes, and play), superego, concept of self, awareness of problems, and intelligence quotient estimate.

Our approach to the psychiatric component of the pentaxial scheme is seen in Table 6-2. In this scheme there are 12 major areas that must be covered systematically: general appearance, affect, object relations, impulse control, reality testing, thought process and cognitive function, speech, identification, defense mechanisms including neurotic, somatic, and character traits, structural aspects of the personality, behavior in various settings, and biological factors. For some of these areas, subheadings further define the area to be evaluated, and each area is provided with descriptors to direct the thinking of the examiner (Appendix B). With constant repetition, these areas for evaluation become automatic, just as the medical student learns to automatically examine the heart in five parameters (size, action, sounds, murmurs, and thrills).

To define the parameters of the mental status examination, however, is not to describe the *manner* in which these data are collected, the questions to be asked, the way the questions must be modified concordant with each child, and his or her age, levels of development, comprehension, and levels of anxiety. Bird and Kestenbaum (1988) and Kestenbaum and Bird (1978)

Table 6-2   *University of South Florida College of Medicine Division of Child and Adolescent Psychiatry: Psychiatric Examination—Summary*

Name _____	Chronological Age _____
Date _____	
1. General Appearance:	11. Behavior (description in various
2. Affect:	settings):
3. Object relations:	
4. Impulse control:	
A. Motor	
B. Emotional	
C. Affective response	
5. Reality testing:	
6. Thought process and cognitive	
function:	
7. Speech:	
8. Identification:	
9. Defense mechanisms:	
A. Neurotic type:	
B. Somatic:	12. Biological factors:
C. Character traits:	13. Diagnosis:
10. Structural elements of personality:	

provided specific questions that may be asked to explore the events and feelings of each aspect of the child's life: school, work, interpersonal relationships, self-concept, anxiety, conscience, anger, reality testing, depression, and fantasy. Such an outline directs the examiner to each area that needs to be explored. The experienced psychiatrist follows the directions dictated by the child, permitting the examination to flow into the direction of the child's needs, exploring each new area as it is revealed, but always keeping in mind the areas to be covered in the examination and returning to each until all are known. This is an open-ended, semi-structured clinical interview. It is the type of interview taught in child psychiatry training programs and it is the type of interview done by most child psychiatrists in daily practice.

The inter-rater reliability and the test-retest reliability of this open-ended, semi-structured examination is demonstrated daily in centers for the training of child psychiatrists. Objective evidence, however, is scant with Rutter and Graham (1968) providing one of the few test-retest and inter-rater reliability studies. The Rutter and Graham (1968) study found a one-half hour interview a valid instrument "to make a provisional judgment on whether or not the child exhibits any psychiatric disorder" (p. 574).

The open-ended, semi-structured clinical interview is not designed to provide quantitative measures. It can be easily modified, however, by carefully defined boundaries for each category, to provide gross measurement of psychiatric impairment (none, mild, moderate, or severe) (A. A. Silver, Hagin, De Vito, Kreeger, & Scully, 1976) and of specific symptoms elicited (i.e., depression). For research purposes, particularly with the emphasis on specific symptom targets in psychopharmacology research, there has been "dissatisfaction with the reliability and validity of traditional diagnostic procedures" (Edelbrock & Costello, 1984). Further, the explicit diagnostic categories of DSM-III-R also demanded a "more standardized approach to assessment of child symptoms." As a result, a series of interview scales are in varied stages of development and use. These scales vary as to target phenomena to be assessed and degree of structure. The Diagnostic Interview for Children and Adolescents (DICA, Herjanic & Campbell, 1977; Herjanic & Reich, 1982), for example, is highly structured with specifications for the order, wording, and coding of all items. The DICA yields information on 185 symptoms and is cross-indexed against DSM-III. The *how* of gathering the data demanded in Table 6-2, at least in terms of the questions to be asked, is also specified. The Kiddie Schedule for Affective Disorders and Schizophrenia (Kiddie SADS, Puig-Antich, Bleu, Mark, Greenhill, & Chambers, 1978; Puig-Antich, Chambers, & Tambrizi, 1983), on the other hand, is designed to assess clinical features associated with depression. There are, however, items dealing with somatization, nondepressive neurotic disorders, conduct disorders, and psychotic disorders. The sections of this scale dealing with symptoms of depression and schizophrenia are also structured with specific wording of questions.

The specific interviews described above are distinct from parent, teacher, and child checklists and rating scales, which vary from specific syndrome scales (such as the Conners Parent-Teacher Questionnaire, Conners, 1973b) to a more general overview of psychopathology (such as Achenbach, 1966, 1978; Achenbach & Edelbrock, 1979, 1983; Quay, 1977; and Quay & Peterson, 1983).

The development of structured interviews for children continues to be encouraged by the National Institute of Mental Health (NIMH). This support has resulted in the relatively new scale, the Diagnostic Interview Schedule for Children (DISC, Costello, Edelbrock, Kalas, Kessler, & Klaric 1982; Costello, Edelbrock, Dulcan, Kalas, & Klaric 1984), a highly structured interview in which the order, wording, and coding of all items was specified. A total of 264 items covers a broad range of symptoms and behaviors that may be collapsed into 27 symptom scales corresponding to diagnostic categories.

Eight such scales suitable for epidemiological and clinical research were described in a report from the Division of Biometry and Epidemiology, NIMH (Orvaschel, Sholomska, & Weissman, 1980). Seven of the eight psychiatric interview scales described in that report, together with the DISC, were reviewed by Edelbrock and Costello (1984) in a study paper for the Center for Studies of Child and Adolescent Psychopathology, Clinical Research Branch, NIMH. Each scale is discussed in terms of its item content, response scaling, administration time, degree of structure, informant, age range, training of interviewer, alternate form, information yield, psychometric properties (reliability and validity), and applications. Orvaschel (1985, 1988) and Orvaschel and Walsh (1984) have also reviewed five of the structured or semistructured interview scales, including the Children's Assessment Schedule (CAS, Hodges, Kline, Fitch, McKnew, & Cytryn, 1981; Hodges, Stern, Cytryn, & McKnew, 1982), DICA, DISC, the Interview Schedule for Children (ISC) (Kovacs, 1983), and the children's version of the K-SADS. The characteristics and content of these schedules are shown in Table 6-3.

In addition to the structured interview schedules reviewed in Table 6-3, this same *Psychopharmacology Bulletin* issue also outlined the Children's Global Assessment Scale (D. Shaffer et al., 1985), the Psychiatry Interview for Children, (Rutter & Graham, 1985), and the Children's Psychiatric Rating Scale (B. Fish, 1985). Edelbrock and Costello (1984) concluded that "much work is needed before structured interviews can be recommended as assessment and diagnostic tools. All . . . are in need of more thorough studies of reliability and validity (pp. 30–31). While the interview scales can discriminate between "disturbed" and normal, a scale for sensitivity and specificity has yet to be developed. Exceptions to this may be the Kiddie SADS and the ISC, which, as we have mentioned above, were developed specifically for research on depression. Interpretation of these scales, however, demands clinical judgment.

For our everyday clinical use, we are left, then, with the open-ended, clin-

Table 6-3   Characteristics and Content of Structured Psychiatric Interviews

Interview Properties	CAS	DICA	DISC	ISC	K-SADS
Number of items	128	267–311	264–302	200 +	200 +
Time period assessed	current or past 6 months	current or ever	past year	2 weeks or past 6 months	current or lifetime
Age assessed	7–17	6–17	6–17	8–17	6–17
Completion time	45–60 min	60–90 min	50–70 min	60–90 min	45–120 min
Structured		X	X		
Semistructured	X			X	X
Symptom oriented	X		X	X	
Category oriented		X			X
Severity ratings				X	X
Pre-coded	X	X	X	X	X
Computer scoring		X	X		
Administration					
Lay interviewer		X	X		
Clinician	X	X	X	X	X
Reliability data	X	X	X	X	X
Axis Disorders:					
Affective Disorders					
Adjustment disorders with depressed mood				X	
Cyclothymia	X		X		X
Dysthymia	X	X	X	X	X
Hypomania				X	X
Major depression	X	X	X	X	X
Mania	X	X	X	X	X
Minor depression					X
Anxiety Disorders					
Avoidant	X	X	X	X	
Generalized anxiety	X				X
Obsessive-compulsive	X	X	X	X	X
Overanxious	X	X	X	X	X
Panic	X		X	X	X
Phobic	X	X	X	X	X
Separation anxiety	X	X	X	X	X

Table 6-3   *(continued)*

Interview Properties	CAS	DICA	DISC	ISC	K-SADS
Behavioral Disorders					
Attention deficit	X	X	X	X	X
Conduct		X	X	X	X
Oppositional	X	X	X	X	
Eating Disorders					
Anorexia nervosa	X	X	X		X
Bulemia	X	X	X		X
Psychotic Disorders					
Psychotic signs (only)	X	X			
Schizoaffective				X	X
Schizophrenia				X	X
Schizophreniform			X	X	X
Substance Disorders					
Alcohol	X	X	X	X	X
Drugs	X	X	X	X	X
Tobacco		X			
Other Disorders					
Encopresis	X	X	X	X	
Enuresis	X	X	X	X	
Gender identity		X	X		
Schizoid	X	X		X	
Sleep terror	X				
Sleep walking	X				
Somatoform		X			
Axis II Disorders					
Borderline				X	
Compulsive				X	
Histrionic				X	
Schizoid				X	
Schizotypal				X	X
Other Content					
Developmental questions		X		X	X
Observational items	X	X		X	X
Stressors		X			
Sexual behavior		X		X	

Note. From "Psychiatric interviews suitable for use in research with children and adolescents" by H. Orvaschel, 1985, *Psychopharmacology Bulletin, 21,* No. 4, pp. 739–740. Material in public domain.

ical interview outlined in Table 6-2. The content of that interview must be complete, exploring all parameters in Appendix B. The structure, however, will vary depending on the circumstances and the age, intelligence, verbal ability, level of development, anxiety, and comprehension of the child.

How the data provided in this psychiatric evaluation contribute to the diagnosis of a child with a learning disorder may be seen in a study of Jay who was 6 years, 2 months of age when seen with the parents' and school's complaint of hyperactivity.

CASE STUDY: JAY

Jay is a handsome, dark-haired, 6-year-old boy. His hands and feet are dirty, his clothes are stained, and, in general, he appears unkempt. He leaves his mother with no overt anxiety. However, he immediately says he would like to sit at my desk and begins to tell the examiner that he does not like school especially when he has to write. He is not hyperkinetic and does not examine objects on the desk or in the room. On questioning he says he has trouble falling asleep. He sees a man's face in the wall and sometimes sees rattlesnakes, spiders, or tarantulas in his room. He hears the devil talking to him saying "vulgar" words. He says he would rather be "in a crib. I can play baby in there and people play with you more." "I know I'm too old for that now, but they [his parents] don't know I like it." He wishes to be a baby when he is asked to do things he feels he cannot do. When he cannot regress, he becomes rebellious, demanding, and repeatedly frustrated. At these times he may hurt himself or has a fantasy of being hit by a car. He feels guilty about the bad things he does. Sometimes he pretends there are no problems, or that he would like to be invisible so that he could scare people or to be a rocket and look about in space. He is pleased that he is a boy but does not think he will be as strong as his father or talk as loud as he does. As Jay felt less anxious in the examination, he was able to leave the examiner's desk and play with the toy cars on the child table.

From this interview we may conclude that Jay does have emotional problems, which, by themselves, could account for his behavior and problems in school adjustment. He is depressed and sometimes discouraged; his object relations vary between being demanding and attention seeking and being clinging and infantile. His motor impulse control in this evaluation is good; his emotional impulse control is poor with a need for immediate gratification; his reality testing and identification are adequate. He is anxious, already feeling that the world is too demanding. He has fears of animals, visual illusions, and even auditory hallucinations. His anxiety makes him restless, even "hyperactive." His personality structure is already rife with guilt.

From this interview alone, however, we do not have a complete picture of Jay and his school problems. The pentaxial evaluation adds further dimensions to Jay's picture. He has superior verbal intelligence but average perfomance ability. Neurologically he has difficulty with fine-motor coordination, in praxis (where his performance is no higher than age 4), and in visual-motor function. His father is demanding, overbearing, and physically and emotionally abusive to his wife, Jay's mother. She, in turn, is self-effacing, mouselike, and browbeaten. On questioning, Jay's father says that Jay has no problems, that Jay is just as he was, that he also had trouble in school because he could not write clearly and that he still dislikes writing.

With these data, a fuller picture of Jay unfolds. There may be a basic developmental delay that is mild and possibly genetic, involving fine motor coordination and praxis. Upon this, however, is superimposed the spectre of a father whom he cannot please and who actually frightens him, a mother who cannot give Jay the support he needs, and now a school that is making demands on him that physically he cannot meet. He reacts with anxiety, hyperactivity, regression, denial, withdrawal into fantasy, depression, and guilt. Dynamically he has not resolved the anxieties of the oedipal phase and has remnants of even earlier psychosexual developmental phases. He is already failing in first grade. In management he needs the cooperation of his school, not only in understanding his high capabilities as well as his poor motor function, but also in offering intervention so that he could overcome his poor function; help for his parents in resolving their emotional difficulties and their impact on the child; and at the very least supportive psychotherapy for Jay himself. Without the understanding of this child's emotional problems, treating him for inattention would not solve his school or behavioral difficulties. Medication was not used in the successful resolution of Jay's difficulties.

NEUROLOGICAL EXAMINATION

The value of a neurological examination for children with learning disorders has been questioned by some educators and even by psychiatrists. In 1980 G. Weiss stated "it is known that children with learning disabilities and/or hyperactive impulse disorders may not have abnormal neurological or EEG findings, and even if they had (aside from the rare treatable neurological conditions, such as brain tumors or frank epilepsy) the findings would make no difference whatever to their educational and psychological rehabilitation or their total management" (p. 349). Kinsbourne and Caplan (1979) broadened the criteria for neurological examination to (a) where there is suspicion of organic disease of the central nervous system, (b) where the examiner has elicited signs "which lend themselves to ambiguous interpretation," or (c) where a satisfactory examination of the nervous system has not been done.

Our position is clearly on the side of Kinsbourne. Although children with "learning disabilities" may not have abnormal neurological or EEG findings, of course, some of them do. In a study of 494 children comprising the entire first grades of seven schools on the East Side of New York City, Hagin, Beecher, and Silver (1982) found approximately 25% of the entire group to have signs suggesting vulnerability to learning disorder. Seventeen percent

(83 children) of the total sample did not have findings on neurological examination other than the specific perceptual deficits of developmental dyslexia, but 5% (21 children) of the total group did have neurological findings. This study was done on an unselected population, a "normative" group to be found in any first-grade classroom in a typical inner city public school in Manhattan.

When dealing with older children who have already failed in academic achievement and who are in classes for emotionally disturbed children, neurological examination is most important and, in our opinion, an evaluation of such children is not complete if it does not include neurological study. In an examination of the first 60 children placed in self-contained classes for severely emotionally disturbed children in a west Florida county (A. A. Silver, 1984b), 18 (30%) of the 60 had evidence of some structural defect of the central nervous system, another 18 (30%) were children with long-standing specific learning disability (dyslexia), and 10 (17%) were suffering from an attention deficit disorder. Tables 6-4 and 6-5 outline the neurological and cognitive findings in these 60 children. In a second study (A. A. Silver, in press) of 32 children between the ages of 12 and 16 who were consecutively referred to our child psychiatry clinic because of academic and behavior difficulty in classes for emotionally disturbed children, electroencephalograms were done on 29. Of these, 19 EEGs were reported as abnormal and 10 as normal. Abnormalities included abnormal focal slowing, multifocal or focal spikes, paroxysmal spikes, or generalized excessive slowing. It was clear that neurological examination and, in selected children, neurological and electroencephalographic examination contributed an important dimension to understanding these children who were having so much difficulty in learning and in behavior.

Table 6-4   *Neurological and Cognitive Findings for Children in Self-Contained Classes for Severely Emotionally Handicapped*

Predominant Diagnosis	School S (n)	School M (n)	Total n	Total %
Attention Deficit Disorder	5	5	10	17
Organic Defect in the Central Nervous System	10	8	18	30
Specific Learning Disability	6	12	18	30
Schizophrenia	1	2	3	5
Borderline Mental Retardation	3	8	11	18
TOTAL	25	35	60	100

Note. From "Children in classes for the severely emotionally handicapped" by A. A. Silver, 1984, *Journal of Developmental and Behavioral Pediatrics, 5,* p. 50. Copyright 1984 by Williams and Wilkins. Reprinted by permission.

Table 6-5   Variety of Neurological Disorders for Children in Self-
Contained Classes for Severely Emotionally Handicapped

Disorder	Total n
Prematurity[a]	3
Cerebral Palsy	3
Genetic (Chromosome Defect)	3
Seizures, Idiopathic	2
Cerebellar Palsy	2
Rh Incompatibility	1
Tourette's Syndrome	1
Unknown Dyskinesia	1
Pb Toxicity	1
Birth Trauma	1
TOTAL	18

[a]One with fetal alcohol syndrome.
Note. From "Children in classes for the severely emotionally handicapped" by A.
A. Silver, 1984, *Journal of Developmental and Behavioral Pediatrics, 5,* p. 50. Copy-
right 1984 by Williams and Wilkins. Reprinted by permission.

Even with younger children, children in the early elementary grades who
are beginning to show signs of a learning disorder, neurological examination can be of importance in guiding the teacher in her work. Generally
children with neurological problems, particularly those with diffuse central
nervous system dysfunction, are more vulnerable to anxiety. Their stimulus
barrier is thin—they have difficulty controlling the impulses that spring
from within themselves, and they are more sensitive, overreacting to stimuli
that impinge upon them. Thus they may be easily distracted and cannot
always sustain attention in the midst of the average classroom. Quiet places
may be necessary. Sensitivity, however, is found not only in their responses
to physical stimuli (children talking, papers rustling, or outside noises), but
they are also sensitive to emotional stimuli and are easily emotionally hurt.
Their response may be aggression or withdrawal. In either event, the teachers' awareness of emotional sensitivity can provide a buffer to emotional
stimuli as well as to the more obvious perceptual ones (see Chapter 14, "The
Organic Group").

From a learning point of view, there are additional problems in children
with organic defects of the central nervous system. Their perceptual deficits
are more resistant to change than are those in children with developmental
dyslexia. In a 12-year follow-up study of children with learning disorders,
children with an "organic diagnosis" did not outgrow their perceptual
defects (A. A. Silver & Hagin, 1964). The same perceptual problems found
at age 8 were found in these people when they were in their 20s. Also these

children have difficulty with memory. What they may learn one day is forgotten the next. In children with neurological findings teaching requires more time, proceeds more slowly, and may have a more guarded prognosis than in children with dyslexia with similar perceptual defects (see Chapters 7, "Principles of Educational Remediation" and 14, "The Organic Group").

Neurological findings, contrary to the opinion expressed by G. Weiss (1980), have much to contribute to educational and psychological rehabilitation. Part of the problem in accepting neurological study is that in children with learning disorders, the classical neurological examination involving static examination, muscle tone, power and synergy, deep and superficial and pathological reflexes, cranial nerves and gross sensory evaluation, must be amplified by the study of soft signs: kinetic patterns in various states; postural responses; the so-called "higher cortical functions" (Luria, 1966)—spatial orientation and temporal organization in visual, auditory, and body image modalities; and the receptive, associative, and emissive aspects of language. Our outline for neurological evaluation is seen in Table 6-6. Findings must then be placed on the background of a normal developmental curve.

Classical neurological examination needs no amplification here. An expanded outline for neurological examination may be found in Appendix C. Soft signs, however, including testing of higher cortical function, do need definition and description.

Testing for Neurological Soft Signs

Soft signs on neurological examination have been defined in two ways.

1. First, as "non-normative performance on a motor or sensory test identical or akin to a test item of the traditional neurological examination, but which is elicited from an individual who shows none of the features of a fixed or transient localizable neurological disorder" (D. Shaffer, O'Connor, Shafer, & Prupis, 1983). These signs may be elicited in three general areas: (a) movement, including spontaneous tremors, tics, synkinesis and choreoform movement: (b) coordination, including dysmetria, dysdiadochokinesis, and awkwardness, and (c) sensory integration, such as stereognosis and graphesthesia. Shaffer's concept of soft neurological signs further states that these signs cannot be related to "any serious postnatal neurological insult that might be expected to leave residual neurological signs" nor may "groupings of soft signs have a pathognomic pattern that would indicate localized structural lesions, generalized encephalopathy, or CNS involvement" (p. 144).

2. Second, as representing the persistence of a primitive form of a response (Kinsbourne & Caplan, 1979), a failure of the child to have

Table 6-6   University of South Florida College of Medicine Division of Child and Adolescent Psychiatry Neurological Examination—Summary

Name: _____   Birthdate: _____

Address: _____   Present Date: _____

Telephone No.: _____   Age Now: _____

School and Grade: _____

Head Circumference: _____

Ectoderm: _____

Gross Posture and Gait _____

Hand used for writing: _____

I. Neurological

1. Extension with counting
   a. adventitious movements
   b. convergence-divergence
   c. elevated extremity
2. Rotation of head
   a. standing
      1. head to left
      2. head to right
   b. sitting
3. Muscle tone
   a. increased-decreased-normal
   b. fluctuating
   c. myoclonic activity
   d. synkinesis
4. Classical
   a. cranial nerves-nystagmus
   b. tendon reflexes
   c. pathological reflexes
   d. superficial reflexes
   e. cerebellar function
5. Patterned motor behavior
   a. gross patterns
      1. hyper-hypo
      2. anti-gravity play
      3. relationship to adult
      4. toe walking
         hopping
         tandem walk
      5. other
   b. Fine-motor coordination
      1. F.F.
      2. F.N.
      3. Praxis:
      4. R 1-3, 1-5, 1-2, 1-4
      5. L 1-3, 1-5, 1-2, 1-4
6. Language
   a. receptive
   b. associative
   c. emissive
   d. Van Alstyne (picture vocabulary)
   e. word recognition (WRAT)
   f. spelling (WRAT)
   g. arithmetic (WRAT)

II. Autonomic Nervous System

1. Pupils
   a. size l. s. n.
   b. shape
   c. position
   d. reaction to L&A.
   e. convergence
2. Ptosis
3. Salivation
4. Vasomotor and Sudomotor
   a. perioral pallor
   b. skin temperature N. Abn.
   c. sweating of palms
   d. other
5. Heart rate

III. Perceptual-Cognitive

1. Visual
   a. discrimination
   b. recall
   c. figure–ground
   d. visual–motor
   e. block design
2. Auditory
   a. discrimination
   b. rote sequencing
   c. sentences
   d. code sequencing
3. Tactile
   a. extinction
   b. stereognosis
   c. finger gnosis

   Single   *Sym. bilat*
   R-1, L-3, L-5, R-4   R2-L2, R4-L4
   Asym. bilat
   R3-L5, R2-L4, R4-L3, R3-L4
4. Body Image
   a. right-left discrimination
      1. in self, R, x'd
      2. in examiner, R, x'd
   b. draw-a-person

matured in a particular function consistent with that expected for his or her age. Such functions may not only be in the motor area, in coordination, and in sensory integration as described in the D. Shaffer et al. (1983) definition, but may also be found in such perceptual functions as in tests of spatial orientation and temporal sequencing. In the motor area, for example, the choreoathetotic movements of the infant as he grasps for a rattle are perfectly normal. The persistence of such choreoform movement in a 10-year-old or in a 7-year-old, even in the absence of an identified neurological disease, suggests that in that child the function of modulation of motor movement is immature. Similarly, in the concept of the body image in space such as in right–left discrimination, praxis, or finger-gnosis, a soft sign means that performance in these functions is not that expected for the child's age. A soft sign thus suggests that the maturation of a particular function is delayed; it is a sign of neurological or neuropsychological immaturity.

The concept of soft signs as an indication of immaturity in development is a concept broader than that delineated by D. Shaffer et al. (1983). It is more consistent with the concepts of Gesell (1945/1969) who described development as proceeding in hierarchical fashion in a continuum of space and time: Functions or behaviors gradually emerge from the latent biological anlage of the trait into behaviors present in dormant fashion and finally into manifest behavior. At any point in space and time, factors within or external to that organism may interfere with the maturation of a particular function, thus interfering not only with its expression but also with functions that stem from it. Some of these interfering factors may lie within the organism itself, such as an idiosyncrasy inherent in the genes; some may result from toxic interference in embyonic development, such as seen in the fetal alcohol syndrome, or from some lesion (i.e., traumatic or anoxic) acquired at birth or in early life (i.e., infection or trauma); and some may occur in children in whom the environmental stimulus needed to transform the available biological anlage into manifest function is inappropriate or insufficient.

In any one child, of course, combinations of these possible origins of soft signs may be found. A child with a genetic predisposition to a specific language disability, for example but a disposition not great enough *per se* to result in language disorder, may experience a birth trauma that can bring out the latent predisposition. As Zangwill (1960) said of reading disabilities, "the ambilateral constitution provides no more than a setting for the interplay of genetic and acquired tendencies in growth and development (p. 26). Contrary to D. Shaffer's statement that "soft signs cannot be related to any serious postnatal insult that may be expected to leave residual neurological signs," our experience and the literature suggest that with perinatal or postnatal events such as perinatal distress, postnatal trauma, or infection, classical neurological signs may be obtunded with age or may indeed be entirely absent so that soft signs or a learning disorder may be the only residuals of such events. In this context soft signs may represent manifestations of definite neurological abnormalities, the behavioral and educational consequences of which may be profound.

What happens to soft signs as the child grows older? Are they simply "transient phenomena that pass with maturation"? Longitudinal studies suggest that they do not necessarily disappear with maturation. As pointed out in Chapter 1, the concept of "developmental lag," as advanced by Gesell and Thompson (1934) and later by L. A. Bender and Yarnell (1940), applied to children whose classical neurological examination was normal. Structural central nervous system defects could not be identified in these children, and functional defects (soft signs) were not considered fixed but to have a potential for maturation. This potential, however, does not mean that the lagging function will accelerate and spontaneously become age appropriate.

Longitudinal studies (Hertzig, 1982; McMahon & Greenberg, 1977; Minde, Weiss, & Mendelson, 1972; D. Shaffer, 1980; D. Shaffer et al., 1983; A. A. Silver & Hagin, 1964; G. Weiss, 1983; G. Weiss & Hechtman, 1986; G. Weiss, Minde, Werry, Douglas, & Nemeth, 1971) demonstrated the consistency of soft signs over time. D. Shaffer et al. (1985) in a follow-up of black male children with soft signs, children originally examined as part of the Collaborative Perinatal Project, found that more than half the children who showed dysdiadochokinesia and mirror movements at age 7 still showed these signs at age 17. Hertzig (1982) reported two examinations, four years apart, on 53 children who were part of an original study of 198 children comprising a sample of children attending a special school for learning disabled and neurologically impaired children. The mean number of nonfocal (i.e., soft) signs did decrease in stepwise fashion from 4.8 in the 9½-year-olds to 2.5 in the 15½-year-olds; however, "the number of children who displayed 2 or more non-focal signs on each examination did not differ significantly on two examinations conducted four years apart" (p. 231). G. Weiss et al. (1971) and Minde et al. (1972) followed the fate of children diagnosed as hyperactive and treated with phenothiazines or dextroamphetamine for 5 years. In general, hyperactive children had significantly higher rates of academic failure and more behavioral problems than the controls. Further, on the Lincoln Oseretsky Motor Development Scale, the hyperactive children actually dropped in their performance from the 31st to the 15th percentile. The results of the WISC, Goodenough Draw-a-Man, and Bender VMGT tests showed no significant change over time.

In a 10–12-year follow-up study, 24 children with a learning disability (21 boys, 3 girls), who were aged 8–10 in their initial examination at the Bellevue Hospital Mental Hygiene Clinic, were reexamined at median age 19 years with the same battery of tests used earlier (A. A. Silver & Hagin, 1964). A control group of 11 children, also referred to the Bellevue Hospital Mental Hygiene Clinic, matched with the reading disability children in age, sex, IQ, socioeconomc status, and psychiatric diagnosis, were also followed. It was specifically noted that some of the tests were modified for use with the older group but were designed to measure the same function studied earlier. In studying visual figure–ground perception, for example, the Marble Board test (Strauss & Werner, 1943) was used for the younger children; to this was added the Gottschaldt visual figure–ground test for the young adults. Findings indicated that, in spite of maturation in some areas, specific reading disability is a long-term problem, the signs of which may be detected in young adult life. The ability to distinguish right and left was improved, but evidence of immaturity in visual-motor function; in figure–ground perception in the tactile, auditory, and visual areas; and in finger-gnosis remained. Also, subjects who as children had neurological evidence suggesting a structural defect of the central nervous system tended to retain in young adulthood the same signs they had as children, while those designated as having developmental learning disabilities recovered partially or developed cues to help cope with spatial or temporal problems.

It appears, then, that there is a constancy of soft signs over time, although they need not be static. The important issue is that although some maturation may be found, the developmental immaturity still persists relative to normal age-appropriate levels of the same function as the child grows older. Tests must be adapted to the age of the child. The ceiling of a test suitable for a younger child will not reveal the defect in an older child. An example of adapting figure–ground tests to age is seen in the previous paragraph. Another example may be seen in tests for right–left discrimination. A 6-year-old with a learning problem may not be able to identify his own right hand. An adolescent with a learning problem may be able to identify her own right hand but cannot identify the right hand of the examiner in front of her, a task that the intact adolescent has no difficulty performing.

Not only must tests for the same function be adapted to age, but also tests for new functions that normally emerge over time must be done. Satz, Rardin, and Ross (1971), Satz et al. (1978), and Satz and Van Nostrand (1973), for example, postulate that in kindergarten children in whom learning disabilities will develop later there is a lag in the development of skills of perceptual discrimination and analysis. These skills are subsumed under the term "sensory-perceptual-motor-mnemonic" ability. By the fifth grade, by age 10, however, these skills, said Satz, will eventually catch up, but there will be a subsequent lag in the conceptual-linguistic skills, which have a slower and later ontogenetic development. The emergence of hierarchical function lags in time is certainly to be expected. However, if the perceptual skills of a 10-year-old with a learning disability are tested in a framework suitable to that age, they may not "catch up" at all, but will reveal telltale evidence of the immaturity foretold by their earlier testing.

A standardized procedure for comprehensive testing for soft signs has not been generally accepted. L. A. Bender has generally been credited with viewing soft signs as evidence of immaturity of the central nervous system. Her techniques for eliciting soft signs are included in her extensive publications, but these techniques have lacked systematic studies of reliability and validity. Nevertheless, students who have worked with her have evidence of their clinical reliability in their daily work.

Attempts have been made to structure the neurological examination for soft signs by the Collaborative Perinatal Study (Nichols & Chen, 1981), by the Psychiatric and Neurological Examination for subtle signs (PANESS, Close 1973, revised by Denckla, 1985), by Rutter, Graham, et al. (1970), by Hertzig (1982), and by A. A. Silver and Hagin, (1972b). A timed motor coordination battery, along with sample norms, is included in the Denckla (1985) revision. Nevertheless, procedures for comprehensive testing for soft signs generally vary among investigators. Not only may different investigators examine different functions, but also, even when different investigators study the same functions, the method for studying that function may vary. Table 6-7 compares methods that have appeared in the literature for testing soft signs.

In testing for stereognosis for example, the CPP study uses a bottlecap, nickel, and button which the child must, with eyes closed, identify by touch. Those who fail are given a "more gross" test using a key, marble, and ¾″ block. The directions as given in Nichols and Chen (1981) are not clear, but it is presumed that each hand is tested separately and the children's responses are verbal identifications. In the scored neurological examination (Close, 1973; Denckla, 1985), a coin, ring, safety pin, and key are used; in the Rutter, Graham, and Yule (1970) protocol a rubber (eraser), matchbox, key, and penny are used; Hertzig (1981) uses a comb, key, quarter, and penny. These subtle differences make comparisons uncertain. Tests for finger-gnosis are even more variable. The CPP examination uses "abnormal tactile finger recognition." Children were asked to identify fingers that were lightly touched when the fingers were out of their sight. Each of the ten fingers was tested with a single stimulus and results were quantitatively coded by number of errors. It is not clear whether the identification was verbal, by number or by name of the finger, or simply by indicating by gesture which finger is touched. Rutter, Graham, & Yule (1970), PANESS (Close, 1971; Denckla, 1985) and Hertzig (1982) do not test for finger-gnosis. A. A. Silver and Hagin (1972b), however, make finger-gnosis an important part of their study for spatial orientation of the body image. They use a sequence of developmental skills: first single stimuli, then bilateral simultaneous symmetrical stimuli, and finally bilateral simultaneous asymmetric stimuli. It is interesting to note that as far back as 1959, Benton stated that "the methods employed to assess right–left discrimination and finger local-

Table 6-7 Protocols for Examination of Soft Signs

	CPP 1982	PANESS 1973	PANESS 1985 Revision	Rutter et al. 1970	Hertzig 1982	A. Silver and Hagin 1972(b)
Motility						
Abnormal Movements	Thumb and forefinger opposition	Extension of arms, eyes open and closed	—	Extension of arms, squeeze, bulldog clip	Prechtl movements	Extension of arms
Primitive Reflexes	—			—	—	TNR & NR, toe walking, antigravity play
Coordination and Synergy						
Fine Motor	Tying shoes, buttons, zippers, writing	Finger tapping, foot tapping, coordinated finger, foot taps		Tying shoelaces, stringing beads	Foot taps	Finger to finger testing
Finger-Nose	Eyes open and closed	Eyes open and closed	Eyes closed	Hand to nose and to examiner's finger		Eyes open and closed
Heel to Knee	Eyes open and closed	Eyes open and closed	—	—		
Gait and Synergy	Hopping, walking, running	Tiptoe, heel walk, hopping	Toe walk, heel walk, everted gait, tandem gait, steadiness		Standing, hopping, tandem walk	Observed tandem walk
	Toe walking, heel walking, hopping	Tandem walk, Romberg	Balance on leg, hopping			Standing on one foot, Romberg, diadochokinesis
Other	—	Eye movements (nystagmus)	Tongue protrusion	—	—	
Timed Coordination	—		Foot tapping, heel toe rocking, hand	—	—	—

Muscle Tone	—	—	patting, hand pronation and supination, finger to finger, tongue wiggles	Flapping hands, bending fingers, flexion and extension at elbow	Ala Rutter and biceps	Biceps, finger extension, quadriceps
Sensory-Perceptual						
Visual	Bender-Gestalt	—	—	—	—	Discrimination, recall, visual-motor
Auditory	—	—	—	—	—	Discrimination, sequencing memory
Language	—	—	—	Verbal commands, comprehension, phonics and rhythm	—	Quality, content, syntax
Body Image	Finger-gnosis, single stimulation	—	—	—	—	Finger-gnosis, (single, bilateral stimulation), praxis right/left discrimination
Kinesthetic	Stereognosis: nickel, bottle cap, button, position sense	Coin, ring, safety pin, key graphesthesia	—	Rubber, matchbox, key, penny	Comb, key, quarter, penny graphesthesia	As indicated
Praxis	—	Face-nose	—	Reproduce match stick designs	—	Imitation of fine finger movements
Extinction	—	—	—	—	—	Face-hand, wrist-wrist
Lateral Preferences	—	—	Eye-foot-hand	—	—	Arm extension

ization in patients have been so diverse that the findings of various clinical investigators are not comparable" (p. 162). Diversity among methods in examinations for soft signs, which renders comparisons difficult, is still true.

Equally important for most of the functions studied, age norms are sadly lacking. How many Prechtl movements of the outstretched hands, for example, are normal and at what age? At what age do synkinetic (mirror) movements tend to diminish? Quantitative data for this type of soft sign is generally lacking and the examiner is left to rely on clinical experience and judgment. For sensory-perceptual tests, however, norms may be established. The problem here is that except where standardized neuropsychological batteries are used (e.g., Reitan), idiosyncratic examination techniques make norms useless for general application.

Table 6-7 outlines various schemes for the evaluation of soft signs. The CPP (1982) bases its evaluation on the classical neurological examination but in addition stresses motor coordination and synergy, the presence of abnormal movements, sensory-perceptual evaluation of position sense, stereognosis, and finger-gnosis. PANESS (Close, 1973) consists of 43 items to be scored, involving tasks of motor coordination and synergy: finger to nose (items 1–4), heel to shin (items 5–8), walking tiptoe (item 21), heel walking (item 22), hopping (items 23–24), tandem walking (items 25–26), tongue extrusion (time able to extend) (item 30), arms extended, eyes open (item 31), arms extended, eyes closed (item 32), standing on one foot (items 33–34), Romberg (items 35–36), finger tapping (items 37–38), foot tapping (items 39–40), synchronous finger and foot tapping (items 41–42); sensory-perceptual (graphesthesia, items 9–16), stereognosis (items 17–20), two-point discrimination (item 29), face hand test (item 27), face nose test (item 28) and opticokinetic nystagmus (item 43). The revision of the 1973 PANESS (Denckla, 1985) deletes items that were reported to be cumbersome, ambiguous, or unreliable or to be scored abnormal in less than 4% of the subjects: these items included eye tracking (item 43), stereognosis (items 17–20), extinction (items 27–28), and synergy (items 1–8). Other items were added to amplify the 1973 items involving station, gait, and rapid coordinated movement. A timed motor coordination battery replaces the more static examination involving hopping, balancing, and alternating movement. Rutter, Graham, and Yule (1970) add to the tests for motor coordination and synergy, and to sensory-perceptual status, an evaluation of language and speech involving comprehension, phonics and rhythm, and production of language. They also evaluate muscle tone in a number of ways—flapping hands by holding the lower forearm, flexing the wrist, supinating and pronating the arm, bending fingers back, and flexing and extending the elbow.

Inclusion and exclusion of items in these schemes depend not only upon the interest of the examiner, but also upon the purpose for which soft signs were studied. Nichols and Chen's (1981) protocol was to understand the place of soft signs along with learning disability and hyperkinesis in the syndrome of minimal brain dysfunction. The scored neurological examination was formulated to provide a standard for the study of psychopharmacological effects; the Isle of Wight study (Rutter, Tizard, & Whitmore, 1970) was "to detect the presence of neurological disorder rather than to diagnose the nature of pathogenesis or to form part of an assessment for treatment purposes (p. 27).

Our examination was formulated to aid in understanding children with disorders of learning. It is formulated with two principles in mind: (a) a neurological examination including that for soft signs is an essential part of the pentaxial evaluation; (b) a study of soft signs must include an evaluation of the functions of spatial orientation and temporal organization, skills which our experimental evidence and clinical experience lead us to believe are basic for the learning of academic skills of reading, spelling, and arithmetic. (Table 6-6 outlines the neurological evaluation used in our clinics. Appendix C details this examination.) This evaluation stems from the work of Schilder (1935), which was applied to children by L. A. Bender (1956) and modified by one of us (A. A. Silver) to include testing for spatial and temporal organization. The examination has been quantified for use with children aged 5 years, 3 months to 6 years, 7 months (A. A. Silver & Hagin, 1981), and has been used in its qualitative form since 1960 (A. A. Silver & Hagin, 1960) in a study of children with learning disabilities referred to Bellevue Hospital Mental Hygiene Clinic. Its reliability has been assessed by examination of children by generations of child psychiatry fellows supervised by one of us (A. A. Silver).

The examination for soft signs is thus part of our routine neurological evaluation. For convenience, our neurological examination (Table 6-6) is divided into three general parts: (a) the classical neurological evaluation, including motor coordination, tone, power and synergy, cranial nerves, deep and superficial and pathological reflexes, and gross sensory evaluation; (b) autonomic nervous system stability; and (c) perceptual-cognitive functions. Soft signs include evaluation of overall motility, adventitious movements, synergistic movements, synkinesis, primitive postural responses, right–left discrimination, praxis, finger-gnosis, double simultaneous stimulation, testing for extinction phenomena, displacement of sensory stimuli; and visual and auditory perceptual tests relating to visual spatial orientation and auditory temporal organization.

While the classical neurological examination needs no expansion here, there are unique features of this evaluation that do require description.

Arm Extension Test The child stands with his arms extended in front of him, palms down, fingers spread, feet together, eyes closed. He is asked to count for 30 seconds or, if he cannot count, his attention is distracted for 30 seconds. Normally by age 5, the child is capable of following directions for this test. Normally also by age 5, one arm gradually rises slightly

higher than the other and adventitious movements and gross postural sway-
ing of the body are minimal. An occasional Prechtl movement at that age is
normal. By age 7, even that should disappear and the posture is stable with
one arm held slightly higher than the other. While the child is standing with
his arms extended and his eyes closed, his head is gently passively turned by
the examiner first to one side and then the other. By age 6, the body does
not turn to maintain the head, neck, body alignment (neck righting
response) and tonic neck positions are not elicited.

The arm extension test stemmed from two sources: (a) the early work of
Gesell (1938) and Gesell and Thompson (1934), in which the direction of
the tonic neck reflex (TNR) successfully predicted handedness in later life;
the TNR is one of the earliest manifestations of hemisphere asymmetry and
may offer clues to the establishment of hemisphere asymmetry and later lateralization of function; (b) the observation of L. A. Bender (1947, L. A.
Bender & Freedman, 1952) that motility in schizophrenic children is based
upon tonic neck and neck righting responses; the neck righting response is
referred to in the literature as the "whirling test." In our own work, the arm
extension test followed by rotation of the head was, at first, used to detect
the remnants of primitive postural responses such as the TNR and the neck
righting responses. However, the test has come to yield other important
information. Adventitious movements, myoclonic movement, and choreoform and athetotic motility are dramatically visible on extension of the arms.
Tremors are readily visible and tics seem to emerge.

In addition, in examining every child in the first grade of a public school
in New York City ($N = 171$), it was noted that in approximately 25% of all
first-graders, there was a discrepancy between the elevated arm and the
hand used for writing. Normally, in right-handed children, it is the right
hand that is elevated on the extension test. However, in right-handed children with specific language disability (dyslexia), the right arm does not rise
above the left; the left arm may be slightly higher than the right, or neither
arm is elevated, or there may be a fluctuation in the elevated extremity, at
one moment the left, and then the right. In determining which extended
arm is raised higher than the other, the examiner stands directly in front of
the child, viewing the extended arms at their level and judging arm elevation
at the wrist. There appears to be no advantage in quantitative measurement
of the degree of elevation. Further correlation studies (A. A. Silver and
Hagin, 1972a) revealed a strong positive association between this task and
the functions on our examinations relating to spatial and temporal orientation. In left-handed children with dyslexia, the evidence is not so clear-cut
and the elevated extremity may be either arm. We have extrapolated from
these data the suggestion that in right-handers, in the absence of peripheral
orthopedic defect or centrally induced paresis, the elevated extremity is governed by the increased tone of the hemisphere specialized for language. In
other words, the right-handed child's elevation of the right arm suggests a

left hemisphere specialized for language. If the left hand is elevated, or if neither arm is elevated, then hemisphere specialization has not yet been established. Some support for this interpretation is found in Kline and Kline (1976).

A relationship between the extension test and oral reading and reading comprehension was suggested by an experimental study done by A. A. Silver and Hagin (1972b) in the late 1960s and reported to the Carnegie Corporation in 1972. In this study, 76 boys ranging in age from 7 to 12, coming from the first through sixth grades, with full scale IQ (WISC) ranging from 80 to 132, all with intact homes, were referred to the Bellevue Hospital Mental Hygiene Clinic because of learning failure and/or behavioral difficulty. These boys were matched for age, IQ, reading ability, neurological signs, and psychological impairment and were randomly assigned to one of two groups.

The experiment was designed to study the effect of perceptual stimulation of deficit perceptual areas on perception, on reading, and on measures of cerebral dominance for language. The design was a crossover one planned for 1 year, in which, for the first 6 months, group I received perceptual stimulation while group II received compensatory remedial reading. For the second 6 months, group I received compensatory reading while group II received perceptual stimulation. The boys were tested at the beginning of the experiment (T1), at the end of 6 months (T2), and at the end of a year (T3). In this crossover research design, both within-group (Table 6-8) and between-group (Table 6-9) comparisons could be made.

In between-group comparisons (Table 6-9), at T1 the groups were not significantly different on the extension test (chi-square = .05, NS). At T2, however, measuring improvement in the extension test, a significant value for chi-square was obtained (chi-square = 15.31, $p < .01$). At this point only group I had received perceptual stimulation; thus there is a suggested relationship between perceptual training and normal response on the exten-

Table 6-8   Arm Extension Test: Comparisons Within Groups

	T1	T2	T3	χ^2	p
Group I					
Normal	7	27	20	26.00	.01
Abnormal	26	6	11		
Group II					
Normal	5	6	17	17.09	.01
Abnormal	16	15	4		

Note. From "Effects of perceptual stimulation on perception, on reading and on the establishment of cerebral dominance for language" by A. A. Silver and R. A. Hagin, 1972, *Report to the Carnegie Corporation,* New York.

Table 6-9   *Arm Extension Test: Comparisons Across Groups*

| | Group I | | Group II | | | |
	Normal Response	Abnormal Response	Normal Response	Abnormal Response	χ^2	p
T1	7	26	5	16	0.05	NS
T2	27	6	6	15	15.31	.01
T3	20	11	17	4	1.65	NS

Note. From "Effects of perceptual stimulation on perception, on reading and on the establishment of cerebral dominance for language" by A. A. Silver and R. A. Hagin, 1972, *Report to the Carnegie Corporation*, New York.

sion test. At T3, chi-square was again not significant (chi-square = 1.65, NS). At T3 both groups had received perceptual training and if the extension test is responsive to such training, both groups would show improvement at that time. Within-group comparisons show a shift to the normal extension test during the perceptual training phase in each of the groups, regardless of the order in which perceptual stimulation was given. These results suggest that spontaneous maturation did not occur, but that perceptual stimulation may have influenced the direction of the elevated arm to normal.

Mean oral reading scores for groups I and II combined, obtained before the training phase, and the mean combined reading scores, obtained after the training phase, were dichotomized in accordance with posttraining normal or abnormal findings on the arm extension test (Table 6-10).

The group of children in whom the response to the arm extension test was normal following the perceptual stimulation phase earned a pretest mean of 2.68 and a posttest mean of 3.48 in oral reading. The difference between these means was found to be significant (t = 5.49, p < .001). For the same group, the pretest mean in reading comprehension was 2.22 and the posttest mean for the same measure was 3.02. The difference between these means is also significant (t = 4.68, p < .001). On the other hand, the group with abnormal response to the extension test, following the perceptual stimulation phase, earned a pretest mean of 2.70 and a posttest mean of 3.33 in oral reading. On the reading comprehension test, their pre- and posttest means were 2.31 and 2.82, respectively. Computed t-ratios for the difference between these means were 2.65 for the oral reading measure and 2.07 for the reading comprehension, neither ratio reaching the level of significance set for this experiment. This suggests that there is a relationship between reading and the arm extension test.

In summary, the arm extension test gives valuable information about motor impulse control. When combined with passive rotation of the head, it may elicit remnants of primitive postural responses. Further, the elevated

Table 6-10 *Extension Test: Relationship with Oral Reading and Reading Comprehension, Groups I and II Combined*

Extension Test Response	Oral Reading			Reading Comprehension		
	Test Mean Preexperiment	Test Mean Postexperiment	t-ratio	Test Mean Preexperiment	Test Mean Postexperiment	t-ratio
Normal (n = 44)	2.68	3.48	5.49 (p < .001)	2.22	3.02	4.68 (p < .001)
Abnormal (n = 10)	2.70	3.33	2.65 (p = NS)	2.31	2.82	2.07 (p = NS)

Note. From "Effects of perceptual stimulation on perception, on reading and on the establishment of cerebral dominance for language" by A. A. Silver and R. A. Hagin, 1972, *Report to the Carnegie Corporation*, New York.

extremity in right-handed children may be an index of hemisphere specialization and appears to be related to success in beginning reading.

Spatial Concept of the Body Image   As seen in Table 6-7, the skills of right-left discrimination, finger-gnosis (including the extinction phenomenon), and praxis are not stressed in examinations for soft signs in learning disorders other than in our routine protocol. Historically, disorders of the body schema were described by the early twentieth-century neurologists (Pick, 1908; Schilder, 1931, 1935), particularly in adult patients with aphasic disorders and disorders of "symbolic formulation and expression" (Head, 1926, 1963) and by Gerstmann (1924, 1927, 1930), who related right–left disorganization to focal disease in the parietal-occipital region of the dominant hemisphere. Associated with this spatial disorganization, Gerstmann described a syndrome including finger agnosia, acalculia, and agraphia. Head (1926) postulated the existence of a mental schematic "model of the surface of the body," the integrity of which was a prerequisite for correct localization of body parts. The Gerstmann syndrome was descriptively a disturbance of the body image. Benton reviewed (1959) the early history of the body image concept as it relates to right–left discrimination and finger localization, and Schilder (1935) described the importance of body image in relation to psychiatric integrity and to psychopathology. As indicated in Chapter 3 ("Patterns of Neuropsychological Dysfunction"), the development of an age-appropriate concept of the body image in space is a necessary function upon which to build skills in reading, writing, and arithmetic.

Right–left discrimination attempts to tap the stability of body image in space. Right–left discrimination was part of the original Binet-Simon test (done in 1908): 75% of Parisian schoolchildren of that time were able to identify their right hand and left ear by age 7; all 8-year-olds passed both items (Binet & L. Simon, 1916). In 1916, Terman placed the identification of right hand, left ear, and right eye at a 6-year-old level. It was dropped from the 1937 revision probably, said Benton, because it did not discriminate between mental age levels as well as other tests. Piaget noted that a 6- or 7-year-old can identify right and left in his own body but not in a person facing him (Piaget & Inhelder, 1958). Benton (1959) studied right–left discrimination with a protocol of 32 items involving verbal commands (20 with the subject's eyes open and 12 with eyes closed): pointing to single lateral body parts, execution of double-crossed and uncrossed commands, pointing to lateral body parts on a schematic, front-view representation of a person (obviously eyes open), and execution of double-crossed and uncrossed commands involving lateral body parts of both subject and schematic representation. Benton did not require immediate response and spontaneous corrections were permitted but noted. In 158 children, 6 to 9 years of age, representing IQs between 85 and 115, and of average socioeconomic level, "right–left discrimination showed a progressive development. . . . the growth of this skill begins at about age 5 years; the 9-year-old has . . . a level of performance somewhat below that . . . [of] the average adult. The performance of the average 12-year-old child is virtually the same as that of the average adult" (p. 27). However, the representation of a person facing a child is more difficult than identification of own body parts, and performance is not significantly greater with eyes open than with eyes closed (Benton, 1959).

In 6-year-olds, there was a tendency to make an ipsilateral response to crossed commands. Benton stated that where the age factor (and mental age) is controlled, there is no significant difference between boys and girls in the development of right–left discrimination.

Our examination (Table 6-11) uses eyes-open verbal commands to identify the child's own right and left hands (4 items), double simultaneous ipsilateral commands (i.e., right hand on right eye) (4 items), double-crossed, contralateral commands (i.e., right hand on left ear) (4 items), and the identification of right and left in the examiner facing the child, uncrossed (2 items) and crossed (1 item), for a total of 15 items. This examination uses a portion of the protocol of Benton's form A of his right–left discrimination battery, using 15 of his 32 items and eliminating the items done with the subject's eyes closed. Benton's form V, which requires the child to *name* lateral body parts, is not used in our evaluation.

For the 5- and 6-year-olds, our protocol has been modified into a 10-item

Table 6-11   Protocol for Right-Left Orientation

I. Single commands
    A. Show me your left hand.
    B. Show me your right eye.
    C. Show me your left ear.
    D. Show me your right hand.

II. Double simultaneous ipsilateral commands
    A. Put your left hand on your left ear.
    B. Put your right hand on your right knee.
    C. Put your left hand on your left knee.
    D. Put your right hand on your right ear.

III. Double simultaneous, contralateral commands
    A. Put your left hand on your right ear.
    B. Put your right hand on your left knee.
    C. Put your left hand on your right knee.
    E. Put your right hand on your left ear.

IV. Examiner facing child
    A. Which is my left hand?
    B. Which is my right ear?
    C. (examiner's arms crossed) Now which is my right hand?

---

test for which norms are available for inner city, suburban, and private schools. Quantification of results in this 10-item test, and its use on a battery to detect potential learning disabilities in kindergarten, is discussed in Chapter 10 ("Prevention of Learning Disorders").

Our experience shows that average 5-year-olds in kindergarten can identify their own right and left hands; 6-year-old first-graders have ipsilateral double simultaneous skills; and 7-year-olds have contralateral double simultaneous recognition. It takes 8 years to correctly identify right and left in the examiner facing the child. Some children with learning disability (see Chapter 3, "Patterns of Neuropsychological Dysfunction") have not developed skills in right–left orientation, and it is not infrequent to find adolescents with reading problems still hesitant in correct identification of their own right and left hand. Systematic reversals—that is, consistently identifying right for left and left for right—and hesitations in response are considered as immaturity in the development of spatial orientation. It is interesting that while Benton did not classify systematic reversals as failure in his testing, and while children with systematic reversal did not show defects in finger localization or in arithmetic skills, they did have "impressive" impairment in the development of language functions (Benton, 1959).

Finger-gnosis is the ability to localize correctly by touching, showing, or naming tactile stimulation of the fingers, or by localizing fingers correctly in the subject or in the pictorial model of the hand, in response to verbal commands designating the fingers by name or number. Along with right–left discrimination, it is part of the central representation of the model of the body, the schemata of Head (1926), and the body image as described by Schilder (1935). It is said to require the integrity of the parietal-occipital area of the dominant hemisphere. Disturbance in finger-gnosis, i.e., finger agnosia, implies that in spite of intactness of the somatosensory functions of touch and kinesthesia and in spite of the ability to understand verbal directions, the stimuli to the fingers cannot be age-appropriately localized.

Essential to the study of finger-gnosis is the method of testing for it. Benton stated (1959, p. 13) that "finger localization, like right–left discrimination, comprises a variety of types of performance related to the awareness of the finger schema, which differ greatly with respect to complexity and level of difficulty." Gerstmann's early studies (1924, 1927, 1930) asked for indicated fingers to be named and named fingers indicated. Benton (1955a, 1955b, and 1959) used a 50-item battery assessing (a) with the aid of vision, identification of single fingers that have been touched, (b) without the aid of vision, identification of single fingers that have been touched, and (c) without the aid of vision, identification of pairs of fingers subjected to simultaneous tactual stimulation. The stimulus on that part of the battery "without the aid of vision" was made on the subject's fingers. The identification of that stimulus was made on a pictorial, two-dimensional model of the hand and fingers by means of pointing, naming, or number of the fingers. A verbal response was not required. The subject had to project the mental schema of his own fingers to that of a model. Satz and Friel (1973) and their associates used a similar procedure: shielded unilateral stimulation with identification by subject pointing to his own fingers and to a corresponding diagram of a hand, shielded stimulation of the back of the hands, bilateral and unilateral, shielded unilateral stimulation and then bilateral stimulation of fingertips with the subject recalling the number of the finger or fingers stimulated. Satz's battery required a verbal mediation.

Kinsbourne and Warrington (1962, 1963), in their original study of finger agnosia in 12 adult neurological patients, used a different procedure with five separate components:

1. *In-between test*—two fingers of one hand are simultaneously touched. The patient is asked to state the number of fingers "in-between" those touched.

2. *Two-point test*—touching the same finger or two different fingers of the same hand. The patient designates whether one finger or two fingers are touched.

3. *Matchbox test*–one or two matchboxes are placed between the fingers. The response designates awareness of the sides of the fingers. This portion of the Kinsbourne-Warrington battery is similar to earlier studies of Elthorne, Piercy, and Crosskey (1952).

4. *Finger block test*—the patient's hands are molded around a test block and the patient is required to pick out a corresponding block.

5. *Finger strip test*—requiring strips of paper, which have the names of fingers written on them, to be arranged in sequence.

Kinsbourne and Warrington concluded that finger agnosia involves "specific difficulty in relating fingers to each other in correct spatial sequences."

Pontius (1983) studied representation of the fingers in different cultures (New Guinea, Indonesia, and western Europe) by the pictorial representation of the fingers as seen in a drawing of the human figure. Pontius, a foremost proponent of an ecological (cultural) evolutionary neuropsychiatry (ECEN), found that there is a quantitatively inaccurate pictorial representation of the fingers in 78% of the New Guinean islanders and in 70% of Indonesians living in remote areas as compared to 16% in western Europe. "A specific link" is noted between low skills in arithmetic and inaccurate pictorial image of the fingers. Pontius theorizes that because the counting system of New Guinea is done concretely by looking and touching the hands, fingers, and other lateral parts of the body "no mental representation of the fingers appears to be necessary and no concept of number is employed as a symbol."

Kinsbourne and Warrington (1963) stated that by age 7½ the criteria for finger-gnosis was met by more than 95% of children. Using the same group of 158 children examined in his study of right–left discrimination, Benton (1959) studied them with the 50-item protocol described in the preceding paragraphs. He found that (a) total score rose progressively from ages 6 to 9; (b) the level of performance of 6-year-olds was considerably above chance expectations, indicating that initial development of the finger schema begins in early childhood; (c) the level of performance of 12-year-olds was roughly that of adults; (d) finger-gnosis under visual guidance was relatively easy (this finding is in contrast to right–left discimination where performance under visual guidance does not appear to be significantly better than when the hands are hidden); (e) double simultaneous discrimination was difficult even for 9-year-olds; and (f) mental age played an important role in developing accuracy of finger localization but not as great as in accurate right–left discrimination.

In contrast to the methods described for testing finger-gnosis (those of Gerstman, Benton, Kinsbourne, & Warrington, and Satz & Friel) in which the child is asked to identify fingers touched with eyes open and with eyes closed or for which a verbal mediation is required or needed to identify fingers by number in a pictorial representation of the hand, we have adopted a protocol that is relatively simple to give but which we find encompasses a developmental sequence in maturation of the finger schema (Table 6-12). The child sits across the table from the examiner, her hands placed

Table 6-12   Protocol for Finger-Gnosis

Single stimulus (5 years or under)
  R1
  L3
  L5
  R4
Bilateral symmetrical (6 years)
  R2–L2
  R4–L4
  R5–L5
Bilateral asymmetrical (8 years)
  R3–L5
  R2–L4 .
  R3–L4
  R4–L3
Score:

Single stimulus	number correct × 1 =
Bilateral symmetrical	number correct × 2 =
Bilateral asymmetrical	number correct × 3 = _____
Total Score	

Note: Adapted from: A. A. Silver and R. A. Hagin. *Search,* 1981, 2nd edition, p. 55. New York: Walker Educational Books.

upon the table, palms down fingers spread apart, eyes closed. The examiner says, "I will touch some of your fingers while your eyes are closed. Then you will open your eyes and point to the fingers I touched. Would you close your eyes please?" The examiner touches lightly the middle phalynx of each finger to be tested. Three groups of stimuli are used: (a) single stimuli (R1, L3, L5, R4); (b) double simultaneous, bilateral symmetrical stimuli (R2–L2, R4–L4, R5–L5); and (c) double simultaneous, asymmetrical stimuli (R3–L5, R2–L4; R3–L4 and R4–L3) are used for children 10-years-old or older. A developmental sequence may be found: 5-year-olds can easily identify single touch on digit 5 or digit 1; 6-year-olds identify double simultaneous bilateral symmetric stimuli of digit 5 and digit 1; the 7-year-olds identify double simultaneous bilateral symmetrical stimuli of digit 2 and digit 4. It is not until 8 or 9 years of age that children can identify double simultaneous bilateral asymmetrical combinations of digit 4 and digit 2, and not until age 10 can children identify the digit 4–3 combinations. In scoring, weighted credits are given—1 point for each correct single stimulus, 2 points for each correct bilateral symmetrical stimulus, and 3 points for each bilateral asymmetrical stimulus. Quantitative norms for kindergarten and first-graders in various educational settings are included in the *Search* manual (A. A. Silver & Hagin, 1981).

Table 6-13 summarizes the finger schema norms for kindergartens in three different settings: highly selective private independent schools ($N = 384$), inner city schools ($N = 311$), and suburban schools ($N = 949$). In

Table 6-13 **Finger-Gnosis in Kindergarten Children in Three Different Socioeconomic Settings**

	Distribution of Scores in a 14-Item Test: Number of Items Correct		
Stanine	Private Independent ($N = 384$)	Inner City ($N = 311$)	Suburban ($N = 949$)
9	14	14	14
8	14	14	14
7	12–13	13	12–13
6	10–11	11–12	10–11
5	9	9–10	9
4	7–8	8	7–8
3	6	6–7	5–6
2	4–5	4–5	4
1	0–3	0–3	0–3

Note: From "Spatial orientation and temporal organization in three socioeconomic groups" by A. A. Silver and R. A. Hagin, 1989, presented at the annual meeting of the American Academy of Child & Adolescent Psychiatry, October 11–15, New York, N.Y.

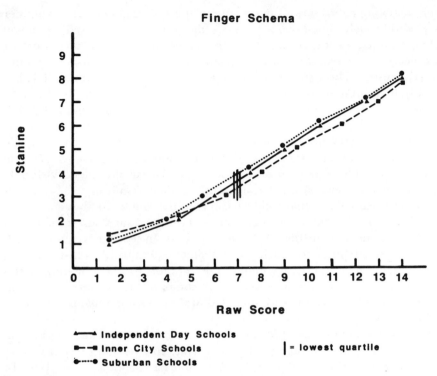

Figure 6-3   Finger Schema in 5- and 6-Year-Olds
There is no significant difference in distribution of scores among the three socioeco-
nomic groups; the lowest quartile is the same for all groups.
Source: Silver & Hagin (1989). *Spatial orientation and temporal organization in three socioeconomic*
groups. Presented at annual meeting, American Academy of Child and Adolescent Psychiatry,
New York City, October 1989.

spite of the superior IQs of the children in independent schools and the
socioeconomic differences in the three settings, the development of finger-
gnosis abilities in 5- and 6-year-olds appears to be independent of these variables (Figure 6-3). It will be recollected that in the A. A. Silver-Hagin follow-
up study (1964) finger-gnosis along with visual finger–ground perception
was resistant to spontaneous maturation.

In the management of the clinical examination for finger-gnosis, while
the child is sitting across from the examiner, hands on the table, eyes closed,
it is a simple matter to test for *extinction phenomena.* Extinction means that
in the double simultaneous stimulation test the subject reports only one of
the two stimuli. Thus, a definite impairment in perceptual awareness is present. However, if the same areas are stimulated separately and singly, the
stimulation will be perceived. The extinction phenomenon has also been
described as "inattention" (Critchley, 1964). Oppenheim in his examination
of adult neurological patients reported that "in certain brain diseases which

cause unilateral disturbance of sensibility . . . stimulate simultaneously two symmetrical points. The patient will . . . detect it only on the sound side, whereas in single tests he may detect every stimulation of the affected side." M. B. Bender (1952, 1970; Bender, Fink, & Green, 1951) has adopted this technique in a series of investigations with Hans Teuber, involving penetrating wounds of the brain, adult patients with a variety of neurological disease, children with cerebral palsy, and normal adults and children. The technique of double simultaneous stimulation has been applied in various perceptual modalities—visual, auditory, tactile, and haptic. It is the basis for studies of hemisphere specialization including dichotic listening testing in which different verbal stimuli are applied to the ears simultaneously and in which there is a normal suppression of stimuli from one ear.

In our examination we use tactile sitmulation. In effect, in our double simultaneous stimulation of the fingers, as we test for finger-gnosis, we have already tested for extinction phenomena. We have used double simultaneous symmetrical (i.e., homologous) stimuli and double simultaneous asymmetrical stimuli. Two additional stimulus sites, however, are specifically directed at the study of the extinction phenomena: double simultaneous stimulation of homologous areas of the wrist (wrist-wrist) and double simultaneous stimulation of the forehead and the wrist (wrist-head). With the child's eyes closed, the dorsa of the wrists are lightly touched. The child is asked to open her eyes and point to the places where she is touched. The wrist and lateral aspect of the forehead are then touched and the question is repeated. In the wrist-head test, both ipsilateral (right wrist, right forehead; left wrist, left forehead) and contralateral (right wrist, left forehead; left wrist, right forehead) stimuli are used. In testing for extinction, several variables must be considered: intensity and duration of the stimulus, type of stimulus, sensory area to be tested, and age and general intelligence of the subject. Increasing intensity or duration can push the stimulus into awareness and extinction phenomena may be obliterated. In our examination for extinction, the wrist and forehead are lightly brushed and the stimulus is applied for only a fraction of a second.

Just as in the development of finger-gnosis, there is a maturation in the ability to distinguish both the wrist and forehead stimuli on the face-hand test. M. B. Bender et al. (1951), using a slightly different method for examination, found that 90% of normal children aged 3 to 6 ($N = 56$) responding to contralateral face-hand stimulation would identify only the face stimulus, and in normal children aged 7 to 12 ($N = 76$) only 38% correctly reported both stimuli. In all there was the relative dominance of sensation in the face over the hand.

In our work a similar developmental pattern was observed. Half the children in kindergarten reported only the head stimulus on the face–hand test, but by the first grade (ages 6 to 7) at least 75% of the children in the entire first grade were able to report both stimuli. Extinction of the wrist stimulus in second-graders was considered abnormal. There was, however, an additional important finding: in approximately 20% of the 5-year-olds, either the head stimulus was displaced to the homologous contralateral side (allesthesia) with extinction of the point of the head stimulus, or the head stimulus was referred to both sides (synchiria). These phenomena, allesthesia and synchiria, were also observed in older children where there was evidence for an organic disturbance of the central nervous system. The possible relationship of the direction of displacement to the development of hemisphere specialization has yet to be studied.

Praxis is "the ability to carry out purposeful movements by an individual who has normal motor strength, reflexes and coordination and has normal comprehension of the act to be carried out" (Hecaen, de Ajuriaguerra, & Angelergues, 1963). Liepmann (1920) described apraxia as a dissociation between the idea of the movement and its motor execution. It is conventional to describe three types of apraxia: (a) *ideomotor,* the disruption of simple gestures used to convey symbolic meaning—i.e., to wave good-bye, stir coffee with a spoon, or hammer a nail; here the response to the verbal command is disrupted while the response to imitate gestures may be preserved; (b) *ideational apraxia,* the disruption of complex gestures which together make up a coordinated act; although the individual elements of the act can be performed, there is "disruption in the logical and harmonious succession of separate elements" (Hecaen, 1963); and (c) *constructional apraxia* (Kleist, 1934), "a disorder of formative activities in which the spatial part of the task was disturbed although single movements were not affected" (Hecaen, De Agostini, & Monzon-Montes, 1981, p. 264). This may be seen clinically in the inability to reproduce by drawing a design, for example, a cube or a simplified drawing of a house. Rutter, Graham, and Yule (1970) used reproduction of matchstick designs in their test for praxis. Constructional apraxia may also be seen in the visual-motor tasks that are in common use in batteries of neuropsychological tests and which we also use in our routine examination. The meaning of visual-motor difficulty may not be so clear, however. It may suggest defects at any point from problems in visuospatial discrimination, through difficulty with the ability to establish or sequence a program for a desired action, to difficulty with the motor execution of the task. Visual-motor function is thus a complicated task that requires careful analysis.

As part of our routine examination for praxis we use a test that Schilder (1931) called constructive finger praxis, the ability to imitate positions of the fingers given an intact voluntary motor apparatus. With the subject standing facing him, the examiner successively touches his own thumb to digit 3, digit 5, digit 2, and digit 4, first with the right hand then with the left. As each finger is touched, the subject is asked to imitate that motion. Just as the test for finger-gnosis does, this requires the development of a central schema of the fingers. It is more difficult than our test for finger-gnosis in that the child must be able to visualize the correct spatial representation of the examiner's fingers, transfer that spatial image into her own body schema, and then correctly execute the movement of the fingers. According to Schilder the inability to indicate fingers on command (finger agnosia) is related to a defect in the angular gyrus. The inability to name the fingers (finger aphasia) is related to a defect of Wernicke's area. Visual finger agnosia (an inability to identify the examiner's finger) is related to a posteriorly placed occipital lesion; apraxia of finger choice (an inability to move fingers on command), and constructive finger apraxia are related to defects in the region of the supramarginal gyrus. At any rate, our examination for praxis appears to measure related but different functions of the body image, including elements of visual finger agnosia and constructive finger praxis. In young children ages 5 to 6 years, 6 months old (kindergarten and first grade) the pencil grip is taken as a measure of praxis.

These tests—right–left discrimination, finger-gnosis, double simultaneous stimulation, and praxis—are manifestations of the development of the concept of body image in space and as such are an important part of our theoretical formulation that spatial orientation is an essential foundation for academic learning.

Visual Discrimination and Visual Recall of Asymmetries The examination for soft neurological signs is not complete without evaluation of visual discrimination and recall of asymmetric figures, visual-motor function, and auditory temporal sequencing. In addition, although not specifically included in the protocols for examination of soft signs (Table 6-7), the receptive, associative, and emissive aspects of language are informally evaluated and studied more intensively as indicated.

Our own routine testing for visual discrimination and recall of asymmetric figures is based on the Lamb Chops Test: the ability of the child to match the orientation of asymmetric figures (the lamb chop) as the axis of the figure is rotated 90, 180, 270, and 360 degrees in random fashion. The test requires the child to match stimulus cards, each containing an asymmetric figure in various degrees of rotation, with response cards from which the child must select the correct orientation. In the matching part of the test the child is given unlimited time to make his choice. In the recall part the stimulus is flashed for a limited time (4 seconds for 5- and 6-year-olds), and the child must *recall* the position of the stimulus figure by indicating its orientation on the response card. Norms for children ages 5 through 6 years, 6 months appear in *Search* (A. A. Silver & Hagin, 1981): three or four correct matching responses of eight trials and two or three correct recall responses of eight trials are normal for these ages. It is of interest that the number of correct responses of children from inner city schools on these tests is not significantly different from those of children from highly competitive independent day schools (Figure 6-4).

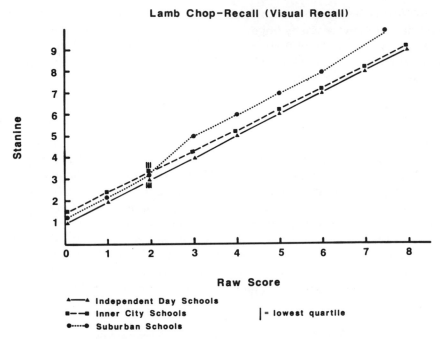

Lamb Chop–Recall (Visual Recall)

▲——▲ Independent Day Schools
■——■ Inner City Schools | = lowest quartile
●·····● Suburban Schools

Figure 6-4   Visual Recall in 5- and 6-Year-Olds
There is no significant difference in distribution of scores among the three socioeco-
nomic groups; the lowest quartile is the same for all groups.
Source: Silver & Hagin. (1989). *Spatial orientation and temporal organization in three socioeconomic*
groups. Presented at annual meeting, American Academy of Child and Adolescent Psychiatry,
New York City, October 1989.

Bender Visual Motor Gestalt Test

One of the most frequently used techniques involving the ability of the child
to copy written patterns is the Bender Visual Motor Gestalt Test (VMGT).
Although the visual-motor function involves many functional elements
(visual perception of spatial relationships, praxis, and fine motor coordination), it is a basis for writing and is a skill needed for written work in school.
Bender (1936) wrote that "the visual-motor gestalt function is a fundamental function associated with language ability and closely associated with various functions of intelligence such as visual perception, manual motor ability, memory, temporal and spatial concepts and organization or
representation" (p. 112). This test had its origins in the work of Max Wertheimer (1923), a German psychologist, who used a variety of line drawings
and configurations as stimuli for his subjects to elicit verbal descriptions of
their perceptions. L. A. Bender adapted these figures. She first used them
to elicit drawings from otherwise inaccessible, mute schizophrenic women
at Springfield State Hospital in Maryland. When she moved to New York

City, she realized the potential of this drawing technique in her work with children. In describing gestalt psychology L. A. Bender wrote (1938) that it "teaches that whatever we perceive, we experience as a global whole or gestalt. The organized whole is more immediately experienced than any of its parts or details, which are recognized later by a process called differentiation" (p. 5).

Published in 1938 as a monograph of the American Orthopsychiatric Association, Bender's VMGT is a well-defined method for evaluating the gestalt function, i. e., "that function of the integrated organism whereby it responds to a given constellation of stimuli as a whole, the response being a motor process of patterning the perceived gestalt" (p. 3). The aim of the test is to determine the individual's capacity to experience visual-motor gestalten in a spatial and temporal relationship.

Test administration is relatively simple. The examiner presents cards containing nine figures, one at a time, and asks the child to copy them. The examiner is asked to discourage turning of the cards ("I have to show them to you this way") and to encourage but not to insist on drawing the first figure in the upper left-hand quadrant of the page. However, instruction should be noncommittal, with no time limit indicated. This is a clinical technique in which formalization would destroy its function. The aim of the test is to obtain a record of the perceptual-motor experience that is unique and often retains its characteristic quality over the years.

L. A. Bender's manual (1938) and later writing (L. A. Bender, 1970) described the principles that determine maturation of visual-motor perception. The first of these principles is vortical movement, which is biologically determined and gives rise to the most primitive circles and loops. Movement is always present and always directional. At first this movement in space may be clockwise or counterclockwise; later, as the child works in the horizontal plane, it takes on sinistrad or dextrad directions. As control of vortical movement emerges at about age 3, the child begins to produce closed circles and arcs. These figures help her organize the foreground and background aspects of the visual field. Gradually, boundaries of the figures are delineated. At about age 5 the phenomenon of verticalization in drawings appears. Gradually crossed lines and diagonals emerge at a later level of maturation, usually at ages 7 and 8.

The "niceties" of the perceptual-motor relationships of the Bender VMGT are not usually completed until about age 11, but the main principles are recognizable in the normally developing child certainly by age 8. L. A. Bender (1958) also drew on the field of embryology to relate perceptual-motor development to the principle of plasticity. On the VMGT this principle is represented in the lack of stabilization of form, particularly with those figures of the test that consist of a constellation of dots. Plasticity is the state of being as yet undifferentiated, but capable of being differentiated. Plasticity has both negative and positive implications for development.

Table 6-14   Ages of Mastery of Figures
of the VMGT

Figure	Age
A	7 years (75%)
1	9 years (75%)
2	10 years (60%)
3	11 years (60%)
4	10 years (80%)
5	7 years (65%)
6	10 years (60%)
7	11 years (75%)
8	7 years (60%)

In the negative sense it may appear in the tendency to revert to more primitive forms, while in the positive sense it may represent the promise of increased maturation.

The VMGT standardization data include cross-sectional studies of 800 normal children. These data show characteristic drawings of the figures at ages 5 through 11 (L. A. Bender, 1938), as well as the ages at which a majority of children produce a mature figure. Table 6-14 is based on these cross-sectional studies. As can be seen from this table, age of mastery of the figures range from 7 through 11 years.

Unfortunately some of the current clinical uses of the VMGT violate the theories of gestalt psychology and the rationale on which the test was based. Examples of four of these misuses described below indicate the attempt to use the VMGT as a cookbook, rather than as the thoughtful consideration of developmental parameters intended by the test's author:

- The "30-second squint" in which the drawings are viewed hastily and then pronounced as "a good Bender" or a "bad Bender." This method of interpretation is without documentation and is, of course, of little use in understanding the child's problem.

- The use of the VMGT to determine the presence of brain damage. Koppitz (1975) and L. Small (1980) listed peripheral behavior characteristics that are "indicators of brain damage," giving the mistaken impression that the Bender test is sort of a poor-man's neurological examination.

- The futile attempt to force the VMGT into a psychometric mold. There have been complaints that the VMGT is not an acceptable measure to use with learning disabled children because it lacks statistical evidence of test-retest reliability. L. A. Bender has stated repeatedly that she did not intend the VMGT as a psychometric measure but as a developmental technique.

- Minute examination, sometimes even with a protractor used to measure angles, to detect errors that are then summed to obtain an age score. Given the range in age of mastery of the test figures (as shown in Table 6-14) and also the large standard deviations of the means of the error scores of one such scoring method (Koppitz, 1975) the lack of validity of this approach is obvious.

Even more significant to the clinician who seeks to understand a child's learning disorder through the use of the VMGT is the fact that these misuses fail to take into account the gestalt—the global nature of the task. L. A. Bender (1938) wrote cogently to this point in the manual of instructions to the VMGT: "However a child produces the gestalt test, it is a perfect, complete, and correct projection of that child's experience at that time and at the level of his total maturation, including whatever personality, maturation, and organismic problems he may have. A child cannot make an error in reproduction."

Based on Bender's formulation of the development of gestalt function in children, the following questions can be used to guide the interpretation of VMGT drawings:

- What is the motor pattern of the gestalt along which the figures of the test are organized?
- What signs of circular movement and plasticity are present?
- How are directional orientation of figures and directionality handled?
- What signs of verticalization of diagonal lines are present?
- How are angles and parts of figures differentiated?

Examples of VMGT drawings in children with various learning disorders are seen in Figures 6-1, 13-1, 13-2, 14-1, 14-4, 14-5, 15-1, 15-3, 15-4, 15-5, and 15-6 in this book.

Auditory Rote Sequencing

Auditory rote sequencing assesses the extent to which the child has memorized commonly heard verbal sequences and to which he can order the elements within these sequences. Ten items are included in the sequencing test used for kindergarten and first-grade children (Table 6-15).

The scoring for this test varies with the developmental difficulty of the item so that the items involving the capacity to order sequences are weighted. Of the 15 possible points a child could earn on this item, norms for ages 5 to 6 years, 6 months and for specialized groups (independent day

Table 6-15   Auditory Rote Sequencing

	Value	Score
1. Count my fingers as I touch them.	(1)	
2. What number comes after 5?	(1)	
3. What number comes before 3?	(2)	
4. What number comes after 6?	(1)	
5. What number comes before 9?	(2)	
Examiner says:		
Today is ———		
6. What day will tomorrow be?	(1)	
7. What day was yesterday?	(2)	
8. Name the days of the week starting with Sunday.	(2)	
9. What day comes after Monday?	(1)	
10. What day comes before Thursday?	(2)	
	Total Weighted Score	15

school, suburban, and inner city) appear in *Search* (A. A. Silver & Hagin, 1981). It is on this test, which requires verbal mediation, that experiential factors are most important, with distribution of scores of the inner city children far below that of suburban children who, in turn, are significantly lower than those from the independent day schools. Of a possible 15 items correct on this test, the lowest quartile of the inner city kindergarteners falls at 3 correct, the suburban children at 6 correct, and the independent day school at 8 correct. A similar discrepancy appears in first grade with no improvement in distribution of scores for the inner city children (lowest quartile at 3 correct), while the suburban first graders are significantly improved (lowest quartile at 9 correct) (Figure 6-5).

INTEGRATION OF DATA OF THE PENTAXIAL EXAMINATION

While the description of the neurological examination for children with learning disorders in this chapter may appear to indicate that each detail of the examination exists independently of all the others, in practice each bit of data has its place in completing the comprehensive profile of the assets and deficits we are building for each child. Each bit of data adds to the picture, which, in sum, is greater than any of its parts. In Charles, the child reported as a case example at the beginning of this chapter, the soft neurological signs dramatize the difficulty he has in orientation of the body image in space (finger-gnosis, praxis, and extinction phenomenon). The spatial disorientation may well be the biological basis for his visual-motor immaturity, which, in turn, portends poor written work and resistance to demands for him to do such work. His immaturity in the placement of

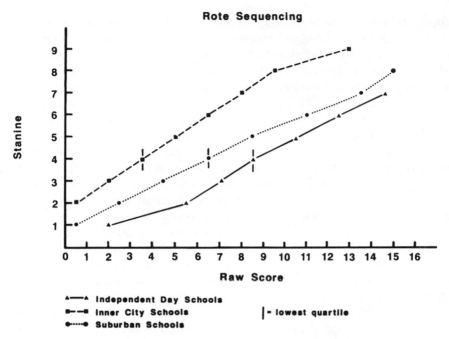

Figure 6-5   Auditory Rote Sequencing in 5- and 6-Year-Olds
There is a wide difference in distribution of scores among the three socioeconomic
groups; the lowest quartile is significantly different for each group.
Source: Silver & Hagin. (1989). *Spatial orientation and temporal organization in three socioeconomic*
groups. Presented at annual meeting, American Academy of Child and Adolescent Psychiatry,
New York City, October 1989.

sequences in time may be the biological underpinning to putting sounds in
proper sequence to make words—thus his reading difficulty. And all of
these signs are seen against a background of diffuse disorder in impulse control and in motor coordination, a lowered threshold for anxiety, and a less
than supportive family and, unfortunately, a less than understanding school.
Charles illustrates the need for pentaxial study at least for each child whose
learning problem has not responded to educational measures. Of course, it
would be optimal for each child with a learning disorder to have the advantage of such a comprehensive evaluation before he or she is long on the road
to failure, and the data thus obtained needs to be integrated into an appropriate plan for management.

SUMMARY

Psychiatric and neurological examinations are part of the pentaxial scheme
for evaluation of children with disorders of learning. The psychiatric examination explores the content, dynamics, genesis, and structure of the child's

thoughts, wishes, conflicts, and reactions to stress; it evaluates the supports and stresses of the environment and the development and structure of the child's personality. The clinical interview most commonly in use assesses affect, object relations, impulse control, reality testing, identification, thought content, defense mechanisms, and behavior. There is increasing use of a more standardized approach to assessment with a series of structured interview scales. Eight of these are described in this chapter.

The neurological examination investigates the integrity of the central nervous system and the level of its maturation and integration, including neuroperceptual function. It is an important component of the pentaxial scheme and of the examination of children with disorders of learning. The classical neurological evaluation is here supplemented by study of soft neurological signs, including kinetic patterns; postural responses; the so-called higher cortical functions, such as spatial and temporal organization in visual, auditory, and body image modalities; and receptive, associative, and emissive aspects of language. Soft signs are viewed as an index of maturation in the central nervous system, responsive to genetic laws of maturation, modified by factors from within or from the environment that may interfere with such maturation. Soft signs may not spontaneously disappear with maturation, and the lagging function may not spontaneously became age-appropriate. A standardized procedure for testing is only now beginning to evolve. Procedures for standardized examination are described for the arm extension test, right–left discrimination, finger-gnosis, and praxis. The arm extension tests offers clues for the establishment of hemisphere specialization; right–left discrimination, praxis, and finger-gnosis are components of the awareness of the body image in space, a function frequently impaired in children with learning disorders. Visual discrimination and recall tests visual spatial orientation; the Visual Motor Gestalt Test relates to the ability to reproduce the spatial orientation of visual symbols and as such is a basis for writing; auditory rote sequencing assesses the function of temporal organization.

The neuropsychiatric examination completes the sequence of study of the child with a learning disorder—academic achievement, educational opportunity, sensory acuity, cognitive function, and neuropsychiatric-neuropsychological evaluation.

CHAPTER SEVEN

Principles of Educational Remediation

Although the etiologies of learning disorders are varied and the diagnosis is multidisciplinary, the responsibility for remediation is primarily educational. Inevitably, whether children learn to listen, speak, read, write, spell, and do mathematical calculations depends on what they are taught in school. While the chapters of this book dealing with the various learning disorders focus on specific educational provisions for each of these disorders, this chapter deals with general educational issues: (a) organizational patterns for delivery of services, (b) evaluation of special education placements, (c) models of intervention approaches, and (d) recommended intervention principles.

ORGANIZATIONAL PATTERNS FOR DELIVERY OF SERVICES

As might be expected, the Education for All Handicapped Children Act (P. L. 94-142) and the state plans that implemented it have had a strong influence on the organization of services for children with learning disorders. Before this law was passed, the outlook was dismal for children with learning disorders unless their families were able to provide private services for them. In 1974 the U.S. Comptroller General's report to Congress stated that 60% of the nation's handicapped children were not receiving appropriate schooling. Although some progress had been made in providing services to children with mental retardation, sensory handicaps, and orthopedic impairments, few districts provided services flexible enough to meet the needs of children with less visible problems like learning disorders. Where programs existed, services were often fragmented, with restrictive eligibility requirements and grudging administrative support.

By 1970, however, changes in public attitudes toward people with handicaps and strong pressures from parent and professional groups were being felt by state and national legislators. Some states (notably Massachusetts) were moving ahead on their own with laws to provide public school programs for children with special educational needs. For the first time, learning disabilities were acknowledged to be a handicap and children with learning disabilities[1] were included among the groups eligible for services. The passage of P. L. 94-142 provided strong federal leadership for these increasing efforts. This law had major impact on every school in the country through the state plans that it required.

P. L. 94-142 placed some revolutionary responsibilities on local school districts in terms of the education of children with learning disorders. In

---

1 Note that the term *learning disability* is used in discussions on legislation and research where that term has been used in the original source. We prefer the broader term *learning disorders* for reasons discussed in Chapters 1 and 2.

order to be in compliance with this law (and, incidentally, to share in its financial benefits) school districts must:

1. identify all learning disabled children through individual multidisciplinary studies (no simple task, in view of the continuing definitional problems)
2. write individual educational plans (IEPs) to meet their special educational needs
3. provide a "continuum of alternative placements" for meeting these needs
4. place children in "the least restrictive environment" within the continuum of placements
5. provide "related services" that are required for children to benefit from special education
6. establish procedural safeguards that protect parents' rights to due process, confidentiality, nonbiased assessment, and informed consent.

That school districts met these responsibilities at various levels of compliance is not surprising. Considering where the field was in 1975 when the law was enacted, that it was implemented *at all* probably constitutes a minor miracle.

Two key provisions, the continuum of alternative placements and the least restrictive environment, brought marked organizational changes as school districts sought to provide the education guaranteed by the law to all handicapped children. The range of placements available in individual school districts, or through cooperative arrangements between school districts, or with private schools or agencies is apparent in Table 7-1. Placement for learning disabled students is distributed among all the alternatives but tends to cluster among the least restrictive organizational models. The following text gives an interpretation of this table.

Regular Classes

More than 16% of students classified as learning disabled were in full-time regular class placements. Presumably these children receive indirect services based on consultation between classroom teachers and special education consultants. The roles of consulting teachers vary but may include such services as demonstrating teaching in regular classes, team teaching with the regular classroom teacher, providing assistance in implementing educational recommendations in the regular classroom, assisting students in making the transition from special education to regular classes, and others. West and Cannon (1988) have used a Delphi technique to identify 47 different

Table 7-1 *Percentage Distribution of Handicapped Persons 3 to 21 Years Old Receiving Special Education Services by Educational Environment: 1984/85*

Type of Handicap	All Environments	Regular Class	Resource Room	Separate Class	Separate School Facility		Residential Facility		Correction Facility	Homebound/ Hospital Environment
					Public	Private	Public	Private		
All conditions	100	26.9	41.6	23.7	3.5	2.1	1.0	0.4	0.3	0.7
Learning disabled	100	16.2	60.7	20.9	1.1	0.8	–	0.1	0.2	0.1
Speech impaired	100	64.8	26.3	4.9	1.0	2.5	–	–	–	0.5
Mentally retarded	100	4.8	28.1	53.0	8.4	2.1	2.6	0.4	0.2	0.4
Emotionally disturbed	100	11.8	34.3	33.3	8.6	4.8	1.7	2.4	1.6	1.6
Hard of hearing and deaf	100	21.3	23.6	30.5	7.3	4.7	10.9	1.1	0.1	0.5
Orthopedically handicapped	100	18.2	20.7	33.6	13.1	5.5	0.8	0.7	–	7.4
Other health impaired	100	23.5	25.5	32.8	4.0	2.0	0.7	0.6	–	10.9
Visually handicapped	100	32.7	29.6	18.7	4.1	3.3	9.8	1.0	0.2	0.6
Multihandicapped	100	2.8	13.7	44.1	18.3	10.1	6.4	2.5	0.4	1.6
Deaf-blind	100	4.6	15.8	23.7	16.6	5.0	28.1	4.5	–	1.7

Note. From *The Condition of Education* (p. 57), by National Center for Education Statistics, 1987. Data calculated from U.S. Department of Education, Office of Special Education and Rehabilitative Services, *Ninth Annual Report to Congress on Implementation of Public Law 94-142* and unpublished tabulations. Washington, D.C.: Government Printing Office.

[1]Less than .05%

competencies essential for collaborative consultation by special educators. This model has value in that it keeps learning disabled children in the regular classroom activities, provides the language stimulation that so many learning disabled children need, and does not isolate them socially from their peers.

Some studies show this model to produce an educational impact that is superior to other placements. For example, based on an analysis of eleven empirical studies, Wang and Baker (1985/1986) found that "mainstreamed learning disabled students are consistently found to have outperformed non-mainstreamed students with comparable special education classifications" (p. 518). However, the model's effectiveness depends upon the skills of the consultant and the willingness of the classroom teacher to individualize instruction and use the services of consultants.

Tutoring

One-to-one tutoring to supplement regular classroom work is a model about which very little is written, although it may be one of the most frequently used services for children with learning problems. For the most part, schools do not provide for such a model because it is regarded as too expensive. Usually tutoring is arranged on an informal, private basis by the child's family. Tutors may work on their own or in association with other professionals. Cowen (1985) has described a nonprofit organization in Massachusetts called the Tutoring Network that offers screening and matching of educational therapists with students. Because of the private and individual nature of these services, there is little efficacy research on this model. It may be significant, however, that so distinguished an educator as B. Bloom (1984) has recommended that schools experiment with innovative strategies that use the one-to-one tutoring model. What appears on the surface to be an expensive model may in the end turn out to be one of the more cost-effective methods.

Resource Rooms

Sixty-one percent of the children classified as learning disabled received resource room services. These youngsters were enrolled in regular classrooms for the major part of the day but went to the resource room for remedial services in specific skill subjects (reading, language arts, or mathematics) usually through small groups or individual instruction. This model demands a wide range of competencies and organizational skills on the part of the resource room teacher who must be able to conceptualize and implement educational plans for at least five different students each hour of the school day. It is not surprising that one youngster described it as "sort of like a study hall where we do our homework." At its best, under the direction of a knowledgeable and energetic teacher, the resource room can focus on special educational needs while encouraging achievement in the regular classroom. At its worst, it can become a place for humdrum workbook exercises unrelated to individual needs and a source of alienation from classroom activities. For example, a 6-month analysis of remedial activities in four schools found that "remediation consisted of students completing skill lessons in workbooks or worksheets managed by the teacher. Most activities were not congruent with classroom tasks" (Allington, Stuelgel, Shake, & Lamarche, 1986). In contrast, D. L. Friedman, Cancelli, and Yoshida (1988) found positive outcomes for the resource rooms they studied in the increased amount of engaged time spent in academic work and in the decrease in disruption. Systematic classroom observation showed that whereas the learning disabled children were engaged an average of 55% of the time in the regular classrooms, in the resource rooms the same children were engaged an average of 79% of the time. During instruction directed by the teacher, the children were more apt to be engaged (73%) than when they were working independently (56%).

Self-contained Classrooms

Approximately 21% of the children classified as learning disabled were placed in self-contained classrooms with limited enrollments. The names for these classrooms vary from state to state and the composition of the classes may be either categorical (consisting only of students with learning disabilities) or cross-categorical (containing a range of classifications). Where appropriate, some of these children are integrated into regular classrooms for instruction in content subjects and for special activities such as art, music, gym, assembly, and lunch. Because of the principle of least restrictive environment, self-contained class placements are less frequently chosen for learning disabled children; if such placement is effected, it may be because of either a severe degree of learning disorder or problem behavior that cannot be managed in less restrictive settings.

Most literature reviews of self-contained versus regular class placement fail to reveal any clear-cut support for either alternative. Carlberg and Kavale (1980) used the techniques of meta-analysis to reanalyze data from existing studies of these contrasting placements in terms of a common metric, Effect Size *(ES)*. This statistic enables the investigator to combine the findings of many studies and examine them simultaneously. Carlberg and Kavale calculated a measure of Effect Size, defined as the mean difference between experimental and comparison groups divided by the standard deviation of the comparison group ($ES = (X_e - X_c)/SD_c$) for 50 primary research studies of special versus regular class placement. No great differences were found between means for outcome measure of achievement and social adjustment. However, the category of exceptionality revealed differential placement effects. Slow learners and educable mentally retarded children experienced negative consequences associated with special class placement, but learning disabled and behavior disordered students exhibited positive effects from the special class placement. There were no dramatic findings either for or against special classes.

Separate Schools

Two percent of the students classified as learning disabled attended special public or private schools. Only a very few school districts maintain special schools for children whose primary classification is that of learning disability. However, in some cases courts have decided that a specific child's educational needs could not satisfactorily be met by the existing public school programs and that child should receive private school services at public expense.

Less than one-half of 1% of the learning disabled were placed in more restrictive settings such as residential treatment centers, correctional facilities, hospital schools, or home-bound instruction. Where learning disabled children received such placement one might expect that the placement decision had resulted from the combination of learning disability with other handicapping conditions. These generally more restrictive placements should not be seen as an easy or permanent solution. The inevitable question of return to the educational or vocational mainstream cannot be postponed indefinitely. The more restrictive a placement has been, the more difficult it will be to accomplish this reintegration.

EVALUATION OF EDUCATIONAL PLACEMENTS

While the quantitive data provided in the Annual Reports to Congress show that there are a variety of service models available to handicapped children in public schools, these data tell us little about qualitative issues in the education of handicapped children. Trusdell (1985) surveyed 50 states, the District of Columbia, four territories, and the Bureau of Indian Affairs to obtain information on the nature of service delivery models in use with learning disabled children. Supervisors responsible for programs for learning disabled children were asked to describe and rate the effectiveness of existing models on a five-point scale. Resource room models were the most frequently used (91%) and received the highest mean rating, 4.15 (with a range of 2–5), from the supervisors. The consulting teacher model was only slightly behind with a mean effectiveness rating of 4.04 and use reported by 79% of the respondents. Self-contained and modified self-contained classroom models were rated less effective with learning disabled students (mean rating 3.48, range 1–5). Some respondents judged this model to be more effective at the elementary than at the secondary school level. Multicategorical classes, consisting of children classified as learning disabled, emotionally disturbed, or mentally retarded, received the lowest effectiveness ratings of all, except when they were organized at the secondary school level. This result is especially interesting, because recent years have seen a strong trend toward "generic" organization of classrooms in which children of various diagnoses are grouped together as "mildly," "moderately," or "severely" handicapped on the basis of their current levels of educational progress.

The Collaborative Study of Children with Special Needs, a 5½-year research effort funded by the Robert Wood Johnson Foundation (1988), provided salient information on the overall impact of P. L. 94-142. The major research question in this study was what differences the law had made in the lives of handicapped children, their families, their teachers, and their nonhandicapped classmates. Answers were sought in five large metropolitan school districts: Milwaukee, Houston, Charlotte-Mecklenburg (NC), Santa Clara County (CA), and Rochester (NY). Reviews of school records and interviews with children, parents, teachers, and key informants representing a sample of 2,000 elementary school special education children constituted the data base for this study.

The Collaborative Study of Children with Special Needs resulted in both positive findings and what was called "an unfinished agenda." The procedural guarantees of P. L. 94-142 were found to be securely in place. The report saw as one of the law's most profound effects the schools' acceptance of their role of therapeutic agent and their commitment to the principle of the least restrictive environment.

Variations in local practices and in the frequency with which different handicapping conditions were identified were noted. For example, the percentage of learning disabled children identified in the five school districts ranged from 31 to 58%. Specific placements may depend on many factors, some of which are independent of the child's needs: economic conditions within the district, the child's level of social adjustment, and the wish to avoid certain stigmatizing classifications. Learning disability was one of the conditions that showed the highest degree of variation in placements among the five cities studied. The majority of special education students were mainstreamed, attending regular schools and spending at least part of the day with regular classes.

The review of the cost basis for the various placements indicated that the mainstreaming ideology supported the least-cost approach. The report cautioned against the application of mainstream placements because of the economic rather than the educational benefits it promised.

The investigators conducted a 2-year follow-up study of 1,184 students from the original pool (Walker, Singer, Palfrey, & Orza, 1988). There was very little movement back to regular classes, with 72% of the children remaining in the same classification and 12% receiving placements in different categories. Only 17% (generally children with speech and language problems) had returned to the regular educational program.

Parents' Responses to Special Education Services

Although the Collaborative Study of Children with Special Needs offers reassurance that the organizational structure mandated by P. L. 94-142 has been implemented, even cursory contact with parents and professionals in the field leads to a sense of uneasiness about the quality of educational services. Satisfactory ratings were given by 80 to 85% of the respondents on such variables as social integration, school administration and teachers, facilities, transportation, and related services, but only 60% rated the academic progress of their learning disabled children satisfactory. This finding is particularly striking in that it is precisely for increased academic progress that these children were placed in special education programs in the first place. Some parents show this discomfort in a lack of trust in their relationships with school personnel. Results of diagnostic studies and triennial reevaluations are viewed with suspicion; relationships at educational planning conferences take on a legalistic, sometimes adversarial tone. The IEPs parents are asked to approve may be lists of canned computerized behavior objectives that bear little relationship to what their children tell them happens in the classrooms every day. Their worries about educational and vocational outcomes for their children leave them vulnerable to promises of magic cures through unconventional interventions unsupported by rational theory and research (L. B. Silver, 1987).

Administrators' and Teachers' Responses to Special Education Services

Policy makers and administrators in the schools also express a sense of discomfort. At times they seem more worried about complying with the letter than with the spirit of 94-142. Those who have dealt adequately with compliance issues may face the budgetary problems involved in financing these services. As the number of children with special needs grows, these leaders become concerned not whether children are being taught well, but whether there has been "overidentification" in the category of learning disability.

The concept of overidentification provides a facile solution to the large numbers of children identified as learning disabled. While policy makers might hesitate to investigate the general educational effectiveness of schools or to entertain the idea that there just might be that many children with learning disorders, the thought that someone was identifying too many children was an attractive one. The blame could easily be displaced to a visible group, the school diagnostic teams.

Using a series of clinical vignettes and naturalistic observations Ysseldyke (1983) raised questions about the ability of diagnostic teams to differentiate learning disabled children from other special education classifications and to make educational plans on the basis of clinical data. Ysseldyke summarized his findings and predicted dire (and as yet unrealized!) consequences:

> *We believe at present, there is no defensible system for making service delivery decisions about students failing in school. We believe asking questions about definitions of the names we apply to these students is clearly the wrong way to proceed. Frankly, we believe it is time to ask a different set of questions; for example, what system of service delivery for students failing in school makes sense? Clearly the one currently growing at an unacceptable rate does not make sense and will likely not be tolerated as public policy for much longer. (p. 13)*

Other studies of team decision making have not confirmed Ysseldyke's results. In a similar simulation study, Pfeiffer and Naglieri (1983) found that teams exhibited significantly less variability in placement decisions than the same specialists acting independently, thus "supporting the efficacy of the multidisciplinary team." No one profession dominated the decision process in their sample of 86 professionals, representing 22 teams. Cummings, Huebner, and McLesky (1986) also failed to replicate Ysseldyke's simulation experiment. In reporting their own and five additional team decision-making studies, these investigators commented that their subjects "were reluctant to label the child as *handicapped* and to recommend special class placement. Rather these psychologists made decisions reflecting a least restrictive environment." Strangely enough, in a kind of Gresham's law transplanted from economics to education, the Ysseldyke findings are more often cited than those of the other investigators who found positive qualities in the deliberations of diagnostic teams.

Teachers and other members of the special education teams feel overwhelmed by the bureaucratic structure and the accompanying paperwork involved in services for children with special needs. The documents that IEPs have become take many hours of work. The computerized objectives that the parents find so impenetrable have become their responsibility. Written in the language of behavior objectives, imperatives such as the following appear on the IEPs:

> *The student will*
>   *RO11 R050320F say sound value of 11 consonant blends in word form, given*
>   *24 words 19/24 correct*
>   *Evaluation method: teacher observation*
>
>   *RO14 RO59335F decode unfamiliar words containing digraphs, be given passage to read, maximum 2 errors*
>   *Evaluation method: teacher observation*

These objectives isolate skills from the normal process of teaching children to read. Furthermore with their built-in expectations of error, they seem to lack confidence in the child's ever achieving mastery of these very basic phonic elements.

Teachers are also frustrated in their attempts to work with children with learning problems who are not specifically referred for special education services. Opportunities for informal consultations with special services personnel are frequently limited because school psychologists, social workers, and learning disability consultants are responsible for referrals to special education and are not available for services to other children. In recent years some districts have attempted to remedy this situation by organizing teacher assistance teams and pre-referral preventive programs, a practice very much to be encouraged.

A final source of confusion to the teacher responsible for work with children with learning disorders is the mixed messages received from investigators in the field of learning disorders. The lack of synthesis of information useful to the practitioner is illustrated in a paper written by a well-trained resource room teacher who makes an effort to keep up with current writings and meetings in the field: "As I read through the journals, I find information contrary to what I learned at my workshop in neuropsychology, which, of course, contradicted information received in my course in neurolinguistics. . . . I heard Dr. Frank Vellutino disclaim visual perception processing as a cause of learning disabilities. Among other things Vellutino concluded that there is a memory or linguistic problem" (Chisholm 1983, p. 180). But then she remembered that "a recent research article by Lyon and Watson (1981) showed that an empirically derived subgroup indicated reading impairments which are due to deficiencies in visioperceptive capacity rather than language-based deficits" (p. 180).

Further on she described teaching implications of Witelson's work on hemisphere specialization: "Dr. Witelson reviewed a study using dichotic listening tests with dyslexic children and a normal control group. [She concluded that in children with learning disabilities there is]—more unitary, gestalt processing, and a bias for cognitive, nonsequential processing" (p. 180). Chisholm commented that this explanation made sense to her as a special educator ". . . when I discovered—in literature written by the neuropsychologists—that there is no behavioral method of determining left/right brain persons, and that dichotic listening tests are nonsense" (p. 181).

Although these comments might be dismissed as naive, they illustrate the kind of messages one well-intentioned educator received from research in the field of learning disorders. Research often seems to be an end in itself, with little potential impact for the classroom. An example of this alienation between research and practice is seen in Lyon's and Moats's (1988) discussion of critical issues in the instruction of the learning disabled. On the basis of what they described as "a selective rather than an exhaustive review" of the literature, they reached the following conclusions:

- Theory-based instruction is a necessary but not totally sufficient condition for improved academic outcomes.
- Even the most efficacious instructional approaches rarely totally remediate academic deficits.
- Instructional outcomes are difficult to quantify accurately because remediation may not lead to changes in cognitive and academic functioning.
- The outcomes of instructional decisions evade understanding through conventional research designs; to address these questions in a meaningful way will require research methodologies that are "dynamic, fluid, flexible" (pp. 832–833).

According to these investigators, the field of learning disorders should not look to current research for guidance: current research in the field of learning disabilities seems to lead only to more research.

Why is it that all these serious, enlightened, well-intentioned efforts do not lead to more clear-cut answers on how to teach children with learning disorders? One reason may lie in the growing gap between research and practice. Although researchers and practitioners may use the same words, they do not speak the same language. Because of gaps in communication, the lag between what is learned through research and what is applied in the classroom is often wide.

The vast, varied constituency of classroom teachers makes decisions on educational methodology more often on the basis of expediency than on rational consideration of the research literature. The latest "in-service workshop," the sample materials left by salesmen, the sales pitches in the advertising, and the exhibit booths at conventions—all offer quick solutions. Decisions cannot be postponed until the research results are clarified, for the children are there in school to be taught.

Nor is the lot of educational researchers a happier one. In contrast to investigators in other fields, they lack control over many of the variables that may have major influences over the outcomes of their studies. Attempts to control for broad situational and historical variables threaten the generalizability of findings. Because of the length of time required for the effects of educational experiments to be observed, ethical considerations may prevent the use of placebo conditions. Finally, even variables like teaching methods that would appear to be controllable by experimenters can be subject to different levels of intensity, timing, interpretation, and teaching competence.

MODELS OF EDUCATIONAL INTERVENTION

While the Education for All Handicapped Children Act gives firm direction about *where* and *when* this education is to take place, it is less specific about *what* and *how* it should be taught. The range of choices of both content and method is wide, and, given the heterogeneity of the children with learning disorders, no one approach can be expected to be appropriate for all children. Choice of a particular set of educational interventions would depend on: (a) one's point of view about the nature of learning disorders, (b) the needs of the specific child to be taught, and (c) the resources, both in terms of professional services and supplies and equipment, available in the educational setting. One additional condition, not to be minimized, is chance—the serendipitous combination of human factors, timing, and specific educational services that produce the appropriate match for a given child. This luck of the draw may account for mixed results of outcome studies (Spreen, 1988).

Processes by which a given set of interventions are provided to a particular child are not easily examined. Even when clear directions are given in psychoeducational reports, there are gaps in translation into educational interventions. D'Amato and Dean (1987) investigated the agreement among the needs identified in psychoeducational reports, IEPs, and daily lesson plans for 45 children in special education programs. Across all areas, the probability was 22 in 100 that recommendations made in the psychoeducational reports would be implemented in daily lesson plans. There was a higher probability of utilization of recommendations for work in content-related areas (reading, spelling, and mathematics) than for other areas (problem solving, auditory skills, sequencing, memory, and coping behaviors). Situational reasons—such as number of students, limited school resources, and the nature and background of skill-ability areas recommended—were offered to explain why recommendations were not always followed. This sample of teachers apparently perceived their role as a narrow one, confined to reteaching academic subjects despite the broader needs diagnostic study had shown in their students. Unfortunately, this study focused only on the content areas appearing in the daily lesson plans and did not explore the methods used by the teachers in the sample. Studies of both the *what* and the *how* of teaching would do much to increase our understanding of the values and shortcomings of special education.

The following discussion of intervention models focuses on the area of reading for a number of reasons. First, reading is the skill area that presents problems for the greatest proportion of children with learning disorders. Lerner (1988) estimated this figure to be 80%. Second, difficulties in reading soon impact upon other curricular areas, so that their effects are inescapable. Third, reading is a complex task that is probably the most difficult one our culture asks in the education of young children. Finally, the complexities of the reading process have engaged the interests of a large number of investigators, so that differences in conceptual frameworks can be discussed along with the instructional models represented.

Skilled reading is a complex, multilevel system that includes letters, graphophonemic patterns, words, and syntactic and semantic units. The divergence among theoretical models of the task of reading lies in the weight and relationships ascribed to these components by various investigators. Inevitably, these theoretical models of the task of reading influence the materials and methods that find their way into classrooms. One theoretical dichotomy is that of the bottom-up versus top-down models of reading. The *bottom-up* model is based on the idea that the analysis of smaller units (such as graphophonemes and words) is essential to processing of larger conceptual units. In contrast, the *top-down* model assumes that readers use knowledge of higher-order language structures to anticipate oncoming text. Goodman (1967) described this process as the "psycholinguistic guessing game." An additional formulation, somewhere between the two extremes, is the *parallel interactive* model that suggests that all sources of information—from signal cues of the perceptual features of words to syntactic and semantic information—are used simultaneously.

These models can be used to classify the instructional methods represented by the major classroom approaches to teaching reading, although it should be acknowledged that few methods are applied in the "pure" sense. The bottom-up approach is best illustrated by phonics methods that teach grapheme/phoneme relationships, encourage the synthesis (or blending) of sounds into words, and use phonetically regular text insofar as it is possible to do so in English. Linguistic approaches that provide simple phonetically regular text ("Dan can fan. Can Dan fan?") on the assumption that learners will discover for themselves generalizations about sound-symbol relationships can also be described as bottom-up approaches. The top-down model is exemplified by language experience approaches in which sentences often dictated by the children are introduced as meaningful wholes, with later practice with matching and identifying individual words by referring back to the original sentences. Little work is done with the smaller components of the text, because it is assumed that the correspondence between the text and the child's own language will provide adequate word recognition cues.

Conventional basal reader approaches used in typical classroom instruction represent the parallel-interactive model. These approaches expect the learner to learn approximately 200 words as "sight" words on the basis of signal cues in the visual configuration of the words and language and contextual cues from the story content. Most teachers supplement this work with workbooks or worksheets dealing with phonic generalizations. However, unlike the synthetic phonics methods, these practice materials require the child to apply generalizations to visual manipulation (copying or underlining) of words already met as sight words.

The Job Analysis of Reading (described in Chapter 5, Table 5-3) represents the model of reading used in this book. This model posits four skills areas for effective reading: prereading, word attack, comprehension, and study skills. The child with a learning disorder may experience difficulties with any aspect of the reading process and may require directive teaching of subskills that other children learn from casual experiences. This is particularly true of the prereading skills of visual and auditory perception and directionality. Meta-analyses of the relationships between perceptual skills and reading support the inclusion of visual and auditory perception:

> *The comprehensive perspective provided by the statistical integration of a variety of molecular studies indicated that visual perception is an important correlate of variables related to reading achievement. Therefore, a complete description of factors predictive of reading ability should consider perceptual skills. (Kavale, 1982, p. 51)*

> *The statistical integration of individual study findings indicated that auditory perception is an important vector in the complex variables related to reading ability. It should be considered, therefore, for a complete description of factors correlative of reading achievement. (Kavale, 1981, p. 545)*

The variety of word attack skills include versatile use of sight, context, language, phonics, and structural cues, all of which are necessary because of the phonological and orthographic variations of written English. Comprehension skills draw on oral vocabulary for literal comprehension, inferential reasoning, and appreciation of meaning. Study skills comprise the strategies necessary for locating, selecting, organizing, and retaining the content one reads. Each of the interventions described below is analyzed in terms of its contributions to the comprehensive model of the reading tasks in Table 5-2.

Interventions Using Regular Classroom Methods

Interventions using regular classroom methods have their basis in the belief that learning disorders are primarily pedagogic in nature, that children with learning disorders are not very different from the range of children within the regular classroom, and that their learning problems result from inadequate and ineffective teaching. It would follow that these problems can be remediated through more intensive, effective reteaching of the same content.

Grade Repetition   Recommendations for a child to repeat a grade are the most obvious application for this approach. This provision may help in cases where the child has not had appropriate opportunity to attend school (because of chronic illness, family mobility, or disorganization, for instance), but its efficacy in improving the academic fate of children with learning disorders has yet to be documented. Nonpromotion also carries with it emotional burdens of guilt and loss of self-esteem.

Administrative Procedures   A number of administrative procedures have been developed in connection with the dyspedagogic point of view. Transitional classes to intensify instruction have been tried with limited success. New York City's well-known "Gates Program" is an example that has continued for a decade. Cross-class grouping for reading instruction, peer tutoring, cross-age tutoring, and buddy-reading are all examples of experimental measures to meet the needs of low-achieving children within regular classrooms. These programs, too, need careful evaluation.

Oral Reading Techniques   Some specific techniques use regular classroom materials but focus on specific skill deficits in reading fluency. Moyer (1982) developed a technique she calls *multiple oral rereading (MOR)* in rehabilitation work with a patient with acquired alexia. Materials are chosen at a level that presents little difficulty in word recognition for the reader. The selection is read once at a pace that permits a high degree of accuracy. The selection is then repeated, usually three or four times, with speed increasing with each repetition. Moyer says that "daily practice with MOR has consistently resulted in an increase in the rate of reading new material" (p. 619). Repeated reading in remedial instruction provides the degree of redundancy necessary to extract the system of correspondence between the written and spoken language. Other methods also draw on the principle of redundancy for their basic premise. The neurological impress method (Hechelman, 1969) uses choral reading by student and instructor. Massive oral decoding (R. J. Johnson, Johnson, & Kerfort, 1972) uses the repetition of phonetically regular text.

The simplicity and economy of these methods is attractive. However, all three methods are designed to encourage fluency in reading only *after* the learner has acquired some word attack skills. Moreover, no objective data are presented to indicate their effectiveness.

Reading Recovery   The reading recovery program developed by New Zealand educator Clay (1985) is a more broad-based application of regular classroom procedures. This approach targets the lowest 20% of the first-grade children identified by their teachers and by a diagnostic survey that includes six measures:—letter identification, word test, concepts about print, writing vocabulary, diction test, and text reading level—on which the teacher keeps a "running record" of the child's oral reading performance.

In addition to their regular classroom activities, target children are provided daily one-to-one 30-minute individual tutoring sessions by specially trained teachers. Instructional activities include (a) reading easy stories read previously, (b) reading a story independently while the teacher makes a running record of errors, (c) working on letter identification and use if the child has a limited knowledge of letters, (d) constructing a written message in the child's own writing book, (e) reconstructing the written message after it has been transcribed on a strip and cut apart, (f) talking about a new book selected to support the child's strategies, and (g) reading a new book with assistance by the teacher (Pinnell, 1985). Results of the Reading Recovery program in New Zealand reported by Clay (1988) indicate that children at risk for failure made accelerated progress while receiving individual tutoring. "After an average of twelve to fourteen weeks in the program, almost all Reading Recovery children had caught up with their peers and needed no further help. Three years later the children still retained their gains and continued to make progress at average rates" (p. 2). Reading Recovery has been replicated in the United States through Ohio State University and has been selected as an exemplary program by the U. S. Department of Education's National Diffusion Network on the basis of data on educational impact in model programs in Ohio.

Regular Education Initiative An even broader based program is the Regular Education Initiative advocated in 1986 by Will who was then Assistant Secretary for the Office of Special Education and Rehabilitative Services in the U. S. Department of Education. This program advocates major restructuring of the education of "mildly" handicapped children (the learning disabled, educable mentally retarded, and behavior disordered). It delivers systematic and organized intervention in the regular classroom through individualized programs in which special-needs students receive instruction tailored to their needs. The initiative was designed to serve not only regular class and "mildly" handicapped students but also the disadvantaged students in Chapter 1 programs, limited English–proficient students in ESL programs, Native American children in Indian Education Programs, and children from families of migrant workers. Will urged local education agencies be given time-limited exemptions from certain special education regulations to avoid loss of funding while they conducted experimental trials of these restructured programs.

The Regular Education Initiative questions the efficacy of special education for such reasons as the following:

- Efficacy studies have not proved that the educational practices associated with special education classifications lead to improved outcomes in the classroom (Biklen & Zollers, 1986).

- Although there has been overidentification of learning disabilities, many children who are not eligible for services remain without services in regular classrooms (Will, 1986).

- Pull-out programs (like the resource rooms) result in disjointed education and divided responsibility (Will, 1986).

- Classification in special education programs stigmatizes children and results in lowered academic and social expectations (Will, 1986).

- There is no clear evidence that "real" subtypes describable in neurological terms exist and indicate distinctive educational approaches (M. C. Reynolds, 1988).

Three studies have reported results with the Adaptive Learning Environments Model (ALEM), the model most frequently cited for implementing the initiative (Wang & Birch, 1984; Wang, Peverly, & Randolph, 1984; Wang & Walberg, 1983). Although the ALEM model is characterized by providing support and services from specialists within the general educational setting, no information is given about how these services are used. Although two contradictory components—highly structured guided learning and exploratory, student-managed learning—are proposed, their classroom application, as opposed to their theoretical descriptions, is not presented. Also there is very little description of the characteristics of the handicapped children who participated in these programs beyond their general category of exceptionality. Finally the number of handicapped children included in the experimental samples is very limited: 33 learning disabled in a sample of 31 classrooms in one study, 69 special education students in a sample of 26 classrooms in a second study, and 11 special education students in a sample of 108 children in ALEM classes in a third study. Hallahan, Keller, McKinney, Lloyd, and Bryan (1988) did a detailed analysis on the methodological shortcomings of these studies and concluded that a more robust foundation was needed before a policy that could affect the education of large numbers of children could be considered for adoption.

In the long run, the controversy over the Regular Education Initiative may contribute to the improvement of education by focusing on issues of educational quality in both regular and special education. This common ground is implicit in the very reasonable position statement of the Association for Children and Adults with Learning Disabilities (ACLD) on what was called the Regular Education/Special Education Initiative:

ACLD, Inc. applauds the U. S. Department of Education's interest in an attempt to provide appropriate services in the regular classroom for students with a wide range of needs. At the same time, ALCD Inc. respectfully points out that, when intervention in the regular classroom is unsuccessful for a trial period, those students who have not been properly identified as handicapped should be considered for special education evaluation and their eligibility for special education services determined. (ACLD, 1986, p. 1)

Models Emphasizing Language Development

The relationship between general language abilities and reading achievement has been recognized for some time. The apparent logic of this relationship was confirmed early in correlational studies (Artley, 1950; Peake, 1940; W. E. Young, 1936). In a clinical study contrasting groups of retarded and nonretarded readers from a population of children with behavior disorders matched in terms of age, IQ, and sex, Hagin (1954) found clear-cut differences between the groups in a number of measures of language. The groups differed significantly in their perception of verbal stimuli as assessed through measures of auditory discrimination—auditory blending, rhyming, and matching initial sounds of words. Measures of verbal fluency—as assessed through word association, articulation, and measures of sentence length and complexity in oral language samples—also differentiated the groups, as did conceptual use of language through the use of oral opposites, analogies, and level of abstraction on a sorting test. Finally the groups differed on breadth and accuracy of oral vocabulary definitions, but not on a vocabulary test that required a pictured response.

Language Enrichment Programs Most textbooks on learning problems are rich sources of methods for enhancing language development in young children (D. J. Johnson & Myklebust, 1967; Lerner, 1988). Dudley-Marley and Searle (1988) offer guiding principles for enriching language environments for students with learning disabilities: (a) provide a physical setting that promotes talk, (b) provide opportunities for children to interact and use language as they learn, (c) provide opportunities for children to use language for a variety of purposes and for a variety of audiences, (d) respond to student talk in ways that encourage continued talk. These principles characterize a very different classroom setting than do those in which children sit at their desks writing in workbooks in solitary silence.

During the 1960s interest in the language of minority children resulted in the development of language stimulation materials for use with inner city children. The four Peabody Language Development Kits (Dunn & Smith, 1965, 1966, 1967, 1968) were among the best conceived of these sets of materials. A few years later Blue and Beaty (1974) categorized all the activities of the Peabody kits in terms of the components of a major language battery, the Illinois Test of Psycholinguistic Abilities (ITPA) so that they could be accessed more conveniently in work with children with learning disabilities.

Illinois Test of Linguistic Abilities There has been much discussion of the ITPA by its authors (Kirk & Kirk, 1971; Kirk, McCarthy, & Kirk, 1968;

McCarthy & Olson, 1963); its supporters, and its critics. ITPA divides global language behavior into chartable subskills for analysis and remediation. The experimental edition published in 1963 and a revised edition published 5 years later generated wide clinical application and research inquiry. Concurrent, construct, and predictive validities have been shown to be adequate, but factor analytic studies have not demonstrated a high degree of subtest purity (Weener, Barritt, & Semmel, 1967). This last finding has raised questions about the use of the language subskills in approaches to remediation, particularly since research findings generated by the ITPA were mixed. On the basis of a gross categorization (+ or 0) of intervention effects in 39 published studies, Hammill and Larsen (1974a) concluded that the idea that psycholinguistic constructs, as measured by the ITPA, could be trained was not validated. A subsequent critique by E. Minskoff (1975) described 10 methodological errors in the Hammill and Larsen review, including oversimplification, grouping of noncomparable subjects and failure to consider length and intensity of experimental treatments. More rhetoric followed the critique, with Hammill and Larsen reaffirming their original position, a review of the original 39 studies by another group of investigators (Lund, Foster, & McCall-Perez, 1978) and finally a meta-analysis (Kavale & Forness, 1985) showing a mixed picture overall but a substantial effect-size for expressive language components in 24 studies analyzed. Unfortunately, the fine points of these papers did not feed back into general practice in the field, and the gross generalizations of the 1974 study continue to be quoted most frequently.

Whole Language Approach   The classroom instructional strategy called the whole language approach has been recommended by Brand (1989), who believes it can alleviate some of the difficulties of learning disabled children including problems of memory, cognition, anxiety, inadequate self esteem, locus of control, attentional problems.

The whole language approach requires the teacher to establish a literate environment in the classroom, demonstrating how language is used for real communication in recreational and functional activities. There is emphasis on free choice reading and student authorship, so that reading instruction is integrated in natural ways with the other language arts of listening, speaking, and writing. Reading and writing always involve communication that is meaningful to the students. Organized so that the physical, intellectual, and social-affective components of the setting emphasize communication, this environment contrasts with the classroom that emphasizes isolated worksheets, memorized rules, and skill tests (Duffy & Roehler, 1989).

All of which sounds ideal for children with learning disorders, until one considers how this approach accomplishes the teaching of word attack skills, one of the major difficulties these children encounter. Duffy and Roehler (1989) explain this in their textbook on reading methods. Teachers are told to teach children to recognize sight words by having them read the words to be learned in phrases from flash cards "until students instantly recognize the word." For some children with learning disorders this lesson might last for a long time. With otherwise unfamiliar words, the student is encouraged to use context cues (guessing on the basis of the words around the unknown word) or structural analysis (using its structural units such as prefixes, suffixes, roots, and inflectional endings). As a last resort the student might use phonics to "sound out" the unknown word, but Duffy and Roehler apparently have a dim view of these methods: "Phonics is the slowest of the three decoding methods because it requires that each separate letter-sound unit be retrieved from memory and then blended together. . . . Further, phonics is not always reliable because letter sounds are not always consistent and predictable" (p. 108). This point of view about phonics is maintained in the face of a substantial body of research to the contrary (Chall, 1983; Stanovich, 1986).

The Duffy/Roehler textbook, intended for use in the training of teachers, makes few suggestions for adaptations for children who have trouble learning to read. About "special students" they write: "Sometimes teachers have the expectation that such different students require different instruction. This is not so. You must adapt your instruction to the level at which such students are working, but your basic instructional techniques remain the same" (pp. 76–77).

Thus, this textbook appears inflexible in relation to teaching children with learning disorders. The whole language approach has merit in its emphasis on the natural interrelationships of language skills, its recognition of the importance of meaning in the development of communication skills, and its adaptability for use with the word-processing systems as microcomputers become part of regular classroom equipment. However, because of its inadequate provision for teaching word attack skills, the whole language approach does not offer much promise for success in teaching learning disordered children.

Fernald Tracing   Fernald's tracing technique is a venerable remedial method that also uses student authorship and language context to teach beginning reading (1943/1988). Fernald developed this method in a clinical setting with bright retarded readers, described its use, and documented it with painstaking case studies. The steps in its use are as follows:

- The student writes a brief story without any assistance.
- The student and the teacher rewrite the story, making corrections in terms of capitalization, punctuation, and grammar.
- As misspelled words are encountered, they are rewritten in large cursive writing by the teacher on paper approximately 4¼ by 11 inches.

- The student traces each word with his or her finger, saying the word (not individual letters) aloud.

- When the student feels the word has been learned, he or she writes the word from memory on a small piece of paper and then compares it with the large copy written by the teacher.

- If the student wrote the word correctly, it is then written in the copy of the story that is being rewritten; if it was not correct, the tracing is resumed until the word can be written correctly from memory.

- The large copies of words are filed to serve as an informal dictionary for the student as other stories are written.

- Rewritten stories are typed, to be used as text for oral reading.

The reasons for the effectiveness of this technique with some children has not been established. Fernald's hypotheses about the effects of kinesthetic-tactual stimulation seems improbable in the light of more recent information about brain function. It may be that the use of language generated by the student provides more salient contextual cues to the beginning reader than text like "Come, Spot and Puff, come." It may also be that the tracing and rewriting impose detailed, directionally accurate inspection of the words, so that the student is given more cues and more practice than with the conventional "look and say" classroom approaches to initial reading instruction. Whatever the reason, the Fernald tracing techniques appears to be one of the few "top-down" methods that holds promise for children with severe reading disorders.

Models Emphasizing Sound-Symbol Correspondence

There is probably no aspect of reading instruction that has given rise to greater controversy than that dealing with phonic analysis in word attack. Orton cited this controversy in the Salmon Lectures in 1937:

> There has been in recent years a striking swing toward the use of the sight or flashcard method of teaching reading and away from the use of phonetics. The writer is not in a position to offer an opinion as to the efficacy of either of these methods as a general school procedure but their effect on children suffering from varying degrees of strepho-symbolia has come under his immediate attention and he feels that there can be no doubt that the use of the popular flash method of teaching reading is a definite obstacle to children who suffer from any measure of this disability. (Orton, 1937/1989, p. 104)

The subject of diatribes [*Why Johnny Still Can't Read* (Flesch, 1981)], carefully reasoned research analyses [*Learning to Read: The Great Debate* (Chall, 1983)], and policy statements [*Becoming a Nation of Readers: The Report of the Commission on Reading* (R. Anderson, Hiebert, Scott, & Wilkersen, 1985)], the question whether phonics should be taught is not debatable at this time. Few self-respecting school administrators would admit that any beginning reading approach used in their districts did not teach phonics. Lerner (1988) listed nine different phonics programs designed for this purpose currently in use in schools.

Orton-Gillingham Approach Despite the continuing concerns about the teaching of phonics to improve reading competence, the description Orton wrote more than 50 years ago is equally true today: "the hallmark of specific reading disability or strephosymbolia is a failure in recognition of the printed word even after it has been encountered many times" (1937/1989), p. 175. Orton described the teaching of sound-symbol correspondences in the Language Research Project at Neurological Institute in New York City:

- use of kinesthetic-motor patterns to teach graphic forms of letters
- teaching phonetic equivalents of printed letters through cards containing the printed letters
- teaching the process of blending auditory sequences of such equivalents to produce the spoken form of the written word
- using associative linkages of vision, audition, and kinesthesis to ensure transfer to written spelling

With admirable restraint he added: "We have tried to avoid overstandardization lest the procedure become too inflexible and be looked upon as a routine method applicable to all cases of nonreaders, which would be clearly unwise in view of the wide variation in symptomatology and hence in training needs which these children exhibit" (p. 175).

These procedures were developed with Gillingham who later organized, expanded, and recorded this approach so that it could be used by other teachers (Gillingham & Stillman, 1956). These modest beginnings, now known as the Orton-Gillingham approach, have influenced a large number of teachers and inspired many related teaching systems (S. B. Childs, 1973; Cox, 1977; Enfield, 1988; E. T. Hall, 1976; R. E. Saunders, 1973, Slingerland, 1971; Traub, 1972). The sample lesson components of Cox's Alphabetic Phonics approach (1985) provide a specific example of typical content in a current program:

- an alphabetic activity to strengthen automatic use of the sequence
- new learning of one of the 98 graphemes through multisensory methods: tracing, writing, saying orally
- review of graphemes previously taught through rapid exposure of sound cards

- written review from dictation of sounds previously learned
- reading and spelling practice, requiring application of sound-symbol knowledge
- handwriting practice
- verbal expression focusing on vocabulary, syntax, semantics, and auditory processing
- listening to good literature

Progress in the Alphabetic Phonics Program is assessed through Bench Mark Measures (Cox, 1977), which are criterion-referenced measures in the following skills areas: alphabet and dictionary; reading accuracy of words and paragraphs; spelling and sentence dictation; and handwriting. It has been emphasized that Orton-Gillingham is an approach, rather than a standardized program. While specific applications of the approach may differ, there are common themes deriving from the principles elucidated in Orton's early work.

Despite the widespread application of this approach, there has been little educational research to assess its efficacy or to compare it with other interventions. What research has been done is open to question because of methodological flaws. For example, Kline and Kline (1975) did a follow-up study of 216 dyslexic children from a clinical sample, comparing outcomes for children who had regular school services. However, the fact that the investigators did not explain how judgments of improvement were determined, did not control for length of time in tutoring, did not control the interventions given to the comparison group, and did not make random assignment of subjects weakens the impact of their findings. Kline (1977) has himself commented on the lack of research in this area.

Experimental interest may eventually provide a different kind of validation for code-based teaching approaches. Stanovich (1982) pointed out that, while higher level memory processes and text-level comprehension processes account for some of the variance in reading ability, there is research evidence that decoding processes at the word or subword level must be considered and that across a wide number of studies, the correlations between the speed and accuracy of word recognition and reading comprehension range from .50 to .80. A. A. Silver and Hagin (1964) in a 10-year follow-up study of children with reading disabilities, found that rho coefficients between freedom from errors on a battery of tests of visual, auditory, and body image perception and oral reading was .25, in contrast to a rho coefficient of .71 between the same perceptual ratings and reading comprehension. These correlations suggested to them that individuals with severe problems in perception become so involved with the task of decoding written symbols that their interpretation of meaning of text was impaired. La Berge and Samuels (1974) and Perfetti and Hogaboam (1975) stated this hypothesis more positively in their conclusions that as decoding becomes more automatic, attention is freed for higher level cognitive processes.

Phonological Awareness The recognition of the significance of decoding to the reading process has resulted in research focus on phonological processes. J. P. Williams (1984) pointed out that two decades ago this area was known as *auditory skills*: today some of the current terms used in this connection are as follows: phonological awareness, linguistic awareness, linguistic insight, phonemic segmentation, phonemic synthesis, phonemic analysis, sound segmentation, phonological processing, phonological recoding in lexical access, and phonetic recoding in working memory. As can be gathered from this list, terminology is not clear-cut. In addition, some complex terms are used to designate familiar processes; for example, "phonemic synthesis" is used to describe the activity most teachers call "blending" and "phonological recoding in lexical access" is used to designate what teachers call "sounding out words." Whatever terms are used, they indicate studies to understand how children learn to identify and use correspondences between letters and sounds in reading. To do this, the child must be able to identify the units, *both graphic and phonetic*, and to blend these units in accurate temporal sequences into recognizable words. These processes of analysis and synthesis are complex because of the variations and irregularities of sound-symbol correspondences in the English language.

According to J. P. Williams (1984), some of the earliest work relating phonemic analysis to reading was done by two Russian psychologists. Williams noted that in 1963 Zhurova found that many children between the ages of 3 and 6 could not isolate the first phoneme in simple words and, when attempts were made to teach this skill, many such children failed to learn it. Zhurova predicted that these children would have difficulty learning to read. Similarly, Elkonin (1973) taught children to identify the number of phonemes within words by using discs to represent separate phonemes. When the discs were replaced with letters these children "showed improvement in various aspects of literacy" (J. P. Williams, 1984, p. 219).

In the following decade a number of investigations focused on relationship of various aspects of phonological processing to reading: developmental trends and predictive accuracy (Calfee, Lindamood, & Lindamood, 1973); differences in the development of syllable segmentation and phoneme segmentation (Liberman, 1973); sound deletion and language arts achievement (Rosner & Simon, 1971); and ceiling levels at age 4 for word and syllable segmentation and at age 6 for phoneme segmentation (Fox & Routh, 1975). All found significant relationships between phonological skills and word recognition in reading. Bryant and Bradley (1983), using an "odd word out" paradigm, found that, when asked to recognize or to produce rhymes, "backward readers" in English schools had more difficulty than younger children who were reading at the same achievement level. They concluded that these difficulties resulted from phonological weakness.

While these studies demonstrated positive relationships between reading and phonological awareness, the implications for teaching remain a question. L. Bradley and Bryant (1985) studied the impact of training in phonological processing over a 2-year period with groups of 13 children treated with one of four conditions: (a) categorizing words on the basis of their sounds—i. e., recognizing rhymes and alliteration, (b) categorizing words by concrete sound—recognizing rhymes and alliteration but, in addition, demonstrating shared sounds among words by spelling them out with plastic letters, (c) categorizing words by conceptual categories, and (d) no-treatment control conditions. At the end of 2 years the difference of 4 months in reading between the sound categorization and the conceptual categorization groups was not regarded as reliable. The concrete categorization group— which received sound categorization plus letter demonstrations—had an average advantage of 9 months in reading and 17 months in spelling. The reliable difference in achievement may indeed have resulted from phonological training. However, an alternative hypothesis suggested by the data is that the visual form of the letters may also have played a role and that the intermodal (auditory and visual cues) or spelling cues in addition to the phonological training made this condition the most powerful intervention.

J. P. Williams (1984) conducted one of the most carefully designed and evaluated training studies in a decoding program that included lessons in phonemic analysis and blending. Evaluation after training showed that the program children were able to decode both familiar words and nonsense combinations, indicating transfer effects of the skills taught. The results suggested to her that phonemic training made instruction more effective, but she added the caution that it was impossible to evaluate the effects of phonemic training apart from the effects of all the other components of the experimental program. Thus, while this work is valuable in that the experiment was placed within the natural context of reading instruction, additional research is necessary to focus on the contribution of specific phonological skills.

Williams's caution is a reasonable one, especially if one considers a series of experiments that used an interference condition to isolate visual and phonological skills as children solved two matching tasks, one involving rhyming and the other involving conceptual grouping (Baron, 1979). The interference condition, which blocked out use of phonological cues, interfered with reading and recognizing rhymes but did not interfere with reading and doing the conceptual task. The investigators concluded that in the early stages of reading many children adopt a visual strategy that takes them directly to the meaning of words without having to build them up from their phonological elements—without translating symbols into sounds at all. The paradox is that while normal readers seem to acquire the skills of phonological analysis as part of their language development, they seem to be able to read without using these skills. In contrast, children with reading disabilities have difficulty acquiring these skills and usually need a word attack approach embodying phonological skills for success in beginning reading.

It seems premature to suggest, as Wagner (1986) did, that phonological factors are causal. At least two alternative hypotheses suggest themselves. The first is that there may be a circulat effect; while phonological awareness enhances the process of learning to read, knowing how to read enhances one's awareness of phonology. This interaction might explain why the phonemic segmentation of words does not develop fully until age 6, when children have had some experience with the sound-symbol correspondences in beginning reading. Studies by L. Bradley and Bryant (1985) and Liberman, Cooper, Shankweiler, and Studdert-Kennedy (1967) suggest this point.

A second hypothesis is that the difficulties with phonological tasks may be part of general difficulties in the associative aspects of language, in spatial orientation, and in temporal sequencing that children with learning disorders experience.

Models Emphasizing Neuropsychological Interventions

Recent interest in neuropsychological techniques for assessing brain–behavior relationships has influenced the field of learning disorders. Telzrow and Speer (1986) have offered some general suggestions for maximizing instruction for children with learning problems based on their observation that children with learning disabilities demonstrate many of the characteristics symptomatic of chronic neuropsychological dysfunction, such as attention and concentration problems, memory deficits, uneven learning patterns, and difficulties in generalizing and solving problems.

There remains considerable skepticism about the relevance of neuropsychology to educational intervention (Sandoval & Haapanen, 1981; Senf, 1979). Criticisms have focused on the validity and discrepancy in results of neuropsychological tests of children. However, one of the major concerns centers around the practical significance of neuropsychological data for instruction. The evidence thus far accumulated for systematic interaction between learner characteristics and teaching approaches has not been encouraging (Cronbach & Snow, 1977). Reviews of intervention approaches designed to match modality strengths have also been less than impressive (Arter & Jenkins, 1977; Tarver & Dawson, 1978). Investigators have concluded that the studies they reviewed offered little insight applicable to prescriptive teaching.

Hartlage and Telzrow (1983), however, offer three fundamental objections to some of the original studies on which these reviews were based. First, methodological weaknesses include such flaws as unmatched samples, too brief intervention conditions, and inappropriate statistical treatment.

Second, the aptitudes and treatments studied were highly specific in nature and were isolated from the classroom in laboratory-like settings. Cronbach and Snow (1977) urged the investigation of aptitude-treatment interactions in natural educational settings in the belief that such studies would produce outcomes more relevant to teaching. Third, it is not clear whether the aptitudes investigated in the studies were meaningful from a neuropsychological perspective. While Cronbach and Snow assumed that nearly any attribute might be used to predict educational responses, the studies they reviewed examined such traits as state anxiety, field independence, and masculinity. While these variables may influence learning, they are different from the kinds of learner characteristics usually assessed in neuropsychological examinations.

The neuropsychological model most frequently applied in the treatment of learning disorders is the functional dichotomy of simultaneous/successive information processing. These concepts originated in Luria's (1966) clinical examinations of persons with cortical lesions. *Simultaneous processing* refers to the synthesis of separate elements into holistic, unitary representation. Measures of simultaneous processing include tasks of spatial organization, reading tasks in which words are perceived as wholes, and language tasks in which semantic relationships among separate linguistic elements must be identified. *Successive processing* refers to the synthesis of separate elements of information into a sequential, temporally-dependent order; elements of this synthesis remain independent of each other, accessible from their preceding elements through temporal order. Measures of successive processing include sequential memory tasks, analysis of the sequence of sounds in a word, and comprehension of syntactic structures in language. Luria found that lesions in the occipital-parietal area were associated with disturbances in simultaneous processing and that lesions in the frontal-temporal region were associated with disturbances in successive processing.

These functions were first described by Das, Kirby, and Jarman (1975, 1979) in relation to learning problems in children. The use of this model has increased with the appearance of the K-ABC, a psychological test designed to assess simultaneous/successive information-processing styles (see Chapter 5). The authors recommend that the test be used in planning educational interventions by matching teaching methods with children's preferred information-processing styles. In two of three remediation studies comparing interventions based on processing strengths with those using conventional teaching procedures, Kaufman and Kaufman (1983) reported significant gains in reading comprehension for the experimental group.

Other investigators have replicated the Kaufman's findings, but Fisher, Jenkins, Bancroft, and Kraft (1988) failed to do so in a carefully focused study that was designed to examine the effects of sequential, simultaneous, and mixed remedial strategies on word recognition skills. Although the results of this study indicated a consistent pattern supporting the predicted aptitude-treatment interaction, the differences were small and not of a magnitude suggesting statistical or practical significance. In their discussion of the reasons for these conclusions, Fisher et al. (1988) questioned the manner in which the preferred mode of processing was determined by the K-ABC and the validity of the construct. Using Das's test battery for determining information-processing mode, measures of language, and reading processes and reading achievement, Kirby and Robinson (1987) found that reading-disabled children used simultaneous processing in reading tasks (word attack and syntactic analysis) that normally require successive processing. These investigators suggested two possible explanations for the use of the inappropriate processing mode: either a deficit in the skill of successive processing or an unwise choice of strategy. They concluded that the latter explanation would suggest the need for remediation aimed at improving the child's ability to select and use the appropriate strategy for the task at hand. In contrast, the former explanation would imply the need for training to improve the defective skill or to design alternative forms of instruction that emphasize simultaneous processing, the preferred processing mode seen in these children.

Because large numbers of children with learning problems demonstrate strengths in the simultaneous processing mode, some investigators such as Jorm (1979) have recommended that methods of reading instruction should capitalize on "look-say" approaches to reading. The idea may be logically derived from existing neuropsychological data, but it runs counter to major currents in educational research and practice. It should also be remembered that the simultaneous/successive-processing paradigm is relatively new. Considerably more research is needed to determine its robustness as a psychological phenomenon. When more is known about it, particularly its development in normal children, and when it can be demonstrated reliably, then it will be appropriate to use as a basis for selecting teaching methods.

Another neuropsychological intervention model is the one that emphasizes compensatory approaches. Drawn from the rehabilitation of adults with brain damage, this approach draws on methods that use such alternative strategies as sign language, rhebus text, braille, recorded books, and Kurzweil readers for teaching reading or hand calculators for teaching mathematics. As can be seen, these approaches imply a guarded prognosis in terms of independent learning. They may be appropriate for a small number of children, especially those with acquired brain damage, but they are too restrictive for most children with learning disorders.

There have also been interventions based on concepts of hemisphericity. The analysis of the tasks being taught is often oversimplified and the purported brain site of the function purely hypothetical. At any rate, the results of such educational applications have not been impressive (Kershner, 1979). This is not to imply that the modification of hemisphericity is not an intriguing intervention approach. Bakker and Vinke (1985), for example, reported experiments with hemispheric stimulation as a means of increasing reading achievement with some types of dyslexic children. The ill-lateralization seen in many children with learning disorders has yet to be explained, however (see Chapter11, "Specific Language Disabilities"). There are many possibilities: (a) a disconnection-like condition that results in less specialization of each hemisphere, (b) overconnection that results in too much interplay between the hemispheres, (c) unbalanced arousal and activation of hemispheres, and (d) metacognitive mismanagement. Applications in interventions must await clearer understanding of brain function.

Interventions Using Microcomputers

As with many aspects of American life, microcomputers have influenced the teaching of children with learning disorders. Lerner (1988) observed that computers offer the child with learning problems "privacy, patience, and practice." Informal observation and at least one research study indicate that they offer something else—the opportunity to start even (Hearne, Poplin, Schonemann, & O'Shaughnessy, 1988). Responses of 56 randomly selected junior high school students were compared with those of 56 junior high school students classified as learning disabled on the Computer Aptitude, Literacy, and Interest Profile (CALIP). The four aptitude subtests (Estimation, Graphic Patterns, Logical Structures, and Series) produced standard scores for the two groups that were compared by analysis of variance techniques. There was no significant difference in scores earned by students with learning disabilities and those of their peers with no learning disabilities. These findings suggested that learning disabled students were not different from their peers in their readiness for a full range of computer activities and that they had the potential for complex work with computers that goes far beyond remedial practice in a computer-assisted-instruction (CAI) paradigm.

The CAI paradigm characterizes the most frequent instructional use of computers in programs for children with learning disorders (Cosden, Gerber, Semmel, Goldman, & Semmel, 1987). Software from both commercial producers and public domain sources has proliferated to the extent that nearly every content and skill area in the school curriculum has been tapped. The range in quality is also wide. Teachers rated the following features as essential: (a) simple readable directions, (b) alternative means of presentation available (graphics vs. text), (c) uncluttered screens, (d) minimal keyboard skills required, (e) frequent feedback after responses are entered, (f) frequent opportunity for review of content, and (g) direct teaching of learning strategies that nonlearning disabled students learn incidentally. On examination of currently available software, Lee (1987) reported that he did not find these characteristics consistently present. The teachers also expressed a need for well-developed tutorials, rather than the simple drill and practice type programs that are currently predominating in the commercial software market.

At its worst, software can be little more than an electronic flash card. Once the novelty of computer use has worn off, the student using a poor-quality or inappropriate program will become bored with the repetitiveness and may find ways of faking by manipulating the responses without actually reading the material. At their best, software programs used for drill can provide the opportunity for private, unhurried practice sufficient for the mastery and fluency readers need as a basis for adequate comprehension. One excellent application to develop fluency in decoding skills in reading is the use of software programs with voice synthesizers (Jones, Torgeson, & Sexton, 1987). Another program called the Reading-Writing Connection (Hartley) provides flexible cues to help students learn to use mature syntax and sentence structure.

Microcomputers also have excellent capabilities as word processors. There are obvious advantages in terms of convenience, opportunities for easy revisions, spelling checking, the positive reinforcement provided by the good quality of the printed copy, and for some the interactive quality of word-processing programs that frees one to get ideas on paper much more easily than with pencil and paper or conventional typewriters. With younger children, voice synthesizer programs are especially helpful in encouraging composition work. These relatively inexpensive adaptations can be set to read letters, words, or the entire story as they are written. However, it should be remembered that the computer does not do the job of teaching all by itself. Teacher direction is needed to offer structure, guidance, and quality control to the students' composition lessons.

Tutorial programs are a different microcomputer application in which the computer program has a more active instructional role, to teach a specific skill such as typing or use of a word-processing system.

Authoring programs are appearing to permit teachers to make modifications of programs for individual students with special needs. Modification of commercial software programs is usually rendered impossible by protection devices built into programs to prevent unwarranted duplication.

Finally, some computer programs are designed as simulations and problem-solving activities. These programs are often more creative applications of computer capabilities that permit the student greater control over the learning tasks. Reasoning skills programs and use of computer languages like LOGO are examples of these newer developments (Collins & Carnine, 1988).

Interventions Involving Strategy Training

Interventions involving training in cognitive strategies are being used to improve academic functioning, particularly with students at the secondary school level. Many students, despite the goals of academic competence, independent learning, and intrinsic motivation set for them in earlier school programs, have failed to realize these objectives by the time they reach secondary school. Many (Deshler, Schumaker, Levy, & Ellis, 1984) reach a plateau in skill development at approximately a fifth-grade level. Deshler's group, finding that these students had been in programs with a strong remedial emphasis for several years, felt the need to explore other than the traditional approaches.

These adolescents had been described as "inactive learners," who failed to attend selectively, did not know how to organize material to be learned, did not use mnemonic strategies in learning, and had difficulty maintaining on-task behavior (Ryan, Short, & Weed, 1986). Despite these maladaptive strategies, some investigators found that the students could behave strategically if they were taught how to do so. Indeed, once they were taught many of these youngsters could use effective learning strategies (Palinscar & Brown, 1987; Torgesen & Houck, 1980).

The purpose of the strategies approach is to enable learning disabled adolescents to use their existing academic skills in a strategically optimal fashion. These students are taught task-specific strategies for such activities as monitoring errors in written work, test-taking skills, retrieval of information from textbooks, and self-questioning and paraphrasing as aids in reading comprehension. The following acquisition steps are used in the Deshler group's work at the University of Kansas Institute for Research in Learning Disabilities:

1. *Task-related pretest.* This step establishes the need for the strategy to be taught by assessing the student's current achievement with that specific task. Results of the pretest are discussed with the student so that he is aware of his instructional needs.

2. *Rationale.* The teacher provides a rationale for using the skill and a description of its use in current school activities.

3. *Modeling.* The teacher models the skill with appropriate demonstration and explanation.

4. *Verbal rehearsal.* The student rehearses the skill verbally, listing the steps involved in the skill to the level of mastery.

5. *Controlled practice.* The teacher provides practice material at the student's instructional level, so that practice can occur without interference caused by content difficulties.

6. *Advanced practice.* When the student is able to apply the strategy with material at a modified level, she is given grade-level material for further practice.

7. *Task-related posttest.*

These teaching methods have been validated with 90 learning disabled students in grades 10 through 12 (Deshler et al., 1984). Results were seen in increased scores on classroom tests and district competency examinations, improved course grades, and positive teacher perceptions of students. One caution is offered in the use of strategy training: The students must have some basic reading competencies (approximately fourth-grade level) if they are to profit from this kind of training.

Some investigators have pointed out the need for modifications of strategy training in order to ensure more opportunity for generalization of strategic approaches. One method for doing this is through self-instruction methods. Self-instruction is based on Vigotsky's theories of internalization of self-guided speech into thought, in which the learner moves from other-regulation to internalized language of self-regulation. During this process, which starts with the task being modeled by the teacher, the student gradually takes over the task through overt and gradually covert verbalization (Meichenbaum & Goodman, 1971).

Another approach to the problem of generalizability has been taken by Ellis et al. (1989), who developed and tested a methodology for increasing the ability of students to generate new strategies or to adapt existing task-specific strategies for meeting varying demands in the regular classroom. Instructional methods include the use of cue cards listing the steps of the substrategies and an overarching acronym, SUCCESS. Evaluation was done through a multiple baseline design that showed "dramatic increases in the subjects' verbal expression of metacognitive knowledge and ability to generate task-specific strategies" (p. 108). There were also increases in regular class grades, although the procedures seemed to be more effective with students who were marginal than with those who were already failing in their coursework.

One of the most important applications of strategy training has been with memory. Since learning and memory are inseparable, it is not surprising to find memory problems associated with learning disabilities. Gelzheiser et al. (1983) have provided a rationale for teaching memory strategies to learning disabled students. Three processes are involved in memory strategies: mnemonics (i.e., categorization, rehearsal, and elaboration); monitoring; and evaluation. Successful learners apply these strategies without specific training.

Gelzheiser, Solar, Shepherd, and Wozniak (1983) also hypothesized that cognitive resources are finite and, therefore, that central processing is limited. Differences between novices and experts in memorization may be due to differences in the way they allocate limited central processing capacity. The proficient memorizer organizes a plan and remains conscious of the goal as work continues. Often learning disabled individuals are found to be deficient in planning how to deal with a memory task; they also tend to remain at the stage of consciously directed practice for a longer period of time. It may be that they need more practice (opportunity for overlearning) in order to reach the stage of automaticity.

As can be seen from these descriptions and the limited research on strategy training, this approach represents very thorough and efficient teaching and very precise analysis of the tasks to be taught. It may be helpful in teaching students with learning disorders to use, maintain, and generalize the study skills that many other students devise and use on their own.

Interventions Through Social Skills Training

Bryan and McGrady (1972) showed that teachers perceive the child with learning problems as less socially adept, less task oriented, less facile verbally, and less organized and responsible with schoolwork than their normally-achieving peers. Findings from a number of studies can be summarized by the following generalizations:

- Children with learning disabilities display less positive behavior (attending and positive social interactions) than their non–learning disabled classmates (Bryan & Wheeler, 1972; McKinney & Feagans, 1984).

- High activity level does not seem to differentiate learning disabled children as a group and no correlation was found between distractability and hyperactivity (Lahey, Stempniak, Robinson, & Tyroler, 1978).

- Teachers respond differently to students with different achievement levels. They use more drill, more control statements in their management, and more positive reinforcement with low-achieving students (Brophy, 1979).

- Initiations of learning disabled children were more frequently judged as inappropriate (McKinney & Feagans, 1984); sometimes such initiations were ignored by both teachers and peers (Bryan & McGrady, 1972).

These findings have resulted in an explosion of investigations of ways of intervening with these social skill deficits. Three possible sources for the social skill deficit have been hypothesized (Gresham & Elliott, 1989). One view is that deficits result from the neurological dysfunctions that are responsible for academic problems. Gresham and Elliott discount this explanation because of the lack of data to support the position that localized brain dysfunction results in specific forms of social skills deficits and the fact that all learning disabled children are not similarly affected. Another view is that the socially maladaptive behavior is a secondary result of the academic problems learning disabled children experience. Gresham and Elliott also discount this explanation because they feel the only supporting evidence is correlational. They feel the most effective explanation lies in the third view, that social skills deficits result from failure to *acquire* social behaviors because of the lack of opportunity to learn the skill or the lack of exposure to models of appropriate social behaviors. A social performance deficit results from the lack of opportunity to *perform* social skills and/or lack of reinforcement for socially skilled behaviors (Gresham & Elliott, 1989).

Although there are currently only scant data to indicate which, if any, social skill deficits are *unique* to students with learning disabilities, there has been an explosion of intervention programs in this area in recent years. Earlier efforts used a relatively few interventions (such as contingent or negative reinforcement) to control specific behaviors (for example, to extinguish calling out in class). More recent efforts address broader goals such as positive changes in social competence and increased peer acceptance. Intervention strategies are more varied, including instruction, modeling, rehearsal of specific behaviors, performance feedback using videotape, and social cognitive problem solving. Typical skills targeted in these programs include eye contact, rate of peer interaction, self-expression, initiating social interaction, controlling negative behaviors, assertion, friendship-making, giving feedback, offering support, greeting, joining, conversing, sharing, problem solving, extinguishing inappropriate behaviors such as bossing and tattling, and getting along with authority figures.

Some questions have been raised about whether the behaviors targeted in the training will indeed lead to the realization of the goals intended. For example, the target behaviors of some programs (i.e., maintaining eye contact or appropriate greeting behavior) may not be crucial in the social repertories of children with learning disorders. J. N. Hughes (1986) believes that the way behaviors are chosen for intervention is important in determining their appropriateness. She analyzed 32 studies published between 1980 and 1984 along the dimensions of social validity and individualization. She used the term social validation to refer to the relationship between a given skill and socially significant outcomes. This dimension was assessed to determine the extent to which the researchers had selected the behaviors to be taught on the basis of empirically validated criteria. The studies were also judged to determine if individuals selected for training were actually deficient in the targeted cognitive or behavioral skills. The criterion of individualization would seem to be a basic principle in any educational intervention. Applied in the case of social skills training, it would mean that not only should researchers verify that the student lacks the targeted skills, but also they should make efforts to ascertain individual characteristics that may contribute to or explain the reasons for the observed skill deficit.

Only 8 of the 32 studies met the two criteria of social validity and individualization. In more than half of the studies, social skills were selected on a nonempirical basis. Selection of skills was justified in some studies through research with noncomparable age groups. A majority of the studies did not indicate an attempt to verify that individuals lacked the specific skills to be taught in the intervention programs. Only 12 studies reported selecting children based on preintervention observation of their performance on the targeted skills. Fourteen studies met neither standard for social validation or individualization (J. N. Hughes, 1986).

These interventions are clearly at a developing stage. More research attention must be focused on the kinds of behaviors that can be changed and at what cost. The effects of changes in specific behaviors must be evaluated in terms of their long-range effects on social competence. Developmental issues need more attention than they have received; social competence at latency is a very different matter from social competence at adolescence.

The programs themselves must be compared with existing interventions to determine what they contribute to the remediation of children with learning disorders. Measurement issues must be dealt with. Although it is easy to recommend multiple measures, well-standardized measures in this field are few. Much of the current information in the field now comes from soft measures (that is, from teacher ratings of social adjustment and sociometric devices of social acceptance).

Hughes's criticisms of program content must be taken seriously if the 32 studies she analyzed are in any way representative of the state of the field. Her results demonstrate that thoughtful attention must be directed not only to *what* is targeted in social skills training, but also to *whom* such intervention is directed.

PRINCIPLES OF EDUCATIONAL INTERVENTION

Thoughtful consideration of organizational patterns in intervention models inevitably leads to the conclusion that there is no single structure or model that can be regarded as suitable for every child in the vast, heterogeneous population of learning disorders. There is no one "best" model that will work in all cases with all children. Furthermore, there is no way of borrowing the "double-blind" design from pharmacology to set up comparisons of intervention models and placebo conditions to find the "teaching method of choice" for children with learning disorders. The independent variables in such a research would be so variable and the dependent variables so difficult to measure that such an experiment would be difficult to conduct and results, if any, impossible to interpret.

This is not to suggest that results of the study of intervention models are irrelevant to educational planning—far from it. Studies that highlight the strengths and weaknesses of the various models available to the field are especially helpful in guiding appropriate educational choices. The intervention models discussed in this chapter all possess strengths and limitations. Table 7-2 presents these strengths in terms of the Job Analysis of Reading. It shows the possible contributions of each of the interventions discussed in the chapter to each of the subskill areas of reading. This kind of analysis of

Table 7-2 Job Analysis of Reading: Instructional Emphases of Intervention Approaches

	Prereading Skills			Word Attack Skills					Comprehension Skills		Study Skills		
	Visual	Auditory	Directional	Sight Words	Language Cues	Context Cues	Phonics	Word Structure	Oral Vocabulary	Interpretation	Selecting	Organizing	Retaining
Regular Classroom Methods													
Grade Repetition				+	+	+			+	+			
Peer Tutoring				+	?	?			+	?			
Oral Reading Techniques				++	+	+		?					
Neurological Impress				++	+	+							
Reading Recovery				+	?	?	?		+	+			
Regular Education Initiative				?	?	?	?	?	?	?	?	?	?
Language Development Models													
Language Enrichment Programs				+	+	+			++	++			
ITPA	+	+							++				
Whole Language Approach				++	++	++			++	+			
Fernald Tracing	+		?	++	+	+			+				
Sound-Symbol Correspondence				+	+	+							
Orton-Gillingham Approach		++		+	+	+	++	++					
Phonological Awareness		++					?						
Neuropsychological Approaches	+		+	+									
Computer Approaches	+	?	++	?	?	?	?	?		?	?	?	
Strategy Training									+	++	+	++	++
Social Skills Training									+	++	+	++	++

Key: ++ Marked Instructional Emphasis
       +   Instructional Emphasis
       ?   Possible Instructional Emphasis

skills addressed by an intervention is most important if one is to match children's educational needs appropriately within the wide range of possible educational interventions. This kind of analysis is also useful in that it defines the limitations of each of the interventions, so that one can guard against unreasonable expectations from any one specific method. In short, intervention decisions are best made with a broad understanding of the potential contributions of all existing models. The following principles have guided us in our work.

Understand the Child

Educational planning based on systematic multidisciplinary diagnostic study of the child increases the chances for successful intervention. Chapters 5 and 6 dealt with the basic components and rationale for these examinations. The decision tree (Figure 2-1) suggests priorities for the most parsimonious management of the diagnostic questions.

In addition to the examination components that supply answers to the major diagnostic questions, we have found that informal assessment of specific cognitive, perceptual, and motor skills is helpful in planning educational intervention. These tests are not a formal battery, but, rather, a menu from which we select measures to follow up on hunches that may have developed from clues during the formal diagnostic testing. The choices among these measures depend on the subjects' ages, the educational problems presented, and the strengths and deficits that have been elicited in previous or current evaluations. Examples of selections at different age groups are shown in Table 7-3.

Analyze the Task to Be Remediated

Understanding the task to be taught is as important as understanding the student's strengths and needs. Task analysis of the steps in learning a given skill is essential if the teaching plan is to be successful. The unrealistic recommendation to teach a child with auditory processing problems to read by using a purely visual approach is an example of the failure to understand the task. Inspection of the job analysis of reading should convince one that the task of reading (except in the case of a profoundly deaf person) involves *both* visual and auditory skills. Task analysis should also be applied to workbooks and other independent study materials in order to determine exactly what skills these materials teach. For example, many beginning reading workbooks purport to teach sound-symbol associations—phonics—by the use of picture pages. The page will be organized with the letters to be taught at the top of the page and under them, some pictured objects. The child is directed to "draw a line between the letter and the picture that has that

Table 7-3   Supplementary Tests to Assess Effective Educational Intervention

Preschooler, Kindergartener, or First-Grader	Elementary-School Child	Secondary-School Student or Adult
Search	Figure Drawing	Writing Sample
Figure Drawings	Writing Sample	Bender Visual Motor Gestalt Test with recall
Kinetic Family Drawing	Bender Visual Motor Gestalt Test	Trailmaking
Preschool Language Scale	Head's Clock Drawing	Stroop Color-Word Test
Vineland Social Maturity Scale	Stroop Color-Word Test	Rote Sequencing
	Trailmaking	Phoenecian Spelling Test
	Auditory Discrimination	Purdue Pegboard
	Rote Sequencing	Directionality
	Rhyming, Matching Initial Sounds	Finger Schema
	Phoenecian Spelling Test	
	Purdue Pegboard	
	Directionality	
	Finger Schema	
	Key Math	

beginning sound." Apart from the niceties of definitions of letters, sounds, phonemes, and graphemes and the several signalling systems involved, it is questionable whether this kind of work teaches sound-symbol associations, since the child has been given a purely visual task. If she happens to know how to spell the word, the line might be drawn correctly from, for example, the letter *H* and the picture of the house. However, having named it as the letter *H*, the child would have no clue for this sound or, worse yet, an incorrect association if he recognized the picture as a *cabin*. A further example of the need for task analysis are the reading kits that really teach secondary school students to answer multiple choice questions when their teachers think they are learning to comprehend text.

Plan Remediation Within the Total Context of Language

Learning disorders can be expected to affect every aspect of a child's language functioning—listening, speaking, reading, handwriting, and composition. Seldom is the problem confined to a single aspect of the sequence. Short-term plans that address only the current problem without reference to the other parts of the sequence will not be effective in the long run.

Realize the Importance of Decoding

The weight of the evidence is accumulating that not only is a strong decoding emphasis important in beginning reading, but also fluency in decoding is probably necessary for high level comprehension skills. In addition, the mature reader and writer should have a variety of word attack skills available. Versatility in word attack is the ideal.

Make Provisions for Overlearning

Overlearning (i.e., drill) is an embarrassment to many teachers who feel their time is being wasted unless their students are involved in abstract concept development. Yet many children with learning disorders need the opportunity for mastery through overlearning. Strong plans can provide for this practice by designing alternative modes of presentation and drawing upon appropriate computer programs.

Consider Age and Skill Levels Carefully

Plans must take into account the student's school history—the previous attempts at remediation and the amount of exposure to the same remedial methods. While many publishers are providing content materials with a high-level of interest but a low level of readability for elementary grades, such provisions are not always made with teaching methods in the secondary grades. The productive work in teaching strategies that help secondary school students make optimal use of the skills they have merits careful consideration by educational planners. At the other end of the age range, let us hope that equal care will be taken in planning appropriate innovative teaching methods and content for the young developmentally delayed children who will soon be in school.

Encourage Lifelong Planning

With the possible exception of learning disorders resulting from poverty and inappropriate stimulation, most learning disorders can be expected to be lifelong conditions. This does not mean that one cannot be optimistic about outcomes for these children, but rather that provisions and accommodations may be necessary throughout schooling and adult life. Thus these children and their families need to be provided with accurate information about the nature of their problems and guidance in lifelong planning for the best use of their abilities. Support is particularly important at decision points and in negotiating major transitions for further education and vocational plans. In this connection, the compensatory activities that may have been regarded as hobbies (interests in computers, sports, creative arts, and part-time jobs) during the early years, may serve as directions for vocational interests in young adulthood.

Ensure Follow-up for Student and Teacher

Reevaluation is valuable for the student and his family in that it gives them an opportunity to assess results of intervention. It also serves the planner by providing an opportunity to assess the efficacy of the plans made for the individual, as well as the overall outcomes of the intervention activity itself.

SUMMARY

Although the etiologies of learning disorders are varied and the diagnosis is multidisciplinary, the responsibility for remediation is primarily educational. Federal laws for the education of the handicapped have in the past decade expanded services and set procedural guidelines for many aspects of educational diagnosis, planning, and intervention.

Two key provisions of P.L. 94-142, the continuum of alternative placements and the least restrictive environment, have shaped the organization of these services. Because of these provisions, schools must provide a range of possible placements so that children with learning disorders can be educated in the settings that provide the greatest opportunity for contact with students in regular educational programs. Annual reports to Congress by the Office of Special Education and Rehabilitative Services show that these programs are in place and that learning disabled children are receiving services in regular classes, resource rooms, self-contained classrooms, and separate schools in increasingly large numbers. There is, however, little information available about the quality of these programs. Concerns expressed by administrators and policy makers center around (a) the large numbers of children who are being identified as learning disabled, (b) the bureaucratic procedures and accompanying paperwork that consume professional time that might better be spent with students, and (c) lack of clear communication between researchers and practitioners.

Models for the education of children with learning disorders range widely. Some are adaptations of regular classroom practices; others use "top-down" methods that draw upon overall language functioning; still others use "bottom-up" approaches that deal first with phonemic elements of the language. Methods inspired by neuropsychological theories are making their way into classrooms and clinics. Microcomputers are being used effectively for practice, tutorials, word processing, simulation, and problem-solving activities. Strategy training to help students with learning disorders make optimal use of their skills shows great promise as a means of ensuring their success at the secondary school level.

Given the variations in the children with learning disorders, it is overoptimistic to expect that any model or method of instruction would turn out a uniform product. It is suggested that instructional planning should be based on understanding the student's needs with a clear statement of learning goals and careful monitoring of results.

CHAPTER EIGHT

Drugs Affecting Learning and Memory

In 1973, at a symposium on the biochemical correlates of learning and memory, Nakajimo and Essman noted that "the enhancement of intellectual function by drug administration has been one of the most formidable tasks presented to the student of the function of the brain" (p. 1). In spite of advances in the use of medication in child psychiatry since that time, there is still no practical way of increasing intelligence by use of drugs and it is only within the past 5 years that controlled studies of a new class of drugs, the nootropic drugs, suggest that piracetam may have a specific effect in facilitating verbal memory.

Medication is of course available for the relief of symptoms that may be associated with some learning disorders. Chapter 13 of this book describes the successful use of stimulant drugs (dextroamphetamine, methylphenidate, and pemoline) in reducing overactive, inattentive, and impulsive behaviors in children with attention deficit hyperactivity disorder, and improving performance in tasks that require sustained attention. Antidepressant medication has been helpful in restoring affective balance in depressive children; anticonvulsive medication has been effective in abating seizure discharges; and psychotropic medication such as phenothiazines and butyrophenones have helped bring the psychotic child back into this world. Where the symptoms of each of these conditions (ADHD, depression, seizures, or schizophrenia) contribute to impairment in learning, relief of the symptoms may free the child to learn. There is no evidence, however, that these drugs have a direct effect on the processes of learning and memory themselves. There is as yet no compelling evidence that medication is effective as a treatment of disorders involving the neural processes that accompany learning and memory.

One reason for this is that only within the past two decades are we beginning to understand the molecular events that accompany learning and memory. Although clinical reports of the amnesias and the agnosias have been available for over 100 years, only in the past 20 years have the complex connections and interconnections among neural structures involved in the storage and retrieval of memory been traced.

ANATOMY OF MEMORY

Learning is defined as the process of acquiring new information; memory is the persistence of learning in a state that can be retrieved at a later time. Memory involves a persistent change in the relationship among neurons through structural modification, or through biochemical events within neurons, that change the way neurons communicate. Learning most often originates as sensory impressions, gathered by peripheral sensory receptors and transmitted via neural pathways to primary areas, specialized for the reception of the particular sensory stimulus, in the cerebral cortex. For example, visual stimuli are gathered by the retina and are transmitted via the optic nerve and tract to the lateral geniculate body and from there to the primary occipital visual cortex. Similarly, auditory stimuli are transmitted from the cochlea to the auditory nerve, to the central cochlear nuclei, and then via the acoustic striae and trapezoid body to form the opposite lateral lemniscus that courses through the superior olivary nucleus to reach the posterior quadrigeminal and the medial geniculate body. From there impulses are transmitted to the primary auditory cortex in the superior temporal gyrus. Each primary cortical area reflects a systematic image of the peripheral sensory field, and each small region of the field activates a distinct cluster of neurons in the cortex. But from each primary cortex, impulses are transmitted to secondary and tertiary cortical stations; the visual, for example, to the inferior temporal cortex, the posterior parietal cortex, and the angular gyrus. While individual neurons in the striate cortex respond selectively to a single stimulus presented at a specific location in the visual field, the inferior temporal neurons receive data from large segments of the visual world, suggesting that information is processed at each station, becoming progressively more comprehensive in complexity of the information they admit, until at the final station, a complete representation of the stimulus is synthesized. This progression has been traced for response to visual, auditory, and tactile stimuli. The posterior parietal cortex also has a visual role, receiving impulses from the primary visual cortex, but mediating visual spatial relationships. The role of the posterior parietal cortex in mediating the body image has long been known (Schilder, 1935), but only recently have positron emission studies linked this area to brain activity in tasks related to vision.

The neural circuits involved in memory, however, do not stop at the secondary and tertiary cortical relay stations. Information from patients undergoing brain surgery and from experimental surgical, pharmacological, and behavioral studies (particularly in primates), have indicated that medial temporal structures, diencephalic structures, and prefrontal cortical areas are involved in the transformation of short-term learning to long-term memory. In 1953, a patient, H. M., now classic in the literature of learning and memory, became amnesic as a result of bilateral surgical excision of the medial temporal region to relieve severe epilepsy (Scoville & Milner, 1957; Corkin 1984). This amnesia had three characteristics: (a) it was global, involving memory from experiences of all senses; (b) it was anterograde; and (c) there was a patchy retrograde amnesia extending for approximately 3 years before surgery, but his early memories were retained clearly and vividly.

H. M. had normal language skills and a good vocabulary; he could perform tasks he had learned before surgery; and his IQ on the WAIS was 118. Yet when tested 13 years after the surgery he was virtually unable to recall or to learn any new verbal or visual material. He could manage short-term memory. He could learn material if it were within his short-term memory span, but he could not remember that material. For example, he could retain the digit span of six that he had preoperatively, but he could not increase the length of that span even with repetition. If given a series of 10 words, he could not recall the words at the beginning of the list but could recall only those from the end of the list. He could rehearse and keep material in mind for several minutes, but no longer. "He forgets the episodes of daily life as rapidly as they occur" (Squire, 1987, p. 138). H. M. stated that "Every day is alone in itself, whatever enjoyment I've had, whatever sorrow I've had. . . . At this moment everything looks clear to me, but what happened just before? That's what worries me. It's like waking from a dream. I just don't remember" (quoted in Rozin, 1976, p. 6).

These findings are interpreted to indicate that short-term memory was spared, provided the information does not exceed immediate-memory capacity, but that short-term memory could not be transformed into long-term memory. The medial temporal structures, particularly the hippocampus, are essential for the development of long-term memory. In primates, surgical destruction of both hippocampus and amygdala are needed to produce a global anterograde amnesia (Mishkin, 1982). In humans Mishkin and Aggleton (1981) suggested that the severity of memory loss may vary in proportion to the amount of damage sustained jointly by the amygdala and the hippocampus.

The hippocampus and amygdala, however, do not function in isolation. Efferent fibers from each course to the dorsomedial nucleus of the thalamus and to the mammilary complex. In turn, nuclei from these structures send fibers to limbic structures and then to specialized areas of the cortex. Long-term memory may be interrupted at any of these stages. The hippocampus and the amygdala, the thalamus and the hypothalamus, normally participate in memory storage without being the site of that storage.

A case illustrating the role of the dorsomedial nucleus of the thalamus is reported by Squire (1987). The patient, N. A., sustained a penetrating wound of the brain when a fencing foil was accidentally thrust through the right nostril and entered the left forebrain, producing an initial right-sided paresis and a right oculomotor weakness. The paresis subsided and he was left with a mild paresis of upward gaze, a mild diplopia, and a severe memory impairment for verbal and conceptual material. He now has difficulty remembering the events of each day. For example, he forgets what he has just done and whom he has just seen. It is as though his memory is intact up to the time of his accident: his past extends up to that time only. In 1981, 21 years after the accident, his IQ was 124 on the WAIS and he earned superior scores on vocabulary and visual-motor function. He has an obsessive concern with keeping everything in his house in fixed locations, and his personality is rigid—"single-minded" and inflexible in thought. On examination CT scan revealed a small lucency in the position of the left dorsomedial nucleus of the thalamus. He has a severe anterograde amnesia. His mother says, "you've got to have a memory to remember."

Clinical and experimental data thus have identified neural stations within the brain, in which sensory information is processed from elementary units into global perception of the information and from short-term information to long-term memory. Children with learning disorders may have impairment at any one point of these pathways. In specific developmental reading disability, for example, subgroup studies have identified varied patterns of information-processing deficit. We also stress the importance of temporal organization in the auditory-verbal area and spatial orientation in the visual and body-image area. The problem for these children is not in long-term memory but in the correct perception of their world. The recent findings of abnormality in the cellular patterns of the temporal lobe in specific developmental reading disability would suggest that the functions normally subsumed by these cortical areas are impaired. These functions relate to decoding information. Our remedy should attempt to correct these basic functions rather than approach remediation at higher levels of memory. On the other hand, children with structural damage of the central nervous system resulting, for example, from hypoxia or from birth trauma may well have, in addition to perceptual impairment, difficulty with higher levels of memory, with long-term memory, and with retention and retrieval of stored information. Brain damage occurring in early development may alter the pattern of relationships among surviving neurons. These children need help over and above the basic perceptual remediation. In children with attention deficit hyperactivity disorder, who do not have the perceptual distortion of the specific developmental disability, the emphasis in remediation need not be educational but the modulation of poor impulse control and the difficulty with sustaining attention so characteristic of these children.

MOLECULAR MECHANISM(S) OF LEARNING AND MEMORY

Cellular Mechanisms

Although there is general agreement about the anatomy of learning and of long-term memory, the molecular mechanisms of these events are only now beginning to be defined. Work on vertebrate systems such as the isolated spinal cord and skeletal muscle of chickens and on higher invertebrates such as *Aplysia* (Kandel et al., 1983; Kandel & Schwartz, 1982)), *Hermissenda* (Farley & Auerbach, 1986), and *Drosophila* (Dudai, 1985, 1988) identified cellular mechanisms for short-term learning, as in habituation and sensitization, and for longer term memory, as in conditioning.

Hawkins and Kandel (1984) summarized the common features of these findings as follows. Elementary aspects of learning are not diffusely distributed in the brain but can be localized to the activity of specific nerve cells. Learning produces alterations in membrane properties and synaptic connection of these cells. Memory storage lasting days and weeks in the systems studied have not involved formation of new synaptic contacts but result from changes in already existing contacts. These profound and prolonged changes in synaptic strength can be achieved by modulating the amount of chemical transmitter released by presynaptic terminals of the neurons (presynaptic facilitation). Finally, in several instances the molecular mechanisms involve cyclic nucleotide second messengers and modulation of specific ion channels.

In *Aplysia,* sensitization involves activation of facilitator neurons that synapse on the terminals of sensory neurons and use serotonin as the dominant neurotransmitter. Activation of serotonin receptors on the sensory cell initiates a series of biochemical events, the result of which is to phosphorylate a membrane protein, which closes a particular type of K^+ channel, increasing the duration of the action potential, and increasing the influx of Ca^{++}, thus permitting an increase in transmitter release. The biochemical cascade involves the activation of an adenylate cyclase in the terminals of the sensory neuron, increasing the level of cyclic adenosine monophosphase (cyclic AMP), which, in turn, activates a second enzyme, a cyclic AMP-dependent protein kinase, by combining with its regulatory unit, thus freeing its catalytic unit for protein phosphorylation. In turn, the change in protein closes K^+ channels and opens the Ca^{++} channel. Classical conditioning is described as resembling sensitization, in that a response to stimulus in one pathway is enhanced by activity in another, leading to selective enhancement of responses to stimuli (the conditioned stimulus) that are temporarily paired with the unconditioned stimulus. Hawkins and Kandel (1984) stated that the mechanism(s) of learning used by lower forms of animals may be a cell-biological alphabet to be put together by higher forms: "Where individual neurons may possess only a few fundamental types of plasticity that are utilized in all forms of learning, combining the neurons in large numbers with specific synaptic connections . . . may produce the much more subtle and varied processes required for more advanced types of learning" (p. 391).

Protein Synthesis

While the biological cascade described for *Aplysia* may be a basis for elementary "learning," the relationshp between this mechanism and long-term memory still needs to be explored. In long-term memory, terminals of the sensory neurons undergo striking morphological change, increasing the number and size of active zones. It is generally agreed that for the experiences of short-term memory to be encoded into long-term memory, new structural proteins, underlying any permanent changes in synaptic connections and/or in axonal or dendritic morphology, are required. Evidence for a macromolecular change in long-term memory is gathered from three major sources: the plasticity of the neuron responding with structural change to stimulation and to deprivation; the increase in neuronal RNA and the change in base ratio of RNA in cells involved in training; and the interference with long-term memory by inhibitors of RNA and protein synthesis.

Neuron Plasticity Morphological changes in brains of rats reared in a stimulating environment with toys and interaction with other animals, in contrast to those reared in standard laboratory cages, show an increase in gross cortical weight and thickness, in size of neurons, and, most important, in the number and length of dendritic branches and dendritic spins (Greenough, 1984; Rosenzweig & Bennett, 1978; Turner & Greenough, 1985). The terminals of the dendritic spines also undergo striking morphological changes: The sites on the axon terminals from which neurotransmitter vesicles are released undergo a marked increase in number and sensitivity (Bailey & Chen, 1983). Conversely, where there is a deprivation of stimulation there is a decrease in complexity and number of dendrites and dendritic spines (Valverde & Ruiz-Marcos, 1970). Riesen (1970) kept newborn monkeys in the dark for the first 3–6 months of their life and found that when they were brought into a normal visual world, they could not discriminate even simple shapes. Direct evidence that sensory deprivation in early life can alter the cellular structure of the cerebral cortex was obtained by Hubel and Wiesel (1979). In a series of ingenious experiments, Hubel and Wiesel found that in depriving a newborn monkey of vision in one eye for 6 months by suturing the eyelids closed, that eye will have permanently lost useful vision when the sutures are removed. Electrical recordings from the retina of that eye and from cells of the lateral geniculate body that received projections from the eye were normal. Electrical recordings from the visual cortex corresponding to those projections, however, were not obtained. Further, the cellular architecture of the visual cortex corresponding to the occluded eye was altered, with the size of the ocular dominance columns reduced. There appears to be abundant evidence that stimulation is necessary for function and that stimulation can change the morphology of the cortex, the number and complexity of dendritic conections, the number of sites for neurotransmitter release, and the sensitivity of receptor sites. These changes require new macromolecules.

The development of ultraviolet microspectographic and microelectrophoretic techniques (Hyden & Egyhazi, 1962) to determine the quantity and base percentages of RNA in single neurons dissected from the mammalian brain, contributed to the evidence that macromolecular change accompanies long-term memory. In one of their early experiments, Hyden and Egyhazi (1962, 1963) found total RNA to be significantly increased in cells of the vestibular nucleus of rats trained to obtain food by balancing on a 1-meter steel wire set at an angle of 45 degrees. Control animals subject to passive vestibular stimulation without having to learn to balance also showed increased RNA in the vestibular nucleus. Control animals, who did not undergo the learning or the stimulation experience, did not. RNA base composition changes, however, were seen only in the learning group and there only in neuronal and glial nuclei. The finding that RNA was increased during stimulation was confirmed by others (Booth & Sandler, 1967; Zemp, Wilson, Schlesinger, Boggan, & Glassman, 1966). The base composition changes, increases in adenine (35.7% in experimental animals and 21.0% in controls), and decreases in uridine (4.4% in experimental animals and 21.3% in controls), however, seemed to be specific to the learning process. Using a different species (goldfish) and a different paradigm (the fish had to learn to overcome being forced to swim upside down), Shashoua (1968) found the cytosine/uridine ratio to double because of decreased uridine after the learning experience. These data suggested that in learning the functional site of the gene is permanently altered, thus directing the formation of new proteins that are theorized to act in altering the excitability characteristics of the neuron.

Neuronal RNA   At about the time the RNA and RNA base composition experiments were reported, a startling series of observations appeared, in which a learned conditioned response in one animal could be transferred to another animal by extracts of the brain of the trained animal. In a series of reports, McConnell (1966) described the transfer of a light-shock conditioning to untrained planaria that had cannibalized trained worms or in which was injected a crude RNA extract of the trained worms. These phenomena were repeated in intraperitoneal injection to untrained rats of donor (trained) rat brain homogenates, from animals conditioned in various paradigms (Albert, 1966; Fjerdingstad, 1971; Reinis, 1965; Ungar, 1970, 1971). That RNA was the active ingredient for this transfer was suggested by the inability of planaria to be trained after they had been in a solution of ribonuclease for 10 days. Also, if the synthesis of RNA were blocked with actinomycin D, the transfer was unsuccessful. Similarly, ribonuclease injected into the hippocampus of rabbits and rats will inhibit their training in food-gathering. What was surprising in these experiments is not that training could be transferred by brain homogenates from trained animals, but that the *specific* learned experience could be transferred. By the early 1970s, however, a review of approximately 250 investigations of this phenomenon (Dyal, 1971) found that fully half of them failed to demonstrate the transfer of training. It was suggested that RNA is not the only substance extracted from brains of trained animals: DNA, proteins, peptides, and complex carbohydrates may also be found. These substances themselves may activate the synthesis of RNA in untrained animals. Although a specific peptide effective in transfer experiments was later reported by Ungar, Desiderio, and Parr in 1972, the hypothesis that specific information is encoded in correspondingly specific molecules is not now generally accepted. The death of Ungar in 1977 and the demise of the *Worm Runner's Digest* in 1979 stilled active proponents of the specific molecule for specific training theory. Rejection of the specific encoding hypothesis, however, does not reject the importance of protein synthesis for the formation of long-term memory. As Rosensweig and Bennett (1984) stated, researchers are "convinced that there is one obligatory process: the formation of long-term memory requires synthesis of proteins" (p. 264).

Protein Synthesis Inhibitors   Evidence that protein synthesis is necessary for long-term memory also stems from studies that use protein synthesis inhibitors. The basic design of these studies, recapitulating the early work of J. B. Flexner, Flexner, and Stellar (1963), involves brief training of the animal; retests done at varying times after training; administration of a protein synthesis inhibitor at varying times after training; and comparison of test performance of experimental and control animals. It was expected that memory of the training would be retained at the retests. In the early studies in the 1960s and early 1970s, puromycin, a drug that becomes incorporated into the carboxyl ends of growing polypeptides, was used in goldfish (Agranoff, 1970, 1981; Agranoff, Burrell, Dokas, & Springer, 1978; Agranoff & Klinger, 1964) and in mice (Barondes & Cohen, 1966, L. B. Flexner, Flexner & Stellar, 1965). The toxic and side effects of this drug, including the induction of abnormal hippocampal EEG's, clouded interpretation of results. Puromycin was soon replaced by cyclohexamide, acetocyclohexamide, actinomycin D, and anisomycin. Antibiotic memory loss of a learned discrimination (Squire and Barondes, 1973), of passive avoidance (H. P. Davis & Squire, 1984), and long-term habituation (Squire & Becker, 1975), all in mice, have been reported. A retention deficit for a motor task, active avoidance learning, and tasks that are interpreted as requiring memory storage are reported in goldfish (Shashoua, 1968). Anisomycin, which blocks protein synthesis at the level of translation, is reported to be markedly less toxic than the other protein-synthesis inhibitors mentioned above and can produce 80% inhibition of protein synthesis in the brain for about 2 hours (Bennett, Rosenzweig, & Flood, 1977). Thus it can be repeated at 2-hour intervals and can extend the inhibition to 14 hours.

Using the repeated injection paradigm it was found, in rodents, that the stronger the training, the longer the inhibition had to be maintained to prevent the formation of memory for a one-trial passive avoidance training (Flood, Bennett, Orme, & Rosenzweig, 1975). The timing of the inhibiting injection relative to the time of training suggested that "under appropriate training conditions, protein necessary for establishing long-term memory can be synthesized within minutes after training" (Bennett et al., 1977). With chicks the inhibitor can be administered as long as 20 minutes after training and still be amnesic. The conclusion from the time interval studies is that once a brief critical period is past (and its exact time course may vary with task and species), even prolonged subsequent administration of aniso-mycin will not prevent formation of memory.

The effect of protein synthesis blockers in "animals (fish, mice and chicks) under the influence of a block in brain protein synthesis demonstrated [acquired] the learned behavior as do uninjected controls. On subsequent testing, however, they are partially or totally amnesic" (Agranoff, 1978, p. 623). Thus protein synthesis selectively block the formation of long-term memory or perhaps accelerate the forgetting process. Other protein synthe-sis inhibitors have also been shown to block retention. Camptothecin, which blocks synthesis of ribosomal RNA; alpha amanitin, which blocks RNA poly-merase II; and 5 bromoturberciden, an adenine analog, which blocks mRNA and rRNA—all have amnesic action. There is evidence that protein synthesis inhibition in the entire brain is not a requisite for memory deficit. Small amounts of cyclohexamide injected bilaterally into the hippocampus, amygdala, or striatum of mice after training impaired memory formation, whereas injection into midbrain reticular formation, thalamus, and cortex did not (cited by Agranoff et al., 1978).

Increasing RNA

There have also been attempts to facilitate memory by increasing the syn-thesis of RNA. An early report by Cameron and Solyom (1961) that the memory of geriatric patients could be improved by oral administration and by intravenous injection of RNA stimulated the search for improvement of memory by administration of ribonucleic acid. At that time Cameron was a well-respected figure in psychiatry, director of the Allen Memorial Institute of Psychiatry and chairman of the Department of Psychiatry at McGill Uni-versity. The 1961 paper received much attention. Forty-one patients, 19% of them suffering from what was diagnosed as "brain arteriosclerosis," 8% of them as "senile dementia," were orally given slowly dissolving RNA tab-lets in doses from 3 to 18 grams daily for an average period of 6½ months, for a total mean dose of approximately 1,200 to 1,300 grams. Unfortunately this group of patients was also given intravenous injections of RNA for a total of approximately 164 grams. The effectiveness of oral RNA alone is not clear. A second sample of 43 patients from a geriatric ward of a provin-cial mental hospital were divided into medication and placebo groups. The paper is scant in the details we now expect. The authors concluded, how-ever, that RNA has a favorable effect in general upon memory retention failure in the aged because it increased alertness, interest, initiative, and confidence. Unfortunately the Cameron and Solyom results could not be confirmed clinically, and results of animal experiments were equivocal. Research using this direct approach has faltered. High doses of brewers yeast, however, a source of ribonucleic acid, is still a folk remedy to improve impaired memory.

In 1966 Glasky and Simon reported that magnesium pemoline (Cylert) increased the activity of RNA polymerase *in vitro* and *in vivo*. This effect could not later be confirmed by Stein and Yellin (1967) in the same laboratories. Clinically, magnesium pemoline is used in the treatment of attention deficit hyperactivity disorder. Its effects parallel those of methylphenidate in improving attention span and in reducing impulsive behavior. It does not improve academic performance unless that performance is impaired by the attention deficit itself. Experimental studies on learning in mice and in the effectiveness of pemoline in attenuating the amnesia produced by electroshock have been equivocal. However, two studies have found pemoline to improve cognitive performance. Conners (1972) found that, in a heterogeneous group of 81 hyperactive children aged 6 to 12, both pemoline and dextroamphetamine improved spelling, reading, perceptual abilities, and visual-motor function at the end of 8 weeks of treatment. The improvements in cognitive function were later (Connors & Taylor, 1980) found to be modest, although significant, in improving full scale and performance IQs. The consensus in the literature, however, is that pemoline, just as methylphenidate, does not appear to have any long-term effect on improving academic performance. This drug, along with methylphenidate and dextroamphetamine, is considered in more detail in Chapter 13. It may well be that pemoline exerts its action through its mildly sympathomimetic activity and not by its action on RNA polymerase at all.

MODULATION OF LEARNING AND MEMORY

The formulation of a memory trace thus appears to involve basic processes in which the stimulus induces molecular transformation as it goes from short-term perception to memory and recall.

Simultaneously with learning, however, there are neurohumeral and hormonal changes that persist into the posttraining period and which may influence learning consolidation and storage: "These agents do not affect the direct process of protein synthesis but may act by facilitating or inhibiting the transmission of neural impulses and circuits involved in processing information leading to memory formation" (Rosenzweig & Bennett, 1984, p. 275). These agents are the neurotransmitters and hormones released in the "affective states" (Kety, 1976) that accompany learning, the reaction to the stress of learning, and the homeostatic responses that accompany change. Peripheral hormones (epinephrine and cortisol) peripheral norepinephrine, pituitary hormones (vasopressin and oxytocin), and endogenous opiates and central neurotransmitters (particularly but not exclusively, cholinergic, catacholamine, and GABA transmitters) have been studied as agents modulating learning and memory. Performance may thus be affected by many exogenous and endogenous factors. The concept of modulation denotes that "in addition to the neural systems within which the content of memory is preserved, other systems may be involved in the memory process by serving a more trophic function" (M. Gallagher, 1984, p. 368). The concept of modulation does not depend on a single integrating system but on an interrelationship among systems, an "endogenous state dependency" (Izquierdo, 1984). Within this concept, the specific pattern of arousal present in the brain at the time of training may become an integral component of the stored information, "to promote the persistence of those circuits that have led to reward or the relief of discomfort" (Kety, 1976, p. 323). Search for the underlying mechanism(s) of modulation are in their early stages.

The Acetylcholine Hypothesis

In 1954, Krech, Rosenzweig, and Krueckel at the University of California at Berkeley reported the cholinesterase activity of the visual cortex of the rat to be 20% lower than that of either the somatosensory or the motor cortex. They questioned whether or not a high concentration of cholinesterase in sensory areas make for a generally more adaptive (that is, more intelligent) animal and whether high concentration of cholinesterase in specific areas of the brain had relevance for the mode of adaptation the animal used. In a series of investigations with rats solving spatial and visual mazes, they concluded that learning capacity is related to levels of acetylcholine and of cholinesterase, so that, within limits, the greater the amount of functioning acetylcholine at the synapse, the greater the efficiency of transmission and consequently the greater the learning ability (Rosenzweig, Krech, & Bennett, 1960). While this conclusion has proven to be an oversimplification of the effect of cholinergic activity on learning, two major lines of evidence have implicated acetylcholine as having, at least, a modulating role in learning and memory. The first is finding in repeated studies in mice, dogs, and human volunteers that, in general, drugs that increase acetylcholine levels in the brain (choline, arecoline, physostigmine, and diisopropylphosphofluoridate) increase retention of learned responses, while drugs that block acetylcholine receptor activity (atropine and scopolomine) decrease retention. These generalities may be modified by such variables as drug dose (where low doses of cholinergic drugs may potentiate and high doses may inhibit retention learning), relationship of time of administration of the drug to the time of training and testing, the type of training task, the method of drug administration, and the subject animal used. For example, the specific effect of physostigmine may facilitate or impair learning, depending on how long after training the drug is administered (Squire, 1987). If given 3–14 days after training it will facilitate, but if given between 30 minutes and 5 days after training it will impair learning. Cholinergic drugs, said Squire (1987) "are the only ones [studied] that have been reported to have opposite effects, either facilitating or impairing, depending simply how long after training the drug is administered" (p. 47). That these effects are central rather than peripheral is suggested by a report of Drachman and Leavitt (1974), who compared the effect of scopolomine, which crosses the blood–brain barrier (1 mg subcutaneously), with that of methscopolomine, which mimics only the peripheral effects of scopolomine, and with physostigmine, which does cross the blood–brain barrier. The subjects were 20 men (volunteers, aged 19–25) and 20 controls; the test was that of immediate memory (digit span), storage, and recall (free recall of lists of words, and then writing lists of remembered words). While no difference among groups was found in immediate memory, the scopolomine-treated subjects were significantly impaired in measures of word storage and recall, whereas the methscopolomine subjects showed no more impairment than the controls. When the subjects were given a small dose (1 mg) of physostigmine, they performed equal to or slightly better than controls but were definitely impaired when a higher dose of 2 mg was used.

The second line of evidence implicating the cholinergic system relates to the anatomical and chemical findings in Alzheimer's disease, where profound and selective degeneration was found in the cholinergic neurons of the nucleus basalis of Meynert (Whitehouse et al., 1982). Similarly, a 60 to 90% loss of choline acetyl transferase activity was found in the areas receiving the cholinergic projections from the nucleus basalis, namely the hippocampus, neocortex, and entorhinal cortex. While there is evidence that other transmitter systems (loss of noradrenergic cells in the locus ceruleus, loss of serotonogenic cells in the raphe nuclei) are linked to Alzheimer's disease, the importance of the cholinergic system in the dementia of Alzheimer's disease appears undisputed. Attempts to improve memory in Alzheimer's disease by use of acetylcholine precursors such as choline and lecithin (a source of choline) and by acetylcholine agonists, however, have not been successful (Jorm, 1986). One study however (Summers, Majovski, Marsh, Tachiki, & Kling, 1986), reported that tetrahydroaminoacridine (THA), a potent cholinesterase inhibitor that penetrates the blood–brain barrier and has a high margin of safety, improved the cognitive function of 17 patients (mean age 71) with moderately severe Alzheimer's disease. The drug was given in doses up to 200 mg/day along with 900–1200 mg of lecithin for 4–6 weeks. Unfortunately the effect lasted only for 8–10 hours after each dose and the drug did not affect the course of the disease. THA has been known since 1907, about the time Alzheimer described the disease that bears his name. Although the Summers et al. study has been criticized for its methodological faults (Crook, 1988), a large multicenter study to determine the safety and efficacy of THA in Alzheimer's disease, is now underway. On the other hand, in the memory impairments that may accompany the use of anticholinergic drugs when given to patients on neuroleptic regimes, discontinuation of the anticholinergic drug has yielded improved performance on the Wechsler Memory Scale (Fayen, Goldman, Moulthrop, & Luchins, 1988).

Thus the cholinergic system is implicated in learning and in memory. Just what that role may be is still unclear. The cholinergic system may function as a modulator, or it may be important because of its synapses in those areas of the brain (the hippocampus, amygdala, and cortex) that are important in memory.

An attempt has recently been made to ameliorate the course of cholinergic nerve atrophy by using a nerve growth factor. This experiment was done in aged rats and has no clinical relevance as yet (Fischer et al., 1987).

The Norepinephrine System

The norepinephrine system is involved in modulation of memory, as the following facts show:

1. *Posttraining treatments alter norepinephrine function and thus affect retention of recent learning.* Sympathomimetic drugs such as amphetamine or metaraminol can attenuate the memory impairments produced by antibiotics (A. J. Dunn, 1980). Conversely, peripherally administered adrenergic receptor antagonists will enhance the memory impairments induced by antibiotics and will render ineffective other drugs, such as vasopressin, which attenuate such antibiotic-induced impairment. The destruction of norepinephrine projections from the locus ceruleus by 6-hydroxydopamine will also intensify memory impairment induced by antibiotics. The effects of norepinephrine on memory are related to dosage: There is an optimal level for maximum effect; above or below that level the effect is decreased along the familiar inverted U curve fashion.

2. *Norepinephrine may serve to enhance neuronal communication in which the primary information is carried by other transmitters.* For example, when norepinephrine is applied iontophoretically to a neuron (Waterhouse, Moises, & Woodward, 1980), the responses of the cell to other inputs, excitatory or inhibitory, are often enhanced. The probability of lateral geniculate cells firing in response to electrical stimulation of the optic nerve is increased by application of norepinephrine to the recording site (Rogawski & Aghajanian, 1980). Long-term potentiation of lateral geniculate cell firing may be enhanced by peripheral injection of amphetamine or epinephrine (Delanoy, Tucci, & Gold, 1983). Norepinephrine has also been found to affect long-term potentiation in the hippocampus (Goddard, Bliss, Robertson, & Sutherland, 1980). These findings suggest that the threshold necessary to establish long-term memory may be reduced by adrenergic agonists and raised by adrenergic antagonists. Gold (1984) stated that the effect of norepinephrine on long-term memory appears to be mediated by peripheral alpha-2 receptors.

3. *Central norepinephrine may interact with endogenous opioids to affect memory.* There is a depth of experimental evidence to indicate that memory in

rodents, as assessed in a variety of training tasks, is modulated by posttraining treatments affecting opiod receptors. Retention is generally impaired by posttraining administration of opiate receptor agonists (such as morphine and beta-endorphin) and enhanced by opiate receptor antagonists (such as naloxone and naltrexone) (McGaugh, Introini-Collison, & Nagahara, 1988). These affects appear to be central, since retention is not affected by posttraining intraperitoneal naltrexonemethylbromide, which does not readily pass the blood-brain barrier. Propranolol will block the enhancing effect of naloxone on memory (Izquierdo & Graudenz, 1980). This finding suggests that since opioid peptides inhibit norepinephrine release, opioid antagonists such as naloxone may enhance memory retention by releasing norepinephrine from the inhibitory effect of opioid peptides. McGaugh et al. (1988) reported that the anatomical site for such interaction to enhance memory lies in the amygdala. Propranolol blocked the memory-enhancing effect of naloxone when it was injected into the amygdala but not when it was injected into the caudate or into the cortex dorsal to the amygdala. That both beta-1 and beta-2 receptors may be involved is seen in the blocking of the naloxone effect on memory by the beta-1 adenoreceptor blocker, atenolol, and by the beta-2 blocker, zinterol. Conversely, the posttraining intra-amygdala administration of the alpha-1 antagonist, prazosin, or the alpha-2 antagonist, yohimbine, did not attenuate the memory-enhancing effects of systemically administered naloxone.

4. *Central norepinephrine appears to mediate the influence of hypophyseal peptides on the process of memory consolidation.* In 1965, De Wied found that removal of the posterior and intermediate lobes of the pituitary in rats interfered with the maintenance of shuttle-box avoidance behavior. This behavior could be reversed by injection of pitressin or by purified vasopressin. In intact animals, a single injection of vasopressin, administered during the acquisition or the extinction period of shuttle-box avoidance behavior, resulted in a long-term, dose-dependent, inhibitory effect on the extinction of that behavior—that is, memory persisted. This effect persisted beyond the actual presence of the peptide in the body (De Wied, 1971, 1976). There appeared to be an association between concentration of vasopressin released during critical periods of avoidance learning and retention and memory consolidation. The memory effect of vasopressin was dissociated from its peripheral endocrine effects. Subsequent studies revealed that vasopressin and related peptides could prevent or reverse the amnesia for a passive avoidance response in rats induced by CO_2, by electroshock, or by pentylenetetrazol. Vasopressin could also reverse the puromycin-induced amnesia for a maze-learning task in mice. Oxytocin appears to have an effect on memory, opposite to that of vasopressin. With both vasopressin and oxytocin, the familiar inverted U shape, dose related, curve on memory, was found. Systemic or intracerebroventricularly administered vasopressin will enhance norepinephrine turnover in the hypothalamus, thalamus, and

medulla. Conversely, destruction of the cerullotelencephalic norepineph-rine pathway by 6-hydroxydopamine prevents the facilitory effect of vaso-pressin, if the vasopressin is injected immediately after the learning trial but not if injected prior to the retention test. Intracerebral vasopressin affects other transmitter systems, however, facilitating dopamine turnover and decreasing serotonin concentration in the mesencephalon and the septum but not in the hippocampus, hypothalamus, or striatum (De Wied, 1984).

Evidence from these four sources thus appears to implicate the adren-ergic systems, at least in the modulation of processes involved in learning and memory, influencing them either directly or indirectly through the effect of endogenous opioids and of hormones of the posterior pituitary.

From this evidence it is to be expected that drugs which stimulate the release of norepinephrine would facilitate learning and memory and that those which block its action would impede learning and memory. There are reports that beta blockers do indeed impair short-term verbal memory in nonpsychiatric hypertensive patients (Solomon et al., 1983). As with other drugs used for specific indications in psychiatric patients, however, if the specific symptom is inhibiting learning, the overall effect of the drug may actually enhance the ability of the child to focus attention on learning. Pro-pranolol, although in itself an inhibitor of learning, may so relieve anxiety and impulsivity that the net effect is improvement in attention and behavior. There is no conclusive evidence, however, that beta blockers or the widely used adrenergic drugs, directly affect the basic biological cascade involved in learning or the transformation of macromolecules needed for memory consolidation.

The adrenergic agonists, methylphenidate, pemoline, and dextroamphet-amine, are discussed at length in Chapter 13. Dextroamphetamine is an indi-rectly acting sympathomimatic, releasing biogenic amines from storage sites in the nerve terminal. The dextroisomer is three to four times more potent than the levo. Dextroamphetamine significantly counteracts the amnestic effects of anisomycin even when given as late as 90 minutes posttraining. By that time, consolidation of learning into long-term memory is probably over. Interestingly in rodents, amphetamine will not enhance retention when injected intracerabrally but will do so when injected intraperitoneally. That its effect may be mediated peripherally is seen in using 4-hydroxyamphet-amine, which, although it does not penetrate the blood-brain barrier, mim-ics the d-amphetamine effect on retention of memory in anisomycin-treated animals.

Clinically, the effect of dextroamphetamine in normal children was stud-ied by Rapoport et al. (1978). In 14 normal prepubertal boys of normal IQ, with no learning problems and without attention deficit disorders, the administration of a single dose (0.5 mg/kg, mean dose approximately 16 mg/day) of dextroamphetamine resulted in decreased motor activity, generally improved attention with faster reaction time, improved immediate recall, and improved vigilance. However, a marked behavioral rebound, consisting of excitability and talkativeness, occurred in about 5 hours. These boys were included in another study (Rapoport et al., 1980), which also involved hyperactive boys and young adult college men and the administration of a single dose of dextroamphetamine or a placebo. The college sample was divided into low- and high-dose d-amphetamine. All four groups responded to the drug with decreased motor activity, the hyperactive boys most of all, a trend to increased scores on a verbal learning test, and a tendency to increase verbal output. Both groups of the prepubertal boys reported "feeling funny." The adults had the feeling of increased energy and decreased fatigue. The effects of amphetamine may result from its cortical and possibly reticular-activating system stimulation. It should be noted that in doses of amphetamine higher than 30 mg/day, dopamine is released from nerve terminals; in still higher doses, serotonin is released. Disturbances in gait and perception and in the development of tremor and stereotype behavior may result.

Methylphenidate and magnesium pemoline also have adrenergic effects, blocking the reuptake of catecholamines from the synaptic cleft by the presynaptic nerve terminals. The blocking effect, however, is not on norepinephrine alone, but it is nonselective, influencing the reuptake of dopamine also. The effectiveness of dextroamphetamine, methylphenidate, and pemoline in modulating impulsivity and in enhancing attention, as well as their lack of effect in enhancing learning, memory and academic achievement, is documented in Chapter 13, "Attention Deficit Hyperactivity Disorder." The general conclusion is that these drugs are not recommended for improving learning or academic achievement in children with specific language disability. The drugs do have their use in some children with attention deficit hyperactivity disorder whose learning disorder is the result of their impulsivity.

Clonidine, an alpha-2 agonist, is having increasing use in child psychiatry with reports of its effects on attention deficit hyperactivity disorder and in Tourette's syndrome. Studies on the effect of clonidine on learning and memory are scant. In a case report (G. Fein, Merrink, Davenport, & Buffreon, 1987), a depressed 74-year-old diabetic man is said to have had "significant" short-term memory loss on 0.1 mg of clonidine b.i.d., with low scores on immediate recall and in recall after a 5-minute delay, on an object memory test. No deficits were found in adolescents (Falkner, Koffler & Lowenthal, 1984), while facilitative effects of clonidine on cognition of primates are reported (Arnsten & Goldman-Rakic, 1985). There is one clinical study reporting improvement in memory of patients with Korsakoff's syndrome (McEntee & Nair, 1980). At this writing, the effects of clonidine on academic achievement are unknown.

Tricyclic Antidepressants and Learning Like the adrenergic stimulant drugs, the tricyclic antidepressants have been effectively used in modulating the activity and attention of children with attention deficit hyperactivity disorder. Like those drugs, too, they block the reuptake of norepinephrine from the synaptic cleft. However, they also block the uptake of dopamine and serotonin. The potency and selectivity of the tricyclics for inhibition of neuronal uptake varies, with desipramine a most potent blocker of norepinephrine uptake but less potent for serotonin; amitriptyline inhibits uptake of norepinephrine and serotonin but is less potent for dopamine; clomipramine and fluoxetine are potent and selective blockers of serotinin uptake. In addition, tricyclics and the newer antidepressants have anticholinergic properties, blocking muscarinic cholinergics with a potency of $\frac{1}{20}$ to $\frac{1}{80}$ that of atropine in inhibiting the effect of acetylcholine on guinea pig ilium. In practice this effect is not inconsiderable since the therapeutic doses of tricyclics are higher than the effective doses of atropine. In theory, then, the tendency of anticholinergics to inhibit learning conflicts with the tendency for adrenergic drugs to facilitate learning. Of the tricyclics, desipramine is least potent in its anticholinergic activity; while amitryptyline, with its strong anticholinergic activity, impaired short-term memory in adult nondepressed volunteers (Liljequist, Linnoila, & Mattila, 1974; Mattila, Liljequist, & Seppela, 1978).

In children, while imipramine and desipramine appear to be effective in modulating impulsive behavior (see Chapter 13) there is little effect on cognitive performance (Rapoport, 1965; Waizer, Hoffman, Polizos, & Englehardt, 1974; Werry, Aman, & Diamond, 1980). Rapoport found no improvement in cognition in tests of 29 hyperactive boys given imipramine in a mean daily dose of 80 mg/day for 6 weeks; Waizer (1974) found a statistically significant impairment in recalling digits forward in 19 hyperactive boys receiving imipramine in a mean dose of 174 mg/day; Werry, administering imipramine in a dose of 1–2 mg/kilo/day for 3 weeks to hyperactive children found improvement on a continuous performance test. In short, the effects of imipramine in cognition in hyperactive boys paralleled those seen with the stimulant drugs.

It is said (Quinn & Rapoport, 1975) that no adverse effect on long-term use of imipramine in a mean dose of 65 mg/day was found in cognitive or intellectual functioning. The long-term effect of the drug on receptor sensitivity should be considered, however. Long-term use, and just how long long-term is, is not clear, may result in desensitization of presynaptic alpha-2 adrenergic receptors, increased neuronal responsiveness to alpha-1 adrenergic agonists and to serotonin and decreased numbers of serotonin receptors and beta adrenergic binding sites (Gilman, Goodman, Rall, & Murad, 1985). Certainly enhancement of learning and memory, and improvement of academic learning, is no indication for use of tricyclics.

Caffeine and Theophylline   Among the stimulant drugs that are said to increase vigilance, caffeine, a methylxanthine, is said to mediate its effects by presynaptic release of norepinephrine. It may elevate cyclic adenosine monophosphate by inhibition of phosphodiesterase. Parents will frequently ask about the effects of coffee and cola drinks on activity level and on learning. A series of 10 studies, reviewed by Elkins et al. (1981) revealed little or no benefit on the vigilance and behavior of "hyperkinetic" children when caffeine was given in a daily dose of 3–12 mg/kilo. Elkins et al. (1981) studied the effect of a single dose of high (10 mg/kilo) and low (3 mg/kilo) doses of caffeine on the mood, activity, evoked potential, reaction time, memory, and sustained attention in 19 "normal," prepubertal boys whose mean age was 10 years, 6 months. There was a significant increase in vigilance on the high dose of caffeine measured by both a decreased median reaction time and a decrease in omission errors on the Continuous Performance Test. However, there was an increase in commission errors in that test, suggesting that although vigilance was enhanced with the single high caffeine dose, impulsivity was not modulated, total motor activity increased significantly, and recall scores in the memory test worsened. The low dose of caffeine, approximating a moderate to heavy daily dietary caffeine intake, had minimal or no behavioral effects.

The adverse effect on school performance by theophylline in therapeutic doses was cited by Rachelfsky et al. (1986). After review of the data in the literature on theophylline and learning, the Pulmonary-Allergy Drugs Advisory Committee of the Food and Drug Administration (FDA) concluded that present data do not support the adverse effect of theophylline on the academic performance of schoolchildren. However, the FDA (1988) concluded that further well-controlled studies are needed. A subsequent report found no adverse effect of theophylline (Theo-Dur tablets, 14–16 mg/kilo/day) on 27 measures of performance, behavior, and attention in 17 children receiving the drug in a crossover design (Rapaport et al., 1989).

The Dopamine System

While this section has so far emphasized the role of the adrenergic system in learning and memory, there is evidence to indicate a crucial role for the dopamine system in the learning and memory of spatial discrimination in rats and primates. Injection of 6-hydroxydopamine injected bilaterally into the lateral septum of rats induced selective depletion of dopamine concentrations in the septum without damaging noradrenergic or cholinergic cell bodies. This injection into the lateral septum interfered with spatial memory in rats (Simon, Taghzouti, & Le Moal, 1986). Iontophoretically applied dopamine into the prefrontal cortex of primates enchanced a task involving spatial short-term memory. Fluphenazine and haloperidol attenuated the learning of spatial short-term memory, whereas sulpride had no effect (Sawaguchi, Matsumura, & Kuboto, 1988). Neonatal dopamine in rats, depleted at 3 and 6 days of age with intraventricular 6-hydroxydopamine, resulted in deficits in tasks requiring spatial alternation behavior, when tested from day 15 through day 29. Dopamine depletion appeared to result in a significant impairment in the ability to use spatial cues during ontogony (Feesner & Raskin, 1987).

Dopamine Blockers

These findings raise the question of the effect of frequently used dopamine blockers on learning and memory. Phenothiazines and butyrophenones have a direct effect on learning and memory by the sedative effect of these drugs, by their anticholinergic action, and by the various clinical conditions for which the drugs are prescribed. In general, neuroleptic drugs selectively inhibit the learning of conditioned avoidance behaviors in animals: motor responses are fewer, slower, and smaller and vigilance of human subjects on tapping-speed tests is impaired. On the other hand, neuroleptic drugs do not significantly impair function on digit-symbol tests. In adults, in normal volunteers and in schizophrenic patients, no significant effects on short-term memory as measured by immediate recall of words lists, random numbers, and visual designs were found. Also the ability of schizophrenic patients, hospitalized for the long term, to recall recent, mid-past, and distant events was not impaired with chlorpromazine in doses of 25 to 900 mg/day. What was related to impaired memory, however, was the serum anticholinergic level induced by low potency neuroleptics and not by the serum level of the neuroleptic drug at all.

In children, neuroleptic medication has been used in management of symptoms of hyperactivity, aggression, heterogeneous conduct disorders, Tourette's syndrome, schizophrenia, autism, and mental retardation. The major concern in studies investigating these populations was on the target symptoms and not on learning and memory at all. For example, a 1966 placebo-controlled, double-blind clinical trial of chlorpromazine in hyperactive children of normal intelligence with a mean age of 8 years, 5 months was done by Werry, Weiss, Douglas, and Martin, with the focus on hyperactivity and attention. On a mean daily dose of 106 mg of chlorpromazine, hyperactivity and attention were improved but at the end of 8 weeks of treatment, cognition, as seen in the comprehension subtest of the WISC and on the Bender-VMGT was depressed. Psychomotor activity was slowed in a group of 12 aggressive, hospitalized patients aged 7 years, 8 months through 12 years, 10 months, receiving 3 mg/day of haloperidol. On the other hand, haloperidol in doses of 0.05 mg/kg/day for 6 months did not adversely affect a battery of tests measuring scholastic achievement and intellectual function (Wong and Cook, 1971). Werry, Aman, and Lampen (1975) found that the adverse effects of haloperidol on measures of cognitive function in hyperactive, aggressive children, was largely a function of the dose of the drug; low doses (0.025 mg/kg/day) reduced the number of false responses in a continuous performance test. Compared to the placebo and to methylphenidate, high doses (0.05 mg/kg/day) of the drug impaired performance on both a continuous performance test and a short-term memory test. On an even higher dose (mean 0.096 mg/kg/day) of haloperidol, given to hospitalized children diagnosed as having conduct disorders, there were no significant effects on a matching familiar figure test, short-term recognition memory, or the Stroop test. Thus in the hyperactive children of normal intelligence and in disturbed aggressive children, haloperidol, in doses that decrease target symptoms, may also depress some aspects of cognition.

Since the time Fish, Campbell, and Shapiro (1970) found that chlorpromazine in autistic children was sedating in doses that had little effect on symptoms, attention has focused on the use of an alternate drug, haloperidol, in this group. Two reports coming from the New York University laboratories are relevant to learning and memory. In the first (Campbell et al. 1982a), the effect of haloperidol in doses of 0.5 to 4.0 mg/day was compared with a behavioral intervention focusing on language acquisition, and on the results of a combination of both treatments (drug plus behavioral intervention) in a group of 40 autistic children aged 2 years, 6 months to 7 years, 2 months, hospitalized at Bellevue Psychiatric Hospital. While haloperidol alone was effective in decreasing stereotopies and withdrawal, the combination of the drug and contingent reinforcement facilitated language acquisition in the 12-week study. There was no effect on cognition as measured by a cognitive battery. The most common untoward effect was sedation, which was a function of dosage. In reviewing this detailed paper, contingent reinforcement schedules were clearly more effective than the noncontingent schedules in enhancing language, even in the placebo-treated children. The differences between the haloperidol and the placebo groups and the effectiveness of language training in enhancing language were not statistically significant. The haloperidol-contingency reinforcement group, however, showed an acceleration in language acquisition in the second half of the project, and it is this acceleration that turned the tide. It must be mentioned, however, that language acquisition was still primitive, consisting of shaping of immature speech by successive approximation. The paper does not tell us how many children mastered that skill, going on to identification of objects, two-word chains, concepts, responsive speech, and predictive identification. The overall rates of learning (number of words mastered/the number of sessions) were 1.61 for the haldol-contingency reinforcement group, 0.77 for the placebo-contingency group, 0.46 for the haldol-noncontingency group, and 0.32 for the placebo-noncontingency group. Unfortunately details of the language acquired are not given.

In the second study (L. T. Anderson et al., 1984; Campbell et al. 1982b) the question of whether haloperidol facilitates learning because of improved attention was addressed. In this study 40 children (29 boys, 11 girls) ranging in age from 2 years, 3 months through 6 years, 9 months, mildly to profoundly retarded, were given haloperidol or a matching placebo tablet in a double-blind crossover design, in doses individually regulated to yield optimal behavioral response with minimal sedation. The effect on learning of discrimination tasks was determined in a structured environment, in an automated operant conditioning paradigm in which correct responses to discrimination tasks were automatically rewarded with an M&M candy. The discrimination tasks were visual, flashed on the computer screen. Behavior such as hyperactivity was also automatically recorded in the structured environment by means of pressure-sensitive switches mounted every 6 inches under an indoor-outdoor carpet. The experimental design divided children into two groups: the first received haloperidol for 4 weeks–placebo for 4 weeks–haloperidol for 4 weeks; the second received placebo–haloperidol–placebo. Each treatment condition consisted of 10 learning sessions. The percentage of correct responses for each child and the mean across treatment groups and treatment periods was plotted. Learning tended to improve within each set of 10 sessions, more so in the first two sets. This improvement was seen in both the haloperidol group and in the placebo group; however, an effect in favor of the haloperidol group was seen in the first 4 weeks (first 10 learning sessions) of the study. The effect favoring the haloperidol group became stronger when Gesell language developmental quotients (DQ) were considered: the high verbal DQ haloperidol group performed significantly better ($p = .05$) than the high verbal DQ placebo group. The children receiving haloperidol performed as well as children on the placebo who at the beginning of the study scored 20 points higher on the Gesell verbal DQ. Also in that same treatment period (group I haloperidol, group II placebo), 71% of the children receiving haloperidol achieved a performance score higher than an arbitrary determined cut-off score on the discrimination tasks in contrast to 39% of the placebo group. Only two variables, verbal developmental quotient and drug, significantly accounted for performance in discrimination learning. Hyperactivity and stereotypy did not appear to affect such performance adversely, suggesting that "the effect of the drug on learning was not a function of its [effect on] decreasing maladaptive behaviors, but was possibly a function of its more directly affecting attentional mechanisms" (L. T. Anderson et al., 1984, p. 1200). It is still not clear, however, what the biochemical mechanism of haloperidol-induced enhancement of discrimination learning in these autistic children might be. Certainly the work of the New York University investigators needs confirmation. At this writing, therefore, the use of dopamine antagonist is not recommended for treatment of specific language disabilities nor for enhancement of learning in populations other than in autistic children, and even in autistic children the effect of dopamine antagonists on learning is equivocal.

Glutamic Acid, Glycine and the GABA System

There have been numerous attempts at enhancement of learning with drugs that modify the availability of gamma-amino-buteric acid (GABA) in the central nervous system. Basing their work on the fact that 1-glutamic acid is oxidized *in vitro* by the brain (Weil-Malharbe, 1936), Zimmerman and Ross (1944) suggested that feeding 1-glutamic acid might enhance intelligence. Indeed feeding 1-glutamic acid to rats for 2 weeks facilitated maze learning in these rats. Clinical application of this study followed. Zimmerman, Burgemeister, and Putman (1947) reported that the intelligence quotients of retarded and epileptic children were enhanced by feeding them 1-glutamic acid for 6 months, but this work was not subsequently confirmed. By 1966 Austin and Ross had reviewed 33 studies on the effect of glutamic acid on intelligence in humans; only 6 of these were controlled studies of children with mental retardation; 14 used no control group at all. In general, the studies were criticized for lack of adequate control groups, the neglect of double-blind methodology using placebo controls, and the difficulty in controlling for effects of environmental stimulation. Practically, also, the task of ingesting the recommended dose of bulky 1-glutamic acid (6 gram/day) for long periods of time, with its attendant gastric irritation, created problems in compliance. The use of glutamic acid to increase intelligence has fallen into disuse.

A number of central nervous system stimulants have had use in "tonics" and in management of regressed geriatric patients. Strychnine particularly in the form of the tincture of Nux Vomica, was a turn of the century ingredient in "tonics" intended to "improve the appetite . . . amelioration of subjective symptoms . . . special senses rendered more accurate" (Edmunds & Gunn, 1937). Strychnine is a potent central nervous system stimulant and a convulsant that selectively blocks inhibition in the central nervous system and interferes with normal postsynaptic inhibition mediated by glycine. Gillman, Goodman, Rall, & Murad (1985) stated that "strychnine has no demonstrated therapeutic value despite a long history of unwarranted popularity" (p. 582).

Picrotoxin, bicuculine, and pentylenetetrazol are also potent convulsant drugs that stimulate the central nervous system. Picrotoxin antagonizes gamma-amino-buteric acid at all levels of the central nervous system; bicuculine is a true GABA antagonist, and pentylenetetrazol also inhibits GABA-inhibiting activity. They obviously have no place in treatment of learning disorders in children.

Nootropic Drugs

Within the past 10 years a group of drugs has been said to enhance learning and memory in children with specific reading disability (developmental dyslexia). This group has been classified by Giurgea (1972) as "nootropic" drugs (from the Greek, *noos* = mind, *tropein* = toward) as drugs acting on the central nervous system, acting "directly on higher, integrative brain mechanisms by enhancing their efficiency, thereby resulting in a positive, direct, impact on mental, noetic, function" (Giurgea, 1978, p. 67). Thus the nootropic drug is said to:

- facilitate learning acquisition
- reduce the adverse effect on memory of such factors as electroshock and cerebral hypoxia
- enhance transcallosal transfer of information

In addition, these drugs do not cause sedation or affect the autonomic nervous system, and they have minimal toxicity. The nootropic drugs are claimed to have possible specific effects on the left-hemisphere language function, including vigilance, coding, short-term verbal memory, naming, and verbal learning (Dimond & Brouwers, 1976) but not on spatial ability of children with developmental dyslexia. These are the functions said to be subserved by the cerebral cortex dominant for language. Piracetam, the first drug of this class, chemically 2-pyrrolidinone acetamide, is chemically related to gamma-amino-buteric acid. Its mechanism of action is reported to be an activator of brain adenylate cyclase, and it is reported to enhance cerebral perfusion in dogs with induced cardiovascular insufficiency. An analog of piracetam, oxiracetam has been synthesized.

Two major studies of the effect of piracetam on the learning of children with specific reading disability have been reported. The first, a 12-week multicentered double-blind trial, involved six centers and 257 boys with dyslexia defined as a "specific written language difficulty." The subjects were otherwise normal, with average or above IQ; good school, social, and language opportunities; no visual or auditory acuity problems; and no neurological or psychiatric disturbances. Piracetam is reported to have increased their reading fluency (speed of reading) without sacrificing accuracy. In children with poor short-term memory, piracetam increased their digit span score but did not improve reading comprehension (Di Lanni et al., 1985). Encouraged by this study, a 36-week double-blind, multicentered study to test the effects of long-term administration of piracetam was initiated. The five sites for the study were the New York Columbia-Presbyterian Psychiatric Institute (R. Rudel, principal investigator), Washington, D.C. Children's Hospital (C. K. Conners), University of North Carolina (L. Feagans), Minneapolis Washburn Child Guidance Clinic (L. Hanvik), and San Diego Children's Hospital (P. Tallal). The study involved a total of 225 children (153 boys, 73 girls) ranging in age from 7 years, 6 months through 12 years, 11 months. The criteria for acceptance into the project were similar to those of the 12-

week project. On the average, the children were 3.4 grades below expectancy in reading as measured by the Gray Oral Reading Test. The project involved double-blind placebo controls, with the experimental group receiving 3.3 mg of piracetam administered in two doses of 5 ml each, one in the morning and one in the evening. Careful monitoring of physical status, including hematology, blood chemistry, and urine analysis, was done. At 12 weeks, 24 weeks, and 36 weeks into the project, two general areas of reading achievement were evaluated: reading accuracy (WRAT, Gilmore oral reading, Gray oral reading), and reading comprehension (Gilmore oral passage reading test, Gray oral passage reading test). Two hundred children completed the project.

Results have been reported with all centers combined (Wilsher, 1987) and by the individual centers. The report of the Columbia group is representative (Helfgott, Rudel, Koplewicz, & Krieger, 1987). Their major finding was improvement of the piracetam-treated children on the reading comprehension scores on both the Gilmore and Gray oral passage reading tests. On the Gilmore test of reading comprehension, improvement was significant at 36 weeks of the project. On this test, piracetam-treated children increased their comprehension 1.5 grade levels, while the placebo-treated children increased 0.7 grade level. As measured with the Gray oral passage reading test, comprehension of the piracetam group was significantly improved when compared with the control group at 12 and 36 weeks of treatment. On the other hand, while single-word reading accuracy, as measured by the WRAT and by the Gray oral reading test, improved after 12 weeks of treatment with piracetam, the improvement at the end of 24 weeks and at 36 weeks was not different from that of controls. On the Gilmore oral reading test no significant difference between placebo and piracetam groups was found. The authors cautioned, however, that because the pretreatment comprehension scores of their children were about 1.75 grade above their accuracy scores, studies should be done with children whose comprehension scores are as low as their accuracy scores.

Slightly different results are reported by the San Diego group (Chase & Tallal, 1987). Here improvement in word recognition skills and in number of words per minute read accurately was found. In contrast to the pilot 12-week study, however, improvement was not noted until 24 weeks on the WRAT and until 36 weeks on the Gilmore. Reading comprehension improved only as measured by the Gilmore oral passage reading test, but not on the Gray paragraphs.

The differences in results among sites are expected to disappear into the combined results obtained from all five sites (Wilsher, 1987). At one of the project sites, however, the baseline differences between control and experimental group reached statistical significance. Accordingly, group data were calculated both with and without data from that site. Of the 225 children entering the study, 25 left before the study was completed. The mean age of the original group was 10 years; 205 were white, 15 black, and 5 other. Their average full scale IQ on the WISC-R was 104 (performance IQ of 106, verbal IQ of 100). All the children were randomly assigned to piracetam or control groups: 11 black children, 99 white, and 3 other were assigned to the control group; 4 blacks, 106 white, and 2 other were assigned to the piracetam group. Results of the total study, excluding those from the site with the baseline difference data, showed significant differences favoring the piracetam group in the Gray Oral Reading Test at 12, 24, and 36 weeks, the Gray total comprehension score at 12 and 36 weeks, the Gilmore oral reading comprehension score at 36 weeks, and the WRAT-R reading score at 24 weeks. No differences between the groups were found on the WRAT-R score at 12 weeks and at 36 weeks, the rate and accuracy of reading as measured by the Gilmore oral reading test and the Gray comprehension score at 24 weeks. One of the project sites found a significant difference favoring the placebo group on the Gray oral total passage score at 36 weeks. The major finding of the study appeared to be an overall improvement in reading comprehension seen in the piracetam-treated group compared to the controls.

Wilsher also dichotomized the entire sample by median age. The older group (10–13 years) proved to be homogeneous in baseline differences and in treatment by investigator interactions. This group demonstrated increased overall reading ability (WRAT, at 24 and 36 weeks, Gray oral reading at 36 weeks, Gilmore oral reading accuracy at 36 weeks, and Gray oral comprehension at 12 weeks). In contrast, the younger group was not homogeneous and the only significant improvement was found in the Gilmore oral reading comprehension test. Wilsher (1987) states that "it is possible that piracetam acts differently in different age populations, i.e., increasing comprehension in the young group but increasing overall reading ability in the older group" (p. 106).

Side effects to the drug were minimal, with three piracetam children complaining of irritability or nervousness, compared to none for controls and one child in the San Diego study with elevated liver enzymes after 60 days of treatment.

What is disturbing about this multisite study is the lack of information on the educational experiences of the children during the 36 weeks. Detailed data about intervention other than medication is needed.

The studies on piracetam are reported here in some detail because of the obvious importance of nootropic drugs on understanding the mechanism(s) of learning and memory, and the apparently specific effects of piracetam on the verbal processing deficit of children with specific language disability. At this writing, piracetam is not ready for use as a therapeutic modality in the treatment of specific language disability. Educational intervention is still the way to go.

This chapter has reviewed the effect on learning and memory of various classes of drugs that are currently being used in the management of emotional and behavior disorders in children. Unfortunately many of these drugs have an adverse effect on learning and others, although used to influence academic achievement, do not do so. As our knowledge of the anatomy and biochemistry of the processes of learning and memory increases, our knowledge of the effect of drugs on these processes will also increase, offering promise of designing drugs to influence these processes. The nootropic drugs with their chemical relationship to GABA and their effect on brain adenylate cyclase may be the first class of drugs to do so.

We have not considered in this chapter, the anticonvulsant drugs, which are discussed in Chapter 14, "The Organic Group."

SUMMARY

Learning is defined as the process of acquiring new information; memory, the persistence of learning in a state that can be retrieved at a later time. Memory involves a persistent change in relationship among neurons through structural change or through biochemical events within and between neurons. The structures of the medial temporal lobe (particularly the hippocampus, amygdala, and dorsomedial nucleus of the thalamus) are essential neural stations for processing sensory information into memory. Molecular mechanism(s) by which a change in neurons may occur have been identified. For long-term memory the synthesis of proteins is required. Attempts to improve learning and memory by direct administration of RNA or by increasing the activity of RNA have not been successful.

Although they do not directly affect protein synthesis, there are drugs that may act by facilitating or inhibiting the transmission of neural impulses or the circuits involved in processing information leading to memory. Historically, levels of *acetylcholine* and of *cholinesterase* have been implicated in learning; a greater amount of acetylcholine at the synapse enhances learning. Thus choline, arecholine, physostigmine, or diisopropyl phosphofluoridate increase, while atropine and scopolamine decrease, retention of learned responses. Attempts to improve memory in Alzheimer's disease with choline and lecithin, however, have not been successful. THA, a potent cholinesterase inhibitor, is under investigation. Experimentally, *sympathomimetic amines* (norepinephrine) enhance, while *adrenergic antagonists* inhibit cell excitability. The adrenergic response is enhanced by *opioid receptor antagonists* that appear to activate the beta 1 and 2 receptors. *Hypophyseal peptides* (vasopressin) facilitate norepinephrine activity on memory retention. Clinically, beta blockers (propranolol) impair short-term verbal memory; however, the adrenergic agonists (methylphenidate, pemoline, and dextroamphetamine) while blocking the amnestic effects of antibiotics do not enhance learning, memory, or academic achievement. The effects of clonidine, an alpha-2 antagonist, on memory are as yet unknown. Caffeine and theophylline do not enhance learning and memory. *Tricyclic antidepressants,* which block the reuptake of catecholamines, but which also have anticholinergic properties, have not enhanced learning but, just as with the stimulant drugs, when given to hyperactive boys tricyclic antidepressants may improve attention.

Dopamine depletion during ontogony interferes with the ability to use spatial cues. Dopamine blockers have an effect on learning because of their sedative and anticholinergic actions. In children, chlorpromazine depresses cognition, while the effect of haloperidol varies directly with the dose: low doses appear to enhance learning, while high doses impair performance on a continuous performance test and on a short-term memory test.

Overall, *glutamic acid* has been unsuccessful in increasing cognitive function in retarded children, while GABA blockers (picrotoxin, bicuculine, and pentylenetetrazol) are too toxic for use.

The one group of drugs that shows promise for facilitating learning is the *nootrophic* group. Piracetam is said to improve reading comprehension, oral reading, and, in some studies, reading fluency. This group of drugs holds promise for having specific effects on the left-hemisphere functions.

CHAPTER NINE

Principles of Psychotherapeutic Management

SPECTRUM OF PSYCHOLOGICAL REACTIONS TO LEARNING DISORDERS

In the Child

The child with a learning disorder does not leave his psychological problems in the classroom. He carries them home, into his relations with parents and peers; they pervade the adjustment of the adolescent and reach into the social, emotional, and vocational adjustment of the adult. Unless the disorder is adequately and appropriately treated, the child will not outgrow it. He may learn to compensate for it, however, and ultimately it may affect his entire life.

How the individual adjusts to a learning disorder—what emotional and behavioral defensive patterns she develops—depends on a multitude of factors: the cause, extent, and severity of the disorder; the temperamental and intellectual endowment with which the child was born; the presence of complicating factors such as hyperactivity, attentional deficits, problems in fine and/or gross motor coordination; and, most important, the adequacy and appropriateness of the support the child receives from parents and school.

Management of the child with a learning disorder must begin with an evaluation of all these factors, a comprehensive evaluation along the pentaxial scheme described in Chapters 5 and 6 (principles of interdisciplinary diagnosis).

While the psychiatric reaction to learning disorder is thus an idiosyncratic response, there are certain common problems with which all children with learning disabilities must cope. These problems deal with the results of the basic biological immaturities that learning disorders impose upon the child, with "deviant performance in perceptual, linguistic, sequencing, and intersensory integrative abilities" (Benton and Pearl, 1978, p. 468). In Chapter 3 ("Patterns of Neuropsychological Dysfunction") we described the neuropsychological deficits of the child with a learning disorder and how most of these deficits may be understood as an immaturity in spatial orientation and temporal organization—an immaturity in the concepts of space and time, the inability to perceive accurately symbols in space and sounds in time.

While these skills are basic to learning, they also form the basis for the hierarchical steps needed for more advanced skills. Delay in temporal sequencing, for example, leads to a difficulty in the storage of sequences. As a result, there must occur lacunae in the retrieval of information; problems with word finding; the presence of expressive reversals; and difficulty in organizing tasks, planning projects, scheduling and establishing priorities, and organizing and sequencing ideas. Persistent problems in spatial orientation are seen in problems in right–left orientation, in concepts of distance and map reading, in telling time or being aware of time sequences, and in understanding nonverbal communication—gestures and facial expression.

The academic disorder itself thus is but the tip of the iceberg, the outcome of a more basic neuropsychological dysfunction in the central nervous system in which the child's sense of his own identity may be involved. Piaget (1954) stated that reality is constructed out of one's multimodal contact with the external world. The child with confusion in spatial orientation and temporal organization must perceive reality in a distorted frame. His construction of the world is distorted, and if to this distortion we add immaturity in right–left discrimination, praxis, and finger-gnosis, the concept of his own body image in relation to the world must also be askew.

The child with a learning disorder, however, is not exempt from the emotional problems of growing up with which all children must cope. The problem here is that her biological substrate is different, her neuropsychological apparatus immature, and her vulnerability to anxiety increased. Our task is to understand how this biological difference influences the child's feelings, thoughts, and behavior—to understand that there are emotional reactions to the real problems created by the learning disorder.

The learning disordered child's problems may be apparent in preschool and kindergarten. At this level, visual-motor difficulties are seen in the child's inability to copy a circle or to color within lines; he may not be able to recognize asymmetric letters, tell a coherent story, or understand directions. The pattern of failure and frustration thus is set very early. School becomes a confusing and perhaps a painful experience, something to be avoided by refusing to leave mother, crying, or complaining of stomachaches or, on the other hand, to be passively accepted by simply withdrawing, regressing, and behaving much like someone with the "learned helplessness" (Seligman & Groves, 1970; Seligman & Meier, 1967) of animals who, after repeated, unescapable electric shocks, fail to initiate responses to escape the shocks when they are freed. Other preschool children may become actively aggressive, clowning, disobedient, or negativistic.

The patterns established in the preschool years are intensified and aggravated in the elementary grades when academic demands cannot be met. Word recognition in reading, phonic sequences needed for spelling, and motor control and praxis needed for writing may be lacking. Academic failure is the consequence, and frustration once again surrounds the child. She now is convinced that she is stupid and cannot learn. Some children blame themselves for the failure, that somehow they are "bad," that they are being punished. Others project the blame to teachers, parents, and peers. The patterns of defense begun in kindergarten are clearly evident: Submission, somatization, depression, regression, negativism, clowning, and aggression are seen. Some children try very hard to conform, developing ritualistic behavior. In all, however, the normal progression of psychological maturation is interrupted, the anxiety engendered is not adequately managed, and neurotic-type symptoms may emerge in fears, obsessions and compulsions, nightmares, and eating and toileting problems.

By early adolescence new educational demands are placed on the child. Education now emphasizes the ability to abstract, to gather and identify information, and to impart what has been learned in sequential written form. College preparatory courses require foreign languages. Remedial programs are no longer concerned with neuropsychological processes but with tutoring. Cognition is expected to evolve into formal operations. Social needs also change. The adolescent is expected to understand social judgments. If by high school reading has somehow been improved, the rate of reading is generally slow and comprehension impaired. Reading and writing are burdens, and outlining sequential material is difficult. Moreover, the consistent classroom teacher of elementary school becomes a series of academically oriented taskmasters. In adolescence the learning disordered child is more capable of acting out emotions in sexual and aggressive behaviors. This pattern is more readily seen in children who come from homes where aggression, antisocial behavior, and drugs are the social milieu. The pattern for delinquency emerges: early school failure, frustration, acting out, truancy, apprehension, more frustration, development of poor self-image, alienation, and finally being pushed out of school or dropping out as a response to an overwhelming sense of defeat (Poremba, 1975). The high prevalence of learning disability in adolescents in juvenile detention centers has repeatedly been documented. Compton (1974), for example, studied adolescents committed to the Colorado Department of Institutions between 1972 and 1973 and found 90.4% to have a clinically diagnosed learning disability. In New York City Juvenile Court, Peck, Harrower, and Beck (1950) found 84% of the children referred were 2 or more years retarded in reading. Lewis, Shanok, and Bella (1980) and Lewis, Shanock, Pincus, and Glaser (1979) found that more than one-third of the adolescents in detention centers have a learning disorder. Of course there are other variables, such as socioeconomic ones, related to delinquency. In a major study, however, Elliot and Voss (1974) found school failure in the early grades to be the single, most statistically significant variable predicting later delinquency.

It seems apparent that all children who have repeated unexplained absences from school and those who are truant deserve a comprehensive study to understand the reasons behind their school absence. All studies suggest that a majority of these children are suffering from severe learning problems. Not all of these problems are in the category of specific language disability; some children have borderline intelligence or a subtle organic defect of the central nervous system. But even in these children with low intelligence, an unrecognized language disorder may contribute to their low IQ. A 1982 article in the *Tampa Tribune,* for example, bemoaned the fact that truants are placed in detention centers. Although it indicated that more counselors are needed for these children, it made no mention of the need for comprehensive evaluation for these children and for remedial measures appropriate to those findings. Also glaringly absent is mention of earlier recognition and treatment of these children, perhaps as early as in kindergarten.

Truancy, school drop-out, drugs, and delinquency, significant as they are, are but one end stage in the natural history of learning disorders and their emotional consequences. A learning disorder is the most frequent finding in classes of severely emotionally handicapped children (A. A. Silver, 1984a). Most of the children in this study had already internalized intrapsychic problems and were severely anxious with low self-esteem, depressed, obsessive-compulsive, or phobic; many had conduct or behavioral problems—they ran away from school or were oppositional and aggressive. L. B. Silver (1989) emphasized that "emotional, social and family problems are . . . the result (not the cause) of the frustrations and failures experienced by the individual plus the frustrations and failure experienced by the parents" (p. 319). To this we add the frustrations experienced by the teachers.

In the Parents

We have so far been concerned with the direct effect of a learning disorder on the child. Equally important are the psychiatric implications of a learning disorder on the parents. With the identification of a learning disorder in their child, often there is in parents an immediate reaction of denial. This is true of families at all levels of the socioeconomic scale and at all intellectual levels. Those with high intellectual function, with their tendency to project their own needs onto the child, have great difficulty in accepting the child's deficits. Those on the lower socioeconomic scale proclaim how well they have done without education. In both groups a common reaction is "He is just as I was when I was a boy. He will grow out of it." As a result of denial, many parents do little to obtain help for their child. Some devote time, money, and energy in pursuit of an "expert" who will tell them what they want to hear, namely, "the child will outgrow it."

As problems continue, denial, suppression, or nonacceptance of the child's difficulty are replaced by depression and guilt in the parents: depression that the child is impaired, that the future is uncertain, and that the child cannot fulfill their wishes for him; guilt to find at least one indiscretion in themselves to account for their learning disordered child. Inevitably in their search for the cause of the learning disorder and perhaps as a way of relieving their own guilt, parents will project the blame onto anyone other than themselves: the obstetrician who delivered the child, the pediatrician who cares for him, the schools that have failed him, the psychologist who tested him, and finally the psychiatrist or neurologist who examined him. Anger is directed at all who are involved with the child, at the spouse, and at the child himself. With some parents, the resentment is focused in complaints of the money spent for remedial help, special schools, and special tutoring. At times, the anger is suppressed, and, with a mechanism of reaction formation, the child may be overprotected and infantilized. Such overprotectiveness may not only inhibit the child's independent function but also disrupt the balance of authority in the household so that the spouse and siblings are relegated to subsystems, which, in turn, generates resentment, usually directed against the learning disordered child whose overprotection labels her the "sick" one. She then becomes the scapegoat, responsible not only for the reality problems of her disorder but for all other problems within the family: the father's job, the daughter's boyfriend, and the mother's isolation. As a result of not accepting the child as she is, parents do not give the child the support she needs, adding to the child's feeling of worthlessness and guilt that she cannot seem to please even her parents.

By the time the child reaches adolescence, parents usually have made some adjustment to the affects evoked in them by their child with a learning disorder. Some of these adjustments are supportive: the acceptance of the learning disorder, realistic appraisal of goals, cooperative effort with schools, and special remedial help. Some are not so supportive, continuing the defeating patterns of affect and behavior, undermining the child's confidence in himself, preventing him from developing trust, stirring up conflict with schools and other professionals, and, above all, making the family a dysfunctional system.

Further, the patterns of behavior the child develops at home are carried with her wherever she goes: the helplessness or the aggressive anger and the control over the household. Each may be reflected in attempts to control the school, demanding the teacher's attention, finding excuses for the child's behavior, and blaming the teachers. All of these behaviors are disruptive to academic performance and behavior and serve only to feed back increasing frustration, failure, and resentment.

In the Schools

The psychiatric implications of a learning disability, however, are not restricted to the child and parents. The school is also involved, both teachers and administration. There is still a tendency to think of a child who does not learn as stupid or lazy or negativistic; to think of the child with a behavior problem as "bad." True, there are stupid, lazy, negativistic, and rebellious children, but it is the wise teacher who is not threatened by a lack of success with this particular child and who asks what the cause of such behavior or poor learning may be. In many cases the answer is a specific language disability, perhaps complicated with hyperkinesis, attentional deficit, poor motor coordination, or even more specific signs of organic insults to the central nervous system.

The identification of a child as learning disordered, however, is only the beginning of the school's responsibility. Can the school modify the curriculum so that it can support and encourage the child's strengths but make little academic demands on his or her deficits? Can the school provide the training so that the deficits may be overcome? Can the school provide appropriate remedial help? In terms of sheer numbers of children with learning disorders, this is a formidable problem of logistics, money, and emotional involvement.

MANAGEMENT OF EMOTIONAL AND BEHAVIORAL PROBLEMS

Professional to Function as an Ombudsman

While remedial educational help is the basis for management of most children with learning disorders, management of the complex emotional interrelations between child and parents, parents and school, and child and school may make the difference between educational success and failure, social adjustment and maladjustment, and vocational gratification and vocational lack of achievement. As we have repeatedly stressed, comprehensive evaluation will yield information on the psychiatric, biological, cognitive, environmental (parental), and educational dimensions. As the data unfold the parameters for help are identified and management becomes a task of dealing with each of these parameters. In our experience it is helpful if one person takes the job of coordinator and synthesizer of all these data; one person becomes the contact person, the ombudsman to impart information to all concerned, including the child and parents, and to coordinate management. Just what professional should undertake this job is not the major issue. No matter in what discipline this professional is trained, he must have knowledge, not necessarily expert, in all the skills implied in the comprehensive data base. All too often this information is fragmented, or never obtained, and thus imparted in fragments; remedial measures are uncoordinated, so the child and family appear in the psychiatrist's office with a heavy load of behavioral problems, academic difficulty, and, frequently, a blanket of hostility.

A clear explanation to the family and to the child within the capacity of her understanding is a first step in practical management. These explanatory visits help lay out the problems and clear the air for further help. To the parents and to the child, these visits provide a comprehensive overview and an intellectual understanding of the problem. They define the relationship between specific neuropsychological deficits and academic difficulty. They detail the overall assets and capabilities of the child and suggest educational help needed. They confront the parents with their psychological defenses, and they offer continued support of a knowledgeable professional.

Practically, one of the most immediate problems requiring help is management of school adjustment. Here the family and the child need help in evaluating the appropriateness of the school and its curriculum for the child. In addition, however, the academic goals of the parents may be forcing the child into a no-win situation. The needs of the school, the desires of parents, and the abilities of the child must be reconciled.

CASE STUDY: EVAN

A 15-year-old boy, a 10th-grader in an academically demanding, college preparatory school, was beginning to fail the five classes he was taking. His parents complained that he was not studying, was rebellious, and had no friends. On examination, he was a small, thin child with a face covered with acne. He was truculent, grandiose, and negativistic, replete with mechanisms of denial. However, he was very depressed and anxious. He had severe perceptual problems, with visual discrimination and recall of asymmetric figures, visual-motor function, and auditory sequencing all at an 8–10-year level. His performance IQ on the WISC-R was 65, verbal 105. Academically he could recognize words at the sixth-grade level, but his rate of reading was slow and his comprehension was poor. Written work was an impossibility. He blamed the school and his parents for his problem, but inwardly he was overwhelmed, with little self-esteem or hope for the future. Discussion with the school revealed their inability to individualize their curriculum to modify the demands made on the child.

Discussion with the parents helped them see the child's real difficulties and to accept his placement in a small school for learning disordered children. Incidentally, in the year after he was relieved of the consistent pressure of classical academic demands, he grew at least two inches, and his acne responded to treatment. The parents, however, need continued visits to help them cope with their rapidly shifting expectations, varying from grandiose high-level profession to despairing low-level clerk. Now, 5 years after his leaving high school, this young man did manage to get a high school equivalency diploma and is graduating from a small college with a degree in criminal justice. He is seriously considering graduate school. During these years he has had intensive remedial educational help and continued psychotherapeutic support.

Therapy for Parents

It is difficult, however, to separate effective educational modification and remediation from the emotional problem of the child and parents. It is essential to recognize, however, that, although psychotherapy of whatever type for the child and parents will not cure the learning disorder and although education is still a basic component of any management plan, the emotional tensions within the child, within the parents, and between the child and parents cannot be neglected.

The resolution of the psychological and behavioral dysfunction within the family of the learning disordered child is thus essential for successful social, vocational, and even academic outcome of the learning disordered adolescent. Practically, how can this be done? As suggested above, work with parents starts with the explanation of the nature of the learning disability, its impact on academic achievement and social adjustment, and its impact on the family and their reactions to it. As a rule, behavior and attitudes do not change with the one-visit explanation. As with all psychotherapy, what further work is done depends on the individual situation and on the training and experience of the therapist. Periodic visits with the parents, family group meetings involving parents and the learning disordered child with or without siblings, and even individual therapy for parents have been advocated (Abrams & Kaslow, 1977). Learning disordered families, with their tendency toward overprotection, enmeshment, lack of conflict resolution, and scapegoating and rigidity, resemble in many ways the "psychosomatic families" described by Minuchin, Rosman, and Baker (1978). Family therapy has been an effective, relatively economical way of relieving the dysfunctional tensions within such families.

Whatever the technique, involvement of parents and families of the child with learning disabilities is an important component of management. The goal is to encourage conflict resolution by developing appropriate communication between parents and child and between parents.

Parents, however, have additonal groups with which to identify and within which to work for support of specific learning disordered programs within the community. There are, by now, local chapters of the Association for Children and Adults with Learning Disabilities (now called the Learning Disability Association) and of the Orton Society. These groups have been helpful in helping parents understand that they are not alone with this problem, helping them find appropriate educational programs for their own child, maintaining lists of qualified special education teachers who are available for private tutoring, and making them part of a group to encourage community understanding and overcome community prejudice. The Learning Disability Association may be reached at 4156 Liberty Road, Pittsburgh, PA 19234; The Orton Society at 724 York Road, Baltimore, MD 21204).

Therapy for the Child

Although the literature is replete with studies on the use of medication and of the value of various behavior modification techniques in the management of children with learning disorders, there is a singular dearth of reports on the use of psychotherapy in these children (see Adamson & Adamson, 1979; Cantwell, 1975; Fine, 1977; Whalen & Henker, 1980a, 1980b). There are possibly three reasons for this.

1. *Reasons inherent in the nature of psychotherapy.* Psychotherapy is itself an idiosyncratic process, undertaken by personnel of varying degrees of training and experience, administered to individuals who bring to it all varieties of the effects of nature and nurture, which are difficult to define and quantify, and to measure in terms of levels of effectiveness, adequacy, and efficiency. The problems inherent in an evaluation of psychotherapy have been described (Hargreaves, Atkisson, Siegel, McIntyre, & Sorenson, 1975; Parloff, Parloff, & Sussno, 1976), and a study of the value of psychotherapy in depression has been initiated by NIMH (Parloff, 1979). To this is added the scarcity of trained personnel and the duration and cost of such treatment.

2. *Reasons related to the broad spectrum of therapeutic modalities needed to manage children with learning disorders.* Psychotherapy is only one aspect of total management for children with learning disorders, and in most instances it is considered the least important aspect, eclipsed by the dramatic behavioral results that medication may induce in children with ADHD and by the effective educational techniques of compensation for, or stimulation of, the glaring areas of cognitive defect with which these children suffer. However, if we consider psychotherapy as encompassing a spectrum from psychoanalysis, on the one hand, through supportive psychotherapy to counseling, on the other, and if we consider management of the children by their parents and teachers using dynamic understanding also as psychotherapy, we must conclude that virtually every child with a learning disorder requires some form of psychological understanding and management. Just what form this takes unfortunately depends more on the theoretical orientation of the therapist than on the needs of the particular child. This book stresses the reciprocal interaction of biological, psychological, and environmental forces. The understanding of each individual child depends on the levels and potentials of biological and psychological maturation and integration, the content of intrapsychic conflict and its defense, the reality pressures from the environment, and the interaction between the child and the environment. After these are understood, we can allocate intervention strategies, including psychotherapy, rationally and appropriately. As a corollary to this view, accurate diagnosis, or rather comprehensive evaluation, is essential to treatment planning. Such evaluation should include the pentaxial schema discussed in Chapters 5 and 6.

3. *Reasons inherent in the "immutability of brain damage."* A third factor accounting for the dearth of reports in psychotherapy of children with learning disorders may be in the erroneous conception that one cannot alter the behavioral consequences of brain dysfunction by psychotherapy, that behavioral deviations are attributed to "irrevocably damaged neural structures" (Blau, 1936; Bond & Appel, 1931; Kahn & Cohen, 1934; Strauss & Lehtinen, 1947) and therefore are impervious to change. Of course, it is true that, overall, developmental dysfunction may be a lifelong problem,

one that is simply not outgrown in the course of maturation. Nevertheless, there is no one-to-one relationship between the brain dysfunction and the outcome in behavioral, emotional, and cognitive terms (A. Thomas, Chess, Birch, Hertzig, & Korn, 1963). As suggested above, the clinical picture is the resultant of reciprocal interacting forces from biological, psychological, and environmental vectors (Eisenberg, 1957, 1964; A. A. Silver, 1958, 1981). The biological dysfunction itself has infinite variations, and the ultimate prognosis, as we have repeatedly stated, may depend on the nature and extent of the dysfunction, the age of onset, the child's temperamental and intellectual resources, and the nature of the support he or she receives from the environment. On the other hand, as Gardiner said (1979), if we take a stand diametrically opposed to the "immutability" camp and consider all signs and symptoms a manifestation of psychogenic problems, we are bound to pose unrealistic goals for psychotherapy and "likely cause even greater frustration to all concerned" (p. 627). One must make what perhaps is an artificial distinction between primary symptoms of developmental dysfunction and behavioral symptoms of that dysfunction. There are some symptoms, such as perceptual distortions, impulse control, and motor and equilibrium difficulty, that have a basis in structural defect or developmental lag and these require all therapeutic modalities, yet even these, and certainly their affective and behavioral consequences, also require a psychotherapeutic approach.

Thus psychotherapy is but one facet of management in which educational measures, medication, and parental guidance play major roles. Yet as we review our experience with children with learning disorders seen in a private practice of psychiatry and in the public schools of New York and now in Florida, our errors were those of omission. In retrospect, psychotherapy was not offered often enough, intensely enough, or long enough to child and/ or parents and/or teachers, believing that once the biological dysfunction became more normal, the child would automatically regain his self-esteem, lose his anger and depression, stop projecting blame to parents and teachers, and realize his potential. In spite of the best of remedial education this did not always occur, and the affective and behavioral consequences of the learning disorder continued on, in varied forms, into adult life (A. A. Silver & Hagin, 1985). Fortunately, many of these children and their families were tenacious and would call us until we did involve many in therapy.

Obvious indications for psychotherapy include the following cases: (a) where the disturbed affect and behavior interfere with other management measures, e.g., educational; (b) where the child is in emotional pain; (c) where the defenses the child has adapted are maladaptive, getting her into difficulties with parents, teachers, and peers and interfering with psychological maturation, both sexual and social; and (d) where the environment does not offer the emotional support the child needs for maturation and/or where the child becomes the expression of the parent's unconscious needs, and, as a corollary to this indication, where the child's behavior must be interpreted to teachers so that they may work with him successfully.

TECHNIQUES OF PSYCHOTHERAPY FOR CHILDREN WITH LEARNING DISORDERS

What of the techniques of psychotherapy with these children? It has been said (Christ, 1978, 1981; Gardiner, 1979) that the child with a learning disorder does not respond to insight therapy. Well, many of us without a learning disorder do not respond to insight therapy. The goals and theoretical approach of our therapy depend on the needs and abilities of each child. Certainly, one does not start treatment of the child with normal biological development with "insight." One waits for the appropriate time and conditions. However, the biological imprint of a learning disorder demands modification of psychotherapeutic techniques. For example, the literature advises that a clear explanation of the child's problem must eventually be presented to the child and his parents; for the child this means emphasis that he is not unique, that his problems are relatively common, and that he is not stupid or a freak, abnormal, or a "retard," but that he is more than his problems and has skills and assets.

However, the timing and manner of this explanation must be an individual thing. I recollect telling a depressed 12-year-old, with potentially average intelligence, that he was failing in school because his brain just was not hearing sounds in the proper order, and that this was not his fault but that he was just born this way. Rather than reassure him, this explanation only convinced him that his brain was no good and intensified his depression. The explanation must obviously be geared to the capacity of the child for understanding and must be buffered by an emphasis on positive function.

Another example: A first-year medical student could not master the sheer volume of material presented to him. He was falling farther and farther behind in his work, becoming depressed, and was ready to quit medical school. Our examination revealed the persistence of an old specific language disorder, with a rate of reading expected for a seventh-grader. An explanation of his difficulty only convinced him that he never could master the academic demands of medical school and he became more depressed. Only vigorous intervention, including special help in organizing his work, selecting priorities, supportive reassurance from the medical student dean, and supportive psychotherapy enabled him to carry on.

Most important is the awareness in the therapist of the lowered threshold for anxiety in these children, the decreased stimulus barrier, and the specific perceptual and cognitive deficits. For most children with learning disorders, from the youngest preschooler to the older adolescent, stimuli offered must be low keyed and as far as possible in one perceptual modality, avoiding the deficit perceptual areas and attempting to use the intact ones. Many stimuli, such as many toys in the toy chest, paper and crayons on the desk, and ash trays or decorations strewn about, will not only create chaos in the child's perceptual field, but will render him unable to focus on any one stimulus; his attention will leap from one object to the other, producing a hyperactive child out of control. Similarly, the specific cognitive defects will influence the therapeutic technique. For a child with severe visual-motor or visual-perceptual defects but with intact auditory-verbal perception, the therapy becomes verbal while visual-perceptual and visual-motor stimuli are minimized and the intact perceptual avenue is used. The visual problems are most often those involving spatial orientation. Clearly games involving that skill will only invite failure and only convince the child that you, too, are making life difficult. Conversely, the child whose perceptual skills are primarily visual-spatial but who has auditory sequencing problems will only be confused by a verbal approach.

The principle is to use the intact areas in therapy and minimize the deficit ones. In remedial education, the opposite is true; the principle is to stimulate the deficit perceptual areas in training and use the intact ones for teaching and for support. If, as frequently happens, all perceptual modalities are affected, one must select the most intact, using that one for communication and dealing with it at its basic level of ability, repetitiously, with immediate feedback to be sure you are being understood. The approach here is contrary to the so-called multisensory one that offers reinforcing stimuli via all perceptual areas, virtually simultaneously. Such an approach only promotes confusion.

Basic rules so far described in the conduct of psychotherapy for children with perceptual-cognitive immaturities may be summarized as follows:

1. Use the intact perceptual areas in communication.
2. Present stimuli as simply as possible concordant with the child's perceptual and cognitive ability, a single stimulus at a time, repetitiously with immediate feedback.
3. Avoid the chaos of distracting stimuli.

These principles are most important in the preschool and elementary school years, but they are still valid in working with adolescents. These principles also, by protecting the child from stimulus overload, decrease anxiety, help sustain attention, and also help decrease hyperactivity and impulsivity.

These symptoms may be controlled further by structuring the therapeutic session so that it is organized and predictable for the child. For example, in the latency-age child one might start with a quiet time where we review the reality events since our last visit, emphasizing events in space and time. This is followed by feelings about these events, expressed in the manner appropriate for the child—drawing, storytelling, and games to illustrate affect and behavior. After this, the child's time is devoted to his or her specific interests: frequently playing a competitive game, drawing on the chalkboard, or playing with puppets. In all of these structured activities, ideas and feelings are expressed in as concrete terms as possible, and abstractions are avoided. In the exploration of affects, impulses may get out of hand, with the child acting out feelings sometimes directed at the therapist. However, simple release of affect or behavior, letting it hang in the air without control, can be destructive, with the child becoming more disorganized, hyperactive, and disturbed. It is therefore helpful to avoid direct exposure of the child to his affects, not only because they may get out of control but because they are painful to the child. Confrontation of the affect via drawings, dolls, puppets, toys, and stories projects the feeling or behavior onto the third person, and so buffers the child from himself; it places the affect or behavior at a safe distance from the child. This, of course, is the usual device one uses in psychotherapy for children. For the learning disordered child of latency age, it is an essential device. Furthermore, confrontation of affect and behavior must be cautious, titrated against the child's ability to understand and withstand the anxiety induced. In many children, their ability to withstand stress can be read in their autonomic reactivity as well as in the more overt manifestations of anxiety such as hyperactivity. Dilation of pupils, flushing of face, increase in perioral pallor, increase in heart rate, and a sudden desire to go to the bathroom are warning signs that the limit of the child's tolerance is being reached. Attention to the autonomic signs in these children will keep the therapist from treading into dangerous waters.

However, confrontation of affect and behavior, albeit via a third person or object or via transference, is not our therapeutic goal. Most of these children need further help in controlling their impulsive expression of feelings and wishes. Our object is to interpose the control that these children lack. As indicated above, some children attempt to compensate for lack of impulse control by obsessions and/or compulsions. This defense mechanism may indeed function to control the anxiety of neurotic conflict—anxiety that may be present in all of us but here is exaggerated and unmodulated. However, in these children the obsession and the compulsion function as nonneurotic defenses: an attempt to control the world by rehearsal (the obsession) or by ritual (the compulsion), thus avoiding the disorganization of overwhelming stimuli, whether they emanate from external or internal sources. Unless the defense is in itself paralyzing, my choice is to develop and encourage this control. Verbal rehearsal is the basis of Meichenbaum's (1977) "self-instructional techniques" and Santostefano's (1978) "cognitive control therapy." Here, however, the child must be given the words to rehearse and the tools for self-instruction. My own preference is to deal with the affect or behavior in simplistic terms of "good" or "bad," adaptive or maladaptive, functional or nonfunctional. This decision is made by the child, and together we work out ways to avoid the "bad"—i. e., to control the impulse—and decide what the child must tell himself when these feelings arise. This technique does not yet reach the psychodynamic genesis of behavior; in children with a biological immaturity in impulse control, our effort is to interpose new pathways to control, to inhibit, and to modulate. Such control does not, of course, appear overnight. Patient, persistent effort, with endless repetition is the key.

What has been said above is that problems with impulse control, with which the child with a learning disorder struggles, may be helped by structuring the therapeutic situation, by confrontation of affects and behavior within the limits of the child's tolerance, by using the principle of projecting the affect to another person or object, and by interposing a mechanism in which the child may not only attempt to modulate the external stimuli but also the impulses from within. Such a mechanism may be obsessive and compulsive patterns or ritualistic self-structuring.

For those children in whom muscle coordination, posture, and equilibrium immaturities are present, the basic principles described in dealing with perceptual and cognitive dysfunction and the suggestions in psychotherapeutic management of impulse control are valid also. Here, however, the behavioral consequences of deficit areas that must be understood are fear of physical activity, fear of changes in posture, fear of ball playing, fear of height, and the need to cling to physical objects such as a chair or to people such as parents, a teacher, a therapist, or other children. To force these children into such exercises as walking a balance board or into competitive sports will only intensify their anxiety and harden their resistance to change. In therapy, the principle of using intact areas of function applies; the therapist must recognize what is anxiety-provoking and protect the child from these things, but also attempt to find things the child can do—things that give gratification and promote maturation. As psychotherapy proceeds, and as carefully monitored physiotherapy or occupational therapy begins to stimulate the lagging function, then the child can safely be encouraged to reach out without clinging and overprotection, and parents can be encouraged to permit the child more independent activity and assertiveness.

SUMMARY

The emotional and behavioral response to a learning disorder depends upon the cause, extent, and severity of the disorder and the adequacy and appropriateness of support the child receives from parents and school. Failure and frustration may appear very early, in kindergarten where reactive behaviors may be avoidance, passive helplessness, aggression, and disobedience. In the elementary school years, the child may be convinced that he is stupid and bad, with patterns of defiance, begun in kindergarten, evident. By early adolescence the child is more capable of acting out her emotions in sexual and aggressive, antisocial behaviors such as drugs or truancy, finally dropping out of school. School failure in the early grades has been found to be the single, most statistically significant variable predicting later delinquency.

The parents' initial reactions to their child's problems (denial and nonacceptance) is frequently replaced with depression and guilt; some use mechanisms of projection, anger, and scapegoating. The schools, too, may see the child as stupid, lazy, or negativistic and may not understand the child's special educational needs and the need for their own flexibility in meeting those needs.

Management thus begins with a comprehensive evaluation and the selection of an ombudsman to synthesize all the data and coordinate management. Modifications in the school program, including the adequacy of remedial education, are immediate tasks in management. Help for parents, including family therapy and support groups, may be useful. Although educational help is most important, psychotherapy, which may encompass a spectrum from psychoanalysis on the one hand to supportive counseling on the other, is frequently neglected in management. It is much needed, certainly where the disturbed affect and behavior interfere with educational management, where the child is in emotional pain, and where environmental support is inadequate for the child's needs. In psychotherapy with children with learning disorders, communication is best achieved via the child's *intact* perceptual areas, avoidance of sensory overload, careful structuring of the therapy session, imposition of cognitive controls over impulsive behavior, and avoidance of anxiety-provoking motor demands,

CHAPTER TEN

Prevention of Disorders of Learning

Commitment to the primary prevention of learning disorders is reflected more often in exhortations on its value than in data-based demonstrations of its efficacy. This point can be illustrated in the results of computer searches, that were completed in July 1988, of two major data bases ERIC, and Psychinfo. These searches produced a total of 69 references dealing with early identification and prevention of learning disorders. That these references deal more often with prevention in the abstract than with data-based research on specific intervention strategies can be seen in Table 10-1.

Most of the conventional textbooks provide little information about preventive interventions. Two recent volumes on psychoeducational assessment of young children (Lichtenstein & Ireton, 1984; Paget & Bracken, 1983) scarcely mention preventive interventions; Achenbach's (1982) section on prevention in his volume on developmental psychopathology is an admirable exception to this practice.

The content analysis reported in Table 10-1 shows that general discussions of the needs and values of prevention are a frequent type of paper. However, any significant application of prevention to the problem of learning disorders requires more than good intentions. Effective prevention requires judicious selection of goals, as well as specific formulation of principles for targeting, timing, and guiding intervention strategies. It is with these specifics of preventive intervention that the data base is thin. Of the 30 specific projects reported, 17 provide extensive descriptions of methods for selection of participants and procedures, but offer little data on outcomes of these interventions. Five papers provide descriptive and anecdotal data on outcomes, and only eight provide evaluation data to document pro-

Table 10-1   Content Analysis of Prevention Literature Search

Content	Number of References
Discussions of the value of prevention	
Generally favorable	11
Generally unfavorable	3
Methods for early identification	
Recommending	16
Opposing	3
Specific Intervention Projects	
No evaluation data provided	17
Descriptions of favorable outcomes	5
Data on outcomes provided	
Favorable outcome	7
Instructional objectives not met	1
References not relevant to prevention	6
TOTAL	69

gram effects. Ultimately, discussions of the fine points of rationale for an approach or even sophisticated statistical computations of the "hit rate" of a screening instrument are only academic, unless they are part of a total program that achieves measurable results in interventions with vulnerable children.

Interventions for the prevention of learning disorders will be considered here from this pragmatic standpoint. The chapter is organized in terms of (a) general consideration of facilitators and barriers to preventive intervention, (b) instruments to identify potential learning disorders at age 5, (c) experimental programs in early education, (d) administrative strategies in prevention, and (e) specific interventions for children identified as vulnerable to learning failure.

FACILITATORS AND BARRIERS TO PREVENTIVE INTERVENTIONS

A comprehensive description of the need for prevention of learning disabilities through efforts directed at the preschool years was voiced in a position paper offered by the National Joint Committee on Learning Disabilities (1985). The multidisciplinary membership of this committee (NJCLD) represents some of the major organizations in the field, including the Association for Children and Adults with Learning Disabilities, the American Speech and Hearing Association, the Council for Learning Disabilities, divisions of the Council for Exceptional Children concerned with communications disorders and learning disabilities, the International Reading Association, the National Association of School Psychologists, and the Orton-Dyslexia Society. This report emphasized that the preschool years are a critical period during which essential preventive and intervention efforts are most effective. Recognizing that learning disorders are a heterogeneous group of disorders of presumed neurological origin, the report provides a cautionary note that indiscriminate labeling is not warranted because normal development is characterized by broad ranges of individual and group differences, as well as by variability in rates and patterns of maturation. Early identification procedures were defined to include examination of biological, genetic, perinatal, and adventitious risk indicators through systematic observation, screening, and other (unspecified) procedures. The NJCLD paper noted, however, that early identification was only one step and the "identification programs not followed by assessment, intervention, and follow up are futile" (ERIC Document 206544).

The NJCLD paper advised caution in the design of such programs in observing that "traditional readiness activities are often not sufficient to ensure later school success." Periodic evaluation of effectiveness is recommended so that interventions focus not only on ameliorating deficits that affect current functioning, but also develop abilities, skills, and knowledge necessary for later linguistic, academic, and social functioning. Eight areas of need were recommended:

1. systematic identification programs
2. assessment based on interdisciplinary approaches that provide an integrated statement of current status and needs
3. validated models for early intervention available to all preschool children with identified developmental deficits
4. qualified personnel necessary to meet the needs of the identified children
5. assistance to families in participating fully in all phases of identification and treatment
6. public information concerning issues of child development and its disorders
7. response to the unique needs of non-English speaking and limited English-speaking families
8. systematic research to address issues related to provision of services for preschool children with suspected learning disorders

The NJCLD paper presents a clear and enlightened position. If one agrees that prevention of learning disorders is at all possible and desirable, there is little in the NJCLD report that is controversial. It is significant that the nature of preventive interventions is sidestepped completely through the call for "validated models." Whether this joint statement sought to avoid supporting any existing model or to disregard the results of at least twenty years of research in early identification and prevention is not clear. The wastefulness of the second alternative is obvious. However, because of variations in viewpoints among the organizations involved, the neutral first alternative may have been chosen in order to produce a unified statement of support for prevention from the members of the Joint Committee.

Although the NJCLD recommendations seem to offer an unattainable ideal, it should be remembered that the Education for All Handicapped Children Act of 1975, Public Law 94-142, passed 10 years earlier, mandated a "free appropriate public education" for all handicapped children between the ages of 3 and 21. Very specific provisions designed to meet the unique educational needs of handicapped children and their families obligate school districts to identify all handicapped children within the age groups served, to inform parents fully of their rights under the law, to provide comprehensive assessments at least once every 3 years, to develop annually an individual educational plan (IEP) written by a committee that includes a teacher, a school administrator, the child's parent, and other specialized personnel as needed, to provide services as delineated in the IEP, and to see that the services are carried out in the "least restrictive environment" (i. e., settings that ensure contact with the educational mainstream to the extent that it is appropriate for a given child).

The law specified that the IEP should include an analysis of the child's current needs and capabilities, annual goals stating the levels to be achieved during the current year as well as short-term objectives to accomplish the annual goals, evaluation criteria, instructional techniques and their location, and related services (i. e., noninstructional services, such as special transportation, counseling, and physical therapy, necessary for the child to profit from the individual educational plan).

While the model represented in P. L. 94-142 could have been interpreted to include provisions for the primary prevention of learning disorders, its implementation has generally resulted in provision of services only after children have experienced a severe degree of learning failure (see the case study of David, Chapter 1). This result occurred because of economic considerations (which were probably outside the control of professionals working on behalf of children) and theoretical considerations (which probably were not). While P. L. 94-142 recognized the need for early identification and most of the state plans for local implementation provided funds for early screening, financial support for intervention continues to be based on documentation of the need for remediation after failure has occurred.

This choice of remediation over prevention was probably not a deliberate one. The gap between the services mandated in P. L. 94-142 and what existed in most school districts was wide. Personnel needed to be recruited and trained. The sheer numbers of children identified as "learning disabled" and the cost of the services required had not been anticipated. The emphasis on remediation came because the need for services for learning disordered children had not been met for so long that there was much to be done to provide even minimal compliance with the law.

It must be conceded that P. L. 94-142 had not been drafted with the assumption that the federal government would assume all the costs of educating handicapped children. Congress considered that it was a joint responsibility of local, state, and federal governments to share these costs. Unfortunately, the grass-roots implementation of an enlightened law resulted in a special education model that rewards programs that serve children *after* they have failed.

A second reason for the loss of the opportunity to support preventive programs under the Education for All Handicapped Children Act lies in the lack of professional consensus on a definition of "learning disabilities." Federal and state legislators can hardly be expected to fund enabling legislation for services to a group of handicapped children whose characteristics are varied, confusing, and often contradictory. The very people who purport to provide these services cannot agree on a definition, indeed some of them question the existence of a clear-cut etiological group (Beers & Beers, 1980; Sprinthall, 1984).

The debate over definition does a disservice to the cause of prevention. People who would mount preventive projects in the field of learning disorders are faced with the task of justifying interventions to keep from happening phenomena that some of their colleagues argue do not exist in the first place. The vague and variable definitions do a similar disservice to the development of preventive approaches. In the face of the definitional disagreements, the efficacy of successful interventions may be doubted by the compulsive definers who will, in the light of their idiosyncratic definition, dismiss the children who responded favorably to the intervention as not having been "truly learning disabled" to begin with or at least to have avoided learning problems because of mysterious maturational and compensatory processes (Lindsay & Wedell, 1982; Wedell, 1980).

Despite differences in some aspects of the definitions of learning disorders and the methods by which this determination can be made for individuals, there is probably a considerable amount of concordance among professionals concerning the nature of learning disabilities. Ultimately, the definition is one of exclusion in which a learning disability is said to be present when a discrepancy between a child's potential and actual achievement exists despite normal sensory acuity, adequate intelligence, conventional educational opportunities, and appropriate motivation for learning. Preventive programs are organized to reduce the incidence of these disabilities and the emotional and behavioral consequence of such learning failure. The need for preventive programs to deal with the problem of learning disabilities is especially significant because of the long-term effects of school failure on every aspect of personality.

According to Barclay (1984), successful preventive programs have in common three basic components:

1. assessment technology to identify the children at risk
2. a set of intervention procedures
3. sufficient time to assess the results

The success of a program in fulfilling the promise of prevention depends on assumptions that the assessment technology provides a means for identifying the children who are otherwise destined to fail to learn with conventional classroom instruction and that the problems thus identified are modifiable. It further depends on the effectiveness of the match between the needs of an individual child and the intervention strategies. Finally, successful programs require the opportunity for sufficient time for application of the intervention strategies and for follow-up evaluations over time to monitor individual progress and to improve the overall program on the basis of feedback provided by the outcomes of evaluation.

EARLY IDENTIFICATION OF POTENTIAL LEARNING DISORDERS

General Considerations

The prevention of learning disorders in childhood is confounded by the fact that learning failure is but a symptom, one manifestation, stemming from a multitude of factors acting singly or more often in synergistic combination.

As in any complex behavior, learning involves the interaction of biological, psychological, social, and educational factors. Biological factors include genetic variants, developmental lags, and imposed pathological events; psychological factors include cognition, attention, motivation, and emotional influences; socioeconomic-environmental factors involve cultural and economic status, the quality and quantity of stimulation at early ages, and the vicissitudes of life experiences throughout time; educational factors deal with the appropriateness and adequacy of educational exposure. For any child, these factors have varying degrees of influence on learning, but in children with learning disorders all these influences must be considered, for each may play a synergistic and reciprocal role in their learning disorder.

It is reasonable to assume that the first step in the prevention of learning disorders is to understand the specific contribution to learning of each of the risk factors; then, if possible, to remove the causative factor or to avoid exposure to it. If, for example, some specific constellation of factors, unique to cultural difference and economic disadvantage, are actual causal agents for learning disorders, then broad social planning and educational change to modify these factors may be needed. Such conclusions may be drawn from work such as that of Brody and Axelrod (1970); Caldwell, Bradley, and Staff (1984), and Hess and Shipman (1968). If perinatal events such as neonatal hypoxia may be identified as potent contributors to learning disorders, then primary prevention involves the isolation of these events and their modification by new obstetrical and perinatal techniques. The importance of perinatal hypoxia in cognitive development and later learning has been documented (Browman, 1979; Broman et al., 1975; Sarnoff et al., 1981; Siegel, 1983).

On the other hand, there are children with learning failure in whom the causative agent cannot be clearly identified. These are children with so-called specific developmental learning disabilities. In these children there is no history of traumatic physical events of the pre-, peri-, or postnatal periods. They have not suffered social or economic disadvantage; their central nervous system is not marked with focal or even diffuse structural defect; their emotional state and educational experiences are not so different from their peers who do learn; their intelligence is within the normal range, and they do not suffer from defects in visual or auditory acuity. Yet these children do have academic difficulty. We classify these children as suffering from specific developmental learning disabilities. We postulate that before they enter kindergarten these children already have the anlage for disability present in their central nervous system and that there may be a genetic predisposition to that disability.

The list of identified risk factors stemming from social-cultural-economic disadvantage, from pathological events of pregnancy, and particularly from possible genetic influence and from the vicissitudes of life's experience is not only a long one, but one which does not yet lend itself to primary prevention. We are not yet able to eradicate the risk factors—to eliminate poverty and disadvantage, prematurity and hypoxia, genetic defects and developmental lags, inadequate or inappropriate stimulation.

In the prevention of learning disorders we are therefore left with a fallback position—to secondary prevention: the identification of children who we predict will become learning disordered and providing for them appropriate intervention before learning failure has occurred.

Currently, there is a large group of children for whom such secondary prevention of learning disorders is available. These are children in whom the various primary risk factors, be they biological or experiential, leave a mark on the function of the central nervous system such that the psychoneurological processes involved in learning are impaired. Thus, a traumatic or hypoxic birth for example, the inappropriate and/or inadequate stimulation of poverty or cultural deprivation, a genetic predisposition to developmental lags in language in all its ramifications—all of these may be reflected in psychoneurological dysfunction, which makes learning to read, write, spell, or do arithmetic difficult.

For this group of children it is now possible to identify the psychoneurological defects by the time the child is 5 years old, to predict with confidence at the time the child enters kindergarten whether or not that child will fail learning and to offer a program of intervention so that learning failure does not occur. It is clear that the children so identified as vulnerable to learning failure are a heterogeneous group, composed of children who may have been exposed to different risk factors and their combinations. The identification process is thus not a diagnosis but it certainly is a first stage to secondary prevention. We identify these children with a constellation of neuropsychological dysfunction in "one or more of the basic processes in understanding or using written or spoken language" (P. L. 94-142) as being potential learning disordered.

It is recognized that there is a rich literature on the identification of factors within the spectrum of "social-cultural-economic disadvantage" that predispose to learning failure (Caldwell et al., 1984; M. Deutsch, 1965; Hess, 1970; Murphy & Moriarty, 1976; Sameroff & Chandler, 1975; Tableman & Katzenmeyer, 1985; and Werner & Smith, 1982). These factors, their identification, and the social and educational resources that have been interposed between the predisposing factors and learning failure are described in Chapter 12 of this book, "Effects of Poverty and Inappropriate Stimulation." The long-term outcome of the Head Start Program and of early educational programs suggest that prevention of learning disorders for the group of children reared in the culture of poverty is moderately effective. Study of the successful factors in such intervention is still needed, however. The present emphasis on early preschool education for handicapped children will offer further identification of educational techniques effective in preventing learning failure.

This chapter discusses methods for the identification of 5-year-olds vulnerable to learning failure and describes programs of successful intervention.

Ideal Characteristics of Tests to Identify Children Vulnerable to Learning Disorders

Programs for the prevention of learning disorders have three components: scanning, diagnosis, and intervention (Barclay, 1984; A. A. Silver, Hagin, & Beecher, 1978). By scanning is meant the survey of entire populations to detect children who have the functional deviations associated with learning disorders. Effective detection means that the instrument can accurately predict learning failure and learning success; that in the scanning process the incidence of false positives is negligible and of false negatives, minimal; that the test meets the standards for educational and psychological testing as described by the American Psychological Association (1985), and that its content and norms are appropriate for the population studied (A. A. Silver, 1978). Beyond statistical demonstration of validity and sensitivity, however, a predictive instrument should be based on a rational framework that offers conceptual unity with the learning process. In addition, the scanning test must be brief enough to be given to large numbers of children quickly and economically, clear enough to be administered and to be interpreted by school personnel after brief training, and comprehensive enough to identify children who need detailed diagnostic procedures. Finally, it should provide guidance to the teacher in using interventions appropriate to each child's needs.

Scanning is not diagnosis. All scanning can be expected to accomplish is identify a heterogeneous group whose members have only one thing in common: Their function in those parameters assessed by the scanning instrument is immature when compared to their peers.

Statistical Considerations

False Positives and False Negatives   One measurement of the sensitivity of scanning instruments is through assessment of false negatives and false positives. Because learning failure is a symptom that may result from many factors, and which is responsive to the dynamic changes in the child's world, it would be overly optimistic to expect a brief scanning instrument to tap all the variables important in learning and to predict for any child the vicissitudes of time. False negatives (the test score indicates that the child will succeed, but, instead, she fails), are to be expected. False positives (the test score predicts failure, but, instead, he succeeds) are more disturbing, raising the spectre of labeling and creating a self-fulfilling and teacher-fulfilling prophecy. Just what constitutes an acceptable level of false negatives and of false positives is uncertain. Obviously, the fewer of each, the better.

The level of inaccurate predictions, however, may be adjusted by statistical manipulation of the scanning battery. False positives may be decreased by lowering the cut-off score—the score at or below which failure is predicted and above which adequate learning is suggested. Lowering the cut-off score will put fewer children in the vulnerable category. At the same time, however, decreasing the number of false positives will increase the number of false negatives. Conversely, raising the cut-off score will increase the number of false positives and decrease the number of false negatives. Determination of the cut-off point thus becomes an important consideration in the structure of predictive tests. In their original Predictive Index, for example (De Hirsch, Jansky & Langford, 1966), a total score in 3 passing subtests of the 10 subtests in the battery identified less than 50% of the failing readers in the sample, i. e., more than 50% of false negatives. When the cut-off point was raised to 5, the Index correctly identified 71% of the failing readers, with approximately 30% false negatives but 24% false positives, which is certainly an undesirable percentage of false positives.

The global (total score) cut-off point must be derived from component subtests scores. Since the scores in subtests are usually not dichotomous, but represent scores along a continuum, the cut-off point (i. e., the score above which success is predicted and at or below which failure is predicted) for each subtest becomes important. How each cut-off score was derived is not clearly stated in many predictive instruments.

In contrast to this questionable measurement practice, some test authors do clarify their decision-making process on cut-off score. Fletcher and Satz (1984), for instance, stated that for the Florida Kindergarten Screening Battery, "discriminant analysis formed the basis for classifying (predicting) children into reading groups later in school. . . . in essence, this technique computes a weighted linear composite of Kindergarten (predictor) variables that maximally separates subsequent criterion reading groups" (p. 165). A. A. Silver and Hagin (1981) used base rates of reading failure in their samples to set cut-off scores for each of their subtests in their scanning instrument, called *Search*. The total score for any individual was the number of subtests in which the child scored above the cut-off point on each of the 10 subtests comprising the battery. The lowest one-third on the distribution of total *Search* scores identified the child for whom academic failure was predicted. The lowest one-third of the distribution was equal to the base rate for reading failure in schools used for standardization. Jansky and De Hirsch (1972) also defined the cut-off point in the total score of their screening battery in terms of each school's judgment as to what, for that school, constitutes reading failure.

Bayesian theories of probability have been suggested as a way of determining cut-off points that will yield maximum efficiency in correctly identifying true positives and true negatives on psychometric devices (Meehl & Rosen, 1955). These authors stated that in order for a positive diagnostic assertion (a prediction) to be more likely true than false, the ratio of the positive to negative base rates in a sample must exceed the ratio of false positive rates to valid positive rates as attained in the scanning test. If, for example, the base rate for reading failure in a sample is 30% and if the scanning test yields false positive predictions of 5%, then 30/70 (i. e., base rate of failure/base rate of adequate readers) must be greater than 5/95 (i. e., false positive rate/valid positive rate) for the prediction to be more likely true than false. With a base rate of 30%, a false positive prediction of 5% is statistically acceptable. Decreasing the cut-off point will improve decisions only if the ratio of improvement in true positive rate to worsening false negative rate exceeds the ratio of actual negatives (failures) to positives (successful readers) in the population. Meehl and Rosen stated that an inflexible cut-off score should not be advocated for any psychometric device; the base rates of prevalence for any given sample should determine cut-off points. Detailed data on the derivation of cut-off scores would aid in evaluation of predictive instruments.

Criteria for Validation   Criteria used for validation have also varied among scanning tests. The Florida Longitudinal Project, summarized in Fletcher and Satz (1984), used both a classroom-based criterion and test-based criteria. The classroom-based criterion was a checklist in which the teacher recorded the child's instructional level of reading; the test assessment was the Iota Word Recognition Test (Monroe, 1932) at the end of second grade for their initial sample and the Vocabulary and Comprehension subtests of the Gates MacGinitie Reading tests on an additional sample. For grade 5 follow-up, the WRAT was used; in grade 6, the Metropolitan Achievement Test was used. The Silver-Hagin criteria were oral reading on the WRAT and the Word Identification and Word Attack sections of the Woodcock-Johnson Psychoeducational Battery, all at the end of grades 1, 2, and 3; the comprehension test of the Science Research Associates (SRA) basic reading series was added at the ends of grade 2 and grade 3.

The importance of considering carefully the criteria used for validation studies is two-fold. First, comparison among scanning instruments may be confounded by their use of differing validation criteria, which may not be comparable; second, the validity of the criterion measure itself may be questionable. Even when specific comparable criterion measures are selected, there are other variables to be considered. Many tests, for example, are normed in certain months of the school year, i. e., in months of educational exposure. Norms for a test developed for testing in May or June are inappropriate for November or December.

In addition to choice of the criterion measure, a decision must be made as to what level of achievement on that measure constitutes failure. For example, should class expectancy level or median class achievement level be used as a measure of academic success? A. A. Silver, Hagin, and Beecher (1978) found a 4% false negative rate using expectancy criteria of grade 4 at the end of grade 3. If, however, the median class achievement score of 4.6 were used, the false negative rate became 13%. In one school at the end of second grade the expectancy score at grade 3 yielded 9% false positives (*Search* predicted failure, yet the child scored above expectancy). Using the median achievement level lowered the false positive rate to 3%.

Content Considerations

With these caveats, what should be the content of a scanning battery? Unfortunately, there is, as yet, no generally accepted theory as to the nature of the learning processes. The functional precursors to reading, spelling, writing, and arithmetic are not clear, and thus there is no general agreement as to what functions a predictive instrument should evaluate. Also, the skills required of a beginning reader may differ from those of a more advanced reader. It has been said (Farr, 1969) that tests, which practical judgment indicates are related to early academic learning, are most predictive of that learning. Our task in prediction, however, is to find the skills that are needed before the child is exposed to academic learning.

Chapter 3 of this book, "Patterns of Neuropsychological Dysfunction," reviews the variables thought to predict reading failure. Surveys of the literature on such predictive variables as age, sex, socioeconomic status, laterality, visual perception, auditory perception, and intersensory integration conclude that although each single variable contributes to learning (i. e., reading), any one skill is not central to reading and not predictive (De Hirsch, 1971; Jansky & De Hirsch, 1972).

In contrast to sensory modality studies, Blank and Bridger (1966, 1967) found symbolic mediation to be a necessary condition to solve problems involving temporally presented stimuli regardless of modality. Vellutino (1978) is in strong support of this argument. Phonic awareness is felt by the Haskins Laboratory researchers (Liberman et al., 1985) to be an essential skill in learning to read.

We should not be surprised that the single modality research has not been able to predict learning disability with any useful degree of accuracy. Considering the specific developmental reading disability itself, we know that within this group of children there are marked individual differences in distribution of assets and deficits which may appear in all aspects of perceptual, associative, and emissive language function—in all aspects of dysgnosias, dyspraxias, and dysphasias (A. A. Silver & Hagin, 1960, 1972a). Recent multivariable studies (Rourke, 1978, 1985; Rourke & Strang, 1983) of neuropsychological patterns in children with reading disability substantiate this variability. The importance of these variations is that in any correlational study of large numbers of children, individual differences in distribution of function may well cancel each other out and the investigator will dismiss as insignificant some variables that may have crucial importance for some children in the sample. What is needed is a theoretical formulation that would encompass all, or most, of the variations seen in specific developmental learning disorders. The content of predictive instruments thus should not be a collection of extraneous items put together by myth and larceny, but should spring from a conceptual unity of the learning process. A number of such conceptual positions have been advanced.

Satz and his associates of the Florida Longitudinal Project (Satz et al., 1971; Satz & Sparrow, 1970; Satz & Van Nostrand, 1973), postulated that "reading disabilities reflect a lag in the maturation of the brain which differentially delays those skills which are in primary ascendancy at different chronological ages . . . skills which develop . . . earlier during childhood (i. e., visual perceptual and cross-modal sensory integration) are more likely to be delayed in younger children . . . maturationally immature . . . skills which have a slower rate of development during childhood (language and formal operations) are more likely to be delayed in older children developmentally immature" (Satz et al., 1978, p. 319). Thus, this theory predicts that children who are delayed in visual perception and cross-modality skills at ages 5 and 6 will eventually fail in reading. The theory further predicts that these children will eventually "catch up" on the earlier developing skills, but will subsequently lag in conceptual linguistic skills.

Some evidence for the predictive value of sensory-perceptual factors may be seen in an analysis of the early standardization battery of 14 variables used in the testing of 497 white, male, kindergarten pupils in the Alachua County, Florida, public school system (Satz & Friel, 1973) in which factor analysis yielded three major factors: (a) sensory-perceptual motor-mnemonic, (b) verbal-conceptual, and (c) verbal-cultural. In a later paper, Satz (Satz, Morris, & Fletcher, 1985) and his associates described four factors: (a) sensory-perceptual motor-mnemonic, (b) teacher evaluations, (c) conceptual-verbal, and (d) motor. However, as the project developed and additional samples were studied, the number of variables in this battery decreased, and the final Florida Kindergarten Screening Battery (Satz & Fletcher, 1982) consists of five subtests: the Peabody Picture Vocabulary Test, a visual recognition discrimination test (a visual matching to samples of geometric design), the Beery test of visual motor integration, alphabet recitation, and finger localization. This battery introduces language tests, which, although of greater predictive value than the original standardization battery, dilutes the theoretical concept of a lag in sensory-perceptual functions. Further, the concept of developmental lag does not ensure that children will outgrow that lag. Follow-up studies (A. A. Silver & Hagin, 1964) have demonstrated the persistence into young adulthood of the perceptual defects originally found in children 10–12 years old with learning disorders. It appears that perceptual dysfunction does not necessarily mature spontaneously, and that reading disability must be considered a long-term problem.

The concept of a lag in development, in contrast to "brain damage," was advanced by Gesell and Thompson in 1934. Gesell and Thompson asked, "does the infant present specific lags and accelerations among components of his behavior equipment?" L. A. Bender and Yarnell (1941) were the first to apply the term "developmental lag" or "maturational lag" to children with reading disabilities in whom classical neurological examination was normal. L. A. Bender and Silver emphasized as early as 1949 that many of the conditions seen in children, considered at that time to be "organic" or "brain damage," were better understood as maturational delays rather than as structural defects of the central nervous system.

The problem of what functions are delayed in children who will fail in reading is not solved. Studies of subgroups of neuropsychological dysfunction in children with learning disorders have suffered from the perennial problems of disparate samples, definitions, boundaries, and methodology. Multivariate studies have proliferated with most finding variations on the themes of language defect and graphomotor and visual-perceptual deficits, with varied emphasis on the specific deficits present. Doehring (1968) found that the concept basic to subgroups of reading disabilities is impairment in sequential processing abilities; Petrauskas and Rourke (1979) found one group with most difficulty in finger-gnosis and in immediate memory for visual sequences. Satz and Morris (1981) found one group with no impairment in their neuropsychological tests. Is there a concept that can unify the many and varied neuropsychological immaturities that have been found in children with specific learning disabilities?

Position in space and order in time are fundamental functions of the central nervous system. Paul Schilder (1964) emphasized these concepts when he said, "we deal with the fundamental fact that human existence expresses itself in space and in time" (p. 22). In the development of perception, movement (i. e., temporal change) and form in space are both essential and "there is a constant interplay or integration between motor and sensory features which can never be separated" (L. A. Bender, 1958, p. 13). Lashley (1951) emphasized this interrelationship: "Spatial and temporal order appear to be almost interchangeable in cerebral action" and "temporal integrations are especially characteristic of human behavior and contribute as much as any single factor to man's intelligence" (Lashley, 1951, p. 114). Rozin (1976) emphasized the importance of spatial and temporal contexts in human memory: "Events occur in particular spatio temporal contexts, and they are stored in memory with respect to these contexts, so that the past has order, reality and coherence" (p. 15). Further, temporal sequencing structures a series of hierarchies of organization; language involves the ordering of letters and phonemes in a word, words in a sentence, sentences in a paragraph, and, finally, the sequences of logical thought and memory. The body image in space defines the space coordinates of the child's perceptions.

As they reviewed the varied clusters of neuropsychological deficits in children with reading disabilities, A. A. Silver and Hagin (1972b) were impressed that these deficits may be considered as problems with orientation in space and organization in time and that spatial and temporal organization were not age-appropriate in children with specific developmental learning disabilities. These problems may be seen in all combinations of visual, visual-motor, auditory, and body image perception. Thus, there is unity in the diverse deficits in the functions of the SLD child. That unity is disorientation in space and disorganization in time. A. A. Silver and Hagin suggested that, if these deficits could be detected in the 5-year-old as the child enters kindergarten, intervention may take place in the kindergarten and early elementary grades. In the visual discrimination and recall of asymmetric figures, spatial orientation could be tested; in auditory rote sequencing and in auditory memory, temporal organization may be seen; in right–left discrimination, praxis, and finger-gnosis, awareness of the body image in space may be determined; visual-motor function may combine visual perceptual skill and body image awareness (praxis).

These perceptual tasks were included in an intensive examination of all children in the first grade of a school in the Kips Bay area of New York City during the years 1969/70 and 1970/71 (A. A. Silver & Hagin, 1972b). This examination was an intensive individual study involving neurological, psychiatric, psychological, social, and educational examinations of 171 children. These examinations yielded data that detected, with only 1% false positives, the children who would fail in reading 2 years later, at the end of second grade. Factor analysis of the data in this study identified five factors accounting for 61% of the total variance:

    I. auditory-associative factor

   II. visual-perceptual body image factor

  III. psychiatric impariment

  IV. chronological age

   V. general intelligence as measured by the WPPSI

What tended to support the theory of deficit in spatial orientation and temporal organization is that factors I and II contained variables designed to assess these deficits. Further, they were independent of age, IQ, and psychiatric status, and they, together, accounted for 36.5% of the total variance.

Based on the auditory associative and the visual-body image tests with the highest loadings, a scanning battery of 10 subtests was constructed: visual-discrimination, recall of asymmetric figures, visuo-motor function, auditory discrimination, auditory rote sequencing, articulation, intermodal dictation, right–left discrimination, finger-gnosis, and praxis. This battery is designed to detect children whose skills of spatial orientation and temporal organization are immature. Immaturity in these skills may be used to predict reading failure.

A different conceptual approach was used by Jansky and De Hirsch (1972) in the development of their Predictive Screening Index: "The choice of tests . . . was based upon their prognostic usefulness in clinical practice, as well as predictive efficacy established in . . . past research" (p. 45). The following aspects of development were considered: perceptuo-motor organization, linguistic competence in both its receptive and expressive aspects, and readiness to cope with printed symbols. The heavy emphasis on linguistic tests derived from the authors' conviction that "the ability to comprehend and use oral language was of overwhelming importance in learning to read" (p. 45). The final predictive index of six tests was devised from multiple regression procedures based on data from a pool of 19 tests given to a heterogeneous sample of 347 kindergartners. The surviving tests included Letter Naming, Picture Naming, Gates Word Matching, Bender VMGT, Binet Sentence Memory, and Binet Word Recognition. Of these six, five appear to evaluate the use and comprehension of oral language.

The theoretical position of the remaining scanning tests used to predict reading or learning failure is essentially a pragmatic one—the use of probes that most closely resemble the skills that practical judgment says are related to learning. Two of these predictive tests are frequently used. The Meeting School Screening Test (Hainsworth & Siqueland, 1969) uses 15 subtests, 5 in each of three clusters: language, visual-perceptual-motor, and body image and motor control. Each cluster is composed of tests to determine how a child takes in information, processes it, and responds to it. The language cluster includes serial counting, phrases (nonsense syllables and auditory discrimination), articulation, sentence repetition, and verbal reasoning. The visual-perceptual-motor cluster includes copy of geometric designs, visual recognition of abstract forms, directions involving spatial orientation, draw-a-person, and writing name; the body image-motor control cluster includes hopping, clapping, directions, gross motor coordination, and control of hand movements. The Hainsworths have worked for 15 years to develop this predictive instrument, with norms on 2,500 children aged 2½ through 6½. A developmental age equivalent is available for each cluster.

The Slingerland (1968–1977) Screening Tests for Identifying Children with Specific Language Disability are also in frequent use. Three forms are available: Form A for grades 1 and early 2; Form B for grades 2 and early 3; Form C for grades 3 and early 4. Forms B and C are not really early predictive instruments, but rather diagnostic batteries for use after the child has failed to learn to read. Each form consists of eight subtests for the purpose of identifying (a) children with inadequate perceptual-motor, visual, auditory, and kinesthetic skills, (b) children with specific language disability, and (c) children who may need later educational support. Wiig's (1985) review in the *Ninth Mental Measurements Yearbook* cited assets in terms of the tests' simplicity of subtests and observable relationship to the school curriculum. Limitations were seen in the absence of norms to reflect national geographic, ethnic, and socioeconomic representation; the questionable reliability in scoring some items; and the lack of clarity in the definition of specific language disability.

It may be seen, therefore, that the theory underlying various predictive instruments is varied—in most, the tests sample skills presumed to resemble reading. If one examines the name of each subtest, there appears to be much redundancy and overlap between the skills measured by the tests. On closer look, however, the actual manner in which the subtest is given may be completely different among scanning tests so that, even though the identifying name of the test may be the same, the functions measured may be very varied. For example, in the Florida Kindergarten Screening Battery (Satz & Fletcher, 1982), a part of the test for finger-gnosis requires the child to recall and state the number of the stimulated finger. The *Search* battery deliberately eliminates oral language from its test of finger-gnosis.

Predictive Validity Considerations

To date, the scanning tests have largely been designed to predict success or failure in reading rather than to predict learning failure in general. A summary of technical aspects of 19 readiness and screening tests in print is found in Table 10-2. Each test is considered in terms of date of its standardization, the standardization sample, measures of reliability and validity, the manner in which norms are expressed, provision for local norms, and the nature of the predictions made by the test. This review will consider in more detail three of the scanning batteries for prediction of reading failure: the Florida Kindergarten Screening Battery (Satz & Fletcher, 1982), *Search* (A. A. Silver & Hagin, 1981), and the Predictive Screening Index (Jansky & De Hirsch, 1972). These instruments have had major research support: Satz et al. from NIMH, A. A. Silver and Hagin from the U.S. Office of Education,

Table 10-2 Technical Aspects of Readiness and Screening Tests

Test	Date of Standardization	Standardization Sample	Reliability Measures	Validity Measures	Nature of Norms	Provision for Local and/or Age Norms	Nature of Predictions and Cautions
Battelle Developmental Inventory (Newborg, Stock Wneck, Guidubaldi, & Svinicki, 1984)	1982–1983	800 children: newborn–7 years, 9 months; wide socioeconomic range	SE_M = 1.5–3.75; test-retest interrater reliability coefficients .90+; average reliability .81–.95	Content concurrent .78–.93	Standard scores		Identify children at risk for developmental handicaps; identify relative strengths and weaknesses of nonhandicapped children
Boehm Test of Basic Concepts (Boehm, 1969);—Revised (Boehm, 1986)	1968–1969	2,204 children: K–2; representing low, middle, and high socioeconomic status	Split half using Spearman-Brown formula: .81–.91; SE_M = 1.7–2.7	Content	Percentile by grade and SES level	Percentage passing analysis can be done for each classroom; separate norms for grades K–2	Identify children with poor conceptual knowledge. Caution: performance should be viewed in relation to rest of class
The Communication Screen: A pre-School Speech-Language Screening Tool (Striffler & Willig, 1981)	1981	133 children: 2 years, 10 months to 5 years, 9 months; free of hearing impairment, major developmental disabilities; English-speaking homes; wide socioeconomic, ethnic background	Test-retest .91–1.00 agreement	Predictive correlation with scores on PPVT (Form A) and ITPA (4 subtests)	Age at which items should be passed		Early identification of potential speech- and language-delayed children. Caution: gross screening only. Passing the screen does not

Test	Date	Sample	Reliability	Validity	Score type	Norms/Features	Purpose
							preclude subtle linguistic deficits that may appear later in development
Denver Developmental Screening Test (Frankenburg, Dodds, 1968–1981)	1967, 1970	1,036 children: 2 weeks–6 years, 4 months; normal population cross section of SES and race	Agreement among examiners 80–95%	Content validity	Percentage of children at each age passing each item	Age norms given	Detection of developmental delays in infants and preschool years
Developmental Indicators for the Assessment of Learning (DIAL) (Mardell & Goldenberg, 1975); also DIAL-R (Mardel-Czudnowski & Goldenberg, 1983)	1972	4,356 children: average age 4 years, 4 months; stratified for sex, race, and SES in Illinois	Test-retest (no coefficients reported)	Content concurrent (12 Head Start children given test battery—yielded 85.3% agreement); Congruent validity with PPVT; Predictive validity compared stanine scores on standardized tests 2 years after DIAL was administered, correlations ranged from .45 to .73	Percentage of children at each age passing each item		
Early Screening Inventory (Meisels & Wiske, 1983)	1983	465 children: 4 years, 6 months to 6 years; low-lower and middle-class urban predominantly white families	Inter-scorer reliability .80–.91 agreement; test-retest .82 total score (subscales below .80)	Concurrent with McCarthy Scales of Children's Abilities .73; Predictie validity (Metropolitan Readiness .83%)	Percentile	Local cut-off points can be established	Identify children "at risk" for academic problems in early school grades; best used for children aged 4½–5½

(continued)

Table 10-2 Technical Aspects of Readiness and Screening Tests (Continued)

Test	Date of Standardization	Standardization Sample	Reliability Measures	Validity Measures	Nature of Norms	Provision for Local and/or Age Norms	Nature of Predictions and Cautions
Florida Kindergarten Screening Battery (Satz & Fletcher, 1982)	1973, 1976	497 white males Alachua County, Florida, middle- or upper-class SES	Internal consistency (no test-retest)	Predictive-based battery and outcomes of later reading levels; cross-validity (74% accuracy)	Weighted scores divided into four reading categories	Recommended local norming studies	Early detection of reading disability
Gates-MacGinitie Reading Readiness (Gates & MacGinitie, 1968)	1966–1968	4,500 children: grades K & 1; selected by census data	Kuder-Richardson for each subtest, range = .63–.87	Prediction of 1st-grade reading achievement r = .59–.60 with Gates-MacGinitie, Primary A	Weighted scores, stanines, percentiles	Separate norms for kindergarten and 1st grade	Used to find deficit areas of individual children. Use caution in interpreting differences between subtest scores
The Lollipop Test: A Diagnostic Screening Test of School Readiness (Chew, 1981)	1981	69 children: mean age 5 years, 8 months; 50% male; 50% females; 50% white, 50% nonwhite; SES not given	Internal consistency Kuder Richardson 20 = .93	Concurrent validity with Metropolitan Readiness Test, r = .86; with teacher ratings, r = .58	No norms available; guide given to develop local norms	Provisions for developing local norms	Assess readiness for first grade focus on deficit areas
McCarthy Screening Test (McCarthy, 1978)	1972 McCarthy Scales (not separately standardized but based on subtests of McCarthy Scales of Children's Abilities)	N = 100 at each of 10 age levels 2½ years–8½ years; stratified sample	Internal consistency range .41–.80	Predictive validity moderate correlation with Metropolitan Readiness (Naglieri & Harrison, 1982)	Normed from McCarthy Scales percentiles		Identify children 4–6% at risk for educational failure Cautions: not clear how

Test (Author)	Year	Sample	Reliability	Validity	Scores	Uses/Comments
				MST & Peabody Individual Achievement (r = .66)		shorter length of MST affects norms; not standardized on 6-year-olds—norms for MTS interpolated
Meeting Street School Screening Test (Hainsworth & Siqueland, 1969)		494 children: grades K–1st, in East Providence schools	Test-retest (2–4 weeks): for total score r = .85, subtest range of r = .75–.85, Interrater r = .95	Concurrent with ITPA r = .77; with Frostig Predictive: MSST in K, r with readiness score = .66; r with achievement at end of 1st grade = .63; MSST in 1st grade, r with 1st grade achievement = .53; with 2nd grade achievement = .46	Scaled scores	Separate cut-offs for grades K, 1	Identify children likely to have learning disability; in diagnosis use with psychological and personality measures
Metropolitan Readiness Tests (Nuress & McGauvran, 1965)	1964	12,231 children: grade I throughout U.S.; geographically balanced	Odd-even for total score; above .90 SE_M 4.2–4.3 score points	Content based on research and professional judgment. Concurrent r = 80 with Murphy Durrell Readiness; r = .76; with Pintner-Cunningham Primary predictive range r = .58–.73; with Metropolitan Achievement Test Subtest, r = .52–	Percentiles, stanines, readiness, status	Readiness for 1st grade, forming reading groups. Caution: do not interpret individual subtests

(continued)

Table 10-2 Technical Aspects of Readiness and Screening Tests (Continued)

Test	Date of Standardization	Standardization Sample	Reliability Measures	Validity Measures	Nature of Norms	Provision for Local and/or Age Norms	Nature of Predictions and Cautions
Pre-Reading Screening Procedures (Slingerland, 1969)	1969	400 children: aged 5 years, 7 months to 7½ years; in Northwest and in Texas with IQ = 90		.75; with Stanford Achievement Test, Primary Subtests	Scores converted to one of five ratings ranging from high to low		Used with Metropolitan Readiness & Pintner-Cunningham to identify children with potential reading, writing, and spelling difficulty. Caution: note quality of errors
Preschool Screening System (Hainsworth & Hainsworth, 1980)	1980	947 children: in grades K–1; described by sex and ethnicity	Test-retest 2–3 weeks r = .83; SE_M 1.3; Intrarater r = .89; Interrater r = 71	Content: items written by educational specialists. Concurrent: significant chi-square with teacher rating of readiness	Quartiles with 1st quartile the cut-off for further evaluation and special services	Separate quartiles for K and 1	Identify children in need of further evaluation and special services
Psychoeducational Inventory of Basic Learning Experiences (Valett, 1968)					5-point rating scale to indicate strengths and weaknesses		Identify areas of disability that necessitate programming

Reading Aptitude Test (Monroe, 1935)		437 children: aged 5½–8½	Spearman-Brown (odd-even) $r = .87$	Predictive correlation of entering-1st-grade scores with end-of-1st-grade reading achievement (Gray Oral or Iota) $r = .75$	Percentile		Used for reading readiness and diagnosis
School Readiness Screening Test (Haines, Ames, & Gillespie, 1980)	1980	80 children: aged 3–4½; 50% male, 50% females; selected on basis of fathers' occupations to represent US census distribution of occupations of employed men; 92% white	None published by Gesell Institute	None published by Gesell Institute; done by various investigators	Developmental age		To determine readiness for kindergarten at ages 4½–5
Screening Index (Jansky & De Hirsch, 1972)		401 children from five public schools of New York City: sample described in terms of sex and ethnicity		Given in K, the index identified 75% of children who failed in reading at end of 2nd grade (2.2 or lower on Gates Advanced Primary or Gates-MacGinitie Paragraph Reading Test)	Converted scores based on multiple regression analysis	Children are ranked by score; Local cutting point = percentage of 2nd-grade reading failure plus 10%	Used to identify high risk for reading failure. Caution: intervention based on careful diagnostic study (diagnostic battery) should follow
Search: A Scanning Instrument for the Identification of Potential Learning Disability (A. A.	1975	2,319 kindergarten children: aged 5 years, 2 months to 6 years, 7 months; multiethnic	Internal consistency (Kuder-Richardson range .23–.95)	(1) Content validity, (2) Predictive validity, (a) (WRAT), (b) teachers estimates	Stanines based on age at 3-month intervals	Directions for calculations of local norms given	Identification of young children who are vulnerable to learning

(continued)

Table 10-2 Technical Aspects of Readiness and Screening Tests (Continued)

Test	Date of Standardization	Standardization Sample	Reliability Measures	Validity Measures	Nature of Norms	Provision for Local and/or Age Norms	Nature of Predictions and Cautions
Silver & Hagin, 1981—2nd ed.)		population; inner city, suburban, and rural	Test-retest stability coefficients range .28–.97; SE_M of total *Search* score = .89	of reading prediction performance; comparisons place 83% of one sample and 87% of a second sample on follow-up of reading achievement	(63–80 months); specialized demographic norms		disabilities; identify deficits in perceptual areas that form the basis for beginning reading skills

*This is an updated summary by Carol L. Frankel, graduate student in School of Psychology, Fordham University, of Table 17-2, compiled by R. Beecher and N. Goldfluss, in A. Benton & D. Pearl (Eds.) *Dyslexia: An Appraisal of Current Knowledge.* New York: Oxford (1978).

and Jansky and De Hirsch from the Health Research Council of the City of New York. All meet in greater or lesser degree the statistical guidelines of the American Psychological Association.

Florida Kindergarten Screening Battery The Florida Kindergarten Screening Battery (FKSB) is summarized by Fletcher and Satz (1984). Its predictive validity was based largely on a follow-up at the end of grades 2 and 5 of its initial standardization sample of 497 white kindergarten boys in Alachua County, Florida, first examined in 1970. The prediction results are based on a screening battery of four variables (PPVT, alphabet recitation, recognition discrimination, and the Beery Test of Visual-Motor Integration). Finger-gnosis, which is part of the final FKSB as published, is not included. At the end of grade 2, criterion measures included an estimate of the level of reading proficiency by the teachers (the Instructional Book Level), the Iota Word Recognition Test, and vocabulary recognition scores from the Gates-MacGinitie tests. The criterion measures identified four reading outcome groups: severe reading deficiency (12.1 months below expectancy), mild (10.7 months below expectancy), average (3.3 months above), and superior (16.3 months above). The grade equivalency levels, as stated in the manual for criterion measures, were used to place the reading outcome groups.

The battery identified 95 children of the 497 white kindergarten boys as high risk for learning difficulty: 48 of these did have severe reading retardation and 21 had mild reading retardation, but 26 were average readers. Of the 67 children predicted to be at mild risk, 10 had severe reading problems, 26 had mild reading problems, 29 were average readers, and 2 were superior readers. For the total number of children for whom failure was predicted (162), 105 had severe or mild reading problems (true positives); 55 of the children, however, were incorrectly identified (false positives), a false positive rate of 55/162 or 34%.

The battery predicted that 120 children were at low risk for reading failure. Of these 78 were average and 16 were superior readers, but 7 had severe and 19 had mild reading problems. The battery was most successful in the "no risk" prediction. Of the 135 "no risk" predictions, 123 were average or superior readers and 12 were severe or mild poor readers. For the total number of children for whom success was predicted (255), 217 were correctly identified (true negatives), while 38 were not (false negatives); a false negative rate of 16%. The predictions are thus more correct for identifying children who will succeed than in identifying those who will fail. The overall correct classification was 77%. The very high rate of false positives, however, causes concern. Assuming a base rate of reading disability at 20%, the ratio of positive to negative base rates does not exceed the ratio of false positives to true positives ($20/80 < 34/66$).

By the end of grade 5, although many of the children in the standardization sample had moved out of the county, an Instructional Book Level (teacher's evaluation of reading) was obtained on 442 of the original 497 boys. Other criterion measures were not available, so that the predictive utility is based only on the results of teachers' evaluations. In general, the predictive outcomes were similar to those of follow-up at the end of grade 2. The total hit rate was 72% with 36% false positives and 22% false negatives.

At the end of grade 6, a smaller subset (195) of the original sample, who still resided in Alachua County, were administered the Vocabulary Subtest of the Metropolitan Achievement Test. The results were similar to the grade 2 and grade 5 follow-up study. Cross-validation studies were done. One hundred eighty-one children, comprising the total number of white boys in the five largest elementary schools in the county, were tested at the beginning of their kindergarten year in 1971 and again at the end of grade 2 in 1973. This group had a higher socioeconomic level than the original standardization group because of the exclusion of six rural elementary schools. The trends noted in the standardization group persisted here. The overall hit rate was 74% with 33% false positives and 22% false negatives. A second cross-validation study of 28 black children (13 boys, 15 girls), and 104 white children (54 boys, 50 girls), originally tested at the beginning of their kindergarten year in 1974, were evaluated with individual reading measures at the end of grade 2. False negative rates were very respectable (6%), but false positives were very high at 41%.

As these data are reviewed, it is apparent, when base rates of reading are considered, that the FKSB cannot reliably predict which child in kindergarten will later fail in reading; and, except for the false negative rate found in the second cross-validation group, the ratio of false negatives to true negatives does not quite reach the level of statistical acceptance as described by Meehl and Rosen (1955).

Search The objectives of the A. A. Silver-Hagin research group at New York University were in some respects different from those of the group at the University of Florida. Historically, by the mid-1960s, the New York University group had already become aware of the importance of spatial orientation and temporal organization as indicators of the biological immaturity found in many children with learning disorders, and their follow-up studies at that time emphasized the tenacity with which such immaturity persisted into adulthood. In the late 1960s, their attention was focused on developing methods for intervention to train out these immaturities in children with reading disabilities, and by 1972, with a grant from the Carnegie Corporation, such intervention techniques were studied intensively. By 1970, however, it was clear that one did not have to wait for reading failure to occur, but that it was more desirable to find the potential reading failures in kindergarten and intervene with them, bringing their functions of spatial orientation and temporal organization to that point where they could learn to read with classroom educational methods. *Search and Teach* were the outgrowth of this preventive effort: *Search* not only to identify children who will fail, but also to guide the teachers in intervention, and *Teach* to describe intervention techniques that would train out the deficits found in *Search*.

The development of the predictive battery began with an intensive individual multidisciplinary examination over two successive years of every first-grade child in a public school in the Kips Bay section (East Side, 33rd Street) of New York City. The results of these examinations, described in A. A. Silver & Hagin (1972a), were able to predict reading failure by the end of second grade to within 1% false positives and 8% false negatives. These examinations included psychiatric, neurological, psychological, social, and educational evaluations. The examinations were obviously long and expensive, using skills not readily available to the public schools. A scanning instrument with the characteristics described earlier in this chapter was a solution. The 10-subtest content of *Search* was derived from factor analytic study of the variables of the intensive examinations. Standardization data were obtained from a sample of 2,319 children representing the entire kindergarten classes of 31 schools in four school districts. Of these, 1,165 children came from schools in lower Manhattan, New York City, a multiethnic, multilingual area with extremes of socioeconomic clustering. In addition, 410 children came from three largely middle class Brooklyn schools, and 744 came from 22 schools located in semi-rural and smalltown North Carolina. Eighty-seven percent of the standardization group was between 5 years, 6 months and 6 years, 8 months of age.

The base rate of reading failure of the entire group, approximately 30%, guided the cut-off point for each subtest. The resulting Total Score (the number of subtests in which the child exceeded the cut-off score) was used to predict success or failure in reading. It was found that approximately 10% of the entire standardization sample earned a total *Search* score of 0–3; approximately 30% earned between 0 and 5; 60% between 0 and 7, and, of course, 100% between 0 and 10. In accordance with the base rate of reading failure, a Total *Search* Score of 0–5 was said to predict reading failure, a total score of 6 and above predicted success.

The validity of this prediction was studied in five different samples of children who comprised the standardization group. Scores for 1,136 children, all representing intact groups tested over 3 successive years, were examined for false negatives. Four-hundred ninety-four of these children (Sample A) were examined at the end of grade 1; 386 (Sample B) at the end of grade 2, and 256 (Sample C) at the end of grade 3. Two additional samples (Sample D, $n = 40$, and Sample E, $n = 153$) were also available for false negative evaluation. Children were considered successful readers if they achieved reading scores on the reading section of the WRAT at, or above, actual grade placement; conversely, children earning reading scores below grade placement were considered to have failed.

The percentage of false negatives in the 1,136 children in Samples A, B, and C was 5%—that is, 5% of the children for whom *Search* predicted normal progress did not make the normal progress. In Sample D, the rate was 10%; in Sample E, 5%.

False positives were more difficult to obtain because the very fact of intervention is designed to invalidate the original predictions of failure. The *Search and Teach* program was set up to intervene with vulnerable children. Thus, by operating the full preventive program, access to data on false positives was limited.

It was possible to collect data, however, on false positives from two untreated samples. Sample D (*n* = 40) came from a school in which the scanning measure was administered, but intervention was not implemented because of budgetary constraints. Sample E (*n* = 153) came from three schools in which teacher time was available for only half the vulnerable children. In these schools (Sample E) the vulnerable children were randomly assigned to intervention and control conditions. Children who received intervention were excluded from the analysis of false positives. Of the children for whom failure was predicted, 3% of Sample D and 9% of Sample E succeeded in reading when tested at the end of second grade; this is a false positive rate of 3% and of 9%, respectively. Overall, 87% of the children in Sample D and 83% of those in Sample E were correctly placed by *Search*.

The predictive utility of *Search* was also assessed with a different set of measures. The object here was to relate the predictions of *Search* with those obtained from the intensive pentaxial clinical evaluation done with all vulnerable children in the diagnostic phase of the preventive program. One hundred-twenty-four children of a sample of 494 who were scanned with *Search* earned scores within the vulnerable range. Individual neurological, psychiatric, psychological, social, and educational evaluations found five of the children originally identified as vulnerable on *Search* to be normal learners, an incidence of false positives of approximately 4% for that sample. Using Bayes's theory of probability, the ratio of positive to negative base rates exceeded the ratio of false positive rate to valid positive rate; thus, the predictions of *Search* are more likely true than false.

It is noted that *Search* was devised to find children who in their kindergarten year were immature in their spatial orientation or temporal organization abilities. However, it was apparent that clinically the total score obtained on *Search* appeared to have some relationship with clinical evaluation. Accordingly, 171 children comprising all children in the first grades of two schools were given intensive, individual neurological and psychiatric examinations during the fall of their first grade. The clinical diagnosis was correlated with *Search* scores obtained in kindergarten (Table 10-2). It was found that of 22 children with a *Search* score of 0–3, 19 had neurological signs suggesting a diffuse, static encephalopathy, 2 were retarded, and 1 was chronically ill; of 37 children with *Search* scores of 4–5, 23 had a specific reading disability and 6 had neurological signs; of the 43 who scored 6–7, 17 had emotional or family problems, 16 had no deviations that could be found, 7 were SLD's, and 2 had neurological signs; of the 69 children who scored 8–10, 61 had no deviations that could be found, 5 had emotional or family problems, and 1 each had SLD or neurological signs. Thus, with a *Search* score of 0–3, signs of organicity and/or cognitive retardation may be expected; with 4–5, most suffer from specific learning disabilities; with 6–7, emotional or family problems may be expected; and with 8–10, no problems are the rule. Thus, not only was *Search* able to predict reading failure and reading success, but it could also identify children who needed neurological study and/or psychiatric evaluation.

The distribution of successes and failures on the subtests of *Search* offered a profile of the child's abilities and disabilities in those functions. This will be described in the next section of this chapter, providing a guide for educational intervention.

Predictive Screening Index The Predictive Screening Index of Jansky and De Hirsch (1972) stemmed from the pilot investigations of De Hirsch et al. (1966) in which 53 children were given a lengthy battery of 37 tests in the areas of motility, gross and fine motor patterning, body image, laterality, visual and auditory perception, receptive language, prereading, and estimates of behavioral style. This battery was roughly equivalent, except for the neurological-psychiatric evaluations, to the intensive individual exami-

Table 10-3 **Search *Scores and Clinical Diagnosis of All Children in First Grade of Two Schools Over Two Successive Years***

Total SEARCH Score	Chronic. Ill	General Ret.	Organ.	SLD	Emotional Family Problems	No Deviation	Cultural Difference	Total
8–10			1	1	5	61	1	69
6–7			2[a]	7	17	16	1	43
4–5	1		6	23	3	2	2	37
0–3	1	2	19					22
Total	2	2	28	31	25	79	4	171

[a]One child was in our nursery program and so had the benefit of intervention.

Key to Abbreviations

Chronic. Ill	=	Chronically Ill
General Ret.	=	General Retardation
Organ.	=	Deviation on Neurological Examination
SLD	=	Specific Language Disability

nations used by A. A. Silver and Hagin (1972b). The 10 best tests that differentiated between failing and passing readers were selected to constitute a Predictive Index. The Predictive Screening Index evolved from that preliminary study, with the final selection of items derived from stepwise multiple regression procedures. The test sample included a heterogeneous group of 347 kindergartners from five public schools in New York City. The original kindergarten sample included 217 boys and 184 girls; more than half were white, 42% were black, 5% were Puerto Rican, and 3 children were of oriental origin. At the end of second grade, a variety of reading and spelling tests were given, including the Roswell-Chall Auditory Blending Test, the Bryant Phonics Test, Gates Advanced Primary (1958 form) or Gates-MacGinitie Paragraph Reading Test, Primary B (1965 form), Grey Oral Reading Test (1955 or 1965 form), Fluency of Oral Reading, Guessing at Words from Context, and Written Spelling from the Metropolitan Achievement Test for grade 2, Oral Spelling from the Stamford Achievement Test for grades 1–2, Numbers and Letters Transposed and/or Reversed from the Metropolitan Achievement Test, and Number of Words in Written Composition and Percentage of Correctly Spelled Words in Composition. In addition, the effectiveness of teacher competence was noted and choice of textbooks used in the classroom was recorded. With all of these criterion measures, failure in reading was defined as a grade score of 2.2 or lower on the silent paragraph reading test.

Jansky and De Hirsch (1972) stated that "the sober finding should be reported at the outset: in the group of 347 children, 16 percent of the white girls, 23 percent of the white boys, 41 percent of the black girls, and a staggering 63 percent of the black boys had failed to learn to read by the end of second grade" (p. 53). These base rates, while sobering, are not at all surprising.

Overall, the Predictive Scanning Index identified 77% of the children who failed in reading at the end of second grade. There were 19% false positives. Considering only the black and Puerto Rican girls and boys and white boys, the test identified 79% of the failing readers, but had 22% false positives. With white girls ($n = 87$), there were 32% false positives. False negatives are not given.

The overall correct prediction of reading achievement thus ranges from 72% (FKSB) to 87% *(Search)*. As we have pointed out, however, the number of correct predictions is only one part of the problem. The number of incorrect predictions is equally important. To date, of the screening tests in print, the three described above have given more data on false positives and false negatives than the rest. It is clear that there are limits and problems in screening instruments. To maximize the validity of predictions, few test authors suggest that local norms be devised. When the sample numbers 100 or more children, this is feasible.

In spite of the problems of false positives and negatives, in criterion measures used for validation of predictions, and in the general lack of consensus as to the content of a predictive battery, well-studied scanning instruments are available. At this stage of our knowledge, the prediction, in kindergarten, of children who will later fail in reading is certainly possible. Prediction, however, must be followed by appropriate intervention.

EDUCATIONAL INTERVENTIONS FOR THE PREVENTION OF LEARNING DISORDERS

While successful programs have in common the basic elements of assessment, intervention, and evaluation components, the various programs are differentiated in their choice of objectives. This choice depends on the point in what Offord (1982) referred to as "the causal chain" that is selected for intervention. Intervention programs for the prevention of learning disorders usually represent one of two approaches. The first approach consists of efforts to promote social competency and cognitive strengths in broad aspects of functioning, on the assumption that children thus immunized will be less vulnerable to learning difficulties they may encounter in the course of their schooling. These approaches have been described as "enhancement efforts" (Lorion, Work, & Hightower, 1984). The second group of preventive approaches identifies precursors of learning disorders and seeks to target specific skills and competencies regarded as essential to successful learning during the school years. The review of preventive programs is organized in terms of these two kinds of approaches.

Experiments of Early Education

The experimental early intervention efforts of the 1960s are an excellent example of programs with enhancement objectives. These programs with their target population of poor, disadvantaged preschool children, their clearly defined interventions, and their long-term follow-up research culminating in the collaborative report of the Consortium for Longitudinal Studies (1983) meet all of Barclay's success criteria (p. 262 of this book). While each of the programs of the Consortium conducted research and evaluation in its own site, the pooled analyses of data across programs provided a remarkable opportunity for long-term follow-up of the results of early interventions. The independent analytic group, the Foundation for Human Services, describes the remarkable sample organized in 1975 as follows:

> *Every early intervention study that had specific curriculum, focused on children of low-income families, was completed prior to 1969, and had an original sample in excess of 100 subjects was invited to join the Consortium. The investigators of all but one of the 15 eligible studies accepted this invitation. Thus this is not a sample of*

preschool programs but rather is essentially the whole population of large-scale pre-school intervention studies conducted in the United States during the 1960's. Results of the pooled study are generalizable in the same sense a thorough literature review is generalizable—it summarizes the best available data. (Consortium for Longitudinal Studies, 1983, pp. 411–412)

This research opportunity was a fortunate one, for it permitted the evaluation of long-term effects of preschool programs that would ordinarily have required 15 years of longitudinal study to obtain. The social and political climate of the country has changed and with this change had gone the enthusiasm for the promise of early educational intervention. Results of most of the individual evaluation studies were mixed; the findings of a major evaluation attempt of Head Start (Westinghouse Learning Corporation, 1969) were unsatisfactory in terms of both content and methodology. In contrast, the marked increase in enrollments of children from all socioeconomic groups in early childhood programs suggested that many parents continued to believe in their value. The question of the efficacy of early education programs in enhancing the cognitive and affective functioning of children at risk for learning failure remained unanswered.

The participating research sites provided a valid substitute for prospective longitudinal research to answer this question. The members agreed to submit their original raw data to an independent group for analysis, to develop a common protocol for collecting follow-up data from their experimental and control subjects, and to collect the common follow-up data for independent analysis. It was expected also that individual projects in the Consortium would pursue individual research directions in terms of their unique objectives and resources; reports of these studies are included in the Consortium volume (1983). For the purposes of this paper, however, the results based on the pooled data are significant because they document common outcomes from diverse intervention projects, all with the goal of enhancing the cognitive and affective development of young children.

The major research question of the Consortium project was to assess the overall effectiveness of early education programs through primary, secondary, and meta-analysis of data on intelligence, educational achievement, achievement orientation, school competence, and occupational attainment from more than 1,000 subjects. As might be expected, the amount of attrition varied among the projects, with recovery rates ranging from 31 to 100%, with a median of 79%. However, when recovered subjects were compared with lost subjects on four background variables (pretest IQ score, mother's educational level, socioeconomic rating, and IQ score at age 6), the researches concluded that attrition was random and that program and control samples were equivalent.

Standardized tests and measures of social and educational adaptation were used to address the question of the impact of early education. The following conclusions were reached:

1. Developed abilities, as assessed from Binet, WISC, and WISC-R scores and achievement test scores, showed significant differences favoring the program participants up to 4 years after completion of the program. At grade 3, program participants performed better than controls on both mathematics and reading achievement tests when results for four projects were pooled. At grades 4 and 5, pooled results showed program graduates to be significantly higher in mathematics but not in reading. After grade 6, the experimental/control differences had generally disappeared. In the final follow-up, achievement test scores in reading and mathematics for program participants were generally within the 25–30 percentile range.

2. Early education also appeared to foster positive attitudes toward achievement, particularly for young women. Older program participants rated themselves higher on school performance than did controls without preschool experience.

3. Analysis of school competence on the basis of continuing school records showed substantial program effects on special education placement and ingrade retention. Robust differences were found between program participants and controls on the likelihood of meeting the basic educational requirement of their schools by avoiding special education placement or repetition of a grade.

4. A significant differential of 15% was found between the experimental and control groups in the likelihood of obtaining a high school diploma.

5. Overall there were no differential affects in terms of subgroups (IQ levels, sex, family structure) of children benefiting more than others from preschool training.

6. Higher level vocational aspirations, but not educational aspirations, were associated with preschool attendance.

7. Indirect effects, through the intervening variables of school competence and achievement orientation, were seen in employment status, educational attainment, and educational expectations for older program participants.

Lazar, who headed the Consortium group in Ithaca, concluded that "Independently and collectively, the major studies of early intervention with low income children reported in this volume clearly demonstrate positive effects of these programs throughout childhood and adolescent years" (Consortium for Longitudinal Studies, 1983, p. 461).

The Abecedarian project (Ramey & Campbell, 1984) at the Frank Porter Graham Child Development Center of the University of North Carolina is a more recent example of the enhancement approach in prevention. Since 1972 this experiment has been conducted to determine whether systematic early education can prevent retarded intellectual development in a sample of psychosocially defined high-risk children who, in the absence of apparent biological dysfunction, appear to have delayed intellectual development. This experiment aimed to modify environment and to provide preschool experiences to teach skills required for school success.

Unlike many of the earlier experiments, the Abecedarian program identified high-risk families and enrolled their children as infants in order to support optimal development through the preschool years. A high-risk index (based on parental education, family income, history of mental retardation, or school learning failure in the family) was used to identify four cohorts of 28 children each, with approximately half in the experimental group and half in the control group.

These children began coming to day care at age 6 weeks. Intensive, comprehensive services were provided with a staff/child ratio of 1/3 in the nursery and 1/6 in the preschool. Educational intervention was based on the Sparling and Lewis (1981) *Learning Games for the First Three Years* for the day care children and on conventional nursery school activities with a communications skills emphasis in the preschool. To equate the experimental and control groups for physical care, bottled formula, pediatric services, and social work services were provided for all participants, control as well as experimental.

Children were tested on appropriate individual cognitive scales twice a year. Statistically significant differences favoring the educational intervention group appeared on the Bayley at age 1½, on the Stanford-Binet at ages 2, 3, and 4, and on the McCarthy Scales at ages 3½ and 4½. The treatment effect was computed to be approximately 1 standard deviation at ages 2 through 4 years, with control children six times more likely to earn scores within the retarded ranges. These results are impressive. The final assessment of the project awaits data from school follow-up with these children.

The Brookline Early Educational Project (BEEP) is another long-term research effort that follows the enhancement approach. Begun in 1972, the program has sought answers to question of the feasibility of public school–based early education programs. Evaluation data collected as the youngsters reached second grade have been presented by Pierson, Walker, and Tivnan (1983). When enrollment closed in October 1974, 285 families from Brookline and adjoining areas of Boston had responded to the program's invitation for participation as the pilot group. Diverse background characteristics were represented in terms of ethnicity, primary language, maternal age and education, and family structure. Three program components were provided in a special center near the Brookline-Boston boundary: parent education and support, diagnostic monitoring, and educational programs for children.

Families were randomly assigned to one of the three levels of program cost and intensity: (a) high intensity—the most expensive level (projected at $1,200 per child per year) involved frequent home visits, meetings, and limited child care, each scheduled at least once every 4 weeks; (b) moderate intensity—($800) involved in the same offerings with less frequent appointments scheduled every 6 weeks; (c) low intensity—the least expensive level ($400) involved no outreach through home visits, meetings, or child care, but offered information and support at the BEEP Center, only at the request of the parents. Diagnostic examinations were provided in cooperation with a local medical center, but the purpose of these examinations was for research and monitoring purposes, rather than to provide primary medical care. Beginning at age 2, weekly play groups were held for the children. At ages 3 and 4, BEEP participants were offered a daily morning prekindergarten program in which the curriculum was influenced by the High/Scope Progarm (M. Hohman, Banet, & Weikart, 1979). The emphasis in this program is on "structuring space and materials to afford each child an opportunity to develop a sense of effectiveness, to explore concepts, and to develop mastery and social skills essential for competencies in school."

Evaluation for the results of BEEP has provided multiviewpoint (teacher, parent, independent observer) and multitimepoint data. Results at the end of second grade reflect the children's functioning 3 years after the termination of BEEP services. Attrition rate was approximately 10% per year, with 169 of the original 285 families available for follow-up. A comparison group randomly selected and representative in terms of relevant background variables was observed in second-grade classrooms along with program participants for six, 10-minute intervals by independent observers who were unaware of the group identity of the children. Results of these evaluations indicated that:

1. A significantly smaller percentage of BEEP participants (14.2%) than comparison children (28.4%) were rated by observers as "having difficulty" with classroom learning behaviors such as working independently, following directions, resisting distractions, completing work, and getting along with other children.

2. Assessment of reading levels showed that 19.3% of the BEEP participants and 32% of the comparison children were not decoding and comprehending stories at the high second-grade level, their current grade placement.

3. When program cost levels were related to level of parents' education, a direct relationship between level of services and what was regarded

as adequate reading performance was found with well-educated families; few children of well-educated parents were not reading at grade level.

4. In contrast, with children whose parents were not well educated, high levels of outreach were thought to be necessary. In the program level group in which parents were required to initiate contacts for services, there were no significant differences in the adequacy of reading between BEEP children and the comparison group at the second grade.

The experimenter concluded on this basis "that for families who are not highly educated, greater outreach was required in order to produce lasting effects" (M. Pierson et al., 1983).

The assumption of causal relationship between the level of services to parents and reading achievement appears to go beyond the available data. An alternative hypothesis might be that the children's lack of school progress is associated with their parent's lack of educational skills, which in turn made it difficult for them to initiate requests for services from BEEP. More careful analysis of intervening variables or possibly path analysis similar to that done in the pooled analyses of the Consortium for Longitudinal Studies (1983, pp. 454–455) would appear to be necessary to support the conclusion of a direct relationship between services to parents and reading achievement.

It would also appear that the measures of reading outcomes are gross in view of the other aspects of BEEP's experimental design and the questions for which answers were sought. To regard grade level achievement in reading as "adequate" appears to be setting rather limited goals for the children of well-educated parents. Furthermore, the adequate/inadequate dichotomy does not take into account the range of achievement one can expect by second grade in any normally distributed group of children.

To summarize, early education programs directed toward enhancement of psychosocial competencies have shown themselves to be effective in realizing these objectives. In contrast to comparable control youngsters, a high proportion of program graduates avoid the need for special education placement or for repetition of grades in school and earn fewer scores within the retarded ranges on intelligence tests. They reflect positive attitudes toward education, have a greater likelihood of graduating from high school, and demonstrate more productive behaviors in the classroom. Older program graduates reflect the indirect effects of greater educational and social competency in improved vocational expectations and status. However, these programs seem less effective in producing and maintaining specific educational skills in reading and to a lesser extent in mathematics in about 20% of program participants. This percentage is an interesting one in that it corresponds to the usual incidence estimates of specific learning disability. One is tempted to speculate whether this group may be composed of learning disabled youngsters who require more specific interventions for their special learning problems than enhancement programs provide.

Administrative Strategies to Prevent Learning Disorders

A wide variety of administrative arrangements and innovative programs has been recommended for the prevention of learning disabilities. Unlike the enhancement approaches described in the previous section, these modifications are short-lived and often fall victims to the winds of educational change before clear-cut evaluation of their effectiveness can be accomplished. Preventive intervention programs are particularly vulnerable because of their lack of statutory funding and consequent dependence on administrative whim or experimental funds for survival. These conditions limit the number of preventive interventions suitable for review for the purposes of this paper. Despite these limitations, however, 14 programs provide sufficient data for some analysis of the efficacy of these models.

Departures from the traditional lockstep organization of school grades have been proposed as educational provisions for kindergartners who seem destined to fail in conventional first-grade programs. The pre–first-grade transition class has been proposed by a number of investigators (for instance, De Hirsch et al., 1966) but efficacy data were not provided. More recently, Zenski (1983) compared the language, reading, and mathematics achievement of children who had been placed in a transition class prior to first grade with that of children who had repeated first grade when both groups of children were enrolled in second grade. No significant differences were found between the two groups in any of the achievement measures at the end of second grade. However, Zenski noted that the transition class experiences had provided little practice with the academic skills on which the evaluation was based and speculated whether more definitive results might have been found if more time had passed between the experimental procedures and the evaluation.

A retrospective evaluation of a junior first grade by Kilby (1983) produced very different results from those of Zenski's research. This ex post facto study compared academic achievement and social adjustment in grades 4 through 8 for children who had participated in a junior first grade following their kindergarten year. The achievement and adjustment of the experimental children were more favorable than those of comparable classmates. It was also found that there were fewer referrals to learning disability programs and fewer grade repetitions in the primary grades for program participants. These results led to the conclusion that "the intensive reading instruction in the junior first grade may have had a positive and long term effect" (Kilby, 1983).

Expansion of kindergarten offerings has also been suggested, although mixed results have been reported. Weissman (1985) in a study of the impact of early intervention on special education students' readiness for mainstreaming found that expanded pre–first-grade programs, whether they involved regular education or special education programs, did not discriminate successful from unsuccessful mainstream adjustment. Disappointingly, the socioeconomic level of the child's parents, regardless of the kind of educational intervention, was most closely associated with outcomes.

In contrast, E. Anderson (1984) reported increased educational effectiveness associated with the full-day (as opposed to the half-day) kindergarten. The full-day program resulted in an increase of instructional time from 3 to 4½ hours. The programs in both half-day and full-day kindergartens drew upon similar curriculum content, with the major differences between the classrooms consisting of increased engaged instructional time in the full-day programs. Classrooms were matched in terms of children's ages, socioeconomic levels, sex, and entry level skills on a kindergarten skills inventory. Teachers in the full-day program had the services of volunteer mothers as classroom aides, while the half-day kindergarten teachers had the services of paid aides. Results of the Stanford Early School Achievement Test administered at the end of kindergarten indicated significantly higher scores for the full-day kindergartners in skills, knowledge, and understandings in reading and mathematics. Parental support of the full-day program was high and may have influenced ratings that indicated greater self-confidence, independence, and ability to play cooperatively associated with the experimental program.

Another kind of administrative provision suggested to prevent learning failure is grade placement on the basis of individual patterns of development. This approach is based on the work on school readiness done at the Gesell Institute in New Haven, Connecticut by Ilg and Ames (1965). Their test of school readiness consists of a series of clinical tasks (block construction, copy forms, interview questions, writing of names and numbers, Incomplete Man Test, and assessment of gross motor control). While the test has been normed and widely used, little validation data beyond case studies has been presented. One recent study (Wood, Powell, & Knight, 1984) examined the predictive validity of the Gesell Readiness Screening Test in a sample of 84 kindergartners by using referral for special needs evaluation during kindergarten as the criterion for failure. According to Wood et al., Developmental Age scores on the Gesell Readiness Screening Test were significantly related to the criterion, but the variations in the percentages of false negatives and false positives with only slight changes in the cut-off scores were great enough to raise questions about the basic statistical characteristics of the measure. Nevertheless, this measure has had considerable use by school personnel in making decisions for the grade placement of children. In some cases use of the test has resulted in the decision to postpone school admission even though the child had reached the legal age for school entrance.

May and Welch (1984) examined the application of the developmental placement approach as an administrative provision for preventing learning disabilities. They chose a developmental age cut-off score of 4½ years as indicating an "unready child" who will not succeed in kindergarten and will find it stressful. The developmental age concept maintains that 50% of all school problems could be prevented or remedied by placement in terms of developmental ages. Problems later diagnosed as emotional disturbance, learning disability, minimal brain dysfunction, and underachievement are said to result from children's being asked to perform at levels for which they are not developmentally ready (May & Welch, 1984). This approach does not propose a curriculum, but suggests that children take another year to mature in order to handle the regular school offerings.

This theory opposes early intervention based on a child's needs and assumes that waiting a year in a less demanding environment will make a child ready for success in the conventional program. May and Welch tested the outcomes of predictions made on 222 children in grades 2 through 6 of a suburban New York school district by locating children for whom the developmental ages they had earned as kindergartners placed them in one of three groups: (a) children earning developmental age scores below 4½ years whose parents accepted the recommendation to "buy a year" (i. e., to postpone kindergarten entrance), (b) children earning developmental age scores below 4½ but whose parents did not accept the recommendation to buy a year and who, according to the theory were "overplaced," and (c) children whose developmental age scores were greater than 4½ and who were placed according to their chronological ages.

The investigators found no significant differences among the three groups in numbers of referrals for special education placement, speech and language services, remedial services in reading or mathematics, or counseling. Two children from each of the three groups had been recommended to repeat a grade and a few more of the "buy a year" group (significant at .05 level) had been referred to adaptive motor and resource room programs. May and Welch concluded that these results do not show greater difficulties for the overplaced group and that maturation alone will not make a child ready for schooling. These data are congruent with our own.

These studies suggest that administrative arrangements by themselves do not hold much promise for the prevention of learning disabilities. The exceptions may be in modifications that increase engaged time (as in the full-day kindergarten) to the extent that a better match between the child's educational needs and the educational program takes place.

Projects for the Prevention of Learning Disabilities

The design of most successful intervention projects is based on an underlying rationale that focuses on the nature of the tasks to be learned and the specific links in the causal chain that the intervention will address. As might be expected, rationales differ in terms of the professional orientation of the investigator and the age of the population to be served. Variations are great because of complexities in the nature of the learning disability.

Skarda (1974) and her associates viewed learning disabilities in terms of delays in language development. Thus communication skills became the focus of their model preventive program whose objective was to develop life-oriented language skills in language delayed children. This group provided a 2-year early oral language intervention program in public schools in Wisconsin. Complex case finding procedures involved referrals, prekindergarten screening, individual needs assessment through parent interviews, observation of children in naturalistic settings, and multidisciplinary team evaluations. Interventions involved "structuring the auditory environment, reinforcing essential behaviors, and fostering home-school communication" (Skarda, 1974). Curricular emphasis was on art, physical movement, and music activities, with extensive use of audiovisual aids. Evaluations based on parent interviews, language tests, and case studies provided evidence that language functions were improved. However, follow-up data on the relationship of these gains in terms of later school achievement is not available.

R. S. Weiss (1980) also designed a preventive project with language as a central focus. INREAL (Inclass Reactive Language), located in Colorado, served children of hispanic background who had limited English proficiency (LEP). The objectives of this project were to increase language development of LEP children and to prevent later language-related learning problems. Intervention consisted of "non-stigmatizing methods using inclass service delivery, thus redefining the role of the speech-language pathologist" (R. S. Weiss, 1980). Evaluation using matched INREAL and control groups showed that the experimental program effected highly significant improvement in language skills. A follow-up study 3 years after the conclusion of the original project ended showed that INREAL participants needed fewer remedial services (remedial reading or speech-language services) and were less likely than the control subjects to be retained in grade. A cost effectiveness study showed that an original investment of $175 per pupil in INREAL produced savings of $1,283.76 to $3,073.16 that might have been required for special services to program participants.

The sequencing and timing of educational activities is another preventive focus proposed by some investigators (Ainscow & Tweddle, 1979; G. A. Lindsay & Wedell, 1982; Stott, 1974). These writers are critical of predictive measures and diagnostic procedures as offering little guidance for educational intervention. They argue that learning disabilities result from unproductive learning styles and strategies rather than from some inherent disability. This educationally-focused intervention model would use classroom-based screening by the teacher, followed by the setting of appropriate objectives for the children identified as having problems at that time. According to Ainscow and Tweddle (1979), there is no implicit assumption that these children will fail academically in 1 or 2 years' time; the focus is on present skills, using current evidence of functioning. This approach requires considerable training of teachers so that they can task analyze educational content into smaller steps, constituting a more detailed sequence of specific educational objectives. Such objectives provide criteria for on-going monitoring of children's progress. The sequence of objectives used to monitor the child's acquisition of basic skills also serves as a means of tracing the child's performance back to establish a starting point for modifying the teaching.

It is unfortunate that, despite Lindsay and Wedell's critical appraisal of most early identification efforts on both substantive and statistical grounds, they have not provided research evidence of the efficacy of the objectives approach to prevention. The assumption that all children can be helped to cope with the regular instructional program if teachers learn to monitor their performance appropriately may be questionable. At least in the case of some children, this approach would merely defer provision of services until the child has failed, thus making the matter one of remediation rather than prevention.

While this approach has value in that it places responsibility for educational management with the classroom teacher, it may expect higher level planning skills in sequencing objectives than many teachers are able to offer, given the constraints of time and class enrollments that prevail in the typical school. To a great extent the efficacy of the objectives approach to prevention would depend upon the quality of implementation of the model. In turn, the quality of implementation would depend upon the professional skills, educational resources, time, and level of motivation of the classroom teacher.

The importance of quality of implementation of program models is illustrated in the case of a preventive program designed and validated in a school district in Illinois. Evaluation data presented to the Joint Dissemination Review Panel of the U.S. Office of Education and the National Institute of Education met the standards of educational impact, replicability, and cost effectiveness that qualified the project for membership in the National Diffusion Network. Patrick, Kimball, and Crawford (1984) reported the disastrous replication of this highly successful original project. Their evaluation of the replication in 68 schools of a second school district in another state found no significant differences in achievement test scores for schools where the program had operated and those in which it had not. In fact, a small negative correlation was found between the number of minutes of treatment in the program and achievement test scores. These strange results prompted the evaluators to study the replication process. They surveyed implementation in the schools in which the program operated and found that the extent and quality of implementation varied considerably. Only 78% of the teachers in these schools reported knowing how to implement the experimental program, 63% were able to implement the program, 48% used the one-to-one or small group structure, and 49% used the modality centers that were part of the design. The evaluators concluded that there was no way to know if the fully implemented program was effective from the data they elicited in their study. Thus, even well-designed models may fail to be effective in settings that do not assure adequate quality in their implementation.

Preventive approaches that draw upon the neuropsychological subskills basic to reading have engaged the attention of a number of investigators and clinicians. Serwer (1971) designed an experiment that contrasted these intervention strategies with conventional classroom approaches involving the direct teaching of skills as advocated by the skills-oriented approaches. Sixty-two first-graders identified as being at risk for later learning difficulties were assigned to either of two special classes or were distributed through regular first-grade classes. Experimental treatments consisted of direct teaching of reading (using supplementary phonics and language experience activities, indirect teaching (perceptual-motor training), combined direct and indirect teaching approaches, and control condition (classroom instruction using a basal reader approach). Phase I of the program involved group instruction within treatment conditions, and Phase II involved individualized instruction within the same treatment approaches. Major findings were that low but statistically significant correlations between treatment method and posttest achievement existed: The indirect and combined treatment groups showed better achievement than the direct and control groups. Serwer commented that results may have been affected by the limited age range in the group and the limited intervention time spent on the intervention conditions (½ hour per day). Although research designed to contrast differing intervention approaches is needed, very few studies like Serwer's are reported. This lack of definitive studies results from a number of conditions, including difficulties in maintaining experimental treatments uncontaminated in the natural atmosphere of the classroom, the reluctance to withhold intervention in order to preserve a control condition, and the lack of commitment of resources and funding for experimental research in schools.

These barriers to development of preventive interventions were overcome in a fortunate collaboration between a learning disorders unit in a medical school department of psychiatry and an urban school district in an interdisciplinary program using the *Search and Teach* model. Based on work begun in 1969, this model has attempted to prevent learning disabilities and their emotional consequences through an interdisciplinary, school-based model that locates children vulnerable to learning failure and provides diagnosis and appropriate educational and clinical intervention in the child's own school.

The first step in the preventive program is to locate children vulnerable to learning failure. This is done by means of the scanning test, *Search* (A. A. Silver & Hagin, 1981). This test is based on the rationale that delays in the acquisition of skills in spatial orientation and temporal organization are marker variables for learning failure in young children. These delays may appear in various combinations, and each child may be expected to have a unique pattern of strengths and needs. By surveying all the children in the kindergarten with *Search*, the program attempts to identify children who are vulnerable to learning failure but who have not yet failed.

Search evolved from clinical experience with children with learning problems, culminating in intensive clinical examinations of all first-graders at an elementary school in Manhattan for two successive years, during which time parameters of psychiatric, neurological, psychological, and educational functioning relevant to school learning were studied (A. A. Silver & Hagin, 1972b). Factor analysis of these data defined *Search* components and located the most powerful measures of each component. Statistical characteristics of the test are described in detail in the test manual. Relevant here is the test-retest reliability (.80) and the standard error of measurement of the total *Search* score (.89 of a raw score unit). The manual also describes predictive validity studies of *Search* against educational and clinical criteria. Prediction-performance comparisons show rates of 5–10% false negatives and 1–9% false positives.

The second step in implementing the preventive model is to provide diagnostic examinations for children identified on *Search*. These diagnostic services were the responsibility of the clinical staff of the learning disorders unit, who represented the disciplines of psychiatry, psychology, and special education. Results of *Search* and the diagnostic examinations were pooled in case conferences attended by the school and unit staffs in order to clarify the learning needs of individual children and to plan appropriate intervention strategies.

The third element of the preventive program is provision of educational intervention. These activities are designed in *Teach* (Hagin, Silver, & Kreeger, 1976)—a prescriptive approach designed to build foundation skills necessary for progress in reading and the language arts. It provides directed activities to teach accuracy of perception within single modalities and intermodal skills to relate the input of several modalities. The scanning and diagnostic data are used to set teaching priorities and to formulate individual teaching plans. Educational plans are implemented through tasks selected from *Teach*. These tasks proceed through three stages of increasing complexity: matching, copying, and recall. Practice continues until mastery criteria appropriate for each task have been reached. Teaching logs, completed with the child during *Recap* at the end of each teaching session, record progress with the intervention plans.

All services were provided in classrooms located in the child's own school. Educational intervention was provided by Board of Education teachers and educational assistants under the supervision of the Learning Disorders Unit staff. Children were taught individually or in small groups three to five times a week in sessions lasting 30 minutes. Although services are structured as a 2-year program for kindergarten and first grade, or for first and second grades, the children's progress is monitored through the elementary grades.

The model was validated by the Joint Dissemination Review Panel of the U.S. Office of Education on the basis of data on its educational impact, replicability, and cost effectiveness. The evaluation provided for a control group design with two consecutive groups, children born in 1970 (BD 1970) and in 1971 (BD 1971) as subjects. In the BD 1970 group ($n = 126$) children were randomly assigned to either intervention or no-treatment control groups. For BD 1971 ($n = 91$) children were assigned to one of two cohorts varying in duration of intervention. Cohort 1 received intervention for the entire school year; Cohort 2 received intervention only during the second half of the school year. This design permitted comparison of perceptual status (assessed by retesting on *Search*) and reading skills, including oral reading, word attack, and reading comprehension.

Results of the analyses of variance for the BD 1970 group showed that the intervention group made significant gains relative to equally vulnerable controls on the *Search* retest, $F(1,124) = 31.52$, $p < .0001$; in word recognition, $F(1,124) = 7.58$, $p < .01$; and in word attack, $F(1,124) = 5.51$, $p < .02$ at the end of first grade. Data at the end of second grade produced even more striking contrasts between the intervention and control groups in the results with oral reading and word attack measures. In addition, reading comprehension scores for the intervention group were significantly different from those of controls $F(1,76) = 25.18$, $p < .001$).

For BD 1971, children were assigned to one of two cohorts varying in duration of intervention. This design permitted comparison of perceptual and reading skills at the end of first grade. Data were analyzed by ancova, which statistically equated the groups for initial differences in perception and WPPSI verbal IQs by using these measures as covariates. Cohort 1 exceeded Cohort 2 on *Search* retest and all reading measures. These contrasts were less striking than comparisons for the BD 1970 first-graders, when a true no-treatment control group was possible, but were nevertheless statistically significant: *Search*, $F(1,89 = 12.339$ $p < .05$; word identification, $F(1,89) = 5.54$, $p < .02$; word attack, $F(1,89) = 3.96$ $p < .05$. At the end of second grade the differences between the cohorts continued to be significant on the word recognition measures and on reading comprehension, $F(1,52) = 4.51$ $p < .038$). These educational gains have also been associated with signs of normal behavioral adjustment in the upper elementary grades (A. A. Silver, Hagin, & Beecher, 1981) and a lowering of the incidence of nonpromotion from a rate as high as 12–17% to 1–3% over the 12 years in which the preventive program operated (Hagin, 1984).

CURRENT NEEDS

The state of the art of preventive interventions with learning disabilities is not as bleak as first impressions of the research literature may suggest. While more gaps exist in practice than in theory, there are lessons to be learned from work that has already been done in the field:

1. Both legal and theoretical foundations for prevention of learning disabilities already exist.
2. A variety of methods for the identification of vulnerable children have been developed and researched.
3. The values of early education have been demonstrated through careful analysis of extant data from the early experimental projects of the 1960s. The enhanced social adjustment and increased educational competence of the program participants over comparison groups was reflected in lower rates of nonpromotion, referrals for special education, and noncompletion of high school. However, the atypical learners may require special intervention projects addressed specifically to learning disabilities.
4. A number of administrative provisions have been proposed as preventive interventions. However, results of implementation of these innovations have been mixed. The most promising are those that provide increased amounts of quality instructional time.
5. Interventions with a variety of program emphases have been designed: communication skills, sequencing of educational objectives, and neuropsychological. Research aimed at comparing the relative merits of each of the emphases will probably be less useful and may result in further fragmentation of an already divided field. A more constructive approach would relate assessment to intervention approaches so that more appropriate matching of individuals with the programs most suitable for their needs could be made.

To best serve the prevention of learning disorders, research and training should be directed toward refining early identification and diagnostic methods so that they can be closely related to educational intervention in the natural setting of the school. The interdisciplinary collaboration involved in such work would provide a rich source of data for the improvement of the education of young children.

SUMMARY

Heterogeneity in the population of the learning disabled, lack of professional consensus on a definition of "learning disabilities," and the enormous financial and professional demands in treating children who have already failed in learning all have combined to set a low priority for programs for the prevention of learning disorders. Yet there are programs that meet Barclay's criteria. The technology exists to identify children for whom learning failure is predicted, as they enter kindergarten; a set of intervention procedures to prevent that failure is available, and follow-up studies have documented the success of such preventive programs. While it is not yet feasible to *eliminate* the long list of factors that place the child at risk for learning disorders, it is possible to identify children in whom the primary risk factors have left a mark on the function of the central nervous system such that the psychoneurological functions involved in learning are impaired. We can detect the *beginnings* of the defects in central processing that are considered basic to learning; we can identify the defects by age 5, years before the child has failed in learning. Such identification programs should be able to accurately predict learning failure and learning success, that in the process, the incidence of false positives is negligible, and false negatives minimal and that the identifying instrument meets the standards for educational and psychological testing as described by the American Psychological Association. Ideally, the predictive instrument should be based on a rational framework that offers conceptual unity with the learning process and can guide the intervention procedures. Three such predictive tests (the Florida Longitudinal Project, *Search,* and the Predictive Screening Index) are discussed in detail and the technical aspects of 19 screening tests in print are listed in Table 10-2. The correct prediction of reading achievement in these tests ranges from 72 to 87%, with the best false positive results in the 3–9% range, the best false negative around 10%. Although there are problems in numbers of false negatives and false positives, in criterion measures used for validation, and in a general lack of consensus as to the content of the predictive battery, well-studied instruments are available.

Intervention programs offer two general approaches: efforts to promote social competency and cognitive strength (enhancement) and efforts to target specific skills and competencies considered essential to successful learning. Major studies of early intervention with low-income children (in Head Start programs) demonstrate positive effects throughout childhood and early adolescence, fostering positive attitudes for achievement and avoiding special education placement or repetition of a grade and long-term effects in employment and educational attainment. Although achievement test scores favored participants in these programs, differences between experimental and control groups disappeared after grade 6. More impressive results were attained in other preschool programs.

A variety of administrative strategies—pre–first-grade transition class, junior first grade, and expansion of the kindergarten day from half day to full day—have been tried. Results suggest that intensive reading instruction in the "junior" first grade and the expanded kindergarten day were most effective, resulting in fewer referrals to learning disability programs. An alternative approach, that of not permitting entry into kindergarten unless the child has a developmental age of 4½ years, has not changed the numbers of children referred for special education, speech and language services, remedial math or reading and counseling.

Most successful intervention projects focus on the nature of the specific skills and abilities considered essential to successful learning. Just what these skills are is a matter of professional debate, and programs vary accordingly. Whatever the approach, the professional skill, educational resources, time and level of motivation of the classroom teacher, and the problems of each child are important in determining outcome. A significant study found intervention based on "indirect" teaching (i. e., perceptual training) was more effective than direct teaching of reading in reading achievement of first-graders identified as being at risk for learning disorders. An effective intervention program based on providing directed activities to teach accuracy of the perceptual dysfunction found in a screening test is described.

PART THREE

CLINICAL PATTERNS IN DISORDERS OF LEARNING

CHAPTER ELEVEN

Specific Language Disability

Among the children with learning disorders, the most prevalent in the classroom are those with specific language disability. This group has been described as having developmental dyslexia (Critchley, 1964), strephosymbolia (Orton, 1928, 1937/1989), congenital word blindness (Hinshelwood, 1895, 1896, 1900, 1907, 1917), congenital auditory imperception or congenital word deafness (Worcester-Drought & Allen, 1929), and psychoneurological learning disability (Myklebust, 1968; Myklebust & Boshes, 1960). Specific language disability is equivalent to the primary reading (learning) disability of Rabinovitch (1968; Rabinovitch et al., 1954), the pure dyslexia of Denckla (1978), and the specific reading retardation of Rutter (1978a, 1978b). The term minimal brain dysfunction (Clements, 1966) has also been used to include this group, but, because of its imprecise definition and its implication of brain pathology, that term has outlived its usefulness.

We have chosen to use *specific language disability* (see Table 2.1) because it focuses on the *one* major area of defect, namely language, and because it does not have etiological implications, which, at this point, are a matter of speculation. The term "language" is used here in its broadest sense: the processing of symbols from all modalities, including decoding, association, retention, retrieval, and expression. In educational terms, this includes the language sequence of listening, speaking, reading, handwriting, spelling, composition, and mathematical concepts. This chapter describes children with specific language disability, summarizes relevant research in neuropsychology, neurophysiology, genetics, and neuropathology, and outlines our experiences in clinical management.

CHARACTERISTICS OF CHILDREN WITH SPECIFIC LANGUAGE DISABILITY

The essence of the problem of specific language disability lies with the ability to deal with symbolic formulation and expression. For example, parents report that the acquisition of language may be delayed and that as beginning readers children with specific language disability may not remember what words look like—they may not remember the appearance of a word from two lines before. The process of word analysis is learned with difficulty and may remain so laborious a task that it interferes with fluent reading and comprehension. In later childhood, the syntax of language does not become automatic: SLD children may fail to sense the meter and rhyme of poetry and they have difficulty organizing information in sequential fashion in content subjects. Even as accomplished adults, associative problems may be found in metalinguistic difficulties. Such discrepancies are not due to any of the other etiological factors listed in Table 2–1. These children are not hyperactive or clumsy and they do not have abnormal findings on classical neurological examination, are not mentally retarded, and do not have defects in sensory acuity related to learning failure. Although their emotional state may be reactive to their learning disabilities, personality factors are not basic causes of these difficulties. In fact, parents of these children have been heard to report, "He was such a nice child before he went to school."

It is recognized, of course, that children with specific language disability may indeed have attention deficit disorder, hyperactivity, or motor clumsiness and that, in most discussions of learning disability, these motor and attentional problems are considered part of the learning disability. In this book, however, we do not consider attention deficit disorder or motor clumsiness as part of the SLD syndrome. In this course, we agree with the designation, "dyslexia pure," which Denckla (1978) gave to the child who corresponds to our specific language disability group. Our position is also supported by Witelson (1976) who considered the SLD child "to be a different type of learning-impaired child, than those described as "hyperactive" or as having "minimal brain dysfunction" (p. 239).

We make this distinction to identify a group that is as homogeneous as our current knowledge permits. Certainly there are children who are hyperactive, who have attention deficits, and have problems with learning but who do not have the characteristic processing problems that mark the child with SLD. In short, they are not *specific* language disabilities at all. The learning problems of the hyperactive child may be due to his or her difficulty with attention and with control of impulses. Factors other than those causing the specific language disability may be operating to cause the attention deficit disorder and the hyperactivity.

We make this distinction also because treatment of our SLD children and their generally favorable outcome with appropriate intervention is different from the guarded prognosis of attention deficit disorder (ADD), with or without hyperactivity. Furthermore, the incidence of children who have both SLD and ADHD is small when contrasted to the incidence of the pure SLD group. In our studies (Hagin, Beecher, & Silver, 1982), for example, 17% of the total population of all first-graders in seven schools on the East Side of New York City were diagnosed as SLD; only 2.4%, however, had specific language disability associated with ADD, hyperactivity, or motor clumsiness. In the Collaborative Perinatal Project, also, it was found that less then 1% of the sample with abnormal "minimal brain dysfunction (MBD) factor scores," had a learning disability associated with hyperactivity or impulsivity (Nichols and Chen, 1981). In that study, contrary to anecdotal reports, the association of specific language disability with attention deficit hyperactivity disorder was not high. This conclusion is in contrast to the reports of Halperin, Gittleman, Klein, and Rudel (1984) and of L. B. Silver (1981, 1989) who found that 15 to 20% of children identified as having learning disabilities also had attention deficit hyperactivity disorder. The discrepancy in findings may be the result of the perennial problems of research in this field: the variations in samples and the lack of clear-cut definitions and sharp boundaries in the diagnoses. For example, we may find that restlessness and inattention are a consequence of the learning disability itself, and a child with these characteristics is not considered to have an attention deficit hyperactivity disorder. This issue is considered at length in Chapter 13, "Attention Deficit Hyperactivity Disorder."

Although, by definition, the diagnosis of specific language disability has many exclusionary qualifications, its inclusionary characteristics are equally important. All children with a specific language disability demonstrate dysfunction in the central nervous system. For each child, however, the dysfunction is unique and may appear in any combination of the various neuropsychological functions that were described in Chapter 3, "Patterns of Neuropsychological Functions." These functions may be found in all aspects of language considered in its broadest sense, resulting in the following symptoms:

- Such children may be slower in reaching the developmental milestones for using words and sentences.

- Oral inaccuracies may persist in their speech longer than that of other preschoolers and then mature spontaneously.

- They often do not enjoy the playful rhyming that many young children do spontaneously.

- In the primary grades their oral language may be less complex than their age and intelligence would indicate.

- They have difficulty generating rhymes and matching initial sounds.

- They have difficulty remembering the names of people and common objects.

- Vocabularies may be more limited than age, intelligence, and background experiences indicate.

- They sometimes mix up the order of syllables within words and produce spoonerisms.

- Longer than most first-graders, they will continue to reverse or rotate letters and numbers when they write.

- They continue to confuse right and left directions and the orientation of the body in space.

- When they are learning to do cursive writing they find it hard to remember the motor patterns of letters.

- They have trouble remembering the arbitrary sequence of letters, months, and measures.

- They have trouble relating sounds to written symbols and blending these sounds into known words.

- Written expression will be simple even though they may have complex ideas to express.

As seen in Chapter 3, clusters of these functions do appear, however—clusters of auditory-verbal defects and clusters of visual-spatial-graphomotor defects—although in many children, the dysfunctions are mixed. The diversity of clinical pictures has led to the conclusion that specific language disability is itself a heterogeneous group. The following two case studies illustrate the basic clusters: auditory and spatial.

Richard is an example of a child with a specific language disability, whose major deficit is in the auditory processing of information and in associative learning.

CASE STUDY: RICHARD

Richard was first seen at age 6 years, 7 months when he was in the first grade of a demanding private school. The major complaint was behavioral, "he has not adjusted to first grade" said his mother. He clowned, and became physically aggressive to his classmates when he did not get their attention. The teacher reported that he seemed to lack the understanding necessary to discuss his problems with peers or with teachers. At home with two young siblings aged 3 and 2, his mother reported Richard to be "hard driving, persistent, difficult to handle, and jealous of his brothers." His father, a physician, was preoccupied with his profession and at home preferred to retreat into an easy chair to read, with little verbal communication. His mother was attentive, concerned, and verbal, but she had to manage the home and the children with little support.

On examination, Richard was found to be a good-sized and handsome, brown-eyed child, who came into the examining room with little overt anxiety and began immediately to play with the toy trains. He was attentive, cooperative, and motivated, but his verbal responses were laconic, with short sentences and simple sentence structure. On the WISC-R he earned a full scale IQ in the average range (92), but there was a significant discrepancy between verbal IQ of 69 and performance IQ of 121. His strengths were in Picture Completion (scaled score 14), in Picture Arrangement (17), Coding (13), and Mazes (14). His greatest weaknesses were in Information (5), Similarities (2), and Arithmetic (2). Richard's difficulty appeared to be in auditory processing and in associative learning. It was noted that when questions were difficult for him, he would frown, hold his head in his hands, even grind his teeth, but would never say he did not know the answer. On the PPVT he scored in the 40th percentile. The ITPA further delineated Richard's auditory processing deficits, with auditory memory 1¾ years below chronological age, auditory association 1½ years below chronological age, and auditory reception 1 year below chronological age. He could not sequence the days of the week. On the

Aphasia Screening Test of the Halstead Reitan Neuropsychological Battery there was difficulty naming objects, and mild finger agnosia.

Classical neurological examination was within normal limits. There was, however, immaturity in right-left discrimination, in finger-gnosis, and in praxis. On the extension test, the left hand was elevated in this right-handed boy, suggesting that hemisphere specialization for language was not yet established (see Chapter 6, "Principles of Psychiatric and Neurological Diagnosis"). Electroencephalogram and audiometric examinations were normal.

In short, this was a child with a specific language disability whose major area of deficit was in auditory reception, in temporal sequencing of auditory information, and in the recall of that information. He was already reacting to his frustration with anxiety and with demands for attention and temper outbursts when his demands were not met. He could not cope with the high expectation of the school that he was attending. Accordingly, Richard was placed in a special school for children with learning disabilities where he was given specific training for his auditory and associative deficits. By fourth grade he was doing well in a reasonably demanding private school. His father received psychotherapeutic assistance. Examination of a younger brother when he reached kindergarten age revealed the same pattern of deficits with which Richard struggled.

In contrast to Richard, Victoria is an example of a child with specific language disability whose major areas of immaturity are in spatial orientation and in the orientation of the body image in space.

CASE STUDY: VICTORIA

Victoria was 14 years, 9 months of age and in the ninth grade of a challenging private school when she was referred because she was depressed. She had lost interest in schoolwork, in friends, and in equestrian training, which she had previously enjoyed. Her father is said to be a "slow" reader. On psychological testing she earned a full scale IQ of 107 on the WISC-R (verbal 111, performance 102). Her oral reading (WRAT) was eighth grade, spelling sixth, and arithmetic sixth. Classical neurological examination in this right-handed child was essentially within normal limits. Visual perception, however, was markedly impaired with difficulty in accurate reproduction of angles where stellate angles and the presence of the primitive tendency to verticalization were found. She was able to recognize her visual-motor errors, but when she attempted to correct them her performance actually became worse. Less impaired but also immature was her functioning on visual discrimination and on visual recall of asymmetries. There was still difficulty with right-left orientation, immaturity in finger-gnosis with difficulty in recognizing bilateral asymmetric stimuli, and immaturity in praxis. Auditory perception, on the other hand, was intact in discrimination, temporal sequencing, and in immediate auditory recall. Her depression stemmed in part from the increasing academic difficulty she experienced as she went from elementary to secondary grades where there were increasing demands for written reports and on the comprehension of difficult reading material.

Fortunately her school was willing to modify their demands for written reports, permitting verbal reports and examinations and allowing additional time for written work. In addition to these compensatory efforts, Victoria had the advantage of direct training of her deficit perceptual functions.

The very diversity in clinical findings, has also led attempts to find a principle, a unifying concept, that underlies the diverse neuropsychological defects. (A review of these subgroup studies is found in Chapter 3.) Vellutino and Scanlon (1985) felt that a unifying concept may be limitations in coding the structural or purely linguistic attributes of the spoken word; Liberman et al. (1985) found "ineffective use of phonological strategies needed for lexical access and representation in short term memory" (p. 163). While these concepts are useful for some of the children, such as Richard, they do not encompass the entire group of children designated as having specific language disabilities because they offer no explanation for the visual-motor and body image difficulties many of these children have. An alternate proposal, one that encompasses all the neuropsychological defects found in reading disabilities, is that the child with a specific learning disability is immature in his or her abilities to process information requiring age-appropriate spatial orientation and/or temporal sequencing: He or she has problems with space and/or time. These functions are inherent in the fundamental skills needed for beginning reading and are the basis for the hierarchical development of the language skills described by Vellutino and by Liberman, for the "naming" problems described by Denckla (1977), for the intermodal associations described by Birch and Belmont (1965), and for the metalinguistic abilities felt to be important by Blank and Bridger (1967). Although the unifying concept of spatial orientation and/or temporal organization has been criticized (see Chapter 3), the concept has been useful in developing a test battery for children with learning disorders and in developing an instrument to identify 5- and 6-year-olds for whom reading failure is predicted.

RESEARCH IN THE ETIOLOGY OF SLD

It must be noted that the neuropsychological deficits found in children with specific language disorders and the concept of spatial orientation and temporal organization that attempts to relate these defects with each other are not the *cause* of specific learning disabilities. The cause or causes are still obscure; investigators continue to uncover deeper levels in the search for origins. It is as though the academic difficulty itself is but the tip of the iceberg, the apex visible to all; the neuropsychological defects are the next layer, hidden just beneath the surface, and made accessible by test probes, which appear to be related to spatial orientation and temporal organization. The neuropsychological defects, in turn, may be the behavioral expression of the underlying abnormality in the biological substrate. For instance, it has been said that awareness of spatial orientation and temporal organization depends on asymmetry of the perceiving system—an animal whose brain is bilaterally symmetrical cannot differentiate between stimuli arriving from homologous points (Mach, 1959). Kephart (1971) also pointed out that an internal spatial coordinate system must be established before directionality in space may be appreciated. These concepts suggest that the asymmetrical brain is needed to establish the functions of spatial orientation and temporal orientation and that hemisphere specialization of function is needed for age-appropriate performance of these skills.

Studies on Hemisphere Specialization

While the relationship between language and cerebral lateralization was documented by Marc Dax in 1836 (published in 1878) and later rediscovered, apparently independently, by Broca in 1861, it was not until 1917 that James Hinshelwood related "congenital word blindness" to a focal agenesis of the left angular gyrus. To Orton (1928, 1937/1989), the problem of hemisphere specialization was central in understanding the group of developmental language problems that included reading, writing, and spelling disabilities, "word deafness," motor speech delay, and developmental apraxia. He attributed these disorders to failure to establish the physiologic habit of working exclusively from the engrams of one hemisphere, that is, the failure to establish a dominant hemisphere. Orton reasoned that visual symbols are represented in each hemisphere, oriented correctly in the dominant hemisphere but as a mirror image in the nondominant side. Normally the nondominant image is elided from awareness. In developmental language disorders, said Orton, suppression of the nondominant engram does not occur. The competing engrams result in twisted symbols or "strephosymbolia," creating the one symptom "common to the entire group (of developmental language disorders) . . . a difficulty in repicturing or rebuilding in the order of presentation, sequences of letters, of sounds, or of units of movement" (Orton, 1937/1989, p. 145). Orton felt there was an increased incidence of left-handedness, incomplete handedness, and/or crossed eye and hand dominance in these children.

While the Orton explanation of confusing mirror-images in specific language disability has not been substantiated, and more recent research has failed to find a relationship between "mixed" eye-hand preference and specific language disability (Hagin, 1954), there has been continuing study of the adequacy of hemisphere specialization, particularly in children with specific language disability. Such studies have been spurred by the development of noninvasive neuropsychological techniques, techniques in which two different perceptual stimuli within the same modality are simultaneously presented to the left and the right sensory fields. Stimuli from the right sensory field normally are represented predominantly in the left hemisphere; those from the left sensory field in the right hemisphere. "Any asymmetry in hemisphere processing of particular stimuli may be reflected in response asymmetry to left vs. right stimulation as measured in accuracy or reaction time" (Witelson, 1976, p. 235). Such stimuli may be in the auditory (dichotic listening), visual (visual half fields), or tactile-kinesthetic (dichotomous tactile stimuli) areas and involve both linguistic and nonlinguistic processes. Unfortunately, these techniques and the studies using them are not without their problems. Thus, unequivocal resolution of the question of hemisphere specialization in developmental language disorders by means of these techniques is still not available.

Dichotic Listening Studies   The dichotic listening techniques were initiated by Broadbent (1954) and applied clinically by Kimura (1961, 1963) at the Montreal Neurological Institute. By then the Montreal Neurological Institute was already known for the pioneering work of Penfield and Roberts (1959) in localizing, by direct electrical stimulation of the brain, areas subserving language. In addition, the Montreal Neurological Institute was known for locating the side of the brain subserving speech by the unilateral intracarotid injection of sodium amytal (the Wada Test, Wada & Rasmussen, 1960). The sodium amytal test is useful in determining which hemisphere controls speech and language, independent of the handedness of the patient. From studies of this procedure it was found that 95% of all right-handers without history of early brain damage have speech and language controlled by the left hemisphere and 5% are controlled by the right hemisphere; 70% of left-handers are left-brain dominant for speech, 15% have speech controlled by the right hemisphere, and 15% have bilateral speech control. For those who have a history of left-brain damage early in life, 70% of right-handers and 19% of left-handers have right hemisphere–controlled or bilateral speech. Results of the Kimura dichotic listening tests parallel, but do not entirely coincide with, results on the sodium amytal test—i.e., all patients who are left-brain dominant do not necessarily show a right ear advantage on dichotic listening (Kimura, 1961).

The technique of the Kimura dichotic listening tests includes using pairs of different spoken digits presented simultaneously via headphones to each ear in groups of three pairs. The subject is to recall in any order as many of the digits as possible. Control subjects reported the digits presented to the right ear more accurately than to the left (right ear advantage, REA): The stimuli reaching the left hemisphere are more accurately reported than those to the right hemisphere. This has also been found for words, nonsense syllables, pairs of consonant-vowel syllables formed with the stop consonants *(b, d, g, p, t),* Morse code, and processing and ordering temporal information (Noffsinger, 1985). On the other hand, when musical chords and melodies are used instead of digits or words there is a left ear advantage (LEA), suggesting that musical symbols are more accurately perceived with the right hemisphere. Using sets of dichotic nonsense syllables as stimuli, Noffsinger (1985), found that in adults the ear advantages revealed are often small, the listening tasks are demanding, and the tasks require many stimulus presentations to establish advantage. Normally also, the size of the ear advantage is not consistent across subjects. Moreover, in any one subject, no ear advantage at all will be found in approximately 27% of the trials.

In children with specific reading disability, no clear-cut pattern of ear advantage emerges, although there is a tendency for REA to be less in older (ages 11–15) boys with learning disability than in good readers of the same age. Zurif and Carson (1970) and Witelson and Rabinovitch (1972), for example, found no significant REA in the learning disabled groups as contrasted with controls and, indeed, they found a nonsignificant trend in favor of LEA in the learning disability groups. Using digit pairs as the auditory stimulus, Witelson (1976) found that although the overall accuracy increased with age for both reading disabilities and controls, and that each group had a significant REA, the overall accuracy was significantly greater for the normal group. These findings are consistent with the theory that learning disabled children have "some dysfunction" in the left hemisphere.

Similar, although less significant, results were found by Sparrow (1969) and Sparrow and Satz (1970) in 40 learning disabled boys, aged 9–12, when they were compared to a matched control group in a dichotic listening task using four-pair digits. In these studies REA was found for both groups, but almost four times as many dyslexic boys had LEA. When groups of younger boys were studied at ages 5, 7, and 12, Darby (1974) found that in the control group (normal readers matched with the dyslexic boys), the magnitude of ear asymmetry increased with age, with increasing REA, which, however, was statistically significant only at age 12. By contrast, the dyslexic groups revealed no significant REA at any age, although there was a trend for REA at age 12. The general conclusion from these studies suggests that, normally, the magnitude of REA increases with age (to age 12) with the trend to REA observable by age 5. Normal readers tend to demonstrate a greater magnitude of REA than do children with learning disabilities particularly at older ages, at early adolescence. Satz, however, specifically stated that children with learning disability "reveal a lag in the development of ear asymmetry with no significant REA at any age level" (Satz, 1976, p. 282). This finding was used to lend support for the theory that, in disabled readers, functional lateralization of the brain matures at a slower rate than normally. The general conclusion of less adequate REA in poor readers as contrasted with adequate readers is reflected in a review of dichotic listening studies (Bryden, 1988) in which 20 of 35 studies report weaker lateralization in poor readers, 5 show greater lateralization, and 10 report no differences in lateralization between poor and adequate readers. Beaton (1985) however, stated that "most experiments have shown a REA for verbal material among disabled as well as normal readers. . . . what is in doubt is the magnitude of the asymmetry in each group of readers and how this relates to age" (p. 208).

Recent advances in the ability to determine blood flow in various regions of the human cortex have been used to study the relationship of blood to frontal, temporal parietal, and occipital areas in subjects undergoing dichotic listening tests (Coffey, Bryden, Schroering, Wilson, & Mathew, 1989). Cerebral blood flow measurements were estimated by the $^{133}X_e$ inhalation technique. A mixture of $^{133}X_e$ (5.7 MCi/mm) and room air was administered through a face mask for 1 minute with clearance of the isotope from the brain for the next 10 minutes, monitored with a system of 32 scintillation detectors mounted on a helmet, and applied to the scalp. A two-tone pitch discrimination task (Gregory, Efron, Divenyi, & Yund, 1983), the ear advantage for which was determined in pre $^{133}X_e$ trials, was used to determine whether the ear advantage was associated with increased regional cerebral blood flow (RCBF) in the contralateral temporal cortex. Fourteen strongly right-handed medical students (mean age 23 years), screened for active medical neurological or psychiatric conditions, had significant ear advantage on the two-tone dichotic listening tests. Nine of the 14 had LEA and 5 had REA. A small, low significant increase in mean RCBF to the temporal cortex contralateral to the ear advantage was found. Those with REA showed activation over the left temporal region, while those with LEA exhibited activation over the right temporal region. A trend toward increased blood flow in the frontal regions (left greater than right) was also found in the group with LEA. The authors stated that "these are the first data to provide a direct indication that perceptual asymmetry on a dichotic listening task is associated with regional asymmetries in brain functional activity measured by the RCBF" (Coffey et al, 1989, p. 50). The analytic strategies used by the subjects in solving the dichotic listening test were not documented. The authors stated, however, that because of (a) the small number of subjects, (b) the confounding effects of variables inherent in dichotic auditory testing, and (c) the possible metabolic changes in subcortical structures, these results are to be considered preliminary.

In a different paradigm, regional cerebral blood flow was studied in 14 adult men with "severe developmental dyslexia" and a control group (Rumsey et al., 1987). When given a simple cognitive task, no difference in regional cerebral blood flow was found. With tasks involving reading and comprehension, however, the dyslexic group showed more activity than controls in the left hemisphere of the brain, suggesting that dyslexics do not process information as efficiently as controls.

Visual Half-Field Presentation Studies   Studies on visual half-field presentation, just as those with dichotic auditory presentations, also suffer from technical and theoretical problems. The hemifield tachistoscopic technique is based upon the anatomic arrangement of fibers from the retina, in which fibers from one-half of each visual field reach the occipital cortex, contralateral to the stimulated side. Stimuli from the right visual half field, striking the nasal half of the right retina and the temporal half of the left retina, are ultimately carried to the left visual cortex, while those from the left visual half field impinge upon the nasal portion of the left retina and the temporal portion of the right and are ultimately processed in the right occipital cortex. The technique requires the subject to fixate his or her gaze on a specific point positioned on a screen in front of the subject. This may create a problem since poor readers may be less likely than normal readers to fixate appropriately when told to do so. Tachistoscopic presentations are made to the right or left visual half field, or bilaterally and simultaneously. The presentation must take less than 180 msec (the time to initiate and saccade in the direction of presentation), usually 100 msec or less. The size of the stimulus must be 1 degree or more to avoid the bilateral macular projections, and the presentations to each half field must be random so that the subject cannot predict the field stimulated. Presentation of words is confounded by scanning habits. Because in English we scan from left to right, a word presented in the left visual half field is further away from the fixation point than a word in the right. Requiring a subject to read words presented to the visual half field may also be a problem since it may not be visual field asymmetry that is being studied, but simply the reading disabled subject's difficulty in reading the word no matter in which half field it is presented. Interpretation of results may also be criticized in that differences in hemifield recognition may relate more to style of information processing than to a proposed lateralization of function. Beaton (1985) stated that, of visual field studies, "there is a surprising lack of sophistication in attempting to understand the cognitive processes which are deficient in cases of reading retardation" (p. 206).

Nevertheless, using this technique in normal adults, Kimura (1969, 1973) found superiority in right visual field recognition for English letters or words. Other studies described left visual superiority in normal adults for recognition of complex forms, recognition of dot figures, recognition of overlapping figures, face recognition, and line orientation (see E. Zaidel, 1985). D. W. Zaidel stated (1985) that "it is by now commonly agreed that letters, words or digits are better recognized in the right visual field than in the left visual field" (p. 147) and that the "left visual field [is superior] for recognition of complex forms, recognition of dot figures, recognition of overlapping figures, face recognition and line orientation" (p. 148). However, unlike consistent right visual field superiority for recognizing verbal material such as letters and words, left visual field superiority for recognizing nonverbal stimuli is smaller in comparison and in general is less consistent.

Because of the singular lack of information about the development of visual field superiority in normal children, however, there are problems in interpreting visual field studies in children with learning disabilities. McKeever and Huling (1970), presenting four-letter nouns, found right visual field advantage (RVFA) in recognition of words in both normal children and those with severe reading retardation. Mean age for both groups was 13 years. No difference in hemifield asymmetry between normal and reading disabled children was also found by Keefe and Swinney (1979). Marcel and Rajan (1975) also found significant asymmetry in the right visual field for word and letter reports in both good and poor readers, but the absolute difference between left and right hemifields was greater for the good readers. This study included both boys and girls, of whom all except two, were right-handed, aged 7 years, 6 months to 8 years, 7 months. A methodological procedure confounds this study since the mean duration of exposure was much longer for the disabled readers than for the normal controls. Significantly elevated thresholds in the right visual field than in the left were found by K. Gross, Rothenberg, Schottenfeld, and Drake (1978). Reduced hemifield asymmetry for four-letter words presented bilaterally was found in 19-year-old poor readers (Kershner, 1979) and in 12½-year-old poor readers (Pirozollo & Rayner, 1979). Yeni-Komshian, Isenberg, and Goldberg (1975), however, found a significant asymmetry in the right visual field for both numerals and vertically presented words in a group of black children, boys and girls, aged 11–13, only in *poor* readers. Finally, Witelson (1976) in 83 "dyslexic" and 86 normal boys, aged 6–14, did not demonstrate a right visual half field asymmetry for both groups. The stimuli in this study were two upper-case letters which were similar or different. The subjects were required to indicate whether the letters were the same or different but not to name them. When pictures of people were used, however, the normal group obtained significantly different scores for each visual field, with greater accuracy in the left visual field, whereas the dyslexic group, did not obtain significantly different scores for each visual field. Witelson stated that "the lack of significant behavioral asymmetry for the dyslexic group could be suggestive of a lack of right hemisphere specialization for spatial processing in the dyslexic group" (p. 245). A review of 14 visual hemifield studies (Bryden, 1988) found 8 of them to confirm the conclusion of less lateralization in poor readers than in adequate readers. Four of the studies, however, found equal lateralization and two found poor readers more adequately lateralized.

The Witelson study was part of a larger one in which she proposed to evaluate hemisphere specialization in children with dyslexia. This project, carefully planned and implemented, studied 85 right-handed boys, aged 6–14, with reading disability, who had performance IQ scores of at least 85 on the WISC, difficulty in reading since grade 1, a discrepancy of at least 1½ grades in reading between reading level on the WRAT and chronological age, with no detectable neurological damage or primary emotional disturbance, adequate sensory acuity, educational opportunity, and English as the first and main language. A control group of 156 normal boys was used. Hemisphere specialization was studied by (a) tactile stimulation (nonsense shape test and a letters test); (b) lateralized tachistoscopic stimulation using pictures of people; and (c) a dichotic listening test using digits.

Dichotomous Tactile Tests The suggestion of impaired right-hemisphere specialization in dyslexics was reinforced by Witelson's results on tactile stimulation tests. The first of these, a dichotomous tactile stimulation test, was designed to be nonlinguistic. It required spatial perception of pairs of competing nonsense shapes through touch. The subject was required to choose the two test stimuli from a visual recognition display of six shapes. In 100 nondyslexic boys aged 6–14, greater accuracy was observed for shapes felt by the left hand, whereas for 49 dyslexic boys the differences between the left- and right-hand scores were not significant; the right-hand score of dyslexics was significantly greater than that of the controls, however. A second dichotomous tactile stimulation test used letters (three-dimensional, presented in 10 sets of two pairs) instead of nonsense shapes with the same groups of dyslexic boys and controls. The groups did not differ significantly in overall accuracy. For the normal group, the right-hand score was significantly greater than the left-hand score; for the dyslexic group, the left-hand score was significantly greater than the right. In addition, the left-hand score of dyslexics was significantly greater than the left-hand score of normals.

Witelson concluded (1976) that "in contrast to the normal pattern of right hemisphere specialization for spatial processing, it is suggested that dyslexics have a bilateral representation of spatial functions. . . . This hypothesis is based on the dyslexics' lack of left field superiority on the spatial touch test and on the visual spatial test and on their atypical pattern of left hand superiority on the 'linguistic' touch test. There appears to be an association between the syndrome of developmental dyslexia and two possible neural abnormalities; a lack of right hemisphere specialization for spatial processing and a dysfunction in left hemisphere processing of linguistic functions" (p. 251).

Conclusions concerning hemisphere specialization arising from dichotic and tachistoscopic studies, however, have been challenged. First, visual and auditory measures of lateralization are not highly correlated with each other

(Eling, 1981; Fennel, Bowers, & Satz, 1977; Hiscock & Kinsbourne, 1982). Second, reliability of the tests is low (Blumstein, Goodglass, & Tartter, 1975; McKeever, 1974). Such variability may mean that the laterality tests are tapping functions that can shift over brief intervals of time. Special strategies adopted by subjects and attentional biasing may contribute to performance (Gregory et al., 1983; Hiscock & Kinsbourne, 1982). Third, these tests underestimate the incidence of left-hemisphere speech in right-handers as determined by the sodium amytal test. If, as determined by the sodium amytal test, the estimated prevalence of left-brain speech in normal right-handers is 95%, and 70% of that right-handed sample show a right ear advantage on a dichotic listening test, then the probability of right-brain speech when a left ear advantage is found in right-handers is small. This raises the issue of validity of these tests as measures of cerebral dominance for language.

Lastly, the basic inference that peripheral sensory advantage relates to contralateral specialization for that function may be an oversimplification, neglecting the transfer of information from one hemisphere to the other, the "callosal-relay" (E. Zaidel, 1985). It is possible that complex cognitive tasks call for complex hemisphere transfer. Further, certain experimental conditions can shift hemispheric control over a task as the processing requirements change.

It is clear that the problem of hemisphere specialization in children with specific language disability is far from resolved by the techniques of dichotomous sensory presentation. Normative development of the functions revealed by the behavioral techniques of dichotic listening, visual field presentation, and dichotomous tactile stimulation has yet to be uncovered. Floor and ceiling effects of the tests used must be considered. Studies using comparable groups of children, well studied in the diagnostic parameters discussed in this book, comparable in handedness and reading level as well as in chronological age, and comparable test techniques are needed. Use of a laterality measure independent of overall accuracy is suggested by Bryden and Sprott (1981). With all these caveats for dichotomous sensory presentation, however, the concept of inadequate cerebral specialization of function continues to be advanced in an attempt to conceptualize the mechanism underlying the dysfunctions found in children with specific language disability.

Interpretation of Lateralization Findings Two major hypotheses have been advanced to explain the putative anomalous lateralization of function in children with language disabilities: the developmental lag hypothesis and an abnormal cerebral organization hypothesis.

The Developmental Lag Hypothesis L. A. Bender and Yarnell (1941) were the first to use the terms developmental lag or maturational lag for children with reading disabilities in whom the classical neurological examination was normal. By developmental lag is meant there is no known structural defect of the brain, but only a physiological immaturity, particularly in development of those areas of the brain related to language. Some evidence for this is that the angular and supramarginal gyrus, an association area integrating information from many sensory modalities, develops late in ontogony and is one of the last cortical areas to myelinate. The developmental lag hypothesis was amplified by Satz and Sparrow (1970) who felt that in reading disabled children the rate of lateralization of functions of the left and right hemispheres is slower than in normal children. Thus it would be expected that on dichotic listening tests, normal (i. e., non–reading disabled) children would have a greater right ear advantage than would reading disabled children. As we have seen, this was found to be true for children aged 11–12 but not for those aged 7–8. Bakker (1987), in discussing his proposed division of impaired readers into the L-type (using left-hemisphere strategies) and P-type (using right-hemisphere strategies), stated that the primary subservience of reading switches from the right hemisphere to the left at some point in the process of learning to read. P-type children may fail to make the hemisphere shift; L-type children, on the other hand, skip the right-hemisphere processing of the learning to read process and, because they have "no eye for the visuo-perceptual features of script, substantive errors are relatively frequent" (p. 31). Witelson's conclusions, based on her study of dichotomous presentations in the visual, auditory, and haptic fields (1976), also relate to anomalous hemisphere specialization a possible "lack of right hemisphere specialization for spatial processing and a dysfunction in left hemisphere processing of linguistic functions" (p. 254).

The early work of Lenneberg (1967) suggested that, at birth, the two cerebral hemispheres are unspecialized and have equal potential for subserving language; that lateralization is a process of increasing specialization of language by the left hemisphere in parallel with decreasing involvement of the right hemisphere; that this process may be identified as beginning at about age 2, at the time the brain has developed the biological capacity for language, and as lasting until puberty; and that cerebral dominance for language is the key to brain–behavior relationship in understanding lateralization, because such lateralization is tied to language acquisition. In short, according to Lenneberg, there is a biologically determined developmental sequence to brain laterality. More recent work, however, has indicated that "at no time from birth on, do the two hemispheres appear to be equipotential for language on any interpretation of the term equipotential" (Curtiss, 1985, p. 101). Anatomical asymmetries of the infant brain resemble those in the adult, with the temporal speech region larger on the left than on the right (Witelson & Pallie, 1973). Entus (1977), combining nonnutritive sucking with a dichotic listening paradigm, for example, found hemispheric asymmetry in processing dichotically presented speech and nonspeech stimuli in infants 20–140 days of age. Molfese, Freeman, and Palermo (1975), and Molfese and Molfese (1980) found that infants as young as 1 week of age manifest strongly lateralized electrophysiological responses to speech and nonspeech stimuli. A. E. Davis and Wada (1977) found strong lateralized evoked potentials to flashes and clicks in infants as young as 2–10 weeks of age. It is pointed out, however, these laterality effects may come about as a result of unknown variables (Beaton, 1985). The general conclusion of the infancy studies, however, is that although speech may not begin until age 2, lateralization of function may be observable in the first weeks of life and that the neural substrata of certain human cognitive function is lateralized long before the cognitive functions themselves are measurable. This is, in general, the position of Kinsbourne (Hiscock & Kinsbourne, 1982). It is unfortunate that the early death of Lenneberg has prevented a modification of his conclusions in the light of current knowledge. The principle of "developmental invariance" in hemisphere specialization does not rule out the concept of developmental lag. Specialization of the cerebral hemispheres at birth does not mean that the *degree* of specialization does not increase during childhood. Maturation still occurs; function evolves in response to maturation and in response to appropriate and adequate stimulation at critical ages. The developmental lag hypothesis simply implies that in children with specific learning disabilities, for a reason or reasons yet unknown, the functions needed for reading or spelling or writing or arithmetic have not reached an appropriate level for those skills to be learned.

The concept of delay or lag in the maturation of hemisphere specialization in children with specific language disability, with its implication of plasticity, offers the optimistic outlook that these delays may somehow be made up. This is not necessarily so. The neuropsychological dysfunctions may not mature spontaneously and the specialized functions of the central nervous system may not accelerate. We cannot wait passively for such maturation to occur. (The long-term stability of the deficits and the long-term effects on academic achievement and on vocational and social adjustment are discussed in Chapters 3 and 9.) Further, the concept of maturational lag implies that the problems are functional, not morphological. This concept may require modification in the light of the morphological abnormalities found by Galaburda (1983, 1985) in the brain of dyslexics.

The concept of a maturational anomaly in the development of hemisphere specialization does not tell us the *cause* of such anomalous function; it offers only a theoretical mechanism to explain the processing immaturities found in the child with a specific language disability.

The Abnormal Cerebral Organization Hypothesis　Although in its ultimate result, delayed hemisphere specialization will yield an anomalous organization of hemisphere function, the abnormal cerebral organization hypothesis implies a qualitative rather than a quantitative dysfunction, "a dysfunction in the structure of cerebral organization either prenatally or during early postnatal development" (Obrzut, 1988, p. 585). The abnormal cerebral organization hypothesis is "concerned with conceptualizing how the cerebral hemispheres act together as a unit in performing multiple cognitive processes concurrently, how the hemispheres work together, collaborate and integrate their processes" (Kershner, 1988, p. 528). Two possible mechanisms for disruption in this dual-processing system are advanced: the neurological model and the resource model. The neurological model is an elaboration of the selective attention theory of hemisphere processing advanced by Kinsbourne and Caplan (1979), that normally the expectation of a verbal task, for example, selectively activates the left hemisphere with concurrent suppression of the right hemisphere. In poor learners, however, this reciprocal balance of excitation and inhibition is impaired. As a result, neurons involved in the processing of a function are unprotected by inhibitory barriers, and there is a "structural interference between subprocessors" (Kershner, 1988, p. 529) resulting in inadequate conceptual differentiation among tasks. The resource model contends that each hemisphere acts as an independent processor, with a specific capacity for performing the functions needed in learning. Where this capacity is exceeded by the demands of a task, poor learning will occur. Capacity, the resources mobilized for a task, may also be less efficient than demanded by the task or it may be out of phase with the demands of the task. In each of these models, abnormal asymmetries in hemisphere activation may cause learning problems.

Just as in the maturational lag model, the dual-processing model does not offer a cause for the specific language disability. It too, offers a mechanism attempting to explain the neuropsychological defects found in these children.

Genetic Factors and Laterality Specialization

Genetic factors have been implicated as important in the development of hemisphere specialization and presumably in the anomalies of hemisphere specialization that are inferred from the behavioral studies of children with specific language disabilities. The family and twin studies of dyslexic populations are discussed in the next section of this chapter; this section reviews theories involving genetic influence on hemisphere specialization. Genetic models of handedness and laterality were described early in this century (for review see J. Oppenheimer, 1977). More recently, Levy and Nagylaki (1972) proposed a model of genetic variation according to Mendelian principles. On the other hand, an extreme environmental, cultural explanation was offered by Blau (1946) who stated that right-handedness and presumably left-brainness is a learned response to a right-handed bias in our environment. Blau was a psychoanalyst who felt that faulty education or negativism could lead to left-handedness. His was an era in which it was the rule to explain behavior in psychodynamic terms. As with most extreme positions, such as the strict Mendelian versus the strict psychodynamic, there is a bit of truth in each of them, so that a combination of the positions may best represent the data. Annett (1981) proposed that although there are unsystematic environmental influences, most people inherit genetically determined right-handedness (left brain to control the right hand), which she calls a "right-shift" factor. The absence of this genetic factor will lead to inconsistent handedness (ambilaterality). Corballis and Beale (1976) believed that the right-shift is not encoded in the genes, but that there is a genetically controlled expression of a more fundamental underlying gradient that normally favors more advanced development on the left hemisphere. Both right-handedness and left cerebral control of speech in humans are specific manifestations of the same gradient. There appears to be abundant evidence from studies of acquired aphasia and from the sodium amytal test that 95% of right-handers have speech control lateralized to the left hemisphere.

The relationship between eyedness and handedness and presumably to cerebral lateralization is not nearly so clear. About one-third of the population uses the left eye in sighting. Thus it is not uncommon in the normal population to find mixed hand and eye preference, i. e., right hand–left eye. Hiscock and Kinsbourne (1982) stated that "there is little or no correlation between the two measures" and that "laterality measures other than handedness contribute little to our understanding of cerebral lateralization" (p. 199).

A mechanism for the genetic influence on hemisphere specialization was suggested by Geschwind (1983) and Geschwind and Behan (1982), who found an association between left-handedness, autoimmune disease, and dyslexia. On the basis of a questionnaire that included questions related to handedness, and personal and family histories, Geschwind was able to identify 500 strongly left-handed and 900 strongly right-handed individuals. Forty (8%) of the left handers and 25 (2.8%) of the right handers had a history of autoimmune disease, most frequently that of the gastrointestinal tract (regional ileitis, ulcerative colitis, and coeliac disease). Learning disorders were found in 10% of the left-handers and in 1.1% of the right-handers. Learning disorders and autoimmune diseases were more frequent in relatives of left-handers. One implication of these data is based on a Geschwind syllogism; (a) Left-handedness is more common in males than in females; (b) learning disorders occur predominantly in males; (c) there is a higher frequency of learning disorders among left-handers than among right-handed children. According to Geschwind there is something in the development of the male fetus, different from that of the female fetus, which encourages left-handedness. By implication, this factor leads to increased growth of the right hemisphere. Such a factor is testosterone, which the male fetus produces in large quantities during intrauterine life.

Geschwind (1983) stated that "it is reasonable to raise the possibility that it is testosterone that is slowing the growth of the left hemisphere" and "when the quantities (of testosterone) are elevated, it is more likely to produce left-handedness and in extreme cases lead to alterations in the left hemisphere which are responsible for the childhood learning disorders such as dyslexia" (p. 34). Because testosterone affects the development of the immune system, and because testosterone also slows the development of the left hemisphere, the relationship of dyslexia to autoimmune disease is explained by Geschwind. One bit of evidence for this theory is that Galaburda has succeeded in producing in mice disturbance of the migration of nerve cells similar to those found in dyslexics. Satz and Soper (1986), reviewing these data, however, found only marginal support for Geschwind's theory, which, they said, contains potentially misleading claims about left-handedness. Satz and Fletcher (1987), in an additional study, found no relationship between left-handedness and reading level, cognitive function, birth history, or parental achievement in two unselective samples of 571 white boys who were followed from kindergarten to the end of grade 2. Although Pennington, Smith, Kimberling, Green, and Haith (1987) also found no significant association between handedness and autoimmune disease in 87 "dyslexic" and 86 "nondyslexic" members of 14 three-generation kindreds, they did find 10% of their dyslexics had autoimmune disease (for example, lupus or rheumatoid arthritis) contrasted with 1.5% in their nondyslexics.

Whether or not the Geschwind hypothesis proves to be true, a genetic factor in the establishment of right-handedness and in left-hemisphere specialization for language appears to have support. As with most human function, however, a biological basis for that function, genetically wired, still requires appropriate and sufficient stimulation at critical ages for that function to be manifest.

Family and Twin Studies

"There are bountiful data attesting to the familial nature [of specific language disability] and strong presumptive evidence that this familial distribution is due at least in part to genetic factors, [but] assessment of specific hypothesis concerning modes of inheritance has been confusing and inconclusive" (McClearn, 1978, p. 287).

Family Studies   The familial nature of SLD is said to have been recorded first by C. J. Thomas in 1905 when he described congenital word blindness in two brothers and in another boy with similarly affected sister and mother. More recent and sophisticated studies (Finucci, Guthrie, Childs, Abbey, & Childs, 1976; Hallgren, 1950; Owen, 1978; Owen, Adams, Forrest, Stolz, & Fisher, 1971), including those from the Colorado family reading study (De Fries, 1985; De Fries, & Baker, 1983) have reinforced the same finding. Hallgren, carefully defining his criteria for selection of cases for "specific dyslexia," found 81 children belonging to 77 families from the Psychiatric Clinic of the Karolinske Institute in Stockholm, 22 additional children from a junior high school in Stockholm, and an additional 9 children with "specific dyslexia" from a control population sample, to fit his criteria. Ninety of his 112 cases had families with one affected parent and one or more affected sibling; 12 had no affected relatives, and 10 had both parents affected and, in some, other relatives in addition. In the 90 children with one affected parent, assumed to be heterozygous for the affected trait, the ratio of affected children to nonaffected was 45.7%, which was consistent with his theoretical assumption of an autosomal dominant mode of inheritance. The overall sex ratio of probands was 3.3 males:1 female. This study has been criticized because of Hallgren's failure to consider genetic heterogeneity among his 90 families (B. Childs, Finucci, & Preston, 1978) and because the diagnosis of "dyslexia" for at least some of the children and most of the adults was made on historical evidence alone. However, the Hallgren study was the first to provide presumptive evidence of familial transmission of specific language disability.

The high prevalence of specific language disability within families is documented in more recent studies. Owen et al. (1971) and Owen (1978) screened children in a special remedial program for the educationally handicapped in the Palo Alto California Unified School District who were 1½ to 2 years below grade-level expectancy in spelling and/or reading with a full scale IQ of 90 or above on the WISC and who had same-sex siblings of school age. Successful academic children with their appropriate siblings were the controls and were matched with the poor readers/spellers. When 76 matched sets of EH (educationally handicapped) and successful academic (SA) children were compared, it was found that:

1. The reading and spelling of the EH siblings were significantly lower than those of the controls, with the EH siblings slightly below grade-level expectancy in reading, while the SA siblings were almost a year above grade-level expectancy. In spelling, too, the EH siblings were almost a year below grade-level expectancy.

2. The WISC subtest scores of both EH children and their siblings were highly correlated on tests that involve verbal ability requiring conceptualization and verbal expression, namely comprehension and similarities subtests; for SA children and their siblings, this correlation was not significant. On the WISC performance scale, object assembly and coding scores were significantly correlated with reading and spelling for both SA and EH groups but were slightly higher for the EH pairs.

3. The parents of EH children had had academic problems in the language area in their school career. These problems persisted "to some

degree" into adulthood. Mothers of EH children obtained the lowest scores.

4. Impairment in auditory tapped patterns, right–left discrimination, extinction to double simultaneous tactile simulation, and fast-alternating finger and hand movement tests were found in both EH children and their siblings.

Owen concluded that "certain types of dyslexia may be transmitted through multifactorial inheritance" (1978, p. 283) in which the trait may be determined by a large number of genes, the expression of which would be a function of the genetic predisposition and environmental experiences. This view is supported by McClearn (1978).

The Colorado reading project has as its long-range objectives the identification, characterization, and validation of etiologically distinct subtypes of reading disability. The project includes four components: psychometric assessment/family study, twin study, reading and language processes, and patterns of electrophysiological activity. The psychometric assessment/family study section was concerned with the assessment of possible reading deficits in parents and siblings of children identified by the project as reading disabled and was designed to study the transmission of reading disability in families of the index reading disabled children (probands).

Both probands and matched controls were referred by local school districts in Colorado. Criteria for reading disability included the following: an IQ of 90 or above as measured by a standardized intelligence test, reading achievement one-half grade level below expectancy or lower as measured by a standardized reading test, age 7.5–12 years, residence with both biological parents, no known emotional or neurological impairments, and no uncorrected defects in auditory or visual acuity. Control children, those who were reading at grade level or above, were matched on the basis of age, sex, grade, and home environment. Siblings (7½–18 years of age) and parents of probands and controls were also tested.

The study included 125 reading disabled children (96 boys, 29 girls) and their immediate families matched with 125 control children and their families for a total of 1044 subjects. Data from the family study are based upon results of seven tests: the reading recognition, comprehension, and spelling sections of the PIAT; a Non-Verbal Culture–Fair Intelligence test; the Spatial Relations Test (for Primary Mental Abilities); the Coding subtest of the WISC, and the Colorado Perceptual Speed Test. A principal component factor analysis with Varimax rotation of the resulting correlation matrix yielded three dimensions: reading, symbol-processing speed, and spatial reasoning. Symbol-processing speed had its highest loadings on the WISC Coding subtest and on the Colorado Perceptual Speed Test; spatial reasoning was loaded on the Non-Verbal Intelligence and the Spatial Relations tests. In the Colorado study, the principal components analysis of families of probands, families of controls, probands only, and control children only were highly congruent. But there were significant group and gender differences on multivariate analysis of reading, symbol-processing, and spatial-reasoning scores, for each of the three comparison samples. A summary of the results of the family study included:

1. *Comparing probands versus controls:* Composite reading score was over 2 standard deviations lower; symbol-processing speed and spatial reasoning were 0.7 standard deviations lower. Girls obtained higher scores on symbol processing and boys scored higher on spatial reasoning, but the reading disabled girls were no more or less impaired than the reading disabled boys.

2. *Comparing brothers of probands versus brothers of controls:* Reading score was about 1 standard deviation lower, and significant differences were found in symbol-processing speed and in spatial reasoning.

3. *Comparing sisters of probands versus sisters of controls:* Reading scores were about 0.4 standard deviations lower.

4. *Comparing parents of probands versus parents of controls:* Scores were lower for each of the three measures, somewhat greater for fathers (0.8 sigma) than for mothers (0.5 sigma).

These results demonstrate the familial nature of reading disability. The Colorado Reading Project, however, provides additional evidence of family influence on test scores of their children:

1. A 5-year follow-up of 69 matched pairs of children revealed that initial test scores of probands were less predictive of subsequent reading performance than initial test scores of controls. If the parents' initial test scores were added to the prediction equation, however, there was a "significant increase in the squared multiple correlation for reading performance of probands" (DeFries, 1985, p. 117).

2. In a review of longitudinal data, the contribution of family influence on the magnitude of longitudinal stability in reading scores differed for families of controls and for those of reading disabled children. In the case of families of controls, parental influences accounted for less than 1% of stability over time, whereas in the families of reading disabled children, over 60% of longitudinal stability could be attributed to parental influence. Family influence (genetic and/or family environment) was also seen in symbol-processing speed and in spatial reasoning. Thus the accuracy for long-term prognosis for reading disability may be improved by considering parental reading abilities.

3. Parental self-reported reading status is a factor that contributes to the risk of a child developing a reading disability. Self-reported reading

status was obtained from parents of 174 probands and 182 control children. Using a 5% prevalence rate for reading disability, sons of fathers who have reported problems learning to read have about a 40% risk of developing a reading disability (about 7 times greater than if the fathers do not report reading problems). Sons of reading disabled mothers have a 35% risk (5 times greater than sons of mothers with no reading problems) of developing reading disabilities. For daughters of parents reading disabled by their own report, the risk is lower (17–18%) than for sons, but still it is 10 to 12 times the risk for daughters of parents who do not report having reading problems.

In general, the results of family studies "conclusively demonstrate the familial nature of reading disability, but no single-gene model was found to account adequately for transmission of the disorder. Little or no evidence for sex-linkage was obtained and complex segregation analysis of the total data-set provide no evidence for autosomal major-gene influence. . . . [When, however,] data from only families of female probands was analyzed, the hypothesis of single-gene recessive influence could not be rejected" (De Fries, 1985, p. 112).

Pennington and Smith (1983) and S. D. Smith, Kimberling, Pennington, and Lubs (1983), however, found nine families in whom the presence of a developmental dyslexia was traced in over three generations and in whom the mode of inheritance appeared to be autosomal dominant. Deviation in the heteromorphism (A and C banding) in this group was significant, suggesting that in one form, at least, of dyslexia, there is an autosomal dominant locus on chromosome 15. In families in whom this chromosome variation was found, the likelihood that this association with reading disability was a chance one was improbable ($p < .001$) (S. D. Smith et al., 1983). It is worthy of mention, however, that with new data this result could not be replicated (Kimberling, Fain, Ing, Smith, & Pennington, 1985).

Twin Studies   Twin studies provide further evidence for an inherited component for specific reading disability. Pennington and Smith (1983), reviewing the literature (Bakwin, 1973; Hermann, 1959; Hermann & Norrie, 1958) found 47 monozygotic twins of whom 30 were concordant (both members of the pair are similarly affected) for dyslexia. Only 20% of 64 dizygotic twins were concordant. Sex of the twins was not reported. In the Bakwin study, there were 31 pairs each of monozygotic (MZ) and dizygotic (DZ) twins with at least one dyslexic child per pair. Concordance for MZ twins was 84% and for DZ twins it was 29%.

Twin studies were also a component of the Colorado Reading Project. The major objective of the twin study was "to delineate how environmental and genetic factors may contribute to individual differences in the expression of reading disability" (Decker & Vandenberg, 1985, p. 124). Sixty pairs of twins (30 MZ and 30 DZ) in which at least one twin in each pair was diagnosed as having a reading disability, and control pairs matched to the reading disabled twin pairs on the basis of age, sex, and zygosity, were studied. Concordance rates are presented for 40 pairs of twins (20 MZ, 20 DZ). Using a cut-off reading level at or below the 41st percentile, 16 of 20 MZ pairs were reading at or below that level in contrast to 9 of the 20 DZ pairs. There was, however, variability in the MZ twins who scored at "normal" levels, with two of the four pairs earning reading scores at the 43rd and 44th percentiles. Additional criteria were applied to determine concordance. Using the PIAT for reading recognition, reading comprehension, and spelling; the verbal and performance IQ from the WISC-R; and mothers' reports of whether or not children were having difficulty reading, the concordance rate for MZ twins was 85% and for DZ twins 55%, a difference significant at the .05 level.

Thus, while family and twin studies point to a familial prevalence for a specific reading disability, the genetic mode of inheritance is still elusive. Overall findings point to a heterogeneous mode of transmission, with evidence for a polygenic, multifactorial, autosomal-dominant mode and, in female probands, a possible autosomal-recessive mode. However, only between 25 and 50% of the children identified as having a specific reading disability may demonstrate familial transmission. The problems of clear definition of probands, and their heterogeneity in etiology and in patterns of deficits, continue to plague genetic studies.

Electrophysiologic Studies Electroencephalographic studies have attempted to correlate EEG abnormalities with dyslexia. As J. R. Hughes (1985) pointed out, these studies are plagued with the same generic problems already mentioned in Chapter 1, problems related to definition and classification of dyslexia—that is, to the imprecise boundaries of samples under study and to the fact that dyslexia is a heterogeneous group with components differing in etiology, symptoms, and even prognosis. To these fundamental problems are added the reporting of questionable EEG abnormalities, the relatively high prevalence of positive EEG findings in control groups, and the lack of agreement as to the "abnormality" of some of the reported EEG findings. Conners (1978, 1987) added more specific criticism to EEG–dyslexia correlation studies: that most studies employ nonblind readings of unknown reliability; that they do not, for the most part, rule out associated conditions such as behavior problems or neurological abnormalities; that matching of control samples is usually poor. When matching was good, as in the early study of Myklebust and Boshes (1969), no difference between any EEG variable between controls and learning disability subjects was found. In that study, the greater degrees of EEG abnormality were associated with the milder degrees of reading disorder. Denckla (1978) further criticized EEG studies that do not describe or control for the psychophysical conditions under which the EEG is recorded and that use what she called "naive statistical analysis."

With these caveats, J. R. Hughes (1985), in a review of 10 studies using the standard clinical electroencephalogram and that include 530 children designated as "dyslexics," found an overall mean of 45% (ranging from 27 to 88%) in prevalence of abnormal EEG in these children. This percentage is in contrast to that found in the few studies in which control groups were used, in which the percentage of abnormal EEG's ranged from 7 to 29%.

The EEG patterns that have been described in children with "dyslexia" are essentially four different types: positive spikes; excessive occipital, sometimes temporal, slow waves; generalized, diffuse abnormalities; and epileptoform discharges. Positive spikes in the 6–7- and the 14-second range are considered by some to be a normal variant. J. R. Hughes, however, feels that positive spikes are a significant indication of abnormality; he found (1971) positive spikes in 20% of 214 academic underachievers compared to a 1% prevalence in controls. Bosaeus and Selladen (1979) found positive spikes to be the most common EEG finding in 743 children; although these children were initially considered behaviorally "normal," when a sample (222) of them were subjected to intensive neuropsychiatric examination, they were found to have some type of behavior disorder and "other clinical symptoms." J. R. Hughes cited this paper apparently to suggest that positive spikes, so prevalent in the "dyslexia" population, may not be normal at all. An additional report adds to that suggestion. W. L. Smith, Philippus, and Guard (1968) found that patients with positive spikes showed significant improvement in verbal and full scale IQ when treated with ethosuxamide, an anticonvulsant. This clinical result raises questions about the "purity" of the dyslexia in this sample.

Excessive occipital slow waves have been correlated with impaired visual-motor performance (J. R. Hughes, 1971; Pavy and Metcalf, 1965), but have also been correlated with behavior disorders (Cohn & Nardini, 1958). Excessive occipital slow waves, however, may be so difficult to distinguish from the occipital slow waves so frequently found in children under 15 years of age that they are considered normal. J. R. Hughes nevertheless found a statistically significant difference in the prevalence of slow waves in academic underachievers when compared with those in controls. Slow waves encompassed 27% of all EEG abnormalities found in reading disabled children. Diffuse or generalized abnormality, most often slow waves, has varied from 3 (J. R. Hughes & Park, 1968) to 50% (Caputo, Niedermeyer, & Richardson, 1968). The prevalence of epileptiform discharge, too, has varied with reports from 4 (J. R. Hughes & Park, 1968) to 67% (Ingram et al., 1970) to "the most common EEG abnormality found in patients with dyslexia" (Torres & Ayers, 1968). It is to be noted that the Ingram sample was "highly preselected," the majority of whom had been examined in the neurological and speech clinics of the Royal Hospital for Sick Children in Edinburgh.

In addition to the reports of deviations of EEG patterns in children with reading problems, differences in frequency of different spectral bands in dyslexia are reported. In general, in normal maturation, there is a decrease in numbers of slow waves (delta and theta) and an increase in the alpha and beta range, at all scalp locations, up to age 15. In children with "dyslexia," there has been reported a selective increase in low frequency and a decrease in higher frequency activity. Colon, Notermans, de Weerds, and Kap (1979) and Hanley and Sklar (1976) found the alpha effects inconsistent, but there was decreased beta activity in the bilateral central, parietal, and mid-temporal leads. Fuller (1978) found that when the child was engaged in a task, there was decreased variation in alpha activity, not the attenuation of alpha that occurs normally with the active processing of information. In this connection, the contingent negative variation (a wave form found where there is an expectancy that a given event is about to occur) was reported to be reduced or even absent in children with a learning disability (J. Cohen, 1980).

In spite of the numerous reports relating EEG abnormality to reading disability, the conclusion about that relationship is much the same as Benton and Bird (1963) reported over 20 years ago: A specific association between EEG and reading disability has not been demonstrated. Benton (1978) stated that "few conclusions about the nature of the relationships between electroencephalographic abnormality and specific reading retardation can be drawn from the large body of data which includes a number of suggestive findings, but at the same time so many conflicting results" (p. 465). From his own work and from a review of the literature, however, Hughes concluded that "dyslexics" show a higher prevalence of positive EEG findings than do control groups, but that the kind of EEG patterns found in individuals with reading disabilities are not of one variety (J. R. Hughes, 1978). Studies are still needed on groups of children homogeneous for etiology of their reading disorder and for the distribution of their perceptual deficits, controlled for age, sex, and handedness.

Event-Related Potentials Electrophysiological studies of the relationship between reading disorders and brain waves, however, have advanced beyond the direct visual reading of the standard clinical electroencephalogram that records electrical potential from the scalp under conditions of "passive recording" with the subjects' eyes closed. Research strategies are now attempting to evaluate the EEG quantitatively and to record the dynamic changes in the EEG under conditions in which the brain is challenged by tasks requiring active processing of information. The resulting wave forms, called event-related potentials, are processed by computer to yield quantitative information. Two of the pioneers in this development are F. H. Duffy at the Children's Hospital Medical Center in Boston and E. R. John at New York University College of Medicine.

The Duffy technique reduces the complex wave forms obtained in the EEG in response to different testing conditions into their frequency components (spectra) and the quantity of the forms with that frequency (power). The result is a power spectrum plot for each frequency at each electrode. This technique reduces the complex data of the EEG into a set of four single numbers (a power for each spectral band) for each electrode. Topographical maps of the head, representing the power of each spectrum band, may now be drawn and displayed on a computer-driven color video screen. This technique, called brain electrical activity mapping (BEAM), has been widely adopted so that now it is available at many centers. The effect of sensory stimuli and of tasks requiring active processing of information on the topographical maps may be studied over time in a sequential display of images. Duffy has developed statistical methods (statistical probability mapping) to delineate regions in which brain electrical activity from an individual subject differs from that of a referenced population. In addition, differences between groups—such as those between dyslexics and controls—may be studied by comparing each point on the topographical maps evoked for each test in the control and dyslexic groups. The significance of differences between values for each point is determined by the standard two-sample t statistic, which is then transformed into a "percentile index," which is, in turn, converted into a topographic image.

Two papers report the findings of these techniques for dyslexic boys. In the first (F. H. Duffy, Denckla, Bartels, & Sandini, 1980), with 8 dyslexic boys and 10 "normal" boys aged 9 to 11, topographic mapping revealed four discrete regions of differences between the two groups, involving both hemispheres, the left more than the right. The eight dyslexics fulfilled the criteria for "dyslexia-pure," and full scale IQ scores (WISC-R) ranged from 94 to 114. Two of the children were left-handed, two were ambidextrous, and four were right-handed. The controls came from a similar socioeconomic group to that of the dyslexic children. Two controls were left-handed, one was ambidextrous, and seven were right-handed. The EEG was recorded during 10 different tasks, 2 of which involved "simple resting brain activity" with eyes opened and eyes closed and 8 of which were designed to activate either the left hemisphere (speech and reading) or the right hemisphere (music and geometric figures) and both hemispheres together (paired visual-verbal associations). In addition, 2 evoked-potential tasks (visual and auditory) and 1 requiring a difficult phonological discrimination were given. Significant percentile index differences between the two groups were found in four regions: bilateral medial frontal (supplementary motor); left antero-lateral-frontal (Broca's area); left mid-temporal (auditory associative); and left postero-lateral quadrant (Wernicke's areas, parietal associative areas, visual associative areas). The authors concluded that "dyslexia-pure may represent dysfunction within a complex and widely distributed brain system, not a discrete brain lesion" (F. H. Duffy et al., 1980a, p. 417). In addition, there were greater mean alpha in response to event-related tasks in the dyslexic group, a finding in agreement with that of Fuller (1978), and which may signify underactivation of frontal systems in dyslexic boys. Of the test challenges, a sound-symbol association test and a phonetic discrimination test produced the greatest differences between groups. In the evoked-potential challenges, positive waves at 282 msec after visual stimulus (flashes from a strobe light) were found in the dyslexics, but negative waves at 282 msec were found in the controls; for the auditory evoked-potential differences, usually positive waves were found in the dyslexic children, whereas negative waves in the controls appeared at 114, 198, and 342 msec.

The BEAM data obtained in this study of 18 boys were used to identify diagnostic rules for dyslexia and were tested against similar data gathered from an additional group of six boys (three normal and three dyslexic). The 183 measures obtained in F. H. Duffy, Denckla, Bartels, Sandini, and Kiessling (1980b), were statistically reduced to the 55 that differentiated between control and dyslexic groups, and these, in turn, were reduced to the 24 best discriminating features. Multivariate analysis, in which each subject was represented by the 10 highest ranking features, separated the dyslexic and normal groups. The combined analysis of EEG and evoked-potential features was superior to analysis of either alone. Ultimately two features, the auditory evoked-potential task involving a difficult phonological discrimination and the auditory evoked-potential task involving clicks, were used to correctly identify five of the six test groups (all three normal and two of the three dyslexics), a diagnostic success of 80%. When all 24 subjects are considered (the 18 previously tested boys plus the 6 additional), a correct classification was obtained in about 90%. These diagnostic rules have yet to be applied to a larger number of children. Preliminary results involving brain maps obtained with the BEAM technique of 44 "dyslexia-pure" boys are reported by Denckla (1985). While differences in bilateral frontal regions characterized all dyslexia groups when compared with controls, the extent and magnitude of differences also are found in three dyslexic subgroups: The global language disordered group had the greatest difference, followed by the anomic subgroup; fewer differences were found in the dysphonemic-sequencing disordered group.

The group at New York University Medical School (John, Prichep, Fridman, & Easton, 1988) derived a set of equations that transforms data obtained from the resting EEG and from waves resulting from 58 tasks that challenge sensory, perceptual, and cognitive functions into standardized (Z statistics) form so that they may be compared with data obtained from a normative group. This technique is called *neurometrics*. The normative data from subjects from age 6 to 90 include univariate and multivariate descriptions of absolute power, relative power (power for each frequency band divided by total power across the frequency bands), mean frequency, and coherence and asymmetry between homologous leads for both monopolar and bipolar derivations, all for delta, theta, alpha, and beta frequency bands. Evoked potentials and event-related potentials are recorded within 10 msec latency intervals for 500 msec after stimulus onset. "With these data an individual neurometric profile may be construed for each patient, describing the statistically deviant measures and the regions in which they deviate from normal values" (J. R. Hughes, 1985, p. 81).

The normative data for children are based on 600 "normally" functioning children, aged 6–16. Approximately half of these are Swedish subjects, aged 1–21, whose normative data for 16 EEG features were described by Matousek and Petersen in 1973. To this group, John et al. (1980) added the same EEG features they found in 306 "healthy, normally functioning" American children aged 6–16. The resulting 32 absolute power features were normalized as a relative power for each derivation, transformed so that the features could be expressed as Z scores. The range of values is reported to correspond well with that obtained from normal children in other countries.

The neurometrics technique was able to identify abnormality in approximately half of three different diagnostic groups: those at risk for neurological disorder, learning disordered children with generalized disabilities, and learning disorded children with specific learning difficulties. Studying more specific learning disabilities, comparing normal children with verbal underachievers, with arithmetic underachievers, and with a group of "mixed" underachievement, John et al. (1988) found children with different patterns of underachievement to have different neurometric profiles.

The verbal underachievers had visual evoked potential amplitude differences in the left parietal and central areas, occurring at 200–350 msec after stimulus; the arithmetic underachievers had excess theta at the parieto-occipital locations; the mixed group had excessive delta and theta at the posterior regions. Differences in amplitude of visual evoked potential were seen in two domains, the 100–200 msec and the 200–300 msec. These domains presumably are related to perceptual (at 100–200 msec) and cognitive processes (at 200–300 msec). This report of the New York University group is supported by the finding that, using visually presented discrete word stimuli, reading disabled children appeared to have two peaks between 200–300 msec in the ensuing wave form, in contrast to one peak for normal readers.

Conversely, when the different neurometric profiles were examined, the theta-excess group showed poor performance on tasks requiring sustained attention, including reaction times and digit span; the delta-excess group had deficits in Digit Span and the Trail-Making test; the auditory evoked-potential asymmetry group had more errors on Color Naming, and Trail Making and longer delays on the Digit Span test. As John et al. (1988) pointed out, however, most of their reading disordered children came from a special education facility and did not meet the criteria for "dyslexia pure." One other report (Yingling et al., 1986) described a low incidence of abnormal neurometric findings on a sample of pure dyslexics.

The work of the BEAM group in Boston and the neurometric group in New York is reported in some detail because of the promise it holds for future electrophysiological studies of reading. When correlated with behavioral, neurological, and neuropsychological measures and using tasks that require ongoing processing of different types of information, these approaches may become useful instruments for meaningful subgrouping of children with learning disorders.

Although the past 25 years have seen over 100 papers other than those of F. H. Duffy and John dealing with the electrical activity of the brain that accompanies visual, tactile, and auditory stimulation (evoked potential and event-related potential), few have been primarily concerned with learning disabled children. Of those that have been concerned, most suffer from the methodological problems cited earlier in this section, so that Shagass, Ornitz, Sutton, and Tueting (1978), in an early review of event-related potentials and psychopathology, stated that "they cannot be properly evaluated," and Conners (1987) enumerated 10 methodological flaws that are frequently found. Nevertheless, research on the normative reaction of the brain as it receives and actively processes information is, of course, essential basic data against which changes occurring in reading disabled children may be compared. This section will not review the studies on "normal" data. A review of event-related potentials that accompany the phonological, contextual, and semantic tasks of language may be found in Molfese (1983).

A number of event-related potential studies have shown differences between reading disability children and controls. In an early study Conners (1970), measuring the evoked potential to light flashes in 27 "poor readers," 8–12 years old, found an attenuation of amplitude in a negative wave derived from the left parietal area that appeared 200 msec after stimulus. This attenuation was not found in recording from the right parietal or from occipital regions. This finding was confirmed on nine 10-year-old disabled readers (Preston, Guthrie, & Childs, 1974). Conners (1978) also reported one family in whom all members with a reading disability had an attenuated N200 wave. However, Sobotka and May (1977) found reading disabled children, in contrast to controls, had an *increased* amplitude to unattended stimuli at parietal electrode sites (P140-N200) and at occipital sites (N200-P280) and slower reaction time to attended stimuli at the same sites. Stelmack, Saxe, Noldy-Cullum, Campbell, and Armitage (1988) concluded that there has been "little success in distinguishing consistent ERP [event-related potential] differences between normal and disabled readers with a visual event related potential component that emerge within 250 msecs of stimulation" (p. 186).

Studies examining auditory event-related potential of reading disabled subjects suggest that disabled readers may be differentiated from controls by a *reduced* amplitude of the positive wave appearing 500 msec (P300) after stimulation, in tasks requiring the discrimination or detection of unexpected or significant semantic elements. These findings are not robust (Holcomb, Ackerman, & Dykman, 1985; Ollo & Squires, 1986). Stelmack et al. (1988) explored the recognition memory for words in 7 reading-disabled boys and 10 control subjects at 7–12 years of age. The task was to read, silently, words presented on slides (visually) and to try to remember as many as possible in a subsequent memory test. There was an enhanced amplitude of the P200 component but a decreased amplitude of the N400 wave in both the acquisition and the memory tasks in reading disabled children compared with the controls. These findings suggest differences in the early sensory stage of encoding and retrieval (P200) and semantic or memory search (N400). The N400 wave appears to be a sensitive indicator of the semantic relationship between a word and the context in which it occurs (Kutas & Hillyard, 1980).

A different approach using an event-related potential probe technique was taken by Shucard, Cummins, Gay, Lairsmith, and Welanko (1985). This study, part of the Colorado Reading Project, actively engaged subjects in an ongoing information-processing task and, while subjects performed these tasks, pairs of task-irrelevant auditory tone pips were presented to them binaurally over headphones. Two experimental conditions, letter sounds and letter-shapes, are described. The former required a visual-phonemic transfer; the latter a visual-shape processing. In both conditions, the pattern of auditory event-related potential amplitude asymmetry found for disabled readers was opposite to that for normal readers, with reduced right-hemisphere responses for disabled readers, suggesting that these tasks involved "different cerebral processes" in the two groups studied (Shucard et al., 1985). This study is important because it is part of the Colorado Reading Project whose electrophysiological findings may be integrated with neuropsychological and genetic ones.

In spite of the methodological problems, the electrophysiology of event-related potentials and the quantitative study of neurometrics and of BEAM offer an additional parameter in which to study the brain as it is challenged with tasks that require the processing of information. When electrophysiology is correlated with neuropsychological and clinical data, the results will add another dimension to our understanding of learning disorders.

Morphological Studies

Although gross morphological asymmetries of the mammalian brain have been known for many years, the relationship between these asymmetries and specific language disability has only recently been unfolding. In 1968 Geschwind and Levitsky found, in routine autopsies of unselected brains, that in approximately 65–70% of the brains examined the left planum temporale was larger than the right, whereas in approximately 10% it was larger on the right, and in 20–25% there was no difference in planum size. Broca's area, too, has been found to be asymmetric, with the posterior third of Broca's region on the left containing greater surface area than the right. Also those areas of the angular gyrus related to language show the left brain larger than the right in most cases.

These gross anatomical findings of asymmetry in areas related to language in these unselected brains are reflected in cytological differences as well. Microscopic evidence of a greater number of cells was found in the left Wernicke's area (area designated as Tpt) and in that portion of the left angular gyrus (designated Pg) than in the right (Eidelberg & Galaburda, 1982, 1984; Galaburda, Sanides, & Geschwind, 1978).

Many of the gross and microscopic anatomical asymmetries described in the brains of adults and children are present, too, in the fetal human brain (Witelson & Pallie, 1973). Witelson and Kigar (1988) found that the midsagittal area of the human corpus callosum obtained from postmortem measurement varied with tested hand preference: It was larger by 11% in left-handed and ambidextrous people than in those with consistently right-handed preferences.

The relationship of these findings to dyslexia has not yet been documented. The first anatomical study in dyslexia was done by Drake (1968) on the brain of a 12-year-old boy who died of a cerebellar hemorrhage. Although this child had defects in reading, writing, and calculation, there were complicating problems with the diagnosis. Hyperactivity, "dizzy spells," and blackouts that were reported in the history raise questions about the purity of the dyslexia and thus render the relationship of the anatomical findings to dyslexia questionable.

Galaburda approached the problem of the anatomical substrate for dyslexia on the basis of several questions:

- What is the evidence of an unusual brain underlying dyslexia?
- Could anatomical studies produce a description of the brain that would explain the observed behaviors in dyslexia?
- If a different architecture of the brain is demonstrated, what might be the cause of the change? At what level of development was this change initiated? (Galaburda, 1989)

Observations were based on autopsies of eight people (six males and two females) diagnosed as dyslexic by experts in the field. Ages ranged from 12 to 88 years and included right-handers, left-handers, and ambidextrous individuals. All had earned IQs within the 100 to 130 range; all had had opportunities to learn to read. None had a significant psychiatric history. Galaburda acknowledged that this group may not represent the full spectrum of the disorder, but he was confident that they are all dyslexic individuals. Galaburda also had access to a normative collection of other brains for comparison.

The first of the two major phenomena Galaburda observed relates to symmetry in language areas. He regards this symmetry as an anatomical characteristic rather than an abnormality. Among unselected brains, only 20–25% are symmetrical; in *every one* of the eight dyslexic brains, however, the planum temporale is symmetrical. Galaburda (1989) concluded that this is a strong association statistically and that symmetry, a variation from the expected structure, is significant in the dyslexic brain.

Further studies were directed toward describing the nerve-cell networks that underlie processing in these brains. Galaburda hypothesized that in unselected brains naturally occurring regressive events in neurogenesis cause a decrease in the number of neurons in the right hemisphere although the number of neurons in the left side does not change significantly. In other words, a differentiating characteristic of the dyslexic brains is that they have "too much language on the right." The normal asymmetries are observable early in human development, as early as 4 to 5 prenatal months. They can also be observed in studies of the development sensory cortex of animals in the laboratory (Galaburda, 1989, p. 74).

Galaburda speculated on the functional effects of hemisphere specialization. He believes that the elimination of neurons is a physiological process observable in Type I neurons in response to environmental requirements. When too few are eliminated (as in the case of the dyslexic brains he examined), there is a less precise match with environmental requirements, as well as differences in connections that determine functional properties. Galaburda and others in his laboratory inferred from animal studies of the development of asymmetries that the dyslexic brain may be excessively connected *between* the two hemispheres and not well enough connected *within* each hemisphere. The significance for language development, as Galaburda sees it, is that the dyslexic lacks the connectivity of structures within the left hemisphere to deal with the various subprocesses involved in language (Galaburda, 1989).

The second phenomenon Galaburda observed in the eight dyslexic brains in his laboratory concerns evidence of ectopias, collections of neurons appearing outside of expected locations and associated with distortion of the architecture of the brain. These evidences of *microdysgenesis* are focal and multiple, and they vary in the brains in both number and distribution. What is least variable about these foci is that all the brains have involvement in the anterior language area.

In addition, two of the male brains and both female brains contain a cluster of abnormalities that are dramatically different from the microdysgenesis described above. These findings are little scars that first were thought to be the results of minor strokes that occurred during the life of the person. However, staining of the scars indicated that they contained myelin, a finding that placed the scars early in the development of these individuals. The significance of these scars to language development is not clear from present observations. However, the presence of such scars in a strain of autoimmune laboratory mice (New Zealand Black mice) has led Galaburda to consider the contribution of autoimmune disorders to these anatomic findings.

Galaburda's findings, if indeed the eight brains in his laboratory are at all representative of the population of people with dyslexia, have very special significance for the field of learning disorders. As with any new research, these formulations need to be considered in relation to what has already been learned about dyslexia in previous behavioral research and clinical observations.

The finding that the brains of the dyslexic sample were consistently more anatomically symmetrical than those in an unselected sample is consonant with the results of a variety of investigations showing that people with dyslexia are not well lateralized. Studies of dichotic digits, visual half fields, and tactile discrimination have all reached this general conclusion. Studies of cerebral blood flow suggest inefficient processing within the language hemisphere; this, too, would be consonant with the implications of disturbances in connectivity. The suggestions that these differences in brain architecture are pervasive and manifested early in life is also not inconsistent with the results of genetic studies.

The ectopias and the evidences of early scarring are also not inconsistent with results of clinical research. The variation Galaburda found in both number and distribution of these foci could account for some of the variation nearly all investigators report within the group designated as dyslexic. The almost obsessive preoccupation with subgroup studies in current research is evidence of the variation in the responses of individuals to a wide range of clinical probes. For people who have done longitudinal research, the intra-individual variations are equally interesting, not only as clinical phenomena, but also as demonstrations of the plasticity and reorganization of which the developing human brain is capable. Researchers and practitioners will continue to look to Galaburda's laboratory for increasing understanding of the biological substrate underlying this most puzzling disorder of learning.

MANAGEMENT OF SPECIFIC LANGUAGE DISABILITY

All the foregoing data represent results of studies from many disciplines. While the cause (or causes) of specific language disability (or disabilities) is still elusive, these studies have broadened the breadth and increased the depth of our understanding of the central processing problems of the child and the adult with SLD. Nevertheless, we are faced with the practical problem of identifying the child with SLD, providing appropriate and sufficient treatment, and following him through the years of his life. These practical problems have already been addressed in previous chapters of this book: diagnosis in Chapters 5 and 6, management in Chapters 7, 8, and 9, and long-term outcomes in Chapter 3. This section uses two case studies to apply recommended management guidelines.

Rawson (1968) wisely observed that "the many, many people who fit the broad general designation of dyslexia are notable, first of all, for their seeming likeness to everybody else. Their ranges in age, IQ, and social and other circumstances are just as wide, and in every sense of the word 'normal.' Their learning and skill problems are specific to language" (p. 179).

In some ways, their very normality creates problems for the children with specific language disability. Nearly a century since it was first identified clinically and 50 years after Orton wrote about it so insightfully, dyslexia is still regarded as a myth by some writers who say these children are just like all the other poor readers and even not very different from mentally retarded children. This could be an interesting theoretical debate, except that some of these writers are educators whose writing can have grave consequences for the educational interventions available to children with specific language disabilities.

Although the presenting symptom (reading difficulty) may be similar in all these cases, the etiology, clinical course, and prognosis are different. This book is based upon that understanding. Even brief clinical experience should convince the most obstinate critic, but research evidence is also available in an aptly entitled paper, "Is There a Thing Called Dyslexia?" (Aaron et al., 1988). These investigators provide sound evidence that children with dyslexia are different from those they call "garden variety retarded readers." Furthermore, if Galaburda's dyslexic brains are in any way representative of the population of dyslexics in general, these children are different in the way they develop the brain functions that serve language. Each new set of language symbols and each step in the language arts sequence holds new hazards for them. Most of the time, conventional classroom methods will be ineffective for them.

CASE STUDY: JANE

The following progress notes from her teachers recount the sad school history of Jane, a bright, seriously depressed youngster who was seen at age 13.

Progress Report: End of Grade I

Jane is a student of fine ability. She has insatiable curiosity. She thinks rapidly and logically. Her ability to reason and draw conclusions is superior. She is ever alert and strove to do her best this year, but there were areas beyond her reach because of her level of developmental maturity. Initially, Jane required a period of extended readiness for formal reading instruction. Now, although Jane has made progress, her skills have not reached grade level, nor has she reached her potential. My recommendation is to retain Jane in first grade, which I feel would be the most appropriate placement at this time.

[Translation: We don't know what we did wrong, but we want to do it over again.] The parents did not agree to nonpromotion. Reading achievement test score: 14th percentile.

Progress Report: End of Grade 2

Jane has been working a bit harder lately and is showing improvement in all academic areas, particularly math. Jane still does not show as much interest in reading as she must in order to be able to be a more proficient reader. She struggles with words, even in a primer, and becomes restless when her small reading group is at the reading table. She likes to look at the other children while they are reading when she should be following along in her book. She looks at the pictures for clues much too often at this time of year. She should have broken away from that rather questionable reading aid by now. In my professional opinion, Jane has not made sufficient progress in reading this year to ensure success in third grade where so much additional reading will be required. Jane is a bright youngster who deserves a chance to be the best she can be. I recommend retention in second grade.

[Translation: I don't know how to teach her either, but I think whatever it is that is wrong is your fault, because you should have let her repeat first grade.] The parents agreed to having Jane repeat second grade. Reading achievement test score: 9th percentile.

Progress Report: End of Grade 2 (repeated)

Jane has successfully completed second grade this year. Her math has improved tremendously. She is still having difficulty with her reading, but hopefully this also will continue to improve. Jane is a very creative and imaginative girl as exemplified by her writings, drawings, and storytelling. She is very outgoing and friendly. She usually has a very good relationship with her classmates. Jane still needs to work on increasing her self-confidence. When she feels she is "smart," things go well. When she feels she is "dumb," she starts having difficulty in all areas.

[Translation: Since we can't teach her to read very well, let's work on self-confidence, now that we've taken that away by having her stay back.] Reading achievement test score: 25th percentile.

Progress Report: End of Grade 3

Since Jane is still experiencing difficulty with her classroom work, she will continue remedial reading classes in order to support Mrs.————'s efforts.

[Translation: We've given up.] Reading achievement test score: 15th percentile.

Records do not contain further end-of-year reports. However, the reading achievement test score for fifth grade was recorded at the 16th percentile.

The records show that the typical administrative approaches (retention in grade and remedial reading consisting of reteaching the basal reading series used in the classroom) did not help Jane read better. Even more striking is the emotional attrition from failure. In 3 years the interested, motivated youngster became acutely sensitive to slights about her intellectual abilities, which even in her depressed state at age 13 were respectable (WISC-R: full scale IQ, 116, verbal IQ, 106, performance IQ, 124). After third grade she was placed in a resource room program under special education auspices. That the combination of workbook exercises and homework helping she received there was not particularly effective is indicated by achievement test scores at age 13:

WIDE RANGE ACHIEVEMENT TEST	PERCENTILE
Oral Reading	1
Spelling	8
Arithmetic	6

Woodcock-Johnson Psychoeducational Battery

	GRADE SCORES	PERCENTILE
Reading Cluster	3.0	5
Mathematics Cluster	3.4	7

Despite daily sessions in the resource room, she has not mastered decoding skills. When she met an unfamiliar word, she guessed at it on the basis of its visual configuration and initial grapheme. Thus *form* was read as "from," *grunt* as "garnet," and *theory* as "through." The Phoenician Spelling Test showed that she was uncertain of the short vowels but knew most consonant blends and digraphs. She did not know such serviceable generalizations as the long vowel/silent e rule or the closed syllable rule, but she knew r-controlled vowels, and soft g and c; she reversed the letter b twice.

Jane: Phonecian Spelling Test

WORD DICTATED	RESPONSE	WORD DICTATED	RESPONSE
mag	mag	muttin	motin
fid	fed	noy	nowy
vol	val	tort	tort
pub	pud	cim	cim
plat	blat	theet	thet

WORD DICTATED	RESPONSE	WORD DICTATED	RESPONSE
chim	chen	gem	gem
cred	cred	bode	bod
cade	cad	quell	qwel
bine	bin	dard	bard
seld	seld	sow	sow

Decoding and encoding skills were so limited that it was difficult to assess Jane's reading comprehension and writing skills. It is not surprising that she felt lost and discouraged when faced with classwork in a large suburban middle school.

The discouraging outcome with Jane illustrates how her normality and reasonableness did her a disservice. Had she demonstrated some problem behavior, she would have called attention to her problems and perhaps received more effective assistance. Her defense was one of withdrawal and self-devaluation.

Not all youngsters with specific language disabilities respond as Jane did (see Chapter 9): Some youngsters respond with anger and hostility; others become dependent and passive; some use denial and isolation; some become almost sociopathic in their skill at cheating on tests, copying homework, and beating the system. When these children get to the clinician's office, the diagnostic problem is complicated by the need to separate the primary problem from the defensive system the youngster has had to construct to survive.

Therefore, a major management principle is the need for early, comprehensive, multidisciplinary diagnosis. On the basis of information elicited, an intervention plan should be developed so that one professional becomes responsible for intervention strategies. This kind of individual educational plan is mandated by special education legislation in the schools; it is no less necessary in the private practice of psychiatrists, educators, and psychologists working with children with specific learning disabilities. This disorder is a lifelong condition. A brief diagnostic conference or a few months of tutoring to "catch up" in a subject area will not suffice. While direct services may be necessary at some critical times in an individual's development, at other times they may need consultation at pivotal decision points (such as with a change of schools or vocational plans), or support in documenting the history of a learning disorder in order to have accommodations such as extended time on tests available for various qualifying examinations.

This plan should be arrived at in cooperation with the parents and the youngster involved. Effective implementation of the plan depends upon consensual agreement and commitment of all the people involved. The most important people in the implementation of the plan are the youngsters, who may if they have had experiences like Jane's in the past, express some reservations about any plan for remediation. Time spent dealing openly with those reservations and in building understanding of the intervention plan is certainly time well spent. It may be that some students who bear the scars of many previous unsuccessful interventions will require some negotiation before they agree. Setting a time-limited trial period is one method of providing such youngsters the control they feel they must have before they can make commitment to an intervention plan. One can understand students' reluctance to trust still another program that promises to teach them to read, having felt disappointment in the past. This is particularly true when students have some doubts about their ability to learn; they may be reluctant to make a great investment in a program that will prove, in the final analysis, that they really do not have the ability to learn to read.

Once the intervention plan has been agreed on and the responsibilities for intervention have been assigned, the program is ready to begin. Whether it is a relatively modest arrangement for tutoring, a resource room program, a special class, or a special school, it should be understood that educational decisions are under the control of the teacher. Although they may be therapeutic in effect, these programs differ markedly from psychotherapy in this respect. Rapport in this setting is based upon the teacher's designing the work in such a way as to give the student opportunity for successful learning. This sense of accomplishment will be a most powerful motivating force. Used successfully, it will make rewards in the form of extrinsic motivation unnecessary.

For the child with a specific language disability, the program activities should be embedded in the total language sequence. Content of the lessons should be based on the child's level of development in that sequence and move on from there. Although students may request it, help with school homework is not very useful unless it is appropriate to the level and the type of skills being taught. Frequently, homework assignments will be far beyond the actual language skills the student needs work with. Sacrificing the time needed for practice with these skills to complete what may be inappropriate busywork is an unwise choice. This problem can be met by asking that homework requirements be modified by the teacher in terms of the child's actual educational needs. One exception to this advice might be the use of the textbooks in the content subjects when reading comprehension strategies are being taught. For example if the SQ3R comprehension technique (survey, question, read, review, recite) is being taught, using the child's science or social studies textbook will improve transfer of the technique to real-life requirements.

Particularly at the secondary level, other accommodations in the school program may be necessary. This might mean the substitution of one type of skill for another (i. e., the substitution of a computer language for a traditional foreign language requirement) or the choice of a more phonetically regular foreign language (i. e., Spanish, Russian, or Hebrew rather than

French). The use of the word processor (and spelling checker) for written compositions is an important skill for secondary school students to learn and to use with regular assignments.

The major problem with most students with specific language disabilities is in the area of decoding. Teachers working with them should not assume that all aspects of these skills are in place, no matter what the age of the student is. A careful survey of the student's skills through examination of oral reading, formal spelling, and a spontaneous writing sample is essential. Any aspects of these processes that have not been mastered should be given major priority in intervention. Reading comprehension is seriously hampered by word attack skills that are not automatic; written expression is constricted if the student must take time from expressing her ideas in order to select words she can spell and avoid those she can't.

Finally, the teacher of the child with dyslexia should be alert for special abilities the child may have that are not addressed by the current school program. In our descriptions of the language problems of these children, it is easy to lose sight of their strengths. These talents may begin to show up in art and design, in mechanical abilities, in mathematics, in leadership and management skills, in computer applications, in sports abilities, and in countless other fields. During the school years they represent a respite from the drudgery of learning to deal with the language. However, as the youngster enters adolescence, these interests may assume a more important role than that of hobby or compensatory activity. They may point the direction for vocational choice in adult life.

CASE STUDY: MATT

The case of Matt illustrates some of the principles just discussed in educational intervention with a boy who has a specific language disability.

Matt was referred for psychological testing and educational planning by a child psychiatrist whom his family had consulted because of Matt's lack of progress in learning to read. Matt's family was acquainted with dyslexia, because his older brother had similar problems. In addition, his father, although he had graduated from an Ivy-League college and was now a successful professional man, had had difficulty in learning to read. The signs were recognized early in Matt and help was sought when he was a 7½-year-old second-grader in a challenging independent school. He was first seen in January 1974.

On the WISC Matt earned a full scale IQ of 124, placing cognitive functioning at the 94th percentile. The performance IQ of 135 (99th percentile) was superior to the verbal IQ of 110 (75th percentile), although one of the highest scores on the record occurred with the verbal scale test of Vocabulary. The only significantly low score was with rote sequencing of digits.

WISC Scaled Scores

Information	12	Picture Completion	12
Comprehension	11	Picture Arrangement	20
Arithmetic	11	Block Design	15
Similarities	12	Object Assembly	15
Vocabulary	16	Coding	13
Digit Span	8		

In addition to Vocabulary, Matt also did well with the subtest tapping the building of a story sequence from pictures. On this test he showed skill in sequencing ideas and insight and alertness to the subtle behavioral cues in the pictures. This easy sequencing of ideas contrasted with his difficulties with the arbitrary sequences of digits, on which he was only able to handle a sequence of four digits forward and three digits reversed.

Matt related well in the session. He was honest with himself about what was hard for him. He tended to undervalue his efforts, however, and needed encouragement to improvise with items on which he was not completely certain of the answer, particularly with manipulative or numerical items.

Because of Matt's superior cognitive resources, his educational expectancy was estimated to be at the high third-grade level at the time of testing. This expectancy estimate is a rough standard that can be compared with the scores he earned on the educational tests listed below:

WIDE RANGE ACHIEVEMENT TEST	GRADE SCORES
Oral Reading	1.4
Spelling	1.6
PEABODY INDIVIDUAL ACHIEVEMENT TEST	GRADE SCORES
Mathematics	3.2
Reading Recognition	1.2
Reading Comprehension	(untestable)

As can be seen from the above scores, learning of mathematics is appropriate to expectancy. The only difficulties he experienced occurred with such arbitrary verbal sequences as measures (inches, pints, quarts, etc.) and with place values of some numbers.

Oral reading places at the beginning reading level on both the PIAT and the WRAT. Matt has some idea of phonic analysis, but did not associate all sounds and symbols accurately. Furthermore, phonic knowledge was not used with any consistency in reading. When Matt met an unfamiliar word, he was apt to guess at it on the basis of its configuration, rather than to use sounds even when he knew them.

Spelling reflected the same mixed approach. It was not possible to assess reading comprehension at that time because Matt recognized too few words. The impression, however, was that once he learned to decode the words, he would have no trouble dealing with the ideas.

On assessment of perceptual skills, Matt found auditory tasks easier than the visual and visual-motor tasks. His articulation was precise. He blended sounds into words well but had difficulty matching initial sounds and recognizing or supplying rhymes. The Bender VMGT was difficult for him, with integration and orientation of figures somewhat below his age level. Even when the motor aspect was removed from the task (as it was on the Lamb Chop Test) he tended to rotate the figures. He was able to indicate right and left on himself, but not on the examiner. He was also uncertain of the finger schema. Our arm extension test suggested that for Matt laterality for language had not been firmly established.

Despite superior cognitive abilities, a diagnosis of specific language disability was made and tutoring was recommended along the following lines:

1. training in prereading skills to build a basis for beginning reading:
   a. visual motor
   b. visual orientation
   c. rhyming
   d. locating sounds within words
   e. finger schema
2. when perceptual skills permit, teaching of independent word attack skills with emphasis on a code-based approach and use of phonetically-regular text
3. written language activities to teach accurate mechanics and to encourage fluent written expression

The first step in tutoring was goal setting. Added to the original three instructional goals was an additional one, that of reaching consensus with Matt, his parents, and his school about the recommended intervention program. Matt's parents were intelligent, sensible, and supportive. Matt himself had not experienced devastating failure and, although he may have had some reservations, he went along with the plans quietly. His school was also cooperative, albeit overoptimistic about what Matt had accomplished with the conventional program. Exchange visits were arranged so that we had some idea of classroom activities and his teacher had an opportunity to observe a tutoring session. Responsibilities were apportioned so that some skills that required daily practice (i. e., Rhythmic Writing on the chalkboard) could be done at school. Observation of the reading lesson at school indicated that some modification of the basal reader sight-word approach was needed to reinforce the code-based approach used in the tutoring sessions. The suggestion for this change required tact, but it was received and implemented with materials already available in the classroom.

The first work with Matt centered around building the prereading skills. Matt enjoyed Rhythmic Writing on the chalkboard, adapting himself to the precision in motor control required by the task, even inventing motifs of his own to be added to the collection we were getting ready for publication in *Teach*. The purpose of Rhythmic Writing was to provide practice with directional orientation and to help him overlearn the motor patterns needed for handwriting. The latter purpose was crucial because his school curriculum made the transition from print to cursive writing at the end of second grade. It was important to Matt to keep up with his classmates with this skill, although it was not easy for him; he often complained that he could not remember "how the letters went." These handwriting techniques (and the neuropsychological principles underlying them) have been described (Hagin, 1983).

Work with rhyming provided a supportive skill for learning phonic analysis. The idea of rhyming was taught using paired associate learning, practice with games (such as Concentration and Rhyming Dominoes), and poems. This skill needed to be automatic if it were to be of any use in word attack. Matt enjoyed this work, seeming to find comfort in its repetitiveness. He soon began trying his hand with writing simple rhymes like this one that turned into a valentine after much help with the spelling:

> A valentine heart
> In my best art.
> Made for you
> With paper and glue
> Because
> Parents are
> Good skiers
> &
> Sight see-ers
> Great cooks
> And they help us with books
> And tons of fun
> Your happy son
>
> Matt

Work in decoding reviewed all consonant sounds to mastery and began introducing various phonic elements, more or less in the sequence presented in Gillingham's *Jewel Box*. Activities in this area included (a) rapid review of sound cards from previous lessons, (b) introduction of the new sound element, (c) dictation of words containing a high frequency of the sound element being taught with much emphasis on Matt's blending sound elements as he wrote them, (d) oral reading of the dictated words, (e) rapid silent reading of the dictated words in response to a Guessing Meanings game, and (f) reading aloud from phonetically regular text (i. e., from such series as the SRA Basic Reading Series). This pattern of activities (called *DOMinate*) was used to teach all phonic elements. As word attack skills were mastered, there was gradual introduction of natural text from conventional remedial materials and, with them, generalizations and procedures for syllabication. This work was not accomplished easily or rapidly; it spread over 4 years, with many frustrating hours for Matt as the sound-symbol associations almost mastered at one session eluded him completely on his return.

When dealing with words he could decode, Matt had little difficulty understanding meaning. His exceptionally broad vocabulary was enriched by the many travel experiences his family provided and by the broad-based, sometimes very challenging curriculum at school. The first book Matt read independently was in fourth grade in connection with a history unit on the Middle Ages at school. We had found a simplified version of *Men of Iron*, and he set to work enthusiastically. During the next session he explained the game-plan he used on each chapter: "First I read the words; then I read it to see what it says; then I close the book and think about what happened." An effective, if rudimentary study strategy!

Spelling and written composition work moved most slowly of all the goals. There was such a gap between Matt's ideas and his ability to deal with the written language code that many of his early efforts were almost unreadable:

wen we went ot apan we had fund and do you
know wut the most fun wun sking.
and my big ——— got a ——— fi ——— ———
and I tride tem on but theaye did mot fot
and I wuz sad.

Using the Fernald tracing technique (Chapter 7), Matt rewrote the story:

    Aspen
When we went to Aspen, we had fun. And do you
know what was the most fun? Skiing.
My big brother got a pair of moon boots
and I tried them on, but they did not fit.
I was sad!

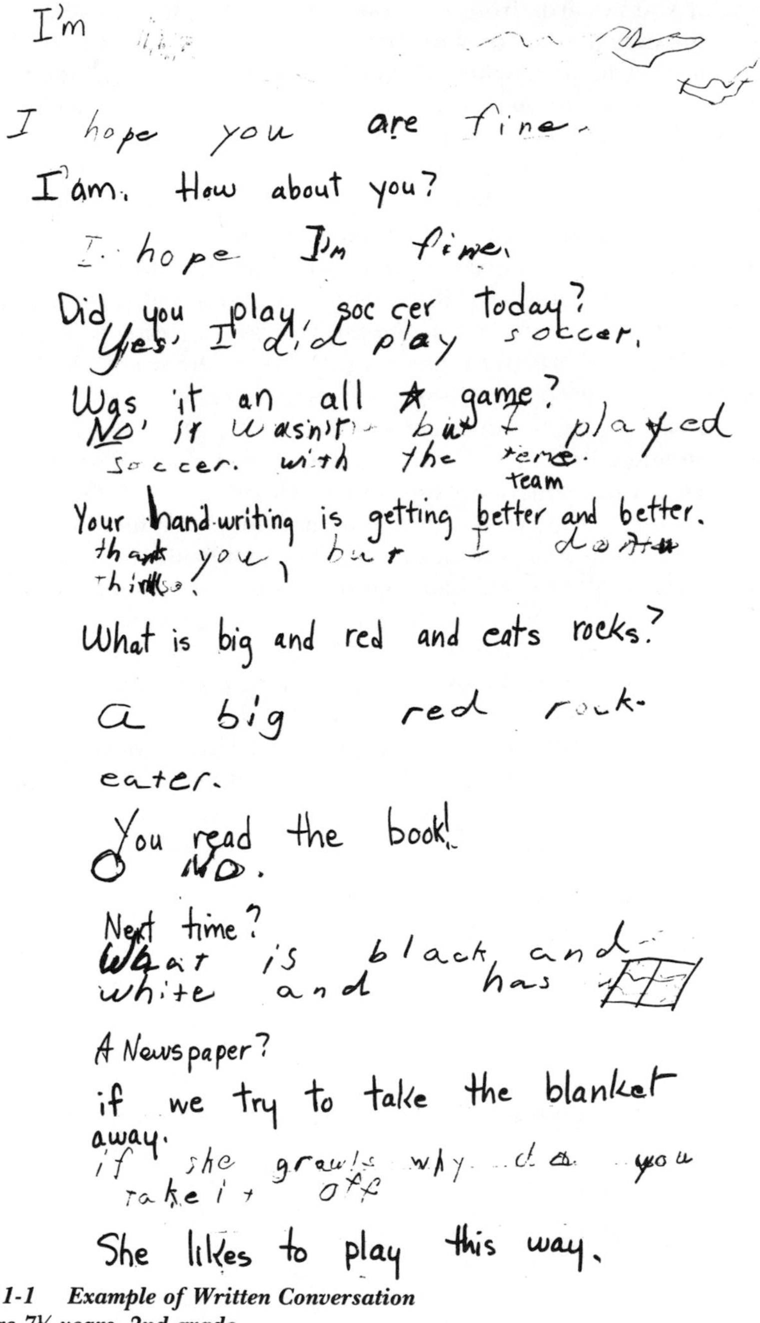

I'm

I hope you are fine.

I am. How about you?

I hope I'm fine.

Did you play soccer today?
Yes, I did play soccer.

Was it an all ★ game?
No, it wasn't but I played
soccer with the team.
                              team

Your hand-writing is getting better and better.
thank you, but I don't
think.

What is big and red and eats rocks?

a big red rock-

eater.

You read the book.
NO.

Next time?
What is black and
white and has

A Newspaper?
if we try to take the blanket
away.
if she growls why do you
take it off

She likes to play this way.

Figure 11-1   *Example of Written Conversation*
Matt: Age 7½ years, 2nd grade

Fernald tracing helped Matt build a private dictionary of words he used in his own writing. We also used written conversations (see Figure 11-1), rehearsals of letters he would be writing from camp, and letters to other children, thank you notes—any and all excuses were used to give Matt functional use of communication skills. Eventually, spelling generalizations were taught in the sessions. Matt's school allowed him to substitute the Plunkett speller for the one used in the classroom because the former was more consistent with the code-based approach we were using in his tutoring sessions.

Reevaluation of educational progress was an integral part of the work. It helped Matt gain confidence in his ability to learn and it helped us assess the effectiveness of the teaching approach. This information was shared with parents and school staff, as shown in the letter in Figure 11–2.

Dear Mr. and Mrs. Blank:

    This is a progress note on Matt's work with me. I am enclosing a copy in order that you can share it with Mrs. Jones and Miss Smith at Matt's school.

    Matt did retests of reading and spelling this month. The scores are listed below together with results on the same measures six and twelve months ago:

	1/74	6/74	2/75
Wide Range Achievement Test			
Oral Reading	1.4	2.5	3.4
Spelling	1.6	2.2	2.4
Peabody Individual Achievement Test			
Reading Recognition	1.3	2.4	3.1
Reading Comprehension	untestable	2.0	3.1

As you can see there is progress in all areas since last year, although Matt has not reached the level that his cognitive abilities predict.

    Matt has made progress with the basic perceptual skills underlying reading and spelling. One area in which he will continue to need work is with Rhythmic Writing, which Miss Smith continues to do at school. This is most important work in making cursive writing motifs automatic. As you probably have noticed, Matt still complains about "forgetting how the letters go." I've noticed this with the formation of cursive capitals. Other perceptual skills have been learned and are being used to support word attack in reading.

    It has been very helpful to hear from Miss Jones from time to time in order to coordinate our efforts. I have noticed such a difference since Matt has been working with the code-based series at school also. In addition to this growth in cracking the code, Matt is also making better use of contextual cues in reading. This was especially apparent in his work on the PIAT comprehension section and his comments about whether what he reads "makes sense."

    I have added some composition to our regime here, so that Matt can build a core vocabulary to use in written work. He has a second set of his "word file" at home--his own idea, I might add. Words are added each week, taught by multisensory cues. The entire file is reviewed and alphabetized to incorporate the week's new words.

    Matt's motivation is improved. He is gradually becoming more confident in his ability to learn and to try new skills. This confidence will, of course, facilitate further progress.

    I will continue to keep you informed concerning our work. Please let people at Matt's school know I appreciate hearing from them and look forward to continued cooperative planning on Matt's behalf.

                    Sincerely yours,

Figure 11-2   Example of Report to Parents

Matt's achievement continued to improve, so that by the end of sixth grade the following scores were earned on the Woodcock Reading Mastery Test:

Woodcock Reading Mastery Test

	GRADE SCORES	PERCENTILE
Letter Identification	6.2	50
Word Identification	11.0	80
Word Attack	12.9	83
Word Comprehension	11.2	79
Passage Comprehension	8.7	64
Total Reading	9.6	82

Tutoring was concluded at that point, although informal contact was continued with him and his family. When he applied for admission to boarding school at grade 9, acceptances were received from all schools to which he made application. He chose a rigorous one and worked hard through the 4 years. He met the foreign language requirement with Spanish, managing to survive with the help of tutoring during the summer. At this point, he has completed college and is working in a small law office and reviewing for the Law School Admissions examinations.

Matt's case makes a number of points about the clinical management of specific language disability. It documents the positive outcomes when the problem is identified early and when appropriate support is provided as long as the youngster needs it. Matt was fortunate in his family's choice of schools; these schools, in turn, offered him challenges that he met without any attempt to avoid hard work. Finally, it illustrates that specific language disability does not inevitably doom the individual to learning failure and emotional distress.

SUMMARY

The essence of the dysfunction of specific language disability lies in the brain's ability to process, store, and retrieve symbols when this dysfunction appears to be the result of a developmental process (other than general cognitive retardation, autism, or schizophrenia), the cause of which has not yet been identified. Although, in general, the dysfunction relates primarily to the processing of information from visual, auditory, and tactile modalities, and although the majority of children with SLD appear to have auditory processing deficits, the pattern of dysfunction for any individual child is unique, so that clinically the SLD group itself appears to be heterogeneous.

The academic difficulty is but the tip of the iceberg; the neuropsychological deficits are just below the surface. To offer a mechanism for the neuropsychological deficits, the concept of an abnormality of hemisphere specialization has been advanced. Studies of lateralization of brain function have been spurred by the development of noninvasive neuropsychological and neurophysiological techniques. Asymmetry in processing bilateral, simultaneous presentations of auditory, visual, and tactile stimuli have, in general, suggested that hemisphere specialization in children and adults with specific language disability is not as well developed as in normal controls. This inference, drawn from dichotic listening, visual half field, and bilateral symmetrical tactile studies, has been challenged. Nevertheless, the concept of developmental or maturational lag in the neuropsychological functions necessary for learning reading, spelling, writing, and arithmetic continues to be advanced as an explanation for the deficit functions. This concept does not necessarily mean that maturation will spontaneously occur, and there is evidence that unless the disorder is adequately and appropriately treated, processing deficits persist into adult life. An alternate concept, that of abnormal cerebral organization in SLD, is concerned with how the cerebral hemispheres act together as a unit. A neurological model proposes that abnormal cerebral organization occurs when the reciprocal balance of excitation and inhibition in processing information is impaired, resulting in inadequate conceptual differentiation among processing tasks; a resource model of abnormal cerebral organization states that in SLD the "capacity" of each hemisphere to deal with information is less than that required to master that task, so that poor learning results.

Neither the developmental lag hypothesis nor the dual-processing model offers a cause for the central nervous system dysfunctions of SLD. Genetic factors to account, at least in part, for SLD have been advanced. Family and twin studies offer strong presumptive evidence of a genetic factor in the expression of SLD. There is a high prevalence of SLD within families, and twin studies demonstrate a significantly higher prevalence of SLD in monozygotic twins than in dizygotic twins. The genetic mode of inheritance, however, is still elusive.

Morphologically, the normal pattern of asymmetry in the cerebral cortex does not appear to be present in specific language disability, and microscopic findings consistent with cell dysplasia and ectopia, particularly in the left temporal lobe, were found in the few patients studied. Computerized tomography scans also find the more usual pattern of cerebral asymmetry to be absent or reversed in the brains of "dyslexics." Electroencephalographic studies have revealed many different patterns in children with SLD. The relationship between each of these wave patterns and SLD is controversial. EEG patterns have been studied with computer assistance so that plots of the wave frequencies (spectra) and their quantity (power) may be obtained for each electrode position on the scalp and then displayed on a computer screen (brain electrical area mapping, BEAM). Such maps have revealed suggestive differences between SLD and normal readers. The study of event-related potentials in relation to aspects of language processing in children with specific language disability is still in its early stages. Case studies are presented to illustrate principles of management.

CHAPTER TWELVE

Effects of Poverty, Cultural Differences, and Inappropriate Stimulation

CASE STUDY: WYN

Wyn was already 16 years old when he was referred to us from the juvenile justice system with a history of having been involved in an armed robbery. He had been on homebound instruction because he could not be contained in a day care program for children with severe behavioral and learning difficulty, and even on homebound, he refused to be available for his tutoring sessions. He was involved with drugs, sex, and behaviors that his father said will "either get him killed or him killing someone else."

Wyn has a long, distressful history of aggression and learning disorder going back to his first grade. Repeated psychological testing revealed a full scale IQ on the WISC-R in the low normal–borderline range with a verbal IQ of 75 and a performance IQ of 94. Psychological study revealed an impoverished vocabulary but no specific areas of defect. Although he received remedial services in grades 1 through 3, his oral reading level at age 16 years (WRAT) was grade 4.0 and his spelling grade was 3.0. Neurological and electroencephalographic examinations were normal. Perceptual study revealed good visual discrimination and recall of asymmetric figures, poor visual-motor function with primitive verticalization, and body image immaturity in right–left discrimination and in praxis. The major area of defect, however, was in auditory perception, with difficulty in auditory discrimination and auditory rote sequencing. It was questionable whether these were actual auditory perceptual defects or a function of his black dialect reaction to standard English. On psychiatric examination he was verbal and appeared intelligent and cooperative, but he was a hedonistic personality with no guilt over his behavior. He has never learned to control his impulses and beneath his overt cooperation was a readily mobilized anger. He projects his anger to his parents, stating that they do not love him, never did love him, and thwart his every wish. He says that he becomes angry when he is restricted unfairly or when someone talks about him. There is a mild paranoid flavor in his thinking. He says his father talks about his school problems, and everyone knows about them. He would very much like to learn in school, but he feels he does not understand the teacher's instructions.

He is one of seven children, the oldest four of whom are in difficulty with the law. His background is one of poverty and disadvantage. His father, a broad-chested man, appearing physically powerful, has not worked for years because of a "back injury." His mother has always worked, according to Wyn, and is emotionally distant from him. The relations at home are mutually distrustful. The image of his father is a macho one, a powerful male whom Wyn is trying to emulate; the image of his mother is vague and nonsupportive.

Can Wyn's behavior and academic difficulty be dissociated from the social reality of the environment surrounding him?

READING DISORDER AND SOCIOECONOMIC "DISADVANTAGE"

The preponderance of evidence points to the determining influence of poverty and impoverishment on the development of learning disorders. More than 20 years ago, Eisenberg (1966) found that 28% of the children in an inner city school were 2 or more years retarded in reading. In contrast, in schools with parents who were predominantly white-collar workers, 15% of the children were similarly retarded and, in suburban public schools, 3% were. In independent private schools, whose students were carefully chosen, there was no child 2 or more years retarded in reading. Where data permitted race to be studied, especially in the predominantly white-collar workers' schools, 12% of the white children, in contrast to 36% of the black children in the same schools, were 2 or more years retarded in reading. While the tests used for criterion measures were not the same across schools, the trend was clear: Reading retardation was more prevalent among children from lower than from upper socioeconomic groups and among black than white children.

Rutter, Tizard, and Whitmore (1970), studying the population of the Isle of Wight, predominantly whites, found that 82% of all children retarded in reading came from the socioeconomic groups represented by the manual, semi-skilled, and unskilled occupation of their fathers. Comparing two populations—all the 10-year-olds living in an inner London borough with all the 10-year-olds living on the Isle of Wight—Berger, Yule, and Rutter (1975), Rutter (1984), and Rutter et al. (1975), found that both psychiatric disorder and reading retardation were more than twice as common in the London children. There was a significant difference between the two populations in prevalence of family discord and disruption, parental deviance, social disadvantage, and school characteristics (rates of teacher turnover and pupil turnover). Van Doornick (1978) found 43% of children from economically disadvantaged families, in contrast to 7% of children from high socioeconomic families, to have school problems, with high rates of academic failure and low scores on reading and mathematics tests.

Longitudinal studies such as the Collaborative Perinatal Project of the National Institute of Neurological and Communicative Disorders and Stroke also stress the potent influence of socioeconomic status and include maternal educational level as a significant factor in the developmental outcomes of the child (Broman et al., 1975). In reviewing the behavioral fate of all children born on the Island of Kauai in the State of Hawaii in 1955, Werner found "poor early environment" to be a determining factor in the outcome of children who initially suffered from prenatal and perinatal stress (Werner et al., 1968, 1971; Werner & Smith, 1977, 1982). The term "disadvantaged children" arose to identify those exposed to social, cultural, and economic handicaps (Birch & Gussow, 1970).

Where the effects of poverty and social disadvantage were compounded by race, educational achievement was particularly low. A report on educational achievement of black pupils primarily from low socioeconomic levels (*Youth in the Ghetto*, Harlem Youth Opportunities Unlimited, 1964) revealed that more than half of the poor black children in academic high schools and 60% of those in vocational high schools dropped out of school. In a more recent survey, Comer (1988) found as many as 50% of minority children do not complete high school. Furthermore, Harlem children at grades 6 and 8 were 2½ years below national norms in reading comprehension, word knowledge, and arithmetic. By grade 3 they were already one grade behind national norms. The Coleman report, *Equality of Educational Opportunity* (Coleman, 1968), dramatized the educational plight of minority groups and spurred impressive socioeducational changes such as busing to equalize racial representation in schools and early compensatory education programs such as Head Start. The Coleman report was not primarily designed to study the effect of social disadvantae, and, as a result, comparisons among ethnic groups, and even within ethnic groups, are confounded by socioeconomic variables. Nevertheless, by first grade, the scores of minority groups (blacks, Indian-Americans, Mexican-Americans, and Puerto Ricans) on standard achievement tests were already 1 standard deviation below the national norms. By 12th grade, scores of minority groups on the same type of verbal and nonverbal skills fell even farther below the national norms. Coleman did report, however, that for all minority groups at grade 6, the economic level of the family had the highest relationship to achievement scores, whereas for the majority group of whites, the parents' educational level had the highest relationship to achievement scores (summarized in Hess, 1970, pp. 512–513).

The importance of socioeconomic status over ethnic factors in level of achievement may be seen in the study of Lesser, Fifer, and Clark (1965). Middle- and lower-class samples of first-grade children in four different ethnic groups (Chinese, Jewish, Puerto Rican, and blacks) were studied with a specially constructed scale to yield ratings on verbal ability, reasoning, numerical ability, and conceptualization of space. For the entire sample, the middle-class children were significantly superior to the lower-class children on all scales and subtests. The pattern of abilities, the distribution of assets and deficits, however, differed among ethnic groups. In verbal ability, for example, Jewish children rated first, followed by blacks, Chinese, and Puerto Ricans. On numerical ability, however, the Chinese children rated first. Social-class differences were most striking in black children where there was a greater difference in scores between middle- and lower-class blacks than between social classes of other ethnic groups. Lesser et al. concluded that, while the *pattern* of abilities tested may vary with ethnicity, the *level* of scores is affected by social-class status (Stodolsky & Lesser, 1967).

Research from the Institute for Developmental Studies underlined the effects of both social status and race on cognition and learning. M. Deutsch (1965) and C. P. Deutsch (1973) further emphasized the concept of a "cumulative deficit" in children of "disadvantaged" socioeconomic groups: the fact that, as these children move into higher grades, they fall farther and farther behind their peers in academic achievement. The concept of cumulative deficit is seen as early as preschool where Klaus and Gray (1968) described "progressive retardation," a progressive decrease in IQ scores in children who remain in what Klaus and Gray referred to as nonstimulating environments.

While there may be many reasons for cumulative deficit, (for example, the academic tasks may be progressively more difficult for the child's cognitive abilities; the educational system may not provide appropriate and sufficient intervention; emotional factors, including resistance to learning, may have developed; there may be a greater frequency of birth difficulties in the disadvantaged), most studies and practical experience point to socioeconomic disadvantage as a factor in learning failure. (A review of such studies may be found in Birch and Gussow, 1970, Rutter and Madge, 1977, and Sameroff and Seifer, 1983.) The evidence is abundant: Children reared in poverty have, in general, more difficulty with academic learning than do their middle-class peers.

Conditions of Socioeconomic Disadvantage in Relation to Learning

It is not sufficient, however, to implicate social-cultural and economic disadvantage as a potent determinant of later educational failure. What is it in the setting of such disadvantage that predisposes to failure? Does the statistical association represent a causal connection, or are there possible alternative explanations, such as heredity or the effect of the child on the family and on the school, and not the family and the school on the child?

R. D. Hess (1970) posed the questions that need to be asked:

What are the *conditions* of the external social and cultural world in which the child lives?

What are the *adaptive consequences* which adults in the environment acquire in their interaction with the system?

In what *specific forms* do these *adult orientations appear in interactions with children?*

What are the *behavioral outcomes* of these experiences in children? (p. 463).

In short, what is there in the setting of disadvantage that predisposes to failure?

Hess (1970) stated that, "powerlessness is one of the central problems of the poor" (p. 465). It limits the poor's ability to influence their own lives and to make changes within their community, and it encourages dependency on society and on chance. Their poverty offers few resources with which to face disaster and restricts the range of alternatives to action. Their relationships tend to be structured in terms of power. Their own low status and inability to command their own lives evokes a low self-esteem and a sense of inadequacy and passivity. Their lifestyle is said (B. Bernstein, 1960) to show a preference for the familiar and a simplification of the external world. There is a low-level skill and experience in obtaining and evaluating information about events and resources that might affect their lives.

In general, "disadvantaged" poverty-ridden homes have more than their share of family discord and disruption: single-parent or many-fathered homes, child neglect, possible abuse, many different caretakers, exposure to crime, low levels of parental educational achievement, lack of role models relating to education with consequent poor motivation for academic success, possible poor nutrition, general patterns of disorganization within the home, depression and discouragement in the mother, physical illness, and large family size with overcrowding and lack of adequate and appropriate stimulation at critical ages, to name a few. Murphy and Moriarty (1976) emphasized that in poor households there is a general lack of appropriate stimulation and feedback. The houses are characterized by bare walls, with no patterned visual stimuli; mobiles, if present, are not within range of vision. There is no variety in the environment, no suitable toys within reach. There is nothing to explore or discover. Most important, however, there is no response to individual differences, few individual tolerances to stimulation, and inappropriate auditory feedback. There is little response to need cues from the infant.

The grim reality of the environment of minority group poverty is described by Kondracke (1989): "Besides abysmal education, illegitimacy, welfare-dependency, unemployment, bad housing, insufficient health care and crime, the black underclass is being raked by drugs, AIDS and an upsurge in child abuse connected to drug addiction" (p. 20).

The difficulty in isolating these various socioeconomic factors as predictive of learning disorders is further complicated by the finding that prenatal and perinatal complications are more frequent in populations that are both poor and black. Pasamanick and his associates (1956) found that the proportion of infants having some problem associated with pregnancy and labor increased from 5% in the white upper social class to 15% in the lowest white socioeconomic group to 51% among blacks. Parenthetically, the studies of Pasamanick, implicating the effect of poverty and minority group status on learning, earned for him recognition by the American Psychiatric Association in 1986 as an outstanding contribution to the prevention of emotional disorders in children.

While retrospective studies have tended to implicate all the above characteristics of poverty and impoverished culture as contributing to learning, prospective studies have not fared so well, since "traumatic" events, which appear to produce disability in some children, are also found in large numbers of children without learning disorders. In short, statistical prediction is not case specific. This finding, of course, should not be surprising. Reading and learning are complex behaviors and it is hardly likely that there will be a one-to-one linear correlation between environmental events and later outcome. As Escalona stated (1974): "That external circumstances and events may have widely different significances for different individuals, at various stages of development is axiomatic in the realm of clinical psychiatry" (p. 42). Rather than adapt a mechanistic model, interpreting development as a linear chain of causes and invariant effects, an organismic interpretation, viewing "children and their environments as undergoing regular restructuring," "discontinuity rather than continuity" (Sameroff & Chandler, 1975, p. 189) appears to be more consistent with reality. This model is an interactional or transactional view in which there is a reciprocal interaction between the child and the environment, each influencing the other by strengthening the weakness, developing skills, and aiding adaptation or, on the other hand, by perpetuating the weakness, offering little support, and contributing to self-doubts and poor object relations. The transactional model attempts to understand the interrelationship between the environment and the biological organization of the child.

The Continuum of Caretaker Casualty and Its Assessment

Just as the long-range effect of *biological* insult depends on the nature of that insult, its extent, severity, and location; the time in an individual's life in which the insult occurs; and the environmental support he receives, so do the long-range effects of *environmental* factors vary in the nature of the traumatic events, the ability of the environment to adjust to and support the child's needs, and the "goodness of fit" in Chess and Thomas's items (Thomas & Chess, 1980). To carry the parallel further, just as there is a "continuum of reproductive casualty," so there is a "continuum of caretaking casualty" (Sameroff & Chandler, 1975; Sameroff & Seifer, 1983). The continuum of reproductive casualty describes the range of deviant pregnancy outcomes from perinatal death through sublethal cerebral palsy and epilepsy to minor motor, perceptual, intellectual, learning, and behavior disabilities; so the continuum of caretaking casualty runs "from lethal conditions in which the child dies from abuse or neglect, through sublethal variations such as battered children, and infants who fail to thrive, to more subtle manifestations of mental retardation and psychiatric disturbance" (Sameroff & Chandler, 1975, p. 190).

Attempts have been made to derive some quantitative way of evaluating the continuum of caretaking casualty. These have included gross social status indices such as parental occupation, family income, education, family size, home crowding, and family disruption and direct observation of maternal–child interactions at the child's home or in an observation nursery. M. Deutsch (1965) related gross social status to intelligence test scores and to academic achievements. The Kauai study (Werner & Smith, 1982) identified several demographic and social variables that characterize children in a low-income population who did *not* have learning or behavior problems: family size fewer than four children, sex (girls had fewer problems than boys), mothers with more than an eighth-grade education, and intact families. These variables, however, only indirectly suggest the quality and quantity of social, emotional, and cognitive support that the child receives.

A generation of parental questionnaires, structured and semistructured interviews, and most important, direct observations of the home have been developed to tap such information. A brief review of the development of scales for assessment of the environment is contained in Caldwell et al. (1984). As early as 1954 Barker and Wright described a narrative account of objects and actions occurring in the child's life during a given time frame. The accounts are subsequently coded into a scheme of categories depending on the requirements of the investigation. The Barker-Wright method was used in the Harvard Preschool Project to analyze the role played by the person interacting with the child (Human Interaction Scale) and the child's involvement with objects in the environment (Object Interaction Scale). In the Harvard studies, for well-developing children in contrast to the poorly developing one, the sheer quantity of interaction between child and parent was greater, more time was spent with the children in intellectually valuable activities, and participation in the activity was more common with more overt encouragement.

A parallel series of investigations was based on the theoretical structure offered by B. S. Bloom (1964) for the development of questionnaires for the measurement of environmental processes. Dave (1963) constructed a 63-item interview along six process dimensions: achievement press, language models in the home, academic guidance provided in the home, stimulation provided to explore aspects of the larger environment, intellectual interests, and activities and work habits in the home. This scale had a correlation of .80 with academic achievement scores and .60 with IQ in fourth-grade students selected by stratified random sample from each social class. Marjoribanks (1972a, 1972b) devised an 188-item, six-point rating scale to assess eight environmental characteristics: achievement, activeness, intellectuality, independence, English language usage, second language usage, mother dominance, and father dominance. Marjoribanks's measures accounted for a large percentage of the variance in verbal, number, and total ability scores of 185 eleven-year-old boys on the Primary Mental Ability Test. Henderson devised a 25-item interview scale (the Henderson Environmental Learning Process Scale, HELPS) consisting of five clusters: extended interest and community involvement, valuing language and school-related behavior, intellectual guidance, providing a supportive environment for school learning, and attention. Two of the factors, valuing language and providing a supportive school environment, were significant in predicting first-graders' performance on both the Boehm Test of Basic Concepts and The Stanford Early School Achievement Test ($R = .72$).

M. Deutsch (1965) defined six variables that were put together to form a Deprivation Index: housing dilapidation, educational aspiration of parents, number of children in the home, dinner conversations, number of cultural experiences, and attendance in kindergarten. The multiple correlation relating the six variables of the Deprivation Index to reading was .49 for the fifth-grade level.

Hess (1970) and Hess and Shipman (1968) were concerned with the differences in styles of information processing in children and with relating these styles to maternal and child interactions. Three major aspects of maternal behavior were examined: modes of social control, modes of communication, and encouragement of achievement. These variables were assessed by interviews in the home, by testing, and by observation of mother and child in a structured teaching situation. Studying 163 black families representing four social status levels ranging from families with mother on public welfare to families with college-educated fathers, Hess and his group found that the use of "external control and authority . . . is related . . . negatively to the development of verbal behavior, performance on cognitive tasks, and to reading readiness as measured by standard tests" (Hess, 1970, p. 516). Working class mothers use such control to a greater extent than do middle-class mothers.

Yarrow, Rubenstein, Peterson, and Jankowski (1973) at the National Institute of Child Health and Human Development derived a scale involving time sampling of five categories of behaviors: level of stimulation, variety of stimulation, positive affect, contingent response to positive vocalization, and contingent response to distress. Using this scale with 41 black infants and their families, Yarrow et al. found moderate correlations were obtained between the observed family behaviors and motivation (i. e., goal orientation, reaching and grasping) in the children.

In their review of research on relationships between the environment and development, Caldwell et al. (1984) theorized that the environmental characteristics likely to influence early development include the following: frequency and stability of adult contact, amount of developmental and vocal stimulation, need gratification, emotional climate, avoidance of restriction on motor and exploratory behavior, available play materials, and home characteristics indicative of parental concern with achievement. With these characteristics as a guide, the Home Inventory for Measurement of the Environment (HOME) was developed (R. H. Bradley, 1982). There are three such inventories: one for families of infants and toddlers (to age 3), the second for preschoolers (ages 3 to 6), and the third, still not fully developed, for families of elementary-age children. Each requires a home visit. The infant and toddler scale, in use the longest, contains 45 items, each of which is scored as present or absent, yes or no. The 45 items are grouped into six subscales: emotional and verbal responsivity of parent, acceptance of child's behavior, organization of physical and temporal environment, provision of appropriate play materials, parent involvement with child, and opportunities for variety in daily stimulation.

HOME scores obtained at 6, 12, and 24 months of age are said to be better predictors of the Binet IQ at 54 months than the Bayley Infant Development Scores and a better predictor of IQ than standard social indices (R. H. Bradley & Caldwell, 1981). In a black sample, for example, HOME scores accounted for approximately three times as much variance in IQ than did socioeconomic status alone. This predictive validity was higher for low-income and minority populations than for higher income groups (R. H. Bradley, 1982; R. H. Bradley & Caldwell, 1981). However, a discriminate function composed of HOME scores at 6 months is reported to predict retardation (IQ below 70) at 3 years with 71% correctly identified and to predict average to above-average IQ (above 90) at 3 years with 70% accuracy. Twelve-month HOME scores also were more efficient predicators of school achievement than were indices of socioeconomic status.

The HOME inventory for preschoolers (ages 3 to 6) consists of 55 items clustering into eight subscales: learning stimulation, language stimulation, physical environment, warmth and affection, academic stimulation, modeling, variety in experience, and acceptance. While the number of investigations completed on the preschool version of HOME is less than that for the infant version, HOME preschool scores appear to be significantly related to measures of cognitive development during early childhood and the primary grades. The total HOME score attained between 3 and 5 years of age had correlations ranging from .51 to .58 with SRA Achievement Test scores in reading, language arts, mathematics and in composite achievement score obtained between 6 to 10 years of age. The HOME subscale score that showed the strongest correlation with academic achievement was toys, games, and experience ($R = .41$ to .49).

The HOME observation requires a home visit of at least 1 hour. For more rapid study, Coons, Gay, Fandal, Ker, and Frankenberg (1981), using HOME as a basis, developed a multiple-choice, fill-in-the-blanks, yes/no questionnaire that may be completed in about 20 minutes. Called the Home Screening Questionnaire (HSQ), it is a parent-answered questionnaire designed to sample social, emotional, and cognitive aspects of the home that relate to a child's growth or development. Correlations between total score on the HSQ and HOME inventory is .81 (Coons et al., 1981). A concurrent measure of HSQ validity was obtained through the ability of HSQ to correctly identify sibling school status: special class placement, one or more grades repeated, low achievement test scores, failures in core subjects, and repeated concerns expressed by teachers. The HSQ was 75% accurate in identifying problems and 44% accurate in identifying no problems, with 28% false positives and 13% false negatives.

Attempts have also been made to assess the risk factors of socioeconomic disadvantage together with those arising from perinatal distress, prematurity, and low birth weight. Tableman and Katzenmeyer (1985) described the Borgess Interaction Assessment (BIA) derived from the Michigan programs in prevention of emotional disorders. The BIA is based on previous infant scanners such as the Neonatal Perception Inventory (Broussard, 1979), which compares the mother's perception of her baby at 1 day after birth and at 1 month in items such as crying, spitting, feeding, elimination, sleeping, and predictability. A negative perception was related to abuse, neglect, injury related to lack of care, and failure to thrive. The Borgess Interaction Assessment (named for the hospital in which it was developed) has three sections: the first, a situational section with 16 items, contains information on the condition of the infant at birth (Apgar rating and irritability) and on the mother's experiences that may impair bonding (i. e., single parent, age of mother, family employment, history of mental illness, drugs, retardation, and family support systems). The second section of 7 items is concerned with the mother's response to the infant immediately after delivery; the third section of 12 items looks at the mother's interaction with the infant during the hospital stay. Tableman and Katzenmeyer reported on 1,062 successive live births. The BIA identified 19.5% of the infant–mother dyads as at risk for later emotional problems; of these, more than one-half were related to situational factors. At the end of 1 year the BIA achieved a correlation of .86 with the HOME inventory. The Michigan study did not study their subjects beyond 1 year, thus its predictive validity for learning disorders is still uncertain. Siegel (1982, 1983) also developed a risk index based on demographic, reproductive, and perinatal factors to predict test scores on selected scales (the Bayley, Uzgeris-Hunt, and Reynell scales of language development) at age 5.

Returning now to our original question about the relationship of socioeconomic and cultural factors to Wyn's learning disorder: The evidence suggests that we cannot dissociate his learning disorder from his environment. We find no evidence for a structural defect of the central nervous system. There is evidence for the specific spatial disorientation and temporal disorganization that underlie the neuropsychological dysfunction of the specific learning disability. Wyn grew up in an atmosphere in which academic achievement was unimportant; where his role model skirted the fringes of and frequently encroached on the law; where life was hazardous; and where drugs were seen as one way out of poverty and helplessness. He was sporadic in school attendance at best. As the fourth of seven children, in a poverty household with the mother working, it is questionable how appropriate and adequate were the affection and cognitive stimulation he received during his early years. Using the strict definition of learning disability of P. L. 94-142, Wyn is *not* classified as learning disabled; yet if any child needed help in learning, it is Wyn. Although his learning disorder was recognized early, his behavioral problems led him into classes for the emotionally handicapped and consistent remedial education was not offered. It was clear that the schools could not overcome the lifestyle that Wyn was born into.

The Language of Social "Disadvantage"

Wyn raises an additional problem, namely why his score on the verbal scale of the WISC-R was 19 points lower than his performance score. It might be argued that a hereditary factor, a genetic predisposition to language dysfunction, may contribute to this discrepancy. As Rutter (1984) pointed out, however, "in no case is the hereditability of psychological attributes so high that there is no room for environmental effects" (p. 295).

As early as 1960, B. Bernstein described differences in "language facility" between two extreme social groups. He described these differences in what he called an "elaborated" and a "restricted" code or style of language. Bernstein stated (1960) that the "differences in language facility result from entirely different modes of speech found within the middle class and the lower working class. . . . the organization of the two social strata is such that different emphasis is placed on language potential which orient the speakers to distinct and different types of relationships to objects and persons, irrespective of intelligence" (p. 27). Middle-class, or elaborated, speech facilitates verbal elaboration of subjective intent, has complexities of syntax at command, is aware of semantic nuances, and has a large vocabulary and experiential store upon which to draw. The "working class," however, has a limited, restricted form of language that discourages elaboration of subjective content and orients the user to descriptive rather than abstract concepts. B. Bernstein's formulations stemmed in part from his early work in which he compared 61 "working class" boys, aged 15–18, with 45 "public school" boys on Raven's Progressive Matrices and on the Mill-Hill Vocabulary Scale and found a significant difference on each of these measures between the two groups.

The 1960s and early 1970s saw intensive studies of the language of lower socioeconomic status groups. Major contributions came from the Institute for Developmental Studies, headed by M. Deutsch (see C. P. Deutsch, 1973). A core sample of 292 children and an extended sample of 2,500 children were available. A cross-sectional study of first- and fifth-graders found that by first grade the groups with lower socioeconomic status were associated with poorer scores on intelligence tests (tests of verbal identification) which require abstract reasoning, on CLOZE tests, on several rhyming and fluency tests, and on verbal explanations than the groups with middle socioeconomic status. By the fifth grade, additional tests involving association and manipulation of language, syntactical control, and logical sequencing further revealed poverty of language. If race were added to low socioeconomic status, additional problems (word knowledge and sentence fluency) were also apparent. M. Deutsch (1965) summarized as follows:

> *As complexity of language increases from labeling to categorizing, the negative effects of social disadvantage are enhanced. . . . the cumulative deficiency is failure in development of an elaborated language system that has accurate grammatical order and logical modifiers, which is mediated through a grammatically complex sentence structure which has frequent use of prepositions and impersonal pronouns and a discriminative selection of adjectives and adverbs. This gives direction to thinking. The restricted code of the lower [socioeconomic status] is grammatically simple, often unfinished sentences; poor syntactical form; simple and repetitive use of conjunctions; inability to hold a formal topic through speech sequences; a rigid and limited use of adjectives and adverbs (p. 84).*

Labov (1969), in an extensive longitudinal study of language development in elementary-school children, found differences in the complexity of language used by lower-class and middle socioeconomic groups.

These cumulative studies have led to the conclusion that, when ghetto children have a verbal deficit, this deficit does not allow for the expression of complex or logical thinking, and it is a major cause of poor performance at school. If this is indeed the case, then language compensatory programs are clearly indicated.

Some studies, however, suggest that the nonstandard language of the poor is not a nonstandard form of the prevailing language at all, but it is a separate dialect, capable within itself of the same logical abstractions and thought of the prevailing language. This concept has support from the work of Chomsky (1967), which argues that language learning is innate, a species universal, which, given adequate biological substrata, will proceed with even minimal stimulation. Tizard et al. (1983), for example, recorded the conversations of 40 four-year-olds at home and at school. While there were no significant social-class differences in the frequency and length of spontaneous conversations at home and at school, there were in the lower socioeconomic status groups three times as many adult–child conversations at home than at school, and exchanges were twice as long at home. The language of the working-class child was more limited in usage at school and there were significant social-class differences in frequency of complex language, but almost all criteria for complex language appeared in the talk of working-class mother and child. These complexities included comparisons; similarities or differences; recall of events; future plans; linking at least two events in time; describing purpose of objects; giving reasons, explanations, purposes, or results of actions; reasoning and inference; and conditional concerned and hypothetical events.

The importance of this concept—that the English of poverty or social disadvantage is not an "inferior" language, but a different dialect, capable of mediating complexities of thinking and reasoning—has led some (Baratz, 1969; Baratz & Shuy, 1969) to resist forcing these children with nonstandard English into a standard middle-class system in school. A *difference* model, rather than a *deficit* model in teaching working-class children is the logical outcome (Baratz, 1969). Labov (1969) decried the ignorance of nonstandard English rules on the part of teachers and text writers, and W. A. Stewart (1969) has advocated dialect-based texts. This philosophical approach has broad practical implications for bilingual education.

When the effects of disadvantage are combined with perceptual defects similar to those found in children with a learning disability, as in the case of Wyn, the synergistic effect is academically and socially disastrous. These children comprise a problem of magnitude and importance and in management require the combined efforts of the social welfare, educational, and mental health systems.

EDUCATIONAL PROGRAMS FOR THE "DISADVANTAGED"

Overall, solutions to the educational problems of children of poverty and of social-cultural disadvantage have yet to be found. A 5-year collaborative study of children with special educational needs (Robert Wood Johnson Foundation, 1988) found that more than one-third of the children served in special educational programs are poor and that more than one-third of their mothers have not completed high school. In their study of five large metropolitan school districts (Milwaukee public schools; Houston independent school district; Charlotte-Mecklenburg, North Carolina, schools; Santa Clara County, California, schools; and the Rochester, New York, school district), Palfrey, Singer, Walker, and Butler (1986) found that in schools that serve poorer children, the diagnosis of "emotionally handicapped" is made more often than that of "learning disability." This placement may reflect the exclusionary criteria for SLD, but, as we have pointed out, placement in classes for the emotionally handicapped may deprive the child of the remedial education that may make the critical difference in keeping him in school and in his subsequent academic, social, and vocational adjustment. Further, more than half the poor black children in the Robert Wood Johnson study did not complete high school.

An urban and suburban county in the west-central portion of Florida reflects the national norms, with blacks and hispanics comprising one-third of the total number of students who dropped out of the regular program and for whom no alternate educational program was available. The *Ninth Annual Report to Congress on Implementation of the Education of the Handicapped Act* (National Center for Educational Statistics, 1987) revealed that in 1986/87 a total number of 4,373,000 children (11% of the total school enrollment) received special education services; of these 1,914,000 (4.8 percent of the total school enrollment) were considered learning disabled and 383,000 (1%) were seriously emotionally disturbed (see Tables 4-2 and 4-3).

Clearly our combined educational and social reforms of the 1960s and the 1970s have not solved the educational problems of children reared in poverty whose environmental stimulation was inappropriate for the development of verbal skills sufficient for learning, for the development of social skills needed for interaction with teachers and peers, and for the motivation to learn what the schools can offer. The problem, of course, is not only that of the educational system. It is estimated that in 1987 appoximately 45% of our black children, compared to 15% of our white children, were living below the poverty level (Kondracke, 1989) and that the problem is growing. Even if the estimate of 45% seems high, the social, educational, and vocational problems of poor black children are enormous. It is clear that education is but one force in the solution of these problems; nevertheless, it is a potent force. Modifying the educational system to attract and maintain the interest of these children, to overcome the frequent antieducational bias of their culture, and to remediate their linguistic and specific learning defects is a dramatic need. Four general approaches have been made to satisfy that need:

1. modification of the environment of the first 3 years of life in Head Start and in early education programs (see Chapter 10, "Prevention")
2. the identification, no later than in their kindergarten year, of children for whom academic failure is predicted (see Chapter 10, "Prevention of Disorders of Learning")
3. modification of the early elementary school–home cultural gap
4. provision of special services within the span of elementary, junior high and senior high years

The Head Start and Early Education Programs

Broad social and educational planning, attempting to modify the environment of the first 3 years of life, to alter the effects of poverty and inappropriate stimulation on the child, have been made in the Head Start program (Cicirelli, 1970; Datta, 1969; M. S. Smith & Bissell, 1970) and in the early education programs such as those of Bereiter (1972), Bereiter and Engelmann (1966), the Perry Preschool Project (Weikart, 1967, 1972), the Early Training Project (Klaus & Gray, 1968), and the Comparative Urbana Illinois Study (Karnes, Hodkins, & Testa, 1969). A critical review of these programs appeared in Meier (1987), and a 20-year outcome study was reported by Gray, Ramsey, and Klaus (1982). The Gray et al. study, following 86 children who were in the Early Training Project in the 1960s, suggested that the intervention program did have a measurable lasting effect, more enduring, however, on school requirement indices than on standardized tests. Insofar as school performance was concerned, however, the favorable effect reached statistical significance only in the females.

The experimental early intervention efforts of the 1960s are an excellent example of programs with enhancement objectives. These programs with their target population of poor, disadvantaged preschool children, their clearly defined interventions, and their long-term follow-up research culminated in the collaborative report of the Consortium for Longitudinal Studies (1983). A review of the programs of early intervention appears in Chapter 10 ("Prevention of Disorders of Learning") of this book.

To summarize, early education programs directed toward modifying the environment of the first 3 years of life by enhancement of psychosocial competencies have shown themselves to be effective in realizing these objectives. In contrast to comparable control youngsters, a high proportion of program graduates avoid the need for special education placement or repetition of grades in school, and earn fewer scores within the retarded ranges on intelligence tests. They reflect positive attitudes toward education, have a greater likelihood of graduating from high school, and demonstrate more productive behaviors in the classroom. Older program graduates reflect the indirect effects of greater educational and social competency in improved vocational expectations and status. However, these programs seem less effective in producing and maintaining specific educational skills in reading and to a lesser extent in mathematics in about 20% of program participants. This percentage is an interesting one in that it corresponds to the usual incidence estimate of specific learning disability. One is tempted to speculate whether this group may be composed of learning disabled youngsters who require more specific interventions for their special learning problems than enhancement programs provide.

How the children of the poor will fare under P. L. 99-457 has yet to be determined. At this writing P. L. 99-457 is designed to provide appropriate education for handicapped children from ages 3–5 and creates a new federal program (Handicapped Infants and Toddlers Program) that provides financial assistance to states for service to 0–2 year olds. As such, children with severe language delays and language immaturities and those with more obvious organic central nervous system defects will be eligible. What is needed is the recognition that poverty itself is a handicapping condition and that our educational, social, mental health, and physical health systems must lower their bureaucratic barriers to combine resources and skills in a unified effort at cutting the present cycle of poverty, school failure, and recurrent poverty.

Programs for Early Identification and Intervention

Programs for the prevention of learning disorders are clearly indicated. Preventive programs involve three major components: (a) reliable and valid identification of children, no later than at age 5 or 6 years, in kindergarten or in first grade, for whom learning failure is predicted, (b) evaluation of these children, and (c) introduction of a successful intervention for these children so that failure does not occur. The identification system must be a practical one so that it may be implemented on a large scale, able to scan large numbers of children quickly, able to be administered and interpreted reliably by school personnel with minimal training. It must meet the statistical constraints set by the American Psychological Association with a minimum of false positives and false negatives, be based on a documented theoretical foundation, and be integrated with the intervention part of the program. Identification alone is not enough. Intervention is essential. The intervention program, just as the identification component, should have a firm theoretical base and be tested in school-based projects with sufficient longitudinal observation to prove its effectiveness. Well-researched identification and intervention programs are available. These have been discussed in Chapter 10 ("Prevention") of this book.

What has impeded the implementation of these programs is not their success in preventing learning failure, but the resistance of school systems in the introduction of new programs. There must be a willingness to commit resources of money and staff, a willingness to accept the training a new program requires, and the patience to work out the kinks that must inevitably develop. The ultimate cost for the education of the learning disabled child and for the emotionally/behaviorally impaired child is immense compared to the cost of a preventive program. The average annual cost for education of a learning disabled child is approximately $6,000, in contrast to the annual cost of approximately $2,000 for the average child. There are currently approximately 2 million children in the public schools of the United States who receive special services because of "learning disabilities." Assuming a savings of $4,000 per child were their learning disability prevented, the annual savings would be close to $8 billion! Further, the dollar cost of the emotional, behavioral, social, and vocational burdens of learning disorders cannot be estimated.

Preventive programs are particularly important for children of poverty who have not had the opportunities of the middle-class child. It seems self-defeating to wait until the poor, minority-group child has failed, has developed emotional reactions to academic failure, is already a behavior problem by the time she is in third grade, and by sixth or seventh grade is already effectively dropping out of school. An effective program for the prevention of learning disorders, in predominantly poor, minority children has been described by Hagin (1984) and by A. A. Silver et al. (1981). Educational gains, demonstrable by second grade, have been associated with normal school adjustment by the end of fifth grade and by a lowering of the incidence of nonpromotion from 12.2% to 1–3% over 12 years.

Programs Modifying the Social Environment of the School

In addition to programs that focus on the basic skills needed for reading, writing, and arithmetic, there are programs that build on the development of supportive bonds which draw together children, parents, and school. The concept behind such programs is stated by Comer (1988): "The contrast between a child's experiences at home and those at school affect the child's psychological development, and this in turn shapes academic achievement. . . . the failure to bridge the cultural gap between home and school may lie at the root of poor academic performance" (p.43). The attitudes, values, and behavior of the family and its social network affect the development of social, emotional, moral, and cognitive values in the child, values critical to academic learning. The child of a poor black family may already resent the mainstream white (and even mainstream black) attitudes the school represents; his or her parents, resentful and/or defensive, also avoid contact with the school staff. Thus a basic problem is the correction of the "sociocultural" misalignment between home and school, the mutual distrust between home and school.

A school-based intervention project growing from these concepts was initiated in 1968 by the Yale Child Study Center and the New Haven school system. Two model schools were chosen—one with 300 children from kindergarten through fourth grade, the other with more than 350 children from kindergarten through fifth grade. In both schools 99% of the children were black and more than 70% were from families receiving Aid for Families With Dependent Children. In an attempt to involve parents, a governance-management team was initiated. The function of the team, in addition to offering parent involvement, was to provide cohesiveness and direction in school policy and teaching. The team, led by the school principal, was made up of elected parents and teachers, a mental-health specialist, and a member of the nonprofessional support staff. It involved parents in shaping policy, and it encouraged them to participate in school activities by supporting programs and attending school events. In addition to the management group, a mental health team of psychologist, social worker, and special education teacher worked together in reviewing and managing troublesome behavior among the children, teasing out what the school might be doing to decrease the incidence of such behavior, and in recommending policy changes to the governance team. Behavior problems were viewed as resulting mainly from unmet needs, not necessarily from "willful badness," and steps to meet those unmet needs were undertaken. Special projects (such as a discovery room for children who have lost interest in learning), social activities, and parent involvement as teachers' aides round out the program.

Within 10 years of the initiation of the project, the two elementary schools, once ranked lowest in academic achievement among the 33 elementary schools in New Haven, now had children in the fourth grade who had caught up to their grade level, and by 1984 fifteen years after initiation of the project, pupils in the fourth grade in the two schools ranked third and fourth highest among the 33 elementary schools in the Iowa Test of Basic Skills. Attendance rates were high, first or second in the city, and there were no serious behavior problems. By 1980, twelve years after initiation of the project, the program was fully integrated within the schools and the Yale group was able to leave the schools and develop their program in other sites. The program has been replicated in Prince Georges County, Maryland; Benton Harbor, Michigan; Norfolk, Virginia; Lee County, Arkansas; and Leavenworth, Kansas.

Programs of Special Services for Specific Groups Within the Span of Elementary and High School Years

While the Yale school intervention project dealt with early elementary age, poor, predominantly black children, a school-based mental health program, administered by the Children's Hospital National Medical Center's Department of Psychiatry, is aimed primarily at refugee children and families from Central America. The program is under contract with the Multi-Cultural Services Division of the Washington, D.C. Commission on Mental Health. There are approximately 85,000 Central Americans, most from El Salvador, now living in Washington, D.C. Their problems are at least threefold: academically delayed, traumatized by war, and adjusting to a strange country. In many cases families are separated. The program attempts to combine the mental health system with the school system, offering a wide range of services that include direct patient care; prevention; mental health consultation to the schools; and working with children, families, and teachers in school, in home visits, and at the Children's Hospital. The services of the program staff are directed at children and their families who are referred by the school staff in need of help. Thus in contrast to the Yale program, which deals with systems in an entire school, the Children's Hospital project is directed at individual "cases." Since 1987, 160 children from four participating schools have been referred. The psychiatrist directing this program, Edgardo J. Menvielle, believes that a key to working with the Central American refugee group is having an understanding of the families and of their culture.

In contrast to the provision for the services for the immigrant refugee sample in Washington D.C., a program, broad in concept, to address the problems of all children in the school district who, because of emotional and/or behavior problems, could not be contained in the mainstream was introduced in the State of Florida. While these children were not primarily diagnosed as learning disabled, a sampling of the classes for severely emotionally disturbed children revealed that at least 70% of them were functioning at an academic level 2 or more years below their grade placement and while they were not primarily directed at serving the poor and minority group children, at least one-third of children in the classes for emotionally handicapped came from the lowest socioeconomic groups. The special classes are fulltime programs, most housed in a wing or in portables, physically a part of a school for "normal children." They comprise the severely emotionally disturbed (SED) classes. Comprehensive neurological, psychiatric, psychological, educational, and social evaluations of samples of these classes revealed them to be comprised of a heterogeneous group of children, differing in diagnosis and in function, demanding for comprehensive management the cooperative efforts of many disciplines, particularly the educational and the mental health systems (A. A. Silver, 1984b).

Accordingly, a joint program, the cooperative product of the state Department of Education and the state mental health system (Health and Rehabilitation Service) was initiated to strengthen the multiagency network to integrate the school systems, social service-welfare systems and the mental health providers in services to severely emotionally disturbed children and to extend the facilities of the multiagency network to those counties in which networks have not been developed. Initially the state provided $150,000 for each of 3 years to each social service administrative district to develop the mental health and school network. The state legislature, however, has continued funding beyond the 3 years, and it appears that such funding will continue.

Administratively most social service districts encompass a vast geographic area, rural and urban, possibly involving a number of counties each. The school administration of one of the counties accepted responsibility for acting as fiscal agent, a steering committee composed of a representative from each school district and a psychiatrist from a mental health center (in this case a medical school) comprised the governing body. The mental health component was to provide a comprehensive evaluation for each child and his family in the program, to mobilize the team needed to develop and implement a comprehensive treatment plan for each child, to prescribe medication as needed and follow the effects of the medication, to offer psychotherapy to selected children, to meet with individual parents and with parent groups, to help teachers in the management of crisis situations, and to be available to them for inservice training. To accomplish these tasks, a psychiatrist was to devote one-half day each week throughout the school year, directly in the classroom; family workers were to devote full time to the SED centers; psychologists and social workers, employees of the school system, were to be assigned part time to each center. A school coordinator was responsible for each center, and, overall, the SED funding was to enable a school coordinator to be responsible for the entire SED program within each district. Essentially the SED network brought together the skills of mental health with those of special education to work in a coordinated team in school-based projects. The success of this integration may be judged by continued funding by the state legislature.

While these special programs are being developed, the school system itself has developed alternative programs to capture the children who are drop-outs or potential drop-outs, to try to interrupt the vicious cycle of poverty, drop-out, poverty with all that this implies. In one county in Florida (Hillsborough County) with its 125,000 children in public schools, the state has funded approximately $5 million in 1987–88 to develop such alternative programs. The county school district has six such programs for adolescents:

1. intensive learning programs for potential drop-outs in 16 junior high schools to offer individualized academic support and counseling to improve self-concept and attitude toward schools

2. intensive learning programs for potential drop-outs in senior high schools parallel to the junior high school intensive learning programs

3. programs for pregnant teenagers, designed to keep students in a school program and to work with them toward the most feasible way to complete their education

4. intensive English in secondary schools for students whose English proficiency is limited

5. non-school-based programs. There are seven sites for adolescents who are runaways, dependent, delinquent, or adjudicated. The objective is to provide education for children in those centers

6. alternative school programs for adolescents who cannot function in the regular school. Those classes are similar to the SED classes for younger children

Thus, there is nationwide recognition of the academic, emotional, social, and behavioral problems of the poor, particularly of the child from a minority ethnic group. Programs to address these problems range from the preschool age in the enrichment programs of Head Start and the preschool early education social intervention to programs designed to redirect the focus of early elementary schools into a cooperative society to bridge the cultural gap between home and school. Programs to prevent the development of learning disorders, to permit the ego a strong point around which to rally, are available and need only the will and the effort to be disseminated throughout school systems. Past the point of kindergarten and first grade, where children have already failed, the integrated efforts of mental health, social, and school systems are being mobilized in a network of special services designed to bring the child back into the mainstream and to function to the limits of his or her potential.

Yet in spite of these advances and innovations, there is much to be accomplished. Not only is there no decline, nationwide, in the drop-out rate, but there is a decline in the number of black high school graduates going to college, from 34% in 1976 to 26% in 1985, a drop of 15,000 students. Of the few blacks who do enter college, only 42% graduate. Yet the economic reality is that in this day and age, a high school diploma is not a "ticket out of poverty" (Kondracke, 1989). Twenty-seven percent of black high school graduates earned no more than the poverty level in 1987. Clearly, more intensive thought and effort is needed to move the poor black child into a "kinder and gentler America."

CASE STUDY: JOEY

Joey, whom we have been able to follow from age 3 through age 18, illustrates a positive outcome with a family that experienced the complex problems associated with urban poverty. It points up the need for coordinating services and agencies: medical and psychological treatment, appropriate educational services, and long-term support from interested professionals.

Joey was referred by The Bellevue Hospital Social Service Department because at age 3, he was speaking very little. His mother (who was seen for treatment by the social workers) had great difficulty managing him. He entered the playroom with some reluctance, but soon headed for the toy shelves. He examined the toys quickly, losing interest in each one he picked up after a very short time. Single words and a few short, unelaborated sentences were used in a mixture of English and Spanish. There was minimal cooperation in any play or aspects of the psychiatric examination. Joey was no more enthusiastic about psychological examination, although over several sessions the Stanford-Binet Intelligence Scale, Form L-M was completed. He earned a mental age of 2 years, 10 months and an IQ of 72. He earned a social quotient of 80 on the Vineland Social Maturity Scale. These scores were regarded to be a minimal estimate of his abilities.

Joey is the only child of Sara and Angel. His birth history as obtained from hospital records revealed normal parturition and neonatal course. Little is known about Angel, although he is reported to have been a waiter. Sara said he was abusive to her and that he left her soon after Joey was born. There is, on the other hand, much information about Sara. Her parents were separated when she was 8 years old; her father, now dead, is said to have been an alcoholic. At the time Joey came to our

Unit, Sara and Joey were living with Sara's mother in a small apartment. Sara has two siblings: Milagros, who is deaf and mute, and Manuel, a mentally retarded resident at one of the large state institutions. Sara is reported to have had meningitis at age 6. At age 11, Sara had a grand mal seizure. She is being followed at the Neurology Clinic and is receiving various seizure medications that control the grand mal seizures. Psychological study done when she was 11 years old placed her functioning within the moderately retarded range (WISC full scalle IQ, 50, verbal IQ, 48, performance IQ, 61). Because of aggressiveness, self-abusive behavior, and what were called "anti-social tendencies," Sara's mother requested that she be placed at Willowbrook State School for retarded children. Although Sara remained at Willowbrook for more than 10 years, little is known about her treatment there because Sara refuses to talk about it. The discharge summary from Willowbrook describes her as "cheerful and affectionate, but craving attention, sulky, and quarrelsome." She appeared at the Walk-In Clinic at Bellevue at age 23 and has remained in contact with various Bellevue services since that time.

Despite his mother's traumatic history, the Unit staff felt that Joey had a normal intellectual potential and that his delayed language development might be due to inappropriate stimulation and ineffective management. Strengths were seen in the good physical care he had received and Sara's active search for help for her son. It was decided to admit him to the Unit's nursery so that his development could be observed over an extended period of time in a program that provided intensive social, language, and perceptual stimulation. It was also decided that Sara would work with the Unit's social worker to make some consistent plans for the household and to learn more effective parenting with Joey.

Joey adjusted well to the nursery group. The teacher noted that he related well and freely to the adults. He liked group activities and entered dramatic play with the other children, although he did not talk much. He was sometimes aggressive, hitting out hard over a toy or a coveted role. However, he would accept adult intervention and compromise solutions and rarely held a grudge. His language was more limited than that of other children in the group. He could name familiar objects and had some simple concepts (big–little, night–day), but did not use any adjectives without help. He had difficulty in drawing forms: He was able to draw a circle but had trouble getting his hand to make a circular motion. He seemed to be left handed, but switched occasionally to his right. Joey continued in the nursery, although attendance was uneven often because Sara overslept.

There were signs that Sara was beginning to trust us, but building an ongoing relationship with her was not easy. Minor crises occurred. Joey was denied admission to kindergarten. Sara had failed to register him during the kindergarten round-up because she was unable to read the announcement. The Unit staff members found an alternative kindergarten and taught Sara how to get there with Joey by public transport until an additional kindergarten class was organized in Joey's neighborhood school. The housing problem was a recurrent one; Sara's mother neutralized gains Sara was making in managing Joey and dealing with issues of independence. As a result, the Unit staff wrote to the Department of Welfare on Sara's behalf, documenting the need for a separate apartment. Through some minor miracle, the request was granted. The next task for the social worker was to prepare Sara for the responsibility of housekeeping on her own. As it turned out, Sara took on these responsibilities easily and, apart from minor setbacks, continues to the present time to discharge these responsibilities very well.

Joey made progress, although it was not rapid. Reevaluation at the beginning of first grade showed marked improvement in both expressive and receptive language. On the WPPSI he earned a full scale IQ of 87, with a verbal IQ of 77 and a performance IQ of 100. Slight immaturity was seen on the neurological examination, but no real dysfunction was noted. When his class was scanned with *Search*, he earned a score of 5, which falls in the vulnerable range. His teaching plan provided perceptual stimulation activities in the Auditory Sequencing, Auditory Discrimination, Visual Recall, Visual-Motor, and Body Image areas. All tasks were completed by the middle of his second-grade year and a code-based approach to reading (SRA Basic Reading Series) was begun in the classroom. By the end of second grade, he was reading at the beginning second-grade level. Joey was well integrated in the school setting and there were few complaints about behavior. Even his attendance improved. By the end of third grade, his reading was approximately at grade level and he earned an oral reading score of 4.0 on the WRAT.

Sara continued her contact with the Unit, although she no longer saw the social worker on a regular basis. Rather, she would initiate contact with the Unit when she had a specific problem or concern. These concerns ranged widely. Her mother threatened to take Joey away from her. (Unit Staff assured her that we would offer evidence of her good care if any court action was brought.) She did not have enough money for presents at Christmas time. (She was put in touch with some of the hospital charities). She had sent Joey to camp but could not find the address. (A call to the agency helped locate him). There was a PTA fashion show for children at school and she wanted Joey to participate. (A word to the organizing committee helped open this opportunity). As time went on, there were less frequent crises or, at least, Sara was better able to handle life's trials on her own. When Joey graduated from sixth grade, he did not earn any special academic honors, but the Unit staff was pleased to see his name listed with nine others who had also achieved perfect attendance that year.

Sara's contact with the Unit staff became less frequent when Joey entered junior high school. At one point, Sara decided he must have a problem because he was so quiet. A telephone call to his guidance counselor indicated that all was well—in fact, he was one of the students the counselor called in when she needed a group of boys to help with some project. The last follow-up occurred in the spring of Joey's senior year in a chance meeting on the street. Sara said that he was graduating and that he was "filling out the papers to go to college downtown." Her information was vague, but it turned out that she was referring to a 2-year community college that prepared people for civil service jobs in the city.

SUMMARY

The preponderance of evidence points to the determining influence of poverty and inappropriate and/or inadequate stimulation on the development of learning disorders, with poor minority children having the lowest scores on academic achievement tests. As these children move into higher grades, they fall farther and farther behind their peers in academic achievement, a "cumulative deficit." The conditions of disadvantage that appear to predispose to failure are, in general, the lack of appropriate stimulation and feedback. A "continuum of caretaker casualty," the environmental characteristics likely to influence early development, include: frequency and stability of adult contact, amount of developmental and verbal stimulation, gratification of needs, emotional climate, avoidance of restriction on motor and exploratory behavior, available play materials, and home characteristics of parental concern with achievement. Inventories to measure these characteristics have been developed, with inventories for toddlers, preschoolers, and elementary-age children. Some studies suggest that the verbal deficit seen in some ghetto children does not allow for expression of complex or logical thinking. On the other hand, there is evidence that the English of poverty or social disadvantage is not an "inferior" language but a different dialect, capable of mediating the complexities of thinking and reasoning.

Broad social and educational programs have attempted to modify the environment of the first 3 years of life. Contrary to early reports of Head Start's ineffectiveness, the Consortium of Longitudinal Studies, reviewing long-term pooled data of Head Start programs, "clearly demonstrated positive effects of these programs throughout childhood and adolescent years." Long-term studies of preschool programs other than Head Start also yielded favorable outcomes.

At the elementary school level, programs to bridge the "cultural gap" between the demands of the school and the experiences of the home, special programs for refugee children, and comprehensive programs to develop a multiagency network for emotionally disturbed children have functioned with reported success. At the junior and senior high school levels, a variety of alternative programs are mobilized to keep potential drop-outs in school. Although there is a national recognition of the academic, emotional, social, and behavioral problems of poor children, the academic problems of that group are still with us. The integrated efforts of mental health, social, and school systems are needed if these problems are to be solved. A case study illustrates how this might occur.

CHAPTER THIRTEEN

Attention Deficit Hyperactivity Disorder

CRITERIA FOR DIAGNOSIS

Although the term *hyperactive* was codified in DSM-II in 1968, the term *attention deficit disorder* (ADD) emerged with DSM-III in 1980, which stated that "the essential features are signs of developmentally inappropriate attention and impulsivity. In the past, a variety of names have been attached to this disorder including: Hyperkinetic Reaction of Childhood; Hyperkinetic Syndrome; Hyperactive Child Syndrome; Minimal Brain Damage; Minimal Brain Dysfunction; and, Minimal Cerebral Dysfunction" (American Psychiatric Association, 1980, p. 41). The most recent diagnostic criteria for ADD with hyperactivity (APA, 1988) may be seen in Table 13-1. Ricky is an example of such a child.

CASE STUDY: RICKY

Ricky was a chubby 9-year-old, red-haired, freckle-faced boy. This year, in fourth grade, he was placed in a class for severely disturbed children because of problems with attention, keeping to the task at hand, getting along with classmates, staying in his seat, and generally following the rules for classroom conduct.

On examination, Ricky was able to contain his behavior for a few minutes during which, although he did sit in his chair, he was generally restless, fidgeting, and shaking his legs rhythmically. After about 5 minutes, however, he could not sit still; he wandered about the examining room, touching and playing with objects in the room—toys, pencils, paper, crayons—picking them up and discarding them just as quickly. He opened and shut the desk drawers, opened and closed books, yet all this time answered questions reasonably and relevantly, and cooperated in the examination.

Neurological examination was within normal limits except for gross choreoform movements on extension of the arms, moderate synkinesis, and abnormally cold hands. There were also perceptual problems, particularly in visual-motor functioning where there was mild verticalization and a difficulty with immediate auditory recall. His auditory problem appeared to be related to his rapid shifts in attention. Emotionally, he was aware of his difficulty in sitting still. He escaped into a fantasy world populated with robots, spacemen, and members of a "galactic patrol." His parents state that they never considered Ricky's behavior to be a problem.

Ricky represents a child whose problems with learning stem from his inability to sustain concentrated attention to a given task and from his difficulty controlling his motor impulses to conform to requirements of the classroom.

It would appear that the evaluation of such a child by observation using the diagnostic criteria of attention deficit hyperactivity disorder as prescribed by DSM-III-R, should be a simple task. Such is not the case.

Table 13-1   Diagnostic Criteria for Attention Deficit Hyperactivity Disorder

Note: Consider a criterion met only if the behavior is considerably more frequent than that of most people of the same mental age.

A. A disturbance of at least six months during which at least eight of the following are present:

1. Often fidgets with hands or feet or squirms in seat (in adolescents, may be limited to subjective feelings of restlessness)
2. Has difficulty remaining seated when required to do so
3. Is easily distracted by extraneous stimuli
4. Has difficulty awaiting turn in games or group situations
5. Often blurts out answers to questions before they have been completed
6. Has difficulty following through on instructions from others (not due to oppositional behavior or failure of comprehension), e.g., fails to finish chores
7. Has difficulty sustaining attention in tasks or play activities
8. Often shifts from one uncompleted activity to another
9. Has difficulty playing quietly
10. Often talks excessively
11. Often interrupts or intrudes on others, e.g., butts into other children's games
12. Often does not seem to listen to what is being said to him or her
13. Often loses things necessary for tasks or activities at school or at home (e.g., toys, pencils, books, assignments)
14. Often engages in physically dangerous activities without considering possible consequences (not for the purpose of thrill-seeking), e.g., runs into street without looking

Note: The above items are listed in descending order of discriminating power based on data from a national field trial of the DSM-III-R criteria for Disruptive Behavior Disorders.

B. Onset before the age of seven.

C. Does not meet the criteria for a Pervasive Developmental Disorder.

Criteria for severity of Attention Deficit Hyperactivity Disorder:

Mild: Few, if any, symptoms in excess of those required to make the diagnosis and only minimal or no impairment in school and social functioning.

Moderate: Symptoms or functional impairment intermediate between "mild" and "severe."

Severe: Many symptoms in excess of those required to make the diagnosis and significant and pervasive impairment in functioning at home and school and with peers.

Note. From *Diagnostic and Statistical Manual of Mental Disorders* (DSM-III-R) (3rd ed. revised), (pp. 52–53), 1988, Washington, D.C.: American Psychiatric Association.

First of all, DSM-III-R criteria describe only a cluster of behaviors, a group of symptoms. These symptoms may arise from different causes. In this respect, although ADHD is an advance over the broad concept of minimal brain dysfunction (MBD), it carries the same burdens. Attention deficit disorder with or without hyperactivity is not a discrete disorder; it is a heterogeneous group, containing clusters of children with similar symptoms but which may differ in etiology, course, and treatment. The problem of heterogeneity is reminiscent of the problems in the definition and diagnosis of "learning disabilities." "Learning disability," too, is composed of heterogeneous groups. We have attempted, along with others (Denckla, 1978; Keogh, 1971, 1980), to define a more homogeneous group of "specific language disability," or "dyslexic-pure," by excluding from our population children with all the other possible etiological factors outlined in Table 2-1.

Similarly, exclusionary criteria have been applied to the hyperactive child:

Hyperactivity refers to a child's frequent failure to comply in an age appropriate fashion with situational demands for restrained activity, sustained attention, resistance to distracting influences and inhibition of impulsive response. So at least for research purposes it may be wise to exclude children under age 6 or over 12 years of age, as well as those with mental retardation, unequivocal evidence of brain damage, chaotic family situations or accompanying (other) psychiatric disorders. Specific learning disabilities, conduct disorders and "soft" or equivocal neurological signs are not unusual among hyperactive children; however these traits are not necessary to the definition of hyperactivity. (Routh, 1980, pp. 56–57)

It should be noted that DSM-III-R criteria call for onset before age 7. Clinically, however, the onset may be traced into the preschool years.

In our clinical experience with impulse-driven children who have difficulty with sustained attention, we, too, separate children with mental retardation, those with unequivocal and even presumptive evidence of structural defects of the central nervous system, children with autism, schizophrenia, Tourette's syndrome, and severe personality deviations, and those with severe anxiety from causes other than ADHD. Specific language disability itself may cause restless and fidgety behavior that teachers may find disturbing. The difficulty of the academic task may not match the child's abilities, development, or cultural background. There may be inadequate motivation or inappropriate reinforcement (D. Shaffer & Greenhill, 1979; D. Shaffer et al., 1983, 1985). Table 13-2 lists possible causes for sustained attention problems with or without hyperactivity.

Thus we can see that children who are restless and whose attention wanders do not all have an attention deficit hyperactivity disorder as defined by DSM-III-R. The symptoms may arise from many causes ranging from being born "temperamentally impulsive" (A. Thomas & Chess, 1980) to severe

Table 13-2   Causes of Sustained Attention Deficits and Hyperactivity (not in order of prevalence)

1. Task too boring or too difficult
2. Specific language disability
3. Anxiety
4. "Conduct disorder" (DSM-III-R)
5. Structural defect of the central nervous system
6. Cognitive retardation
7. Depression; manic-depression
8. Inappropriate or inadequate early object relations
9. Severe developmental disorders (severe language lags, autism, pervasive developmental retardation)
10. Schizophrenia
11. "Attention deficit hyperactivity disorder" (DSM-III-R)
12. Temperamental impulsiveness
13. Tourette's syndrome
14. Toxic substances (i. e., lead)
15. Hearing impairment

psychiatric disorders. There remains, however, a group of children, like Ricky, in whom no etiological factor for their impulsivity can be found. These are the children we consider to have attention deficit hyperactivity disorder, in compliance with DSM-III-R criteria. As Ostrom and Jenson (1988) pointed out, "the new ADHD label, if taken literally, has limited meaning. . . . it lacks a clearly conceptualized research base, and clearly articulated definitions of the primary components of attention deficits, impulsivity and hyperactivity" (p. 263), and "ADHD may not be a unitary condition defined by an attention deficit, but [may include] a more loosely defined set of common childhood problem behaviors . . . non-compliance, academic difficulties, social skills deficits, aggression, overactivity and attentional deficits" (p. 264).

Even with these exclusionary and restrictive factors, there is no certainty that the residual group of children represent a homogeneous entity or that ADHD constitutes a valid syndrome. The validity of a distinct hyperkinetic syndrome was questioned by D. Shaffer and Greenhill (1979). The diagnosis of ADD with hyperactivity, they stated, tells us little about etiology, does not offer generalizations about the clinical state, and has little predictive validity. While observational studies find a clear differentiation between normal and hyperactive children in the hyperactivity dimension (see Luk, 1985, for a review of 25 studies of direct observation of hyperactive behaviors), characteristics that one may logically consider to be related are not. In individual children, for example, activity level is not significantly related to measures of attention. Prior, Sanson, Freethy, and Geffen (1985) found only minimal sustained attention deficits in hyperactive children when auditory and visual vigilance were studied in tasks of 25–30 minutes duration. Lahey, Schaughency, Strauss, and Frame (1984) compared 30 children with attention deficit disorder (10 with hyperactivity, 20 without hyperactivity), whom they selected from a population of 625 children in grades 2 to 5, with matched normal control children. On a battery of teacher ratings, peer ratings, and self-report measures, they found markedly different patterns of characteristics for the two ADD groups:

> *Children with ADD with hyperactivity exhibited aggressive conduct disorders and bizarre behavior, were guiltless and very unpopular, and performed poorly in school. In contrast, ADD children without hyperactivity were found to be anxious, shy, socially withdrawn, moderately unpopular and poor in sports and school performance. Both groups exhibited depression and poor self concepts . . . these different patterns suggest that ADD/H and ADD/WO are dissimilar syndromes and perhaps should not be considered to be sub-types of the same disorder (Lahey et al. 1984, p. 302).*

Loney, Langhorne, and Paternite (1978) also subgroup hyperkinetic children on a behavioral criterion—as aggressive or nonaggressive.

The direction of research is to define further symptom clusters or subgroups along behavioral, situational, or psychophysiological dimensions and to use objective laboratory measures in these definitions. Porges and Smith (1980), for example, used heart rate in a psychophysiological study of sustained attention. Normally, inhibition of heart rate, motor activity, and respiration accompanies sustained attention; the inability of the child to evoke such behavioral inhibition characterizes one group of children designated as hyperactive.

ADHD Rating Scales

The diagnosis of attention deficit disorder with or without hyperactivity is further confused by the use of varied techniques through which diagnosis is made. As the Lahey et al. (1984) study illustrates, the diagnosis is frequently made on the basis of questionnaires completed by parents, teachers, clinicians, peers, and perhaps even the child. The Conners Hyperactivity Rating Scale, with separate scales for parents and for teachers, and the Revised Peterson-Quay Child Behavior Checklist are typical of such questionnaires. Repeated studies, however, (Langhorne, Loney, Paternite, & Bechtoldt, 1976; Sandberg, Rutter, & Taylor, 1978) have demonstrated that rating scales of the hyperactive dimension that have been obtained from different sources, such as from parents and from teachers, correlate poorly with one another. Correlations on the hyperactivity factor between parent and teacher versions of the Conners scale, for instance, have ranged from .18 to .36 with a cross-study average of .26 (Sandberg et al., 1978). The reasons for this lack of agreement, as Henker and Whalen (1980) and Rutter (1983) pointed out, may be in a number of factors: (a) Situational or environmental variations may generate differences in the child's behavior; (b) different observers may have different expectations for the child, different tolerances for the child's behavior, or different interpretations of the questions asked on the scales; (c) the scales themselves may have low reliability and/or validity. Actually all of these factors may be relevant.

Situational Factors Children may exhibit varying degrees of attention and activity in different situations. Porges and Smith (1980) stated that "a description of behavior that constitutes hyperactivity is not meaningful without reference to a situational content" (p. 80). Certainly, clinicians have experienced the variations of activity and attention of children as the children are tested and examined in their office.

Whalen, Henker, and their colleagues (1980) created experimental situations, "provocative ecologies," in the classroom. In one paradigm, two classroom settings, each involving 16 boys, aged 7–11, attending a summer school program of 5 weeks duration, were systematically subjected to varying test situations. Of the 16 boys in each class, 10 had no history of serious school or social problems and 6 were considered hyperactive by their referring physicians. Three of the hyperactive boys were on methylphenidate and three were on a placebo. The classroom environment was systematically varied in a two-by-two design in which two combinations of variables (easy/difficult; self-paced/other-paced) produced four experimental classroom conditions. Task attention rates for all groups dropped during the difficult/other-paced period, but the hyperactive children on placebo had a greater disproportionate drop in attention during that time. Significantly, during the least challenging periods, there was no difference between the hyperactive/placebo group and their peers. Hyperactive children also demonstrated "dysfunctional social behaviors" in familiar and comfortable settings in contrast to their appropriate behavior in a novel social situation. Zentall (1977, 1980, 1985) and Zentall and Zentall (1983) also found hyperactive and normal children influenced by the setting. Hyperactive children showed greater "changes in position" and production of "weird sound" in a "formal" classroom setting in contrast to an "informal" one. Behavior of the hyperactive children was more disruptive in familiar settings. While there may be a "trait" for attention deficit hyperactivity disorder, it is clear that "state" influences the expression of that trait.

These findings have implications for both diagnosis and management. Diagnostically, the identification of an attentional deficit or a hyperactivity trait must be made over time and in different situations. A series of observations of behaviors averaged over time distinguish "situational" from "pervasive" hyperactivity. Results suggest that "classroom ecologies" may be devised to bring out the child's optimal functioning.

Behavioral Factors   Similarly, the expectations for the child's behavior of those completing questionnaires may be dramatically variable. Ricky, the child described at the beginning of this chapter, was in constant motion in the examining situation. His teachers also found his activity level too disruptive for a mainstream classroom, yet his parents reported no problem at home. Even having them come in the examination room to observe Ricky evoked their impression that he was "just a normal boy." What may be tolerated in the home may be disruptive in the classroom.

Scale Factors   Items on the test scales themselves may be subject to different interpretations and emphasis. It has been suggested (Sandoval, 1981) that rather than a general question, that requires subjective judgment (such as, is the child restless or overactive?) more specific wording should be used (such as, does the child sit still at a desk during work periods?).

Equally important for diagnosis is that the rating scales be designed to identify a set of symptoms that are present in a particular child in greater (or lesser) degree than in the group of children on which the scale was normed. Diagnosis made only on the basis of rating scales indicates either that the child has the attentional deficit hyperactivity syndrome because he has attentional deficits or that she is hyperactive because the scale says she is hyperactive. As Rutter (1983) pointed out, "it is of no avail to assert that what differentiates the hyperkinetic syndrome is the presence of hyperactivity, or what differentiates the attentional deficit syndrome is the presence of attentional deficits" (p. 274). Yet we still persist in circular type of reasoning. Ostrom and Jenson (1988) concluded that "the use of behavior checklists and interviews with parents and teachers does provide a range of important information about the child, but is inadequate for the identification of specific deficiencies of attentional processes" (p. 259).

Thus, while it is recognized that there is a group of children with difficulties in attention with or without hyperactivity, in whom no etiological factor may be found, this very group itself appears to be a heterogeneous one. The diagnosis is further compounded by the variability of the child's behavior in different situations and by different interpretations of the criteria in DSM-III-R. Rating scales, so frequently used by teachers and parents, only describe a set of behaviors as *interpreted by the observer*. That these considerations are real may be seen in that ADD is diagnosed nearly 50 times more often in North America than in Great Britain. Linden (1971) said, "In my personal experience in a university [psychiatry clinic] 50 percent of latency-age children fall into the MBD category; in a county clinic receiving a large fraction of school referrals approximately one-half to two-thirds fall into this category" (p. 61). Some (Huessy & Cohen, 1976) reported a prevalence of hyperactivity as 20% of the school-age population (see Chapter 4, "Prevalence of Learning Disorders"). In contrast, in the first grades of a normal school population ($N = 637$), we (Hagin, Beecher, & Silver, 1982) considered only 1.2% of children falling into the ADD/hyperkinetic category. This prevalence in the general population is similar to that found by Rutter, Tizard, and Whitmore (1970). Zametkin and Rapoport (1987), however, pointed out that this difference in rate of diagnosis of ADHD between the majority of reports from the United States and that of the United Kingdom may be more apparent than real; that the difference may be due to the different criteria used, International Classification of Disease, 9th edition, in the United Kingdom, and DSM-III in the United States. In our opinion, diagnosis of this syndrome, as any other syndrome in child psychiatry, must use the comprehensive pentaxial approach as described in Chapters 5 and 6 of this book.

RELATED BEHAVIORAL, COGNITIVE, AND PSYSIOLOGICAL CHARACTERISTICS

Recognizing the problems in identification and classification of the child with attentional problems with and without hyperactivity, investigators have attempted to understand the constellation of related behavioral, cognitive, and physiological characteristics that such a child demonstrates and to identify such characteristics in an objective manner. Quantifiable and objective baseline data are also important in the evaluation of response to medication. The use of objective measures to identify attentional deficits and hyperactivity appears definitely indicated. Yet in his review of 210 studies of hyperactive children, Barkley (1982) found that 64% of them used no specified criteria other than the opinion of the observer in classifying a child as hyperactive. In a survey of 131 school psychologists in New York State, McClure and Gordon (1984) found that only one of them used a direct measure of either attention or impulsivity in evaluating children referred for "hyperactivity."

Difficulty in objective measurement may be a reflection of the difficulty in conceptualizing "attention" and "attention deficit." Attention may be composed of a number of components—alertness, selectivity, and processing capacity—which among themselves may be discrete attributes with weak correlation with each other. Berlyne (1970) identified two essential characteristics of attention: an intensive factor (alertness) and a selective factor (selection of stimuli for further processing). Douglas (1983) and Douglas and Peters (1979) felt that a primary problem in ADHD is in sustaining and organizing attention and that hyperactive children have difficulty with impulse control and with poorly modulated arousal.

Objective tests, however, may suffer from ambiguities in interpretation (i.e., it is possible to infer different processes from the same task), from the need to be adequately normed, or to be "developmentally appropriate" (i.e., responses may vary with age of the child), and from the need for eco-

Table 13-3   Tests of Attention and Cognition to Measure ADHD Behavior

   I. For Tasks Involving Vigilance and Reaction Time
      A. Continuous Performace Test (CPT) (Rosvold, Mirsky, Sarason, Bransome, & Beck, 1956)
      B. Reaction Time and Delayed Reaction Time Tasks (DRT)
      C. Response to Specific Auditory Signal (Hoy, Weiss, Minde, & Cohn, 1978)
  II. For Tasks Involving Perceptual Search
      A. Matching Familiar Figures Test (MFF) Kagan, Rosman, Day, Albert, & Phillips, 1964)
      B. Embedded Figures Test (EFT)
      C. Subject-Paced Viewing Tasks (Ain, 1980)
      D. Picture Recognition Task (PRT) (Sprague & Sleator, 1977)
      E. Recall of videotaped lessons (Barkley, 1977a)
 III. For Tasks Involving Perceptual Discrimination and Retention

 IV. For Tasks Involving Logical or Conceptual Search
      A. Demands for Sustained Strategic Effort
         1. Extended Digit Span
         2. 34-word list
         3. Categorization Learning Task (CLT) (Kinsbourne, 1977)
         4. Paired-associative learning (Benezra, 1980)
      B. Concept-Discovery and Rule-Learning
         1. Wisconsin Card Sorting Test (Parry, 1973)
         2. Diagnostic Problem Solving (Niemark & Lewis, 1967)
   V. For Tasks Involving Avoidance Learning, Inhibitory Control & Pull of Immediate Award
      A. Lykken Maze Test (Lykken, 1957)

Note. Adapted from, "Attentional and cognitive problems" (pp. 280–329), by V. I. Douglas, 1983, In M. Rutter (Ed.), *Developmental Neuropsychiatry*, New York: Guilford Press.

logically valid behavior in the classroom. With these caveats, tests of attention in ADHD children, which differentiate between hyperactive and normal children, have been devised. Although the use of these tests in research is an advance over rating scales, their psychometric characteristics should be carefully considered before using them for clinical decisions concerning individuals. These tests are listed in Table 13-3, and the following discussion of them is based on the review by Douglas (1983).

   I. Vigilance and Reaction Time Tasks

      A. *Continuous Performance Test (CPT) (Rosvold, Mirsky, Sarason, Bransome, & Beck, 1956.* The CPT is used for studying sustained attention, selective attention, and impulse control. Children must pay close attention to relatively simple visual or auditory stimuli, often over extended periods of time, and respond to the appearance of specific stimuli as they appear. Hyperactive children make more errors of ommission (failing to respond to correct stimuli) and commission (responding to incorrect stimuli).

The CPT "requires the subject to establish a response set for designated stimuli, concentrate on responding quickly, maintain a readiness to respond to designated stimuli over time and inhibit responding to inappropriate stimuli" (Ostrom & Jenson, 1988, p.261). Children with specific learning disability who are not hyperactive, in contrast to children with specific learning disorder and hyperactivity, do not show deficits in sustained attention as measured by the Continuous Performance Test (O'Dougherty, Nuechterlein, & Drew, 1984, Tarnowski, Prinz, & Nay, 1986). A modified CPT has been developed by Gordon (1979), and Gordon and Mettelman (1987), and Gordon, McClure and Post (1986) and is described by the authors as a measure of the ability to delay responding in the presence of feedback. In the Gordon Diagnostic System (GDS), the child is instructed to press a response button after a specific sequence of numbers appears on the screen. It has been normed for six age groups between the ages of 6 and 14, with a total of 1,266 children in the normative sample. The GDS is sensitive to the effects of stimulant medication (Barkley & Edelbrock, 1986); it is said to be able to differentiate ADHD from reading disabled, overanxious, and normal children. A distractibility component, flashing digits in two outer portions of the display, has been added to the GDS.

B. *Reaction Time Tasks and Delayed Reaction Time Tasks (DRT).* Mean latencies are generally slower but more variable with hyperactive children, and responses are generally more inappropriate to the task demands (pushing the response button before the signal; responding to the warning signal before the action signal is given; pushing the response button more than once in response to the reaction signal) in hyperactive children. Hyperactive children also have difficulty in *withholding* a response to obtain candy rewards (Gordon, 1979).

C. *Tapping in response to specific auditory signal (Hoy, Weiss, Minde, & Cohen, 1978) as a measure of sustained attention,* found that hyperactive children give a greater number of incorrect responses than do the controls. Over time, and on repeating tasks, hyperactive children become more restless and their performance becomes worse. On the other hand, hyperactive children respond to reinforcement schedules. Douglas and Parry (1983) found that continuous reward reduces mean reaction time and reaction time variability in both normal and hyperactive children. The performance of hyperactive children to *randomly delivered* positive reinforcement, however, deteriorates in contrast to that of normal children.

II. Tasks Involving Perceptual Search.   Scanning a visual or an auditory field in an organized, purposeful manner or conducting a search for critical attributes of the task stimuli.

   A. *Matching Familiar Figures Test of Reflection-Impulsivity (MFF) (Kagan, Rosman, Day, Albert, & Phillips, 1964).*

   B. *Embedded Figures Test of Field Dependence-Independence (EFT).*

   C. *Subject-Paced Viewing Tasks (Ain, 1980):* These tasks involve placing pictorial stimuli representing several levels of complexity, incongruity, or familiarity in a carousel projector and allowing subjects to self-pace presentation of the pictures. The hyperactive group look significantly longer than normal controls at incongruous stimuli during the first trial, but only on the first trial, suggesting that there is no support that hyperactive children have unusual preference for novelty. But hyperactive children are less accurate than controls in recognizing pictures of scenery they had viewed before.

   D. *Picture Recognition Task (PRT) (Sprague & Sleator, 1977):* Arrays of 3–15 pictures are presented to the subject. Each array is followed a few seconds later by a test picture which the subject must decide whether or not appeared in the array immediately proceeding it. Accuracy and speed of response are recorded.

   E. *Recall of videotaped lessons (Barkley, 1977a):* Children are measured on accuracy of retention and success in processing visual and auditory material. Hyperactive children make more mistakes than controls.

III. Perceptual Description and Retention.   No differences between hyperactive and control children were found in the Wepman Test of Auditory Discrimination, on Picture Completion subtests of the WISC, in tests to detect small differences in visual stimuli, on visual-spatial memory, or in verbally presented stimuli. In contrast, it will be recollected that the child with specific language disability may have marked problems with these tasks.

IV. Tasks Involving Logical or Conceptual Search. The discovery of underlying concepts, meaning, or relationship in solving related complex problems.

   A. *Tasks involving demands for sustained strategic effort:*

      1. Extended form of Digit Span

      2. Memory of a 34-word list

      3. Categorization Learning Task CLT (Kinsbourne, 1977), in which a child is shown pictures of several animals and is told that each of the animals is to be assigned to one of four zoos.

The task is to learn the particular zoo with which each animal is associated

4. Paired-associative learning (Benezra, 1980)

Each of these tests except the perceptual tests presents greater difficulty to hyperactive children than to the normal controls. If no initial difference is found, then the hyperactive children gain information at a rate slower than that of the controls.

B. *Concept-discovery and rule-learning tasks*

1. Wisconsin Card Sorting Test (Parry, 1973). Hyperactive children make fewer correct choices, more "perseverative" errors, and more "unique" responses than control groups. One-third of the hyperactive children use only one of three possible scoring categories. However, the performance of hyperactives and normals does not differ when they are reinforced on a continuous 100% schedule for choosing correctly. Also, with continuous reinforcement, there is good transfer of learning from one problem to the next.

2. Diagnostic Problem Solving (Niemark & Lewis, 1967). In specific games and situations, the ADD group children are less likely than normal or reading disabled children to perceive all of the possible classifications of the presented game (Tant & Douglas, 1982). The ADD lack "a basic understanding of how to solve the matrices effectively."

V. Tasks Involving Avoidance Learning, Inhibitory Control, and the Pull of Immediate Award. The Lykken Maze Test (Lykken, 1957) consists of an array of four vertical rows of light, each row a different color. The task is to push buttons corresponding to the colored lights in the horizontal row to discover a set sequence by which the subject can progress from the top to the bottom of the maze. Positive feedback is made for correct choices; "punishment" is given for incorrect choices. Results of that study are interpreted by Freeman (1978) to suggest that there is an avoidance deficit in hyperactive children.

In summary, these studies suggest that "attentional problems represent one of a constellation of closely related deficits, all of which have far reaching effects on the children's behavior, academic achievement and cognitive functioning. A tentative list of defective processes includes: (1) the investment, organization and maintenance of attention and efforts; (2) the inhibition of impulsive responding; (3) the modulation of arousal levels to meet situational demands; and, (4) an unusually strong inclination to seek immediate gratification" (Douglas, 1983, p. 28). Further, these primary deficits may lead to secondary ones: limited development of higher order cognitive schemata, impaired metacognition, and diminished affective motivation.

Modulation of Motor and Emotional Impulses

Problems in the modulation of impulses from within the child and of stimuli from without may be conceptualized as a defect in the function of the stimulus barrier. The stimulus barrier is a metapsychological construct that is defined by its function (A. A. Silver, 1984a): to modulate, within limits tolerable to the organism, the impulses coming both from within and from the world around him; to prevent him from being overwhelmed by stimuli; and to enable him to achieve a dynamic equilibrium between his own needs and the capacity to satisfy those needs. It thus functions in the modulation of psychological and physiological stimuli. In the modulation of physiological stimuli, the stimulus barrier regulates the *milieu interieur* (Bernard, 1858), homeostasis (Cannon, 1939), and "the constant satisfactions and dissatisfactions which occur in a polyphasic colloidal solution" (Stunkard, 1932). In modulation of physiological stimuli, there is a balance, with feedback mechanisms allowing physiological variability within limits tolerated by the organism.

Psychologically, Freud conceived of the stimulus barrier both as a protection against external stimuli and as a modulator of internal drives. As a protection against external stimuli, he said (1920/1955): "The perceptive apparatus of our mind consists of two layers, an external protective barrier against stimuli whose task is to diminish the strength of excitations coming in, and of a surface behind it which receives the stimuli." Freud felt that failure of the protective barrier against external stimuli was clinically important in the development of anxiety and the traumatic neurosis. As a modulator of internal drives, Freud later (1940) considered the stimulus barrier as a significant function of the ego, a "special organization to act as an intermediary between the id and the external world" (p. 15). Of the stimulus barrier, Frosch (1983) stated that "it incorporates multiple ego functions such as the capacity for reality testing, judgement and delay among others. All of these not only facilitate the mastery of stimuli but also defensively control the impact on the psychic apparatus" (p. 287). Silverman proposed (cited in Frosch, 1983) that the very development of defenses and the methods of coping with stress is phase related to the development of the stimulus barrier.

Individual differences in the stimulus barrier may be detected early in a child's development (Brazelton, 1973; R. S. Paine, 1965; Prechtel and Beimtema, 1964). These observations find individual differences in "state" of the infant—differences in state of consciousness with variations from deep torporous sleep (Gesell, 1945/1969) to an alert, bright look with a focus on the source of stimulation. Brazelton (1973) suggested that "the pattern of states, as well as the movement from one state to another, appear to be important characteristic of infants in the neonatal period and this kind of evaluation may be the best predictor of an infant's receptivity and ability to respond to stimuli" (p. 5). In the mid-1940s, Fries (1944) filmed a series of neonates demonstrating a constitutional activity level characteristic for each child. Wolf (1959), observing neonates for protracted periods in the first few days of their life, found specific but characteristically different reactions appearing in regular or irregular sleep, with the infant demonstrating temporally organized or rhythmical motor patterns, an autochthomous clock for serial ordering of adaptive function. Individual variability in temperament was described by A. Thomas and Chess (1980) in nine different categories: activity level, rhythmicity of biological function, approach or withdrawal to new stimuli, adaptability to new or altered situations, the sensory threshold of responsiveness to stimuli, the intensity of the reaction, quality of mood, distractibility, and attention span and persistence. These characteristics really describe functions of the stimulus barrier, including the rhythmicity of autonomic function and impulse control.

The genetic capability of the stimulus barrier, however, may be modified by a number of factors: organic insult to the central nervous system, experiential factors that prevent full potential of the stimulus barrier from being attained, manic-depressive disorder, and elusive syndromes that we call severe developmental disorders, including autism, and schizophrenia (see Table 13-2). Organic insult may vary as to cause, severity, extent, and time of life of its occurrence. Its effect may depend on all these variables and on the support and understanding the child receives from her environment. Experiential factors—stimulation from the environment appropriate to the needs of the child—are essential for the normal development of the stimulus barrier. Biological maturation and genetic potential by themselves are not sufficient for it to function; appropriate and adequate stimulation impinging upon the biological substrate is necessary. Thus, an infant deprived of maternal interaction at the time she is beginning to separate herself as distinct from her mother at about 5 months to about 18 months of age, does not develop a barrier to her primitive drives or impulses. She does not develop an inner modulating structure. She demands immediate gratification. Her behavior is impulsive, hyperactive, demanding, and clinging. She cannot form meaningful object relations. She does not anticipate danger and does not learn from repeated failure. Such a child is suffering from primary maternal acathexis, an affectionless psychopathy due to initial failure of bonding. Earlier such a child was said to have a psychopathic personality (L. A. Bender, 1953); more recently, she is termed a borderline personality (E. R. Shapiro, 1978).

The child with an attention deficit disorder also suffers from a thin, or deficient, stimulus barrier. As we have defined ADHD, its cause must be found in factors other than in structural insult to the central nervous system or in experiential factors. Gorenstein and Newman (1980) found a parallel in the behavior of hyperactive children and the behavior of "psychopathy, hysteria, antisocial personality and alcoholism," all of which belong to a group of disorders they label as "disinhibitory psychopathy," which has a parallel in the syndrome produced in animals by lesions of the septal-hip-pocampal-frontal system.

POSSIBLE CAUSATIVE FACTORS

Genetic Factors

There is some evidence, certainly not as strong as that for specific language disability, that there is a genetic factor in the syndrome. A review of genetic and constitutional factors in hyperactivity concluded the following:

- There is a connection between hyperactivity in children and alcoholism, antisocial personality, and hysteria in their adult relatives.
- Hyperactivity in childhood may predispose people to these psychiatric disorders of adult life.
- Hyperactive children tend to have parents, uncles, and aunts who were hyperactive themselves and *vice versa*.
- There is a direct evidence for genetic determinants of hyperactivity. (M. A. Stewart, 1980, p. 160.)

These conclusions, however, are tentative, based upon too few studies with small samples.

More recent evidence for a genetic component to ADD is reported by Heffron, Martin, and Welsh (1984) who found, as did Cunningham and Barkley (1978) and Lopez (1965), concordance in monozygotic twins. Heffron et al. (1984) reported three pairs of monozygotic twins all concordant for ADD, but they also cautioned that twins have greater prenatal and natal risk, factors that may increase vulnerability to psychiatric disorders.

The question arises whether attention deficit disorder with hyperactivity is an extreme position of "temperamental hyperactivity," as described by Thomas, Chess, and Birch (1968), or whether it is a pathologic entity in itself. Is clinical hyperactivity simply a point on a developmental continuum on which genetic vulnerability, the genetic strength of the stimulus barrier, is inadequate to cope with the demands of the environment? Or is clinical hyperactivity a pathological state of central nervous system functioning? "Most investigators believe that in ADHD they are dealing with a developmental disorder, characteristic symptoms of which change with maturation" (S. E. Shaywitz, Shaywitz, Cohen, & Young, 1983 p. 334).

Biochemical Factors

There is recent evidence to suggest that an immaturity in the maturation of neurotransmitters may be the developmental basis of the ADHD syndrome and that these neurotransmitters may be monoaminergic mechanisms. Wender (1973), for example, impressed with the behavioral parallel between the behavior disorder of post-von Economo encephalitis in children and the behavior disorder of ADD, postulated a defect in catecholamine, particularly dopamine metabolism, in each of these conditions. In adults, Parkinsonism, a clearly defined lesion of dopaminergic neurons, may follow von Economo encephalitis. In children a similar lesion may yield the hyperkinetic, impulse disorder of childhood (see review in Chapter 1, "The Problem of Definition").

S. E. Shaywitz et al. (1983) pointed out that, although our present understanding of the anatomy of brain monoamines is fragmentary, there is evidence to suggest significant variation in both catacholaminergic and indolaminergic mechanisms with normal maturation. For example, norepinephrine mechanisms tend to increase with age during childhood and adolescence, and dopamine activity appears to decrease as the organism matures, whereas serotonin either declines or stays relatively consistent. Serum dopamine beta hydroxylase (DBH), urinary MHPG (3-methoxyl-4-hydroxphenylglycol), and urinary VMA (vanillylmandelic acid) increase with age in childhood; platelet MAO (monoamine oxidase) decreases. Cerebrospinal fluid concentrations of 5-HIAA (5-hydroxyindoleacetic acid) appear to be stable throughout the life cycle. Girls tend to have lower accumulations of dopamine metabolites and a higher accumulation of serotonin metabolites than boys do. S. E. Shaywitz et al. (1983) stated that "these findings suggest that girls tend to have a relatively more mature or modulated CNS functioning, particularly in relation to central inhibiting mechanisms" and "it is possible that variations in disease prevalence [i.e., ADD, autism, and Tourette's syndrome occur more frequently in boys than in girls] might relate to observed differences in monoamine concentrations" (p. 336).

The question, of course, is the relationship of these findings to ADHD. Is there indeed a difference in concentration of neurotransmitters and/or their metabolites in the central nervous system of children with this syndrome? The evidence so far is mixed, plagued by technical difficulties in measurement, in understanding the source (whether it is central or peripheral) of the metabolites measured, in ethical considerations in experimental procedures with children, and in diagnostic heterogeneity. When compared to normal controls, urinary MHPG, for example, is found to be decreased (Shekim, De Kirmenjian, & Chapek, 1977; Shekim, De Kirmenjian, Chapek, Jand, & Davis, 1979), increased (Kahn & De Kirmenjian, 1981), and no different (Rapoport, Mikkelson et al., 1978; Wender, 1971). Comparisons of platelet MAO-B in normal and hyperactive children are also inconclusive, because they have been determined to be both lower (Shekim et al., 1982) and, perhaps in excess (G. L. Brown et al., 1984). The finding of decreased platelet serotonin found in early studies has not been replicated and indeed was later found to be increased (Irwin, Belendink, McCloskay, & Freedman, 1981). Plasma 5-HIAA was reported to be low. No difference in urinary HVA or 5-HIAA was detected between normal and hyperactive children, and there was no relationship between DBH and hyperactivity. Spinal fluid studies, which may more accurately reflect CNS monoamineric function than do urine and plasma studies, are still in preliminary stages. B. A. Shaywitz, Cohen, and Bowens (1977) using techniques of probenecid loading, found concentrations of HVA relative to probenecid significantly reduced in the cerebro-spinal fluid of 6 hyperactive boys, aged 5–9, over that in the 20 controls, aged 2–16. Levels of 5-HIAA were not altered.

Zametkin and Rapoport (1987) reviewed the evidence for "pharmacological dissection" of possible neurotransmitter abnormality in hyperactive children. Dopamine agonists (L-dopa, amantadine, and pirabidel) have not obtunded the symptoms of ADHD, while dopamine antagonists (chlorpromazine, haloperidol, and thioridazine) do decrease the inappropriate motor activity and inattentiveness. These actions appear to be additive with methylphenidate. The importance of norepinephrine in ADHD is suggested by the decreased urinary excretion of MHPG with drugs effective in decreasing hyperactivity and inattention (i.e., dextroamphetamine and desipramine). It is noted, however, that fenfluramine, which also decreases urinary MHPG, is without benefit in ADHD. Fenfluramine also depletes brain serotonin. Increasing serotonin with L-tryptophan results in no behavioral change. Thus it appears that a single neurotransmitter hypothesis is no longer tenable. That urinary MHPG decreases in responders but not in nonresponders to d-amphetamine (Shekim, Javid, Davis, & Bylund, 1983) and that decrease in MHPG, VMA, NE, and total NE turnover correlates with improvement with MAO inhibitors suggests that norepinephrine may be a necessary but not a sufficient condition for understanding the biochemical mechanism for the ADHD syndrome.

Breese and his associates at the University of North Carolina School of Medicine (1981) agreed that hyperkinesis may not have a single pathophysiological base, but that, chemically, hyperkinesis is a heterogeneous syndrome which may involve, in varying combinations, dopamine, norepinephrine, and serotonin systems. These opinions are based on both clinical and laboratory evidence. Clinical data show that the *serum* levels of methylphenidate in hyperkinetic children who do not respond therapeutically to that drug are no different from levels in those who do; laboratory data, examining the mechanism of action of stimulant drugs in rats, suggest that *all* monoamine transmitter systems are involved in the action of d-amphetamine, so that it is impossible to identify any specific monoamine as the vehicle for the therapeutic action of d-amphetamine.

MEDICATION TO MANAGE THE ADHD SYNDROME

The use of medication in the management of the child with ADHD has a long clinical and experimental tradition.

It is over 50 years since C. Bradley (1937) reported on the effect of Benzedrine on the behavior of 30 children, aged 5–14, of normal intelligence, hospitalized at Emma Pendelton Bradley Hospital for severe behavior disorders of varied etiology. Fourteen of his patients were "dramatically improved." Six years later, L. A. Bender and Cottington (1943), picking up the thread of Bradley's work, treated 40 children, aged 5–13, all inpatients at Bellevue Psychiatric Hospital, with amphetamine sulfate (Benzedrine). Thirty of these children with "neurotic diagnosis" improved, and aggressiveness diminished in four children with "psychopathic personality." Since that time, literally hundreds of reports on the use of stimulant drugs in hyperactive, impulsive, and aggressive children have appeared, and recently additional classes of drugs, tricyclic depressants and MAO inhibitors, have been reported to be effective. Reviews and summaries of these papers have appeared in R. A. Barkley (1977b); D. F. Klein, Gittleman, Quitkin, and Rifkin (1980); Rapoport (1983); D. Shaffer (1977); E. Taylor (1984); Werry (1978); J. M. Wiener (1977, 1985), and Zametkin and Rapoport (1987).

Stimulant Medication

The effect of medication on Greg is typical of the effect of stimulants in the majority of children with ADHD.

CASE STUDY: GREG

Greg was 7 years, 9 months of age, a first-grader, when he was first seen in our clinic. He was a thin, wiry, red-headed child, alert and verbal, who said his mother wanted us to see him because he gets angry easily and throws blocks. He said he liked to get angry, that he thought violent things, but that he had these thoughts only when he played with his toys or when he "just thinks." He had violent dreams: "Ryan [his friend] came over. I kicked him. His mom came over. I kicked her in the butt. His father came over, I kicked him." Another dream: "A Tyrannosaurus came after me. I ran into the flowers. I got out my shotgun and shot the Tyrannosaurus. I was 14 years old."

His anger and aggression covered a frightened child who felt that the world was a difficult place for him, that growing up was dangerous, that his parents were not giving him the protection and care he needed, and that school was unreasonable in asking him to sit still and do his work. He earned a full scale IQ of 115 on the WISC-R with a verbal IQ of 108 and a performance IQ of 120. A selective weakness within the verbal scale occurred in Arithmetic (scaled score of 7) and Digit Span (scaled score of 4), both of which subtests are sensitive to attention and concentration. When tasks were difficult for him, he tended to give up quickly. On examination he was friendly and verbal, but definitely hyperactive—unable to sit still, squirming in his chair, moving to another chair, which he then would spin about. His speech was high-pitched and under pressure. Aside from these findings, classical neurological examination was intact. Perceptual examination revealed difficulty with visual-motor function with an impulsive, although accurate, performance on the Bender VMGT. He had mild praxic difficulty but no other body image immaturity. His electroencephalogram was normal.

It was felt that Greg was suffering from an impulsive hyperactivity with difficulty in sustaining attention, the cause of which was unknown. Many of Greg's emotional problems were in part a reaction to his inability to control his impulses and to attend to his academic tasks. He did respond to methylphenidate, which was gradually increased to 10 mg b.i.d., with a marked reduction in hyperactivity and an increase in attention. By 9 years, 4 months methylphenidate had been reduced to 5 mg b.i.d., he "hardly dreams any more," and his academic work was higher than grade level. His speech, however, was still high-pitched and under pressure; a slight synkinesis was noted, and visual-motor function was under better control. It was felt that methylphenidate was definitely helpful in reducing this child's impulsive motor behavior and in enabling him to gain a measure of control over his feelings. By 9 years, 5 months methylphenidate was gradually discontinued. There was a mild increase in restless behavior, but, in the 6 months since discontinuing medication, he was able to maintain concentration at school and he performed well academically with no return of the anxiety dreams and the volatile anger that had disturbed him 2 years earlier.

There is general agreement that, with stimulant drugs:

- In the short term (the exact limits) of which are unknown, amphetamines and related drugs are of established potency in reducing overactive, inattentive, and impulsive behaviors and in improving laboratory tests requiring sustained attention.
- The improvement in inattentive and restless behavior is not matched by clear evidence of improvement in academic learning (Barkley & Cunningham, 1978).
- Beneficial efforts of long-term (2 or more years) treatment are "inconclusive and disappointing" (E. Taylor, 1984, p. 451).
- The incidence of side effects, such as drug dependency and abuse, growth retardation, tics, and emergence of Tourett's syndrome, is still obscure.

Barkley (1977b) in a review of 39 studies involving 2303 children (15 studies with 915 children who received amphetamines; 14 studies with 866 children on methylphenidate; 2 studies with 105 children on magnesium pemoline; 8 studies involving 412 children on placebo) reported the percentage of hyperkinetic children responding or not responding to stimulant drug treatment as judged by various reporting services: "On the average 74 percent of the hyperkinetic children given amphetamines improved, while 26 percent did not change or whose symptoms were exacerbated by the drug" (p. 139). The percentage of improvement ranged from 44 to 96%. Similar rates were found for methylphenidate and magnesium pemoline (ranges of 51–94%). An average improvement rate for placebo treatment was 39% (range of 8–67%). Bradley pointed out that what is meant by "improvement" may vary among studies. Thus, he said (1977) that "it is no longer adequate to report merely the percentage of various degrees of improvement. It is necessary to measure objectively a variety of specific variables to ascertain just how the hyperactive child's behavior is or is not altered by stimulant drugs" (p. 139). Such measurements may be found in psychophysiological parameters, in behavior rating scales, in psychological tests, and in specific measures of activity, vigilance and attention (see Table 13-3).

Whereas most studies report an increase in heart rate and/or in blood pressure with stimulant drugs, Porges and Smith (1980) found an interesting change in heart rate or in variability of heart rate in one group of hyperactive children who received methylphenidate and were exposed to a task requiring active, sustained attention. Passive reflective attention or short-term attention (the first 5 seconds of preparatory set) normally evokes an initial decrease followed by an increase in heart rate. Hyperactive children did not respond differently from "normals" in this set and methylphenidate had no effect. On the other hand, where active, sustained attention was required, there was normally a decrease in heart rate and a decrease in variability of heart rate along with decreased motor activity and respiration rate. One group of hyperactive children were deficient in an active sustained-attention task. With methylphenidate they tended to improve, and with improvement there was a concomitant decrease in heart rate and heart rate variability. Porges and Smith suggested that performance on the task of sustained attention may be used to divide hyperactive children into two subgroups. However, ratings of improved social behavior in the classroom did not parallel improvement in physiological response to stimulant drugs.

Conflicting findings were found in galvanic skin responses, frequency and amplitude of the alpha activity on EEG, and average evoked-potential responses. Although Barkley (1977b) stated that stimulant drugs may help stimulate both CNS inhibitory systems as well as excitatory systems, no clear-cut pattern emerges. Further, Barkley and Jackson (1977), in a study of 24 boys (12 of whom were hyperactive, 12 controls), found that methylphenidate did not produce significant effect on autonomic activity as measured by galvanic skin resistance, heart rate, and respiration taken across four experimental settings. There was also no relationship between psychophysiological activity and objective measures of hyperactivity in both normal and hyperactive children.

As we have indicated, rating scales have been a favorite instrument for evaluating behavior change. Most studies have found rating scales to indicate better functioning along activity, attention, and aggression dimensions with medication. Objective measures of activity level also suggest that an important impact of stimulant drugs is reduction of activity across various situations. However, the change in activity is not the same across *all* situations, and results will vary depending upon the type of activity measured and the way that activity is assessed.

Results obtained in rating scales are paralleled by results found in more objective measures of vigilance, reaction time, perceptual search and conceptual search measures, all of which have been outlined in Table 13-3. In the past 10–15 years these measures have been the subject of intensive study. Barkley (1977b) stated that "it is apparent from these results [on measures of vigilance, reaction time, and cognitive and logical search] that the primary impact of stimulant drugs on hyperactive children is increased concentration or attention span, or improvement in ability to stop, look and listen" (p. 152).

Stimulant Medication and Learning

In spite of the effect of stimulant medication on the improvement on laboratory measures of attention and on the observed ability of the ADHD child to contain his restless motor activity, these changes are not reflected in improved academic performance. H. E. Rie, Rie, Stewart, and Ambuel (1976a, 1976b) found that the academic achievement of children receiving methylphenidate for 6 months was no different from their achievement during a control period on placebo. Sixty-one children with learning problems without hyperactivity were studied by Gittleman-Klein and Klein (1976) over a 12-week period using random assignment to placebo and methylphenidate. Measures of academic achievement were no different for the two groups. Performance on tests that required speed of "mental processing" was improved, but performance on untimed complex verbal tasks was not. In a later study, Gittleman, Klein, and Feingold (1983) combined methylphenidate or a placebo with remedial reading or "academic tutoring." Sixty-six children (boys outnumbering girls 2 to 1, mean age 10 years, with IQs ranging from 90 to 115) were randomly assigned to three groups: group 1 received reading remediation and the placebo; group 2 received academic tutoring and the placebo; and group 3 received reading remediation and methylphenidate. The drug was given at a mean daily dose of 1.19 mg/kg up to 60 mg/day for 18 weeks. At 2 months and 8 months after treatment, there was no difference between groups in basic reading skills, in reading achievement, or in academic skills other than reading. Gittelman et al. concluded, as did Douglas in 1983 and Swanson and Kinsbourne in 1976, that the use of stimulants in conjunction with a training program was problematical.

These conclusions were underlined by Aman and Werry (1982), who compared the effects of methylphenidate and diazepam in 15 children aged 6 years, 8 months to 12 years, whose IQs ranged from 81 to 135 and who were at least 2 years retarded in reading relative to their mental age. In a crossover design, each drug was given for 6 days followed by 1 day washout between conditions. The methylphenidate dose was 0.35 mg/kg/day; that of diazepam, 0.10mg/kg/day. Each child was given a series of behavioral and learning tasks. Significant reductions in omission errors in the continuous performance test were found with each drug. No effects were seen on a manifest anxiety scale, in matching familiar figures, or in audiovisual integration. A slight, nonsignificant improvement was found in letter recognition, in the meta-analysis of reading, and in a psycholinguistic analysis. Word recognition actually deteriorated. Aman and Werry concluded that "drug-related changes occurred mostly in areas unrelated to basic cognitive deficits" (p. 36).

A number of studies reporting improvement in academic achievement in children with hyperactivity, behavior problems, and academic difficulty, however, have appeared since the early optimistic data of Bradley. Two of these papers are early ones (Connors & Eisenberg, 1963; Connors, Eisenberg, & Sharpe, 1964) and three appeared in 1985 (Pelham; Pelham, Bender, Coddell, Booth, & Moorer; Pelham & Murphy). In a placebo-controlled study of 42 children, mean age 10 years, whose primary complaint was some form of learning disorder, Connors (1964) found that d-amphetamine given at a dose of 10mg/day over a 4-week period improved arithmetic achievement, but there was only a nonsignificant trend in reading improvement. Connors noted, however, that his d-amphetamine group had improved performance on the Porteus maze, in ability to copy geometric designs, and in ability to sequence phonemes to make words. Pelham et al. (1985), using a double-blind, controlled crossover design, tested methylphenidate in doses of 0.15, 0.3, and 0.6 mg/kg/day in a 7-week summer day program. There were 24 boys and 5 girls ranging from 5 years, 5 months to 11 years, 5 months of age; 26 of these children were diagnosed as having ADHD, 3 as having ADD. Eight had additional conduct disorders. Pelham stated that during the methylphenidate phase there was increased performance in number of arithmetic problems done and attempted and an increased proportion of comprehension of questions answered correctly. In contrast to the findings of Sprague and Sleater (1977), however, Pelham found that a dose higher than 0.3 mg/kg/day was needed to obtain improvement in these parameters.

In their review of six studies on the effects of stimulant drugs on learning, Aman and Werry (1982) summarized: "While most investigations can be faulted on diagnostic heterogeneity, dose or duration of medication, it seems reasonable to conclude that at present, stimulants have no clear role to play in [improving] learning disabilities" (p. 37).

Tricyclic Drugs and MAO Inhibitors

In addition to the adrenergic stimulant drugs, there have been recent ongoing studies using other agents for children with ADHD. These agents are the tricyclics and the monoamino oxidase (MAO) inhibitors. The use of desmethylimipramine, clorgyline, and tranylcypromine is reviewed by Rapoport, Zametkin, Donnelly, and Ismond (1985), while the use of imipramine and desipramine, specifically in adolescents, is reviewed by Gastfriend, Biederman, and Jellinek (1985). Rapoport et al. (1985) studied 29 boys aged 6–12, who had been referred to a day hospital program because of their hyperactive, impulsive, and inattentive behaviors, in a 3-week, random assignment, double-blind, placebo-controlled paradigm. Sixteen boys received desipramine at one dose per day up to 125 mg/day for 14 days; 12 boys received the placebo. Five of the group are reported as having a learning or language disorder. Between baseline, day 3, and day 14 testing, there was a significant decrease in the Connors Abbreviated Teacher Rating Scale in the drug group, but no difference in the Continuous Performance Test. Clinical improvement was seen by the third day of treatment; clinical effects did not correlate significantly with plasma concentration of desipramine or its metabolite. Decrease in urinary MHPG, however, paralleled improvement in behavior.

MAO inhibitors (Rapoport et al., 1985) clorgyline (MAO-A inhibitor) and tranylcypromine (A and B inhibitor) were studied in 14 boys, mean age 9 years, 2 months ± 1 year, 5 months, in a 12-week, double-blind crossover design in which 2 weeks of placebo were followed by 4 weeks of the active drug. After a 2-week washout period another 4 weeks of the drug was received. With each of these drugs there was an immediate reduction in impulsive, hyperactive behavior, comparable to d-amphetamine. Deprenyl (MAO-B inhibitor), however, was less effective than clorgyline, tranylcypromine, or d-amphetamine. While the use of desipramine appears practical in children with attention deficit disorders, the use of MAO inhibitors, with their need for controlled diet and the possibility of adverse reaction with other drugs, makes their practical use problematic.

Unfortunately, in these studies comprehensive evaluations of these children, with data on neurological signs, soft signs, and distribution of perceptual assets and deficits were not given. As we have repeatedly emphasized in this book, learning disorders are a heterogeneous group. As E. Taylor (1984) stated: "Improvement in ability to attend would only be of overall benefit if it were the limiting factor in achievement. The results of studies so far agree that attention deficit is not usually the limiting factor in school learning. . . . It is certainly possible that there is a subgroup of children with learning disabilities for which attention deficit is a specific and crucial problem but this has not been established" (p. 449). It appears clear, however, that when a specific language disability as we have defined it is accompanied by an attention deficit disorder, medication alone will not cure the language disability. Specific educational management, as described in Chapter 7 (Principles of Educational Management), is needed.

Side Effects of Medication

Medication also is not without its problems. Barkley (1977b) reviewed 29 studies that have reported side effects of stimulant medication. The most frequently noted are insomnia or sleep disturbances, decreased appetite, weight loss, irritability, and abdominal pain. Less frequent are headaches, drowsiness, sadness, dizziness, nausea, proneness to crying, euphoria, nightmares, tremor, dry mouth, constipation, lethargy, tics, anxiety, and suppressed gain of height and weight. Although most of these side effects are more annoying than dangerous, and may be temporary and respond to decrease in medication, some are potentially serious. A number of reports have associated the emergence of Tourette's syndrome with stimulant medication (Denckla, Bemporer, & MacKay, 1976; Lowe, Cohen, Detlor, Kremenitzer, & Shaywitz, 1982; E. Mitchell & Matthews, 1980). The tenacious and disturbing symptoms of Tourette's syndrome demand careful monitoring for emergence of tics. In our clinic, even a family history of chronic tics is reason enough for not giving stimulant medication (see Chapter 15 for discussion of stimulant drugs and Tourette's syndrome).

Effects on growth have been a concern since the report by Safer, Allen, and Barr in 1972, in which was described a dose-related decrement in rate of growth on children receiving methylphenidate or amphetamine over the school year. No growth suppressant effects were found, however, when the daily dose of methylphendiate did not exceed 20 mg. A special committee of the FDS Psychopharmacological Drug Advisory Committee (Roche, Lipman, Overall, & Hung 1979), reviewing reports on the long-term effect of stimulants on growth, concluded that there appears to be a decrease in weight gain and in rate of growth during the first 2 years of medication. By the third year a tolerance appears to develop so that there is no effect on long-term (adult) stature or weight. In contrast to the FDA committee, however, Safer and Allen (1973), found that no tolerance to the height and weight effects developed. They recommend discontinuing medication during the summer months. When medication was discontinued during the summer a "rebound" effect on weight was found during that time.

Growth suppression in hyperkinetic boys has been found with all three of the stimulant drugs used: d-amphetamine (Greenhill, Chambers, Rubinstein, Helpern, & Sacher, 1981), methylphenidate (Mattes & Gittleman, 1983), and pemoline (Dickinson, Lee, & Ringdehl, 1979). Greenhill (1981) reviewed the literature to 1981. The Columbia group found that 13 boys receiving a mean daily dose of amphetamine of 21 mg/day (10–30 mg; 0.84–0.1 mg/kg/day) for 1 year, lost 16 percentile points in weight and 10 percentile points in height. During this time, mean sleep-related prolactin concentrations fell significantly during treatment, but there was no change in growth hormone secretion. These findings persisted in a subgroup of eight children followed for 21 months. Mattes and Gittleman (1983) found inhibition of growth (height velocity) when methylphenidate was given in doses of 1.3 mg/kg/day for prolonged periods up to 4 years. Greenhill et al. (1984), however, found that in 10 boys receiving a mean dose of methylphenidate of 1.3 mg/kg/day (mean amount 39 mg/day) for 1 year, there was a loss of 13 percentile points in weight but only a 3 percentile point loss in height. Mean sleep-related prolactin concentrations were unchanged, although there was a 34% increase (drug related) in mean sleep-related growth hormone. In a study of the acute effects of methylphenidate, Gualtieri et al. (1981) and Gualtieri et al. (1982) found that 1 hour after a single dose of either 0.3 mg/kg or 0.6 mg/kg, significant elevations of growth hormone were found, whereas prolactin was significantly depressed only at the higher dose of methylphenidate. Greenhill et al. (1981) suggested that the short half-life of melthylphenidate as contrasted with d-amphetamine may be related to the lesser growth-inhibiting effect of methylphenidate. Growth inhibition in stimulant treated children may be the result of inhibition of somatomedin, thus altering cartilage metabolism.

Whatever the cause, it is not only prudent to monitor the height and weight curves of children receiving stimulant medication but also to prescribe the lowest dose possible over the shortest period of time to attain the desired therapeutic effect.

There has been concern that children who receive psychostimulants become "addicted" to stimulants as adolescents or may more readily become drug abusers as they grow older. Published evidence suggests that such is not the case, with only one report (Goyer, Davis, & Rapoport, 1979) of a young adolescent abusing a prescribed stimulant. This 13-year-old boy had been receiving methylphenidate for approximately 3 years for hyperactive and behavioral difficulties. He responded to 10 mg t.i.d. Within a year, however, he required a dose of 20 mg t.i.d. He began to take medication more often so that before admission to NIMH he had been taking 40 mg approximately every 2 hours. He claims the drug made him feel "high" or gave him a "numbness" or a "buzz." There was absence of dysphoria following the drug. In fact, such reports that are available (Beck, Langford, MacKay, & Sum, 1975; Blovin, Bornstein, & Trites, 1978) found less drug use in adolescents who had received stimulants in childhood than in a so-called "normal group." There is one report, however, of the mothers of two children abusing the methylphenidate prescribed for their children (Fulton & Yates, 1988). The authors pointed out that where "alcoholism, substance abuse and antisocial personality disorder" exist in families of children with attention deficit disorder the structure for misuse of the presribed drug exists. The $5.00 street value of a 10 mg methylphenidate tablet, in contrast to the prescription price of 35 cents, may also encourage such families to attempt to get multiple prescriptions for the drug.

There are more subtle stimulant drug effects. Whalen and Henker (1980b), in a paradigm involving peer interrelationships and social communication, found that some hyperactive children on placebo seemed happier, were less self-derogatory, and gave more positive feedback to peers than when on medication. Whalen and Henker (1980b) described the "emanative" effects of psychostimulant medication as a series of concentric circles, starting from the inner direct effect of medication, spreading to the psychological effect on the child, family, teachers, and peers, outward to include institutional, subcultural, and societal effects. Medication modifies the child's perception of himself and the way others view him; it conveys the message that the child's problems are biologically based and may interfere with attempts to modify personal effort, intrafamily tensions, and educational aspects of management. The short-term effects of these drugs may also increase the tendency to label a child as hyperactive, may obscure many of the situational influences on behavior, and may perpetuate the fallacy that because a child responds to a drug he is classified as having an attention deficit disorder. A series of studies extending over a 2-year period at the National Institute of Mental Health (Rapoport, Buchsbaum, et al., 1978) compared the response to a single dose of d-amphetamine of normal prepubertal boys, hyperactive boys, and normal college-age males. The college-age subjects were divided into two groups: one given the same per weight dose as was given to children, the second half given a per weight dose to approximate the absolute dose given to the children. In summary: all groups (except the high-dose adults) tended to decrease motor activity and increase vigilance, but the hyperactive children had a greater response to medication. In one task requiring sustained attention, the hyperactive group improved significantly in contrast to the other three groups. Affectively, adults experienced "euphoria" on the medication, whereas children reported feeling "funny" or "tired." In a double-blind, crossover design, using methylphenidate and a placebo given to a group of boys, aged 6–12, with a variety of conduct disorders, all showed positive changes in ratings of behavior and in tests of attention when on stimulant medication (E. Taylor, 1983). Thus, the effect of stimulant drugs is nonspecific and is not confined to a particular pathological state; there does not appear to be a diagnostic specificity in the use of stimulants.

It has also been a frequent practice to titrate the dose of medication with its effect on hyperactivity. However, ratings of attention and behavior responded differently to varying doses of methylphenidate. The error rate on a continuous performance test improved on low doses (10–20 mg) but progressively deteriorated with higher doses, while the teacher rating scales showed decreased hyperactivity and improved behavior with higher doses. In the average preadolescent boy, a dose of 10–20 mg/day appears optimal for cognitive tasks. The target for treatment should help define the dose.

Allergy and the Feingold Diet

In 1974, Feingold, emeritus chief of the Department of Allergy at the Kaiser-Permanente Medical Care Program in San Francisco, published an anecdotal report of role of allergy as a precipitating factor in what he called the Hyperkinetic Learning Disability Syndrome. Feingold specifically indicted salicylates, food colorings, preservatives, and additives. The foods containing proscribed salicylates included a long list of fruits and two vegetables (tomatoes and cucumbers), foods containing synthetic (artificial) color or flavor included most of the foods we buy in supermarkets, "junk" foods, manufactured candy and ice cream, and practically all pediatric medication and vitamins. Eliminating these foods makes up the Feingold or the KP (Kaiser-Permanente) diet.

Objective studies of the effect of food additives have centered largely on eight synthetic food dyes, certified as safe by the Food and Drug Administration: Red #46, Yellow #5 and #6, Red #3 and #4, and Blue #1 and # 2, and Green #3. These substances share no one particular chemical component that might be identified as precipitating behavioral symptoms. Kinsbourne (1984), reviewing the few objective studies, concluded that "a reasonable summary . . . admits that food colors can impair some hyperactive children's ability to learn. However, we regard the therapeutic efficacy of the Feingold diet as still lacking corroboration. . . . the demonstrated effects occurred only after high doses of colors, contrary to the often heard clinically based assertions that 'trace amounts upset the children' (p. 495)." Two types of studies led to this conclusion. In one, diet comparison studies, the effectiveness of an additive-reduced diet is compared to a control diet. In the second, "challenge studies," response to a food dye is compared to that of a placebo. In a diet comparison study, Goyette, Conners, and Petti (1978), reported 10 mothers of 10 preschoolers who rated the children improved on the experimental diet. B. Weiss et al. (1980) found an adverse response to additive diet in 2 of 22 children, aged 2 years, 8 months and 3 years. Harley, Matthews, and Eichmann (1978), failed to find any adverse effect of reintroduction of food dye into diets of children who had previously benefited from an additive-free diet. Conners (1980) and Conners et al. (1976), in a study involving 142 hyperactive children, found that when children were on an additive-reduced diet, about half had a significant improvement as measured by the Conners Rating Scale. Just as did Harley et al. (1978), however, they found no clear pattern of response to reintroduction of food dyes. What was of interest was that, when the additive-reduced diet was given first, there was a decrease in symptoms of hyperactivity, but in the control diet phase symptoms did not return. When the control diet was given first, decrease in symptoms also occurred; but when the additive-reduced diet was then given, symptoms were further reduced.

Results of challenge studies reflect the dose of additive used. With low doses of tartrazine (Yellow #5) there was little support of the Feingold hypothesis (Kinsbourne, 1984, p. 492, 493). With higher doses, however, Swanson and Kinsbourne (1980), in a carefully controlled study, found significant impairment in a paired associate learning test in 20 of 40 children, 1½ and 3½ hours after ingestion of the dye. These 20 children also responded to stimulant drugs, while the 20 children who did not react to the dye also did not improve with medication. In a 1-year follow-up study, Swanson, Kinsbourne, Roberts, and Zucker (1978) found 8 of 25 children had a long-term benefit from the Feingold diet. The beneficial effects of this diet have been attributed to its low sugar content. No objective challenge study of the effect of sugar on hyperactivity has been done to date.

While the efficiency of the Feingold diet as a treatment for hyperactivity is still under scientific consideration, families do ask for it and some may indeed be able to follow this diet without psychological trauma to the child or to themselves. It should not be rejected out of hand, but after considering the psychological effects of diet on family relationships, take its place in the therapeutic possibility for specific children and their families.

EDUCATIONAL MANAGEMENT

The diagnosis of ADHD implies some specific educational considerations. The teacher's understanding not only of the disorder itself, but also of his or her own reactions to the child, is crucial. It is very easy for teachers to lose patience with ADHD children. The difficulties their impulsiveness precipitates; their loud presence in the classroom; the persistence of their questions, comments, and demands—all can render them very unpopular members of the classroom group. Especially in the elementary grades, if the teacher responds punitively to this apparent misbehavior, it becomes a model for other children. The ADHD child is then set up for the role of scapegoat, the brunt of jokes, and the target of tattletales. With older students, punitive reactions on the part of the teacher can produce a series of public confrontations between the ADHD child and the teacher; the other students join as spectators to these contests, thus reinforcing the very behavior the teacher was trying to extinguish.

The teacher must understand that much of the impulsive behavior is not intentional, not part of a plan to defy educational authority. The high activity level, annoying as it is to the people around the youngster, is not always under voluntary control. The teacher will learn, probably on the basis of some unfortunate experiences, that the most effective management strategy for the behavior problems resulting from ADHD is prevention. What can't be prevented sometimes will be best handled by ignoring it.

Some people have used behavior modification approaches successfully with ADHD youngsters, particularly with specific behavior patterns, such as calling out in the classroom and failing to keep on task. Some of the cognitive behavior management approaches are also productive and may have greater generalizability. Self-talk approaches that make use of language as a mediator of behavior are based on sound psychological principles. If the ADHD children can be taught to use verbal rehearsal strategies, they will have a powerful self-management tool.

The fast/inaccurate approach frequently characterizes the learning style of the child with ADHD. If the correction of errors is not to become an exchange of mutual recriminations, the teacher must devise tactful and interesting methods for pointing out mistakes. The spelling checker that accompanies most word processing programs is helpful, also the use of a hand calculator as an alternative method after the problems have been computed by hand is recommended for correction in mathematics.

A related complaint that many teachers have about ADHD youngsters has to do with their apparent inattention. Like Rick in the case study earlier in this chapter, many of these children will seem not to be paying attention, but will be able to recount all that had been happening accurately. Secondary school teachers report with considerable annoyance: "He just sits there and doodles designs, never taking a note in class. Then, when I give a test, he gets one of the highest grades!" People who teach ADHD youngsters have to become accustomed to nontraditional work habits.

The self-discipline imposed by training in karate and equivalent disciplines can be helpful to some youngsters. This training increases body image awareness and control of movement. Timing is also an important aspect of the training. In addition to these direct results of karate training, there are indirect features: the mystique that this sport enjoys and the opportunity for group identification.

Careful analysis of learning needs is necessary with these youngsters even though the attentional problems and hyperactivity appear so obvious that no further study seems necessary. These problems frequently respond to medication and the child will begin to learn in the regular classroom setting. However, if the child has a specific language disability in addition, educational intervention will be required as well as careful monitoring of the medication by the physician. Teachers can be helpful as the physician adjusts dosages in providing objective, nonpunitive reports of the youngster's behavior in group activities at school.

It is common for people who give advice to teachers on the management of children with attention deficits to say that they "need structure." While it is obvious that most of them lack structure, this need cannot always be filled by having the teacher, counselor, parent, or other adult provide it. ADHD youngsters are often experts at evading, avoiding, forgetting, ignoring, undoing, losing, and confusing our efforts to organize their activities and to set up what may seem to us to be sensible structures for them. A more reasonable long-term goal is to help them build their *own* structure for themselves. This means that the teacher must be aware of the child's background (strengths and needs gleaned for the original diagnostic study), must study the child's learning style in classroom activities, must learn to give the child tasks within the zone of completion, and must teach the youngster how to set *and reach* appropriate goals. Thus the teacher's role with the ADHD child should not be one of stern taskmaster ready to punish or reward, but more that of a respected advisor who works with him or her in a benign structure.

Finally, in terms of interpersonal adjustment, these youngsters are often their own worst enemies. Their difficulties in investing attention in anything for any extended period of time produces tangential relationships with other people. Their apparent inattention to feedback discourages easy interpersonal contact. This increases their remoteness and keeps them from awareness of the socializing skills that children learn from warm interpersonal relationships. This failure to learn from interpersonal experiences may produce adult adjustment that is isolated and self-centered.

CASE STUDY: LANNY

Lanny was restless and active since birth. His parents said that as an infant he slept poorly, squirming and flailing his arms. When he was awake he seemed to require constant holding. Near the end of his first year his head-banging was so persistent that he was treated with phenobarbital. As a toddler, he was constantly in motion, often getting himself into dangerous situations atop china cabinets or on kitchen counters. He talked early, combining words by the time he was 11 months old and, according to his parents, he hasn't stopped since.

At nursery school he was described as friendly, related, and talkative, but very hyperactive. Despite his wanting to be cooperative, it appeared that sitting or standing and concentrating for even a short period of time was beyond him. Both the nursery school teachers and the neurologist the family consulted recommended psychological study.

The psychologist who saw Lanny at nursery school stressed that because of his distractibility and hyperactivity, the test results at age 4 should be regarded as minimal estimates. He earned a mental age of 3 years, 3 months and an IQ of 80 on the Stanford-Binet Intelligence Scale (Form L-M), with scatter ranging from year II through year IV-6. He demonstrated at least age-appropriate language ability and social understanding, but great difficulty in focusing attention and isolating essential from nonessential details. When Rorschach testing was attempted, he was overwhelmed by the stimuli. After testing, he told the psychologist that he "wasn't crazy." This comment suggested to the psychologist that he was potentially brighter than the intelligence test results indicated.

Neurological examination and detailed developmental history were within normal limits, although some clumsiness in gross and fine motor control was noted. During the office visit, Lanny wandered about the room, touching everything. The neurologist commented in his report that even with firm one-to-one attention Lanny required constant supervision. An EEG and laboratory studies (CBC, chemical profile, and metabolic screen) were also within normal limits. The diagnosis of attention deficit hyperactivity disorder was made with the recommendation that Lanny be followed at 6-month intervals.

Lanny came to our attention at age 5 years, 10 months as he was beginning first grade. His neurologist and family requested an assessment of his functioning and recommendations for his schooling. A trial of methylphenidate had been started 2 weeks earlier, but his teacher was finding it impossible to deal with Lanny in the regular first-grade classroom. He was very much as previous reports had described him. He had some sense of his motor problems and attempted to avoid written tasks or, when he found writing unavoidable, clowned about it. Initially he tried to take over the examination, bargaining about which items he would work on and issuing directives to the graduate assistant. Despite this apparent bossiness, he seemed to be trying to do what was expected of him. Often he gave more details than were necessary to answer a question. He recognized the limits that were set for him and, although he tested these limits repeatedly, his behavior never got out of hand.

On the WPPSI Lanny earned scores within the average range (full scale IQ of 93, verbal IQ of 97, performance IQ of 89), but the variability of his record is seen in the subtest scores:

Information	11	Animal House	8
Vocabulary	8	Picture Completion	10
Arithmetic	6	Mazes	8
Similarities	10	Geometric Designs	7
Comprehension	13	Block Design	7
Sentences	9		

As with the testing done when he was in nursery school, these scores appeared to underestimate Lanny's potential. The significantly high score on Comprehension suggested that, despite his misbehavior, he had a good understanding of his social role. Verbal tasks were easier for him and he sometimes used verbal cues in solving some performance tasks (i.e., verbalizing the code of the Animal House subtests). He seemed not as yet to have a preferred hand, but rather used hands interchangeably as he wrote or manipulated performance items. (His parents were both natural left handers.)

Educational achievement tests (PIAT) placed him at the pre–first-grade level. In mathematics he was able to recognize numerals and to count and match accurately. However, several responses were incorrect because of impulsive answers. In word recognition, he was able to match and name letters and to recognize the words *play* and *jump*. Lanny earned a score within the vulnerable range on *Search*. Component scores were as follows:

	Stanine
Visual Components	
Lamb Chop Matching	3
Lamb Chop Recall	5
Designs	2
Auditory Components	
Rote Sequencing	4
Discrimination	7
Intermodal	
Articulation	5
Initials	9
Body Image	
Directionality	7
Finger Schema	2
Pencil Grip	Abnormal

As with the WPPSI, Lanny's response to *Search* was variable. His total score indicated that, despite good verbal abilities, he had not acquired the subskills basic to reading and the language arts.

His parents arranged for one-to-one tutoring focused on the following tasks from *Teach:*

- visual matching and recall cluster (to stress spatial orientation and visual recall)
- visual motor tasks using Rhythmic Writing on the chalkboard (to teach control of fine movement and overlearning of motor patterns of letters)
- finger-number game (to make him aware of the finger schema)
- auditory sequence cluster (to help him overlearn common sequences and to locate elements within sequences)

Tutoring continued for the rest of the school year. In addition, he was followed regularly by the neurologist.

Lanny returned for a follow-up appointment 2 months after he entered a regular second-grade class. He gave a detailed account of schoolwork and also added that they didn't have science books because "they didn't come in yet." Retest on the PIAT showed gains in all academic areas with Mathematics placing at grade 2.5, Reading Recognition at grade 4.1, and Reading Comprehension at grade 3.3. Especially significant was the careful consideration he gave to the several responses for each item before indicating his choice on the PIAT. Problems continue in some areas: he holds his pencil with two fingers and thumb rather than in the pincers grasp; hand preferences are not clear-cut, although the right hand is used more consistently. There were signs that Lanny was better able to focus on tasks and to sustain attention productively in the classroom. His manner was quiet and subdued, unlike the whirlwind that tried to take over the office the year before. The figure drawings (Figure 13-1 and 13-2), both portraits of his sister Samantha, reflect this change in affect.

While the methylphenidate he was receiving contributed to his impulse control, the special educational management he received is considered to be an important factor in his overall congnitive and academic improvement.

Figure 13-1   Figure Drawing
Lanny: Age 5 years, 10 months

Figure 13-2   Figure Drawing
Lanny: Age 6 years, 11 months
Illustrating the improvement in impulse control

THE LONG-TERM OUTCOME OF ADHD

The long-term outcome of children with attention deficit disorder with or without hyperactivity, treated with and without stimulant drugs, is reviewed by Hechtman (1985), Helper (1980), G. Weiss (1983), and G. Weiss and Hechtman (1986). The early studies (Laufer & Denhoff, 1957) suggested that in the course of its natural history hyperactivity tended to wane in adolescence and disappear in adulthood. This optimistic prognosis was modified by later studies. Menkes, Rowe, and Menkes (1967), in a 25-year retrospective follow-up of 18 children with hyperactivity and learning disabilities, found most to have poor outcome: 3 still complained of restlessness, 4 were in mental institutions, and 2 were retarded. Of the 8 who were self-supporting, 4 had spent some time in an institution. This dismal outcome was modified in another retrospective study (Borland & Heckman, 1976) of 20 men who, in their childhood, conformed to the diagnostic criteria for hyperactivity. Using brothers of the subjects as controls, Borland and Heckman found that the majority of the subjects were self-supporting, but fully half of them still had symptoms of hyperactivity and difficulty with attention. As a group they did not attain the social or economic level of their brothers.

G. Weiss and Hechtman (1986) reviewed in detail the series of prospective studies at the Montreal Children's Hospital, following their original group of 104 hyperactive children and 45 normal controls over 5, 10, and 15 years. At the 5-year follow-up with children 11 to 16 years old, the initial symptoms of hyperactivity, distractibility, impulsive behavior, and aggression were generally decreased but still were greater than in the normal controls. Further the hyperactive children, now young adolescents, were considered immature, had diffculty maintaining goals, failed more grades in school, and had lower academic achievement than their matched controls. Twenty-five percent of them were considered antisocial. At the 10-year follow-up 76% of the original subjects and 45 normal controls matched for age, sex, social economic status, and IQ were evaluated. The group was then at mean age 19 years. They were tested on a series of variables including biographical data, psychiatric assessment, physiological measures (height, weight, blood pressure and pulse rate, and EEG) and psychological tests (California Psychological Inventory, a social skills test, Means-End Problem Solving test, cognitive skills test such as matching familiar figures and embedded figures). Of the 76 subjects, 6 had received dextroamphetamine for 6–48 months, 27 received Thorazine for 6–48 months, 9 had received various medications, and 35 had received no drug longer than 6 months. The results suggest that "while few hyperactive children become grossly disturbed or chronic breakers of the law and none were diagnosed as being psychotic or schizophrenic, the majority continue as young adults to have . . . continued symptoms of the hyperactive child syndrome . . . lower educational achievement, poorer social skills, lower self-esteem . . . continued impulsivity and restlessness" (G. Weiss, 1983, p. 428).

At the 15-year follow-up, 63 of the original group and 41 controls were available for examination. As a group the hyperactive children had less formal education than the controls; 44% in contrast to 10% of the control group were considered restless and distractable; 66% vs. 7% were considered impulsive, and 23% vs. 2.4% wee considered antisocial. The hyperactive children, now adults, had "more neurotic" and interpersonal problems. Weiss and Hechtman concluded:

> *The hyperactive child syndrome is a pervasive condition in childhood, affecting behavior, social functioning, learning, and self-esteem. While about half the hyperactive children seem to outgrow the symptoms of the syndrome, half continue to be disabled to a varying extent by continuing symptoms. The childhood condition predisposes to various psychiatric diagnoses (but not to schizophrenia or alcoholism) and to increased symptoms of psychopathology. It leads to Antisocial Personality Disorder in a significant minority of the subjects. (1986, p. 82)*

Unfortunately, the use of stimulant drugs does not alter this prognosis. Drugs, so effective in the short term, were not effective in the long term, with adolescents still failing in school, and having behavior problems and poor self-esteem—in short, still at high risk for academic and social difficulty. G. Weiss (1983) reviewed four reports of the long-term outcome of hyperactive children who received stimulant medication. Blovin (1978) compared hyperactive children with children who had school difficulties without hyperactivity in a 5-year follow-up study. Their conclusion is similar to that of other reports: No beneficial effects of methylphenidate were detected on academic achievement, intelligence tests, or behavioral measures of hyperactivity and conduct disorder. Riddle and Rapoport (1976) followed 72 hyperactive middle-class children, who were "optimally treated" with stimulants or tricyclic antidepressants for 2 years. The outcome was disappointing. Most continued on medication and had continued academic and psychiatric problems. G. Weiss, Kruger, Danielson, and Elman (1975) found that 26 hyperactive children treated with methylphenidate for 3 to 5 years did not have a more favorable outcome in adolescence than did two matched groups of hyperactive children, one group of which had received no medication and the other of which had received chlorpromazine.

In short, stimulants are not miracle drugs for hyperactivity and attention deficit hyperactivity disorders (ADHD). We have tried to stress in this book the fallacy of attempting a diagnosis on the basis of one or a cluster of symptoms, that each child requires careful evaluation, and that intervention be based on the findings of such an examination. These opinions are shared by S. E. Shaywitz and Shaywitz (1988) and by E. Taylor (1984). Taylor pointed out that, although stimulants were prescribed for approximately 1% of all American schoolchildren by the late 1970s (Sprague, 1978), they are rarely used in England. An even more startling statistic is provided by Safer and Krager (1988). Using data from biannual surveys of school nurses, that listed all students receiving medication for "hyperactivity" and/or "inattention," Safer and Krager (1988) found that since the mid 1970s, stimulant use has increased steadily in elementary, middle, and high schools, so that by 1987, 6% of all public elementary schoolchildren were receiving stimulants, primarily methylphenidate, primarily prescribed by pediatricians. S. E. Shaywitz and Shaywitz (1988) were concerned that "methylphenidate is now being prescribed for children who may not require it" and that "rather than reflecting the real strides in our conceptualization of neurobehavioral disorders, current treatment practice represents a return to an antiquated, simplistic approach that views all school and behavioral problems as one" (p. 227). Prescriptions of stimulants should not be a reflex action to a complaint of hyperactivity and/or inattention in children and to teachers' complaints about the children's behavior.

SUMMARY

Just as the term "learning disability" includes a range of heterogeneous conditions, so the attention deficit hyperactivity disorder (ADHD) may also represent a common symptom with many possible causes, ranging all the way from the "temperamentally impulsive child" to one with identified structural defect of the central nervous system. Again, just as there are exclusionary criteria for the diagnosis of specific language disability, so there is a group of children who meet the DSM-III-R-criteria for ADHD, but for whom no etiological factor has been identified. These children are considered as having "pure" or "specific" attention deficit hyperactivity disorder. They too, however, may not represent a homogeneous entity. Attention deficit and hyperactivity are considered by some to be two separate dimensions, with ADHD children exhibiting conduct disorders, and ADD children being socially withdrawn. The use of rating scales and checklists, compiled by parents, teachers, clinicians, peers, and even the child himself, does provide important information and baseline data for follow-up studies including response to medication, but these scales only identify a set of symptoms, do not necessarily correlate well with each other, and will vary with the child's surroundings and the task given. Diagnosis based only on rating scales is therefore discouraged. Diagnosis of the ADHD syndrome requires the comprehensive pentaxial examination described in Chapters 5 and 6 of this book. Objective measurements of attention or of hyperactivity are needed. Behavioral measures include tests of vigilance and reaction time; tests involving perceptual search, perceptual description and retention, and logical or conceptual search; and tasks involving avoidance learning and inhibitory control, all of which have been devised. Modulation of motor and emotional impulses is conceptualized as weakness of the stimulus barrier. The key findings of defective processes in ADHD includes the investment, organization, and maintenance of attention and effort, the modulation of impulses to meet situational demands, and "an unusually strong inclination to seek immediate gratification." These primary deficits may lead to limited development of higher order cognitive schema and diminished affective motivation.

The few family and twin studies available suggest that there is a genetic component to the deviations found in ADHD. Immaturity in the maturation of neurotransmitters may be one mechanism by which the genetic component is expressed. An hypothesized defect in a single neurotransmitter system, however, is no longer tenable, although the decrease in urinary MHPG in responders to d-amphetamine suggests that immaturity in the norepinephrine system may be a necessary but not sufficient condition. There is evidence, however, that in varying combinations, dopamine, norepinephrine, or serotonin systems may be involved in hyperkinesis.

Stimulant medication (methylphenidate, d-amphetamine, and pemoline) will relive inattention and restless behavior in approximately 75% of hyperkinetic children. The primary effect of stimulant drugs is increased concentration, or attention span, with improvement in the ability to "stop, look, and listen." Where academic difficulty is a consequence of restlessness and inattention, stimulant medication may be helpful in improving academic achievement. However, most studies do not find that there is clear evidence of improvement in academic learning. This is particularly true when ADHD is accompanied by the central nervous system dysfunction described for the SLD child where "it seems reasonable to conclude that stimulants have no clear role to play in learning disabilities." Tricyclics and monoamine oxidase (MAO-A) inhibitors, particularly, have also been used to reduce impulsive behavior. While most side effects of stimulant medication are more annoying than dangerous, the emergence of Tourette's syndrome has been reported and evidence for growth suppressive on prolonged (years) administration of stimulants, particularly d-amphetamine, continues to exist. While sleep-related prolactin concentration fell during treatment with d-amphetamine, such change was found with only high doses of methylphenidate. The effect of stimulant medication is not specific to the ADHD syndrome; normal children and young adults, too, incurred decreased motor activity and vigilance. With d-amphetamine, children reported feeling tired. Response to stimulant drugs thus cannot be used as a confirmation of the diagnosis of ADHD. It is also noted that with high doses of methylphenidate, the error rate on a continuous performance test increased. The use of the Feingold diet has not received scientific confirmation.

The synergistic effect of medication, training to remediate specific immaturities in spatial orientation and temporal organization, and appropriate management in his school classes is illustrated in the treatment of a child who had both ADHD and a specific learning disability.

The long-term outcome for children with ADHD is generally disappointing. As young adults in approximately half of the children studied, there are continued symptoms of decreased impulse control, lower educational achievement, poorer social skills, and lower self-esteem.

CHAPTER FOURTEEN

The Organic Group

Traditionally, the diagnosis of structural defect of the central nervous system is inferred from history, clinical examination, and laboratory data. Traditionally, too, the neurological examination includes the classical evaluation of nervous system functioning: muscle tone, power, coordination, and synergy; motor impulse control and kinetic patterns; deep, superficial, and pathological reflexes including the development of postural and righting responses; cranial nerves; sensation of touch, pressure, temperature, pain, joint position, and vibration; and the capacity for age-appropriate modulation of sensory stimulation as seen in the presence of extinction phenomena, allesthesia, and synchiria and in age-appropriate aspects of cortical function involving gnosis, praxis, and language. The neurological examination also includes observation for possible "minor physical anomalies," which are often part of diagnosable congenital disorders. A history of trauma, anoxia, infection, neoplasm, seizures, metabolic disorder, toxicity or prematurity, and low birth weight adds corroborative detail to the clinical examination; laboratory findings (EEG, brain imaging, chemical studies, and chromosome morphology) may further confirm the diagnosis and may aid in identification of focal areas of abnormality.

The question for the child with a learning disorder, however, is how many and how strong must the findings be to make a diagnosis of organic defect of the central nervous system? The problem is compounded by the fact that early neurological signs of organic deficit in children may be obtunded or may disappear entirely during maturation, and the only objective signs of such injury may be found in learning and/or in behavior (Sarnoff et al., 1981). Further, there is increasing evidence that in at least one subgroup of children with specific language disability there is a structural difference in their central nervous system as compared to normal children, and that children with attention deficit disorder may have a functional immaturity in their neurotransmitter systems. Should SLDs and ADDs therefore be considered as "organic"?

Although, in the ultimate sense, there is a biological abnormality in these children, we do not, in this book, consider them to be suffering from an organic defect of the central nervous system. In the first place, these biological abnormalities are still elusive. Second, and most important, the mechanism of the abnormality is different from that of the children we call "organic." The specific language disability may be considered a quantitative variant on the low side of a normal curve in the establishment of a specific function. The "organic" states are pathological entities, qualitatively different from normal.

The question of qualitative and quantitative criteria needed for an organic diagnosis does not lend itself to easy answers. The neurologist will generally insist on some objective evidence on neurological examination and greater or less documented history. The psychiatrist will generally be satisfied with equivocal neurological signs, soft signs (see Chapter 6, "Principles of Psychiatric and Neurological Diagnosis") and nonspecific history. The psychologist may infer brain damage from neuropsychological tests. However, all can agree that in a number of children there is evidence for a structural defect of the central nervous system; that in others the evidence is not so clear, but that there is enough for a *presumptive diagnosis* of organic deficit of the central nervous system. Steve, for example, is such a child.

CASE STUDY: STEVE

Steve was 11 years old, a small, tow-haired, disheveled, and unkempt child, when he was referred to our clinic because of academic difficulty and restless, inattentive behavior. He had gross choreoform movements, very poor fine motor coordination, difficulty with equilibrium, suggestively positive Romberg, hypotonia, mild dysmetria with mild rebound phenomena, and marked difficulty with alternating opposite movements (dysdiadochokinesia). In addition, there were severe perceptual immaturities with difficulty in the visual discrimination and recall of asymmetric figures, in visual-motor function, in auditory rote sequencing, and in right–left discrimination. On the WISC-R he earned a full scale IQ of 88 (verbal IQ of 94, performance IQ of 84). Educational assessment showed his word recognition to be about early third-grade level, his spelling and arithmetic each at beginning second grade (WRAT). He was also emotionally immature. He had a great need for affection. His anxiety was seen in an introjected voice of the devil who, in a lady's voice says, "I'm going to kill you if you are bad." He worried about his grandfather and said, "If he dies, I die. I'll kill myself."

The history reveals that his was a prolonged, difficult labor with mid-forceps being used. He was cyanotic at birth and required resuscitation, but appeared to recover. It was noted that he was a clumsy child, with difficulty feeding himself, physically holding onto his mother even by the time he entered kindergarten. His mother, however, was less concerned with her child than with her three marriages. Steve never did see his own father and was not sure just who his father was. His only stable relationship was with his maternal grandfather.

In short, there was evidence of emotional deprivation and lack of physical support that left this child with an emptiness in the gratification of elementary needs and added to his marked anxiety in relation to the adults in his life. He reacted to rejection with his own aggression. In addition, however, the neurological findings were consistent with a cerebellar palsy, the cause of which was presumed to be his difficult birth. In Steve, there appeared to be ample evidence to describe him as having a structural defect of the central nervous system possibly resulting from perinatal trauma and hypoxia.

Christopher is an example of a child in whom the neurological findings are not as defined as those seen in Steve, yet his neurological status is not normal and offers presumptive evidence that there is a structural defect in the central nervous system.

CASE STUDY: CHRISTOPHER

Christopher was 7 years, 9 months of age and in the second grade of a self-contained class for emotionally handicapped children when he was referred to us. The school reported that he was "constantly on the move, has problems with fine and gross motor skills, and has difficulty adjusting to the routine of the classroom." At school, at age 5 years, 4 months, he earned a full scale IQ of 77 (verbal IQ of 72, performance IQ of 86) on the WPPSI.

On our examination, Christopher was a gamin-like, small child, unkempt, and with festering sores on his left elbow and on the palm of his left hand. He had an upper respiratory infection with enlarged, reddened tonsils. There were many old, healed scars on his face and right forearm. He had an esophoria of the right eye and his ocular pupils were unequal, with the right pupil 1mm smaller than the left. His muscle tone and power appeared normal, but his fine motor coordination (as in finger to finger testing) was so awkward he could not touch his thumb to any designated finger but moved all of his fingers at the same time. His gross motor coordination was also awkward, and he had difficulty maintaining his balance. There were occasional choreoform movements, particularly in his upper extremities; synkinesis was marked. In addition to these neurological signs he had severe praxic difficulty. This finding, however, may not be related to perception at all, but to his very poor fine motor coordination, which may prevent him from executing praxic movements even though he may perceive the spatial orientation correctly. The motor problems were also evident in articulation difficulty, which appeared to stem from a lack of synergy in the movements of the muscles of speech. A major perceptual immaturity, however, was found in the auditory area. Although auditory discrimination was intact, his auditory rote sequencing scored at the lowest stanine of his age group. His capacity for intermodal association was also in the first stanine so that he could not decode any words. His score of the PPVT was at 5 years, 9 months. In all our examinations, Christopher was not hyperactive and maintained attention throughout. Educationally he could name only the single letters of the alphabet and could read no words on the WRAT. Auditory acuity was normal.

In spite of his mispronunciations, he was articulate and could verbalize many of his problems. He was anxious, particularly in relation to his father's aggression. He related specific episodes at home and finally he concluded, "my daddy doesn't like God. He curses." His anxiety was seen when he talked about his parents' arguments. He would like very much to rush to his mother's defense, but feels helpless to do so. Added to his anxiety was a depression. Overall, however, it was impressive how well this child could relate in an open, coherent manner, in spite of his difficult home and limited resources.

Christopher was the third of three children. His mother reported that after a 15-hour labor, a cesarean was done. Although he was jaundiced at birth, he did not require transfusion but was placed under ultraviolet light. His mother stated that, as far as she knew, smoking (two packs/day) and drinking alcohol (unknown amount) were the only abnormalities of her pregnancy. Christopher's electroencephalogram was described as abnormal with diffuse, high-voltage slow waves.

What puts this child in the "organic" category are the unequal pupils, the extremely poor motor coordination, the choreoform movement, and the dysarthria, together with his severe perceptual deficits. The diagnosis of organic nervous system defect, presumptively from the neurological evaluation, receives some support from the history and further consideration from laboratory data. The entire picture is consistent with a nonprogressive defect of the central nervous system.

To treat this child as an emotional problem and/or as a child with borderline intelligence is not to do justice to his real motor handicaps or to the severe auditory sequencing and intermodal association problems he is experiencing. In management, he needs occupational therapy for his motor handicaps and specific educational training for his cognitive deficits. Buffering his anxiety with involvement of this family in therapy would be helpful, but it alone will not reach the underlying biological problems.

There are many children with problems similar to those of Christopher. In the Hagin, Beecher, and Silver (1982) study, 5% of children in a "normal" classroom on the East Side of Manhattan had such signs. The specific neurological problems of these children are generally unrecognized in the classroom. By the time they may have reached fourth grade they have already experienced repeated failure and have developed a spectrum of behavior and academic difficulties. In a study of all 60 children in two self-contained classes for severely emotionally disturbed children, A. A. Silver (1984b) found 18 (approximately one-third of them) to have problems similar to those of Christopher and Steve. Of the 18 children diagnosed as having organic defects of the central nervous system, 3 had a history of low birth weight, of whom one child had fetal alcohol syndrome; 3 had cerebral palsy; 3 had identifiable chromosome abnormality (1 mosaic trisomy 21, 1 fragile X, and 1 Treacher-Collins syndrome); 2 had idiopathic seizures; 2 had cerebellar palsy; and 1 each had Rh incompatibility, Tourette's syndrome, lead toxicity, a traumatic birth, and dyskinesia, unknown cause. It seems clear that a severe learning problem, resistant to conventional educational remediation, demands comprehensive evaluation.

CLASSIFICATION OF NEUROLOGICAL DYSFUNCTION

The causes of neurology dysfunction are many and varied. These may be categorized as to:

- *Time of insult* during pregnancy, at birth, in the neonatal period, in early or mid-childhood, or in adolescence

- *Type of insult*   low birth weight with or without prematurity, hypoxia, trauma, toxic, infectious, nutritional, metabolic defects as a result of genetically determined enzyme defects, seizure disorders, or neoplastic disease

- *Progression of insult*   whether or not we are dealing with a progressive disease in contrast to one in which that damage was done and no further structural damage is incurred over time

- *Severity of insult*   Pasamanik and his colleagues (1956) documented a "continuum of reproductive casualty," a spectrum of defects ranging from the most severe insult, resulting in fetal and neonatal death, to a series of clinical neuropsychiatric syndromes depending upon the severity and location of damage.

- *Location of insult*   A. Towbin (1982), reviewing neuropathological studies in children with cerebral palsy and organic mental retardation, described two main forms of cerebral damage: the deep cerebral lesions affecting the basal ganglia and neighboring structures, and the cortical cerebral lesions affecting mainly surface structures of the convolutions. A mixed type, of course, exists, and the structures involved in each of these general areas of damage may vary. Disorders of the basal ganglia may result in many varieties of dyskinesia; disorders of the cortex will present a variety of symptoms depending upon the area or areas involved. Thorburn et al. (1982, quoted by M. A. Stewart, 1983) reported that ultrasound brain scan has been able to detect hemorrhage in the periventricular region, including intraventricular bleeding, in infants with very low birth weight, a short period of gestation, and serious respiratory illness. Follow-up studies have shown these abnormalities to be associated with neurodevelopmental sequelae (M. A. Stewart, 1983).

- *Appropriateness of environmental support*   This not only includes the reaction of the parents to the child's behavior, motor, and cognitive difficulties, but the adequacy of the school in understanding the child and providing appropriate remediation. The importance of optimal social support systems in permitting optimal compensation for incurred perinatal hazards cannot be overemphasized.

NEUROANATOMIC CONSEQUENCES OF BRAIN "INJURY"

Isaacson (1976) outlined physiological and anatomical consequences of brain injury that influence behavior and cognition. The initial effects of brain damage include actual destruction of cells at the location of the damage, with astrocytic reactions at the border and sometimes well beyond the lesion, phagocytosis and invasion of the lesion by microglia, proliferation of blood vessels about the lesion, edema and the development of irritative reactions at the edge of the lesion. As these events occur, there is disruption of activity in nearby tissues as a result of edema (and/or bleeding) and denervation sensitivity in areas to which the damaged regions no longer send impulses. Later retrograde changes occur in cells whose axons have been destroyed, and there is loss of trophic influence in neurons normally reached by processes from the damaged cells. In further delayed effects, new axon collaterals proliferate into cellular regions that had been supplied by fibers from the damaged regions. If the damage occurs in infancy, aberrant fiber tracts may form and changes in the size and cellular composition of the brain may occur.

Globus (personal communication, 1936) likened the effect of brain injury to a fire on the corner of 42nd Street and Broadway: police and fire trucks rush to the flames; traffic is stalled and is backed up blocks around the fire (edema); electrical conduits may be broken, and no power is delivered to distant buildings (trophic changes and denervation sensitivity). The immediate effects of injury thus go far beyond the initial area of insult. As the fire is brought under control, fire trucks leave, traffic is resumed, and power is restored; what remains is the burnt-out area. This simple analogy is not quite accurate for in the brain the distant effects may have more permanent impact. The proliferation of axons into areas deprived of their normal synaptic input may result in a new and abnormal pattern of synaptic input. This could be helpful in providing trophic influences and in reducing denervation hypersensivity, but it may be deleterious in creating abnormal regulatory influences on remaining systems.

Similarly, with early natal damage, new "sometimes abnormal, sometimes peculiar" (Isaacson, 1976, p. 40) fiber connections may occur, and the nerve fibers in the infant brain may accept unusual sites of termination. On the other hand, damage to one hemisphere may, in the infant, evoke compensations, such as the development of an uncrossed cortico-spinal pathway. Thus, "the permanent consequence of brain damage . . . must include the direct effects produced by destruction of cells at the site of damage and all of the permanent secondary changes as well" (Isaacson, p. 42). Experimental studies, particularly in rodents and primates, suggest, or in Isaacson's words, "it seems clear that damage to the infant brain produces greater anomalies in structure and behavior than are found after damage to the brain of the mature or juvenile animal" (p. 58).

The implication is that recovery or sparing of function is not necessarily greater the earlier in life the lesion occurs. Indeed, Hebb (1949) felt that brain damage early in life is more severe and has more profound effects than that occurring later in life. This conclusion is based on the generalization that an intact and functional cerebrum is important in the development of language and other cognitive abilities, but once language and cognitive skills have been attained, their retention does not require an intact brain. Brain damage in the adult most often produces specific defects, and depending on the area of localized injury, there may or may not be loss in intelligence as measured by standardized tests. In the infant, however, brain damage produces a more generalized defect, which affects overall cognition. Kornhuber, Bechinger, Jung, and Sauer (1985) supported this conclusion, finding that, when brain trauma (bleeding, infarction), occurred in children under 4 years of age, their intelligence was impaired to a greater extent than it was in children in whom trauma occurred after 5 years of age, even though the lesions as measured by CT scan, were the same or smaller in extent and similar in location to the lesions occurring in the older children. Of the 51 children studied, the average age at examination was 11 years, 5 months and the time interval between injury and examination was an average of 9 years, 6 months. Thirty-seven of the children had perinatal lesions. Kornhuber et al., (1985) stated that "possible explanations for lower intelligence after early lesions are: cumulative training deficit in children with early lesions and an internal deficit of stimuli for growth and connectivity" (p. 132). Thus, small differences in early lesions may, in the developing brain, result in large differences in intelligence and behavior. For children who had incurred lesions after the age of 5 years, there was a correlation between extent of lesion and IQ as measured by the Wechsler scale and behavior as tested by the Conners scale: a 1% increase in extent of the lesion corresponded to a decrease of 4 IQ points. Equally important, however, are the specific deficits in the processing of information, which may be found in children who, despite perinatal brain trauma, have normal intelligence.

There does appear to be a difference between adults and children in recovery of language and localized brain damage. Infants and young children with localized brain damage "almost always recover the ability to speak. The reason for this is that early in life, both sides of the brain can subserve language function. Thus with injury to the left side early in life, the right side may take over language functions. The frequency of language related problems after damage to the left hemisphere slowly increases with age" (Isaacson, 1976, pp. 48–49).

A GENERALIZATION OF CLINICAL FINDINGS

It has been stated repeatedly, however, that in any one child, the clinical picture is the resultant of reciprocally acting biological, psychological, and environmental forces. The biological dysfunction itself, the conditions subsumed under the term "organicity," have infinite variations, and the ultimate prognosis depends on the nature and extent of the dysfunction, the age of onset, the child's temperamental and intellectual resources, and, to a great extent, the nature, appropriateness, and adequacy of the support he or she receives from the environment, family, and school. It may be misleading, therefore, to attempt to synthesize or create an artificial composite of the great variety of symptoms that may result from "brain damage," organicity, in childhood. No one finding or pattern of findings is symptomatic of the brain-damaged child (H. G. Taylor, 1987). In general, however, the biological substrate is altered by the imposition of organic defect and the resulting symptoms, clinically observed, may be understood as an interruption in the normal progression of maturation, delay in the acquisition of new functions, and retention of more primitive ones. They may be seen in disorders of perception, cognition and language; problems in the initiation and control of impulses; and problems in muscle tone, coordination and synergy, and posture and equilibrium. While we may examine these areas separately, they really function in concert, each influencing the other, then all contributing to the child's behavior, his response to the environment and, in turn, how the people in his world respond to him. As a group, the functions of perception, motility, and impulse control are part of the autonomous function of the ego (Hartmann, 1964) forming the barrier against excessive external and internal stimulation, action and inhibition.

Perceptual, Cognitive, and Language Deficits

Just as the child with specific language disability has a spectrum of perceptual deficits, so does the child with neurological dysfunction. We have indicated that the characteristic stamp of perceptual immaturity in the specific language disability is seen in spatial orientation and in temporal organization and that clinically these deficits may be found in any combination of dysgnosia, dyspraxia, and dysphasia. The child with neurological deficit who has learning disabilities may also demonstrate these characteristic perceptual deficits. The difference is that, in general, the deficits are more extensive. They involve more perceptual modalities, are more severe, and tend to involve a variety of body image functions: finger-gnosis, praxis, and immaturity on double simultaneous stimulation on the face–hand test. Not only is the wrist stimulus obtunded on the face–hand test, but there is a tendency to displace the face stimulus to the homologous contralateral point (allesthesia) and even to indicate that the face stimulus is felt both at the point of stimulus *and* at the homologous contralateral point (synchiria). There may be difficulty with figure–ground perception in both the visual and tactile fields, frequent dyskinesis, and fine motor coordination difficulty, all of which contribute to the visual-motor immaturities.

The case of Van illustrates the motor and perceptual deficits in a child born prematurely with a birth weight of 3 lb., followed by pneumonia and atelectisis.

CASE STUDY: VAN

Van was first seen at age 5, brought primarily because of unintelligible speech. He was slightly obese at that time, in constant clumsy motion, with a persistent dyskinesia, consisting of choreic and athetoid movements, poor fine motor coordination, increased muscle tone in the left with increased deep tendon reflexes, ankle clonus and questionable Babinski on the left. He was dysarthric. His comprehension of language, however, was excellent. On the Stanford-Binet he earned an IQ of 108. Severe perceptual immaturity was found in all areas: He had difficulty with the visual discrimination of asymmetric figures; he could not draw a recognizable circle; and he could not identify a single tactile stimulus to any finger. On testing for visual figure–ground perception with the marble board, Van's responses were chaotic; he could not even reproduce a straight line. His EEG was abnormal with bitemporal paroxysmal features. Psychologically, he was apprehensive, phobic, clinging, and ritualistic.

Van was one of the children in our follow-up study (A. A. Silver and Hagin, 1985). He had the benefit of an upper middle-class professional home, with great support, speech therapy, private schooling, tutoring in reading, and psychiatric counseling for his parents. Repeat evaluations at age 8 years, 12 years, and 18 years found his overall cognitive ability to improve (Table 14-1): Stanford-Binet at age 8 years, IQ of 119; WISC at age 12 years, full scale IQ of 112 (verbal IQ of 120, performance IQ of 100); WAIS at age 18 years, full scale IQ of 116 (verbal IQ of 128, performance IQ of 98). At the same time, with intensive tutoring his word recognition improved from grade 3.3 at age 12 years, to grade 14.8 at age 18 (WRAT). His reading comprehension at that time was in the 57th percentile (Diagnostic Reading Test). His reading speed, however, was at the 2nd percentile and signs of the perceptual deficits he exhibited at age 5 could be detected at age 17. His Bender gestalt drawings (Figure 14-1) and his Goodenough Draw-a-Person Test (Figure 14-2) each showed little maturation as Van grew older, retaining at age 17 years the characteristics seen in his 8-year-old drawings and actually scoring no higher than 8 years on the Goodenough scale. His visual motor function did

Table 14-1   Van's Changes in Cognitive Function

	Age			
	5 years	8 years	12 years	18 years
	Stanford-Binet	Stanford-Binet	WISC	WAIS
IQ	108	119	112	116
			V120	V128
			P100	P98
Reading, word recognition (grade)			3.3 (Jastak)	14.8 (WRAT)
Reading, comprehension (grade)			4.1 (California, primary)	57th percentile (DRT)
Spelling			2.6 (Jastak)	5.2 (Jastak)
Speed				2nd percentile

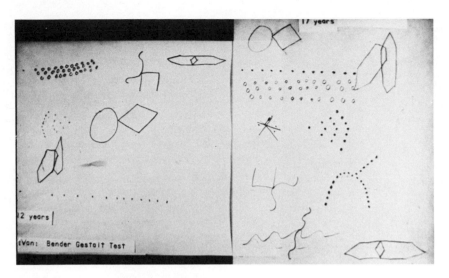

Figure 14-1   Bender Gestalt Drawings
Van: Age 12 years and 17 years
Illustrating persisting difficulty

improve during adolescence. Yet the tendency to verticalization may still be seen (Figure 14-1). With much support, Van was able to complete college and become successful in his own business.

Van illustrates significant and tenacious deficits in perception, together with incoordination in the muscles of articulation and in synergistic movement. His native intelligence and the excellent support he received combined to develop a well-functioning adult. His record also illustrates the significant difference between verbal and performance scores on the WISC, with verbal abilities at least 20 IQ points higher than performance abilities. Although this pattern is sometimes stated as characteristic of a neurological defect, this generalization may be misleading. Organic insult is very capricious in the areas of brain at which it strikes and the expected high-verbal/ low-performance pattern may be reversed in some children. Scott's record illustrates this point.

CASE STUDY: SCOTT

At age 5 years, 9 months, Scott earned a full scale IQ of 82 on the WISC with verbal IQ of 66, and performance IQ of 103. At that age also, the ITPA revealed auditory reception at 4 years, 1 month; visual reception at 5 years, 10 months; visual memory at 5 years, 1 month; auditory association at 2 years, 10 months; auditory

Figure 14-2   Goodenough Draw-a-Person
Van: Ages 8, 12, 14, and 17 years
Illustrating the persistence of body-image immaturity in a child who suffered a low
birthweight and hypoxia in the neonatal period

memory at 4 years, 8 months; visual association at 5 years, 6 months; verbal expression at 2 years, 7 months; visual closure at 4 years; grammatic closure at 3 years, 7 months; and, manual expression at 3 years, 11 months.

A statistical analysis of subtest findings indicated a substantial discrepancy in auditory association skills and in verbal expression. The school psychologist stated in her report that "the total picture suggests a pronounced defect in auditory association that can be perhaps compensated for in some measure by utilizing his relatively strong visual reception skills." Severe perseveration in all testing was noted.

It was not until Scott was 11 years, 1 month of age and in the sixth grade of a class for severely disturbed children that he was referred to our clinic. At that time he was a good-sized 11-year-old, with dark, curly hair and with a head circumference of 23 inches. He wore glasses for myopia. His clothes appeared to have been thrown on him. He had a sad, deadpan expression but became animated when he was more at ease or when affective material was introduced. He exuded a faint urine odor. There was a fresh bruise on his forehead and scrapes on his right elbow.

His gait was clumsy and stiff, and his fine motor coordination was very poor, particularly in the left hand. There were gross choreoform movements with marked synkinesis and a coarse intention tremor. Muscle tone appeared increased in the lower extremities. His deep reflexes were brisk but unequal with increased knee jerk and ankle jerk on the left. Ankle clonus was also present on the left. Cranial nerves revealed eccentric pupils, coarse nystagmoid movements, and a refractive error. A major area of pathology was in emissive speech with scant verbalization, laconic responses, poor vocabulary, mild dysarthria, and respiratory speech dissociation.

There was evidence from his drawings, however, that concept formation was adequate (Figure 14-3). His sensitive use of detail suggested greater cognitive resources than he was able to demonstrate with formal verbal measures. His difficulty appeared to be in finding words for his understanding and his thoughts. Perceptually visual discrimination and recall were intact. Visual-motor function was impaired.

The impairment, however, was different from that seen in the specific learning disability and even in the organic problems that Van displayed. In Scott there were no verticalization errors or angulation immaturities, but his intention tremor made writing difficult. Auditory discrimination and auditory sequencing were both intact. Body image, however, was markedly impaired with severe defects in finger-gnosis and in praxis. He did not demonstrate extinction phenomena. On extension, the arms converged to the point of overlapping. Academically his reading and spelling were about 1 year below his grade placement.

His major problem, in addition to his motor difficulty, was in the storage and retrieval of verbal material. Thus, he had difficulty expressing his thoughts. Unless one was patient, allowing him time to find ways of expressing himself, he became frustrated, angry, and withdrawn. Emotionally, he was already an anxious, sad child who had developed mechanisms of rigidity, withdrawal, compulsivity, passivity, and dependency. His anxiety was great. He had many somatic sensations, and felt he was a bad person with many sins.

Figure 14-3   Figure Drawing
Scott: Age 11 years
(WISC-R verbal IQ 66, performance IQ 103) with severe expressive language difficulty.
His sensitive use of detail suggests greater cognitive resources than are demonstrated
on formal verbal measures.

Past history revealed that he was 10 lb, 5 oz at birth, the product of an unplanned pregnancy, and the oldest of four boys. His mother was a nurse, his father an automobile mechanic. His developmental milestones were slow with delays particularly in language, and he was still eneuritic. At age 4, with a high fever, he had a grand mal seizure, but the sequence of the convulsive pattern was not known. There were three subsequent seizures in his fourth year, this time unaccompanied by high fever. For the next 2 years, he received Phenytoin, but he received no anticonvulsant medication after the age of 6.

Although the history affords only presumptive corroboration of perinatal injury, the findings on neurological examination, the history of seizures, and the EEG places Scott in the organic category. It was noted that he did have a learning disorder, but its nature and extent was different from that seen in a specific learning disability. He did not have the visual, spatial, and temporal problems of SLD. His academic disability relates to his language deficit as well as to his motor incoordination. His placement in a class for severely emotionally disturbed children was inappropriate. He should be mainstreamed and provided with supplementary work in language development. He needed physiotherapy for his motor coordination difficulties, a resumption of anticonvulsant medication, and psychotherapeutic support for himself and his family.

While the perceptual, cognitive, and language deficits in the child with structural damage to the central nervous system are not to be minimized, these children suffer from other effects of the biological damage. There are problems with the initiation and control of impulses and with muscle tone, posture, and equilibrium.

Problems With the Initiation and Control of Impulses

The prototype for problems with the modulation of impulses may be seen in the Moro response, the startle reaction. It is evoked by any sudden stimulus, such as a loud noise or quick passive movement.

Most of us, even as adults, will startle at a sudden loud noise or a sudden change in equilibrium. Our reaction, however, is largely a controlled one, and we restore equilibrium quickly on our recognition of the source and nature of the stimulus. For the child with an organic brain defect, this return is not as rapid. The physiological concomitants of the startle response—increased heart rate, sweating, changes in gastrointestinal tone, pupillary dilation, increased muscle tone, and metabolic changes—all reverberate in persistent waves, which subjectively reach awareness as anxiety.

Theoretically, we can postulate a defect in the ability to screen out and dampen stimuli. Wender (1973) considered this defect to be a major one in children designated as having minimal cerebral dysfunction. He stated the defect as "an apparent increase in arousal, accompanied by an increased activity level and a decreased ability to concentrate, focus attention, or inhibit response to the irrelevant (p. 20)." The defect may well be a decrease in inhibition. Inhibition is a vital function in the central nervous system and is evidenced at successively higher levels of function: from the motor reflex, through the brain stem reticular formation, to the pathways to thalamic, hypothalamic, and cortical areas (Jasper, 1958).

The result, however, is that the organism is flooded with stimuli that it cannot control. This may well be the "predisposition to anxiety," "the physiological sensitivity which heightened the anxiety potential" that Greenacre (1952) described in patients with a history of organic insult at or before birth. She stated that "this is a genuine physiological sensitivity, a kind of increase of reaction to experience which heightens the anxiety potential and gives greater resonance to the anxieties of later life (p. 54)." In Freud's terms, there is a decreased "stimulus barrier" against a flood of stimuli. Clinically, anxiety and social withdrawal in late adolescence were found in children who had soft neurological signs in early childhood (D. Shaffer et al., 1983). Electrophysiologically, Lorente de No (1947) postulated "reverberating circuits" in which a stimulus, once reaching sensory neurons in the diencephalon or in the cortex, maintains a circus rhythm that perpetuates itself. More recent investigation has tended to focus on immaturity in the inhibitory pathways involving neurotransmitters, the catecholamines, and possibly the gamma-amino-buteric acid (GABA) system (Wender, 1973) (see also Chapter 13, Attention Deficit Hyperactivity Disorder).

The stimulus, however, need not always be external, as in the startle response. It may arise from within the organism at any and every level of function from the reflex, automatic level to that involving complex psychic stimuli. At a reflex level, autonomic lability is characteristic of cerebral dysfunction. This can be detected clinically in vasomotor responses, in pupillary responses, and sometimes in visceral responses. The entire homeostatic mechanism is alert and sensitive. In the framework of Selye (1956), this individual is more vulnerable to stress, overreacting initially but reaching the stage of stress exhaustion more readily. The manifestations of homeostatic dysequilibrium (increased heart rate and blood pressure, increased respiratory rate, increase in hippuric acid and steroid hormone excretion, decreased white blood count, and decreased electrical skin resistance) all correlate highly with the factor designated as anxiety (R. B. Cattell, 1963a; Cattell & Sheier, 1961). In addition, these physical sensations of homeostatic dysequilibrium may in themselves create subjective anxiety and perpetuate the physiological response. Hypochondriasis, complaints about somatic sensation, may be a specific clinical manifestation of this dys-equilibrium. When combined with problems with impulse control, the anxiety may be released in aggression. There is some evidence to suggest that interrupting the feedback loop with use of peripherally acting beta-adrenergic blockers will decrease anxiety and help control impulsive behavior in adults with "brain damage."

Problems with impulse control are not only seen in the inability to dampen external sensory stimuli, to control voluntary motor movement, and to maintain autonomic and endocrine homeostasis; impulse control problems are also seen in difficulty in emotional homeostasis, in controlling psychological impulses. As already implied, the child with a dysfunction in the central nervous system is not exempt from the psychological problems of growing up. The difference is that his ego apparatus is immature; it cannot readily inhibit psychological impulses, which may then appear undisguised in thought or action. He may then appear as a primitive personality with incessant demands, immediate gratification, and labile affect. Depression, explosive range, and clinging attachment may appear in response to minor external affective events or in response to tasks that the child feels are confusing or beyond her ability to control. The "catastrophic reaction" of K. Goldstein (1938, 1954), described as a sequel to head injury, may be in this category; this results when unmodulated stimuli impinge on an organism that cannot inhibit overwhelming autonomic and motor impulses, which, in turn, produce overwhelming anxiety. Pathological rage reactions have also been described in children with temporal lobe epilepsy (Lindsay, Ounstead, & Richards, 1979; Ounstead, 1955). D. Lewis et al. (1979) reported a high incidence of "brain disorder" in institutionalized delinquents.

The child does not escape the consequences of his primitive thinking, however. Guilt is a frequent accompaniment and to many children guilt becomes internalized as the voice of the devil versus the voice of God. Clinic experience suggests that the presence of introjections well into latency may be a reaction to a defect at the biological level. Nine-year-old George, for example, with a history of post-measles encephalopathy, could not control his aggressive behavior in school. He told us how he hears the devil talking to him in a low, deep voice, telling him to hit, to throw chalk, and how God tells him not to do it. These voices are heard inside his head, but he is afraid that the devil always wins. In treatment for this child, we must be a substitute for his weakened ego on the spot—the teacher telling him that when he hears the devil he must come to her and she will help him control his feelings. Medication also may be of help. Only when George can feel the strength of his ally can we begin to explore the source of his anger, not only his frustration and feelings of doubt and inadequacy, but also the needs for affection and care that he feels he does not get. With a higher level of personality development than that demonstrated by George, depression after head injury is not uncommon. D. Shaffer et al. (1985) found an excess of affective symptomatology in children with head injuries localized to the frontal and parieto-temporal lobes.

Other children attempt to control impulses by imposing upon themselves the most rigid type of defense: obsessions and compulsions. In discussing the "option of neurosis," Freud speaks of the interaction between "constitutional and accident" factors, i. e., biological and experiential. Organic dysfunction of the central nervous system may be the biological basis for obsessive-compulsive neurosis starting in childhood and continuing into adult life. Schilder (1938a, 1983b) stated this and A. Bender (1956) said that "unsolved impulse problems in childhood may have a more or less outspoken connection with compulsive and obsessive neurosis of later life (p. 25)." From a therapeutic viewpoint, the obsessive-compulsive defense may represent not only a defense against neurotic anxiety but also an attempt to contain the disorganizing effect of poor impulse control. As such, it commands the respect of the therapist and, unless it becomes in itself incapacitating, it should not be interfered with.

The Moro response, then, is the prototype of a reaction from which subsequent anxiety develops, an inability to inhibit or modulate stimuli whether they are external or internal, autonomic or voluntary, motor or psychological. A breaching of the stimulus barrier, anxiety, disturbing somatic sensation, hyperkinesis, primitive lack of instinctual impulses, guilt, introjections, rigidity, obsessions and compulsions may all be psychological consequences.

The symptoms of inattention and hyperactivity have in the past been considered a manifestation of "brain damage" in children and characteristic of the "minimal brain dysfunction syndrome." As pointed out in Chapter 1 ("The Problem of Definition") these behaviors were seen after the influenza pandemic of the 1920s. Reasoning by analogy, children who were hyperactive and inattentive were considered to have some form of "brain damage." While it is true that hyperactivity and inattention may be seen as a consequence of an organic defect of the central nervous system in some children, it is not true of most. The Collaborative Perinatal Project found that children with neurological signs were not characterized by hyperactivity and that the reverse was also true: Hyperactive children did not necessarily have neurological signs (Nichols & Chen, 1981; see also Chapter 13, "Attention Deficit Hyperactivity Disorder). The specific damage induced by specific etiological agents, however, may be an important determinant in the production of hyperactivity. The pathology in the periaquaductal gray regions involved in viral encephalitis, for example, may indeed induce a hyperactivity similar to that of the postinfluenzal child described so many years ago; toxic (lead) encephalopathy yields an impulse-driven child; whereas the child with a head injury with trauma to the superficial cortical areas may not be hyperactive. Indeed, such a child may have an inhibition of activity, although the perseveration he shows indicates that there is a problem with modulation and control of impulses. Involvement of the subthalamic and caudate nuclei, as in Sydenham's chorea, results in an inability to control the characteristic choreoform movements, but also in the frequent development of obsessive and compulsive symptoms (Swedo et al. 1989).

Problems in Muscle Tone, Coordination, Posture, and Equilibrium

Problems in muscle tone, coordination, posture, and equilibrium may be epitomized by the child's reaction to antigravity play. Holding him upside down, swinging him from side to side, and tossing and bouncing him evoke pleasure in the normal child. Disturbance of the equilibrium is normally pleasurable. This is not true of the child with a central nervous system dysfunction. In her, disturbance of equilibrium evokes panic, a clinging, frantic resistance, an attempt to realign the physical orientation of her body with the world. Subjectively and objectively this is fear. Maintenance of posture and equilibrium is a function that is normally performed every minute of our waking hours. It is normally automatic and has an important influence on our muscle tone and even on autonomic functioning. Why should the child with an organic defect of the central nervous system display a precarious orientation in space, and how does this contribute to anxiety?

By the end of the second month of life, equilibrium problems may be found (R. S. Paine, 1964). Holding the child upright and tilting his body forward, backward, and laterally evokes in the normal infant a reflex, depending upon the integrity of the otolith-righting reflexes. Righting responses to linear acceleration, dependent on the labyrinths, are evoked by the sixth month of life. In the child with damage to the central nervous system, these labyrinthine reflexes may not appear until much later and are inconstant and uncertain. Thus, the very biologic apparatus for maintaining head alignment in space is inadequate.

There are problems also in muscle tone relative to spatial orientation. The tonic neck and neck-righting responses are also evoked early; the tonic neck reflex may be found by the second month of life and although normally it is not elicited by the end of the first year, it may be found as late as the third year. The neck-righting response is said by Ford (1937) to disappear by the fifth year, but in our experience, it may persist until the seventh year (A. A. Silver, 1952). As the child develops, these responses are not lost but are buried in the nervous system, constantly exerting their tonic influence, constantly influenced, in turn, by supra-segmental impulses. In the child with central nervous system dysfunction, these tonic neck and neck-righting responses may be clinically persistent, exerting their tonic force and making posture less responsive to volitional command. R. S. Paine (1964) suggested that abnormality in the tonic neck responses is often followed by emergence of motor defect. A persistent tonic neck response may be one of the earliest factors affecting bonding between the infant and her nursing mother. The extended chin extremity that follows rotation of the head to grasp the nipple may be interpreted by the mother as the child physically pushing her away. In reality, it is the persistence of the tonic neck response in a biologically immature infant.

The child with structural brain damage, therefore, has a basic biological problem in maintaining spatial orientation and in muscle tone relative to posture. He cannot automatically and smoothly adjust to changes in posture and equilibrium. Phylogenetically, this is a fundamental necessity for getting food and for defense. The survival of an individual may depend on his ability to orient his head and limbs with respect to the world. Behaviorally, the clinging of the organic child may be understood as an attempt to maintain physical support and to obtain reference points for position in space. Psychologically, the need for physical support could well be the basis for dependency needs, needs that are often so very great that they cannot be met and in themselves then become a source of secondary anxiety (M. Shaffer, 1979).

So important in the consideration of anxiety are postural and equilibrium problems, together with tonic influences of the vestibular apparatus, that

Schilder (1938b) considered these basic to the development of what he called anxiety hysteria in adults. L. A. Bender (1956) stated that "motor problems are a part of development no less important than psychological ones. . . . In psychoanalysis of anxiety neurosis, one often finds recollections of experiences of insecurity in equilibrium from the earliest childhood" (p. 25).

Problems with equilibrium, then, contribute an additional biological impetus to anxiety, leading to a physical dependency that may readily become a lifelong personality trait of dependency and anxiety.

SPECIFIC ETIOLOGICAL FACTORS

With this background to understand the consequences of structural defects in the central nervous system, this section reviews causes of brain damage that are important in the development of learning disorders in children. These causes will include the effects of perinatal and neonatal "injury," seizure disorders, head trauma, *Hemophilus influenzae* meningitis, and radiation. The relationship of otitis media and learning is discussed in Chapter 5.

Effects of Perinatal and Neonatal "Injury"

In the neuropathological studies of neonatal deaths in the Collaborative Perinatal Project, A. Towbin (1980) found the following:

1. Although genetic, metabolic, infectious, and toxic processes appeared in the neonate, they were relatively rare and most cases of cerebral damage in the newborn were due to perinatal hypoxia. Mechanical injury was also common but less significant than hypoxia.

2. Deep basal ganglia damage was observed mainly in the premature neonate, whereas cortical damage was observed mainly in the mature, at term, neonate. The deep form of damage was more frequent than the cortical form.

3. The degree of damage was governed essentially by the intensity and duration of the perinatal hypoxia. Hypoxia may lead to focal necrosis with resulting cavitation and scarring, but even mild hypoxia resulted in cellular damage with patchy or diffuse neuronal loss.

So important is the problem of hypoxia that Skov et al. (1984) stated that "neonatal ischemia is a critical determinant for later neurological and intellectual development and may be the most important single factor" (p. 356). Skov and her associates correlated neonatal cerebral blood flow with behavior at age 4 in a sample of 19 neonates that included 14 prematures. At age 4 children with cerebral blood flow equal or less than 20 ml/100 gram/min had problems with praxis, coordination, muscle tone, tendon reflexes, attention, articulation, understanding of hypothetical questions, visual perception, and memory for numbers—the very problems we may find in a random selection of children with learning disorders. These data implicating ischemia, however, are confounded by the prematurity of most of Skov's subjects.

The importance of perinatal hypoxia in later cognitive development was further documented in the series of reports by Broman and her associates (Broman, 1979; Broman et al., 1975). These reports, based on findings of the National Collaborative Perinatal Project, focus on overall cognitive function as determined by the Bayley scale at 8 months of age, the Stanford-Binet at 4 years, and the WISC at 7 years. These tests are supplemented by a gross motor score on three tests of balance and eye–hand coordination at 4 years and the Bender VMGT at 7 years. Perinatal anoxia is documented clinically by fetal heart rate in the first stage of labor, Apgar score at 1 and at 5 minutes, muconium staining at delivery, primary apnea, single or multiple apneic episodes, resuscitation required during and after 5 minutes, and respiratory difficulty in the neonatal period. Children with these early signs of perinatal hypoxia were compared with those who have no such difficulty, with the groups stratified by ethnicity, sex, and socioeconomic status. Data were studied in a linear multiple regression model with hypoxic variables, along with other predictive variables introduced in a stepwise manner. In a second study, retarded children were retrospectively compared with those with normal IQ, using perinatal hypoxia as the dependent variable.

At age 8 months consistent deficits were found among infants who had respiratory difficulty in the newborn nursery and among those with multiple apneic episodes, with test score differences averaging about 4/5 of 1 standard deviation. At age 7 the test differences were smaller, with a 5.5 IQ point difference on the WISC between hypoxias and controls. At age 8 months, 27% of the white hypoxic sample and 31% of the black had Bayley scores 2 standard deviations below the population mean in contrast to 2–3.6% of the respective control groups. At age 7, 4–7 percent of the white hypoxic sample had WISC scores below 70 (9–13% of which were blacks) compared to 1% in the controls (5% of which were black). Retrospectively, the retarded children at 8 months, 4 years, and 7 years of age had a greater number of hypoxic signs than the nonretarded group. Children with significant errors on the Bender VMGT, as measured by the Koppitz score, had a significantly higher frequency of respiratory difficulty (those with 18 errors had 4–7% frequency of respiratory difficulty vs. 1.5% in the controls; those with 16–17 errors had 11% low (1-minute) Apgar scores vs. 5% in the controls; and those with 16–17 errors had 4% single episodes of apnea compared to 0.4% in the controls).

Broman (1979) concluded that: Anoxic groups, particularly those with a clinical judgment of respiratory difficulty as newborns, one of the most consistently significant signs, had lower cognitive scores than nonanoxic groups in infancy and at age 7. The differences were undramatic at either age but consistent within ethnic, sex, and socioeconomic subgroups. . . . Anoxic groups as a whole were not found to be mentally retarded but the probability of retardation was increased as much as 12-fold in infancy and 6-fold at age 7. Viewed retrospectively, the frequency of most signs of anoxia decreased dramatically as cognitive score levels increased among school children as well as among infants. . . . Research from all analysis indicate that newborns with clinical signs of anoxia are at risk for less than normal development. It is clear, however, that the risk for serious cognitive deficits is greater when other signs indicative of central nervous system impairment are also present. (pp. 51–52).

Broman and her associates have focused on overall, cognitive deficits. Deficits that are less global, however, are equally important in the management of children with learning disorders. J. Hunt (1961), summarizing subsequent developmental problems in low birth weight children, noted a higher incidence of visual-motor problems independent of IQ scores in pre-term children than in full-term children at 4 and at 8 years. Siegel (1982, 1983) found that very low birth weight (less than 1500 grams), pre-term children were found to perform significantly differently from a demographically matched group of full-term children on perceptual-motor tests at 5 years. The variables associated with prematurity appear to be associated with specific impairments of perceptual-motor functioning in childhood. There were no significant differences between the groups on language comprehension. Siegel (1982) went on to state that infant test scores on selected scales (Bayley, Uzgaris-Hunt, and Reynall scales of language development) at 4, 8, 12, 18, and 24 months, together with a risk index based on demographic, reproductive, and perinatal factors, could be used to predict test scores at 5 years.

M. A. Stewart (1983) reported the prospective study of 382 infants, the survivors of 694 infants with a birth weight of 638 to 1500 grams who had been admitted to the neonatal intensive care unit at University College Hospital (London), from 1966–1977. During this time technological improvements to care resulted in improvement in survival from 52% in 1966 to 75% in 1977. Of the 382, 121 infants required mechanical ventilation for respiratory failure and 25 had one or more exchange transfusions. At 2 years of age, 11% of the 382 children (41) had major handicaps; 41 of these 22 (54%) had cerebral palsy, 15 (6%) were mentally retarded, 14 (34%) had sensoneural hearing loss, 4 had hydrocephalus, 3 had retrolental fibroplasia, and 1 had congenital cataracts. At age 3 years, 5 months and at 8 years there was no dramatic group differences in cognitive attainment. However, at age 8 years, 14% of the children, although they attended regular schools, were receiving additional academic help and 5% were in special schools for the mentally or physically handicapped. Twelve percent had perceptuomotor disorders (1 standard deviation below normal on Koppitz scoring of the

Bender VMGT). The proportion of handicaps depended on birth weight, period of gestation, and the presence of respiratory failure and/or convulsions. Twenty percent of the infants who required treatment for respiratory failure and almost half of those who had convulsions in the neonatal period had handicaps at follow-up.

That perinatal events may foreshadow later development should not be a surprise. As early as 1861, Little described the influence of abnormal parturition, difficult labor, premature birth and asphyxia neonatorium on the mental and physical condition of the child. The literature has continued to document the effect of perinatal stress on development. Extensive reviews may be found in Field and Sostek (1983), Field, Sostek, Goldberg, and Shuman (1979), and Tjossem (1976). A review of prenatal and perinatal events specifically relating to reading disability is found in Balow, Rubin, and Rosen (1975–76).

Littman (1979), believing that medical events beyond the neonatal period were also important in the development of the infant, extended the time period of observation of biological events in the life of 126 pre-term infants to the age of 2 years. Four medical events scales (recording obstetric complications, postnatal complications, and pediatric complications at 4 months and at 9 months) were correlated with the Parmelee Newborn Neurological Examination, the Gesell at 4, 9, and 24 months, and the Bayley at 18 and 25 months. Although the only significant correlation between early (prenatal, perinatal, and neonatal) events and developmental outcome was seen in the Bayley motor performance at 18 months, a significant relationship was found between medical events occurring during later infancy and developmental outcomes at 9, 18, and 24 months. Littman (1979) stated that "it is now clear that medical events [of the perinatal and neonatal period] associate themselves with other medical events; and to single out [e.g., low birth weight or hypoxia] in order to relate the impact of its occurrence on development excludes other complications of possibly equal import to the infant" (p. 55).

The importance of these findings is that, not only do perinatal events affect later development, but that the residuals of these events simply do not disappear with maturation alone and that brain function important for learning may be impaired into adult life. As early as 1964, A. A. Silver and Hagin reported a 10-year follow-up of 41 children with learning disorders who initially were referred to the Bellevue Hospital Mental Hygiene Clinic for behavior problems at 8 to 10 years of age. The emphasis of this study was on the maturation of perceptual functions, particularly those relating to orientation in space and sequencing in time. A control group of adequate readers was matched with the learning disordered group for age, sex, IQ, and socioeconomic class. The groups differed in academic achievement and in the presence of the neuropsychological problems described. Within the group of children with learning disorders there were five children, who in

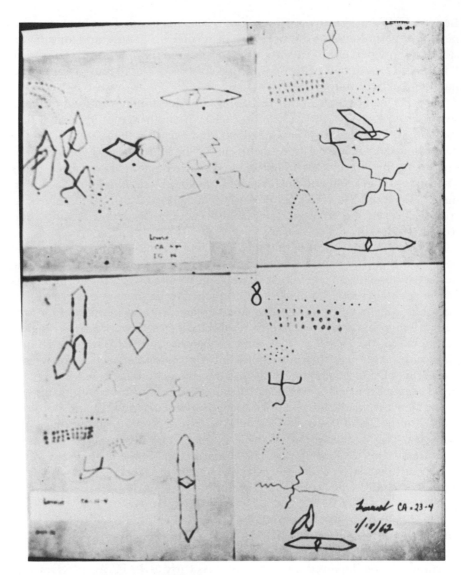

Figure 14-4   Bender Gestalt Drawings
Lennie: Ages 8, 10, 12, and 23 years
Illustrating the persistence of visual-motor problems in a child with gross choreoform
motility when seen at age 8. The upper left drawing illustrates the disorganized gestalt,
the rotations and angulation difficulty at age 8. The upper right drawing at age 10
shows organization improvement but with a dramatic 90-degree rotation of Figure A.
The lower left drawing done in adolescence and the lower right done at age 23 reveal
the same primitive verticalization.
Note. From Silver, A. and Hagin, R. (1985). Outcomes of learning disabilities. In S. C. Feinstein
(Ed.), *Adolescent Psychiatry*, 12. (Reprinted by permission of University of Chicago Press.)

addition to the basic perceptual deviations in spatial and temporal organization, had neurological signs, including marked choreoform motility or poor fine or gross motor coordination.

On follow-up examination 12 years later, when the children had grown into young adults, it was the five with neurological findings who were the least adequate readers and who retained the neuropsychological deficits they had as children. There was no significant perceptual maturation in that group. The persistent defects in visual-motor function are shown in Figures 14-4 and Figure 14-5. Persistent tactile figure–ground problems are shown

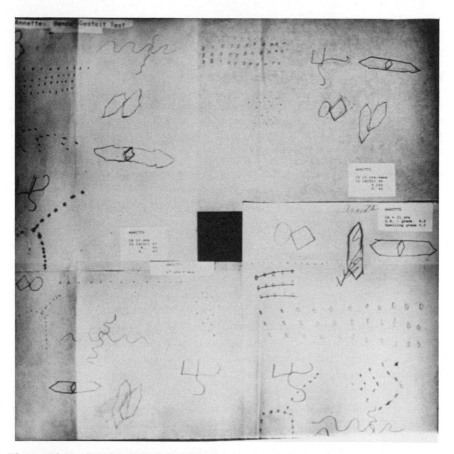

Figure 14-5   Bender Gestalt Drawings
Annette: Ages 11, 12, 17, and 22 years
Illustrating the persistence of visual-motor problems in an individual with grand-mal seizures, history of traumatic birth, and neonatal hypoxia from age 11 (upper left) and age 12 (upper right) to late adolescence (lower left) and young adulthood (lower right). Her verbal intelligence was average. Her oral reading never progressed beyond a grade six level.

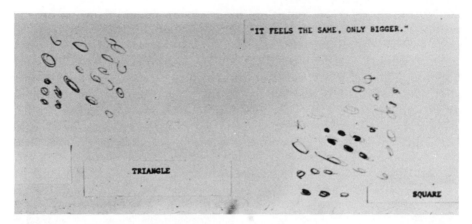

Figure 14-6   Tactile Figure–Ground Test
Annette: Age 21 years
Illustrating the persistence of tactile figure–ground problems. The patient is asked,
with eyes closed, to identify a simple geometric figure of raised rubber thumbtacks in
a field of smooth thumbtacks. The figures are a triangle and a square. Even as an adult
Annette could not perform this task accurately.
Note. From Silver, A. and Hagin, R. (1985). Outcomes of learning disabilities. In S. C. Feinstein
(Ed.), *Adolescent Psychiatry*, 12. (Reprinted by permission of University of Chicago Press.)

in Figure 14-6. These findings led to the suggestion that, for children with organic central nervous system deficit, the compensatory training done was not effective and that direct training of the deficit perceptual areas was indicated.

The relatively poor academic, occupational, social, and psychological prognosis for learning disordered children who have neurological signs has been documented more recently by Spreen (1978a) in a 10-year follow-up of a sample of learning disordered children from a neuropsychological clinic. A. A. Silver and Hagin (1985), with a sample of 79 children drawn from a private practice of psychiatry and psychology, also found that 26% of the 19 children who had evidence for structural deficit of the central nervous system, in contrast to 7% of the specific language disability group, had poor or marginal occupational and educational outcome after 25 years of follow-up. Conversely, 14% of the specific language disability group had excellent outcomes in contrast to 5% of the organic children. All of these 79 children drawn from private practice had the advantage of middle- and upper-income families and received what was then considered optimal treatment.

There is thus a tenacity in the neurological deficits found in the organic child. The old dictum of "he will outgrow it" is outmoded, incorrect, and potentially disastrous for the academic and psychological fate of the child.

Effects of Seizure Disorders

This section does not attempt to provide an exhaustive survey of seizure disorders but focuses on aspects with relevance for learning. It has been estimated that the prevalence of seizure disorders in the general school population may be as high as 0.7% (W. Hauser & Kurland, 1975). Seizure may be secondary, associated with an identified structural central nervous system defect, or primary, occurring without any known structural defect. The term "complicated" is sometimes applied to the former, "uncomplicated" to the latter (Rutter, Graham, & Yule, 1970). Clinical and electroencephalographic data permit classification of seizures as partial or generalized. (Table 14-2). Partial seizures, in turn, include simple partial seizures (generally without impairment of consciousness) complex partial seizures (generally with impairment of consciousness, including temporal lobe or psychomotor sei-

---

Table 14-2   International Classification of Seizures

Partial Seizures (Seizures Beginning Locally)

Partial seizures with simple symptoms (generally without impairment of consciousness)

    With motor symptoms (includes Jacksonian seizures)
    With special sensory or somatosensory symptoms
    With autonomic symptoms
    Compound forms

Partial seizures with complex symptoms (generally with impairment of consciousness; temporal lobe or psychomotor seizures)

    With impairment of consciousness only
    With cognitive symptoms
    With affective symptoms
    With "psychosensory" symptoms
    With "psychomotor" symptoms (automatisms)
    Compound forms

Partial seizures secondarily generalized

Generalized Seizures (Bilaterally Symmetrical and without Local Onset)

Absence (petit mal)
Bilateral massive epileptic myoclonus
Infantile spasms
Clonic seizures
Tonic seizures
Tonic-clonic seizures (grand mal)
Atonic seizures
Akinetic seizures

Unilateral (or Predominantly Unilateral) Seizures

Unclassified Epileptic Seizures (Because of Incomplete Data)

Note. From "Clinical and electroencephalographical classification of seizures" by H. Gastaut, 1970, *Epilepsia*, 11, p.102.

zures). Generalized seizures are bilaterally symmetrical and include grand mal and petit mal seizures. The importance of this classification is to emphasize that seizure disorders may occur without the dramatic appearance of a convulsion.

Seizure disorders as a group may influence learning for any of the following reasons:

1. Children with seizure disorders have the tendency to develop more emotional problems than do the general school population. For example, in an epidemiological survey of the Isle of Wight, Rutter, Graham & Yule (1970) found 29% of 63 children suffering from uncomplicated epilepsy to have "psychiatric disorder" compared to 7% in the general population; this figure rose to 58% in "complicated" epilepsy. Mellor (1977) (quoted in Corbett & Trimble, 1983) found the rate of psychiatric disorder in 308 children with epilepsy from schools in northeast Scotland to be 27% compared to 15% in matched controls. In the past an "epileptic personality"—rigidity, irritability, and impulsive aggressive behavior—was described for these children (Keating, 1961). On the other hand, Corbett and Trimble (1983) felt that psychological disorders of children with seizure disorders are "of similar nature" to those found in nonepileptic children. However, as will be discussed in the use of medication for the control of impulse problems of "organic" children in general, there is evidence that some aggressive, impulsive behavior may indeed be due to complex partial seizures, particularly to psychomotor, temporal lobe seizures (Lewis et al., 1979). Baer, Freeman, and Greenberg (1984) described the "heightened intensity" of feelings and ideas as central to the interictal behavior of individuals with temporal lobe epilepsy; these include increased sensitivity, emotional lability, lowered threshold for anxiety, emotional clinging to teachers, unwillingness to relinquish ideas, difficulty in shifting ideas, compulsive behavior, hypergraphia, and possibly paranoid ideation.

2. Memory, learning, and language functions are frequently affected. With overt seizures, a postictal confusional state, varying in duration is, of course, usual. Memory for events immediately preceding the seizures are effectively erased. In subclinical seizures, too, memory suffers and what may have been recently learned can no longer be recalled. In addition to ictal and postictal memory loss, interictal changes in memory are frequent and are particularly well-documented in temporal lobe seizures. Word-finding difficulty is the most frequent language difficulty experience, although recall of visual spatial material is also impaired. While children with "uncomplicated" epilepsy are said to have a normal distribution of full scale IQ scores (Rutter, Tizard, & Whitmore, 1970), there was a greater variability in the *pattern* of subtest scores, with large verbal-performance discrepancies on the WISC. As a group, by the time children with "uncomplicated" epilepsy

reach the age of 10, they tend to be reading about 1 year behind expectancy. Corbett and Trimble (1983) stated that "this masks the more serious finding that one in five such children are likely to show severe specific reading retardation and that children with complicated epilepsy have even higher rates of reading retardation" (p. 115). What is significant for learning, however, is the memory defect associated with even subclinical seizures and that the pattern of perceptual and cognitive assets and deficits must be determined for each child.

3.   Many anticonvulsant drugs have both overt and more subtle effects on cognition, memory, and attention (E. Reynolds, 1982). Phenobarbital, primidone, phenytoin, ethosuximide and sodium valproate can impair attention, psychomotor speed and performance, memory, and mood: Phenobarbital may cause drowsiness, depression, irritability, and hyperkinetic behavior; phenytoin may decrease psychomotor performance and impair memory; clonazapam may induce drowsiness; and sodium valproate may induce weight gain, decrease platelets and liver toxicity, and impair psychomotor function. Carbamazepine appears to have fewer effects on cognition and memory, but it, too, must be closely monitored for hematological toxicity (E. Reynolds & Trimble, 1981). The effects of these drugs on cognition and memory, are of course, only one aspect of the widespread physical effects they may have. Indications for use of these drugs in the control of seizures will not be considered here. The importance for this discussion is in their effect on learning and memory. The problems described are frequently intensified when combinations of drugs are used in seizures difficult to control. In our experience in a psychiatric clinic where children with difficult-to-control seizures who receive multiple combinations of drugs are referred, the reduction of medication will in selected children improve cognition and mood and may also reduce the frequency of seizures.

Effects of Head Injury

Head injury due to falls and to traffic accidents are common events in school-age children, and accidents at home account for a significant proportion of head injury in preschool children. In closed head injuries, there may be contusion and laceration at the point of impact, with *contre coup* injury most marked in temporal and orbital regions. Subdural bleeding may occur and the events described in the neuropathological section of this chapter ensue. In open injuries with local laceration, intracranial bleeding is generally more severe and involves fracture of the bone. Cognitive and behavioral dysfunction, resulting from head injury and recovery from that dysfunction, is of importance in learning.

   An intensive study of dysfunctions after head injury and their persistence was done on a sample of 5- to 14-year-old children obtained from regional neurosurgical units in southeast England and consisting of consecutive admissions of children with acute head injury (Chadwick, Rutter, Brown, Shaffer, & Traub, 1981; Chadwick, Rutter, Shaffer, & Shrout, 1981; Chadwick, Rutter, Thompson, & Shaffer, 1981; Rutter, 1977, 1981a, 1981b) reviewed by Rutter, Chadwick, and Shaffer (1983). Basing the severity of head injury on the duration of posttraumatic amnesia ((PTA—the period of time following the injury during which recent events are not remembered reliably, consistently, or accurately—the London group found the duration of PTA to be a reasonably good predictor of long-term cognitive, physical, and emotional recovery. Three groups of children were studied, one with posttraumatic amnesia of seven days or more; the second with a PTA of less than seven days but of at least 1 hour duration; and the third a control group of hospital-treated children who also suffered severe accidents but with orthopedic rather than cranial injuries. All children were examined with detailed psychological testing immediately after the accident and then at 4 months, 1 year, and 2½ years after the injury. The study concluded:

1. The intellectual deficit is greatest immediately after acute brain damage, and progressive improvement occurs mostly during the first year.

2. Severe injuries do cause intellectual impairment but mild injuries do not. With a posttraumatic amnesia of less than 2 weeks, there was only one child (of 8) with transient impairment as seen on performance IQ score of the WISC, and none with persistent impairment; transient impairment was characteristic of the children with PTA between 2 to 3 weeks; but persistent intellectual impairment, at 2½-year follow-up, was found in those with PTAs of at least 3 weeks. Other indices of severity (duration of coma or prolonged unconsciousness) also were predictive of residual impairment.

3. Timed visuospatial and visuomotor tests showed more marked impairment and more resistance to recovery 2 years after injury than did verbal tests, regardless of which brain hemisphere was damaged. There was a slight but consistent tendency, however, for all tests of scholastic attainment to show greater impairment with left-hemisphere lesions, and this tendency was more marked in children who were under 5 years of age at the time of injury.

4. The rate of psychiatric disorder in the severe head injury group had markedly increased at the 4-month follow-up period and remained more than double that for the control group over the entire 2½ year follow-up period; the rate of psychiatric disorder in the mild injury group was not significantly different from that of controls over the follow-up period.

5. Although, in general, most psychiatric problems in the head injury group resembled those in the control group, a pattern of social dis-

inhibition, resembling the frontal lobe disinhibition found in adults, was found in children after severe head injury. This pattern included general disregard for social conventions, asking embarrassing questions, and making personal remarks—all behaviors considered socially unacceptable. The early findings of a generalized hyperactivity, impulsive behavior and resistance to discipline as reported by earlier writers (see Chapter 1) was not confirmed.

6. No relationship was found between site of injury and symptoms of overactivity, inattention, aggression, or antisocial behavior. However, there was an association between depression and lesions in the right frontal and left posterior regions.

7. Psychosocial "adversity" when combined with severe head injury increases the vulnerability to psychiatric disorder.

Effects of Haemophilus influenzae *meningitis*

Early reports of the sequelae of *Haemophilus influenzae* meningitis were characterized by high morbidity, with hemiparesis, sensorineural hearing loss, perceptual deficits, and learning and behavior problems found in over 20% of survivors (Sell, Merrill, Doyne, & Zimsky, 1972; Sproles, Azerrad, Williamson, & Merrill, 1969). More recent studies have tempered the pessimistic reports. Follow-up review of subjects and their control siblings found comparable educational achievement and intellectual function (Emmett, Jeffrey, Chandler, & Dugdale, 1980; Tejani, Dobias, & Samburskey, 1982), and in a 1984 study (H. G. Taylor, Michaels, Mazur, Baver, & Linden, 1984), intellectual and neuropsychological outcomes of 24 children, 6 to 8 years after *H. influenzae* meningitis, found these children performed as well as their siblings on individually administered tests of reading, spelling, and arithmetic.

In spite of the adequate academic achievement, however, the postmeningitis children were not without problems. First, although the mean IQ was within the normal range for both postmeningitis and sibling groups, there was significantly lowered full scale IQs and performance IQ, enough to lower the IQ scores for the postmeningitis group relative to that of their siblings. Secondly, there were significant group differences in favor of the sibling controls on the Token test (sequential auditory language), in memory and retrieval of a list of spoken words, and in tasks of fine motor and perceptual motor abilities. Thirdly, in terms of frequency of handicapping conditions, defined as low IQ or academic scores or requiring special educational help, 47% of the postmeningitis children, as compared to 29% of their siblings, were considered midly handicapped. In short, while the academic and behavioral performance of children who had had *H. influenzae* between 1973 and 1975, at an average age of 1 year, 4 months, was similar to that of their siblings, for the most part, these children had subtle neuropsychological deficits for which some compensation, additional school help, was given. Predictors of outcome were a combination of medical variables (age at time of the disease, cerebrospinal fluid glucose and protein levels, and fever duration). The younger the child, the poorer the outcome.

The same 24 children of the 1984 Taylor study were retested by Feldman and Michaels (1988) 4 years later, approximately 10 to 12 years after the original infection. By 1988 the children were at a mean age of 12 years, 7 months, with a grade placement of 6.9; mean age of control siblings was 14 years, 6 months, with a grade placement of 9.8. The postmeningitis children had no greater academic, behavioral, or attentional problems in school than did their control siblings; and, as determined by scores on a child behavior problem checklist completed by parents, they had no greater behavioral or attentional problems at home. Only four postmeningitis children had hearing loss or neurological sequelae. One child with seizures who had tested in the retarded range in the 1984 study remained in a special program for educable retarded children at the time of the 1988 study. There was a general finding, however, that the postmeningitis children received more academic support in school, used more remedial services, and, at home, received more homework help from parents. What is apparent from these studies, is that *H. influenzae* meningitis is associated with persistent neuropsychological sequale, which, although for the most part mild, require comprehensive evaluation and increased academic and family support. Animal studies (Konkol et al., 1987) suggest that *Haemophilis influenzae* meningitis causes a significant elevation of forebrain norepinephrine and dopamine levels in the rat and that the behavioral changes in surviving rats could be explained by "long-lasting perturbation of central monoamine neuronal transmission" (p. 253).

Effects of Radiation to the Central Nervous System

Modern radiation for malignancies in childhood has increased the overall long-term survival rate, so that by now there is a group of children who may be evaluated for the presence of delayed neuropsychologic effects (Meadows & Silber, 1985). This is particularly true for children with acute lymphatic leukemia who have received 2400 RAD of cranial or craniospinal radiation given in combination with five or six doses of intrathecal methotrexate. In a group of 18 children so treated in 1975, reexamination 3 to 5 years after termination of treatment found 11 of the 18 to earn IQ scores 10 or more points lower than their pre-morbid IQ score, with the greatest declines in children younger than 5 years of age and in those with an initial IQ greater than 110 (Meadows et al., 1981). Retrospective studies are consistent with the Meadows' prospective one; treatment with radiation (2400 RAD) to the cranium resulted in lower IQ scores than treatment with intrathecal methotrexate, with or without other agents, intravenous methotrexate, or no central nervous system treatment at all (Copeland, et al., 1985; Rowland, 1984). Radiation also appears to induce cerebral calcification, 5 to 7 years after onset of treatment (Riccardi, Broawers, Dichiro, & Poplack, 1985).

Cranial irradiation for brain tumors may also in the long term contribute to an overall low level of intellectual function with impairment of short-term memory.

What is significant is that the increased survival rate will permit more children who have been treated for acute leukemia, and for brain tumor to return to the classroom. Careful evaluation of their impairment as well as their intact functions is necessary for adequate and appropriate management of their ensuing learning problems.

Effects of Prenatal Exposure to Cocaine

It is estimated that each year in the United States 375,000 newborns, approximately 10% of all live births, will be exposed to their mothers' use of illegal drugs during pregnancy. Of these drugs, cocaine has been found to be the one most commonly detected in the peripartum period, and epidemiological surveys show a dramatic increase of cocaine use in females in their childbearing years, ages 18 to 34 (Hutchings, 1989).

While the use of cocaine during pregnancy has been associated with increased rates of spontaneous abortion, abruptio placentae, pre-term labor, low birth rates, delivery of infants small for gestational age, and specific central nervous system damage, hemorrhagic cerebral infarct has been documented by cranial ultrasound at birth. In one study 38% of 28 cocaine-exposed infants had such lesions. In addition, however, the cocaine-exposed neonate and infant exhibit a range of physiological disturbances, including tremor, irritability, and startle; abnormal cardiorespiratory patterns (greater duration of periods of apnea, periodic breathing, high respiratory rate, and abnormal respiratory patterns in sleep) and poor state control, increased extensor muscle tone, and the persistence of primitive postural responses. State control difficulty may be seen in a variety of behaviors; deep sleep in response to external stimulation; agitated sleep in the labile awake-sleep state with a rapid change from agitated crying to deep sleep; and a "panic state" when awake. Even when awake there are only brief periods of relating to a caretaker before gaze aversion, increased respiration, and disorganized motor activity occurs. The increased and persistent extensor tone interferes with normal motor development and even development of the body image. Other anomalies have been reported in the neonate: dilated tortuous iris vessels; generalized seizures; necrotizing enterocolitis (bowel ischemia secondary to vasoconstrictive properties of cocaine); and congenital malformations (Schneider, Griffith, & Chasnoff, 1989).

It is theorized that these disturbed patterns are a direct response to cocaine and are not a cocaine withdrawal syndrome. Cocaine readily crosses the placental barrier, and is metabolized slowly by the fetus and the neonate; an active metabolic product, norcocaine, readily penetrates the central nervous system. A recycling of norcocaine through the amniotic fluid may permit long exposure to the drug. Cocaine may also be ingested by neonates, when they are breast-fed by cocaine-taking mothers.

Cocaine, a short-acting (15–30 minutes) stimulant of the central nervous system and of the peripheral sympathetic portion of the autonomic system, is a potent blocker of the reuptake of norepinephrine and of dopamine and serotonin from the synaptic cleft, acutely potentiating the catecholamine effects. Activation of the central dopamine system results in stimulation of the central reward system. This effect is abolished by pimozide (dopamine receptor blockade) but not by phentolamine (norepinephrine receptor antagonist); and is reinforced by apomorphine (dopamine receptor agonist) but not by clonidine (alpha 2 agonist), suggesting that dopamine activation is related to the euphoric effect of cocaine. With chronic exposure to cocaine, however, there is a depletion of catecholamines and a compensatory increase in both the number and sensitivity of their receptors. It is postulated that the catecholamine blocked in reuptake is rapidly metabolized by catecol-O-methyltransferase, rendering the catecholamine unavailable for reuse. In addition, cocaine appears to inhibit catecholamine vesicle binding, exposing the catecholamine to intracellular metabolism. A compensatory increase in synthesis cannot overcome the chronic depletion, leading to the hypothesis of catecholamine depletion, particularly dopamine, as a physiological mechanism for cocaine dependency and withdrawal (Extein & Dackis, 1987).

The long-term effects of cocaine on the child exposed in utero, however, are as yet obscure. The effects are complicated by the amount, and frequency of the drug and the time in pregnancy the drug is used, the frequent use of drugs other than cocaine, the general poor prenatal care received by drug abusers, and the lack of consistent and appropriate parenting in an unstable drug-taking household.

It would be reasonable to expect that cerebral infarction will have long-term effects on learning and behavior and that the effects of hypoxia on the central nervous system would not be different from those described in an earlier section of this chapter. Hypothetically, the sensitivity of the neonate to external stimulation certainly suggests an effect of cocaine on sensorineural processing, which may have long-term cognitive sequelae and/or persist as problems in impulse control. The effect of cocaine on the development and maturation of neurotransmitters is still speculative. At this point prospective studies of babies exposed to cocaine in utero have not gone beyond the first 2 years of life. By age 1½ years such babies showed an abnormal affective blandness on separation from their mothers. It is anticipated that studies will be extended to school-age children and that the effect of cocaine on learning may soon be understood.

MEDICAL AND EDUCATIONAL MANAGEMENT

In this section we consider the management of children whose central nervous system pathology is chronic rather than acute, resulting from some type of trauma that occurred early in the child's life or from some acute process (head injury or infection) later in childhood. Both leave some residual imprint upon information processing and/or upon behavior. These children have been described by Carter (personal communication) as suffering from a "static" (i. e., nonprogressive) encephalopathy. Exceptions to this group of children are those with seizures that are, to a greater or lesser degree, controlled with anticonvulsants. In accordance with the position in this book, appropriate and adequate management must rest upon careful evaluation, not only of the etiological factors responsible for the organic state but also of the neurological, emotional, cognitive, social, family, and educational factors within which the child must function; in short, a pentaxial evaluation as outlined in Chapters 5 and 6. Of particular relevance to learning problems is a detailed analysis of the child's abilities and disabilities in dealing with information and of the ability to modulate impulses. In addition, all children with organic defects of the central nervous system deserve at the least an electroencephalogram, which may be of help in consideration of medication.

In general, intervention is indicated to help with the three general groups of symptoms stemming from organic central nervous system defect and discussed in the earlier section of this chapter: the modulation and control of impulses; the processing of information; and the problems with muscle tone, coordination, and synergy. In addition, the emotional reactions and defenses to these basic problems within the child and within his or her family and school frequently require intervention. Psychotherapy, behavior management, medication, physiotherapy, and education all have a place in planning for these children. Psychotherapy for the child and support for the parents were discussed in Chapter 8 ("Principles of Psychotherapeutic Management"). The use of medication and the principles of educational management are of concern here.

Effects of Medication

Except in the presence of seizure disorder, with or without an abnormal EEG, medication is not the first line of management for the child with a structural central nervous system defect who has a learning disorder. Specific remedial education is essential. Effective remediation of perceptual defects, the support of psychotherapy, and an understanding environment will improve academic function and reduce impulsivity so that medication may not be needed. Nevertheless there are children in whom impulse control is so poor that psychopharmacological control is helpful. There are two general groups of symptoms relating to impulse control. Most frequent are children who resemble the child with "pure" attention deficit hyperactivity disorder, except that in the organic child definite or presumptive evidence for brain damage is found. These children appear confused by the perceptual stimuli about them, responding to the slightest change in the environment, the movement of other children, the rustle of papers, and the instruction of teachers. These are the children for whom Cruickshank (1967) devised his "stimulus-free" environment, attempting to protect them from the confusion of the schoolroom by having them work in semi-isolated carrels. The second group of children with problems in impulse control, usually but not always, have the same restless quality of the first group but, in addition, have impulsive outbursts, sometimes aggressive, violent, and destructive, sometimes inconsolable fear or weeping, all evoked by what appears to be minor provocation or indeed appearing spontaneously, seemingly without any provocation. This group is said to be suffering from the "syndrome of episodic dyscontrol," the Intermittent Explosive Disorder of DSM-III that is possibly related to the "catastrophic reaction" of K. Goldstein (1938). There is the question whether these outbursts are associated with undiagnosed psychomotor epilepsy, either as ictal or interictal phenomena. Lewis et al., (1979) and Lewis, Pincus, Shanok, and Glaser (1982) reported that of the 97 delinquent boys they examined, approximately 20% did have evidence of psychomotor seizures. There are reports that the presence of abnormal EEG, even though clinical seizures are not seen, is associated with episodic aggressive behavior (Rickler, 1982). Anticonvulsant medication has been suggested as helpful for this group. Carbamazepine has been reported to decrease disruptive behavior, overactivity, and abnormally elevated mood in mentally retarded adults with or without EEG abnormalities (Reid, Naylor, & Kay, 1981).

In our own clinical experience, admittedly anecdotal, the presence of focal or paroxysmal EEGs suggest the use of anticonvulsants: phenytoin for frontal or diffuse foci and carbamazepine for temporal lobe abnormality. When focal or paroxysmal EEGs are not found, and where psychomotor symptoms are not elicited clinically, the decision for anticonvulsant medication may be more difficult. The presence of diffuse high-voltage slow waves, consistent with "diffuse cerebral dysfunction," adds weight to the use of anticonvulsants. With normal EEGs and with significant clinical symptoms relating to impulse control, beta-adrenergic blockers are considered; where an affective component is present, lithium may be helpful.

Phenytoin, first used for control of seizures by Merritt and Putnam in 1938, has been reported to control aggression (Bogoch & Dreyfus, 1970). Open trial and controlled studies, however, have not found conclusive evidence for the effectiveness of phenytoin in controlling aggressive and disruptive behavior. Unfortunately, it is not clear how many children in these studies suffered from an organic defect of the central nervous system. Looker and Conners (1970), in a double-blind, placebo-controlled, crossover study of 14 children with severe tantrums, found no significant differences between the effects of phenytoin and a placebo. Almost half of the children had abnormal EEGs (41%) and abnormal birth records (47%). It is noted that a small number of children, a number too small to affect group results, did respond "dramatically" to phenytoin. In a later double-blind study Conners, Kramer, Rothschild, Schwartz, and Stone (1971) contrasted phenytoin and methylphenidate in 43 incarcerated delinquent boys and found no therapeutic effect for either drug.

Because of its long history and relative safety in the treatment of seizure disorders, however, phenytoin deserves a closer look when used in children with structural defects of the central nervous system who have clearly defined EEG abnormality. In practice when given orally in a dose of 5–8 mg/kg/day, the drug is slowly absorbed, and several days may be required to attain therapeutic plasma levels of 12–20 μg/ml. Toxicity results from cerebellar and brainstem dysfunction (diplopia, slurred speech, vertigo, ataxia, and headache). Long-term use may produce hirsutism, hypertrophy of gums, and folate deficiency. Peripheral neuropathy has been reported after years on the drug. In animals high doses have resulted in loss of Purkinje cells. In humans, however, Dam (1972) reported that "therapeutic and even toxic doses does not lead to any changes in the density and substructure of Purkinje cells unless the doses are so high that coma with hypoxia results" (p. 234).

Carbamazepine, derived from iminodibenzyl antihistamines and having the ring structure of the tricyclic imipramine, was first used as an antiepileptic in the early 1960s (E. Davis, 1964) and to treat trigeminal neuralgia (Blom, 1962). In the 1970s it was shown to be particularly valuable in partial complex seizures (Dreifuss & Sackellares, 1979), and a review of carbamazepine use in 800 children with behavior disorders (Remschmidt, 1975) found evidence for beneficial effects of carbamazepine on psychomotor function, drive, and mood. Groh (1978) concluded that children with emotional lability, irritability, and paranoia who tended to react violently with minimal provocation were most likely to have favorable therapeutic effect with carbamazepine. Nineteen of the 20 patients studied by Groh had abnormal EEGs. Dalby (1975) found improved mood and behavior and attention in children treated for seizure disorders with carbamazepine. An oral dose up to 25 mg/kg/day will bring the plasma level to therapeutic range, 5–12 μg/ml. Side effects (gastrointestinal complaints, drowsiness, ataxia, and visual-motor disturbances) are dose related. More serious are bone marrow depression (leucopenia or aplastic anemia) and hepatic toxicity. There have been case reports of carbamazepine precipitating a reaction that resembles a paranoid schizophrenia. Although other reports (Rett, 1978) reinforced the effect of carbamazepine in improving impulsive aggressive behavior in children, a clear definition of type of organic defect, its parameters as described earlier in this chapter, together with the type of EEG found, are needed. Such studies should define the indications for the use of anticonvulsants in children with organic brain damage. Recently O'Donnell (1985) stated that "there is as yet no clear basis for treating even severely aggressive conduct disorders with anticonvulsants in the absence of clinical seizure disorder, with or without abnormal EEGs" (p. 274). Yet O'Donnell does state that of a group of 75 children aged 6–13, admitted to an inpatient service, 12 of them (17%) had abnormal EEG (type not stated); 9 of these improved on anticonvulsants, "predominantly carbamazepine," while 4 children with normal EEGs did not significantly improve.

Although propranolol was reported (Elliot, 1977) to be beneficial in controlling outbursts of rage that followed acute brain damage in seven adults and by outbursts in assaultive adults with organic brain disesase (Greendyke, Schuster, & Wooten, 1984), as of this writing, there have been only scattered reports on the effect of *beta adrenergic blockers* on impulse disorders in children with organic brain disorder. As early as 1979 Schreier, found that 100 mg/day of propranolol controlled rage outbursts after acute encephalitis in a 12-year-old. Of four patients Yudofsky, Williams, and Gorman (1981) treated with propranolol, one was an adolescent with "chronic organic brain dysfunction." D. T. Williams, Mehl, Yudofsky, Adams, and Roseman (1982) treated a diagnostically heterogeneous group of 30 patients who had "uncontrolled rage and organic brain dysfunction" with propranolol in doses from 50 to 1,600 mg/day. Of these patients, 11 were children and 15 were adolescents. Diagnostic categories included those with "MBD" and those with a history of uncontrolled seizures. Each had not responded to one or more anticonvulsants, neuroleptics, or stimulants. While propranolol did not control seizures, the overall results yielded a 75% posttreatment improvement in control of rage outbursts. The authors report the duration of treatment with propranolol from 1 to 30 months (median 3–5 months). It is difficult from this paper, however, to understand the factors that correlated with a successful outcome.

While propranolol has both peripheral and central actions, nadolol, a long-acting peripheral beta-blocker, has been reported as effective in reducing aggressive behavior in a 36-year-old retarded man who had been institutionalized since adolescence because of his impulsive, assaultive behavior. Nadolol in a dose of 120 mg/day proved to be more effective than propranolol (Polakoff, Sorgi, & Ratey, 1986). The authors speculated that beta blockers may decrease peripheral somatic reactivity and thus break a "powerful behavioral/feedback loop" (p. 126). This is of interest since the homeostatic lability found in many children with organic brain disorders may promote subjective anxiety and, as pointed out in the review of symptoms section of this chapter, anxiety may be discharged as aggression.

Pindolol has also been reported (Greendyke & Kanter, 1986) effective in management of 11 adults whose impulsive and explosive behavior is said to be a consequence of brain disease or injury. Pindolol does not have the antihypertensive or bradykinetic effect of propranolol.

While *lithium* has been reported to be of benefit in children with cyclic mood swings, manic-depressive illness, and severe explosive or aggressive behavior, the effect of lithium on the impulsive behavior of children with organic brain disorders has not been explored. The chronic impulsive aggression of 66 prisoners aged 16–22, 34% of whom received lithium, was evaluated by Sheard, Marini, Bridges, & Wagner (1976) in a well-designed, placebo-controlled study. The lithium group had significantly fewer aggressive rule infractions than did the placebo group. Fourteen boys aged 7–13 with sporadic, unprovoked physical aggression were maintained on a therapeutic dose of lithium and compared with a matched control group who did not have aggressive behavior (Siassi, 1982). Aggression in the lithium group "declined dramatically" only to return again when lithium was discontinued. The effect of lithium was compared with that of haloperidol and a placebo in reducing the aggressive, explosive, and disruptive behavior of 61 children aged 5 years, 2 months to 12 years, 9 months who were diagnosed in accordance with DSM-III as a conduct disordered, undersocialized, aggressive type, and who were hospitalized at Bellevue Psychiatric Hospital in New York City (Campbell, Perry, & Green, 1984; Campbell et al., 1984). Both lithium and haloperidol were significantly superior to the placebo in reducing the angry affect, bullying, distractibility, fighting, negativism, and temper tantrums. The authors noted that "the primary action of lithium was to decrease explosive affect. . . . Haloperidol merely made the child more manageable" (p. 655). There is some evidence, too, that the aggression of disturbed, mentally retarded adolescents may also respond to prolonged (8-months) administration of lithium (Dostal, 1972). With the exception of three of the retarded boys who had grand mal seizures and two with lower limb paresis, the questions of lithium in organic brain disorders specifically is not considered. It seems clear that this is an area that warrants further investigation.

Educational Principles

Many of the general principles of educational remediation that were discussed in Chapter 7 are relevant to the educational management of children with organic learning problems. However, the nature of their disorder results in some special requirements that the educational planner must keep in mind in order to serve their educational needs appropriately.

Early work in the field of learning disabilities focused on improved methods for teaching these children. Lehtinen's work at the Cove School provided not only an understanding of the nature of their handicaps but also teaching procedures that enabled these children to learn (Strauss & Lehtinen, 1947). Cruickshank, a pioneer in defining the services these children require, continues to offer leadership in the education of children with special learning problems. Cruickshank (1967) and Cruickshank, Bentzen, Ratzeberg, and Tannhauser (1961) demonstrated how instructional variables could be organized in a program within the public school setting to provide for the perceptual and cognitive problems these children experience. Much that is done in special education programs today draws on the work accomplished in these early programs.

As in any planning for educational intervention, it is important that comprehensive, multidisciplinary diagnostic information be available. In the case of children with organic defects of the central nervous system, such information is essential for several reasons. First of all, there is a high degree of variability within the group. Even though their ages and overall levels of achievement may be similar, a program designed for one student may be completely inappropriate for another student because of differences in patterns of functioning. The qualitative information gained from sensitive clinical assessment can contribute information about strengths and needs, personality, and learning styles that is crucial to an effective plan.

Not only are there substantial interpersonal variations within this group of children, but there are also marked intrapersonal variations. For example, organic children frequently have significant interscale variation on the WISC-R. In the case of a child who earns a verbal IQ of 100 and a performance IQ of 70, it creates a completely misleading impression for a psychologist to report the overall level of function as an 84, which falls within the dull–normal range. The generalization does not take into account the significant amount of intrapersonal variation that the test scores demonstrate. The high points these variations signal, as well as the deficits, must be considered in planning.

The student's emotional response to his or her learning problems are another aspect of the diagnostic formulation that has implications for teaching. The emotional lability and tenuous impulse control that characterizes many children with organic learning disorders makes it more difficult for these children to build easy relationships with teachers and other authority figures. The teacher must be able to recognize the effects of these characteristics and to handle them with tact and understanding, rather than to deal with them as behavioral infractions. The pervasive anxiety that is the psychological parallel of the biological substrate must also be recognized.

Awareness of the high level of anxiety that characterizes many of these children can help their teachers understand their mercurial mood swings, their sensitivity to stress, and the fatigue that can be misunderstood as anger and stubbornness. There may be a perseverative quality in their behavior, and teachers may lose patience when the same question is asked for the nth time. Some compulsiveness may also show up in their schoolwork; it may mark the youngster who will become a tenacious student. It also means that these children do not adapt easily to rapid transitions. Teachers will find that a warning about an end of an activity or an impending schedule change may help them adapt to shifts in activities.

The teacher must help these students learn ways of protecting themselves from the intrusion of external stimuli on the educational process. Although each child may have unique patterns of functioning, difficulties with any aspect of information processing—stimulus input, storage, and retrieval— can be expected to occur. It is important for teachers to understand that the child's work requirements may be different from their own and to avoid insisting on procedures that may be comfortable for the teacher but less comfortable for the individual child. For example, some of these students find that background noise or music facilitates concentration; these youngsters actually find the quiet workplace that most adults insist on anxiety producing. With them, teachers should not insist on the quiet workplace they may prefer, when the student really needs the sound of background music to sustain attention to the work.

Fast, inaccurate work styles frequently characterize these youngsters. There is a real question about the extent to which this style can be transformed into the methodical accuracy that many teachers admire in their students. One thing is certain, this transformation will not occur through direct confrontation. Teaching approaches that make use of metacognitive knowledge and skills may be a more appropriate approach. The strategy training procedures developed by Deshler and his associates (1984) are instructional models to be recommended for this purpose.

The level of instruction must take into account the range in abilities these youngsters demonstrate. Some of them may demonstrate superior verbal abilities, but have such poor fine motor control that they write illegibly, uncomfortably, and as infrequently as possible. As the burden of written work increases in the school years, this problem will affect their grades on compositions, their ability to take notes in class, and the fluency with which they express their ideas in written examinations. Understanding the problem and providing typing and word processing equipment at the upper grade levels are essential if these youngsters' written work is to reflect their abilities.

Sometimes specific cognitive limitations must be recognized, particularly among the more severe impaired children in this group. These youngsters may have considerable difficulty in making generalizations, both in terms of academic learning and behavior. They need to be taught many things that other children learn from casual experiences. These children may require much more practice at a given level before reaching mastery. With the rapid pace of many current school curricula, these children experience frustration and failure. As one young woman described her experiences in high school: "I would just begin to understand something and the teacher would go on to something else." Ellen illustrates the problems of a girl with an organically based learning disorder.

CASE STUDY: ELLEN

Ellen was a quiet, dark haired, gentle, 6-year-old girl when we first saw her. She was referred to us because her parents were concerned that she was slow in development of speech and appeared to be clumsy. The history revealed that although she was thought to be 1 month premature, her birth weight was 6 lb, 3 oz. As an infant she slept "constantly." At age 3 months, she had severe croup, became cyanotic, and was hospitalized for a week. The hospital noted repeated episodes of protracted cyanosis. Her developmental milestones were delayed; standing at 17 months, walking at 18 months, single words at 2 years, and still at age 6, having urinary and bowel "accidents" during the day. She had numerous urinary tract infections that required urethral dilatation.

On examination she was alert and cooperative, right-handed but with a grossly abnormal pencil grip, poor fine motor coordination, poor praxis, and visual motor function at just about a 3-year level. Her gait was clumsy, and she had a mild articulation defect. She was not overly active, and the remainder of the classical neurological examination was within normal limits. An electroencephalogram was "abnormal with evidence of paroxysmal slow wave and spike activity appearing in both occipital leads, compatible with cortical alteration in that area and possible convulsive disorder."

Her intellectual functioning ranged from dull–normal to borderline levels, with a full scale IQ of 79, a verbal IQ of 81, and a performance IQ of 81 on the WPPSI. She had severe visual and visual-motor problems, moderately severe body image and auditory sequencing problems, and short-term memory problems. She was then attending a small private school, supplemented with tutoring directed toward teaching preacademic skills. Our impression at that time was that Ellen was indeed suffering from a diffuse, "static encephalopathy," affecting her overall cognitive functioning with specific problems in memory and perception.

Emotionally she was immature and was already reacting to the impatient demands of her intellectually gifted parents. Recommendations for management were made to the school and to the tutor.

When seen for reevaluation a year later, she said "I grewed up. . . . I got bigger." During the year Ellen had made progress with pre-reading perceptual skills, but difficulties in integration of skills in a productive fashion and in comprehension and use of language were now more evident. When Mrs. L was cautioned about expecting too rapid academic progress, she expressed doubts about the structure that the small private school offered. She was encouraged to investigate the newly formed class for neurologically impaired children organized in the local public school.

At the start of the next school year Ellen was enrolled in that class. This class proved to be academically oriented, beyond Ellen's ability at that time. On reevaluation she brought along a basal reader that was difficult for her to read and a towering stack of workbooks—phonics worksheets for a wide variety of sounds she did not recognize, a handwriting workbook, a reading comprehension workbook, Frostig worksheets, and some mathematics worksheets (which she understood best of all the material). Her comment on the schoolwork was to spread her arms out wide and say "I hate it this much." She seemed to handle all this seatwork by making written responses in an indiscriminate fashion, incorrect as often as not. Discussion or verbal rehearsal of directions seemed limited; therefore, Ellen had little opportunity to integrate the skills into her repertoire of responses.

As a result of these generally unhappy experiences, Ellen now 8 years old, began individual weekly tutoring sessions to provide stimulation in oral and written language. Oral language stimulation work started with very elementary work in generating questions. Ellen did not know *how* to find out the things she didn't know; when people did not understand her awkwardly framed questions, she would shrug and say, "Forget it." Language work went on to transforming questions into statements and dealing with conversational exchanges. Manipulatives, such as the Attribute Games were used to deal with logical tasks. Simple reading comprehension materials were used to apply the phonics skills she was working with in school and to give her practice in following written directions. During these sessions her mother was invited to join us for a brief period, either to admire something Ellen had accomplished or to join us in a review game. The purpose of this was to help Mrs. L understand what Ellen could do and to learn to set more realistic goals for her.

A repeat neurological examination at age 8 revealed persistent visual-motor, fine motor coordination, and praxic problems but improvement in gait and articulation. Her EEG was still abnormal with "irregular slow activity over the posterior hemispheres and diffuse peroxysmal slow activity during and after hyperventilation, suggesting diffuse cerebral dysfunction."

The following school year Ellen was placed in a class that gave excellent social stimulation and opportunity for participation in a variety of activities. She began to enjoy school for the first time. In marked contrast to her previous class, there was an underemphasis on academic work and little reinforcement of skills in reading and mathematics. Her language skills had improved and so tutoring in academic areas helped to compensate for the more casual program at school, because it was felt the socialization there was valuable for her.

During the next year, Ellen moved to junior high school where the class offered, as far as could be determined, an ideal program. The class was well-integrated into the life of the school. Educational activities were well-planned and appropriately structured. For the first time it seemed that Ellen felt some responsibility for learning at school. Tutoring was directed toward making the transition to active classwork and self-directed work on her own.

Reevaluation at the end of that school year showed that WISC-R Scores were within the same range as they had been in the past (Full Scale IQ of 80, Verbal IQ of 80, Performance IQ of 82). Thus while there had been no acceleration of IQ, Ellen had held her own within her age group. Her approach to testing was matter-of-fact and uncompetitive. Her subtest scores were less variable than in the past, with high points seen in the Similarities subtest (which taps abstract verbal relationships) and with Object Assembly (a measure of spatial relationships). She exceeded the ceiling for the Illinois Test of Psycholinguistic Abilities with a language age of 10 years (her original score 2 years before had been 7 years, 8 months). Gains had been made in all areas; although grammatical closure was the most difficult subtest for her, even there she had gained 20 scaled score points. Achievement test scores were stable, all placing within the fourth-grade range. Ellen continued in the special education program through her high school years.

After high school, she entered a 2-year vocational program in which she was trained to work as an educational assistant in nursery school. As a young adult, she is poised and outgoing, proud of her productive employment. Her parents are pleased, also. They are comfortable and effective in the supportive role they have taken as sponsors of a social group for young adults with learning disabilities of which Ellen is a part.

Ellen illustrates a number of important principles in the management of children with structural defects of the central nervous system. First, diagnosis was necessary to formulate the unique patterns of Ellen's functional deficits, as well as her strengths. Second, remediation was most effective when it matched her developmental level; it was ineffective when she was overwhelmed by the difficulty and the amount of required activites. Third, the deficits were tenacious, requiring patience and restraint on the part of the tutor and the parents. Fourth, youngsters like Ellen need support, particularly at major life transition points. Fifth, her emotional reactions to pressure for achievement beyond her current level of capability resulted in continued tension within the family.

SUMMARY

Approximately 5% of the children in mainstream first-grade classes have presumptive evidence of a structural defect of the central nervous system. When comprehensive examination, along the pentaxial scheme described in Chapters 5 and 6 of this book, is done on children in self-contained classes for severely emotionally handicapped children, approximately one-third of them will have such evidence. All of these children have some degree of learning disorder. Structural dysfunction of the central nervous system may be categorized as to nature, severity, and location of the insult; the time in the child's life it has occurred; and the appropriateness of the environmental support. Acute effects of injury include destruction of cells at the site of the trauma, astrocyte reaction, proliferation of blood vessels, invasion by microglia, and edema; long-term effects include retrograde axonal degeneration, scarring, loss of trophic influence, and, most important, proliferation of new axon collaterals that may form aberrant fiber tracks. Secondary structural changes with more severe and profound effects on overall intelligence are greater in the infant brain than in the mature or juvenile brain. Following an injury, however, language acquisition and recovery of language after it has developed is more prone to occur the younger the child. In general, behavioral effects after brain trauma are seen in disorders of perception, cognition, and language; in the initiation and control of impulses; and in problems in muscle tone, coordination, and synergy.

In the newborn, infectious and toxic processes are not common, while hypoxia is most significant and more prevalent than mechanical injury. Deep basal ganglia damage was observed mainly in the premature, and is more frequent than cortical damage, which occurred in the mature, at-term neonate. Even mild hypoxia results in cellular damage with patchy or diffuse neuronal loss and is stated to be a critical determinant for later neurological and intellectual development. Infants with clinical signs of anoxia are at risk for less than normal development. Infant test scores on selected scales at 4, 8, 12, 18, and 24 months, together with a risk index based on demographic, reproductive, and perinatal factors can predict cognitive test scores at 5 years of age. Although the effects of neonatal hypoxia are obtunded with maturation and with environmental support, the residuals do not disappear with maturation alone. Seizure disorders may affect learning by memory loss in the post-ictal state and even in subclinical seizures. In temporal lobe seizures a word-finding problem is not unusual and in general there is a variability in subtest patterns with verbal–performance discrepancies in the WISC-R. Even with uncomplicated seizures, there is a tendency for a reading disorder to be evident by the age of 10. Anticonvulsants have a depressing effect on cognition and memory. Emotional problems of the child with seizures—impulsivity and rigidity—interfere with learning. Basing severity of head injury on the duration of posttraumatic amnesia and duration of coma, mild head injury does not cause persistent cognitive impairment; severe head injury, however, may result in marked impairment, particularly in visuospatial and visuomotor tasks. With left-hemisphere lesions, all tests of scholastic attainment may be impaired. Severe head injury also tends to result in an increased rate of psychiatric disorder. Although children who have survived *H. influenzae* meningitis do not as a group suffer academic impairment they appear to need more support, remedial services, and help with homework than their noninjured siblings. Radiation to the cranium for childhood malignancies contribute to a lowered level of intellectual function or impairment of short-term memory. Because of these findings, routine prophylactic cranial irradiation is being phased out.

The management of children with structural defects of the central nervous system must be based on comprehensive evaluation; psychotherapy, behavior modification, physiotherapy, medication, and special education each has a role. Anticonvulsant medication even in the absence of seizure disorder, but in the presence of episodic dyscontrol, has been recommended; propranolol and lithium have also been helpful in reducing aggressive and impulsive outbursts in "organic" children.

A case study illustrates the principles of management of children with a structural defect of the central nervous system: comprehensive diagnosis, matching remediation with the child's developmental level, the tenacity of the deficits, the involvement of parents, and the need for continued support of the child at major life transition points.

CHAPTER FIFTEEN

Gilles de la Tourette's Syndrome

CASE STUDY: ROBERT

Robert was 10 years, 10 months of age in the regular fourth-grade class of a good public school when he was referred to us, 3 months into the academic year. For the past 2 months he had refused to go to school and was becoming increasingly demanding at home—hostile, snarling, negativistic, explosive, and even destructive of objects when his demands were not instantly met. He was an only child, the product of a normal pregnancy and labor with a birth weight of 9 lb. His development, except for delayed speech, was said by his parents to be normal. However, he was described as "always a difficult child," very active and impulsive, so that by age 5 he was diagnosed as "hyperactive." For the next year or more, he received methylphenidate up to 30 mg daily. By age 7, eye blinking and a throwing motion of his arms was added to his hyperactivity. The Valium and Tranxene he received for these symptoms only appeared to increase his agitation and aggressive behavior. Between the ages of 7 and 8 years the tics appeared to increase in severity, with eye blinking, head shaking, shoulder shrugging, and dystonic movements of abdominal and back muscles. He developed vocalizations, grunting and yelling, and episodes of coprolalia in which he kept repeating "son of a bitch." Compulsive behavior—holding his knees together, grabbing his crotch with his right hand, touching and stacking furniture, and touching people as he went by them—was evident.

At age 8 a diagnosis of Tourette's syndrome was made, and since that time he received haloperidol at 1.5 mg daily. This medication did not fully control his symptoms, but increasing the dose to 2.0 mg daily induced drowsiness, extrapyramidal side effects, and akathisia. His EEG and CT scan were reported as normal. The school psychologist reported that on testing at age 8 years, 5 months, Robert earned a full scale IQ of 93 on the WISC-R (verbal IQ of 95, performance IQ of 93). He earned a scaled score of 12 in Information and 10 in Similarities and in Vocabulary, but a scaled score of 6 on Digit Span, 7 in Arithmetic, and 8 in Comprehension. On the performance scale he had marked difficulty with Block Design (scaled score of 6). He refused all graphomotor tasks. He had limited word attack skills in reading and could not go beyond addition and subtraction combinations in arithmetic. Rotation and poor integration of juxtaposed figures were evident on the Bender VMGT.

After the diagnosis of Tourette's symdrome was made when Robert was 8 years of age, he was placed in a class for emotionally handicapped children where, with a combination of haloperidol and support to the family, he was reported to have done well behaviorally but had not progressed academically. Accordingly, for his second and third grades he was placed in a full-time class for children with learning disabilities. The IEP review summary at the end of third grade stated that "significant progress was noted and trial mainstreaming in the third grade appeared successful," and a regular class was recommended for fourth grade.

This proved disastrous. Within a month he refused to go to school. His teacher noted that "because students in fourth grade must work more independently, have fewer oral assignments and increased written assignments, must do copying assignments from the chalkboard involving cursive writing, have increased spelling lists and are more socially perceptive, Robert is experiencing great difficulty. His grades have dropped from A to F, his task completion is greatly reduced, and he has become socially aggressive due to teasing by his peers." At this point he was referred to our clinic.

Examination in our clinic revealed a handsome, slender, 11-year-old boy, with flushed cheeks, perioral pallor, and braces on his teeth. He was in continual motion with tics of the left shoulder and right hand, body torsions, rolling on the couch, lying with his feet in the air, and clearing his throat. The day before the neuropsychiatric examination, psychological testing was to have been done. Robert refused to cooperate on any psychological tests. Reason, coercion, bribery, and threats were all to no avail. Having learned from that experience, the neuropsychiatric examination was conducted in an informal, relaxed manner and as long as he was given no task that would expose his deficits, Robert was affable, pleasant, and verbal and showed the examiner pictures of himself seated in a large bulldozer, gutting a deer he and his father had shot. Except for a rapid, staccato speech, marked synkinesis, and autonomic lability, classical neurological examination was essentially normal. On extension of the arms in this right-handed boy, the left hand was elevated. There was hesitation in responding to tests of right–left discrimination in himself and gross confusion in identifying right and left in the examiner facing him. Praxis, too, was mildly impaired.

Examination of perceptual skills revealed severe visual-motor immaturity (Figure 15-1) with the presence of angulation difficulty, primitive verticalization, and perseveration. He demanded a ruler (which was not given to him) to copy the Bender VMGT figures and became increasingly anxious, finally erasing the designs that were unacceptable to him. He tried very hard, but any written work must be frustrating to this child (Figure 15-2). Auditory rote sequencing was markedly immature, no higher than at an 8-year-old level. He also could not recall the Binet sentences beyond the 8-year-old level.

Emotionally, Robert was under stress. He was emotionally labile, quick to erupt in the face of any stimulus he viewed as threatening, but friendly and reasonable when all went as he wished. There was a sense that one must tread very lightly with Robert. His lability evoked tension in the people around him. There was a cost to his immediate demands, however. Robert felt guilty about all the "bad things" he did, felt he should be punished, and wondered if Tourette's is his punishment. Anxiety was always lurking beneath the surface of his feelings. He feared someone would get into his house—"an insane guy"—to hurt him. He said, "I cannot go to sleep unless I tell my mother to close the closet door. I convince myself that if I hide under the blanket with my dog, I can't be shot by some insane guy." His mother reported that she must sleep in Robert's room, so that he can sleep. Robert said his main problem is that he cannot get to sleep. As a result, how could we expect him to get up in time to go to school? He talked about his school difficulty but blamed

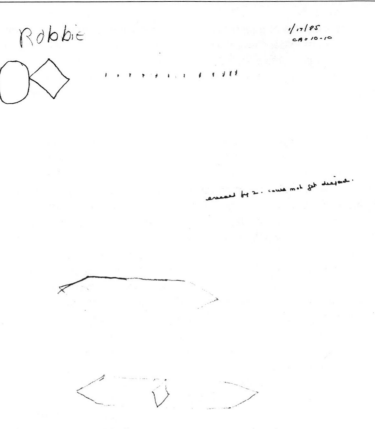

Figure 15-1 · Bender Gestalt Drawing
Robert: Age 10 years, 10 months
Receiving haloperidol (1.5 mg daily) for 2 years for Tourette's syndrome. He had dif-
ficulty with the gestalt drawings and was dissatisfied with his productions, erasing
Figure 2. In addition to verticalization, there were mild angulation difficulties and
difficulty with motor control. He refused to draw the remaining gestalt figures.

it on the school for not having a proper teacher for him. He worried about Tourette's symptoms, saying that he did not know how to get rid of them and if they got worse, "I would do something." He was unsure of the future.

This case vignette is presented in some detail because it illustrates many important issues that must be considered in the diagnosis and management of the child with Tourette's syndrome: the onset of the syndrome; its manifestations and progression; its psychological, social, and school problems; the effect on parents; and the problems of medication and comprehensive management.

Robert

Figure 15-2   Figure Drawing
Robert: Age 10 years, 10 months
His impulsive drawing and his dissatisfaction with his production is seen in the upper
part of this Figure. Finally, he did manage an immature stick figure.

DESCRIPTION OF THE SYNDROME

Tourette's syndrome is described as a neuropsychiatric disorder, "a complex behavioral disorder that is poised between mind and body, governed by innate vulnerabilities and environmental circumstances" (Leckman, Riddle, & Cohen, 1988, p. 112). It is characterized by multiple motor and vocal tics, which may not necessarily appear concurrently; the motor tics are sudden, brief, repetitive, stereotyped, apparently meaningless movements that may be described by their anatomical location, number, frequency, intensity, and complexity. The complex movements may appear purposeful, involving systematic rituals and compulsions, such as tapping, touching oneself, or touching others or objects. At times the touching involves the genital area. The vocal tics may also be simple noises—grunting, throat clearing or coughing, spitting, or sniffing, or they may be complex with echolalia, coprolalia, or sounds that appear to be attempts to hold back words that are socially unacceptable. These tics occur many times throughout the day and, according to DSM-III-R, have their onset before age 21 and must be at least 1 year in duration.

Such was the behavior of the first patient, a Madame de D, described by Gilles de la Tourette in the *Archives de Neurologie* in 1885 (translated by Goetz and Klawans, 1982) and from which is derived the eponym, Tourette's syndrome. (A brief biographical sketch of Gilles de la Tourette is found in *Revue Neurologique, 142,* 801–867, 1986.)

It is recognized now that the syndrome may appear in all degrees of severity, from mild to severe, chronic simple tics to the more complex motor and vocal tics, some manifestations of which are demonstrated by Robert. The variety of the tics is myriad. The problems of the Tourette patient are not confined to tics alone, however, but may be frequently accompanied by obsessive symptoms as well as the compulsive ones, by a rigidity of personality, a tendency to be argumentative, a lability of affect, school and social problems, and, as will be discussed, anxiety. There is controversy as to whether attention deficit hyperactivity disorder is a part of the syndrome (Comings & Comings, 1984) or merely a comorbid symptom, etiologically independent of Tourette's syndrome (Pauls, Kruger, Leckman, Cohen, & Kidd, 1984).

ETIOLOGY

The cause of Tourette's syndrome is still obscure. In 1885 Gilles de la Tourette stated that "as to the underlying lesion we have found no anatomic or pathological cause. One can, by looking to psychology, try to interpret some of the symptoms." Meige and Feindel (1907) referred to tics as "mental infantilism," saying that "tiqueurs are big, badly reared children who never learned to bridle their will and action" and that tics were a "disturbance of motility" (quoted by Mahler, 1949, p. 282).The psychoanalytic authors viewed tics as stemming from an inhibition of motor expression at a period in the child's life when such expression is the principal means of discharge of instinctual tension, particularly aggressive tension. Such inhibition may result in a weakening of the "motility controlling function of the ego" (F. Deutsch, 1947; Fenichel, 1945; Ferenzi, 1950).

Mahler (1949), summarizing 60 cases of tics, recognized *maladie des tics* as a syndrome distinct from "symptomatic tics." The symptomatic tics included transient tics, which indicate tension phenomena, and the tic as a symptom of neurosis in which the tic itself is the symbolic expression of underlying, unresolved instinctual conflict. The *maladie des tics,* described as one type of tic syndrome, corresponds to the "genetic [in a developmental sense], dynamic, structural and economic principles of a systemic organ neurotic disease, with particular affinity for the peculiarities of infantile motor organization" (p. 282). Mahler felt that another type of tic syndrome is the tic as an integral part of an "impulse or character neurosis" (p. 282). The impulse neurosis described by Mahler appears to have the characteristics of what we would now call an attention deficit hyperactivity disorder. Mahler indicated that it is sometimes difficult to distinguish between her impulse disorder and *maladie des tics.* Indeed, as will be described, the impulse disorder may be the beginning of a Tourette's syndrome. The psychodynamic origin of tic syndrome was described by Mahler as the psychological effect of chronic suppression of aggression leading to "general and multifocal tension phenomena in the musculature with restlessness, hyperkinetic or dyskinetic manifestations" (p. 291). Thus "generalized tics" represented an attempted drainage of a chronic state of emotional tension and is the physiological accompaniment of a chronic state of affective tension. While Mahler's description of the personality characteristics of what we now call Tourette's syndrome and her recognition of hereditary or "constitutional" factors in its development are valid and accurate to this day, the emphasis has shifted from psychodynamic factors to biological factors in the cause of Tourette's syndrome.

The shift may have had its impetus in the successful treatment of single patients with haloperidol by Caprini and Melotti (1961) and by Seignot (1961). Although since then more than 50 drugs have been studied in the treatment of Tourette's syndrome and although major advances have been made in the neurosciences, the etiology of Tourette's syndrome is still elusive. In the early 1980s major emphasis was placed on disturbance in the dopaminergic systems located in the midbrain with their projections to the striatum, limbic, cortical, and hypothalamic areas. A hypersensitivity of dopamine receptors or an increased number of dopamine receptors was postulated to account for the sucess of dopamine-blocking agents, particularly in their affinity for D2 dopamine receptors, in the amelioration of Tourette's symptoms.

In recent years it is recognized that a unitary dopaminergic hypothesis is increasingly untenable. The evidence supporting an association between obsessive-compulsive disorder and Tourette's syndrome, and the high incidence of somnambulism in Tourette's syndrome, has implicated serotonergic mechanisms. The higher prevalence in males has suggested gender-specific neuroendocrine disturbance, and the localization of other neurotransmitters in the striatum (GABA, substance P, cholecystokinin, norepinephrine, and endogenous opioids, to name a few), have all suggested that there is a "tightly regulated subcortical system involved with the control of voluntary movement that displays a distinctive ontogenetic progression, is sensitive to stress and to gender-specific hormonal influences and interconnects with a large number of other brain regions including limbic and prefrontal cortical areas" (Leckman, Riddle, & Cohen, 1988, p. 105). Dysfunction of these systems, however, still does not tell us the cause of that dysfunction.

Neuroanatomical study of Tourette's syndrome, reported in only three cases, reveals no definite pathological changes (Richardson, 1982) although in one, the findings are interpreted as a hypoplasia of the corpus striatum, as a failure of neuronal maturation, so that the striatum remained arrested at a stage of development normally found in a young child. Haber, Kowall, Vonsattel, Bird, and Richardson (1986) did not find unique anatomical or cytological neuropathology in one patient with Tourette's syndrome, but on immunochemical study, they did find a decrease in staining for a dymorphin-like protein in the globus pallidus of that patient, with an absence of dymorphin-like staining in the dorsal aspect of the globus pallidus. More recent positron emission imaging studies of brain dopamine receptors did not find increased numbers of DA receptors in Tourette's syndrome patients (T.M. Chase et al., 1984), but there was decreased glucose utilization in the frontal, cingular, and insular cortex and in the inferior corpus striatum.

Nevertheless, while the cause of the syndrome is as yet obscure, there is evidence that both Tourette's syndrome and chronic multiple tics have a familial aggregation (Comings & Comings, 1984; Comings, Comings, Devor, & Cloninger, 1984; Pauls et al., 1984; T. Shapiro, Burkes, Petti, & Ranz, 1978). The importance of genetic factors in this aggregation is seen in a study of 43 pairs of same-sex twins (Price, Kidd, Cohen, Pauls & Leckman, 1985) in whom, for monozygotic twins, there was a concordance of 53% for Tourette's syndrome as contrasted to 8% for dizygotic twins. When the criteria included both chronic tics and Tourette's syndrome, the concordance increased 77% for monozygotic and 23% for dizygotic twins. Pauls and Leckman (1986b), reviewing five studies testing whether a specific genetic hypothesis could account for the mode of transmission, concluded that

Tourette's syndrome and the associated behaviors are transmitted as an autosomal dominant trait with reduced penetrance and variable expressivity, but that there may be a sex-specific expression of specific types of symptoms. The conclusion is supported by a 1986a Pauls and Leckman study in which the segregation data were collected by direct interview of all relatives rather than by relying on family history. Their analysis, done using three diagnoses (only relatives with Tourette's syndrome, then adding relatives with chronic tics, and finally adding relatives with obsessive-compulsive disorder) found penetrance estimates increasing "substantially" as each diagnostic group was added, with the greater penetrance found in males, so that finally, with all three diagnosis included, penetrance for males approached 1.00 and for females, 0.71. In the Pauls and Leckman model, transmission of vulnerability to develop Tourette's syndrome is through a single major autosomal gene. The phenotypic expression, however, is determined only in part by the genetic vulnerability. The final expression may be a function of gender-specific mechanisms (the effect of androgens on the developing brain) or "the presence of comorbid conditions such as attention deficit disorder, migraine, asthma and a host of pre- and postnatal environmental events" (Leckman, Riddle, & Cohen, 1988, p. 111), such as stress and the effects of exposure to pharmacological agents.

NATURAL HISTORY

In reviewing 11 studies encompassing a total of 2,463 patients with Tourette's syndrome, drawn from varied geographic areas, Bruun (1988) found the mean age of onset to be 7 years, 2 months, with a range of 5 years, 8 months to 9 years, 4 months. DMS-III criteria include the ages from 2 to 15 years as age of onset. In a sample of 350 patients drawn from her private practice and from clinics at two large hospitals in New York City, Bruun found that 53% of the patients described an eye tic as their first symptom, either eye blinking or rolling of the eyes; 13% had facial tics, such as grimacing, nose twitching, licking, or biting the lips, as their first symptom, while another 13% had vocalizations, such as (sniffling, throat clearing, coughing, or grunting, as the first symptom. Others described a cephalo-caudal progression of tics (Jagger et al., 1982)).

Robert, described earlier in this chapter, demonstrated an onset and a progression that is being seen with increasing frequency. The onset of tics in Robert's case was preceded by hyperactivity and attentional problems. He is described as having been hyperactive since he could walk, and by age 5 a diagnosis of hyperactivity was made. Methylphenidate was prescribed. Eye blinking and gross choreoform movement of the arms started within two years, at age 7. From that time, even though methylphenidate was discontinued, the progression included more complex truncal tics, including head shaking and shrugging of the shoulders, together with a myriad of vocal tics, such as coprolalia, and complex motor activity in the nature of compulsive grasping with sexual overtones. The progression appeared to be: hyperactivity, to simple motor tics, to complex motor tics, to vocalizations (first simple then complex), to compulsions.

The progression of the disorder, however, is not invariant; symptoms may be static for a long period of time, and characteristically, symptoms may "wax and wane," with spontaneous remissions ranging from 6 months to 3 years. During early adolescence symptoms may appear worse; this is the time when coprolalia may be first manifested (A. Shapiro, Shapiro, Bruun, & Sweet, 1978) and when symptoms change in nature more rapidly (Bruun, 1988). In late adolescence, however, there appears to be a spontaneous trend toward lessening of symptoms (Lucas, 1979). Erenberg, Cruse, Rothner, and Rothner (1987) found that of 58 patients between the ages of 15 and 25 years, 73% reported by questionnaire that tics were diminished or mostly gone as they reached late adolescence or early adulthood. This trend was reported by others. A. Shapiro (1985) found 25% of his adolescent patients to "improve markedly." Bruun (1988) followed 136 patients for 5 to 15 years. Of the 130 of these patients who were treated with medication, 37 of them (all over 18 years of age), were no longer on medication at the time of follow-up. There was also a tendency for the symptoms to become less severe as patients reached early adulthood.

An epidemiological survey in North Dakota, using cases previously identified for calculating prevalence rates, found a prevalence rate of 9.3 per 10,000 for boys and 1.0 per 10,000 for girls under 18 years of age. The rate for adults, however, was 0.77 per 10,000 for men and 0.22 for women. Projecting these figures from the population of the United States in 1980, it was estimated that there were approximately 6,000 men and 2,000 women, 30,000 boys and 3,000 girls, with Tourette's syndrome in 1986. These data support the findings of decreased prevalence of Tourette's syndrome in adults (Burd, Kerbesian, Wikenheiser, & Fisher, 1986). The absolute projections of the prevalence of Tourette's syndrome in this survey may have to be modified in the light of an apparent dramatic increase in the incidence of the syndrome in the past 10 years.

This progression raises the question of whether hyperactivity is an early manifestation of Tourette's syndrome, an inevitable part, for some children, of the natural history in the development of the syndrome? Or is the stimulant drug given for hyperactivity somehow involved in evoking the syndrome in a child already genetically vulnerable to the syndrome? Indeed, can the stimulant drug *cause* Tourette's syndrome in previously unsusceptible individuals? Would Robert have developed full-blown Tourette's syndrome if he had not had methylphenidate? The evidence for answering these questions is mixed. In 1984 Golden described a 9-year-old boy who developed Tourette's syndrome after administration of methylphenidate for the treatment of hyperactivity. This report was followed by a number of similar reports in which tic disorders rapidly appeared after initiation of stimulant drugs, or in which tics, already established, were exacerbated when stimulants were used. Pollack, Cohen, and Friedhoff (1977) in the very title of their paper impute the "precipitation" of Tourette's syndrome "by methylphenidate therapy." In 100 patients with Tourette's syndrome evaluated at Yale University's child psychiatry and neurology clinics, Lowe et al. (1982) described 15 children, 3 to 10 years of age, who developed Tourette's syndrome following administration of stimulant medication for hyperactivity. Symptoms of Tourette's syndrome appeared at variable times after beginning stimulant medication, from several months to 2½ years. Lowe and his associates concluded that "motor tics or diagnosed Tourette's syndrome in a child should be a contraindication to the use of stimulant medication for alleviation of hyperactive symptoms; the existence of motor tic symptoms or diagnosed Tourette's syndrome in the parents, siblings or other family members of the index patient should be viewed as a relative contraindication to stimulant therapy" (p. 1731). Golden (1988) agreed with these conclusions and added that even in the absence of tics and no family history of tic disorder, the appearance of tics after stimulant medication has been given calls for immediate discontinuation of the stimulant drug.

Denckla et al. (1976) reported the development of motor tics in 1.3% of children receiving methylphenidate for attention deficit disorder. Upon discontinuing the medication, tics subsided in all but one child out of the 1,520 children with ADD who were reviewed. However, if the children being treated for hyperactivity and attention deficit disorder had tics before the use of stimulants, 13.3% suffered exacerbation of the tics when receiving methylphenidate. Thus the incidence of full-blown Tourette's syndrome emerging in children who receive stimulant medication for ADHD does not appear to be high. Nevertheless, the huge number of children receiving stimulant medication for ADHD, conservatively estimated at 6% of the estimated 40 million schoolchildren in the United States, or approximately 2.4 million children receiving stimulation medication, and the devastating effect on the individual child who does develop Tourette's syndrome while using stimulant drugs, make this a problem of importance and caution for clinicians. Furthermore, the number of children with Tourette's syndrome who have been treated with stimulant drugs appears to be increasing. Price, Leckman, Pauls, Cohen, and Kidd (1986), for example, found that of 170 patients with Tourette's syndrome, 34 had been treated with stimulant drugs. In our own group of 90 children with persistent motor and vocal tics, 30 of them (one-third) had received methylphenidate or pemoline for hyperactivity and attention problems before the onset of motor and vocal tics.

A differing opinion is expressed by A. Shapiro and E. Shapiro (1988) and by Comings and Comings (1984, 1988). The Shapiros (1988) categorically stated that "in our opinion there is inadequate evidence that stimulants precipitate or permanently exacerbate Tourette syndrome" (p. 277). Comings and Comings (1984), comparing children with attention deficit disorder who subsequently developed motor and vocal tics, found that those who received stimulants had a significantly *longer* time interval between the onset of hyperactivity and the onset of tics than did those who did not receive stimulants. The Comings reasoned that if stimulants are significant in causing Tourette's syndrome or in precipitating tics, then the time interval between onset of ADHD to the onset of tics should be *decreased* in children with ADHD who receive stimulants as compared with the onset of tics in ADHD children who do not receive stimulants. In two successive studies, each involving 250 patients, they found no evidence that stimulant drugs hastened the time of onset of tics and vocalizations. Indeed, the time interval was actually *greater* in the children receiving stimulant drugs. Comings and Comings feel that ADHD is an integral part of the symptom complex of Tourette's syndrome and that the natural history of the majority of Tourette's syndrome cases is to begin as ADHD and then, after an average interval of 2–3 years, to develop tics and vocal noises. In their review of nine studies encompassing over 1,500 patients with Tourette's syndrome, Comings and Comings found that, on the average, approximately one-half of all Tourette's syndrome patients also suffered from ADHD. Further, the more severe the symptoms of Tourette's syndrome, the greater the number of such patients having symptoms of ADHD, with a prevalence of 70–80% of ADHD in the most severe group of Tourette's syndrome patients and approximately one-third of the very mild cases having symptoms of ADHD. The Comings suggested that ADHD may be the first—indeed, the only— manifestation of the putative Tourette's syndrome gene. The findings of Price et al. (1986) also suggest that stimulant medication may not substantially increase the risk for developing Tourette's syndrome. In their study with six pairs of identical twins with ADHD, only one twin of each pair received stimulant drugs, yet both twins developed tics. These twin findings suggest that there may be a genetic vulnerability to Tourette's symptoms in children who develop the syndrome after using stimulant drugs.

The use of stimulant drugs in the *course of Tourette's syndrome* is also controversial. Although they recognize that pemoline, methylphenidate, and dextroamphetamine can exacerbate tics, A. Shapiro and Shapiro (1988) stated that "the increase in tics is short-lived and the potential benefits of stimulants [in reducing symptoms of hyperactivity and attention deficit and in managing the lethargy, dysphoria, and impaired cognition of neuroleptics] often outweigh their disadvantages" (p. 277) and that "stimulants and butyrophenone have overlapping and different effects on tics" (p. 277). Comings, treating 92 patients with Tourette's syndrome with stimulant drugs, stated that in only 7 of these patients were stimulants discontinued because tics could not be alleviated with haloperidol or pimozide. Comings

(1988) said that "judicious use of stimulants, kept at the lowest effective dose, can contribute significantly to overall treatment" (p. 127).

A compromise solution is suggested by some clinicians. Where in the course of Tourette's syndrome, attentional and hyperactivity factors cannot be controlled by environmental intervention or by drugs other than stimulants, clonidine or one of the tricyclic antidepressants such as imipramine or desipramine are used. These drugs have been reported as effective in ADHD, particularly in adolescents, (Gastfriend, Biederman, & Jellinek, 1985; Rapoport et al., 1985)

EMOTIONAL FACTORS

Tourette's syndrome, however, involves more than motor and phonic tics and bizarre compulsive behavior. It affects the feelings and emotional reaction of the child with the disorder both directly and indirectly: directly by the psychological defenses he must build to defend against the frustration of failed impulse control and the vulnerability to anxiety; indirectly by his reactions to the way his family, peers, and teachers respond to his symptoms.

Tourette's syndrome is characterized by an impulse to action. The action is largely involuntary, but the impulse to the action is preceded by an awareness that the particular action will occur, a conscious sensation of specific tension building up within oneself. Bliss (1980) described the feeling as "a compelling though subtle and fleeting itch, the moments before a sneeze explodes, the tantalizing touch of a feather" (p. 1344). Bliss (1980) continues: "Each movement is the result of a . . . capitulation to a demanding and restless urge" (p. 1345).One child in our sample (A. A. Silver, 1988) said "I can feel it when I have to say these [bad] words. They keep coming into my mind. I say them to myself over and over again. I try to stop it, but it has to come out." Even at age 5 the struggle between the impulse to action and the action may be seen. Laura, a verbal, bright, 5-year-old, had a grunting vocalization accompanied by spitting. She said "I know I'm spitting but I can't help it. I think about it and I do it." Brian, aged 10½, had a compulsion to tap his pencil on his mathematics paper. This is done in patterns of three, and is sometimes accompanied by stamping his foot on the floor. He said, "I know it's coming. I can feel it in my hand. It is urging me to put a dot there." Clarence, aged 16, was referred to our clinic because he was disruptive in class. He said, "Tourette's disease just maddens me. Sometimes I would like to holler out loud. I try to hold myself back, but it comes out." The discharge of tension into motor action may for a time be held back by the child, but it invariably escapes voluntary control. For a time this discharge may relieve the tension, only to have it build again. Thus the feelings preceding action may involve not only repetition of words, but also the mental representation of motor pattern. These are attempts at control over the action, but it finally escapes into involuntary behavior. Practically, this struggle is seen in school as the child attempts to conform to the teacher's instructions. The short periods of quiet the child manages to sustain are broken by a sudden dystonic movement or vocalization.

Important as the actual impulsive movement or vocalization is in affecting acceptance by peers, teachers, and even parents, the inability to control his or her thoughts and impulses is equally important to the child's own ego. Charles, aged 9, put it succinctly: "I do not have mind over matter." Two types of response, frequently blurred together in the same child, may appear. In the first, the impulse and the action are projected onto some sinister force that is controlling the child. William, aged 15, said, "It is an affliction of Satan who is trying to take over my life, telling me to do these things." William looks in the mirror and sometimes he sees not his own image but Satan looking back at him. "I looked red and I had a knife. I thought Satan was going to stab me." When Kenny, aged 11, looked in the mirror he sometimes thought that his image was really someone else forcing him to think and say the things he considers bad. Robert, age 10, was afraid that "an insane guy" will come into his house. He said, "I convince myself that if I hide under the blanket with my dog. I can't be shot by some insane guy." (As he told of this fear, Robert stopped and said he sometimes does crazy things that he cannot help doing and that he is afraid of the crazy thoughts he has. He was able to identify with the "insane guy" whom he fears.) The projections of Patsy, aged 12, have become hallucinations of "some evil person telling me to make these faces" (her facial tics).

At the other extreme are children whose impulses are egosyntonic. They blame themselves for the behavior they cannot control. The explosive outburst, the tic, becomes a part of themselves and they are in consistent conflict over the "bad" or evil things, the uncontrolled things they do, and the good things the world expects them to do. Guilt and its consequence, depression, arise from the conflict. Kenny, aged 11, talked to God "a lot." He said, "I pray to be forgiven for all the bad things I do, especially when I curse my mother." He constantly needed God's assurance that he will be forgiven. Michael, aged 13, fought a constant battle between good and evil, between God, who tells him what to do and what not to do, and the devil, who argues with God, telling Michael to steal.

Andy, aged 17, felt his thoughts were so bad that he was afraid to say anything or bad thoughts will emerge. He sat rigidly in the chair, struggling to talk, wanting very much to communicate, yet only capable of looking to the examiner for understanding. Andy's paralyzing obsessions were preceded by a hypomanic episode that lasted for about 6 months, characterized by denial of his gross peri-oral tics, occasional sniffing sounds, and choreoform movements of the arms and shoulders. The denial was abetted by his mother, who refused to accept the diagnosis.

Even when the child has adapted an outgoing, friendly, and apparently relaxed adjustment, the undercurrent of self-blame and depression may be seen. Jennifer, aged 17, was a physically mature lady whose Tourette's syndrome manifested itself in an occasional explosive echolalic repetition of her own affect-charged verbal responses and in an occasional jerky movement of her head. Her outgoing demeanor changed, however, when she said how bad she was or when, in spite of her efforts to prevent it, an explosive, expletive outburst was directed at her mother. Jennifer also has been placed in a class for physically handicapped children, where she says she belongs and is most comfortable.

The lack of balance between impulse and restraint, the difficulty in control of motor tics and vocalization, the constant battle between good and evil, the undercurrent of guilt and depression all evoke additional problems that make socialization difficult. All of the children seen by us were driven by anxiety. The cause of the anxiety, however, may not be clear. Just as the obsessions and compulsions may be multidetermined, the anxiety in these children may also be multidetermined. Anxiety may indeed spring from the conflicts created by the specific consequences of poor impulse control, the guilt, and the depression. In addition, however, the very biological substrate of Tourette's disease may predispose to anxiety, attenuating the stimulus barrier so that it is inadequate to deal with forces from within the organism or with those impinging on it. Physiological as well as psychological homeostasis is precariously balanced, and the child becomes a labile organism, quick to react to any stimulus viewed as threatening, and demanding immediate, sometimes irrational, gratification of needs as he or she perceives them. When these needs cannot be met, as sooner or later they cannot be, the child easily erupts into a tantrum. Robert, age 11, was such a child, tyrannizing his parents, who tried to give in to his every whim. Robert has become a tyrant, controlling his parents and trying to get everyone else in the world to do just as he wishes.

This anxiety may emerge as specific fear. How this occurs may be seen in Kenneth, aged 11. He was afraid to be in his room alone, afraid of ghosts and burglars, so afraid that he had a knife and access to his father's gun. He had terrifying dreams of being attacked and overwhelmed. He dreamed he was "in a trailer or a house, and a big thing came through the door, a wolf. I gave him something to eat but he attacked me"; and "I was living in a trailer on the beach. A big storm came and pushed me into the water." His anxiety, as well as possible ambivalence toward his mother, is seen in another dream: "Some person came and hit my mother and threw her down. They slapped her in the face. I shot this guy, but plenty others kept coming." These dreams were most disturbing to Kenny, especially since he continued to think the dreams would come true.

While the resurgence of anxiety and the emergence of unresolved developmental issues are not unusual in early adolescence, in Kenneth and other children we have seen, symptoms of anxiety are often severe enough to be considered an anxiety disorder. All have difficulty falling asleep and all have similar dreams. Robert, aged 9, said, "I just can't fall asleep. I just sit there and look at the moon." He dreams, "A monster is about to eat me. I took a sword and stabbed him in the side but he ran after me." Charles, a bright 10-year-old said, "I have a wooden sword. If a monster came in, I would cut him in half." Patsy, aged 12, said, "I'm afraid of being in a room by myself. A killer could bust my window with a rock." She described a dream: "White puppy dogs are biting me. I eat them for dinner." Robert, aged 14, heard "noises in the ceiling." This dream evoked panic. All children we have seen attempt to protect themselves by bedtime rituals, such as checking doors, windows, closets, and under the bed, as 13-year-old James felt compelled to do for 15 minutes at a time. James was so afraid of burglars coming into his room that he slept in the linen chest at the foot of his mother's bed.

Compulsions, of course, cannot defend against the recurring anxiety, the feelings of being overwhelmed and hurt. Illusions of a face coming out of the closet or a person emerging from clothing or from the shadows of furniture are not infrequent. Thus their anxiety alone tends to make these children prisoners of themselves: They are afraid to sleep overnight with other children and many resist any change in their own routines. According to some of them (Robert D., age 9; Robert A., age 10; Kenny, age 11; James, age 13; Michael, age 13; William, age 15; Clarence, age 17), their main problem is that they cannot get to sleep. As a result, they ask, how can they be expected to wake up in time for school? This becomes an excuse for refusing to go to school. It also becomes a focal point of tension between mothers and children as they try with increasing frustration to get them out of bed and on the school bus.

Depression is also seen in their low opinion of themselves. They are generally pessimistic about their future. Michael, who earned a full scale IQ of 109 on the WISC-R, feels that his brain is worthless and all he can ever hope to become is a garbage man. Kenneth feels he is ugly and other kids hate him. He has many somatic complaints: headaches and chest pain, "like a sword going through me." Robert says, "If my Tourette's gets worse, I would do something [to myself]." Clarence is concerned about what his disease "will do to my brain in the future." Charles says, "Why do I have to be me? Why is my soul put in this body? Sometimes I think I must be reincarnated."

Tourette's syndrome is more than its behavior manifestations in motor and phonic tics and dystonias. It has a profound effect on patients' thoughts, affects, and attitudes, the way they look at life and themselves, their successes and failures. The basic problem with impulses leads to conscious struggles at control, with obsessive conscious, mental images of the emerging vocalizations or motor acts (D. J. Cohen, 1980; D. J. Cohen, Detlor, Shaywitz, & Leckman, 1982). When tension must be released, there is a feeling of being overwhelmed. The unacceptable thinking and behavior evoke guilt. There are constant battles between the good and acceptable and the bad and unacceptable. Depression and anxiety may be by-products of these ceaseless conflicts, or they may result from the biological substrate, the pathophysiology of Tourette's syndrome, which attenuates the stimulus barrier. Anxiety is seen by day in refusal to go to school, in resistance to change, in extreme rigidity, and in infantile demands and by night in sleep disturbance, in the inability to fall asleep, and, when finally asleep, in the agony of dreams of being attacked and overwhelmed. The stimulus barrier is attenuated, and impulses and drives that normally are more or less mastered erupt in Tourette's syndrome virtually undisguised, adding again to guilt and furthering anxiety. Their self-image is low, and many fear deterioration of their brain. This psychiatric profile may be found, in spite of the heterogeneous nature of the overt clinical manifestations. In addition, most suffer from perceptual problems with consequent difficulty in time-limited, written assignments at school. Similar frustrations are also encountered as these children strive to complete assignments at home.

SCHOOL PROBLEMS

The case vignette of Robert also illustrates an additional problem of the child with Tourette's syndrome—namely, problems in school adjustment and academic achievement. There is by now general agreement that problems in learning constitute a significant problem for children with Tourette's syndrome. Comings and Comings (1988), for example, reported that compared with their control sample, children with Tourette's syndrome are placed in special classes in significantly greater numbers and require greater special tutoring; using their own criteria, "dyslexia"was found in 26.8% of Tourette's patients compared to 4.2% in their control sample. Lerer (1987) reported that "one half of the children with Tourette syndrome have specific learning disabilities, perceptual motor problems, attention deficit disorders, hyperactive behavior and abnormalities of psycho-educational testing." Hagin and Kugler (1988) found that 68% of their sample of 16 children with Tourette's syndrome earned scores below their expectancy in *group* tests of reading, 52% below expectancy in tests of spelling, and 56% below expectancy in mathematics. *Individual* tests of oral reading and *individual* tests of reading comprehension, however, were in the expected range. In an early study, Lucas, Kauffman, and Morris (1967) found "learning disorders" in 9 of 15 children with Tourette's syndrome.

One problem in evaluating these diverse reports is the perennial one of understanding just what authors mean when they use the term "dyslexia," "specific learning disabilities," and "learning disorders." Perhaps more specific questions should be raised: Is there a unique pattern in the academic difficulty and in the patterns of neuropsychological dysfunction characteristic of Tourette's syndrome? Using carefully defined criteria, is the prevalence of specific learning disability greater in Tourette's syndrome than in the "normal" population or in a group of unselected referrals to a child psychiatric clinic?

Despite the small samples of children with Tourette's syndrome who have received careful neuropsychological and psychoeducational examinations, some data are accumulating to answer these questions. There does appear to be a number of academic and cognitive deficits that occur more frequently in children with Tourette's syndrome than in samples of control children.

1. The scores on the *Coding subtest of the WISC-R* fall significantly below the individual's mean scaled scores. In the Hagin and Kugler (1988) study of 26 children with Tourette's syndrome, 40% of the children had Coding subtest scores significantly below their mean scaled scores. Ten of these children, the subjects of an earlier report (Hagin, Beecher, Pagano, & Kreeger, 1982), were recruited from the Tourette Association to identify educational practices. The remaining 16 came as patients to the School Consultation Center at Fordham University, with diverse complaints relating to school placement, academic achievement, and behavioral adjustment. The age of the entire group ranged from 7 years to young adulthood. On the WISC-R, their mean full scale IQ was 104, ± 16 with a mean verbal IQ of 106 ± 18 and a mean performance IQ of 102 ± 15. Thirty-five percent of the group had significantly higher verbal scores and 12% significantly higher performance scores. However, although 36% of the group demonstrated an increased degree of scatter in the subtest scores, no "typical" pattern of subtest scores, with the exception of the Coding subtest, was found. The Coding subtest measures speed and accuracy in associating visual symbols, using a written response. This may reflect a visual-motor-praxic problem. Coding was also the lowest subtest score found by Thompson (1978) in four children with Tourette's syndrome and by Incagnoli and Kane (1982) in 13 children with Tourette's syndrome. Harcherik, Carronara, Shaywitz, Shaywitz, and Cohen (1982) also found Coding (digit symbol B) along with handwriting and with difficulty adapting to changes in speed of the road tracking task, to be the major cognitive deviation from normal in a well-studied sample of 15 children, aged 7 to 15, with Tourette's syndrome.

2. Most studies of neuropsychological function of children with Tourette's syndrome found impairment in *visual-motor function* particularly as seen on the Bender VMGT (Hagin, Beecher, Pagano, & Kreeger, 1982; Incagnoli & Kane, 1982). In a study of 25 consecutive admissions of children with Tourette's syndrome to the Child Study Center at the University of South Florida Medical School, A. A. Silver (1988) found 21 of them to have significant difficulty with visual-motor function. The age of these children ranged from 5 to 17 years; 20 of them earned a full scale IQ on the

WISC-R within the normal range, 2 were borderline, and 3 were in the bright–normal range. The type of visual-motor impairment varied, however, with the majority demonstrating immature gestalt patterns with the persistence of verticalization and angulation. Three records showed perseveration, which took their repetitive dots (Figure 15-3) across the page and onto

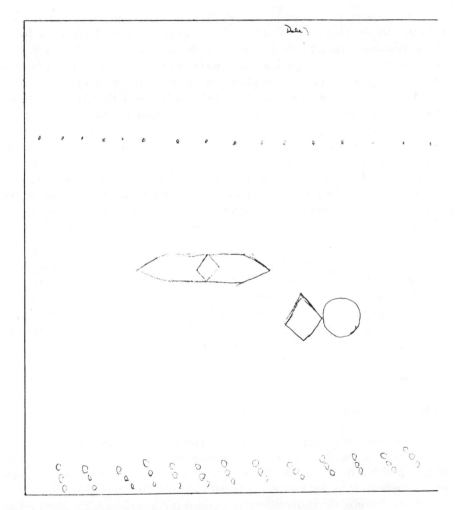

Figure 15-3   Bender Gestalt Drawing
Dale: Age 16 years, 8 months
Receiving 3 mg of haloperidol daily. Tics are well-controlled, but aggressive outbursts have been disturbing. This drawing illustrates perseveration. His gestalt Figure 1 is drawn across the page and continues on to the tabletop. Each line of Figure A and Figure 8 had to be redrawn repeatedly.

the desk; in two children a compulsive pattern—ritualistic counting or tapping—prevented accurate representation of the designs; and in two children the tics presented a jerky, uncoordinated written pattern. The immaturity of the Bender VMGT did not appear to be a visual perceptual one, because the errors were recognized. Rather, it appeared to be a praxic one, with the child's inability to make his fingers do what his eyes conveyed to his brain.

3. In academic achievement, *mathematics* appears to suffer most, although in the Hagin and Kugler (1988) study using the Woodcock-Johnson Psychoeducational Battery, as noted above, 52% scored below expectancy in tests of written spelling, 56% were below expectancy in mathematics, and 68% were below expectancy in group tests of reading. Golden (1984), Incagnoli and Kane (1982), and Joschko and Rourke (1982) also found low arithmetic scores in their patients. Hagin and Kugler (1988) felt that problems in test format itself accounted for the poor performance on *group* tests of reading comprehension. It is the sustained effort over an extended period of time that causes the children with Tourette's syndrome difficulty on that test, not the word attack skills which these children, as a group, do have. The poor spelling and arithmetic result may be due to the basic motor problems of Tourette's children, which result in slow, inconvenient, and poor handwriting, as well as to their praxic difficulty.

4. The presence of *attention deficit hyperactivity symptoms* may be significant in the achievement of Tourette's children. In their study Comings and Comings (1988) found "poor retention" in 41% of their 246 Tourette's sample, as contrasted with 8.3% among a control group. The presence of ADD may be a crucial factor in this finding since the distribution of reading scores in Tourette's syndrome *without ADD* was not significantly different from that found in controls, whereas the distribution of scores of Tourette's children *with ADD* was significantly impaired as compared to controls. Comings and Comings used as their criteria for "dyslexia" the presence of three or more reading problems (letter, number, or word reversals; drops words; reads slowly and has poor retention).

In summary, what appears to characterize most children with Tourette's syndrome is difficulty with Coding, visual-motor-praxic function, mathematics, and handwriting. All of these deficits may be an outcome of visual-praxic immaturities. In a subset, attentional problems may be significant.

The symptoms of Tourette's syndrome may interfere with learning in ways other than by the cognitive effects of that condition. Such symptoms include:

- the tics themselves—the motor tics that make written work uncontrolled, jerky, and sloppy and that make handwriting a physically difficult chore; the vocal tics that accentuate the Tourette's child's difference from other children and call attention to her difference

- the tendency toward restlessness, impulsivity, and hyperactive behavior
- obsessive thinking, which does not permit the child to move freely from one task to another
- compulsive behavior, which traps him into a ritual such as tapping and touching and which keeps him from completing a task
- perseverative behaviors, which may be akin to compulsions or may be one way lack of impulse control is manifested
- increased anxiety, which may be reflected generally in poor sleep habits, morning fatigue, difficulty getting to school, and, finally, refusal to go to school
- the social consequences of these symptoms—teasing of classmates and demands of teachers and schools
- the emotional consequences—poor self-esteem, guilt, and depression
- finally, medication used to treat the symptoms may itself contribute to decreased alertness, sleepiness, and perhaps depression and school phobia.

Thus the cognitive deficits are only one part of the many factors in Tourette's syndrome that interfere with learning. That studies report more than half of their sample of Tourette's children have *some* problems in learning attest to their importance.

It will be noted however that *specific language disability* is not included in the symptoms affecting learning as we have listed them. While it is undoubtedly true that a few children with Tourette's syndrome are suffering from a specific learning disability, as does Robert, the subject of our case vignette, it is questionable whether the prevalence of specific learning disability in Tourette's children is greater than that in the normal population. To date there has been no study, using the generally accepted criteria for specific language disability, to prove that the prevalence of SLD in Tourette's children is greater than that in the normal, unselected school population or even in children diagnosed with other emotional and/or behavioral problems.

The identification of specific language disability in children with Tourette's syndrome is important not only for management of the individual child but also for research studies. SLD and Tourette's syndrome both have a high family incidence (see Chapter 11 for genetic studies of SLD). The genetic mode of transmission for each, however, is not clear. If there is indeed a higher prevalence of SLD in children with Tourette's syndrome than in an unselected sample of their normal classmates, what is the relationship between the two? Is SLD one manifestation of Tourette's syndrome governed by the same genetic fault(s)? Are we dealing with two separate syndromes, which are synergistic? Is there a genetic linkage between the two disorders? These questions are as yet unanswered.

Nevertheless, the recognition of a specific language disorder in a given child with Tourette's syndrome is vital to his or her adjustment. In Robert the SLD was recognized, but it was not treated to the point of mastery and the contributions of his Tourette's syndrome to learning problems was not appreciated. Thus the paper tests he took indicated that he could adjust in the mainstream. The Tourette's symptoms said he could not. As part of the management of his school problems, Robert was returned to the SLD class, to the teacher who was familiar to him and, most important, who understood him. Just as any child with a severe specific language disability, the child with Tourette's syndrome who also has a specific language disability also needs treatment for that disability. We cannot rely on spontaneous maturation to improve perceptual deficits, as the case of Armando shows.

CASE STUDY: ARMANDO

Armando, for example, was 9 years, 9 months of age when he was first seen. In addition to motor and vocal tics, he did not seem to understand verbal questions or verbal directions unless they were presented to him slowly, simply, and even repetitiously. His overall cognitive ability was above average, with no significant discrepancy between verbal and performance scores; his neurological examination was normal, but he had severe perceptual difficulty in temporal sequencing, confusing events in time and being unable to place verbal meaning in proper sequences. He also had severe visual-motor problems characterized by 90-degree rotations on the Bender VMGT. Our findings were conveyed to his school. We did not see Armando for 3 years. Now he is in sixth grade, reading at about the third-grade level. Over the years he had no special help in school, and spontaneous maturation of his skills did not occur (Figure 15-4).

In contrast to the specific language disability Robert and Armando demonstrated, Sam had skills in place but was unable to demonstrate what he knew in the classroom. His were problems inherent in Tourette's syndrome itself.

CASE STUDY: SAM

Sam was referred for an assessment of the educational factors in his troubles at school by the psychiatrist who was treating him. Sam's tics were mild (blinking, shoulder shrugging, and throat clearing), and it was felt that at this point psycho-

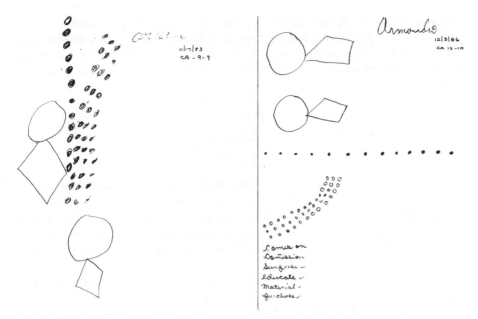

Figure 15-4   Bender Gestalt Drawing
Armando: Age 9 years, 9 months and 12 years, 10 months
Tourette's symptoms mild; not receiving medication; cognitive function high normal;
severe temporal sequencing deficit. Educational remediation was advised but not done.
The primitive features of his gestalt drawing at age 9 years, 9 months are still apparent
3 years later.

first-grader, he arrived clutching a sheaf of dittoed worksheets, most of them incomplete. Early in the session, he became apprehensive about the whereabouts of his mother who was providing a developmental history in a nearby office. When both office doors were opened partially and he was told he could check on her as often as he wanted to, he settled down for the morning's work. He complained bitterly about the work the teacher expected him to accomplish, the notes on his behavior she insisted he take home, and the punishment for noncompletion of his seatwork—the loss of his recreation period or gym class. He asked plaintively, "What do I do if I get tired?"

Psychological study showed Sam to be a bright youngster earning a verbal IQ of 112 (79th percentile) and a performance IQ of 101 (53rd percentile) on the WISC-R. The full scale IQ of 107 was essentially an average of the disparate kinds of functions tapped by the two scales and was in Sam's case not very useful in educational planning. Sam's high score on the Vocabulary subtest reflected his good verbal ability and the wide range of experiences he had had. He used language therapy with Sam and supportive counseling for the parents would be sufficient intervention, without the use of medication. A well-built, red-headed, 7-year-old precisely, often calling on language cues to help himself with nonverbal performance tasks he found difficult. For example, on the Coding subtest he named the different symbols as he located and copied them. It is questionable how much these cues helped, for the Coding subtest was a significantly low scaled score for him. Analyzed according to the factorial structure of the WISC-R, Sam's record appears as follows:

Verbal Comprehension Items	84th %ile
Perceptual Integrative Items	66th %ile
Sequencing and Memory Items	22nd %ile

Sam seemed comfortable at the Center, chatting along about related matters as we completed the test items. There were signs of self-doubts. He found the Arithmetic subtest difficult, but emphasized how much fun it was, as if he was trying to reassure himself. He also wondered aloud several times if his mother "missed" him. When encouraged to go to the office where she was being interviewed, he did so and quickly returned to his work.

In view of the level of functioning seen on the WISC-R, Sam's educational expectancy was estimated to be at the high second-grade level or the 80th to 90th percentile range. When this estimate was compared to his achievement test scores, it was apparent that he was reading appropriately to expectancy. His oral reading was rapid and accurate, placing at grade 4.1, the 96th percentile on the WRAT. That reading was already a tool was seen in his score of grade 3.3 (93rd percentile) on the Comprehension section of the PIAT. He had a good stock of sight words and made good use of contextual cues. Even his errors were intelligent (i. e., the word *pigeons* read as "penguins").

Handwriting was difficult for him. He worked hard to form legible letters, but had great difficulty with organization and spacing. He could spell a few words and write simple sentences. Arithmetic was the hardest skill of all for him, but he was able to handle items dealing with numeration, quantity, and simple addition and subtraction combinations.

The work samples that he had brought from school were much simpler than many of the test items he handled easily in our session. The school seatwork involved such activities as coloring tiny sections of a mosaic-like picture, connecting numbered dots to form a picture, cutting out and pasting words under pictures, and copying text from the chalkboard. It not only did not tap any of the high-level reading skills he showed on tests, but the coloring, writing, cutting, and pasting required fine motor control that Sam just could not manage for any sustained period of time. That Sam's teacher did not appreciate this was apparent from her written comments on some of the pages: "Good, but try to stay in the boxes!" "Why didn't you finish?"

Sam's drawings of the figures of the Bender VMGT are convincing evidence of his difficulties in organization of gestalten, immature verticalization of diagonals, and substitution of simpler figures for more complex ones (Figure 15-5A). On the Purdue Pegboard he had difficulty synchronizing his hands on the bimanual task, and

SAm:
Plate A

Figure 15-5   Bender Gestalt Drawings
(A) Sam: Age 7 years, in first grade, evaluating difficulties in organization with impulsive, primitive qualities. At this time in his life Sam was under great stress in school.

the score for either hand separately fell below the 20th percentile for his age group Right–left discrimination was borderline, accurate on himself and on the examiner but with errors with crossed commands. Symmetrization errors occurred on the finger schema test. Other than these problems in fine motor control and body image, there was little of note on the supplementary tests.

Sam was learning fairly well at school, despite his worries about being called "chicken nose" when his tics appeared in class, his almost phobic concern about fatigue, his dependence on his mother, and the signs of compulsive behavior that were beginning to appear. It was apparent also that his teacher understood neither his strengths nor his deficits, although Sam had been in her classroom for nearly 8 months. Attempts were made to reason with her about Sam's behavior, but these

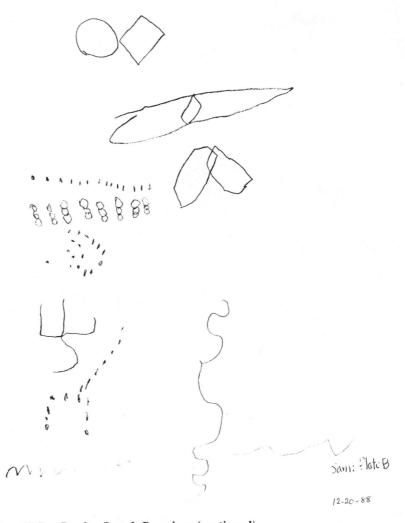

Sam: Plate B

12-20-88

Figure 15-5   Bender Gestalt Drawings (continued)
(B) Sam: Age 8 years, after a year of decreased school demands. The gestalt is improved in organization with decreased impulsivity and fewer primitive elements.

telephone calls deteriorated into a recital of Sam's misdeeds. Sam's test results and general materials about Tourette's syndrome were shared with the school psychologist who promised to work with Sam's teacher on his problems, but she was unable to effect any change in the teacher's management of the boy.

Discouraged as they witnessed the effects of this classroom on Sam's emotional state and disheartened when he was scheduled for placement in a self-contained special class with mixed diagnostic categories for the succeeding year, his parents removed him from school. This decision was precipitated by the IEP, which listed the following as the complete long-term goals the next school year:

The student will
   improve number and numeration skills
   improve operations with whole numbers
The student will
   increase responsiveness and appreciation of classroom structure
   increase the ability to function independently in the classroom
   reduce the incidence of physically disruptive behavior with peers
   improve responsiveness to teacher intervention
   increase awareness of personal thoughts and feelings
   reduce the incidence of disruptive peer interactions
   acquire basic social skills and sensitivities

This decision to remove the child from school was not one to be encouraged since it is in violation of the compulsory education laws, but it can be understood as the response of intelligent, caring, and completely frustrated parents.

Sam did not return to school during what would have been his second-grade year. Private tutoring was provided 5 to 6 hours per week; his parents supplemented this education by taking him on trips to museums and by giving him a membership in the Y that provided socialization in sports, swimming, and craft activities. The family also researched schools and moved to a more hospitable school district where he had been enrolled in the third grade for 4 months when he returned for a follow-up appointment. On retesting, his fine motor control had improved (Figure 15-5B) and his achievement appeared to show no ill effects:

Wide Range Achievement Test
   Oral Reading   grade 6.7
   Spelling   grade 3.7
   Arithmetic   grade 3.6
Peabody Individual Achievement Test
   Reading Comprehension   grade 6.5

Sam's account of his school day, in all its compulsive detail, also seemed to indicate that, at least at present, all was well:

First I unpack my bag and put my books in the desk. Then we pledge allegiance. Then Mrs. A helps me with math or things I don't understand. If I do good, I get a turn at the computer with Math Mansions or I watch some other kid at the computer. Then I go back to my room. I try to listen to what the other kids are doing. If it's interesting, I get involved. Or I read a book. (What do you like to read about?) Oh, lots of things, I'm interested in electricity, coal, Hawaii, rocks. Then we have reading groups, I'm in Stars. Then we get ready for lunch. I go home for lunch. I come back and finish my work. Then we have specials: library, gym, art. I like art best. (How are the other kids in this class?) Friendly—I have two friends, K————and M————. And the nurse, I'm allowed to go to the nurse if I feel tense or tired. (What do you do in her office?) I read this boring book.

Sam's account of his school day illustrates some of the management principles discussed earlier in this chapter. It shows how the classroom provides support as needed, balanced by a challenging level of work in the areas where he does well. While rigid conformity in behavior is not required, social awareness is fostered by the low-key tempo of the classroom. Finally, the nurse's office is available as a temporary refuge.

MANAGEMENT

Medication

While obtunding the symptoms of motor and phonic tics, available medication for Tourette's syndrome does not cure the disorder. Medication, however, is available if symptoms are particularly disturbing, impairing social, education, and/or vocational adjustment. No drug is entirely free of side effects; these—long-term toxicity of the drug, and the meaning of drug use to the child and to his family—must be considered in the decision to use medication as part of the overall management. Nonspecific placebo effects, spontaneous remission of symptoms, and changes in the environment to relieve stress must also be considered in the evaluation of drug effects. Thus the use of medication as part of the management for each child is not automatic but must be based on indications for each individual child, with dosage individually titrated to achieve maximum effectiveness with minimal adverse effects (A. Shapiro & Shapiro, 1988).

In general drugs that are potent *antagonists of the dopamine receptor site* (haloperidol and pimozide) decrease the motor and vocal tics, while those that increase dopamine neurotransmission by increasing the availability of dopamine (L-dopa, sinemet, methylphenidate, amphetamines, and bromocryptine) tend to exacerbate the Tourette's symptoms. Thus, alpha-methyl paratyrosine (an inhibitor of dopamine synthesis), tetrabenazine (which depletes brain stores of catacholamines), and apomorphine (which inhibits dopamine release from nigrostriatal nerve terminals) all tend to decrease tic frequency. Phenothiazines, which also block dopamine receptors, are not as effective as haloperidol or pimozide, primarily, it is theorized, because phenothiazines are more potent blockers of adenylate cylase–sensitive dopa-

mine receptors (D1) with only a weak affinity for the dopamine-2 (3H haloperidol) receptors, while haloperidol and pimozide are potent D2 receptor
blockers, with only weak affinity for D1 receptors. Initial trials of other relatively specific D2 receptor antagonists (sulpride, domperidone and meto-
clopramide) are ongoing (Uhr, Berger, Pruitt, & Stahl, 1985).

A. Shapiro et al. (1978) found that haloperidol improved motor and vocal
tics in 78–91% of 141 patients reported in 41 publications between 1961
and 1975; only 8 to 22% are said to have failed to improve. In a control
study A. Shapiro et al. reported that with an average dose of 5 mg/day of
haloperidol, 80% of his treated patients had decreased symptoms, compared
to 24% in the nonhaloperidol-treated control sample. Shapiro concluded
that 25% of patients have at least 70% reduction of symptoms at low dosage
without significant adverse side effects. Approximately 50% do develop
troublesome side effects to haloperidol, but these can be successfully managed. The remaining 25% are treatment failures. The anti-cholinergic ben-
zotropine mesylate is used routinely (0.5 mg at bedtime) by Shapiro. Haloperidol is increased by 0.25 mg every 5 days until symptoms significantly
decrease or troublesome side effects occur. The dose of haloperidol is
titrated to symptom relief and side effects and is monitored over time. In
Shapiro's hands the effective dose may vary from 2 to 10 mg/day and ultimately averages 5 mg/day.

Pimozide, a diphenylpiperidine, has more specific dopamine receptor–
blocking activity than haloperidol and is reported to have calcium channel-
blocking properties. Although it is as effective as haloperidol in reducing
Tourette's symptoms, pimozide is less sedative and less likely to produce
dystonic effects. In a double-blind, placebo-controlled, 33-day crossover
study of nine hospitalized Tourette's patients, 8 to 28 years of age (mean,
18 years, 7 months), pimozide in a maximum dose of 10–12 mg (given 2 mg
orally as an initial dose and increased 2 mg every other day for 12 days)
reduced motor and vocal tics in six (75%) of the patients (Ross & Moldofsky,
1978). Nomura and Segawa (1979) found that of 31 patients who had not
favorably responded to haloperidol, pimozide resulted in improvement in
90.3% of them. There is no report at this date of haloperidol in pimozide
nonresponders. A. Shapiro and Shapiro (1984) found pimozide to be effective in 80% of 20 patients compared to improvement in 10% of their placebo controls. In contrast to the relatively rapid increase in dose given in
the Ross and Moldofsky study, it is recommended (Moldofsky & Sandor,
1988) that because of the long half-life of pimozide, the drug should be
gradually increased by 1 or 2 mg every 10 days to a maximum dose of 7 to
16 mg/day. Side effects include nonspecific T wave changes and prolonga-
tion of the QT interval on the EKG. Thus a baseline EKG with follow-up
examinations are recommended. Both haloperidol and pimozide have neuroendocrine effects, decreasing the growth hormone and increasing
prolactin.

Because of the adverse side effects of haloperidol and pimozide, leading to noncompliance, or because of their ineffectiveness in some patients, Singer, Trifiletti, and Gammon (1988) recommended the piperazine phenothiazine, fluphenazine, as an alternative. With fluphenazine, a good or fair improvement of tic symptoms was found in 81% of 31 children as contrasted with a similar improvement of 83% in 60 patients receiving haloperidol. Side effects, however, accounted for withdrawal of medication in 19% of the fluphenazine group as contrasted to 33% of the haloperidol group. The mean maximum dose of fluphenazine was 5.1 mg/day. Similar results are reported by Borison, Ang, Hamilton, Diamond, and Davis (1983) and Goetz, Tanner, and Klawans (1989). Drugs more selective in their preferential blocking of D2 receptors in the mesolimbic system are under investigation (Uhr et al., 1985).

Clonidine hydrochloride, an imidazoline derivative used as an antihypertensive, is an alpha-adrenergic agonist that preferentially stimulates presynaptic alpha 2-adrenergic receptors, decreasing centrally medicated vasoconstriction of the peripheral circulation. It also inhibits spontaneous firing in the locus coeruleus, reduces brain norepinephrine turnover, inhibits ACTH and renin secretion, increases growth hormone secretion, stimulates central histamine H2 receptors (Leckman, Walkup, & Cohen, 1988), and is effective in reducing the symptoms of opiate withdrawal. The efficacy of clonidine in relieving Tourette's symptoms is still controversial. First used in Tourette's syndrome by Cohen and associates (Cohen, Detlor, Young, & Shaywitz, 1980; Cohen, Young, Nathanson, & Shaywitz, 1979), its effects, in the hands of the Yale group, are documented by Leckman et al. (1982). Given at a beginning dose of 0.05 mg/day, clonidine is slowly increased in 0.05 mg/day intervals over several weeks until a final dose ranges from 0.15 to 0.30 mg/day. Increasing the total dose may lead to increasing incidence of side effects, possibly because at the higher dose, the action of the drug shifts to increase postsynaptic alpha 1 activity. There is a long latency period of 8–12 weeks between the initiation of clonidine treatment and potential response, with maximum effects seen at even longer intervals, from 6 to 12 months. The Yale experience found a 30% decrease in symptoms during the first 8–12 weeks and a 50% or greater decrease in symptoms over 12 months. The symptom decrease is experienced by the patient as a sense of calm or a decrease in tension, often followed by a decrease in attentional behavioral symptoms and complex tics. Simple tics, said Leckman, Walkup, and Cohen (1988) seem less responsive. Borison et al. (1983) found clonidine to be as effective as haloperidol after a 9-week trial. On the other hand, Goetz et al. (1987) found no objective evidence for the reduction of motor or vocal tics after 12 weeks of clonidine. Side effects of clonidine are reported. Sedation in 10–20% of cases is dose related and may subside with time as tolerance is developed. Orthostatic hypotension, headache, irritability, lability of mood, and sleep difficulties can occur. Electrocardiographic changes (exacerbation of arrythmics) and decreased glucose tolerance require baseline data and monitoring. It is of interest to note that the behavioral symptoms of Tourette's syndrome (impulsivity, attention problems, and complex motor tics resembling compulsions) are said to be responsive to clonidine, whereas the motor and vocal tics appear more responsive to dopamine blockers. The reports of the effectiveness of clonidine on Tourette's syndrome have suggested noradrenergic mechanisms in the pathophysiology of Tourette's syndrome. This has yet to be delineated, since 3H yohimbine binding to alpha-2 receptors in platelets revealed no abnormalities among Tourette's syndrome patients (Silverstein, Smith, & Johnston, 1984); MHPG levels in CSF, plasma, and urine were not consistently different (Leckman et al., 1983); and propanolol was not not effective in reducing Tourette's tics (Sverd, Cohen & Camp, 1983).

Other drugs used in Tourette's syndrome include the following:

1. *Cholinergic.* Since the release of dopamine from the nigrostriatal pathway inhibits synthesis and release of acetylcholine from intrastriatal cholinergic neurons, a dopamine-acetylcholine imbalance was suggested. Stahl and Berger (1982) reported intravenous physostigmine (a cholinesterase inhibitor) to decrease tics in Tourette's syndrome. These results were not replicated by Tanner, Goetz, and Klawans (1982). Choline and lecithin have not yielded significant changes in Tourette's symptoms.

2. *GABA.* Clonazepam, a benzodiazapine that enhances glutamate release, has been reported as effective in relieving Tourette's syndrome (Gonce & Barbeau, 1977), and a direct GABA agonist, progabide, was effective in two of four patients with Tourette's syndrome (Mondrup, Dupont, & Braindgaard, 1985). Levels of GABA in CSF or whole blood, however, did not distinguish Tourette's syndrome patients.

3. *Serotonogenic.* L-5 hydroxytryptophan decreased self-mutilation in one patient with Tourette's syndrome. The positive effect on this patient was not confirmed in other studies when L-5HTP was given in combination with carbidopa. An increase in generalized hyperactivity resulted. However, the effectiveness of drugs that increase the availability of serotonin (clomipramine and fluoxetine) in obsessive-compulsive disorder suggest that these drugs be given intensive trial for use with Tourette's syndrome. Initial data and anecdotal reports have underscored the success of fluoxetine in decreasing severe obsessive-compulsive behavior in children with Tourette's syndrome.

4. *Endogenous opioids.* There are anecdotal reports of the effectiveness of opioid receptor antagonists in Tourette's syndrome.

5. *Calcium channel blockers.* Calcium channel blockers are reported to bring "rapid and dramatic relief in refractory Tourette syndrome" (Alessi,

Walden, & Hiseh, 1989). Anecdotal reports describe improvement in tics and vocalization with nifedipine (R. Berg, 1985; A. Goldstein, 1984; Walsh, Lavenstein, Lincamele, Bronheim, & O'Leary, 1986). The combined use of nifedipine and haloperidol was effective in a 9-year-old boy diagnosed as having Tourette's syndrome, ADHD, and specific learning disorders. Clonidine, haloperidol, pimozide, and fluphenazine were all ineffective or had unacceptable side effects. Neither verapamil nor nifedipine alone produced a major decrease in tics compared to the placebo. Verapamil caused headache, nausea, and dizziness. With the combination of nifedipine (10 mg bid) and haloperidol (1 mg bid) a significant reduction in tic frequency and a marked increase in attention and school performance occurred, "almost immediately" (Alessi et al., 1989).

In reviewing the use of medication in Tourette's syndrome (K.E. Towbin, Riddle, Leckman, Bruun, & Cohen, 1988) reemphasized the need to do the following: start patients on the smallest doses of medication possible, increase doses gradually, ensure an adequate duration of drug trial, use sufficient doses, maintain the lowest effective dose, avoid polypharmacy, and make changes in regimens as sequences of single steps.

Behavioral Modification

Behavioral modification is said to be helpful in reducing the feelings of stress. A variety of techniques of behavior modification for use in Tourette's syndrome have been described by Azrin and Peterson (1988). These include the following:

- *Massed negative practice,* in which the patient voluntarily performs the tic for a specified period of time interspersed with brief periods of rest. The object is to develop a "reactive inhibition," leading to decrease in tic frequency in approximately half of 18 case studies including a total of 24 patients.

- *Contingency management,* an approach based on operant learning theory, using (a) positive reinforcement in nine studies each involving one subject (in one study two subjects were involved) and (b) negative reinforcement in seven studies.

- *Relaxation training,* including muscular relaxation, deep breathing, visual imagery, and verbalizations, led to temporary reduction in tics for short periods. Azrin and Peterson (1988) stated that "patients with Tourette syndrome should be taught relaxation as a general procedure to help reduce tension and decrease frequency and severity of tics" (p. 247).

- *Self monitoring of frequency of tics* has been helpful in reducing tics in three case studies.

- *Habit reversal*, the isometric tensing of muscles opposite to the tic movements (competing response). The opposing muscles are contracted for two minutes immediately on onset of the emission of or the urge to have the tic. This procedure involves self-monitoring, relaxation, and contingency management as well as competing response.

Although each technique has been "somewhat effective" in reducing the frequency of tics, these treatments have been part of multicomponent treatments and thus cannot be evaluated per se. Nevertheless, positive reinforcement, praise and encouragement, may lead to improved motivation and thus improved achievement.

School Practices in Management

In her doctoral disseration, D. Anderson (1984) surveyed the educational services provided for students with Tourette's syndrome in a six-county area in the State of Florida. Sixty-eight percent of the children with Tourette's syndrome in these counties were in the regular public school classes, 10% were in classes for emotionally disturbed children, 9% were in classes for learning disabilities, 1% were homebound, 4% were in special schools for emotional, cognitive, and learning problems, and no report was received on class placement for 8%. There was, however, no clearly defined procedure for management, with a variety of techniques used; the most frequent being a modification in classroom management to accommodate the specific learning and behavioral characteristics of each child.

A survey of positive school practices is reported by Hagin, Beecher, Pagano and Kreeger (1980). Seventy-two responses coming from 19 states, Canada, Australia and Korea, were received in answer to a questionnaire included in the *Tourette Syndrome Association Newsletter*. The responses were organized according to three main headings: educational settings, sources of support, and specific educational practices.

Educational Settings Questionnaire responses emphasized the importance of a moderate classroom structure for children with Tourette's syndrome. The degree of structure, however, elicited a variety of responses. Thirteen replies specifically mentioned a less-structured classroom atmosphere than the traditional setting. This would permit the Tourette's children freedom of physical movement when their symptoms required it, but would also offer appropriate environmental cues to guide their learning.

In contrast to this, two responses mentioned a highly structured boarding-school atmosphere in which "every hour of the day was programmed." These parents mentioned firm structure as being crucial to their children's learning. An additional seven parents mentioned small private schools with "therapeutically oriented," "patient," and "humanitarian" approaches to the pupils. While some advocated special class placements, a number of families firmly supported the mainstream class in which children had opportunities for special provisions, but worked for the major part of the school day with other children of similar ages.

An especially important provision for all the youngsters was some kind of refuge to which the child might go when the symptoms of Tourette's syndrome become severe. The opportunity to leave the class at any time without seeking special permission is an important arrangement between the child and the teacher. A refuge, such as a learning disability resource room, the school clinic, or a nurse's office, are the kinds of provisions mentioned.

While the physical and organizational climate of the school is important, the psychological climate is equally important. Responses mentioned over and over again the need for concerned and active efforts to assist the child to develop his or her full potential. One parent mentioned, "a teacher who never gave up on my son." Another parent mentioned, "the need for the kind of teacher who emphasized the number of correct responses, rather than the errors." The need to learn to ignore the tic and focus on the child is most important.

Sources of Support   A number of parents described ways of informing school staff members about Tourette's syndrome. Fifteen parents mentioned opportunities to explain Tourette's syndrome to the school staff at regular staff meetings. The publications of the Tourette Association were distributed and the film, *The Sudden Intruder,* was used as the focus of these discussions. A film made for children, *Stop It—I Can't,* is a useful starting point for group discussions in classrooms in which children with Tourette's syndrome are enrolled. The publication, *Mathew and His Tics,* has been used by a number of parents as the first step toward peer acceptance of the symptoms of Tourette's syndrome. The importance of an appropriate explanation to the peers of the child or young adult is not to be underestimated. One college student stated that she experienced real acceptance for the first time when she explained to her college professor and the other students the nature of Tourette's syndrome. She said, "They then accepted my condition." Teacher support for the youngster with Tourette's syndrome was mentioned again and again in the questionnaire responses. One wise parent said, "Good teachers don't pity, pamper, or patronize." A youngster commented, "They treated me like a regular student, that helped the most." Another said, "They gave me advanced work to match my abilities." One youngster warned, "Don't let a kid cop out in school; I should have been in college prep."

In many of the reports of school adjustment there was evidence of mature, supportive parents in the background. These parents encouraged peer acceptance, but also made sure that there was adult supervision as needed during the unstructured times at school. It is during unstructured times such as in the lunchroom, in the locker room, and in the play yard that unfortunate incidents can occur.

A variety of school personnel was mentioned as having contributed a good deal to school adjustment. The teacher is a key person, but also included were guidance counselors and school nurses who not only provide teachers with information about the syndrome itself, but also can be helpful in interpreting the responses children may make to medication or to a change in medication. School psychologists were mentioned, as were the Child Study Team as a whole and the Special Education Department.

Private consultants who counseled the family and also dealt directly with the school were another source of support mentioned. Several respondents mentioned the need for careful interpretation of medication effects to school personnel, as well as the need for adjusting homework for children who may be relatively symptom-free.

The parent has a basic role in the support system. All parents should be aware of the child's right to an education in the least restrictive environment as provided in P.L. 94-142, The Education for All Handicapped Children Act. These provisions have been important in a number of cases in which a due process hearing was necessary in order to have a child returned to school after he had been receiving only home instruction for a number of years. One parent pointed out the importance of a basically nonthreatening attitude in relation to the school. She continued, "We have assumed collegiality with those we consider professionals. We know that they are anxious to do their best and we have never been disappointed." Another parent said, "I have tried to maintain good rapport—this is an asset when you are seeking extra help and understanding. As my youngster requires extra help from the teachers, I try to help *them* when they need it as well."

The parent has a broad educational role for the youngster with Tourette's syndrome. This role may involve anticipating the next step educationally and desensitizing the child about possible failure. If long division is coming up soon, the groundwork laid by the parent at home may make it possible for the child to handle long division when the teacher introduces it.

The parent can also have a very helpful role in reviewing for unit tests with the youngster. Careful monitoring of schoolwork is useful so that the parent can fill in the gaps that occur because of attentional and organizational problems. One parent commented, "I taught him to read three times and each time he forgot; now he is an excellent reader." Parents are also helpful to the child in encouraging that they express their feelings which may not be easily expressed in the group at school. The school can help the children by permitting them to take things at their own pace. Time is a major source of stress for youngsters with Tourette's syndrome, and stress exacerbates the symptoms.

Negative points come through in the discussion of school adjustment. Mentioned most frequently was the isolation many children with Tourette's syndrome suffer from in the classroom. Occasionally outright rejection occurs in the form of verbal abuse. One older adolescent mentioned a college professor who called attention to the symptoms. With younger children teasing may occur from classmates in nonstructured settings like the lunchroom, the locker room or the playing field. One parent said, "There have been no positive educational experiences. School meant nothing but harm for my child who was incorrectly diagnosed and placed with retarded children." A more subtle kind of rejection can be seen in the gratuitous advice from school personnel who attribute the Tourette's symptoms to the parents' high expectations. One parent said, "He is classed as a problem child and I am classed as a neurotic mother." Another parent characterized the ineffective and effective teachers in this fashion: "The bad teacher is a martinet who barks out orders; the good teacher is bright and unafraid of bright people. The bad teacher teaches by rote; the good teacher teaches by developing ideas. The bad teacher is rigid; the good teacher is organized. The bad teacher destroys self-esteem; the good teacher guides it. The bad teacher stifles children; the good teacher develops them. The bad teacher takes away the child's sense of self-control; the good teacher builds confidence and self-awareness."

Responses to a questionnaire on positive educational practices sent to members of the Tourette Syndrome Association provided a wide range of information about educational settings and climate, sources of support, and specific suggestions for instructional assistance. While no single educational approach was found to serve all children equally well, responses indicate that many families are dealing with the educational needs of their children effectively and realistically. Running through all responses is the strong conviction that appropriate educational provisions have a vital role for the child with Tourette's syndrome. The courage, supportiveness, and sense of purpose with regard to educational planning is said well in one parent's comment: "We believe so strongly in the importance of schooling that we have jumped many hurdles. It's great fun to conquer these problems; it makes us all feel so smart and so loving."

Specific Suggestions for Instruction   Some specific ideas appeared as suggestions on a number of the questionnaires:

- *One-to-one help* with reading and mathematics is frequently essential. This may be received in a program for children with learning disabilities or in some remedial programs. Whatever the source of the instruction, it should emphasize perceptual cues, sound-symbol associations, and a decoding approach to reading.

- *Small segments* of work should be taught with opportunity for mastery before the child goes on to more complex material.

- *Reasonable goals* are important; praise when they have been reached is essential.

- *The timing of schoolwork* is a critical matter. Like most of us, children with Tourette's syndrome need to work at their own speed.

- *The size of the class* may also be crucial. Like all children, the Tourette's child flourishes when he works in a small individualized class.

- *Peer help* may be very useful. In return, the children with Tourette's syndrome may have the opportunity to help their peers in subjects in which they excel.

- *Specific praise* is an important motivator for continued achievement. No child likes to receive a snow job in response to his efforts, but all youngsters like to have good work recognized.

- *Help in following directions* is needed by most youngsters with Tourette's syndrome. Parents and teachers can help here by underlining significant words in order to draw attention to the sequences of ideas.

- *Handwriting problems* were mentioned in nearly every response to the questionnaire. Some families have solved this problem by requesting that the child be allowed to print. A limit on the requirements of written work is also a contribution. Typing may be a solution for some youngsters, although it has been found to be a source of stress with others. Use of typing would depend on the nature of the tic and whether control would be possible as the child learns the typewriter keyboard. Use of the buddy system to cut down the amount of writing has been suggested. Someone else to help with the writing, perhaps a peer who writes the assignment with a carbon in order to have a copy for the child with Tourette's may be one solution. Use of a classroom aide would also be a possibility. The use of lines, color cues, and plastic pencil wedges all appeared as very reasonable suggestions for use with some youngsters.

- *Exams* represent a critical issue for most older youngsters with Tourette's syndrome. The possibility of taking important examinations like the Scholastic Aptitude Tests in private, untimed administration is one possibility worthy of consideration. Another solution has been to allow the youngster to take a rest break between parts of the examination.

- The importance of a wide variety of *compensatory activities* ran through a number of the questionnaires. One youngster began as a Boy Scout and moved through the ranks so that he now serves as an adult leader. The usefulness of swimming and life-saving training was mentioned by several respondents. A rocket club appeared to be a useful activity for one science-oriented youngster. A number of musicians were reported in the sample: Some youngsters learned to play piano, French horn, and flute, and one youngster became a member of a rock group. One youngster found weight lifting a very important compensatory activity, while another found jewelry making an absorbing hobby.

Summary of Management

Management of the child with Tourette's syndrome thus involves more than control of tics and vocalization; it involves the understanding of all sources of stress, whether they come from the family, from school, or from peers as well as from the Tourette's syndrome itself. With comprehensive attention to each of these sources, the majority of children with Tourette's syndrome can reach their optimal potential academically, socially, and vocationally. Fortunately there is the tendency for the condition to improve by late adolescence. The resurgence of interest and the intensity of research studies to elucidate the cause or causes of the disorder offer hope for new and better methods of treatment.

As we have stressed in the management of all children with other disorders of learning, the first step in management of children with Tourette's syndrome is understanding them and their world; a comprehensive evaluation is in order. At the least this includes psychiatric, neurologic, cognitive, educational, and family study; the content, dynamics, genesis, and structure of the child's thoughts, wishes, fears, and conflicts; the way he or she deals with anxiety in loss of motor and phonic control and in the attenuation of the stimulus barrier; the level of maturation and integration of the central nervous system; the cognitive abilities and disabilities; the academic successes and failures; and the attitudes and behaviors of parents, siblings, and teachers to the child's problem. When all these data are obtained, appropriate intervention may be offered.

A comprehensive plan of intervention involves educational, psychotherapeutic, behavioral, and medication components. Teachers, parents, siblings, neurologists, pediatricians, psychologists, and psychiatrists—the skills of many disciplines—may be a part of the management. With so many disciplines involved, management may become fragmented, and in spite of sincere efforts of each, it may create confusion in parents and exacerbate anxiety in the child. A central coordinator, someone to whom parents and child may turn as problems arise, someone to coordinate the efforts of professionals and agencies, is essential.

After comprehensive study, a meeting with parents helps clarify issues, identifies their own reactions, outlines proposed treatment, and supplies them with someone who is available to them throughout the years. A similar meeting is held with the child, another with teachers and resource people at the child's school. The family most often needs support; in those who may have tics or obsessions or compulsions themselves, their guilt in the thought that they may have transmitted the disease may lead to their own depression, to anger and rejection of the child, or to an overindulgence and overprotection that inhibit the child's emotional maturation. While all families need understanding and support, the extent of family counseling or therapy must be an individual matter.

The child's emotional reaction to the disorder and to the reaction of those about him or her may require individual therapy. The presence of Tourette's syndrome frequently makes the resolution of stage-specific conflicts incomplete and contributes to the development of anxiety and all the defenses mobilized against it. The level and depth of therapy, however, just as with any child, depends on the child's capacity to deal with his or her emotions and may proceed from support in the face of cathartic release, through insight about feelings and behavior, and to resolution of persistent conflict. The ultimate goal is the relief of the stress that aggravates the symptoms of Tourette's syndrome and the promotion of social and vocational adjustment.

SUMMARY

Tourette's syndrome is a neuropsychiatric disorder characterized by multiple motor and vocal tics that vary in location, frequency, intensity, and complexity. Obsessions and compulsions are part of the syndrome; whether attention deficit hyperactivity is intrinsic to the syndrome or is a co-morbid disorder is controversial. The age of onset may vary from the preschool years to early adolescence; frequently the syndrome starts in the preschool years with hyperactivity and progresses from simple tics and vocalization to multiple, complex tics and vocalizations. Classically, coprolalia has been described. The symptoms characteristically "wax and wane," aggravated by stress and tension, frequently spontaneously improving in late adolescence or early adulthood. The syndrome has a strong family aggregation, with greater incidence in monozygotic twins than in dizygotic twins. The male/female prevalence ratio may be as high as 9 to 1 in children and 3 or 4 to 1 in adults. The genetic mode of transmission is still obscure; the mechanism through which the syndrome may be expressed is considered to be an abnormality, possibly developmental, in that part of the subcortical system involved with control of voluntary movement and involving neurotransmitter systems. The effectiveness of haloperidol in control of motor tics suggests a hypersensitivity or an increased number of dopamine receptors as a mechanism. The "unitary dopamine" hypothesis, however, is becoming increasingly untenable as serotonergic, GABA, and other neurotransmitters are implicated.

Tourette's syndrome has a profound effect on the patient's thoughts and feelings. The basic problem with impulse control leads to a conscious struggle to control the impulses, with obsessive mental images and feelings of the emerging tics, vocalizations, and compulsions actually preceding the motor discharge and with a feeling of being overwhelmed when the motor act escapes from voluntary control. The unacceptable thinking and behavior evoke guilt, depression, and anxiety. Anxiety may be severe, seen in phobias, difficulty falling asleep, and dreams of being attacked and overwhelmed. Some children feel they are controlled by something outside of them. Their self-esteem is low; many fear deterioration of the brain, and some think their disease is a punishment for bad thoughts and behavior.

Since medication does not cure the disorder, it should not be automatic but be reserved for symptoms that impair social, educational, and/or vocational adjustment. Side effects must be considered. Dopamine receptor site antagonists (haloperidol and pimozide) are effective in decreasing motor and vocal tics in approximately 75% of patients. There are reports that patients who do not respond to haloperidol may be helped with pimozide. Clonidine, an alpha-adrenergic agonist, has a long latency period (8–12 weeks) before response, with maximum effects seen after months of treatment. The value of clonidine in tic reduction is still controversial. Serotonic uptake blockers (clomipramine and fluoxetine) are receiving attention in their ability to reduce obsessive-compulsive symptoms. Calcium channel blockers are reported to be effective in enhancing response to haloperidol. Cholinergic drugs and GABA agonists have not been significantly helpful in treating Tourette's Syndrome.

School problems are significant for children with Tourette's syndrome. Most of these children have impaired visual-motor-praxic function, coding, mathematics, and handwriting. In addition, the obsessive thinking, compulsive behavior, perseveration, impulsivity, increased anxiety, and poor-self esteem; the tics themselves; and the medication—all contribute to school problems. How many children with Tourette's syndrome have a specific language disability, as defined in Chapters 2 and 11 of this book, is as yet unknown. In school management, the Tourette Syndrome Association recommends that means be found to permit expression of hyperactivity, to allow alternatives to handwriting, to reduce stress, to offer remedial mathematics, and, in general, to increase socialization and self-esteem. The importance of education for the teacher and support for the parents is stressed. A survey of positive educational practices for children with Tourette's syndrome found that a flexibility in educational approach, depending on the needs of the child, was indicated.

CHAPTER SIXTEEN

Autism

CARDINAL SIGNS OF AUTISM

CASE REPORT: DONALD

Donald was 2 years, 10 months of age when he was first seen in our clinic. He was referred by his pediatrician and by the Communicology Department at the University of South Florida where, for the past 4 months he had been receiving a "highly structured language program to increase motor and speech initiation." At age 2 years, 2 months, our communication specialist judged his receptive language skills to be 12 months retarded, while his expressive language consisted of babbling, jargon, and some delayed imitation of single words. During the evaluation by our Communicology Department, however, he did not respond normally to the examiner, with no eye contact, focusing his attention mainly on inanimate objects, and responding to verbal commands, and that inconsistently, only when gestures and prompting were included.

On our examination Donald was a handsome, chubby, 3-year-old boy. His face was full, but pale, with malar flush, perioral pallor, and glistening eyes. He went to the dollhouse, but his play was unorganized, and perseverative, moving a chair from place to place. It was difficult to distract him from that play; he ignored the examiner. He had no spontaneous speech, but he hummed, apparently contentedly, while playing with the dollhouse and while spinning wheels of a toy car. With much prompting by his parents, he identified colors of crayons on verbal command, he recited numbers to 10 and the letters of the alphabet, he read single simple words. He did not use language for communication. His articulation was poor, and it was difficult to interpret what he said. He could only scrawl with the crayons and could not imitate a circle. Physical examination revealed a questionable decrease in muscle tone, primitive postural responses, such as persistent neck righting reflexes (normal at this age), and little anxiety on disturbance of equilibrium. The palate was high, and there appeared to be some clumsiness in movement of his tongue. Classical neurological examination in terms of muscle power, coordination and synergy, deep and superficial reflexes, was with normal limits. No abnormalities were found on brain stem audiometry. Laboratory examination revealed a normal Karyotype 46XY, fragile X was not demonstrated; EEG and CT scan with and without contrast were normal; amino acid screen (urine) using two-dimensional chromatography and quantitative amino acid (serum) values were normal; thyroid function and routine chemistries were normal.

His history revealed that his was a planned pregnancy, the first child of caring parents. There was no history of smoking, alcohol, medication, or fevers during pregnancy. His delivery was normal with a birth weight of 8 lb. Although gross motor development appeared normal, there was colic and fretting in his first 3–4 months, a doughy passivity with little response to his mother, and, of course, the very severe receptive and emissive language delay. There is a maternal uncle who is said to have been a "late talker," a maternal aunt said to be "a little slow, a little weird," and a paternal female cousin, now age 28, in a state mental hospital.

At a repeat examination at age 5, the maturational unevenness, evident at 2 years, 10 months, was dramatically evident. Although now aware of the examiner, he displayed little interest in what was said to him, going immediately to the toy cars, talking to himself, moving the cars in apparently aimless and perseverative fashion. When physically put on the examiner's lap, he permitted himself to be cuddled as an infant, passive, making no effort to leave. At age 5, however, in contrast to his 3-year examination, Donald could more easily be interrupted in his playing and he could respond to verbal commands. He could count by ones, tens, and one-hundreds to 1000, name the days of the week, and sound out words at a fourth-grade level (WRAT). The verbal skills, however, appeared to be rote, in a mechanistic, ventriloquistic tone, and were deficient where responses requiring discrimination and analysis were required. His visual-motor function had not progressed beyond a 3-year level. He could not imitate any praxic tasks. On the Stanford-Binet he was able to attain an IQ of 69; he could name body parts, label single vocabulary items, and string small beads; he could identify which of a group of four drawings was different. The impression, however, was of a mechanical child, responding on a rote level with little spontaneity and little relationship to the adults and other children around him. He was an inner child, happiest when being by himself in his own repetitive play.

At age 6 years, 5 months the picture was moderately improved. His visual-motor abilities were at a 4-year level, he could respond to receptive picture vocabulary tests at a 6-year level, and he was more aware of adults about him. He had developed rituals, was preoccupied with observing himself in a mirror, objected to taking his shoes off, was confused in new situations, and simply sat passively waiting to be dressed. He now talked with his mother, repeating events that had occurred. There was more humanness in this mechanistic child.

During the 3 years, from ages 3 to 6, Donald has been in three programs: at age 3–4 in a county program geared to behavior modification for autistic children; the next year in a small nursery school with much individual stimulation and attention; and now in a special school for children with emotional problems where again he can receive much individual attention and specific training of his deficit perceptual areas. He currently enjoys reading. During these 3 years, too, he has received continued speech therapy, working on appropriate response, to *what* and *who* questions, imitating phrases, and vocabulary. Medication, fenfluramine given in dosage up to 20 mg/day at about age 3, did not appear to effect any change during the 3 months of its trial.

Diagnostically Donald is classified as suffering from an autistic disorder, albeit, a relatively high functioning one, who is making slow but definite progress in maturation of the three areas into which his symptoms may be categorized: in object relations, in language and communication, and in repertoire of activities and interests (Table 16-1). He resembles the 11 children described by Leo Kanner in his classic 1943 paper on "Autistic Disturbances of Affective Contact" and for whom Kanner used the term "early childhood autism" in 1946. Donald appears to have little awareness of adults and children in his environment, he does not relate with

Table 16-1   Diagnostic Criteria for Autistic Disorder

At least eight of the following sixteen items are present, these to include at least two items from A, one from B, and one from C.

Note: Consider a criterion to be met only if the behavior is abnormal for the person's developmental level.

A. Qualitative impairment in reciprocal social interaction as manifested by the following:

(The examples within parentheses are arranged so that those first mentioned are more likely to apply to younger or more handicapped, and the later ones, to older or less handicapped, persons with this disorder.)

1. marked lack of awareness of the existence or feelings of others (e. g., treats a person as if he or she were a piece of furniture; does not notice another person's distress; apparently has no concept of the need of others for privacy)

2. no or abnormal seeking of comfort at times of distress (e. g., does not come for comfort even when ill, hurt, or tired, seeks comfort in a stereotyped way, e. g., says "cheese, cheese, cheese" whenever hurt)

3. no or impaired imitation (e. g., does not wave bye-bye; does not copy mother's domestic activities; mechanical imitation of others' actions out of context)

4. no or abnormal social play (e. g., does not actively participate in simple games; prefers solitary play activities; involves other children in play only as "mechanical aids")

5. gross impairment in ability to make peer friendships (e. g., no interest in making peer friendships; despite interest in making friends, demonstrates lack of understanding of conventions of social interaction, for example, reads phone book to uninterested peer)

B. Qualitative impairment in verbal and nonverbal communication, and in imaginative activity, as manifested by the following:

(The number items are arranged so that those first listed are more likely to apply to younger or more handicapped, and the later ones, to older or less handicapped, persons with this disorder.)

1. no mode of communication, such as communicative babbling, facial expression, gesture, mime, or spoken language

2. markedly abnormal nonverbal communication, as in the use of eye-to-eye gaze, facial expression, body posture, or gestures to initiate or modulate social interaction (e. g., does not anticipate being held, stiffens when held, does not look at the person or smile when making a social approach, does not greet parents or visitors, has a fixed stare in social situations)

3. absence of imaginative activity, such as play acting of adult roles, fantasy characters, or animals; lack of interest in stories about imaginary events

4. marked abnormalities in the production of speech, including volume, pitch, stress, rate, rhythm, and intonation (e. g., monotonous tone, questionlike melody, or high pitch)

5. marked abnormalities in the form or content of speech, including stereotyped and repetitive use of speech (e. g., immediate echolalia or mechanical repetition of television commercial); use of "you" when "I" is meant (e. g.,

Table 16-1   Diagnostic Criteria for Autistic Disorder (continued)

using "you want cookie?" to mean "I want a cookie"); idiosyncratic use of words or phrases (e. g., "Go on green riding" to mean "I want to go on the swing"), or frequent irrelevant remarks (e. g., starts talking about train schedules during a conversation about sports)

6. marked impairment in the ability to initiate or sustain a conversation with others, despite adequate speech (e. g., indulging in lengthy monologues on one subject regardless of interjections from others)

C. Markedly restricted repertoire of activities and interests, as manifested by the following:

1. sterotyped body movements, e. g., hand-flicking or -twisting, spinning, head-banging, complex whole-body movements
2. persistent preoccupation with parts of objects (e. g., sniffing or smelling objects, repetitive feeling of texture of materials, spinning wheels of toy cars) or attachment of unusual objects (e. g., insists on carrying around a piece of string)
3. marked distress over change in trivial aspects of environment, e. g., when a vase is moved from usual position
4. unreasonable insistence on following routines in precise detail, e. g., insisting that exactly the same route always be followed when shopping
5. markedly restricted range of interests and a preoccupation with one narrow interest, e. g., interested only in lining up objects, in amassing facts about meteorology, or in pretending to be a fantasy character

D. Onset during infancy or childhood.

Specify if childhood onset (after 36 months of age).

Note. From *Diagnostic and Statistical Manual of Mental Disorders* (DSM–III–R), 3rd ed. revised, pp. 38–39. Washington, D.C.: American Psychiatric Association, 1988.

warmth or appreciation of the responses of his parents or teachers; his play is isolated, unstructured, and perseverative; his language was delayed in maturation but he has excellent rote language abilities (i. e.; counting and reading). He is only beginning to use language to communicate his needs or feelings; he is developing idiosyncratic although verbigerative verbalization; he requires routines and resists changes. There are other maturational delays in visual-motor function and in motor function of the autonomous ego. His relationships are mechanical and rote, with little capacity for discrimination and analysis.

Donald is typical of one group of children classified as autistic, perhaps 10–15% of the total autistic population. Most, 70–80% of children designated as autistic, function at a lower level, in the moderate to severely retarded range (Sigman, Ungerer, Mundy, & Sherman, 1987) and of these perhaps one third do not use language at all (Paul, 1987). Shane is an example of such a child.

CASE STUDY: SHANE

Shane was a handsome, blond, blue-eyed child of 6 years, 7 months when first seen. He immediately wrapped himself physically about the examiner and literally had to be peeled off. He was attracted to tiny bits of string on the floor, picking them up in a fine pincer grasp, holding his left hand at the side of his face, glancing at his hand out of the corner of his eyes. If there were not strings on the floor, bits of thread from his own socks or from the examiner's clothing would do. The strings were shaken in a fine rhythm or placed in his mouth. Aside from the physical contact, he paid little attention to the examiner. He attended to the tuning fork, and the sound of bells, but not to verbal greetings or commands. His hearing was said by the audiologist to be within normal limits. His verbal communication, however, was nil, but he did make hummming noises to himself and, when given puzzles, attempted to enlist the examiner's help by pulling his arm. Otherwise there was a wandering about the periphery of the room, darting to pick up bits of string. There were moments when he did sit quietly, attempting to do a 4-year-old puzzle without success. His gross motor activity was smooth, fluid, and graceful. His muscle tone was decreased; he enjoyed antigravity play, occasionally toe-walking or spinning about his own longitudinal axis. In spite of his fine pincer grasp, his pencil grip was palmar, with his right hand used for visual-motor scrawling. There were no ectodermal anomalies, but his skin readily flared and whealed on the slightest scratching. On attempted testing with the PPVT, he wriggled off the chair, not looking at the pictures. On the Alpern-Ball test he achieved an overall function rated at about a 2-year level. Laboratory examination revealed normal amino acid screen, a T_4 of 3.8 mg/dl (slightly low), and normal EEG and CT scan.

The family history revealed Shane to be the oldest of two boys, born 1 year after the parents' marriage, having a birth weight of 7 lb., 11 oz. The pregnancy was characterized by nausea and vomiting throughout. He was described as having been a quiet child who would stay awake during the night, just playing. He was disturbed by loud sounds and did not "like anything new." He was noted to be different in his first year of life. There is a history of delayed speech in a maternal aunt.

Now at age 12, Shane is in a group home for retarded children, and attends a county school program for autistic children. He still does not communicate verbally, does not respond to verbal commands, and, in general, has made little progress.

As we contrast the clinical pictures presented by Donald and by Shane, it can be seen that the symptoms of autism span a wide range—from mute to verbal children (but when the children are verbal, their verbalizations are idiosyncratic in content, echoing, inappropriate, and semantically concrete, with abnormal prosody); from children who make no affective relationship and resist physical contact to those who are physically clinging and tenacious; from children who do not respond to perceptual stimuli to those who react with overwhelming anxiety and confusion to perceptual stimuli; from children who are perseverative and "sticky" in their behavior to children who dart from object to object; from passivity to stereotopy; and from children with severe developmental deficits to those with extraordinary reading, mathematic, artistic, or musical skills. Yet these diverse symptoms are tied together by their common developmental delays in object relations, communication and language, and stereotypic behavior. Wing and Atwood (1987) grouped these symptoms into a behavioral triad of "absence or severe impairment of two-way social interaction, non-verbal communication and imagination, and a pattern of activities dominated by repetitive, stereotyped routines." One or another of this triad has been implicated as the core symptoms of the autistic syndrome.

While the interelationship between the areas of defect is still a matter of speculation, the heterogeneity of symptoms requires some organization for an adequate description of the autistic syndrome. Such an organization is seen in the DSM-IIII-R criteria for the diagnosis of "autistic disorder." Another is seen in the criteria proposed by Cohen (1987), in which symptoms are classified into four groups: autistic social dysfunction, gross deficits in language, impairments in communication, and associated features (Table 16-2). The associated feature category includes the many behavioral rigidities, stereotypes, idiosyncratic interests, and deviant response to sensory stimuli seen so frequently in children with the dysfunctions in social relationships and in communication, and language that make up the autistic syndrome.

Social Impairment

Some investigators (i. e.; D. Fein, Pennington, Markowitz, Braverman, & Waterhouse, 1986) considered the social defect as primary in autism. Wing and Gould (1979) subclassified the social impairment into three types: aloof, passive, and active but odd. The *aloof group* corresponds most closely to the "popular image" of the autistic child in whom there is a lack of overt signs of affection and whose communication is impaired with echolalia, pronoun reversal (i. e.; not using the pronoun *I*) repetitiveness, literal meaning, idiosyncratic use of words and phrases, not using speech in social interaction, and having a peculiar intonation. Their play is stereotyped, and they may be interested in whirling objects; their mood is labile, and there may be unusual reactions to sensory stimuli—for instance, they may appear indifferent to pain. Yet, with all this, they may be agile in climbing, and graceful in gross motor activity. The *passive group* may accept the approaches of others, but their relationship is rigid, repetitive, and pedantic, displaying little flexibility and imagination; imitative activity may take the form of echopraxia; they show less resistance to change than does the aloof group. These children are sometimes described as having an "atypical developmental disorder." The *active but odd group* does make spontaneous approaches to others but in a

Table 16-2   *Proposed Criteria for Autism*

1. Autistic social dysfunction: Gross and sustained impairments in socialization and social relations, as defined by impairment in at least two of the following areas:
   a. Attachment
   b. Sociability and social communication
   c. The expression and understanding of emotions
2. Gross deficits in language of either of two types:
   a. Mutism
   b. Peculiar speech patterns, such as echolalia, pronoun reversal, concrete or idiosyncratically metaphorical language use, mechanical intonation
3. Impairments in communication of both of the following types:
   a. Nonverbal communication: impairment in use or understanding of gesture, gaze, vocalization, and facial expression
   b. Verbal communication (when speech is present): impairment in defining the shared topic, establishing rapport verbally, maintaining a dialogue, taking turns, understanding implicit messages in requests, and other aspects of verbal interaction
4. Associated features (one or more of the following associated features may be present):
   a. Resistance to change in the environment
   b. Insistence on doing things in the same way
   c. Oddities of movement, such as posturing, repetitive hand and finger movements (stereotypes), toe walking, peculiar gait
   d. Self-mutilation, such as biting or hitting self or head banging
   e. Excessive fascination with or attachment of inanimate objects
   f. Deviant responses to sensory stimuli (augmented or attenuated behavioral responses to noises, textures, odors, lights, taste)
   g. Absence of imaginative play

Note. From "Issues in classification of pervasive developmental disorder and associated conditions" by D. J. Cohen, R. Paul, and F. Volkmar, 1987 (p. 30) In D. Cohen and A. Donnellan (Eds.), *Handbook of Autism and Pervasive Developmental Disorders.* New York: John Wiley. Reprinted by permission of John Wiley & Sons.

peculiar fashion. Their approach is not for communication but as a way of affording release for their own preoccupations, with repetitive questions, and tenacty in their verbal outpourings, sometimes to the extent of physical clinging. In their early school years, repetitive play is noted, including a preoccupation with maps, space, and time; they are concerned with their own identity and the identity and physical limits of others; there is a lack of understanding of social rules. These children may bear some resemblance to Mahler's (1952; Mahler & Gosliner, 1955) symbiotic child. Their overall skills as measured by IQ tests tend to be higher than those in the aloof group, but here again rote skill, rather than reasoning ability, is manifest.

Volkmar et al. (1989) found that clinical raters using the Wing subtyping scheme could indeed reliably subtype the social interaction of a sample of

149 individuals, 78 of whom were autistic, 34 of whom had atypical pervasive developmental disorders (PDD), and 37 of whom had non-PDD developmental disorders. Lower functioning individuals were most likely to be rated aloof, whereas the highest functioning ones were more likely to be placed on the active but odd group, with the passive group between the two extremes. The younger individuals were more likely to be in the aloof subgroup; the older, in the active but odd group. Although IQ was a "powerful predictor" of subtype assignment, it did not fully account for it. The classification by social interaction subtypes, however, did not correspond to diagnostic categories since non autistic–non-PDD cases were able to be subtyped according to this scheme. Volkmar et al. suggested that "the subtyping scheme may relate more generally to levels of developmental disturbance than to specific diagnostic categories" (p. 85).

D. J. Cohen (1987) emphasized the failure of normal socialization as the "major defining characteristic of the syndrome" (p. 28), a specific impairment not observed in retarded children. This failure may be assessed by performance in three areas: sociability and social communication, attachment, and understanding and expressing emotions. Autistic children may show a greater interest in objects than in people, do not engage people without treating them as objects, do not respond to speech directed at themselves, and exhibit a sparsity of intentional communication acts using either verbal or non verbal means of communication. Their social impairment may be seen in a failure to demonstrate differential attachment to familiar people in contrast with unfamiliar adults—not moving to parents or teachers for reassurance, or wandering away from them as if indifferent to them, for instance. The lack in expressing and understanding emotions in themselves may be seen as an affective blandness or, on the other hand, as an affect unrelated to the situation. They appear to lack a capacity for empathy. The cases of Donald and Shane demonstrate extreme points on the continuum of abnormal socialization.

The Communication Disorder

For some clinicians, the communication deviation seen in autistic children is the root of their abnormal socialization. Paul (1987) stated that "range of early communication functions expressed and the forms used to express these functions are clearly deviant in autism" (p. 65). Very early, preverbal gestures may be delayed, with little or no labeling and acknowledging of others, using functions that do not require attention of others, or using inappropriate expression or self-injury to signal their needs. If and when speech develops, these children are able to represent word meaning in memory but fail to use memory in retrieval or organizational tasks; the semantic function of memory is a problem. Echolalia, both immediate and delayed, has been reported as a classical symptom of autism since Kanner's 1943

report. All autistic children are not echolalic, however, and in the early
stages of language acquisition, echolalia may be found in normal children.
It is now thought (T. Shapiro, 1977) that echoing in the autistic child may
represent the attempt to understand questions and commands for which the
child does not know the appropriate response, an attempt at mastery.
Indeed, comprehension appears to be a significant problem with autistic
children. Tager-Flusberg (1981) (reviewed by Paul, 1987) found sentence
comprehension to be lower in the autistic group than in normal controls
matched for nonverbal mental age. Paul and Cohen (1985) found that autistic children required specific cueing, a concrete structuring of a verbal command, for correct understanding. When the same request was presented in
an unstructured context, the autistic children could not understand the
speaker's request. Even where expressive language has developed, and some
basic intention to communicate exists, there is little skill in communication
involving joint reference or shared topics or participating in supplying new
information relevant to the listener. Thus verbal communication may
become idiosyncratic, rigid, repetitive, and even irrelevant to the situation.
The understanding of a shifting reference, that is the use of the pronoun *I*
in different contexts, is a difficult concept for the autistic child. Vocal patterns, too—intonation, voice quality, and stress patterns—which are frequent in autistic children, may be related to fundamental aspects, as yet
unknown, of the autistic syndrome.

There have been a number of explanations for the linguistic deficits in
autism. Evidence from brain-stem–evoked auditory responses have suggested that the transmission time of auditory stimuli through the brain stem
is longer in autistic than in normal children (i. e., Tanguay & Edwards,
1982), thus interfering with auditory processing in the cortex. L. Bloom and
Lahey (1978), however, pointed out that the processing defect may be the
result, rather than the cause, of abnormal language development. Incomplete hemisphere specialization also has been suggested as relating to
defects in auditory processing of language. Using dichotic listening tasks A.
James and Barry (1983) found autistic children do not show the normally
expected increase in right ear advantage with age, suggesting that, in these
children, language functions are not strongly established in the left hemisphere. As described in Chapter 11 ("Specific Language Disability"), however, there are many problems with the dichotic listening experiment that
make interpretation of results far from clear. Dawson (1983), using the Hal-
stead-Reitan Neuropsychological Battery to compare autistic subjects (IQ
range 52–113; age range 9–34) with a group of similarly functioning subjects and with a group of patients with diffuse brain damage, concluded that
the autistic children under age 13 were more likely than older autistic subjects to "exhibit a pattern typical of left hemisphere dysfunction" (p. 350)
as indicated by deficits in verbal tests. On the other hand, the autistic subjects could not be distinguished from the retarded or neurologically
impaired groups on such subtests as tactile, auditory and visual bilateral

simultaneous stimulation, finger-gnosis (tactile), and recognition of numbers traced on fingertips. An interesting theory related to abnormality in hemisphere specialization suggests that autistic children deal with language in unanalyzed wholes (Prizant, 1983), a gestalt style of processing language, with difficulty in formulating discrete, segmented units. Such a processing style resembles the wholistic functioning of the right hemisphere. It has been pointed out, however, that the wholistic gestalt pattern does not necessarily mean that it is the right hemisphere that plays a dominant role in the language of the autistic child; the rigidity and semantic difficulty of autistic language may result from failure to develop higher levels of mediation.

Frith and Baron-Cohen (1987) also see the problem as one of "higher" cortical function. They conceive of the processing defects of the autistic child not as problems proceeding from the stimulus to its reception in the cortex, a "bottom-up" process, but as problems in cognition—in relating general knowledge to perceptual input and in interpreting input as meaningful—a "top-down" process. The higher level mechanisms may include selective attention, the filtering out of irrelevant information. The bottom-up hypotheses include (a) the sensory dominance hypothesis, in which autistic children are said to make use of the proximal receptors (touch, taste, and smell) in contrast to the distal receptors (vision and audition), (b) the stimulus over selectivity hypothesis, which explains why autistic children may respond to odd, minor features of a stimulus while ignoring other more relevant ones, and (c) the perceptual inconsistency hypothesis (Ornitz & Ritvo, 1968) to account for the unusual stimulus-seeking behavior that is interpreted as an inability to modulate or integrate sensory input as a result of vestibular dysfunction. Experimental evidence does not support these hypotheses. Autistic children show abnormal response to proximal sensation, as well as to distant ones; overselectivity may be found in nonautistic retarded children; and even young and retarded autistic children understand the perceptual constancies of size, shape, and object as well as mental-age matched nonautistic controls (Sigman & Ungerer, 1981). The "top-down," selective-attention hypothesis, on the other hand, is supported by Hermelin (1978) and Hermelin and O'Connor (1970, 1985), who found that at the lower sensory processing levels there is no deficit in any modality that is specific to autism but that only the higher levels of cognitive processing are deficient in autistic children. Frith (1972) also found that the specific difficulty of autistic children is not in *perception* of structure but in the *organization* of structure; this again supports a central cognitive defect as primary in autism.

A Unifying Concept for the Organization of Symptoms

L. Bender (1947, 1955, 1966) proposed a more physiological classification of the symptoms of the autistic syndrome. She viewed the symptoms of infantile autism as a total biological disorder in the regulation and maturation of all the basic behavior functions of children, a maturational lag with primitive (i. e., embryological) features, with plasticity in all patterned behavior in the autonomic, perceptual, motor, intellectual, emotional, and social areas. The children Bender described were, at that time, called schizophrenic in the belief that there is a continuity between the symptoms seen in childhood and the syndrome of schizophrenia as seen in adults.

With the advent of DSM-III, however, the diagnosis of schizophrenia in childhood requires essentially the same criteria as those accepted for adults, namely the presence of a formal thought disorder. As will be seen below, there appears to be one subgroup diagnosed as autism in early childhood that may indeed represent an early onset of the schizophrenic syndrome. This subgroup may consist of relatively high-functioning verbal children capable of expressing hallucinations, delusions, and specific phobias and of revealing thought processes. The importance of Bender's concept, however, is that she underscored the physiological immaturity and plasticity now seen in autistic children, and she related psychological function to physiological immaturity. This was in contrast to the psychodynamic theories of etiology so prevalent in the 1940s and 1950s.

The primitive quality of autistic physiology was seen by Bender (L. A. Bender & Freedman, 1952) in the five areas described by Gesell as typical of the fetal infant: homeostasis, muscle tone, motility, states of consciousness, and respiration. Homeostatic immaturity is seen in autonomic lability, ineffective immune responses, and deviations in neuroendocrine and neurotransmitter systems. Motility is seen in the persistence of primitive motility with the persistence of the tonic neck reflex, neck righting postures, remnants of extensor tone in the lower extremities, and persistent choreoathetotic movement. Muscle tone retains its primitive doughy or molluscous (Gesell, 1945) quality. By states of consciousness is meant the torporous, half-asleep, half-awake characteristics of the fetal infant, the inversion of sleep-awake patterns and the abnormalities in response to perceptual stimuli. Respiration is stated by Gesell as the basis for emissive speech and is the physiological anlage of the later language disturbances seen in autism. Given an organism whose homeostatic apparatus is labile, driven by the rotational force of a persistent neck righting response, whose ability to organize perceptions is unclear, and who has difficulty expressing himself, one can speculate that in such an individual there is an inability to form a stable internal representation of himself and of his boundaries with the outside world. The result in behavior may well be an autistic or a symbiotic relationship with the people about him. D. J. Cohen (1980), stated that "lack of comprehension of the feelings of people is the mirror image of his inability to form a stable internal representation of the connection between his own inner state or sense of himself as the locus of organization of initiative, feelings and thoughts" (p. 385). What Bender has done is define the physiological immaturities that make the development of defined body image in general and ego boundaries in particular most difficult for the autistic child to attain. The cause of the physiologic immaturity is unknown.

ETIOLOGY

The autistic syndrome is hetrogeneous, not only in symptoms but in etiology. Just as there are many causes for the attention deficit hyperactivity syndrome and for the broad category of specific language disability, so there are many causes for autism. The autistic syndrome may represent the final, common pathway for severe, pervasive developmental deviations of childhood. To Cantor (1982) "early infantile autism is a manmade syndrome, useful perhaps for short-hand communication of clinical pictures between mental health professionals or educators, but not a syndrome having a unitary cause or even unitary symptomatology" (p. IV). Two major etiological groups have been described: The first with a known organic or metabolic defect that affects the central nervous system; the second with no known organic defect to relate to the autistic syndrome. The identified organic factors that may yield an autistic syndrome are as follows: metabolic disturbance such as phenylketonuria and histidinemia or disorders of purine metabolism for which genetic markers have not been identified; congenital infections such as rubella, toxoplasmosis, cytomegalic virus and herpes; structural disorders such as tuberous sclerosis, neurofibromatosis, and cerebral lipoidosis; chromosomal disorders such as fragile X, trisomy 21, and XXY (Kleinfelter's) syndrome; and physiological disorders such as infantile spasms (Table 16-3). An increase in uric acid has been reported in an occasional child with autism, and in some there is an increased incidence of prenatal or perinatal abnormal events.

M. Coleman and Gillberg (1985) tabulated diagnosable neurological conditions in 149 cases diagnosed as "infantile autism." Phenylketonuria was most commonly found in 50 cases, rubella in 29. A. A. Silver (1986), reviewing the first 33 children with autistic behavior admitted to a self-contained class in the public school system of Hillsborough County, Florida, found that 12 of them had diagnosable neurological conditions. Of these there were 5 with chromosomal defects (mosaic trisomy 21), 2 with high serum copper with high serum ceruloplasmin (Rett syndrome), 1 with high serum and high urinary histidine, 1 the product of a pregnancy complicated by maternal rubella, and 3 with dyskinesias of unknown cause, but accompanied by abnormal electroencephalograms. Table 16-3 lists central nervous system disorders that have been found to be associated with the autistic syndrome.

The group for which no known organic cause is identified may itself be heterogeneous not only in symptoms but also in laboratory findings and etiology. Research here suffers from the same problems seen in learning dis-

Table 16-3   Disorders Associated With the Autistic Syndrome

I. Metabolic Disturbances
   Phenylketonuria
   Histidinemia
   Hyperuricemia
   Mucopolysaccharoidosis
II. Infections
   Rubella
   Toxoplasmosis
   Cytomegalic Virus
   Viral Encephalitis
   Herpes Encephalitis
III. Structural Abnormalities
   Tuberous Sclerosis
   Neurofibromatosis
   Cerebral Lipoidosis
IV. Chromosome Defects
   Fragile X
   Trisomy 21
   Kleinfelter's syndrome (XYY)
   47XXX
V. Dyskineses of Unknown Origin
   Infantile Spasms
   Idiopathic Seizures

orders, namely the identification of homogeneous groups, with clear boundaries. It may be found that the autistic syndrome (with no known organic factors) may be composed of many subgroups, one of which may be the childhood precursor of schizophrenia in adults: another as the child grows older resembles mental retardation. Rutter (1978a) and Rutter and Bartak (1971) emphasized that approximately one-third of all autistic children will develop seizures by the time they reach adult life. The development of a seizure disorder is taken as evidence that, at the very least, a subgroup of autistic children does suffer from an organic defect, albeit cause unknown, of the central nervous system. Because of the variability in symptoms and in etiology of the autistic syndrome, Wing and Atwood (1987) recommended that a diagnosis of autism should include gross etiology if known, IQ, careful description of behavior, and a careful profiling of other deficits and assets; in short, a description of the child and his environment along the dimensions of the pentaxial scheme (Rutter, 1978a; Chapters 5 and 6 of this book).

In spite of the many organic factors that have been identified as associated with the autistic syndrome, in most children with autistic symptoms a specific organic factor cannot be identified. During the 1950s and 1960s psychodynamic theories of etiology were prominent. In his early papers, Kanner himself felt that the syndrome was a reaction to over-intellectualized, emotionally distant parents. Although the specific nature of the "autistogenic" parent–child relationship was later proven to be untenable, Szurek and Berlin (1973) summarized their concept of the ego defect of the autistic child as resulting from "repressed ungratified infant impulses" with "secondary narcissism of a dissociated human character." Szurek and Berlin based their therapy in the separation of the parent and child dyad to provide the affective needs the child never had. Mahler (1952) felt that a defect in the normal process of separation from the parent and unattained individuation resulted in autistic or symbiotic behavior. An effective nursery in which mother–child interaction was the primary focus was organized. During these early years in definition of the syndrome, the autistic child was believed by some (i. e., L. A. Bender 1947) to be an early manifestation of what would later, in latency or in adolescence, be identified as schizophrenia. A variety of clinical pictures responding to endogenous and exogenous factors may be seen in the natural progression of the syndrome. L. A. Bender believed there was a basic organic defect in the central nervous system of these children, a defect that held development at a primitive embryological level, yet endowing that individual with embryonic plasticity so that areas of accelerated function may be found together with arrested functions. Bender's follow-up studies suggested that the child with schizophrenia would become the adult with schizophrenia.

The confusion in whether a child was autistic or schizophrenic was partially resolved when DSM-III documented discrete criteria for infantile autism and for schizophrenia in childhood. DSM-III classified autism and schizophrenia in childhood as two distinct syndromes, with the criteria for schizophrenia in childhood being the same as that for schizophrenia in adults, namely a clearly defined thought disorder. Rutter (1972) considered the two as separate syndromes, not related to each other, distinguished by a difference in cardinal symptoms, course, intellectual differences, sex distribution, age of onset, and the family history of schizophrenia in contrast to a lack of schizophrenia in families of autistic children (see, however, the section on genetic factors). Kolvin (1971) differentiated the "early onset psychosis" (IP), with onset before age 3, from "late onset psychosis" (LOP), with onset after 5 years of age. The LOP group were distinguished by disorders in the form and stream of thought; disordered thought content; auditory, visual, and somatic hallucinations; and perplexity and "attitude of suffering." The IP group were characterized by severe speech delay, many speech anomalies, echolalia stereotype movements, poor relationships, and gaze avoidance. Green et al. (1984), using DSM-III criteria, were also able to diagnose schizophrenia in children between 5 and 12 years, clearly differentiating that group from the autistic group by its clinical features.

Whether there does exist one subgroup of autistic children who later do meet the DSM-III criteria for schizophrenia is still not convincingly proven. De Myer, Hingtgen, and Jackson (1981) stated that "there is a possibility of a continuum effect with autistic and childhood schizophrenia having the most severe degree of cognitive defect and schizoid and adult schizophrenia population having less severe degree" (p. 393).

At any rate, the emphasis now is not that autism is a result of psychological reaction to inadequate maternal cathexis, but that an organic factor or factors, yet to be identified, is at the basis of the syndrome. As has repeatedly been stated, the autistic group for whom no organic etiology is identified may in itself be a heterogeneous population not only in symptoms but in etiology.

The mechanism through which the organic factor(s) operate is also a matter for speculation and investigation. Theories include causes for aberrant language dysfunction (left-hemisphere dysfunction, right-hemisphere dysfunction, higher "top-down" processing problems), "a cerebral palsy of the limbic lobe" (Damasio & Maurer, 1978; Maurer & Damasio, 1982), and pandevelopmental retardation in an inherited congenital neurointegrative defect (Fish, 1977).

PREVALENCE

The prevalence of autism in the general population is low, estimated to be about 2 to 4 per 10,000, although a prevalence as high as 21 per 10,000 has been found by Wing and Gould (1979) drawn from a relatively small population of 35,000. Where large populations, surveying over 500,000 people were done, the prevalence rates remained at about 0.4 per 1,000. Treffert (1970), utilizing a population of almost 1 million in Wisconsin, found a rate of 3.1 per 10,000. Early epidemiological surveys are reviewed by Smalley, Asarnow, and Spence (1988) and by Zahner and Pauls (1987). The source of variation across studies may be found in the age range of the target population (prevalence is higher in the 7–9 age group), the procedures used to identify autistic subjects, and the diagnostic criteria. Yet with all these variations, there is a general consistency of prevalence across studies.

The most recent epidemiological survey was done by Ritvo et al. (1989) encompassing the approximately 1.5 million population of the state of Utah. Autistic persons less than 25 years of age were found through contact with a network of parents, clinicians, and providers of social services; through voluntary and solicited referrals; and through actual screening records of patients in residential facilities and state hospitals. The criteria for autism as defined by the National Society for Autistic Children, criteria identical to those of DSM-III, was used to diagnose 241 individuals as autistic. Sixty-six percent of these scored in the mentally retarded range (IQ 70 or below), with a higher proportion of females with low scores. (Fifty-two percent of females, and 38% of males earned an IQ less than 50.) The distribution of autism in this population was not correlated with parental occupation, race, or religion. The UCLA–University of Utah study found the autistic group to include three cases of Down's syndrome, two of Sanfilippo syndrome, two fragile X, two Tourette's syndrome, and four of Rett's syndrome. An earlier epidemiological survey (Treffert, 1970) included children with "childhood psychosis" in some of whom an identifiable CNS defect was found.

GENETIC FACTORS

Family history, sibling studies, and twin studies suggest a hereditary influence in this syndrome. Smalley et al. (1988) estimate that 2.7% of the siblings of autistic children also suffer from autism, a rate approximately 60 times that of the general population. Contrasting the rate of autism in siblings of autistic probands with that in siblings of Down's subjects, August, Stewart, and Tsai (1981) found that 2.8% of 71 siblings of 41 autistic probands were autistic, while no siblings of the 38 in 15 Down's probands suffered from autism. If the siblings with language impairment were included, then 11, or 15.5% of the siblings of autistic probands had some language impairment as contrasted with 1, or 2.6% of the siblings of Down's patients. Criteria for language impairment included any one of the following: delay in spoken language beyond age 30 months, gross abnormality in language, specific learning disabilities, and verbal, nonverbal, or full scale IQ less than 80.

Although twin studies have been criticized as being highly selective and not representing random samples; as containing greater numbers of monozygotic (MZ) twins than dizygotic twins in contrast to the greater number of dizygotic (DZ) twins in the population; and as containing opposite sex twins in contrast to the reported sex difference in frequency of autism, the twins studies of Folstein and Rutter (1977) and of Ritvo, Freeman, Mason-Brother, Mo, and Ritvo (1985) are quoted in reviews of the syndrome. Ritvo et al. with a sample of 40 twin pairs (23 MZ, 17 DZ) found a concordance rate of 95.7% in MZ twins and 23.5% in DZ twins. Folstein and Rutter, however, with 21 twin pairs (11 MZ, 10 DZ), found 4 MZ (better than one-third) co-twins diagnosed as autistic, while none of the DZ co-twins met the criteria for autism. However, when, like August et al. (1981), Folstein and Rutter included twins with a cognitive-language defect, 9 of the 11 MZ twins were concordant as contrasted with 1 of the DZ twin pairs. The result suggests that genetic factors may indeed contribute to the expression of autism.

The mode of genetic transmission, however, is still obscure. Assuming an autosomal recessive mode, Spence et al. (1985) studied 34 families with at least two affected children, with 30 standard gene markers, and found no suggestive evidence for linkage. Also by comparing the number of shared HLA haplotypes in autistic siblings, Spence et al., found no evidence for an association of HLA and autism or for linkage with HLA and autism. However, testing of a multifactorial polygenic hypothesis and an autosomal dominant hypothesis on the same sample, Ritvo et al. (1985) found a segregation ratio of 0.19 ± 0.07, results leading to rejection of each hypothesis and tentatively consistent with an autosomal recessive mode in inheritance. Smalley et al. (1988), however, excluded dominant and recessive autosomal modes of inheritance because of (a) the occurrence of 3% in siblings, compared to expected values of 50% for dominant modes and 25% for recessive modes; (b) monozygotic concordance is less than the 100% expected for a monogenetic trait, and dizygotic concordance is less than 50% or 25% respectively; (c) observed sex ratios are not unity. Smalley et al. suggested the possibility of multifactorial and genetic heterogeneity.

Specific chromosome abnormality, a fragile X chromosome, located at Xq27, has been identified as associated with up to 16% of autistic children (Brown et al., 1982), with a range of incidence across studies of 0 to 16%. Goldfine et al. (1985), for example, found no fragile X chromosone in 37 autistic children. Watson et al. (1984) found the incidence of fragile X no greater in autistic children than in a population of severely retarded non-autistic males. The fragile X syndrome is associated with large head circumference, prominent forehead, macroorchidism, prognathism, large ears, and narrow facies. In a subgroup of fragile X retarded children, seizures occurred. Thus while the fragile X syndrome may accompany autism or some autistic features, the relationship of fragile X to the autistic syndrome is still obscure. The variability of autism within and between families with the fragile X site is yet unknown. It has been pointed out also that methodological differences in detecting fragile X in cytogenetic studies may also confound results. There are case reports of autism in 47XXX syndrome and in Kleinfelter's syndrome (47XXY).

NEUROPATHOLOGICAL AND ELECTROPHYSIOLOGICAL STUDIES

The search for identifying specific neuropathological abnormalities in autism has included pneumoencephalography, computerized brain scanning, positron emission topography, and comparison microscopy. Early pneumoencephalography studies reported an enlargement of the left ventricular system in autistic children. More recently, S. L. Hauser, DeLong, and Rosman (1975) found 15 of 17 patients to have enlargement of the left temporal horn, and of the 15 patients, 5 also had enlargement of the right lateral ventricle and atrophy of various brain areas. The authors concluded that left medial temporal lobe dysfunction was an important feature in autism. Computerized topographic scans have in general revealed abnormalities but these differ in anatomical location, are inconsistently present, and have not been confirmed in all studies (J. G. Young, Leven, Newcorn, & Knott, 1987). Indeed, Prior, Trees, Hoffman, and Boldt (1984) found no CT scan abnormalities in a subgroup of highfunctioning autistic children. They stress that in many previous studies, the subjects were a mixed group with a high incidence of mental retardation. The enlargement of the left temporal horn, the most consistent finding on the pneumoencephalogram, is not consistently found on the CT scan. Technical differences in the two techniques may account for these inconsistencies.

Using magnetic resonance imaging, (MRI), however, Courchesne, Hesselink, Jernigan, and Young-Courchesne (1987) and Courchesne, Young-Courchesne, Press, Hesselink, and Jernigan (1988) reported hypoplasia of cerebellar vermal lobules VI and VII in autism. In their 1987 paper, Courchesne et al. found such hypoplasia in one autistic patient who was not retarded, and had no seizures or history of drug use or neurological disease. This paper was followed by another (1988), which contrasted MRI findings of 18 autistic patients (age range 6–30 years, mean age 20.9 years; 2 female, 16 male; verbal IQ from 45 to 111 on the Wechsler scale (mean 77), performance IQ between 70 and 112 (mean 85); 13 of whom had IQs between 73 and 108, with a control group of 12 subjects (aged 9–37, mean age 24.8 years; 3 female, 9 male) who had no symptoms of cerebellar dysfunction. The size of the vermal lobules VI and VII was 25% smaller in 14 of the 18 autistic subjects than in the control group, a difference considered significant. The abnormalities differed from those found in patients with other developmental (i. e., olivopontocerebellar dysgenesis) and acquired (focal lesions) abnormalities of the cerebellum and appear to represent a developmental hypoplasia. Other MRI studies (Gaffney & Tsai, 1987) reported enlargement of the fourth ventricle. Garber et al. (1989), however, did not find anatomical neuropathy in the MRI of 15 autistic patients when contrasted with that of 15 control subjects. In the MRIs of the total 30 subjects studied, Garber reported abnormalities in 3: a smaller than expected cerebellar vermis in a normal 13-year-old control child, a smaller than expected cranial size in an autistic 6-year-old whose mother had cytomegalic infection, and two minimal foci in the left frontal white of an autistic girl age 5 who also had an abnormal EEG. Further there was no significant difference in mean cerebellar glucose metabolism, as determined by positron emission tomography of the cerebellum, between seven autistic subjects and eight age-matched controls (Heh et al., 1989).

The few histo-anatomic postmortem studies that have been done are also inconclusive, with no abnormalities found in four retarded persons with autistic behavior (R. S. Williams, Hauser, Purpura, DeLong, & Swisher,

1980). Ritvo et al. (1986), however, did find lower Purkinje cell counts in the cerebellum of four autistic subjects, and Bauman and Kemper (1985), using a comparison microscope, found reduced neuronal size and increased cell density in the forebrain and amygdala of a 19-year-old retarded autistic man. In this patient there were also abnormalities in the neocerebellar cortex in the roof nuclei of the cerebellum. The histological, pneumoencephalogical, and imaging studies offer tantalizing evidence that there is a biological defect, which, however, may be different in different subgroups.

The EEG and event-related potential findings add an electrophysiological component to this inconsistent evidence. Most studies do report abnormal EEGs in a high percentage of autistic children. De Myer et al. (1981), for example, found 60% of the EEGs in 120 autistic children to be grossly abnormal. However, while 65% of autistic patients in J. Small's (1975) study had spike or spike and wave patterns, so did 54% of hospitalized nonautistic, psychiatrically ill children, 40% of mentally retarded children, and 5.8% of normal controls. However, approximately 25–30% of children diagnosed as autistic develop seizures by age 19 (Deykin & MacMahon, 1979; Rutter & Bartak, 1971). It is in this group that the EEG is helpful in the diagnosis of seizure disorder and its treatment. In general, however, EEG clinical correlations have failed to establish replicable subgroups (J. G. Young et al., 1987). Transmission time of brain stem auditory-evoked potential is reported as delayed (Ornitz, 1985). Recent investigation in event-related potentials suggest that because there is a reduced auditory P300 wave in autistic children, they have a limited or selective capacity to orient to novel information, a function essential to the development of cognitive processes.

NEUROCHEMICAL STUDIES

Neurochemical studies of autistic children have attempted to find differences between autistic and control subjects in levels of neurotransmitters; in their metabolities or in the enzymes involved in their metabolism; in blood, urine, and cerebrospinal fluid; in concentration and activity of psychoactive peptides; and in homeostasis of various endocrines. Relatively few differences have stood the test of confirmation studies. Such differences are worth pursuing, however, because they may offer a mechanism through which etiological factors may exert their effect and provide a rationale for attempts to reduce such differences with medication.

The most consistent and replicated finding is in the *serotonin system*, where approximately one-third of autistic children have elevated blood serotonin (5-HT) levels. This finding, originally described by Schaim and Freedman in 1961, has had repeated confirmation (G. M. Anderson et al., 1987). Blood serotonin synthesized primarily in the intestinal tract is carried by platelets. There is no difference, however, between autistic children and controls in number of platelets, in uptake and efflux of 5-HT, or in the degradation of serotonin within the platelets by monoamine oxidase. Hyperserotonemia is not specific to autism. It may also be found in subgroups of mental retardation, of both known and unknown cause (J. G. Young et al., 1987). It is pointed out also that 5-HT is metabolized principally in the lung and liver by MAO-A in contrast to the MAO-B found in platelets. Kuperman, Beegitly, Burns, and Tsai (1985), studying 34 autistic children and 84 of the first-degree relatives, found a "strong familial resemblance" in blood serotonin levels when adjusted for age, sex, and platelet counts, suggesting a genetic similarity. There appeared to be no relationship, however, between blood levels of 5-HT and urinary excretion of its metabolite, 5-hydroxyindoleacetic acid (5-HIAA). There are conflicting reports of levels of 5-HIAA in the central nervous system, with most studies finding a slight decrease. The problem may not be in the absolute level of CSF 5-HIAA but in the ratio of serotonin to dopamine metabolites (5-HIAA/HVA) with the higher ratio associated with higher functional competence.

The elevated level of blood serotonin found in a large subgroup of autistic children has led to therapeutic trials of drugs that lower blood serotonin levels (Geller, Ritvo, Freeman, & Yuwiler, 1982). L-dopa did indeed reduce blood serotonin but did not affect autistic symptoms. A preliminary study of three autistic children (3 years old; 3 years, 7 months; 5 years, 4 months) found that fenfluramine, a sympathomimetic amine, did induce significant reduction of blood serotonin and was associated with increased social responsiveness and cognition (Geller et al., 1982). Subsequent multicenter, placebo-controlled, double-blind studies of the effects of fenfluramine, involving 150 subjects (aged 2 years, 8 months to 24 years) and involving 18 centers, found a subgroup of approximately 33% of the total to have improved in behavior with decreased irritability, temper tantrums, aggressiveness, and self-mutilation and increased relatedness when receiving the drug. The improvement, however, was not related to initial serotonin levels, nor to degree of lowering of serotonin levels; improvement was found in patients with normal as well as in those with initially elevated serotonin. The results, too, were not consistent across studies, with one center, with 16 subjects, reporting no improvement in IQ or behavior during 4 months of fenfluramine treatment. The long-term effects of fenfluramine—i. e.; neurotoxicity—have not yet been evaluated (Biederman, 1985).

Although *dopamine* antagonists have been helpful in the treatment of autistic children, there is contradictory evidence for increased dopaminergic activity in the central nervous system, with one center reporting slightly decreased or normal CSF homovanillic acid in autistic children (D. J. Cohen, Caparulo, Shaywitz, & Bowers, 1977; D. J. Cohen, Shaywitz, Johnson, & Bowers, 1974) and another, more recent (Gillberg, Suennerholm, & Hamilton-Hallberg, 1983) finding elevated CSF HVA. No significant differences in plasma prolactin (PLR) and homovanillic acid (HVA) levels, urinary homovanillic acid, and dopamine excretion were found in 17 autistic subjects who had been unmedicated for at least 6 months before the study and 20 normal controls having similar age and sex distribution. However, in another report, plasma PLR and urinary HVA were significantly increased, but there was no increase in urinary DA in 23 autistic subjects who had been receiving either phenothiazines, haloperidol, or anticonvulsants for at least 3 months before the study (Mindera, Anderson, Volkmer, Akkernuis, & Cohen, 1989). A decrease in urinary MHPG was found in autistic boys (J. Young, Cohen, Caparulo, Brown, & Maas, 1979), but no conclusive evidence of noradrenergic dysfunction has been found.

In spite of the inconclusive results of chemical studies to implicate the dopamine neurotransmitter system as a mechanism for the emergence of the symptoms of autism, there is by now evidence in children with the autistic syndrome in whom no specific organic etiological factor is found that haloperidol does reduce symptoms of fidgetiness, withdrawal, poor relation to the examiner, other speech deviances and stereotopies and that haloperidol is "an effective therapeutic agent for many autistic children when given in an enriched psychosocial environment" (Campbell, 1987, p. 1227). The effectiveness of haloperidol in facilitation of language learning in a group of hospitalized autistic children is discussed in Chapter 8 ("Drugs Affecting Learning and Memory"). Although it is not unusual for haloperidol to be administered over the long term, in daily clinical practice the effect of long-term administration has not had the benefit of systematic study. Perry et al. (1989) assessed the effects of haloperidol given over a 6-month period to a group of 60 carefully selected children with autism. The children were 2 years, 3 months to 7 years, 9 months of age at the beginning of the study; intellectual function ranged from dull normal to severely retarded. Haloperidol dose ranged from 0.5 to 4.0 mg/day. There were a number of parts to this study:

1. The children were randomly assigned to either a continuous drug schedule in which haloperidol was given daily for 6 months, or to a discontinuous schedule with the drug given for 5 days during the week. By the end of 6 months drug efficacy did not differ as a result of the continuous or discontinuous schedule; intermittent drug holidays did not diminish the long-term effectiveness of haloperidol in lowering target symptoms in these autistic children.

2. A 4-week placebo period followed the 6 months on haloperidol. Approximately 60% of the 59 children who completed the study got worse during the placebo period. Of those who did regress, 80% did so within 3 weeks. Those who did get worse had higher conduct problem factor scores at the beginning of the study and had improved less than those who did not regress by the end of the 6-month study.

3. Of the total group, 71.5% improved at the end of 6 months of treatment, 8.5% were worse, and 20% showed no improvement.

4. The use of haloperidol is not without side effects, however. When administered cumulatively for longer than 3 to 12 months, 22% developed dyskinesia involving the mouth, jaws, and tongue and lasting from 16 days to 9 months (Campbell, Grega, Green, & Bennett, 1983).

While haloperidol has its greatest affinity for dopamine receptors not linked to adenylate cyclase, it has the ability to bind to ^{3}H-spiroperidol receptors in the rat frontal cortex, a measure of serotonin binding activity. Haloperidol may thus exert some of its effect through the serotonergic system.

The decreased pain perception, self-injurious behavior, and poor social relations of the autistic child has prompted a search for abnormalities in the *endogenous opioid* system of the autistic (Panksepp, 1979). Direst tests of the opioid hypothesis, however, have yielded conflicting results: Gillberg et al. (1983) found higher fraction-II endorphin activity in the CSF of 11 of 20 autistic children than in controls, whereas R. Weizman et al. (1984) reported reduced plasma opioid levels in 6 of 10 of their autistic group when compared to age-matched controls. Possible explanations for this discrepancy may lie not only in the heterogeneous etiology of autism but also in the heterogeneity of the endogenous opioid system (Weizman measured humoral endorphin levels using leucine-encephalen as the standard; Gillberg found the increase in a methionine-encephalin) and in the diverse material for sampling (central vs. peripheral opioid systems). Nevertheless, Campbell, Adams, Small, McVeight-Tesch, and Curren (1988) found naltrexone, and opiate antagonist, to be helpful in three of five autistic boys (aged 3 years, 8 months to 6 years, 4 months) in decreasing hyperactivity and aggression and in increasing language production and affective responsiveness. Laboratory studies, including liver enzymes and electrocardiogram, were unchanged. In a subsequent open, acute-dose trial, Campbell et al. (1989) administered naltrexone in ascending doses from 0.5 to 2.0 mg/kg/day to 10 hospitalized autistic children aged 3 years, 4 months to 6 years, 5 months (mean 5 years). Behavioral effects noted as early as one-half hour after the daily dose included increased verbal production, decreased stereotypies, and decreased withdrawal. The use of naltrexone in management of autistic children is being described with increasing frequency in the literature (G. Bernstein, Hughes, Mitchell, & Thompson, 1987; B. Herman et al., 1987; Leboyer, Bouvard, & Dugas, 1988).

It may well be that in a subset of autistic children, increased endogenous opioid activity may be associated with depressed immune function and aberrant immune regulation of autoimmune mechanisms found in these children. A. Weizman, Weizman, Szekely, Wijsenbeck, and Liuni (1982), for example, demonstrated that 13 of 17 autistic patients made an inappropriate cell-mediated response to basic myelin protein, a component of brain myelin. The inhibition of macrophage migration in the autistic group may be evidence of an autoimmune response to brain antigen. The possibility of autism resulting from an autoimmune disorder is further suggested by the finding of an antibody to human brain serotonin receptors, found in 7 of 13 autistic children while none was found in 13 normal children (Todd & Ciaranello, 1985). A link between these findings is suggested by the presence of a serotonin-binding site in myelin basic protein, an immunologically active site. That increased endogenous opioids contribute to autoimmune dysfunction with the possibility of blocking that dysfunction by opioid antagonists holds promise for investigation.

EDUCATIONAL MANAGEMENT

(This section was written by Donna Kimes, M.Ed., formerly behavior management specialist, program for autistic students, Hillsborough County, Florida, Public Schools).

Educational management for children with autism has had a relatively short history but has come a long way since Kanner's study in 1943 first defined infantile autism as a specific syndrome. Remedial approaches that followed over the next several decades frequently emphasized psychoanalytic intervention. Treatment centered on deficiencies in the parent–child relationship, and it was not uncommon for parents to be blamed for their autistic child's problems (Schopler & Reichler, 1971). In fact, parents were sometimes actually advised to remove their children from the home for the child's own good (Szurek & Berlin, 1973). Beginning in the mid 1960s, a trend began to emerge, which shifted focus from the psychoanalytic orientation to the study of specific behaviors in the autistic population. Lovaas, Schaeffer, and Simmons (1965) and others, through their pioneering research, demonstrated that autistic children could be taught by using behavior modification methods. The limitation of many of these early studies was that they often focused on segments of behavior in isolation rather than on the child as a complete human being functioning within the environment. The literature since the 1960s is replete with studies documenting the effectiveness, as well as the limitations, of the behavioral approach. From an educational perspective, it is perhaps best at this point to acknowledge, with respect but caution, the contribution that behavioral technology has offered to the field of education for the autistic child. This technology, however, is only one part of the overall picture of educating this type of student, a tool for the teacher to use as needed. Currently, the function of the whole child in a changing environment is now the key emphasis for educational management (Mirenda & Donnellan, 1987).

This section examines educational management in terms of assessment and curriculum considerations, planning and selecting an educational program, and specialized curriculum planning.

Educational Assessment

Educational assessment of the autistic child requires a multidisciplinary effort. Comprehensive evaluation, along the outlines of the pentaxial scheme described in Chapters 5 and 6, is basic for defining the needs of the autistic child. For the autistic child a developmental history will describe the evolution of the child's behaviors and the reaction of his parents to them; psychological evaluation will provide a base line of current functioning; speech evaluation will document the idiosyncratic language of the autistic child; academic testing through formal and informal instruments will provide data from which an individual education plan may be developed; and direct observation of the child in various environments will offer clues for subsequent management.

Educational Settings

The type of educational programming available for children with autism varies greatly with the service options available in the local community, the needs of the child, the desires of the parents, and the philosophy of the service agency. As with any handicapped child, determining which program provides the most appropriate education in the least restrictive environment is a prime consideration. Thus the educational options for the autistic child may run the full spectrum of programs and service offered to handicapped children.

Residential In terms of program design, residential services may be diagnostic, educational, or, maintenance-oriented. The purpose of the diagnostic residential placement is to provide specialized information to be used on return to a less restrictive community setting. Diagnosing needs in the area of medication management, for example, may require an inpatient stay to evaluate physiological functioning and a child's response over time to prescribed medication. Placements of this type are typically of short duration. On the other hand, educational or maintenance-oriented placements can vary greatly in length of stay. Children who are experiencing particularly severe symptoms, such as intense self-injurious behavior, may need residential treatment to obtain the continuity of intervention that 24-hour care can provide. This type of care would hopefully be short-term in nature, terminating when the problem behavior or situation is eliminated or reduced to a more manageable level.

The needs of older adolescents and adults with autism present a different picture with regard to the requirement for appropriate residential services. The availability of quality, community-based options for living outside the family home is essential for this population as they move into adulthood (Mesibov, Schopler, & Sloan, 1983). Congregate living facilities that are small, situated within the community, and focused on continuing training needs in the areas of socialization, self-care, and independent living are one option. Another model, which more closely approximates a normalized setting for young adults, is the supervised apartment. This allows several young adolescents or adults with autism to share an apartment with supervision provided by rotating staff. The roommates are responsible for maintenance of the apartment, meal planning and preparation, and scheduling and performing of varied household activities. Apartments are located within regular community housing complexes to provide for maximum normalization opportunities.

Self-contained Classroom   The self-contained classroom is the most common type of educational setting for those identified as autistic. This model provides education within the same classroom throughout the day. The autistic student may be placed in a self-contained class with other autistic students, or she may be mixed with other handicapped students of varying exceptionalities. With the exception of resource services (such as: occupational or physical therapy), which may be conducted in specialized rooms, all of the teaching is done within the unit. The advantages of this mode, which make it attractive for the autistic student, are several. First, transitions involving other areas of the school are kept to a minimum. This is helpful for the autistic child who reacts adversely to changes in environment. Second, the ratio of students to staff is generally low, increasing the capability to manage the specialized problems of the autistic population. Last, an increased opportunity for educational consistency is possible within the contained setting. This not only cuts down on stressful changes for the child with autism but also allows the staff to coordinate educational plans and streamline their professional skills. The principle disadvantage of the self-contained classroom is that it limits the amount of contact the autistic child has with his nonhandicapped peers. For this reason, teachers must plan for and implement programs that allow for integrating experiences when this model is selected.

Integrated Environment   Educating autistic children within regular education settings is a small but growing trend that has only recently gained attention as a viable service delivery option for this population. Most often this model is selected after the child with autism has spent some time in a self-contained classrooom and is felt to have developed the skills necessary to function in a less restrictive environment. However, some proponents of the integrated model believe that the autistic child is best educated in the mainstream from the beginning of his educational career unless compelling reasons exist to support a more restrictive approach (Biklen, 1987). In any case, educating the child with autism within the regular classroom requires careful assessment, planning, coordination, and a philosophical commitment on the part of parents and professionals. This type of model may use nontraditional staffing patterns. For example, the regular education teacher may receive assistance from the special education teacher or aide within the regular classroom to meet the needs of the handicapped student. An obvious benefit of this model for the child with autism is the opportunity for regular and ongoing normalized interactions with nonhandicapped peers. It provides training within a more natural environment, which reduces the needs for extensive generalization training. These potential benefits, however, must be weighed against the advantages of the self-contained unit. However, it is anticipated that an increase in innovative integration models combining the best features of regular and special education will emerge over the next few years (Regular Lives, 1988)

A Program Model   Several national models known for exemplary work with the autistic population have been effective. One of these programs, the Princeton Child Development Institute, is discussed here, not only because it offers an impressive model for educating autistic children but also because its several program components can be used to illustrate application of the range of program options discussed.

Located in Princeton, New Jersey, in a state-of-the-art facility, the Princeton Child Development Institute (PCDI) operates a private, nonprofit educational and behavioral treatment program for autistic children, youth, and young adults. Two types of programming are offered by PCDI: an educational day program and residential services.

The day program, which serves approximately 25 children, centers on the dual goals of research and treatment. Children receive intensive one-to-one training coupled with small group instruction across a range of curricular areas including academics, language, gross motor skills, and socialization. Students are taught using the principles of applied behavior analysis, and data are collected for validation of methodology and student progress.

Although the Institute is a self-contained facility, within its walls there exists an atmosphere of movement and flexibility. Students switch location and instructors frequently and seem to do so easily, with practice apparently reducing the anxieties associated with change that typically plague many autistic children. Independence with an emphasis on function is fostered in this open but well-programmed environment, which teaches transition and promotes generalization within the overall framework of a self-contained facility.

Although PCDI does not offer an integrated environment as part of its educational program, efforts are geared to returning the child to public school with two-thirds of their graduates entering local school systems and one-third of these going into regular education. Staff are available to assist with this transition and continue follow-up consultation with both the school and the family after discharge. Obviously, a well-trained staff is needed to perform effectively the duties described; PCDI channels a significant amount of time and effort into ongoing staff development.

PCDI's residential services reflect yet another level of service delivery that confirms the program's goal of developing a continuum of services to autistic individuals from early childhood to adulthood. The Family Focus Program, which includes two group homes, represents the first effort in the country to replicate the Teaching-Family Model home specifically for autistic children and youth. Each group home provides a family-oriented residential and teaching environment for five autistic youngsters. Teaching parents live in the home with their own children, which allows for ongoing integration experiences. As can be seen from PCDI's model, opportunities for integration may be found beyond the confines of tranditional classrooms. Normalized contact with peers can occur within a residential setting, too, when efforts are targeted in this direction.

To complete the continuum of services available to the autistic population, PCDI has begun program development activities in the area of adult services. Research is presently under way to examine assessment, vocational, and transitional issues that relate to the lives of adults with autism. It is expected that services will be developed based on the outcomes of this research.

General Considerations in Curriculum

Parent Involvement   The Education for All Handicapped Children Act, P. L. 94-142, ensures that parents have a right to participate in the development of their child's educational program. Toward this end, parents and professional staff cooperate in planning the child's individual educational plan (IEP) by reviewing assessment data, creating instructional goals and objectives, and building in timelines for subsequent evaluation. Because the child with autism may need to develop skills across many areas, it is most helpful to have the parents participate in prioritizing objectives to receive attention by teaching staff. Periodic review of the child's progress and of priorities that have been set, either formally through revision of the IEP or informally through phone calls and written communication, should be built into the process so that adjustment of educational priorities can be done.

For the autistic child, the need for parental involvement goes beyond the routine participation in planning of the child's individual educational plan. Because autistic children typically have great difficulties in generalizing new information across settings, skills that may be learned in the classroom may not transfer to the home environment without active involvement on the part of the parent. Parents can function as teachers of their own children when provided with appropriate training; parents given training in specific behavioral techniques can be effective in producing behavioral change in their children (Koegel, Russo, & Rincover, 1983; Lovaas, Koegel, Simmons, & Stevens-Long, 1973). Service providers, including public school systems, must coordinate efforts so that parent education is available to interested families. What is realistic for each individual family in terms of the amount of time they can devote to working with their autistic child at home is a personal decision that each family must make. A single parent, for example, with a full-time job and three children may decide to work on a single objective, increasing her child's level of independence when taking a bath. If this is the goal the parent sets for the family, the teaching staff should support the parent with implementation. To enhance implementation, some programs have ancillary personnel available (i. e., a behavior management specialist), who can actually visit the home to provide parent training specific to individual needs and targeted skills.

Prerequisite Skills To begin work in any particular content area or on any particular skill, several basic behavioral prerequisites are required. For the autistic child, this translates into mastering the *attending* skills necessary for the instructional lesson. For most purposes, these skills include the ability to sit quietly, to keep hands quiet until directed, and to look at the instructor or materials on command. These simple behaviors can be taught by demonstrating the skills for the child (or helping him physically if needed) and then reinforcing the appropriate behavioral approximation until the child can perform the targeted behavior. It is easier to teach "hands down" and "look" after the child has mastered the response of sitting down when asked. After these skills are well established in the child's behavioral repertoire, the child is ready to begin more content-related tasks with success because she can attend to appropriate stimuli as presented.

Ongoing maintenance of attending behaviors has additional benefits for the autistic child. Because sitting quietly with hands down is incompatible with many inappropriate behaviors, such as running around, screaming, and hand waving, the differential reinforcement of the attending behaviors actually works to decrease inappropriate behaviors without direct intervention or focus on them. Additionally, the capability of performing attending behaviors upon command can assist the autistic child who is having trouble controlling himself. When the teacher observes this type of situation developing, a quiet reminder of "hands down, sit quietly" can help the child who may be becoming overstimulated to settle himself. An example of the benefit of developing attending skills is seen in the management of Anna.

CASE STUDY: ANNA

Anna, a 5-year-old with a diagnosis of autism, had never attended a day care or school program when she enrolled in a self-contained public school classroom designed to serve autistic students. In fact, Anna and her family rarely went anywhere outside their home unless it was an absolute necessity. The reason for this was Anna's rigid refusal to sit on any chairs or sofas except for those in her own home; she also accepted seating in the family car. Consequently, family drives or trips to the park were the only outings within the acceptable range for Anna. Conversely, a trip to McDonald's that required sitting in one of the restaurant's booths would produce tantrums. To avoid these terrible outbursts, the family, Anna's mother in particular, had become virtual prisoners in their own home.

When Anna began attending school, she was no more amenable to trying out the chairs in the classroom than she had been in other foreign environments. She was allowed to sit on the floor for initial activities while staff worked to gain rapport and collect additional information on potential reinforcers for Anna. Eventually, she was moved to a padded chair at a padded table with staff in continual attendance. As expected, severe tantrums resulted. When Anna periodically settled down to catch her breath, immediate rewards (such as favorite foods, drinks, or bubbles) were offered. At first, she rejected these items and renewed her crying and screaming. Over a period of 2 days, however, she began to accept the reinforcement and showed increasingly longer intervals of appropriate sitting behavior. On the third day, she entered class and took her seat when directed, without incident. The tantruming behavior never repeated itself; further, it was extremely fortunate that Anna immediately generalized her new ability to sit in different chairs. She freely changed seats in the classroom and her parents reported a complete absence of the former behavior in community settings. From this point, shaping Anna's behavior to include the other prerequisite skills of "hands down" and eye contact was relatively easy. Her new adaptive behavior not only increased her opportunities for learning new materials, but also did a great deal to enhance her overall level of functioning.

Age-Appropriateness   Because many autistic individuals are developmentally delayed, there is a tendency to relate to or think of them as perennial children. It is important to remember, when planning content for instruction for the autistic student, to keep activities age-appropriate even when the developmental skills level is below the student's chronological age. This is not a difficult task for the teacher; it requires only an awareness of the student as a total person. For example, when planning music activities for autistic adolescents, the teacher should look to secondary curricula or, better yet, consider current favorites from the radio with which the adolescents are likely to be familiar. Just because autistic teens are delayed, it does not mean they need to be singing nursery rhymes that have become inappropriate to their chronological and physiological age. A sensitivity age-appropriateness when planning curricula will hopefully allow for increased normalization into the family and society.

Functional Curricula Of paramount importance when planning curricula for the autistic child is the issue of keeping the curricula functional. This means that the teacher must be sure that what the child is being taught is *useful*—that the skills being developed can serve some useful function for the child. "Useful" in this context is defined in its broadest sense. For example, it is useful to be able to dress oneself in the morning, to feed oneself, and to take care of personal needs. It is also useful to be able to play with another person using common play materials for the purpose of enjoyment and fun. The basic functional skills are usually associated with the area of self-help and independent functioning. The goal for all handicapped individuals, autistic included, is to become as independent, self-sufficient, and fulfilled as possible. When considering functional skills, teacher and parent must consider both the child's immediate and long-term needs. This does not imply that academic skills are inappropriate for autistic students; this depends entirely on the particular student. What is important is that the emphasis remains functional. A 9-year-old who has been working on sight recognition of letters of the alphabet since age 6 and now consistently recognizes half the alphabet may not be working on the development of a functional skill. Perhaps a related skill with a functional component would be learning to write and recognize name, address, and phone number.

Behavioral and Motivational Needs Because of the dangerous or highly interfering nature of self-injurious or high-frequency self-stimulatory behavior, these are some of the first behaviors to be targeted. One of the most effective methods for reducing behavior involves the building of positive behavior as a substitute through the use of *differential reinforcement*. Nontargeted behavior is reinforced consistently to produce increasingly longer periods of time where the problem behavior does not occur. In situations where the child is a danger to himself, more direct intervention may be required, such as the wearing of a protective helmet to reduce damage from head banging, while behavioral interventions are focused on reducing the self-injurious behavior.

Less extreme than the self-injurious behavior, but highly interfering to the learning process, self-stimulatory behaviors may include hand flapping, rocking, screeching, staring at finger, and spinning of objects, to name but a few. These behaviors are typically idiosyncratic and tend to be the preferred activity of the child. Without appropriate behavioral intervention, many autistic children will spend most of their time engaging in these non-functional behaviors. These behaviors are often disturbing to families and can create an ostracizing effect on the child (Devany & Rincover, 1983). Since the behaviors often occur at a high frequency, it can be difficult to teach the child without reduction of the interfering behaviors.

Stimulus overselectivity will also respond to behavioral techniques (Kanner, 1944; Rimland, 1964). Simulus overselectivity, as identified by Lovaas, Schreibman, Koegel, and Rehm (1971), is believed by some to be one of the major contributing factors to the severity of the autistic syndrome. Stimulus overselectivity is the rigid focus on certain specific features of a stimulus while ignoring other features. Autistic children, when displaying this unusual style of attending, typically respond to a more restricted portion of available stimuli, often ignoring relevant features while attending to incidental components. To illustrate: a child is seated at a table across from the teacher working on a task designed to teach receptive labeling of objects. A toy car and a teddybear are present on the table as the teacher directs the child to "Give me the car" or "Give me the bear." These discriminating stimuli are repeated individually at random throughout the task. For the child exhibiting stimulus overselectivity, relevant information that will facilitate the learning of the correct response, such as key features of the car and bear or the teacher's verbal instruction, may be completely ignored. Instead, the child may respond to an unrelated detail of the task; for example, each time he may select the last item touched by the teacher as she rearranges them on the table. This inability to extract salient features from an instructional lesson will obstruct educational progress unless the teacher, using prompting and differential reinforcement, can guide the child to the desired concept.

A learning characteristic commonly seen in autistic individuals as well as in other populations with organic dysfunction is perseveration. This tendency to "get stuck" in a repetitive behavioral mode can be highly interfering to the learning process, as can be seen with the child who continually selects the object on the right-hand side of the table during a language training exercise simply because that was the point of her first selection. The autistic child must be taught, through systematic application of behavioral techniques, to move beyond this restricted manner of functioning; that is, he must learn to sample other behaviors and patterns so that learning is facilitated. Techniques that use positive reinforcement to shape a child's responses away from a perseverative pattern can be most helpful in broadening the overall behavioral repertoire of the child as well as in facilitating acquisition of specific skills.

Dunlap and Koegel (1980) examined the motivational factors that deserve consideration when planning the educational program for the child with autism. Repeated failures, unstimulating materials, and weak or overused reinforcers will likely result in a lack of motivation to perform. Educational tasks can be planned to counteract these and other motivational inhibitors. Building success, for instance, into a particular activity requires accurate targeting of a child's skills level so she is capable of success; teacher intervention through the use of prompts after a minimal number of incorrect responses ensures that the child will not "get stuck" in the failure mode of repeated errors. Varying instructional materials to pique the child's interest can result in heightened motivation (Dunlap & Koegel, 1980). In a similar vein, selecting materials, including reinforcers, that appeal to the child's favored modality for sensory input may improve interest level and subsequent learning (Rincover, Cook, Peoples, & Packard, 1979). Sensory reinforcers are highly individual and must be matched to each child for positive results to be achieved. One of the best ways to determine individual reinforcers is to observe the child functioning freely in an environment full of stimulating and varied materials. From this observation a list of potential reinforcers can be formulated, with consideration given to planned variation of reinforcers to avoid satiation from overuse.

Normalization   Normalization offers handicapped individuals a pattern of existence that is as close as possible to the mainstream of society (Wolfensberger, 1980). In terms of the curriculum for severely handicapped students including the autistic, providing opportunities for normalization requires both a philosophical commitment and a pragmatic plan for individual implementation. Normalization activities within public school systems are frequently referred to as "integration," which describes educational activities designed to allow and encourage handicapped and nonhandicapped students to learn and interact in shared settings. Settings may include the regular education environment, the special class setting, or other common areas of the school. Planning for integration and normalization should be part of each child's IEP; actual implementation must also be individual with options available that focus on child-centered needs.

Obviously, normalization has educational implications far beyond the confines of the actual school environment. Specifically, normalization activities should include community learning activities such as going to the grocery store, using public transportation, or participating in a "walk-a-thon" to support a community service project. For adolescents, a vocational curriculum that focuses on community-based work experiences provides normalized settings in which autistic youth can receive training.

Generalization and Maintenance   In planning the overall educational program for the autistic child or a specific task in a particular content area, consideration must be given at the onset to generalization and maintenance of skills. The ability to generalize skills to a novel environment is deficient in many autistic individuals (Kazdin & Bootzin, 1972; Lovaas et al., 1973; Rutter & Bartak, 1973). Some have speculated that stimulus overselectivity may contribute to this undergeneralization phenomena. Further, skills that are taught in one particular classroom by one particular teacher do not necessarily transfer to other environments without careful programming. Training sufficient exemplars can be an effective tool for the teacher preparing a generalization plan. This involves training any new skill across a sufficient number of settings and people so that the skill will eventually become generalized across all environments.

After skills learned in the original educational environment are generalized to novel environments, a final but important piece of educational programming remains if the autistic student is to sustain his skills over time. Planning for maintenance can be done in tandem with generalization planning since the two areas are closely associated. To program for maintenance, it is necessary to provide regular opportunities for the practice of the skill to be maintained. This design should include specifics of when, where, and how a skill will be performed and who will evaluate and monitor the maintenance program. Also important in the long-term maintenance of skills and behaviors is careful formulation of a plan for reinforcement of the targeted skill to be maintained. Through the use of reinforcement techniques, motivating factors that provide for the continuation of the skills must be addressed and carefully planned, looking at individual student capabilities, level of reinforcement required, and other similar considerations.

To lend perspective to the need for thorough educational programming in the areas of generalization and maintenance, it is helpful to view these particular areas within the context of long-range achievement for autistic student. In terms of day-to-day instruction, considerable effort goes into the teaching and acquisition of specific skills. Many hours can accumulate while the child works to master a particular skill. With all this up-front effort on skills acquisition, it only makes sense that time spent on ensuring the generalization and maintenance of these skills must be equal in effort and perhaps in time expenditure as well. Long-term durability of learned skills remains a most worthwhile goal in educating the child with autism.

Specialized Curriculum

After the comprehensive assessment is complete and general considerations have been reviewed, it is time to examine the specific goals and objectives that will become the student's Individual Educational Plan. Development of this plan involves all members of the educational team, evaluators as appropriate, and the student's parents. Identifying strengths and weaknesses from the assessment data and tying this information to IEP instructional objectives helps establish a plan that is tailor-made for the needs of the individual student. Actual implementation of the IEP will require additional preparation in terms of planning for specific methods of teaching and selection of materials. Instructional teams should meet before implementation and regularly thereafter to coordinate efforts across disciplines.

IEP development and subsequent implementation focus on skill acquisition in key curricular areas. Although each plan must be individualized, the specialized needs of students with autism provide the framework for the following overview of curricular topics.

Communication   Approximately half the individuals diagnosed as autistic do not develop speech. This alone points out the seriousness of the communication handicap for the autistic. For those individuals who do develop some language, the range of capabilities is extremely broad. Because the communication needs of the autistic student cross all settings, careful coordination must occur between various educational staff and home. Decisions must be made for nonverbal students, for instance, in terms of when to explore alternative communication systems, such as sign language or communication boards. Once the primary mode of communication has been determined, training in language development proceeds along a relatively similar path regardless of the specific type of system chosen (Carr, 1983). When beginning language training, a child typically is shaped behaviorally into producing a single word that has been chosen carefully, based on the child's interests and ability to produce certain sounds according to previously obtained vocalization samples. To illustrate, a child who produces the /b/ sound in isolation *and* who selects a ball frequently for free play activities is likely to be a good candidate to learn "ball" as his first word. A procedure utilizing modeling and reinforcement of successive approximations is used to develop the child's first word. Once the child is approximating the word "ball," he should be given a ball to play with when he emits the word so that he will come to understand the representational aspect of language and its functional use.

As vocabulary building continues, beginning carrier phrases such as "I want . . ." are introduced. Some simple abstractions, "yes," and "no" for example, can also be initiated at this time. "Yes/no" are particularly important concepts from a motivational standpoint since they give the child some power over her environment which hopefully will encourage her functional use of the words. Allowing the child to make decisions in a variety of settings based on his use of language will help him generalize the concepts. From this point, language development continues with the child eventually learning to string two, three, and four words together into simple sentences. Prepositions, pronouns, and adjectives are carefully worked into the program. Depending on the child's overall functioning level, he may or may not go on to more difficult language areas that involve asking and answering questions, higher level abstractions, and more advanced grammatical syntax. Language at the lower skills levels as well as at some higher levels is primarily taught through the same modeling of the appropriate language behavior, prompting as needed, and rewarding finer and finer approximation of the behavior until the terminal language skill emerges. At the same time, teaching the child the functional uses for her language is paramount if the motivation for communication is to become intrinsic. Throughout this entire process, close coordination between the speech therapist and classroom teacher is essential if maximum gains are to be realized for the student in the area of language development.

Socialization   A less educationally traditional but extremely important curricular area for autistic students is that of socialization. Becoming a socialized person in our society is an important prerequisite to having access to normalized opportunities to live in the community, seek employment, and enjoy recreational services. The beginning of socialization training starts with bringing inappropriate, bizarre, or dangerous behavior down to manageable levels. Developing positive social behaviors should occur simultaneously with behavioral reduction. The *what, when,* and *how* to teach socialization skills is entirely dependent on the skill level of each individual child; however, some general comments can be made regarding overall curriculum considerations in this area.

Communication obviously plays a major role in our social development and provides a vehicle for relating to other people. The autistic individual's impaired ability to communicate, therefore, puts him at a disadvantage in terms of developing meaningful interpersonal relationships. Improved communication capability will in all likelihood result in improved socialization as well. For this reason, curricular planning for these two areas must be done in tandem. Not all social relating requires the use of language; learning to play cooperatively with peers is an important part of the socialization curriculum which can be worked on whether or not the child has language. A teacher can begin this type of training by providing a model for appropriate play with a small group of two children. (Using a peer facilitator for this activity would also be most appropriate.) The teacher demonstrates the play behavior, such as building with Lincoln Logs, and reinforces each child for imitating the model with his materials. After the child understands and can perform the skills required in building his own house with Lincoln Logs, the next step is for two children to use one set of materials and build a single house together in a cooperative way. Again, the teacher or peer facilitator demonstrates the behaviors to be modeled, this time not only the play behaviors of building assembly but social behaviors such as taking turns, appropriate communication, and eye contact. Reinforcement is provided for correct attempts to model any play and social behaviors.

Once children develop a repertoire of appropriate play behavior with a variety of materials, learning to play games can be a rewarding next step in the socialization process. The actual teaching procedure is the same as described above. Important to add at this point is that play and related social development for children *should be fun!* If teacher and students are not enjoying the activity, it probably needs some redesigning. Along these lines, the teacher should watch for opportunities to reward and encourage any behaviors related to "having fun." Smiling, laughing, and good-hearted teasing are a few examples.

Expanding and enhancing the child's play behaviors is but one part of the socialization process. Learning skills that give the student behaviors to draw on in social settings can go a long way to help the student and others feel more at ease. The ability to greet another person, for example, is a basic social skill that most autistic students can master. Other skills in this area include maintaining appropriate social distance, discriminating public behaviors (i. e., scratching one's head) from private behaviors (masturbation), learning situation-specific behaviors (i. e., how to behave at restaurants), and use of good manners. Continued refinement of appropriate social skills has a place in the curriculum for autistic students from preschool though adolescence and into adulthood.

Cognitive Development Great variation in cognitive abilities exists among individuals with autism. As a result, curricular emphasis in the cognitive domain should center on the individual child and her specific needs. Generally, developmental models can provide a guide for planning purposes, although cognitive development of autistic individuals does not necessarily parallel normal or retarded development (Sigman et al., 1987). Designing tasks in the area of cognition should balance development of strengths with remediation activities aimed at deficit areas. We emphasize again that the development of an autistic child may not parallel the developmental sequences of the normal child.

Educational tasks in this area can range from performance of simple cause-and-effect activities, such as ringing a bell or pulling a string to obtain a toy, to performance of academic subjects like reading and math. Prereadiness and readiness-level tasks span the area between early developmental functioning and academics. Cognitive skills that require the ability to comprehend abstract concepts are typically more difficult for an autistic child to master. To illustrate, learning the names of the numerals from 1 to 20 is a concrete task—that is, the numerals have a defined shape that does not change over time. The skills required use rote memory and visual discrimination. A child who might master this task within a few days might have a much more difficult time learning that the numeral 3 actually represents three items. Since 3 no longer represents a fixed numerical shape, but now can mean three apples, three boys, or three ants, the child can become confused with the changing nature of the abstraction. Finding creative ways to teach these concepts to the child with autism provides an ongoing challenge.

Self-Help and Daily Living Skills   Functionality cannot be overstressed when considering curriculum options for the autistic population. No area can be considered more functional than the development of self-help skills. Any individual who cannot dress himself, feed himself, toilet himself, and look after other personal needs will have to have this done for him by another. Parents provide this care for their young children routinely; only when the care is still needed beyond certain somewhat flexible timeliness do parents become concerned. For severely handicapped individuals, autistic included, a lack of basic self-sufficiency in the area of self-care can doom them to lives overburdened with some level of institutional care. For this reason, the curricular area of self-help should receive special attention.

The teaching of self-help skills often uses task analysis to make the learning of complex skills sequences more manageable. Task analysis first allows for the division of a task, such as putting on a sock, into step-by-step components (Table 16-4). Next, the teacher plans for the use of a chaining procedure, a behavioral technique used to "chain" the task-analyzed steps together in a cumulative manner until all steps in the sequence can be performed as one complete task. Chaining, which can be done either in a forward or backward progression, offers a most effective method for teaching many self-help skills.

Selecting self-help areas of focus must be done in cooperation with the parent. Parental assistance with follow-up home programs can make the acquisition of the specific target skill come much more quickly. Since the domain of self-help covers activities that typically occur at home, ample opportunities exist for practice and reinforcement.

Related to self-help is the curricular area often referred to as Daily Living Skills. In terms of functionality, this area is perhaps a step removed from the basics of self-help, yet these skills are also important when viewed as part of the progression toward the long-range goal of maximum independence for the autistic person. Skills such as housecleaning, cooking, and caring for one's clothing are customary components of the daily living skills cluster. Application of the behavioral techniques of chaining and shaping assists students in acquiring these skills. Creating ample opportunities at home and at

Table 16-4   Task Analysis: Putting on a Sock

(Note: Tube sock used to avoid need for top/bottom orientation of sock.)
1. Place fingers on sock opening and hold.
2. Pick up sock by opening.
3. Move sock to foot area.
4. Orient sock over toes.
5. Pull sock up to heel.
6. Pull sock up to calf.

school for the ongoing practice of these skills remains an important educational objective.

Prevocational/Vocational Skills Preparing students for the world of work includes analysis of potential job markets, liaison with businesses for placement opportunities, and training of students. Historically, autistic students have had few chances to enter normalized work settings after completing school. In fact, the autistic adult who lands a placement in a limited sheltered workshop slot is often considered fortunate. On the positive side, innovative and precedent-setting programs such as Community Services for Autistic Adults and Children (CSAAC) in Rockville, Maryland, are beginning to offer community-based, less restrictive options for employment for individuals with autism (Juhrs, Brown, & Ingram, 1987). CSAAC's training occurs entirely at the job site thus avoiding some of the generalization barriers that so often impede the autistic. In Rockville, employers using this newly found employment pool state that they are very satisfied with the work provided. Job coaches are assigned to assist the autistic person in adapting to the work environment and in learning the skills necessary to successfully carry out the job. These support personnel remain with the autistic individual for as long as needed.

To prepare autistic students who are still in school for future employment, specific skills can be practiced in the classroom. Creative instructors can canvas the school and the community for meaningful jobs for the students. Collating, pricing, assembly tasks, crafts and sewing, and building and grounds maintenance are just a few examples of work activities that may be done in the classroom and around the school. Building appropriate work behaviors can also contribute to the success of future employment for the autistic individual. Learning how to stay on task, ask for assistance, take a break, and avoid antisocial behaviors are very important requisites to eventual vocational adaptation in the workplace.

SUMMARY

The diverse symptoms of autism may be classified according to abnormalities in object relations, in communication and language, and in stereotypic behavior. These symptoms are seen in impaired social relations, in communication difficulty along a broad spectrum from mutism to echoing, and in inappropriate, concrete, irrelevant verbigeration, with the capacity for rote memory and sometimes with extraordinary rote language. The behavior may vary from stereotypy and perseveration and resistance to change, to overwhelming anxiety and perceptual sensitivity. The primary defect has variously been considered to be impaired object relations and/or the communication defect. The communication defect is seen by some as a problem of higher cortical activity in the ability to organize perceptual structure. A primitive quality of autistic physiology is seen in its plasticity, immature homeostasis, poor muscle tone, motility based on primitive postural reflexes, torporous states of consciousness, and respiratory-speech dissociation and may be responsible for the inability of the autistic child to be aware of himself as a discrete organism.

The autistic syndrome is heterogeneous in etiology. Two major groups have been identified; the first with a known organic or metabolic defect of the central nervous system, the second with no known organic CNS defect. The autistic syndrome may thus be a final common pathway for severe pervasive developmental deviations of childhood. The prevalence of the syndrome is 2 to 4 per 10,000 of the population. Family history and sibling and twin studies suggest a hereditary influence in autism with sibling of affected subjects affected approximately 60 times the rate of the general population and a higher concordance rate found in monozygotic over dizygotic twins. The mode of genetic transmission is obscure. A chromosome abnormality, a fragile X chromosome located at Wq27, has been associated with some autistic children. This marker, however, is also found in a higher percentage of mentally retarded children. Morphologically, enlargement of the left ventricular system has been seen on the pneumoencephalogram; inconstant anomalies on the CT scan; and hypoplasia of cerebellar vermis lobules VI and VII on magnetic resonance imaging. The latter finding is unconfirmed. Histoanatomic studies have also been inconsistent; lower Purkinje cell counts in the cerebellum have been reported. A high percentage of autistic children have abnormal electroencephalograms. Approximately 25% of children diagnosed as autistic develop seizures by age 19, but EEG–clinical correlations have failed to establish replicable subgroups. The transmission time of the brain auditory-evoked potential is reported to be delayed.

Chemically, the most consistent and replicated finding is elevated blood serotonin levels. There appears to be no relationship between blood serotinin levels and urinary excretion of 5-HIAA. Blood serotonin levels may be reduced with fenfluramine, which has been reported to improve social responsiveness and cognition. The fenfluramine effect, however, has no relationship to initial serotonin levels or its degree of lowering serotonin levels. In spite of inconclusive implication of the dopamine system, haloperidol is an effective therapeutic agent for autistic children, facilitating language learning. Naltrexone has been used to decrease self-injurious behavior. The relationship of this finding to increased endogenous opioid activity is under investigation.

Educational management is based on a comprehensive assessment including speech and language and observation of the child's behavior and functional abilities. The emphasis now is not on small segments of behavior but on the whole child as he must adjust to a changing environment. While the education settings may vary from residential, to self-contained class, to integrated classes, and, finally, to mainstream classes, depending on the needs of the child, behavior modification is a major tool in effecting change. Parents, too, are involved in reinforcing the behavioral change and in generalizing the behavior to environments other than school. Mastering the attending skills necessary for instruction and decreasing self-destructive and self-stimulatory behavior are prerequisities for further progress. The curriculum is designed to be age-appropriate (i. e., adolescent music for adolescents) and functional, relating to self-help and independent function. Even academic learning may be done in relation to the skills needed for these ideal goals. Stimulus overselectivity and perseveration may respond to appropriate behavior modification. Generalization and maintenance of the new skills require continued opportunities to practice them.

The prognosis, nevertheless, is guarded.

PART FOUR

FUTURE DIRECTIONS FOR SERVICE AND RESEARCH

CHAPTER SEVENTEEN

Future Directions
for Service
and Research

The imminent arrival of the final decade of the twentieth century, like other endings, invites some introspection about the past and the future of our field. Admittedly, the last 50 years have seen rapid growth not only in recognition of the problems of children who fail to learn in school, but also in legally binding provisions for their education in every public school in the country. Broad-scale research efforts have developed, engaging the skills of investigators in behavioral sciences, medicine, education, health sciences, linguistics, genetics, computer sciences, and neurosciences. If these investigations have not answered all the questions being asked about learning disorders, they have produced a literature that is vast in scope and variety. These first 50 years have been productive, busy, innovative, sometimes acrimonious—what can we expect of the future? If one can judge the future by the past, four major forces can be expected to shape the direction our field takes in the years to come: economic, sociopolitical, educational, and scientific.

ECONOMIC INFLUENCES

Programs flourish or fade sometimes not because of their intrinsic worth, but because of the economic contexts in which they exist. The services needed for children with learning disorders are not inexpensive, even though the consequences of failing to serve these children are much more expensive. Programs to provide those services must bid against other worthwhile (and sometimes not so worthwhile) programs and initiatives. This is an old story, the familiar budget process in a democratic government. However, the economy of our country is changing. Americans are beginning to recognize that the financial resources we have taken for granted for so many years are limited. No longer can we draw on the profits of a leading production-oriented economy. We have become a debtor nation, dependent on capital from other countries. Deficits resulting from military spending affect the stability of our currency at home and abroad. The giddy prosperity of the longest bull market in the history of the stock exchanges is winding down. Other vital concerns—health care, environmental issues, housing, and the deteriorating infrastructure—relegated to a low priority in the recent past, are competing for limited financial resources.

The field of learning disorders will feel the effects of these financial constraints. At the program level, services to children will need clear, data-based evidence of their effectiveness in order to survive in the competition for scarce funds. Research will also feel the effects of the cold winds of economy in greater competition for funding. It may be that there will be greater emphasis on funding of program research in the belief that greater integration of resources in centers makes for more effective and cost-effective investigations. Unfortunately, this trend may limit the opportunities for independent experimentation by people from the applied areas.

SOCIOPOLITICAL INFLUENCES

Sociopolitical influences will also affect the future of learning disorders. Already apparent are the effects on child care practices of the large increase in employment of women outside the home. The future might expect to see a marked increase in the number and comprehensiveness of child care facilities for all children. Emanating from this need is the trend to year-round schools. Relevant also to our field will be the development of diagnostic and intervention programs for young children who show signs of the developmental delays that prevention research has found to be associated with learning disorders. Recent legislation (such as P. L. 99-457) has taken some initial steps, but future directions should see greater expansion of these efforts. Work with infants, toddlers, and preschoolers will require greater interdisciplinary cooperation between educators and child health specialists than now exists in any but the most enlightened settings. The blending of skills may even result in the development of the role of the *educateur* as it exists in some settings in Europe.

The present sociopolitical climate is characterized by a number of grass-roots movements resulting from disenchantment with current leadership in government and business on some specific issues like consumerism, peace, environmental concerns, health issues, and education. Individuals, feeling that solutions for these problems have been too slow in coming through regular channels of government, try to take matters into their own hands by forming organizations to advocate for the causes they value. This is a development that bodes well for the field of learning disorders. It is to be remembered that parent groups, eventually banding together as the Association for Children and Adults with Learning Disabilities, have played strong leadership and advocacy roles in the passage and implementation of current legislation for the education of handicapped children. The continued vigilance of parents like those in ACLD will be important in maintaining and expanding services for children with learning disorders.

A third sociopolitical influence on the field of learning disorders is the pluralistic society in the United States. It can be expected that, because of continuing population mobility, variations in language and culture will be represented in schools throughout the nation. Schools responding to this influence will be required to do more than open a class in which English as a second language is taught. It will mean that all school personnel will need to learn to distinguish between language disability and language differences. School personnel representing language and cultural differences will need to be hired or in some cases recruited and trained. Existing measures need to be examined in terms of bias; in some cases, adaptations of measures need to be developed and standardized (i. e., Hagin, 1984). Clinical personnel, in particular, may need continuing education in this area.

The education problems of poor children demand greater attention. For example, a 5-year collaborative study of children with special needs found that more than one-third of the children in special education are poor and that for more than one-third, their mothers had not completed high school. What is there in the culture of poverty that will finally result in learning failure? Are there specific patterns of central nervous system dysfunction resulting from povery? Are motivational and attentional factors of major importance in this group? If there are neuropsychological patterns resulting from inappropriate stimulation at critical ages of the child's development, how can we interrupt the patterns of failure? How, in the first place, can we prevent them? We know there is an accumulated body of evidence implicating the culture of poverty in learning failure. With all our knowledge, however, there is still a higher percentage of school failure with its attendant emotional, vocational, and social problems among the children of the poor. With rare exceptions, busing has not equalized opportunity and the cycle of disadvantage continues. The linguistic differences found in ghetto and in affluent children need more precise description, and the factors in poverty influencing learning need to be more clearly defined. From a practical point of view, the results of the Head Start programs and of the early childhood intervention programs, particularly those of Caldwell, Bradley, and Staff (1984), need reexamination, refinement, and reapplication to the problems of today. It may well be that in the future, poverty itself needs to be considered a handicapping condition and included in the early education programs mandated under P. L. 99-457 for the handicapped child. Such programs may be a start for offering these children the appropriate stimulation they never received. A closer cooperative effort between the Head Start programs that do exist and the early education for handicapped programs that are currently being formed appears essential. Documented description of the models of instruction and stimulation in these programs, and long term follow-up studies are needed. As it is now (D. L. Friedman et al, 1988) even when children of the poor do have academic problems they are more often placed in classes for emotionally or behaviorally handicapped children than in classes for children with learning disabilities (see also Chapter 1, "The Problem of Definition," case study: Johnny).

EDUCATIONAL CHANGES

The restructuring of *teacher education* through the Holmes Group is a major influence for the future of the field of education. The Holmes Group represents schools of education in leading universities who are working to improve educational standards in order to empower teachers as a major professional group. The curricular pattern includes a 4-year liberal arts degree followed by master's level training in education. Although specific training programs vary among the participating universities, the goal of the program in producing better educated, professional teachers is clear. Close cooperation between university and field-based training sites is seen as a major training strategy that will be helpful for both institutions: The public school will have the opportunity to integrate new approaches and research findings into their curricula; the university researchers will have contact with the realities of the schools. It can be expected that the long-term impact of these efforts to provide better educated teachers will have a salutary influence on the field of learning disorders through improved instruction in the mainstream, earlier recognition of problems, and more effective intervention.

A continuing trend that will probably accelerate in the future is the *broadening of the age groups served* by the public schools. Traditionally, the compulsory education statutes mandated school attendance between ages 7 and 16 years. Legislation for public school services for handicapped children age 3 to 5 years has been passed, and programs for handicapped infants and toddlers are developing. Services for older adolescents and young adults are also developing in public schools, community colleges, and agencies through the transition programs funded through the U.S. Department of Education. These nontraditional older students frequently come back to school for help with learning disorders that were not dealt with appropriately during their school years. Higher levels of literacy are required for vocational competence in our technology-driven workplace. This demand will probably result in expansion of adult education programs well beyond the current basic literacy and GED (general educational development certificate levels) to broad programs of continuing education for all adults.

There are, however, difficulties in introducing a new program into the school system. First is the inertia inherent in a vast bureaucracy. The need for a program must seep through successive layers of bureaucracy, the successive layers of people who would be involved in a new project; the teachers, the principals, the superintendent, the Boards of Education, and, not the least, the parents' and teachers' unions. Then there must be some consensus on how to fill the gap, some decision process as to the solution and how the selected program may be modified to fit the local conditions.

Even when there is an awareness of need, a desire to fill that need, a consensus as to how to fill that need, and even understanding how budgetary constraints may be overcome, there is a psychological barrier to the introduction of a new program, a barrier inherent in the teacher directly involved with its implementation. Keogh (1986) discussed some of the problems inherent in school-based research and in implementation of programs.

She stated that "even where program philosophies or directives are clear and agreed upon, the accuracy of the implementation may not be the same, "that is, in practice, accurate descriptions of what happens between pupil and teacher may not be clear or even be known." To these problems may be added the entrenched involvement of some to a particular method of teaching or intervention, so that new programs are resisted. How a particular teaching method may have evolved, perhaps as a result of unpredictable antecedents, the result of minor perturbations in techniques, or the lack of reliable and valid documentation, may not be an issue to its proponents. Once established, however, the procedures become institutionalized, taught to the teachers who, in turn, develop their own security in its use and are threatened, become anxious, if that security is challenged. Our failure to recognize such resistance will doom a new project at its very beginning. These problems—a bureaucracy difficult to change, never enough money, teachers whose security may be threatened—are, of course, generic problems inherent in the introduction of any change into an unyielding public school system.

DEVELOPMENT IN SCIENCE AND TECHNOLOGY

Perhaps the most rapid expansion in the field of learning disorders is in science and technology. Research is proceeding in at least five fronts.

1. *The genetic.* There is evidence that one subset, at least, of children with specific learning disability does have some inherited defect. Although learning disabilities were thought to be inherited, as long ago as 1905, genetic studies are only at the threshold of knowedge. Twin studies, segregation analysis, and linkage patterns such as that investigated in the Colorado Reading Study, should yield more information. In the future, the geneticist, with her tools of molecular biology, may isolate particular chromosomes and particular areas of chromosomes related to subsets of learning disordered subjects. Advances in the molecular genetics of learning disorders will be carried along with advances in molecular genetics of other disorders and should tell us more than we now know about the cause of specifc learning disability.

2. *The anatomical.* This, too, is an important area of investigation, one in which the Orton Society, with its support of Galaburda's investigations, plays a prominent role. Anatomic studies are also really only beginning. As more material is accumulated, the possible artifacts and the contamination with other brain processes may cancel out, leaving the true morphological structure of the specific learning disability as a residual. Even now correlations are beginning between the gross anatomical asymmetry present in the normal brain and hemisphere specialization. In the brain of individuals suf-

fering from "dyslexia," such asymmetry patterns are altered, and the normal cellular architecture in the left hemisphere is disturbed with dysplasia and ectopia. While such morphological differences appear to be real, confirmation is needed. If anatomical abnormality can be found in dyslexia, we still have the problem of understanding how this change alters function so that learning problems ensue. Further, the presence of anatomical anomaly does not tell us why these changes are there, what has caused them, and how we can prevent them. It is possible that the changes are not specific to SLD at all, but are a final common pathway of expression for many different etiological factors, one of which may be genetic. That early experience also may contribute to the anatomical deviation is not impossible. Gross anatomical patterns may also be studied by other techniques, now becoming almost routine, particularly nuclear magnetic imaging and computerized tomography. With MRI, the surface of the brain may be visualized and gross asymmetrics, particularly in the temporal lobe, may be measured. Cerebral blood flow measures and positron emission tomography are research tools that will undoubtedly be used in future studies.

3. *The Neuropsychological.* Neuropsychological investigations have applied a variety of research paradigms designed to describe differences in children who learn well from those who do not. From most of these studies, there is a general agreement that clusters have delineated subgroups distinguished by deficits in information processing in any or all modalities. The search for a unitary pattern, a single functional defect characteristic of all children with learning problems, is doomed to fail although, in some carefully selected samples, common deficits may be found. The subgroup studies are a necessary contribution to describing the heterogeneity of reading disorders although, with them, we are no closer to determining the cause of each subgroup. Is each subgroup different in its origins, or is each a different manifestation of the same underlying cause? What is the relationship of subgroups to etiological factors? These are some of the questions we hope future research will answer. More immediately, however, there are a number of problems to be considered:

- Aside from the problems inherent in sampling, choice of test probes, and methodology, there exists the question of which of the deficits found are actually related to the reading problem, or, although representing functions of weakness, are these deficits irrelevant to the task of reading? Perhaps the tests used should mirror the normal processes of learning to read. This implies the need to define the normal process of acquiring reading, spelling, writing, and arithmetic skills and how the skills and techniques may differ in normal children.

- Is there a difference in prognosis for children in different subgroups? While some longitudinal studies have suggested that the auditory processing deficits have a better prognosis than the visual-spatial ones (Rourke, 1985), these conclusions require confirmation. Longitudinal studies are indicated.

- Can we relate educational intervention to patterns of subgroups? Can we clearly demonstrate that educational intervention that is related to the individual deficits does make a difference in outcome?

At this writing such questions are unanswered, and educational practice needs to be explored. As Fisk, Finnell, and Rourke (1985) stated: "A systematic, theoretically based approach to the remediation of learning disabled children would seem to be the most useful way of proceeding at this time. . . . Indeed the need to determine subtype by treatment interactions. . . . is the most pressing need in the field today" (p. 338). It is unlikely that school systems will be constrained to mobilize the resources for determining subtypes unless there are convincing, practical reasons to do so.

4. *The electrophysiological.* Research in this area is proceeding in two directions. First, are there quantitative differences in the EEG patterns in children with learning disorders as compared with control groups, as each responds to tasks requiring the brain to process information? Such studies look at the spectral (wave length) patterns, the quantity of those patterns (power), and the coherence and symmetry of patterns in homologous portions of the recording. The result may be expressed in statistically determining deviations from referenced groups and visually displayed in topographic pictures. The second direction of research is in the wave forms (event-related potentials) that appear up to 600 milliseconds or more following specific stimuli that also make demands upon the brain to evaluate and think as information is processed. In addition to identifying gross differences between learning disordered children and normal groups, these studies may be able to define subgroups on the basis of electrophysiological patterns. It will be challenging to determine the relationship between electrophysiological patterns, neuropsychologically derived subgroups, and etiological clusters as outlined in Table 2-1. This field of study needs basic normative data, defining event-related potentials of normal children. What are the electrophysiological events that normally accompany visual or auditory stimuli? What are the subtle differences as meaning of the stimuli is required, as semantic incongruities are introduced, or as arithmetic problems are solved? What is the range of normal? How different are individual differences? These studies are important in understanding brain–behavior relationships. They will become more meaningful when correlated with other aspects of behavior—thinking and feeling. If it can be demonstrated that selected samples of learning disordered children do indeed differ in their event-related potentials, can that potential be brought to normal with training of the spe-

cific function related to the difference? In other words, can it be demonstrated that training alters electrophysiology as it alters function? Here also a collaborative, interdisciplinary effort is needed.

5. *The use of drugs.* A fifth area of research, although it is not directly related to the etiology of learning disorders, may have profound influence in understanding the chemistry of these disorders and in their practical management. This area is the use of drugs in influencing learning. In the past 10 years, a new class of drugs, called the nootropic drugs, have been described. These drugs are said to facilitate learning, to reduce the adverse effects on memory of electroshock and hypoxia, and to enhance transcollosal transfer of information. These drugs may have possible specific effects on the left hemisphere. Piracetam, the first drug of this class, is chemically related to gamma amino buteric acid; its mechanism of action is reported as an activator of brain adenylate cyclase and thus it may enhance the action of cyclic AMP-sensitive protein kinase, which, in turn, will increase phosphorylatin of proteins involved in the acquisition of learning. Results of a multicenter study of the action of Piracetam suggest that this drug increases reading speed without sacrificing accuracy and, as reported in some centers, also improves reading comprehension. Although there was lack of uniformity among the centers in results, and although there are questions about methodology, the overall effect of nootropic drugs on learning is favorable. At present nootropic drugs are still in the research phase. Undoubtedly, research with nootropic drugs will continue. They should be studied in children who do not have learning disorders as well as those who do, and their long-term effects must be carefully evaluated.

THE NEED FOR PREVENTIVE PROGRAMS

There is an additional practical issue, for which we look to the reasonably foreseeable future, for resolution. That is the implementation on a large scale of programs to prevent learning disorders. At present only 29% of children with special needs in our public school system were diagnosed before the age of 5, and these are primarily children with physical handicaps and vision or hearing disorders. Preventive programs for learning disorders are clearly indicated. Preventive programs involve the reliable and valid identification of children, no later than at age 5 or 6, in kindergarten or in first grade, for whom learning failure is predicted, and then the introduction of a successful intervention for these children so that failure does not occur. The identification system must be a practical one to be implemented on a large scale; it must be able to scan large numbers of young children quickly and to be administered and interpreted reliably by school personnel with minimal training. Moreover, the identification system must be appropriate for the population scanned. In its development, it must meet the statistical constraints set by the American Psychological Association with a minimum number of false positives and false negatives, be based on a documented theoretical foundation, and integrated with the intervention part of the program. The intervention program, too, should have a firm theoretical base, be tested in school-based projects, with sufficient longitudinal observation to prove its effectiveness. Although there are many criterion-based readiness scales, there are few preventive programs meeting the criteria of the American Psychological Association and even fewer programs that combine identification with intervention.

A number of well-researched identification programs are available (see Chapter 10, "Prevention of Disorders of Learning"). Replication by investigators other than the developers of a program are needed. What has impeded the implementation of these programs is not their success in the prevention of learning failure, but their failure in the marketing and, almost, the selling needed to have school systems accept them. That these programs will have increasing importance in the near future is suggested by the trend to identifying handicapping conditions even before the age of 5 and providing systematic education for them. From a hard dollars-and-cents point of view alone, prevention makes sense. The average annual cost for the special educational services for the speech-impaired child is about $5,000, about one-third more than the average for each child without handicaps. Annual costs are about $6,000 for each learning disabled child, the emotionally or behaviorally impaired child, and the cognitively retarded child. The dollar cost of the emotional, behavioral, social, and vocational burdens of learning disorders cannot be estimated.

CONSTRAINTS AND OPPORTUNITIES

As the field of learning disorders approaches the twenty-first century, it is not exempt from the economic and social conditions of our society. The demands of these forces, however, are creating new opportunities: broadening the age groups we serve, improving the training of our teachers, implementing prevention, and encouraging the integration of professional skills to serve the "related services" legislated by P. L. 94-142. The new decade should see advances in the scientific base for our understanding of learning disorders: genetics, morphology, neuropsychology, electrophysiology, and pharmacology. What the future needs is the integration of skills and services at every jurisdictional level, involving departments of education and mental health and social services pooling knowledge and financial resources. The child with a learning disorder has multidimensional problems; multidimensional solutions are required.

APPENDIX A

Code of Fair
Testing Practices
in Education

Note. From "Code of fair testing practices in education" by the Joint Committee on Testing Practices, 1988, American Psychological Association, 1200 17th Street, Washington, D.C. 20036

A   DEVELOPING/SELECTING APPROPRIATE TESTS

Test developers should provide the information that test users need to select appropriate test.

Test Developers Should:

1. Define what each test measures and what the test should be used for. Describe the population(s) for which the test is appropriate.
2. Accurately represent the characteristics, usefulness, and limitations of tests for their intended purposes.
3. Explain relevant measurement concepts as necessary for clarity at the level of detail that is appropriate for the intended audience(s).
4. Describe the process of test development. Explain how the content and skills to be tested were selected.
5. Provide evidence that the test meets its intended purpose(s).
6. Provide either representative samples or complete copies of test questions, directions, answer sheets, manuals, and score reports to qualified users.
7. Indicate the nature of the evidence obtained concerning the appropriateness of each test for groups of different racial, ethnic, or linguistic backgrounds who are likely to be tested.
8. Identify and publish any specialized skills needed to administer each test and to interpret scores correctly.

Test users should select tests that meet the purpose for which they are to be used and that are appropriate for the intended test-taking populations.

Test Users Should:

1. First define the purpose for testing and the population to be tested. Then, select a test for that purpose and that population based on a thorough review of the available information.
2. Investigate potentially useful sources of information, in addition to test scores, to corroborate the information provided by tests.
3. Read the materials provided by test developers and avoid using tests for which unclear or incomplete information is provided.
4. Become familiar with how and when the test was developed and tried out.
5. Read independent evaluations of a test and of possible alternative measures. Look for evidence required to support the claims of test developers.

6. Examine specimen sets, disclosed tests or samples of questions, directions, answer sheets, manuals, and score reports before selecting a test.

7. Ascertain whether the test content and norms group(s) or comparison group(s) are appropriate for the intended test takers.

8. Select and use only those tests for which the skills needed to administer the test and interpret scores correctly are available.

B INTERPRETING SCORES

Test developers should help users interpret scores correctly.

Test Developers Should:

9. Provide timely and easily understood score reports that describe test performance clearly and accurately. Also explain the meaning and limitations of reported scores.

10. Describe the population(s) represented by any norms or comparison group(s), the dates the data were gathered, and the process used to select the samples of test takers.

11. Warn users to avoid specific, reasonably anticipated misuses of test scores.

12. Provide information that will help users follow reasonable procedures for setting passing scores when it is appropriate to use such scores with the test.

13. Provide information that will help users gather evidence to show that the test is meeting its intended purpose(s).

Test users should interpret scores correctly.

Test Users Should:

9. Obtain information about the scale used for reporting scores, the characteristics of any norms or comparison group(s), and the limitations of the scores.

10. Interpret scores taking into account any major differences between the norms or comparison groups and the actual test takers. Also take into account any differences in test administration practices or familiarity with the specific questions in the test.

11. Avoid using tests for purposes not specifically recommended by the test developer unless evidence is obtained to support the intended use.

12. Explain how any passing scores were set and gather evidence to support the appropriateness of the scores.

13. Obtain evidence to help show that the test is meeting its intended purpose(s).

C STRIVING FOR FAIRNESS

Test developers should strive to make tests that are as fair as possible for test takers of different races, gender, ethnic backgrounds, or handicapping conditions.

Test Developers Should:

14. Review and revise test questions and related materials to avoid potentially insensitive content or language.

15. Investigate the performance of test takers of different races, gender, and ethnic backgrouns when samples of sufficient size are available. Enact procedures that help to ensure that differences in performance are related primarily to the skills under assessment rather than to irrelevant factors.

16. When feasible, make appropriately modified forms of tests or administration procedures available for test takers with handicapping conditions. Warn test users of potential problems in using standard norms with modified tests or administration procedures that result in non-comparable scores.

Test users should select tests that have been developed in ways that attempt to make them as fair as possible for test takers of different races, gender, ethnic backgrounds, or handicapping conditions.

Test Users Should:

14. Evaluate the procedures used by test developers to avoid potentially insensitive content or language.

15. Review the performance of test takers of different races, gender, and ethnic backgrounds when samples of sufficient size are available. Evaluate the extent to which performance differences may have been caused by inappropriate characteristics of the test.

16. When necessary and feasible, use appropriately modified forms of tests or administration procedures for test takers with handicapping conditions. Interpret standard norms with care in the light of the modifications that were made.

D INFORMING TEST TAKERS

Under some circumstances, test developers have direct communication with test takers. Under other circumstances, test users communicate directly with test takers. Whichever group communicates directly with test takers should provide the information described below.

Test Developers or Test Users Should:

17. When a test is optional, provide test takers or their parents/guardians with information to help them judge whether the test should be taken, or if an available alternative to the test should be used.

18. Provide test takers the information they need to be familiar with the coverage of the test, the types of question formats, the directions, and appropriate test-taking strategies. Strive to make such information equally available to all test takers.

Under some circumstances, test developers have direct control of tests and test scores. Under other circumstances, test users have such control. Whichever group has direct control of tests and test scores should take the steps described below.

Test Developers or Test Users Should:

19. Provide test takers or their parents/guardians with information about rights test takers may have to obtain copies of tests and completed answer sheets, retake tests, have tests rescored, or cancel scores.

20. Tell test takers or their parents/guardians how long scores will be kept on file and indicate to whom and under what circumstance test scores will or will not be released.

21. Describe the procedures that test takers or their parents/guardians may use to register complaints and have problems resolved.

APPENDIX B

Outline for Mental Status Evaluation

Division of Child and Adolescent Psychiatry, University of South Florida, College of Medicine.
Compiled by Archie A. Silver, M.D.

Name: ——————————————   Date: ——————————————

DOB: ——————————————   Current Medication (date): ———

CA: ——————————————   ——————————————————

Psychological Testing Dates—Results: ——————————————

Circle appropriate descriptors.

1. General Appearance:
    1. neat, clean, appropriate
    2. dirty, disheveled, unkempt
    3. gender appropriate
    4. age appropriate

2. Affect:
    1. appropriate
    2. happy, contented, satisfied, hopeful, confident, enthusiastic, joyful, interested
    3. sad, unhappy, disappointed, discouraged, crying, feeling of uselessness, and futility
    4. suicidal thoughts or attempts
    5. elated
    6. fluctuating elation
    7. angry, annoyed, irritated
    8. anxious, fearful, apprehensive
    9. flat
    10. labile

3. Object Relations:
    1. friendly, cooperative, appropriate
    2. obedient, compliant, responsive
    3. passive, unassertive
    4. clinging, dependent
    5. apathetic, withdrawn, autistic
    6. demanding, attention seeking
    7. negative, defiant, hostile
    8. stubborn, bossy, domineering
    9. fearful, anxious, cannot leave parent (separation)
    10. competitive, bragging, challenging
    11. seductive, manipulative, ingratiating
    12. concerned, sympathetic, aware and responsive to feelings of others
    13. responds to affection, expresses affection
    14. suspicious, questioning content, paranoid

4. Impulse Control:
   A. Motor:
      1. Kinetic Pattern
         a. age and situation appropriate
         b. rhythmic shaking of extremities
         c. wriggling, squirming, fidgetiness
         d. markedly overactive relative to situation, moves around room, touching or exploring
         e. not only (d) but increased tempo of activity
         f. underactive, little spontaneous activity
         g. underactive, rigid, anxious, fearful
         h. tics
         i. vocalizations
         j. overt choreoform movement
         k. rhythmic stereotypic movements:
            rocking
            whirling
            head banging
            toe walking
            arm flapping
            observing light through fingers
            exploring periphery of room
            other

      2. Persistence
         a. persists at tasks until completed
         b. needs occasional prompting for completion of tasks
         c. continual prompting for completion of tasks

      3. Distraction
         a. rarely or not at all distracted
         b. occasionally distracted by usual stimuli or distracted by unusual stimuli
         c. distracted by usual stimuli
   B. Emotional:
      1. control of immediate drives and affects, age-appropriate
      2. need for immediate gratification, temper outbursts
      3. physically aggressive to others, "accidental" aggression to self and others, aggressive fantasy, aggression to animals
      4. antisocial behavior—stealing, difficulty with police, drugs, fire setting (see also Behavior)
      5. overinhibited, rigid
   C. Affective response to antisocial and aggressive behavior:
      1. remorse, guilt, feeling of being bad, need to be punished or to punish himself

    2. unconcern to object of aggression or about behavior, concern only with fear of being punished

    3. does not learn from experience

5. Reality Testing:
   1. normal and age-appropriate
   2. tenuous and fluctuating
   3. confused or blurred (lack of insight into reality of fears, hallucinations, delusions)

6. Thought Process and Cognitive Function (also dreams, fantasy, wishes):
   1. relevant, age-appropriate
   2. coherent, logical, sequential
   3. associations rich and relevant
   4. associations loose, thinking dereistic, neologisms, verbigeration, echolalia, blocking, press of speech, circumstantial, irrelevant, fragmented, pronoun immaturity
   5. obsessive

7. Speech (vocabulary, grammar, syntax, comprehension):
   1. Rate: rapid, slow
   2. Pitch: high-pitched, ventriloquistic, unusually loud or soft
   3. Rhythm: respiratory speech dissociation, saccadic smoothness
   4. Articulation: difficult to understand, specific phonic errors
   5. Expressive speech: vocabulary limited (age-inappropriate), word-finding difficulty
   6. Associational problems: (syntax)
   7. Comprehension problems
   8. Auditory perceptual difficulty:
      a. sequencing
      b. discrimination

8. Identification:
   1. age and gender appropriate
   2. concern about sexual attributes, about damage to body, appearance, satisfaction with being his/her own sex
   3. dressing in girls' (boys') clothes, wish to be different sex
   4. concern about sex, reproduction, marriage
   5. feeling of doubt, inferiority, self-depreciation, self-belittlement
   6. identification with parent of same sex
   7. attempts at overcompensation for doubt or fears
   8. grandiose, boasting

9. Defense Mechanisms:
   A. Neurotic Type:
      1. fears:
         a. monsters, ghosts, burglars
         b. animals

      c. injury to family and/or to self

      d. of death, loss, separation

      e. of failure

      f. illusions

      g. nightmares, anxiety dreams

      h. other

  2. obsessions and compulsions:

      a. counting rituals

      b. checking rituals

      c. excessive orderliness

      d. excessive sloppiness

      e. other

  3. introjections and projections:

      a. introjection

      b. transitional objects

      c. hallucinations — visual

                              auditory

                              tactile

                              olfactory

      d. paranoid delusions

      e. ideas of influence and/or of reference

      f. fantasy of special powers

  4. body-image distortions: depersonalization, body changes, macropsia, micropsia, feeling of unreality

  5. general anxiety: fears in specific situations (school, dark, heights, crowds, dates, new people, closed spaces)

  6. repression, denial, withdrawal

  7. sublimation

B. Somatic:

  1. oral-tactile:

      a. eating problems: anorexia, obesity

      b. upper G.I. (peptic ulcer)

      c. passive, dependent

      d. oral aggression, biting, coprolalia

      e. asthma

      f. eczema

  2. motor-kinesthetic:

      a. rocking

      b. head banging

      c. restless activity

  3. anal:

      a. lower G.I. symptoms (soiling, constipation, diarrhea [celiac])

      b. dirty vs. clean and orderly (constipation, compulsiveness, cleanliness)

    4. phallic:
       a. frequent and prolonged masturbation
       b. sexual exhibition
       c. denial of autoerotic activity
       d. enuresis
    5. genital:
       a. regressive to previous levels (see also "identification" above)
    6. general:
       a. allergies
       b. frequent colds
       c. ear infections
       d. headaches
       e. seizures
       f. menstrual data
       g. sleep difficulty
  C. Character Traits

10. Behavior
    1. obedient to authority and rules
    2. lies, steals, destructive, running away, drugs
    3. physically aggressive to others
    4. relationship to peers, siblings
    5. inappropriate sexual behavior
    6. solitary interests, no friends

11. Structural Elements of Personality:
  A. Drives:
    1. age- or phase-appropriate
       a. intensity
       b. range and depth
       c. stability
       d. personal uniqueness
  B. Ego:
    1. capacity to modulate drives
    2. goals, age- or phase-appropriate
       a. range and depth
       b. intensity
       c. stability
       d. personal uniqueness
  C. Superego:
    1. age- and phase-appropriate
       a. ethical values established
       b. ego syntonic
       c. rigid
       d. punitive
       e. weak

APPENDIX C

Outline for Neurological Evaluation

Division of Child and Adolescent Psychiatry, University of South Florida, College of Medicine.
Compiled by Archie A. Silver, M.D. and Gary Pagano, M.D.

Patient ID# _____   DOB _____

Name _____   Present Date _____

Examined by _____   CA _____   Sex _____

I. Time Orientation (mark only if incorrect)

birthday {
    day   O
    month   O
    year   O
}

today's date {
    day   O
    month   O
    year   O
}

II. Appearance and static markers (mark any if present/or abnormal)

head circumference, in cms ( ) O   epicanthal folds   O
interpupillary distance ( )   O   low bridge of nose   O
simian crease   O   attached ear lobes   O
clinodactyly   O   lowset ears   O
abnormal toe spacing   O   high palate   O
dermatoglyphic abnormalities   O   other (describe)   O

III. Autonomic tone (mark if abnormal)

salivation   O   abdominal distention O
perioral pallor   O   sweating   O
skin temperature cold   O   pulse rate   O
skin temperature warm   O   heart rhythm   O
flushed facies   O   abnormal wheal and
                                      flare   O

IV. Perception
    A. Visual

                                                  1 2 3 4
        discrimination (lamb chops) # incorrect 5 6 7 8

                                                  1 2 3 4
        recall (lamb chops)   # incorrect   5 6 7 8
        visual motor:

            Gesell (developmental age years)   1 2 3 4 5 6 7
            Bender Gestalt (mark if present)

                verticalization   O   separation   O
                angulation   O   pressure   O
                loops for dots   O   plasticity   O
                poor impulse control O   chaotic placement   O
    B. Auditory

        discrimination: (Wepman) # incorrect 1 2 3   4   5   6   7
                                               8 9 10 11 12 13 14

        rote sequencing (mark only if incorrect)

count to 10   O   before November   O
after 7   O   months backward   O
before 6   O   days of week   O
months of year   O   after Tuesday   O
after March   O   before Friday   O

     Binet sentences (developmental age)   5 6 7 8 9 10 11 12

C. Body image
    1. Right–Left Discrimination (mark only if incorrect)
       1- R–L: single commands
          a. L hand   O
          b. R leg   O
          c. L eye   O
          d. R ear   O
       2- Ipsilateral, double simultaneous commands
          a. R hand on R eye   O
          b. L hand on L knee   O
          c. R hand on R knee   O
          d. L hand on L eye   O
       3- Crossed double simultaneous commands
          a. Touch L leg with R hand   O
          b. Touch R eye with L hand   O
          c. Touch L ear with R hand   O
          d. Touch R arm with L hand   O
       4- R–L On examiner
          a. Point to my L ear with your R hand   O
          b. Point to my R eye with your L hand   O
          c. Point to my L arm with your R hand   O
          d. Point to my L arm with your L hand   O
    2. Finger-Gnosis (mark only if incorrect)
       a. single stimulus
          (age 5 years or less)

          R1   O   L5   O
          L3   O   R4   O

       b. bilateral symmetrical   c. bilateral asymmetrical

       R2   L2   O   R3   L5   O
       R4   L4   O   R2   L4   O
       R5   L5   O   R3   L4   O
                                          R4   L3   O

      SCORE: a) Number correct × 1 =
               b) Number correct × 2 =
               c) Number correct × 3 =
                   Total finger-gnosis _____

3. Extinction Phenomena (mark errors)

wrist-wrist	○	L face-L wrist	○
R face-R wrist	○	synchiria	○
L face-R wrist	○	displacement	○
R face-L wrist	○		

4. Praxis (mark errors)

R	1-3	○	L	1-3	○	synkinesis	○
	1-5	○		1-5	○		
	1-2	○		1-2	○		
	1-4	○		1-4	○		

V. Arm Extension Test (mark response)
   1. Cerebral Dominance
      a. hand used for writing   R ○   L ○
      b. extremity elevation   R ○   L ○
            alternating ○   equal ○
   2. Hand Posturing

      Fingers maintained spread and extended   ○
      Finger hyperextended   ○
      Fingers flexed   ○
   3. Adventitious Finger Movements

      Prechtl movements   R ○   L ○
      Myoclonic jerks   R ○   L ○
      Choreoathetoid movements   R ○   L ○
   4. Maintenance of Balance

      0. Normal   1. mild   2. moderate   3. severe difficulty
   5. Postural Control
      a) Horizontal drift of arms
         divergence: 0. none   1. mild   2. moderate   3. severe
         convergence: 0. none   1. mild   2. moderate   3. severe

         upward: 0. none   1. mild   2. moderate   3. severe
         downward: 0. none   1. mild   2. moderate   3. severe
      c. Truncal Posturing

         Frontal plane deviation   hyperextention ○
                                            hyperflexion ○

         Lateral plane deviation   ○

VI. Postural Responses and Synergy
    a. Neck righting response and tonic neck response

                                      head to R   head to L
    Standing:

    0.   no movement of lower extremities   ○   ○
    1.   one step taken ("mild")   ○   ○

    2. more than one step taken, but in   O   O
         stop-start pattern ("moderate")

    3. continuous steps taken, no stopping   O   O
         ("severe")

    4. tonic neck posture   O   O

    Sitting:

    0. no movement of torso   O   O
    1. 45° turning of torso ("mild")   O   O
    2. 90° turning of torso ("moderate")   O   O
    3. 100° turning of torso ("severe")   O   O
    4. tonic neck posture   O   O

b. Cerebellar functioning (mark if present)
    1. Finger-Nose   mild difficulty (post pointing)   O
                            intention tremor   O
                            dysmetria   O
                            relieved at rest tremor   O

    2. Rapid alternating movements of upper extremity (20 pairs)
       (mark if abnormal)

       a. Rhythm: Right   Left
          1. slow irregular rhythm, but movement   O   O
             maintained
          2. irregular rhythm with frequent stops   O   O
          3. unable to perform   O   O
    3. Romberg   O
    4. Hypotonia   O
    5. Rebound   O

VII. Cranial Nerves (mark if abnormal)

	R	L		R	L
I olfactory (gross evaluation)	O	O	VII		
II acuity	O	O	ptosis	O	O
visual fields (gross confrontation)	O	O	brow	O	O
			eye close	O	O
			frowning	O	O
disc	O	O	smile	O	O
III, IV, VI			bite	O	O
EOM	O	O	taste (ant. ⅔)	O	O
convergence	O	O	other	O	O
nystagmus	O	O			
Pupils			VIII		
size	O	O	acuity	O	O
shape	O	O	Weber	O	O

position	○ ○	Rinne		○ ○
react to L	○ ○	vesibular		○ ○
react to A	○ ○	(if needed)		○ ○

		IX, X Uvula	○
V		swallowing	○
corneal reflex	○ ○	XI	
sensation of face	○ ○	shoulder shrug	○
masseter and temporalis	○ ○	head to right and to	○
jaw deviation	○ ○	left	
		XII	
		tongue	○

VIII. Motor Function (mark if abnormal)

		Upper Extremities	Lower Extremities
A. Musculature			
1. Mass	R	○	○
	L	○	○
2. Power	R	○	○
	L	○	○
3. Tone			
hyper	R	○	○
	L	○	○
hypo	R	○	○
	L	○	○
fluctuating	R	○	○
	L	○	○
cog wheeling	R	○	○
	L	○	○
other	L	○	○

	R	L
B. Reflexes		
1. DTR		
biceps	○	○
triceps	○	○
quadriceps	○	○
ankle	○	○
other	○	○
2. Superficial Reflexes		
Abdominal	○	○
3. Pathological Reflexes		
Babinski	○	○
confirmatories	○	○

Hoffman	O	O
other	O	O

C. Coordination   (mark if abnormal)

1. Gross Motor

toe walk	O
heel walk	O
tandem walk	O
hopping	O
standing on one foot	O

2. Fine Motor

	R	L
rhythm	O	O
pattern	O	O
pattern	O	O
synkinesis	O	O

3. Pencil Grip

overlapping thumb	O
2 finger grip	O
3 finger grip	O
other	O

D. Motor Impulse Control   (mark applicable description)

1. Kinetic Pattern

a. age and situation appropriate	O
b. rhythmic shaking of extremities	O
c. wriggling, squirming, fidgetiness	O
d. markedly overactive relative to situation, moves around room, touching or exploring	O
e. not only (d) but increased tempo of activity	O
f. underactive, little spontaneous activity	O
g. underactive, rigid, anxious, fearful	O
h. tics	O
i. vocalizations	O
j. overt choreoform movement	O

k. rhythmic stereotopic movements:

rocking	O
whirling	O
head banging	O
toe walking	O
arm flapping	O
observing light through fingers	O
exploring periphery of room	O
other	O

2. Persistence
   a. persists at tasks until completed   ○
   b. needs occasional prompting for completion of tasks   ○
   c. continual prompting for completion of tasks   ○
3. Distraction
   a. rarely, or not distracted   ○
   b. occasionally distracted by usual stimuli or distracted
       by unusual stimuli   ○
   c. distracted by usual stimuli   ○

IX. Language (vocabulary, grammar, syntax, comprehension)
     (mark if abnormal, circle appropriate description)
  1. rate: rapid, slow   ○
  2. pitch: high-pitched, ventriloquistic, unusually loud
                or soft   ○
  3. rhythm: respiratory speech dissociation, saccadic
                smoothness   ○
  4. articulation: difficult to understand, specific phonic errors   ○
  5. expressive speech: vocabulary limited   ○
  6. associational problems: (syntax)   ○
  7. comprehension problems   ○
  8. auditory perceptual difficulty:
    a. sequencing   ○
    b. discrimination   ○

X. Timed Coordination Items Note: Performance quality and simultaneous occurrence of synkinesis. Number of each performed in 20 seconds.

1. foot tap: keep heel on floor and tap toe	L	R
2. foot-heel-toe tap: heel to toe	L	R
3. hand pat (gentle hand taps)	L	R
4. hand pronation and supination	L	R
5. finger tap: tap thumb and index finger together	L	R
6. finger succession (thumb to each finger)	L	R
7. tongue wriggle side to side (time for 10 seconds)	L	R

REFERENCES

Aaron, P. G., Kuchta, S., & Grapenthin, C. T. (1988). Is there a thing called dyslexia? *Annals of Dyslexia, 38,* 33–50.

Abrams, J. C., & Kaslow F. (1977). Family systems and the learning disabled child: Intervention and treatment. *Journal of Learning Disabilities, 10,* 27–31.

Achenbach, T. M. (1966). The classification of children's psychiatric symptoms: A factor-analytic study, *Psychological Monographs, 80,* (7, Whole No. 615).

Achenbach, T. M. (1978). The child behavior profile. I. Boys ages 6 through 11. *Journal of Consulting and Clinical Psychology, 48,* 555–565.

Achenbach, T. M. (1982). *Developmental psychopathology.* New York: Wiley.

Achenbach, T. M., & Edelbrock, C. S. (1979). The child behavior profile. I. Boys ages 12 to 16 and girls ages 6 to 11 and 12 to 16. *Journal of Consulting and Clinical Psychology, 47,* 223–233.

Achenbach, T. M., & Edelbrock, C. S. (1983). *Manual for the child behavior checklist and revised child behavior profile.* Burlington, VT: Thos M. Achenbach.

Ackerman, P. T., Dykman, R. A., & Peters, J. E. (1977). Learning disabled boys as adolescents: Cognitive factors and achievement. *Journal of the American Academy of Child Psychiatry, 16,* 296–313.

Adams, J. (1969). On reconciling the "multidimensional" and "unitary" concepts of brain damage. *Perceptual and Motor Skills, 29,* 579–598.

Adams, P., & Fras I. (1988). *Beginning child psychiatry.* New York: Brunner/Mazel.

Adamson, W. C., & Adamson, K. K. (1979). *A handbook for specific learning disabilities.* New York: Gardner Press.

Adelman, H. S. (1973). The not so specific learning disability population. In J. P. Glavin (Ed.), *Major issues in special education* (pp. 77–83). New York: MSS Information Corporation.

Adelman, H. S. (1979). Diagnostic classification of learning disorders: A practical necessity and a procedural problem. *Learning Disability Quarterly, 2,* 56–62.

Adelman, H. S. & Taylor, L. (1986). Summary of the survey of fundamental concerns confronting the learning disability field. *Journal of Learning Disabilities, 19,* 391–393.

Agranoff, B. W. (1970). Protein synthesis and memory formations. In A. Lajtha (Ed.), *Protein metabolism in the nervous system* (pp. 533–541). New York: Plenum.

Agranoff, B. W. (1981). Learning and memory: Biochemical approaches. In G. S. Siegel, R. W. Albers, B. W Agranoff, & R. Katzman (Eds.), *Basic biochemistry* (3rd ed.). Boston: Little, Brown.

Agranoff, B. W., Burrell, H. R., Dokas, L. A., & Springer, A. D. (1978). Progress in biochemical approaches in learning and memory. In M. A. Lipton, A. D. Mascio, & K. F. Killman (Eds.), *Psychopharmacology: A generation of progress* (pp. 623–635). New York: Raven Press.

Agranoff, B. W., & Klinger, P. D. (1964). Puromycin effect on memory fixation in the goldfish. *Science, 146,* 952–953.

Ain, M. (1980) *The effect of stimulus novelty on viewing time and processing efficiency in hyperactive children.* Unpublished doctoral dissertation, McGill University.

Ainscow, M., & Tweddle, D. (1979). *Preventing classroom failure.* Chichester, U.K.: Wiley.

Akelaitis, A. S. (1940). A study of gnosis, praxis and language following partial and complete section of the corpus collosum. *Journal of American Neurological Association, 66,* 182–185.

Akelaitis, A. S. (1941). Studies on the corpus collosum, VII. *American Journal of Psychiatry, 98,* 409–414.

Akelaitis, A. S. (1942). Studies on the corpus collosum, VI. Orientation (temporal, spatial, gnosis) following section of the corpus collosum. *Archives Neurology and Psychiatry, 48,* 914–937.

Albert, J. D. (1966). Memory in mammals: Evidence for a system involving nuclear ribonucleic acid. *Neuropsychologia, 4,* 79–92.

Alessi, N. E., Walden, M., & Hiseh, P. S. (1989). Nifedipine-haloperidol combination in the treatment of Gilles de la Tourette syndrome: A case study. *Journal of Clinical Psychiatry, 50,* 103–104.

Algozzine, B., & Ysseldyke, J. E. (1986). The future of the learning disability field: Screening and diagnosis. *Journal of Learning Disabilities, 19,* 394–398.

Allington, R., Stuelgel, H., Shake M., & Lamarche, S. (1986). What is remedial reading? A descriptive study. *Reading Research and Instruction, 26,* 15–30.

Altus, G. T. (1956). A WISC profile for retarded readers. *Journal of Consulting Psychology, 20,* 55–156.

Aman, M. G., & Werry, J. S. (1982). Methylphenidate and diazepam in severe reading retardation. *Journal of the American Academy of Child Psychiatry, 21,* 31–37.

Ament, A. (1976). The learning-disabled or hyperactive child. *Journal of the American Medical Association, 235,* 1552–1553.

American Psychiatric Association. (1980). *Diagnostic and statistical manual of mental disorders* (DSM III) (3rd ed.) Washington, DC.

American Psychiatric Association. (1988). *Diagnostic and statistical manual of mental disorders* (DSM-III-R) (3rd ed., rev.). Washington, DC.

American Psychological Association. (1985). *Standard for educational and psychological testing.* (3rd ed.) Washington, DC: American Psychological Association.

Amery, B., Minichiello, M. D., & Brown, G. L. (1984). Aggression in hyperactive boys: Response to d-amphetamine. *Journal of the American Academy of Child Psychiatry, 23,* 291–294.

Anderson, D. (1985). *Educational services for students with Tourette syndrome.* Unpublished doctoral dissertation, University of South Florida.

Anderson, E. (1984, April). *Increasing school effectiveness: The full day kindergarten.* Paper presented at the April annual meeting, American Educational Research Association. (ERIC Document Reproduction Service No. ED 248036).

Anderson, G. M., Feibel, F. C., & Cohen, D. J. (1987). Determination of serotonin in whole blood platelet-rich plasma, platelet-poor plasma and plasma ultrafiltrate. *Life Science, 40,* 1063–1070.

Anderson, G. M., & Hoshino, Y. (1987). Neurochemical studies of autism. In D. Cohen & A. M. Donnellan, *Handbook of autism and pervasive developmental disorders* (pp. 166–191). New York: Wiley.

Anderson, G. M., Freedman, D. X., Cohen, D. J., Volkmar, F. R. Hoder, E. L., Hanson, C., & Young, J. (1987). Whole blood serotonin in autistic and normal subjects. *Journal of Child Psychology and Psychiatry, 28,* 885–900.

Anderson G. M., Ross, D. L., Klykylo, W., Feibel, F. C. & Cohen, D. J. (1988). Cerebrospinal fluid indolacetic acid in autistic subjects. *Journal of Autism and Developmental Disorders, 18,* 259–262.

Anderson, L. T., Campbell, M., Grage, D. M., Perry, R.,Small, A. M. & Green, W. H. (1984). Haloperidol in the treatment of infantile autism: Effects on learning and behavioral symptoms. *American Journal of Psychiatry, 141,* 1195–1202.

Anderson, R., Hiebert, E., Scott, J., & Wilkersen, I. (1985). *Becoming a nation of readers: The report of the Commission on Reading.* Washington, DC: National Institute of Education.

Annett, M. (1981). The right shift theory of handedness and developmental language problems. *Bulletin of the Orton Society, 31,* 103–121.

Anthony, E. J. (1973). A psychodynamic model of minimal brain dysfunction. *Annals of the New York Academy of Sciences, 205,* 52–60.

Applebee, A. N. (1971). Research in reading retardation: Two critical problems. *Journal of Child Psychology and Psychiatry, 12,* 91–113.

Arnold, L. E., Barneby, N., McManus, J., & Smeltzer, D. (1977). Prevention by specific perceptual remediation of vulnerable first graders. *Archives of General Psychiatry, 34,* 1279–1294.

Arnsten, A. F., & Goldman-Rakic, P. S. (1985). Catacholamines and cognitive decline in aged nonhuman primates. *Annals of the New York Academy of Sciences, 444,* 218–234.

Arter, J. A., & Jenkins, J. R. (1977). Examining the benefits and prevalence of modality considerations in special education. *A Journal of Special Education, 11,* 281–298.

Artley, A. S. (1950). Research concerning interrelationships among the language arts. *Elementary English, 27,* 527–537.

Association for Children and Adults with Learning Disabilities. (1986). *Position statement on a regular education/special education initiative.* (Unpublished).

August, G. J., Stewart, M. A. & Tsai, L. (1981). The incidence of cognitive disabilities in siblings of autistic children. *British Journal of Psychiatry, 138,* 416–422.

Austin, A. W., & Ross, S. (1966). Glutamic acid and human intelligence. *Psychological Bulletin, 57,* 429–434.

Ayres, A. J. (1969). Deficits in sensory integration in educationally handicapped children. *Journal of Learning Disabilities, 2,* 160–168.

Azrin, N. H., & Peterson, A. L. (1988). Behavior therapy for Tourette syndrome and tic disorders. In D. J. Cohen, R. D. Brunn, & J. F. Leckman (Eds.), *Tourette's syndrome and tic disorder* (pp. 237–256). New York: Wiley.

Badian, M. (1981). Recategorized WISC-R scores of disabled and adequate readers. *Journal of Educational Research, 75,* 109–114.

Baer, D., Freeman, R., & Greenberg, M. (1984). Behavioral alterations in patients with temporal lobe epilepsy. In D. Blumer (Ed.), *Psychiatric aspects of epilepsy* (pp. 197–228). Washington, DC: American Psychiatric Press.

Bailey, C. H., & Chen, M. (1983). Morphological basis of long-term habituation and sensitization in aplysia. *Science, 220,* 91–93.

Baker, H. J., & Leland, B. (1968). *Detroit tests of learning aptitude.* Indianapolis: Bobbs-Merrill.

Bakker, D. J. (1972). *Temporal order in disturbed reading.* Amsterdam: Rotterdam University Press.

Bakker, D. J. (1979). Hemisphere differences and reading strategies: Two dyslexias? *Bulletin of the Orton Society, 29,* 84–100.

Bakker, D. J. (1984). The brain as an independent variable. *Journal of Clinical Neuropsychology, 6,* 1–16.

Bakker, D. J. (1986). *Electrophysiological validation of L-type and P-type dyslexia.* European meeting of the International Neuropsychological Society.

Bakker, D. J., & Satz, P. (Eds.) (1970). *Specific reading disability: Advances in theory and method.* Amsterdam: Rotterdam University Press.

Bakker, D. J., & Vinke, J. (1985). Effects of hemisphere-specific stimulation on brain activity and reading in dyslexics. *Journal of Clinical and Experimental Neuropsychology, 7,* 505–525.

Bakker, D. J., Leeuwen, H. M. P. Van, & Spyer, G. (1987). Neuropsychological aspects of dyslexia. In D. J. Bakker, C. Wilsher, H. Debruyne, & N. Bertin (Eds.), *Developmental dyslexia and learning disorder* (pp. 30–39). Basel: Karger.

Bakker, D., Wilsher, C., Debruyne, H., & Bertin N. (Eds.) (1987). *Developmental dyslexia and learning disorders.* Basel: Karger.

Bakwin, H. R. (1973). Reading disability in twins. *Developmental Medicine and Child Neurology, 15,* 184–187.

Balow, B., Rubin, R., & Rosen, M. (1975–76). Prenatal events as precursors of reading disability. *Reading Research Quarterly, 11,* 36–71.

Bannatyne, A. (1971). *Language, reading and learning disabilities.* Springfield, IL: Charles C Thomas.

Bannatyne, A. (1974). Diagnosis: A note on recategorization of WISC scaled scores. *Journal of Learning Disabilities, 7,* 272–274.

Baratz, J. C. (1969). Teaching reading in an urban negro school system. In J. C. Baratz, & R. Shuy (Eds.), *Teaching black children to read* (pp. 92–116). Washington, DC: Center for Applied Linguistics.

Baratz, J. C., & Shuy, R. (Eds.) (1969). *Teaching black children to read.* Washington, DC: Center for Applied Linguistics.

Barclay, J. R. (1984). Primary prevention and assessment. *Personnel and Guidance Journal, 62,* 475–478.

Barker, R. G., & Wright, H. F. (1954). *Midwest and its children: The psychological ecology of an American town.* Evanston, IL: Row Peterson.

Barkley, R. A. (1977a). The effects of methylphenidate in various types of activity level and attention in hyperkinetic children. *Journal of Abnormal Child Psychology, 5,* 351–369.

Barkley, R. A. (1977b). A review of stimulant drug research with hyperactive children. *Journal of Child Psychology and Psychiatry, 18,* 137–165.

Barkley, R. A. (1978). Recent developments in research on hyperactive children. *Journal of Pediatric Psychology, 3,* 158–163.

Barkley, R. A. (1982). Guidelines for defining hyperactivity in children: Attention deficit disorder with hyperactivity. In B. B. Lakey & A. E. Kazdin (Eds.), *Advances in clinical child psychology,* Vol. 5 (pp. 137–180). New York: Plenum.

Barkley, R. A., & Cunningham, C. E. (1978). Do stimulant drugs improve the academic performance of hyperkinetic children? *Clinical Pediatrics, 17,* 85–92.

Barkley, R. A., & Edelbrock, C. (1986). *Attention deficit disorder with and without hyperactivity: Empirical corroboration of subtypes.* Paper presented at the 94th annual meeting of the American Psychological Association. Washington, DC.

Barkley, R. A., & Jackson, T. L., Jr. (1977). Hyperkinesis, autonomic nervous system activity, and stimulant drug effects. *Journal of Child Psychology and Psychiatry and Allied Disciplines, 18,* 347–357.

Barnes, K. E. (1982). *Pre-school screening.* Springfield, IL: Charles C Thomas.

Baron, J. (1979). Orthographic and word specific mechanisms in children's reading of words. *Child Development, 50,* 60–72.

Barondes, S. H., & Cohen, H. D. (1966). Puromycin effect on successive phases of memory in mice. *Science, 151,* 594–595.

Barrett, T. C. (1965a). Predicting reading achievement through readiness tests. *Reading and inquiry* (pp. 26–28). Newark, DE: International Reading Association.

Barrett, T. C. (1965b). Relationship between measures of pre-reading visual discrimination and first grade reading achievement. *Reading Research Quarterly, 1,* 51–76.

Barrett, T. C. (1965c). Visual discrimination tasks as predictors of first grade reading achievement. *The Reading Teacher, 18,* 276–282.

Bateman, E. C. (1968). *Interpretation of the 1961 Illinois Test of Psycholinguistic Abilities.* Seattle: Special Child Publications.

Bauman, M., & Kemper, T. (1985). Histoanatomic observations of the brain in early infantile autism. *Neurology, 35,* 866–874.

Bax, M., & MacKeith, R. (Eds.) (1963). *Minimal cerebral dysfunction: Papers from the international study group held at Oxford, September 1962, Little Club Clinics in Developmental Medicine No. 10,* London: William Heinemann.

Bear, D., Freeman, R., & Greenberg, M. (1984). In D. Blumer (Ed.), *Psychiatric aspects of epilepsy* (pp. 197–228). Washington, DC: American Psychiatric Press.

Beaton, A. (1985). *Left side, right side: A review of laterality research.* New Haven: Yale University Press.

Beck, L., Langford W., MacKay, M., & Sum, G. (1975). Childhood chemotherapy and later drug abuse and growth curve. A follow-up study of 30 adolescents. *American Journal of Psychiatry, 132,* 436–438.

Becker, R. D. (1974). Child psychiatry, the continuing controversy. Minimal ceberal (brain) dysfunction—clinical fact or neurological fiction? The syndrome critically re-examined in the light of some hard neurological evidence. *Israel Annals of Psychiatry and Related Disciplines, 12,* 87–106.

Beers, C. S., & Beers, J. W. (1980). Early identification of learning disabilities: Facts and fallacies. *Elementary School Journal, 81,* 67–76.

Beery, K. C., & Buktenica, N. (1967). *Developmental test of visual-motor integration.* Chicago: Follett.

Belmont, I., & Belmont, L. (1980). Is the slow learner in the classroom learning disabled? *Journal of Learning Disabilities, 13,* 496–499.

Belmont, L. (1980). Epidemiology. In H. E. Rie & E. Rie (Eds.), *Handbook of minimal brain dysfunctions: A critical view* (pp. 55–74). New York: Wiley.

Belmont, L., & Birch, H. G. (1963). Lateral dominance and right-left awareness in normal children. *Child Development, 34,* 257–270.

Belmont, L., & Birch, H. G. (1965). Lateral dominance, lateral awareness, and reading disability. *Child Development, 36,* 59–71.

Belmont, L., & Birch, H. G. (1966). The intellectual profile of retarded readers. *Perceptual and Motor Skills, 22,* 787–816.

Ben-Ari, Y. (Ed.) (1981). *The amygdaloid complex.* Amsterdam: Elsevier.

Bender, L. A. (1938). *A visual motor Gestalt test and its clinical use.* New York: American Orthopsychiatric Association.

Bender, L. A. (1947). Childhood schizophrenia. *American Journal of Orthopsychiatry, 17,* 40–56.

Bender, L. (1950). Anxiety in disturbed children. In P. H. Hoch & J. Zubin (Eds.), *Anxiety* (pp. 119–139). New York: Grune & Stratton.

Bender, L. A. (1953). *Aggression, hostility and anxiety in children.* Springfield, IL: Charles C Thomas.

Bender, L. A. (1955). Twenty years of clinical research on schizophrenic children, with special reference to those under six years of age. In G. Caplan (Ed.), *Emotional problems of early childhood* (pp. 503–515). New York: Basic Books.

Bender, L. A. (1956). *Psychopathology of children with organic brain disorders.* Springfield, IL: Charles C Thomas.

Bender, L. A. (1958). Problems in conceptualization and communication in children with developmental alexia. In P. H. Hoch & J. Zubin (Eds.), *Psychopathology of communication* (pp. 155–176). New York: Grune & Stratton.

Bender, L. A. (1966). The concept of plasticity in childhood schizophrenia. In P. H. Hoch & J. Zubin (Eds.), *Psychopathology of schizophrenia* (pp. 354–365). New York: Grune & Stratton.

Bender, L. A. (1970). Use of the Visual Motor Gestalt test in the diagnosis of learning disabilities. *Journal of Special Education, 4,* 29–39.

Bender, L. A., & Cottington, F. (1943). The use of amphetamine sulphate (Benzedrine) in child psychiatry. *American Journal of Psychiatry, 99,* 116.

Bender, L. A., & Freedman, A. M. (1952). A study of the first three years in the maturation of schizophrenic children. *Quarterly Journal of Child Behavior, 4,* 245–272.

Bender, L. A., & Silver, A. A. (1949). Body image problems of the brain-damaged child. *Journal of Social Issues, 4,* 84–89.

Bender, L. A., & Yarnell, H. (1941). An observation nursery. *American Journal of Psychiatry, 97,* 1158–1172.

Bender, M. B. (1952). *Disorders in perception with particular reference to the phenomena of extinction and displacement.* Springfield, IL: Charles C Thomas.

Bender, M. B. (1970). Perceptual interactions. *Modern Trends in Neurology, 5,* 1–28.

Bender, M. B., Fink, M., & Green, M. (1951). Patterns of perception of simultaneous tests of face and hand. *Archives of Neurology and Psychiatry, 66,* 355–362.

Benezra, E. (1980). *Verbal and nonverbal memory in hyperactive, reading disabled and normal children.* Unpublished doctoral dissertation, McGill University.

Bennett, E. L., Rosenzweig, M. R., & Flood, J. R. (1977). Protein synthesis and memory studied with anisomycin. In S. Roberts, A. Lajtha, & W. H. Gispen (Eds.), *Mechanisms, regulation and special functions of protein synthesis in the brain.* Amsterdam: Elsevier/Noth Holland Biomedical Press.

Benson, D. F. (1981). Alexia and the neuroanatomical basis of reading. In F. J. Pirozzolo and M. C. Wittrock (Eds.). *Neuropsychological and cognitive processes in reading* (pp. 69–92). New York: Academic Press.

Benson, D. F., & Blumer, D. (Eds.) (1982). *Psychiatric aspects of neurobiological disorder,* Vol 2. New York: Grune & Stratton.

Benson, D. F., & Geschwind, N. (1970). Developmental Gerstmann syndrome. *Neurology, 20,* 293–298.

Benson, D. F., & Zaidel, E. (Eds.) (1985). *The dual brain.* New York: Guilford Press.

Benton, A. L. (1955a). Development of finger-localization capacity in school children. *Child Development, 26,* 225–230.

Benton, A. L. (1955b). Right-left discrimination, finger-localization and cerebral status. *Acta Psychologie, 11,* 165–166.

Benton, A. L. (1959). *Right-left discrimination and finger localization.* New York: Harper & Brothers.

Benton, A. L. (1961). The fiction of the Gerstmann syndrome. *Journal of Neurology, Neurosurgery and Psychiatry, 24,* 176–187.

Benton, A. L. (1962). Dyslexia in relation to form perception and directional sense. In J. Money (Ed), *Reading disability: Progress and research needs in dyslexia* (pp. 81–102). Baltimore: Johns Hopkins Press.

Benton, A. L. (1975). Developmental dyslexia: Neurological aspects. In W. J. Friedlander (Ed.), *Advances in Neurology, 17,* 1–47. New York: Raven Press.

Benton, A. L., & Bird, J. W. (1963). The EEG and reading disability. *American Journal of Orthopsychiatry, 23,* 92–98.

Benton, A. L., & Pearl, D. (Eds.). (1978). *Dyslexia: An appraisal of current knowledge.* New York: Oxford University Press.

Bereiter, C. (1972). An academic preschool for disadvantaged children: Conclusions from evaluation studies. In J. Stanely (Ed.), *Preschool programs for the disadvantaged* (pp. 1–21). Baltimore: Johns Hopkins Press.

Bereiter, C., & Engelmann, S. (1966). *Teaching disadvantaged children in the preschool.* Englewood Cliffs, NJ: Prentice Hall.

Berg, R. (1985). A case of Tourette syndrome treated with nifedipine. *Acta Psychiatrica Scandinavica. 72*, 400–401.

Berger, M., & Kennedy, H. (1975). Pseudobackwardness in children: Maternal attitudes as an etiological factor. *The Psychoanalytic Study of the Child, 30*, 279–306. New York: International Universities Press.

Berger, M., Yule, W., & Rutter, M. (1975). Attainment and adjustment in two geographical areas: The prevalence of specific reading retardation. *British Journal of Psychiatry, 126*, 510–519.

Berlin, I. N. (1974). MBD: Management of family distress. *JAMA, 9*, 1454–1456.

Berlin, I. N. (1981). Psychotherapy with MBD children and their parents. In R. Ochroch (Ed.), *The diagnosis and treatment of minimal brain dysfunction in children* (pp. 225–240). New York: Human Sciences Press.

Berlin, R. (1887). *Eine besonderer Art der Wortblindheit: Dyslexie*. Wiesbaden: J. F. Bergmann.

Berlyne, D. E. (1970). *Conflict, arousal and curiosity*. New York: McGraw-Hill.

Bernard, C. (1858). *Comptes rendus d L'Academie des sciences, 48*, 245.

Bernstein, B. (1960). Language and social class. *British Journal of Sociology, 11*, 271–276.

Bernstein, G., Hughes, J., Mitchell, J., & Thompson, T. (1987). Effects of narcotic antagonists on self-injurious behavior, *Journal of the American Academy of Child and Adolescent Psychiatry, 26*, 886–889.

Biederman, J. (1985). Fenfluramine (Pondimin) in autism. *Massachusetts General Hospital Newsletter. Biological Therapies in Psychiatry, 8*, 27–28.

Biklen, D. (1987). The integration question: Educational and residential placement issues. In J. D. Cohen, A. M. Donnellan, & R. Paul (Eds.), *Handbook of autism and pervasive developmental disorders* (pp. 653–667). New York: Wiley.

Biklen, D., & Zollers, N. (1986). The focus of advocacy in the learning disorder field. *Journal of Learning Disabilities, 19*, 579–586.

Binet, A., & Simon, T. (1916). *The development of intelligence in children*. Baltimore: Williams & Wilkins.

Birch, H. G. (1964). *Brain damage in children: The biological and social aspects*. Baltimore: Williams & Wilkins.

Birch, H. G., & Belmont, L. (1964). Auditory-visual integration in normal and retarded readers. *American Journal of Orthopsychiatry, 34*, 852–861.

Birch, H. G., & Belmont, L. (1965). Auditory-visual integration, intelligence, and reading ability in school children. *Perceptual and Motor Skills, 20*, 295–305.

Birch, H. G., & Gussow, G. D. (1970). *Disadvantaged children*. New York: Grune & Stratton.

Bird, H. R., & Kestenbaum, C. J. (1988). A semi-structured approach to clinical assessment. In C. Kestenbaum & D. Williams (Eds.), *Handbook of clinical assessment of children and adolescents* (pp. 19–30). New York: New York University Press.

Birkmayer, W. (Ed.) (1975). *Epileptic seizures, behavior, pain*. Bern: Huber.

Black, W. F. (1974). The word explosion in learning disabilities: A notation of literature trends, 1962–1972. *Journal of Learning Disabilities, 7*, 323–325.

Blanchard, P. (1946). Psychoanalytic contributions to the problems of reading disabilities. *The Psychoanalytic Study of the Child, 2*, 163–187. New York: International Universities Press.

Blank, M., & Bridger, M. W. (1966). Deficiencies in verbal labeling in retarded readers. *American Journal of Orthopsychiatry, 36*, 840–847.

Blank, M., & Bridger, M. W. (1967). Perceptual abilities and conceptual deficiencies in retarded readers. In J. Zubin & G. A. Jervis (Eds.), *Psychopathology of mental development* (pp. 401–412). New York: Grune & Stratton.

Blau, A. (1936). Mental changes following head trauma in children. *Archives of Neurology and Psychiatry, 35*, 723–766.

Blau, A. (1946). *The master hand: A study of the origin and meaning of right and left sidedness and its relation to personality and language.* (No. 5). New York: American Orthopsychiatric Association, Research Monographs.

Bliss, J. (Paper edited by D. J. Cohen, & D. X. Freedman). (1980). Sensory experiences of Gilles de la Tourette syndrome. *Archives of General Psychiatry, 37,* 1343–1347.

Blom, S. (1962). Trigeminal neuralgia: Its treatment with a new anticonvulsant drug (G-32883). *Lancet, 1,* 839–840.

Bloom, B. (1984). The search for methods of group instruction as effective as one-to-one tutoring. *Educational Leadership, 41,* 4–17.

Bloom, B. S. (1964). *Stability and change in human characteristics.* New York: Wiley.

Bloom, L., & Lahey, M. (1978). *Language development and language disorders.* New York: Wiley.

Blovin, A., Bornstein, R., & Trites, R. (1978). Teenage alcohol use among hyperactive children: A five year follow-up study. *Journal of Pediatric Psychology, 3,* 188–194.

Blue, C. M., & Beaty, L. L. (1974). Use of the Peabody language development kits in specific language dysfunction. *Journal of Special Education, 8,* 73–79.

Bluestone, C., Klein, J., Paradise, J., Eichenwald, H., Bess, F., Downs, M., Green, M., Berko-Gleason, J., Ventry, I., Gray, S., McWilliams B., & Gates G. (1983). Workshop on the effects of otitis media on the child. *Pediatrics, 71,* 639–652.

Blumer, D. (Ed.) (1984). *Psychiatric aspects of epilepsy.* Washington, DC: American Psychiatric Press.

Blumstein, S. E., Goodglass, H., & Tartter, V. (1975). The reliability of ear advantage in dichotic listening. *Brain and Language, 2,* 226–236.

Boder, E. (1970). Developmental dyslexia: A new diagnostic approach based on the identification of three subtypes. *Journal of School Health, 40,* 289–290.

Boder, E. (1971). Developmental dyslexia: Prevailing diagnostic concepts and a new diagnostic approach. In H. Myklebust (Ed.), *Progress in learning disabilities* (Vol. II, pp. 293–321). New York: Grune & Stratton.

Boder, E. (1973). Developmental dyslexia: A diagnostic approach based on three atypical reading patterns. *Developmental Medicine and Child Neurology, 15,* 663–687.

Boder, E., & Jarrico, S. (1982). *The Boder test of reading-spelling patterns: A diagnostic screening test for subtypes of reading disability.* New York: Grune & Stratton.

Boehm, A. E. (1986). *Boehm test of basic concepts—revised.* New York: The Psychological Corporation.

Bogen, J. E., & Gazzaniga, M. S. (1965). Cerebral commissurotomy in man: Minor hemisphere dominance for certain visuo-spatial functions. *Journal of Neurosurgery, 23,* 394–399.

Bogoch, S., & Dreyfus, J. (1970). *The broad range of use of diphenylhydantoin,* (Vol 1). New York: Dreyfus Medical Foundation.

Bond, E. D., & Appel, K. E. (1931). *The treatment of behavior disorders following encephalitis.* New York: Commonwealth Fund.

Bond, E. D., & Smith, L. H. (1935). Post-encephalitis behavior disorders: A ten year review of Franklin school. *American Journal of Psychiatry, 92,* 17–31.

Bond, G. L., & Dykstra, R. (1967). The cooperation research program in first grade reading instruction. *Reading Research Quarterly, 2,* 1–142.

Bond, G. L. & Tinker, M. A. (1967). *Reading difficulties: Their diagnosis and correction.* (2nd ed.) New York: Appleton-Century, Crofts.

Booth, D. A., & Sandler, M. E. (1967). *Localization of intracranial C14-orotic acid after practice at reaching for food.* Unpublished manuscript cited in D. A. Booth. Vertebrate brain ribonucleic acids and memory retention. *Psychological Bulletin, 68,* 149–177.

Borison, R. L., Ang, L., Hamilton, W. J., Diamond, B. I., & Davis, J. M. (1983). Treatment approaches in Gilles de la Tourette syndrome. *Brain Research Bulletin, 11,* 205–208.

Borland, B., & Heckman, H. (1976). Hyperactive boys and their brothers. *Archives of General Psychiatry, 33,* 669–675.

Bosaeus, E., & Selladen, U. (1979). Psychiatric assessment of healthy children with various EEG patterns. *Acta Psychiatrica Scandinavica, 59,* 180–210.

Bowman, K., & Blau, A. (1943). Psychotic states following head injury in adults and children. In S. Brock (Ed.), *Injuries of the skull, brain, and spinal cord* (pp. 294–341). Baltimore: Williams & Wilkins.

Bradley, C. (1937). The behavior of children receiving Benzedrine. *American Journal of Psychiatry, 94,* 577–585.

Bradley, L. (1980). *Assessing reading difficulties: A diagnostic and remedial approach.* London, U.K.: Macmillan Education.

Bradley, L., & Bryant, P. (1985). *Rhyme and reason in reading and spelling.* Ann Arbor, MI: University of Michigan Press.

Bradley, R. H. (1982). The home inventory: A review of the first fifteen years. In N. J. Anastasio, W. K. Frankenberg, & A. W. Fandal (Eds.), *Identifying the developmentally delayed child.* Baltimore: University Park Press.

Bradley, R. H., & Caldwell, B. (1981). The home inventory: A validation of the pre-school scale for black children. *Child Development, 52,* 708–710.

Bradley, R. H., & Caldwell, P. M. (1980). The relation of home environment, cognitive competency & IQ among males and females. *Child Development, 51,* 1140–1448.

Bradshaw, J. C., & Nettleton, N. C. (1988). *Human cerebral asymmetry.* Englewood Cliffs, NJ: Prentice-Hall.

Brainerd, C. J., & Pressley, M. (Eds.) (1985). *Basic processes in memory development.* New York: Springer-Verlag.

Brand, Shirley. (1989). Learning through meaning. *Academic Therapy, 24,* 305–314.

Brazelton, T. B. (1973). *Neonatal behavioral assessment scale.* London: William Heinemann. Philadelphia: J. B. Lippincott.

Breese, G., Gualtieri, T., Mailman, R., Mueller, R., Youngblood, W., Vogel, R., & Wilson, J. (1981). Developmental neuropsychopharmacology: Preclinical and clinical studies of the hyperkinetic syndrome. In A. Raskin, D. S. Robinson, & J. Levine (Eds.), *Age and the pharmacology of psychoactive drugs* (pp. 63–78). New York: Elsevier.

Brigance, A. H. (1976). *Brigance diagnostic inventory of basic skills.* North Billerica, MA: Curriculum Associates.

Broadbent, D. E. (1954). The role of auditory localization in attention and memory span. *Journal of Experimental Psychology, 47,* 191–196.

Broca, P. (1861) Nouvelle observation d'aphemia produite par une lesion de le moitie posterieure des deuxieme et troisieme circonvolutions frontales. *Bulletin de la Societe Anatomie, 6,* 398–407.

Brody, S., & Axelrad, S. (1970). *Anxiety and Ego Formation in Infancy.* New York: International Universities Press.

Broman, S. H. (1979). Perinatal anoxia and cognitive development in early childhood. In T. M. Field (Ed.), *Infants born at risk: Behavior and development* (pp. 29–52). New York: Spectrum.

Broman, S. H., Nichols, P. L., & Kennedy, W. A. (1975). *Preschool IQ: Prenatal and early developmental correlates.* Hillsdale, NJ: Lawrence Erlbaum Associates.

Brooks, D. (1986). Otitis media with effusion and academic attainment. *International Journal of Pediatric Otorhinolaryngology, 12,* 39–47.

Brophy, J. (1979). Teacher behavior and its effect. *Journal of Educational Psychology, 71*, 733–750.

Broussard, E. R. (1979). Assessment of the adaptive potential of the mother-infant system: The neonatal perception inventories. *Seminars in Perinatology, 3*, 91–100.

Brown, G. L., Murphy, D. L., Langer, D. H., Ebert, M. H., Post, R. M., & Bunney, W. E., Jr. (1984). *Monoamine enzymes in hyperactivity response to d-amphetamine.* Annual meeting, American Academy of Child Psychiatry, quoted by Zametkin & Rapoport, 1987.

Brown, W., Jenkins, E., Friedman, E., Brooks, J., Wisniewski, K., Ragutha, S., & French, J. (1982). Autism associated with the fragile X syndrome. *Journal of Autism and Developmental Disorders, 12*, 303–308.

Bruun, R. D. (1988). The natural history of Tourette's syndrome. In D. J. Cohen, R. D. Bruun, & J. F. Leckman (Eds.), *Tourette's syndrome and tic disorder* (pp. 22–39). New York: Wiley.

Bryan, T. (1974). An observational analysis of classroom behavior of children with learning disabilities. *Journal of Learning Disabilities, 7*, 35–43.

Bryan, T., & McGrady, H. J. (1972). Use of a teacher rating scale. *Journal of Learning Disabilities, 5*, 404–488.

Bryan, T., & Wheeler, R. (1972). Perception of children with learning disabilities: The eye of the observer. *Journal of Learning Disabilities, 5*, 484–488.

Bryant, P., & Bradley, L. (1983). Auditory organization and backwardness in reading. In M. Rutter (Ed.), *Developmental neuropsychiatry* (pp. 289–297). New York: Guilford.

Bryden, M. P. (1982). *Functional asymmetry in the intact brain.* New York: Academic Press.

Bryden, M. P. (1988). Does laterality make any difference? Thoughts on the relation between cerebral asymmetry and reading. In D. L. Molfese & S. J. Segalowitz (Eds.)., *Brain lateralization in children* (pp. 509–526). New York: Guilford.

Bryden, M. P., & Sprott, D. A. (1981). Statistical determination of degree of laterality. *Neuropsychologia, 19*, 571–581.

Burd, L., Kerbesian, J., Wikenheiser, M., & Fisher, W. (1986). Prevalence of Gilles de la Tourette's syndrome in North Dakota adults. *American Journal of Psychiatry, 143*, 787–788.

Buros, O. K. (1978). *The eighth mental measurements yearbook.* Highland Park, NJ: Gryphon Press.

Caldwell, B., & Bradley, R. H., (1978). *Home observation for measurement of the environment: Manual.* Little Rock: University of Arkansas.

Caldwell, B., Bradley, R., & Staff. (1984). *Home observation for measurement of the environment.* Little Rock: University of Arkansas.

Calfee, R. C., Lindamood, P., & Lindamood, C. (1973). Acoustic-phonetic skills and reading—kindergarten through twelfth grade. *Journal of Educational Psychology, 64*, 293–298.

Cameron, D. E., & Solyom, L. (1961). Effects of RNA on memory, *Geriatrics, 16*, 74–81.

Camp, B. (1977). Verbal mediation in young aggressive boys. *Journal of Abnormal Psychology, 83*, 115–153.

Camp, B., Blom, C., Hebert, F., & Doernick, W. (1979). "Think Aloud": A program for developing self-control in young aggressive boys. *Journal of Abnormal Child Psychology, 8*, 157–169.

Campbell, M. (1987). Drug treatment of infantile autism: The past decade. In H. G. Maltzer (Ed.), *Psychopharmacology: The third generation of progress* (pp. 1225–1231). New York: Raven Press.

Campbell, M., Adams, P., Small, A., McVeight-Tesch, L., & Curren, E. (1988). Naltrexone in infantile autism. *Psychopharmacology Bulletin, 24*, 135–139.

Campbell, M., Anderson, L. T., Cohen, I. L., Perry, R., Small, A. M., Green, W. H., Anderson, L., & McCandless, W. (1982a). Haloperidol in autistic children: Effects on learning, behavior and abnormal involuntary movements. *Psychopharmacology Bulletin, 18*, 110–112.

Campbell, M., Anderson, L. T., Small, A. M., Perry, R., Green, W. H., & Caplan, R. (1982b). The effects of haloperidol in learning and behavior in autistic children. *Journal of Autism and Developmental Disorders, 12,* 164–175.

Campbell, M., Grega, D., Green, W., & Bennett W. (1983). Neuroleptic induced dyskinesia in children. *Clinical Neuropharmacology, 6,* 207–222.

Campbell, M., Green, W. H., & Deutsch, S. I. (1985). *Child and adolescent psychopharmacology,* Beverly Hills, CA: Sage.

Campbell, M., Overall, J., Small, A., Sokol, M., Spencer, E. K., Adams, P., Foltz, R. L., Monti, K. M., Perry, R., Nobler, M., & Roberts, E. (1989). Naltrexone in autistic children: An acute open dose range tolerance test. *Journal of the American Academy of Child and Adolescent Psychiatry, 28,* 200–206.

Campbell, M., Perry R., & Green, W. H. (1984). Use of lithium in children and adolescents. *Psychosomatics, 25,* 95–106.

Campbell, M., Small A., Green, W. H., Jennings, S., Perry, R., Bennett, W., & Anderson, L. (1984). Behavioral efficacy of haldoperidol and lithium carbonate: A comparison in hospitalized aggressive children with conduct disorder. *Archives of General Psychiatry, 41,* 650–656.

Campione, J. C. (1989). Assisted assessment: A taxonomy of approaches and an outline of strengths and weaknesses. *Journal of Learning Disabilities, 22,* 151–165.

Campione, J. C., & Brown, A. L. (1978). Toward a theory of intelligence: Contributions from research with retarded children. *Intelligence, 2,* 279–304.

Canadian Commission on Emotional and Learning Disorders (1970). *One million children. A national study of Canadian children with emotional and learning disorders.* Toronto, Canada: Leonard Crainford.

Cannon, W. B. (1939). *The wisdom of the body* (2nd ed.). New York: W. W. Norton Company.

Cantor, S. (1982). *The schizophrenic child.* Montreal, Canada: Eden Press.

Cantor, S., Evans, J., & Pezzot-Pearce, T. (1982). Childhood schizophrenia: Present but not accounted for. *American Journal of Psychiatry, 139,* 758–762.

Cantwell, D. P. (1975). *The hyperactive child: Diagnosis, management, current research.* New York: Spectrum Publications.

Cantwell, D. P., & Carlson, G. A. (1978). Stimulants. In J. S. Werry (Ed.), *Pediatric psychopharmacology: The use of behavior modifying drugs in children* (pp. 171–207). New York: Brunner/Mazel.

Caprini, G., & Melotti, V. (1961). Una grave sindrome ticcosa guarita con haloperidol. *Rivista Sperimentale di Freniatria e Medicina Legale delle Alienazioni Mentale* (Reggio-Emilia), *85,* 191–197.

Caputo, A. J., Niedermeyer, E. F. L., & Richardson, F. (1968). The electroencephalogram in children with minimal cerebral dysfunction. *Pediatrics, 41,* 1104–1114.

Carlberg, D., & Kavale, K. (1980). The efficacy of special versus regular class placement for exceptional children: A meta-analysis. *Journal of Special Education, 14,* 295–309.

Carr, E. (1983). Sign langugage. In R. L. Koegel, A. Rincover, & A. L. Egel (Eds.), *Educating and Understanding Autistic Children* (pp. 142–157). San Diego: College-Hill Press.

Cattell, J. M. (1890). Mental tests and measurements. *Mind, 15,* 373–380.

Cattell, R. B. (1963a). Nature and measurement of anxiety. *Scientific American, 208,* 96–104.

Cattell, R. B. (1963b). Theory of fluid and chrystalized intelligence: A critical experiment. *Journal of Educational Psychology, 54,* 1–22.

Cattell, R. B., & Sheier, I. (1961). *Measurement of neuroticism and anxiety.* New York: Ronald Press.

Centenaire du Syndrome Gilles de la Tourette. (1986). *Revue Neurologique, 142,* 810–867.

Chadwick, O., Rutter, M., Brown, G., Shaffer, D., & Traub, M. (1981). A prospective study of children with head injuries: II cognitive sequelae. *Psychological Medicine, 11,* 49–61.

Chadwick, O., Rutter, M., Shaffer, D., & Shrout, P. (1981). A prospective study of children with head injuries: IV specific cognitive defects. *Journal of Clinical Neuropsychology, 3,* 101–120.

Chadwick, O., Rutter, M., Thompson, J., & Shaffer, D. (1981). Intellectual Performance and reading skills after localized head injury in childhood. *Journal of Child Psychology and Psychiatry, 22,* 117–139.

Chall, J. S. (1983). *Learning to read: The great debate* (Rev. ed.) New York: McGraw-Hill.

Chase, C., & Tallal, P. (1987). Piracetam and dyslexia. In D. Bakker, C. Wilsher, H. Debruyne, & N. Bertin (Eds.), *Developmental dyslexia and learning disorders* (pp. 140–147). Basel: Karger.

Chase, T. M., Foster, N. L., Fedro, P., Books, R., Mansi, L., Kessler, R., & Dichiro, G. (1984). Gilles de la Tourette syndrome: Studies with the fluorine-18-labeled flurodeoxyglucose positron emission topographic method. *Annals of Neurology, 15,* Supplement 175.

Chase, T. M., Geoffrey, V., Gillespie, M., & Burrows, G. H. (1986). Structural and functional studies of Gilles de la Tourette syndrome. *Revue Neurologique* (Paris), *142,* 851–855.

Chew, A. L. (1981). *The lollipop test: A diagnostic screening test of school readiness.* Atlanta, GA: Humanics Limited.

Childs, S. B. (1973). *The child's spelling system.* Cambridge, MA: Educators Publishing Service.

Childs, B., Finucci, J. M., & Preston, M. S. (1978). A medical genetics approach to the study of reading disability. In A. Benton & D. Pearl (Eds.), *Dyslexia: An appraisal of current knowledge* (pp. 301–309). New York: Oxford University Press.

Chisholm, L. A. (1983). Implications of research: Viewpoint of a resource teacher. *Journal of Learning Disabilities, 16,* 180–182.

Chomsky, N. (1967). The formal nature of language. In E. H. Lenneberg, *Biological foundations of language* (pp. 397–442). New York: Wiley.

Christ, A. E. (1978). Psychotherapy of the child with true brain damage. *American Journal of Orthopsychiatry, 48,* 505–515.

Christ, A. E. (1981). Psychotherapy of the adolescent with true brain damage. In R. Ochroch (Ed.), *The diagnosis and treatment of minimal brain dysfunction in children* (pp. 255–271). New York: Human Sciences Press.

Cicirelli, V. (1970). Project Head Start: A national evaluation. Summary of the study. In D. C. Hays (Ed.), *Britannica Review of American Education.* Chicago: Encyclopedia Britannica.

Clarizio, H. F., & Bernard, R. (1981). Recategorized WISC-R scores of learning disabled children and differential diagnosis. *Psychology in the Schools, 18,* 5–12.

Clay, M. (1988). *Reading recovery.* Ohio State University. Unpublished.

Clements, S. D. (1966). *Minimal brain dysfunction in children* (NINDB Monograph No. 3, U. S. Public Health Service Publication No. 1415). Washington, DC: U. S. Government Printing Office.

Close, J. (1973). Scored neurological examination (Psychiatric and neurological examination for soft signs). *Psychopharmacology Bulletin: Special Issue Pharmacotherapy of Children,* 142–150.

Coates, S., & Bromberg, P. M. (1973). Factorial structure of the WPPSI between the ages of 4 and 6½. *Journal of Consulting and Clinical Psychology, 40,* 365–370.

Coffey, C. E., Bryden, M., Schroering, E. S., Wilson, W. H., & Mathew R. J. (1989). Regional cerebral blood flow correlates of a dichotic listening task. *Journal of Neuropsychiatry, 1,* 46–52.

Cohen, D. J. (1980). The pathology of the self in primary childhood autism and Gilles de la Tourette syndrome. *Psychiatric Clinics of North America, 3,* 383–402.

Cohen D. J., Paul, L., & Volkmar, F. (1987). Issues in the classification of pervasive developmental disorder and associated conditions. In D. Cohen & A. Donnellan (Eds.), *Handbook of autism and pervasive developmental disorders* (pp. 20–40). New York: Wiley.

Cohen, D. J., & Donnellan, A. M. (Eds.) (1987). *Handbook of autism and pervasive developmental disorders.* New York: Wiley.

Cohen, D. J., & Shaywitz, B. (1976). Primary childhood aphasia and childhood autism. *Journal of the American Academy of Child Psychiatry, 15,* 604–645.

Cohen, D. J., Bruun, R. D., & Leckman, J. F. (Eds.) (1988). *Tourette's syndrome and tic disorder,* New York: Wiley.

Cohen, D. J., Caparulo, B., Shaywitz, B., & Bowers, M. (1977). Dopamine and serotonin metabolism in neuropsychiatrically disturbed children: CSF homovanillic acid and 5-hydroxyindolacetic acid. *Archives of General Psychiatry, 35,* 545–550.

Cohen, D. J., Detlor, J., Shaywitz, B., & Leckman, J. (1982). Interaction of biological and psychological factors in the natural history of Tourette syndrome: A paradigm for childhood neuropsychiatric disorders. In A. J. Friedhoff & T. N. Chase (Eds.), *Gilles de la Tourette syndrome, Advances in neurology* (pp. 31–40). New York: Raven Press.

Cohen, D. J., Detlor, J., Young, J. G., & Shaywitz, B. A. (1980). Clonidine ameliorates Gilles de la Tourette syndrome. *Archives of General Psychiatry, 37,* 1350–1357.

Cohen, D. J., Shaywitz, B., Johnson W., & Bowers, M. (1974). Biogenic amines in autistic and atypical children: Cerebrospinal fluid measures of homovanillic acid and 5-hydroxyindolacetic acid. *Archives of General Psychiatry, 31,* 845–853.

Cohen, D. J., Young, J. G., Nathanson, J. A., & Shaywitz, B. A. (1979). Clonidine in Tourettes' syndrome. *Lancet, 2,* 551–553.

Cohen, J. (1980). Cerebral evoked responses in dyslexic children. *Progress in Brain Research, 54,* 502–506.

Cohen, J., & Breslin, P. W. (1984). Visual evoked potentials in dyslexic children. In R. Karrer, J. Cohen, & P. Tueting (Eds.), Brain and information: Event related potentials (pp. 338–343). *Annals of the New York Academy of Sciences, 425.* New York: New York Academy of Sciences.

Cohen, N. J., & Douglas, V. I. (1972). Characteristics of the orienting response in hyperactive and normal children. *Psychophysiology, 9,* 238–245.

Cohen, R. L. (Ed.) (1979). Assessment. Section 3. In J. Nospitch (Ed.), *Basic handbook of child psychiatry* (pp. 485–630). New York: Basic Books.

Cohn, R., & Nardini, J. (1958). The correlation of bilateral occipital slow activity in the human EEG with certain disorders of behavior. *American Journal of Psychiatry, 115,* 44–54.

Coleman, J. S. (1968). *Equality of educational opportunity.* Report of the U.S. Department of Health, Education and Welfare. Washington, DC: U. S. Office of Education.

Coleman, J. S., Campbell, G. Q., Hobson, C. J., McPartland, J., Mood, A. M., Weinfeld, F. D., & York, R. L. (1966). *Equality of educational opportunity.* Report of the U.S. Department of Health, Education and Welfare. Washington, DC: U. S. Government Printing Office.

Coleman, M., & Gillberg, C. (1985). *The biology of the autistic syndromes.* New York: Praeger.

Collins, M., & Carmine, D. (1988). Evaluating the field test revision process by comparing two versions of a reasoning skills CAI program. *Journal of Learning Disabilities, 21,* 375–379.

Colon, E. J., Notermans, S. L. H., de Weerd, J. P. C., & Kap, J. (1979). The discriminating role of EEG power spectra in dyslexic children. *Journal of Neurology, 22,* 257–262.

Comer, James P. (1988). Educating poor minority children. *Scientific American, 259,* 42–48.

Comings, D. E., & Comings, B. G. (1984). Tourette's syndrome and attention deficit disorder and hyperactivity: Are they genetically related? *Journal of the American Academy of Child Psychiatry, 23,* 138–146.

Comings, D. E. & Comings, B. G. (1988). Tourette's syndrome and attention deficit disorder. In D. J. Cohen, R. D. Bruun, & J. F. Leckman (Eds.), *Tourette's syndrome and tic disorder* (pp. 119–136). New York: Wiley.

Comings, D. E., Comings, B. G., Devor, E. J., and Cloninger, C. R. (1984). Detection of a major gene for Gilles de la Tourette syndrome. *American Journal of Human Genetics, 36,* 586–600.

Compton, R. (1974). Diagnostic evaluation of committed delinquents. In B. Kratoville (Ed.), *Youth in trouble: The learning disabled adolescent.* San Rafael, CA: Academic Therapy Publications.

Cone, T., & Wilson, L. (1981). Quantifying a severe discrepancy: A critical analysis. *Learning Disability Quarterly, 4,* 359–372.

Conners, C. K. (1970). Visual evoked response in children with learning disorders. *Psychophysiology, 7,* 418–428.

Conners, C. K. (1972). Psychological effects of stimulant drugs in children with minimal brain dysfunction. *Pediatrics, 49,* 702–708.

Conners, C. K. (1973a). Psychological assessment of children with minimal brain dysfunction. *Annals of the New York Academy of Sciences, 205,* 283–302.

Conners, C. K. (1973b). Rating scales for use in drug studies with children. *Psychopharmacology Bulletin Special Issue,* 24–29.

Conners, C. K. (1978). A critical review of the electroencephalographic and neurophysiological studies in dyslexia. In A. Benton & D. Pearl (Eds.), *Dyslexia: An appraisal of current knowledge* (pp. 253–261). New York: Oxford University Press.

Conners, C. K. (1980). *Food additives and hyperactive children.* New York: Plenum.

Conners, C. K. (1987). Event related potentials and quantitative EEG brain-mapping in dyslexia. In D. Bakker, C. Wilsher, H. Debruyne, & N. Bertin (Eds.), *Developmental dyslexia and learning disorders* (pp. 9–21). Basel: Karger.

Conners, C. K., & Eisenberg, L. (1963). The effects of methylphenidate on symptomatology and learning in disturbed children. *American Journal of Psychiatry, 120,* 458–464.

Conners, C. K., & Taylor, E. (1980). Pemoline, methylphenidate and placebo in children with minimal brain dysfunction. *Archives of General Psychiatry, 37,* 922–930.

Connors, C. K., Eisenberg, L., & Sharpe, L. (1964). Effects of methylphenidate (Ritalin) on paired associative learning and Porteus maze performance in emotionally disturbed children. *Journal of Consulting Psychology, 28,* 14–22.

Conners, C. K., Goyette, C., Southwick, M., Lees, J. M., Andrulonis, P. A. (1976). Food additives and hyperkinesis: A controlled double-blind experiment. *Pediatrics, 58,* 154–166.

Conners, C. K., Kramer, R., Rothschild, G. H., Schwartz, L., & Stone, A. (1971). Treatment of young delinquent boys with diphenylhydantoin sodium and methylphenidate. *Archives of General Psychiatry, 24,* 156–160.

Consortium for Longitudinal Studies. (1983). *As the twig is bent: Lasting effects of preschool programs.* Hillsdale, NJ: Erlbaum.

Cooley, E., & Lamson, F. (1983). *A comparison of intellectually average and below average children with learning problems.* Paper presented at the meeting of the Western Psychological Association, San Francisco, CA.

Coons, C. E., Frankenberg, W. K., Gay, E. C., Fandel, A. W., Lafley, D. L., & Kerr, C. (1982). Preliminary results of a combined developmental screening project. In N. J. Anastasio, W. K. Frankenberg, & A. W. Fandal (Eds.), *Identifying the Developmentally Delayed Child* (pp. 101–111). Baltimore: University Park Press.

Coons, C. E., Gay, E. C., Fandal, A. W., Kerr, C., & Frankenberg, W. K. (1981) *The home screening questionnaire reference manual.* Denver: DDM, Inc.

Copeland, D. R., Fletcher, J. M., Pfefferbaum-Levine, B, Jaffe, N., Ried, H., & Maor, M. (1985). Neuropsychological sequelae of childhood cancer in long-term survivors. *Pediatrics, 75,* 745–753.

Corballis, M. C., & Beale, I. L. (1976). *The psychology of left and right.* New York: Halstead.

Corbett, J., & Trimble, M. (1983). Epilepsy and anticonvulsant medication. In M. Rutter (Ed.), *Developmental neuropsychiatry* (pp. 112–129), New York: Guilford.

Corkin, S. (1984). Lasting consequences of bilateral medial temporal lobotomy: Clinical course and experimental findings in H. M. *Seminars in Neurology, 4,* 249–259.

Cosden, M., Gerber M., Semmel, D., Goldman, S., & Semmel, M. (1987). Microcomputer uses within micro-educational environments. *Exceptional Children, 53,* 399–409.

Costello, A. J., Edelbrock, C., Dulcan, M. K., Kalas, R., & Klaric, S. H. (1984). *Development and testing of the NIMH diagnostic interview schedule for children in a clinic population.* (Contract #RFP-DB-81-0027). Rockville, MD: Center for Epidemiologic Studies, NIHM.

Costello, A. J., Edelbrock, C., Kalas, R., Lessler, M. D., & Klaric, S. H. (1982). *The NIMH diagnostic interview schedule for children (DISC).* Unpublished interview schedule, Department of Psychiatry, University of Pittsburg.

Courchesne, E., Hesselink, J. R., Jernigan T., & Young-Courchesne, R. (1987). Abnormal neuroanatomy in a non-retarded person with autism: Unusual findings with magnetic resonance imaging. *Archives of Neurology, 44,* 335–341.

Courchesne, E., Young-Courchesne, B. A., Press, G. A., Hesselink, J. R., & Jernigan, T. L. (1988). Hypoplasia of cerebellar vermal lobules VI and VII in autism. *New England Journal of Medicine, 318,* 1349–1354.

Cowen, C. D. (1985). The tutoring network: A unique nonprofit educational/civic/professional organization. *Annals of Dyslexia, 35,* 209–218.

Cox, A. (1977). *Bench mark measures.* Cambridge, MA: Educators Publishing Service.

Cox, A. (1985). Alphabetic phonics: An organization and expansion of Orton-Gillingham. *Annals of Dyslexia, 19,* 187–198.

Cravioto, J., & Arrieta, R. (1983). Malnutrition in childhood. In M. Rutter (Ed.), *Developmental neuropsychiatry* (pp. 32–51). New York: Guilford.

Crinella, F. M. (1973). Identification of brain dysfunction syndromes in children through profile analysis. *Journal of Abnormal Psychology, 82,* 33–45.

Crinella, F. M., & Dreger, R. M. (1972). Tentative identification of brain dysfunction syndromes in children through profile analysis. *Journal of Consulting and Clinical Psychology, 38,* 251–260.

Critchley, M. (1964). *Developmental dyslexia.* London: William Heinemann.

Crook, R. (1988). Pharmacotherapy of cognitive deficits in Alzheimer's disease and age-associated memory impairment. *Psychopharmacology Bulletin, 24,* 31–38.

Cronbach, J. L., & Snow, R. E. (1977). *Aptitudes and instructional methods.* New York: Irvington.

Cruickshank, W. M. (1967). *The brain-injured child in home, school and community.* Syracuse, NY: Syracuse University Press.

Cruickshank, W. M. (1977). Some issues facing the field of learning disabilities. *Journal of Learning Disabilities, 10,* 57–64.

Cruickshank, W. M. (1986). P. L. 94-142: Its making and its legacy. *Journal of Learning Disabilities, 19,* 388–389.

Cruickshank, W. M., Bentzen, F., Ratzeburg, R., & Tannhauser, M. (1961). *A teaching method for brain injured and hyperactive children.* Syracuse, NY: Syracuse University Press.

Cummings, J. A., Huebner, E. S., McLesky, J. (1986). Psychoeducational decision-making: Reason for referral versus test data. *Professional School Psychology, 19,* 249–256.

Cummins, J. (1979). Linguistic interdependence and the educational development of bilingual children. *Review of Educational Research, 49,* 222–251.

Cunningham, C. E., & Barkley, R. A. (1978). The role of academic failure in hyperactive behavior. *Journal of Learning Disabilities, 11,* 15–21.

Curtiss, S. (1985). The development of human cerebral lateralization. In F. Benson & E. Zaidel (Eds.), *The dual brain* (pp. 97–116). New York: Guilford.

Dalby, M. A. (1975). Behavioral effects of carbamazepine. In J. K. Penry & O. D. Daly (Eds.), *Advances in neurology,* Vol. 11 (pp. 331–344). New York: Raven.

Dam, M. (1972). Diphenylhydantoin: Neurologic aspects of toxicity. In D. Woodbury, J. Penry, & R. Schmidt (Eds.), *Antiepileptic drugs* (pp. 227–235). New York: Raven.

Damasio, A., & Maurer, R. (1978). A neurological model for childhood autism. *Archives of Neurology, 35,* 777–786.

D'Amato, R. C., & Dean, R. S. (1987). Psychological reports, individual educational programs, and daily lesson plans: Are they related? *Professional School Psychology, 2,* 93–101.

Darby, R. O. (1978). *Learning disabilities: A multivariate search for subtypes.* Doctoral dissertation, University of Florida, (University Microfilms No. 79-13, 261).

Das, J. P., Kirby, J., & Jarman, R. F. (1975). Simultaneous and successive syntheses: An alternative model for cognitive abilities. *Psychological Bulletin, 82,* 87–103.

Datta, L. (1969). *A report on evaluation studies of project head start.* Office of Child Development, U.S. Department of Health, Education, and Welfare, Washington, DC.

Dave, R., (1963). *The identification and measurement of environmental process variables that are related to educational achievement.* Unpublished dissertation, University of Chicago.

Davis, A. E., & Wada, J. A. (1977). Hemisphere asymmetries in human infants' spectral analysis of flash and click evoked potentials. *Brain and Language, 4,* 23–31.

Davis, E. (1964). Clinical evaluation of a new anticonvulsant (G-32883). *Medical Journal of Australia, 1,* 150–152.

Davis, F. (1971). *The measurement of mental capacity through evoked-potential recordings.* Greenwich, CT: Education Records Bureau.

Davis, H. P., & Squire, L. R. (1984). Protein synthesis and memory: A review. *Psychological Bulletin, 96,* 518–559.

Dawson, G. (1983). Lateralized brain dysfunction in autism. *Journal of Autism and Developmental Disorders, 8,* 339–353.

Dax, M. (1878). *L'Aphasie.* Paris: Delahaye.

Dee, H., & Fontenot, D. (1973). Cerebral dominance and lateral differences in perception and memory. *Neuropsychologia, 11,* 167–173.

Decker, S. N., & Vandenberg, S. (1985). Colorado twin study of reading disability. In D. B. Gray & J. F. Kavanaugh (Eds.), *Behavioral measures of dyslexia* (pp. 123–136). Parton, MD: York Press.

DeFries, J. C. (1985). Colorado reading project. In D. B. Gray & J. F. Kavanaugh (Eds.), *Behavioral measures of dyslexia* (pp. 107–122). Parton, MD: York Press.

DeFries, J. C., & Baker, L. A. (1983). Colorado family reading study: Longitudinal analysis. *Annals of Dyslexia, 33,* 153–162.

DeFries, J. C., & Decker, S. N. (1982). Genetic aspects of reading disability: A family study. In R. N. Malatesha & P. G. Aaron (Eds.), *Reading disorders: Variations and treatments* (pp. 255–279). New York: Academic Press.

DeFries, J. C., Fulker, D. W., & La Buda, M. C. (1987). Evidence for a genetic etiology in reading disability of twins. *Nature, 329,* 537–539.

DeHirsch, K. (1971). Prediction: Task Force II. In A. Hayes & A. Silver (Eds.), *National interdisciplinary committee on reading disabilities* (pp. 1–64). New York: Ford Foundation.

DeHirsch, K., Jansky, J. J., & Langford, W. S. (1966). *Predicting reading failure.* New York: Harper & Row.

de la Cruz, F. F., Fox, B. H., & Roberts, R. H. (Eds.) (1973). Minimal brain dysfunction. *Annals of the New York Academy of Sciences, 205,* 1–396.

Delanoy, R. L., Tucci, D. L., & Gold, P. E. (1983). Amphetamine effects on long term potentiation of dentate granule cells. *Pharmacology, Biochemistry and Behavior, 18,* 137–139.

DelDotto, J. E., & Rourke, B. E. (1985). Subtypes of left handed learning disabled children. In B. Rourke (Ed.), *Neuropsychology of learning disabilities: Essentials of subtype analysis* (pp. 89–132). New York: Guilford.

DeMyer, M. K., Hingtgen, J. N., & Jackson, R. K. (1981). Infantile autism reviewed: A decade of research. *Schizophrenia Bulletin, 7,* 388–451.

Denckla, M. B. (1972). Clinical syndromes in learning disabilities: The case for splitting versus lumping. *Journal of Learning Disabilities, 5,* 401–406.

Denckla, M. B. (1977). The neurological basis of reading disability. In F. G. Roswell, & G. Natchez (Eds.), *Reading disability: A human approach to learning.* New York: Basic Books.

Denckla, M. B. (1978). Critical review of electroencephalographic and neurophysiological studies in dyslexia. In A. Benton & D. Pearl (Eds.), *Dyslexia: An appraisal of current knowledge* (pp. 241–250). New York: Oxford University Press.

Denckla, M. B. (1985). Revised neurological examination for subtle signs. *Psychopharmacology Bulletin,* No. 4, *21,* 773–800.

Denckla, M. B., Bemporad, J. R., MacKay, M. C. (1976). Tics following methylphenidate administration: A report of 20 cases. *JAMA, 235,* 1349–1351.

Deshler, D. D., Schumaker, J. B., Levy, K., & Ellis, E. (1984). Academic and cognitive interventions for LD adolescents. Part II. *Journal of Learning Disabilities, 17,* 108–118 and 170–179.

Deutsch, C. P. (1973). Social class and child development. In B. M. Caldwell & H. N. Ricciuti (Eds.). *Review of Child Development Research, 3,* 233–82. Chicago: University of Chicago Press.

Deutsch, F. (1974). On postural behavior. *Psychoanalytic Quarterly, 16.*

Deutsch, M. (1965). Role of social class in language development and cognition. *American Journal of Orthopsychiatry, 35,* 78–86.

Devaney, J., & Rincover, A. (1983). Self-stimulatory behavior and sensory reinforcement. In R. L. Koegel, A. Rincover, & A. L. Egel (Eds.), *Educating and understanding autistic children* (pp. 127–141). San Diego: College-Hill Press.

DeWied, D. (1965). The influence of the posterior and intermediate lobe of the pituitary and pituitary peptides on the maintenance of a conditioned avoidance response in rats. *International Journal of Neuropharmacology, 4,* 157–167.

DeWied, D. (1971). Long-term effect of vasopressin on the maintenance of a conditioned avoidance response in rats. *Nature, 232,* 58–60.

DeWied, D. (1976). Behavioral effects of intraventricularly administered vasopressin and vasopressin fragments. *Life Sciences, 19,* 685–690.

DeWied, D. (1984). Neurohypophyseal hormone influences on learning and memory processes. In G. Lynch, J. L. McGaugh, & N. M. Weinberger (Eds.), *Neurobiology of learning and memory* (pp. 289–312). New York: Guilford.

Deykin, E., & MacMahon, B. (1979). The incidence of seizures among children with autistic symptoms. *American Journal of Psychiatry, 136,* 1310–1312.

Dickinson, L., Lee, J., & Ringdehl, I. L. (1979). Impaired growth in hyperkinetic children receiving pemoline. *Journal of Pediatrics, 94,* 538–541.

DiLanni, M., Wilsher, C. R., Blank, M. S., Conners, C. K., Chase, C. H. Funkenstein, H. H., Helgott, E., Holmes, J. M., Lougea, L. Maletta, G. J., Milewski, J., Pirozzolo, F. J., Rudel, H. G., & Tallel, P. (1985). Effects of piracetam in children with dyslexia. *Journal of Clinical Psychopharmacology, 5,* 272–278.

Dimond, D. J., & Brouwers, F. (1976). Improvement in human memory through use of drugs. *Psychopharmacology, 49,* 307–309.

Doehring, D. G. (1968). *Patterns of impairment in specific reading disability.* Bloomington: Indiana University Press.

Doehring, D. G. (1978). The tangled web of behavioral research on developmental dyslexia. In A. Benton & D. Pearl (Eds.), *Dyslexia: An appraisal of current knowledge* (pp. 123–138). New York: Oxford.

Doehring, D. G. (1985). Reading disability subtypes. In B. F. Rourke (Ed.), *Neuropsychology of learning disabilities* (pp. 133–146). New York: Guilford.

Doehring, D. G., & Hoshko, I. M. (1977). Classification of reading problems by the Q-technique of factor analysis. *Cortex, 13,* 281–294.

Doehring, D. G., Hoshko, I. M., & Bryans, B. N. (1979). Statistical classification of children with reading problems. *Journal of Clinical Neuropsychology, 1,* 5–16.

Doehring, D. G., Trites, R., Patel, P., & Fiedorowicz, C. A. (1981). *Reading disabilities: The interaction of reading, language and neuropsychological deficits.* New York: Academic Press.

Dostal, T. (1972). Antiaggressive effect of lithium salts in mentally retarded adolescents. In A. L. Annell (Ed.), *Depressive states in childhood and adolescence.* Stockholm: Almquist & Wiksell.

Douglas, V. I. (1972). Stop, look, listen. The problem of sustained attention and impulse control in hyperactive and normal children. *Canadian Journal Behavioral Science, 4,* 259–282.

Douglas, V. I. (1979). Toward a clearer definition of the attentional deficit of hyperactive children. In G. A. Hall & M. Lewis (Eds.), *Attention and the development of cognitive skills.* New York: Plenum.

Douglas, V. I. (1983). Attentional and cognitive problems. In M. Rutter (Ed.), *Developmental neuropsychology* (pp. 280–329). New York: Guilford.

Douglas, V. I., & Parry, P. (1983). Effects of reward on delayed reacting time task performance of hyperactive children. *Journal of Abnormal Child Psychology, 11,* 313–326.

Douglas, V. I., & Peters, K. G. (1979). Toward a clearer definition of the attentional deficit of hyperactive children. In G. A. Hale & M. Lewis (Eds.), *Attention and cognitive development* (pp. 173–247). New York: Plenum.

Drachman, D. A., & Leavitt, J. (1974). Human memory and the cholinergic system: A relationship to aging? *Archives of Neurology, 30,* 113–121.

Drake, W. (1968). Clinical and pathological findings in a child with a developmental learning disability. *Journal of Learning Disabilities, 1,* 468–475.

Dreger, R. M. (1964). A progress report on a factor analytic approach to classification in child psychiatry. In R. Jenkins & J. Cole (Eds.), *Research Report No. 18.* Washington, DC: American Psychiatric Association.

Dreifuss, F. E., & Sackellares, J. (1979). Treating epilepsy in children. *Current Prescribing,* 63–77.

Dudai, Y. (1985). Genes, enzymes and learning in *Drosophila. Trends in Neuroscience, 8,* 18–21.

Dudai, Y. (1988). Neurogenic dissection of learning and short term memory in *Drosophila. Annual Review of Neuroscience, 11,* 537–563.

Dudley-Marling, C., Kaufman, N. J., & Tarver, S. G. (1981). WISC and WISC-R profiles of learning disabled children: A review. *Learning Disability Quarterly, 4,* 307–319.

Dudley-Marling, C., & Searle, D. (1988). Enriching language learning environments for students with learning disabilities. *Journal of Learning Disabilities, 21,* 140–143.

Duffy, F. H., Denckla, M. B., Bartels, P. H., & Sandini, G. (1980). Dyslexia: Regional differences in brain electrical activity by topographic mapping. *Annals of Neurology, 7,* 412–420.

Duffy, F. H., Denckla, M. B., Bartels, P. H., Sandini, G., & Kiessling, L. S. (1980). Dyslexia: Automated diagnosis by computerized classification of brain electrical activity. *Annals of Neurology, 7,* 421–428.

Duffy, G. G., & Roehler, L. R. (1989). *Improving classroom reading instruction.* New York: Random House.

Dunlap, G., & Egel, A. (1983). Motivational techniques. In R. L. Koegel, A. Rincover, & A. L. Egel (Eds.), *Educating and understanding autistic children* (pp. 106–126). San Diego: College-Hill Press.

Dunlap, G., & Koegel, R. L. (1980). Motivating autistic children through stimulus variation. *Journal of Applied Behavioral Analysis, 13,* 619–627.

Dunn, A. J. (1980). Neurochemistry of learning and memory: An evaluation of recent data. *Annual Review of Psychology, 31,* 343–390.

Dunn, L. C., & Markwardt, F. C. (1970). *Peabody individual achievement test.* Circle Pines, MN: American Guidance Service.

Dunn, L. M., & Smith, J. O. (1965, 1966, 1967, 1968). *Peabody language development kits.* Circle Pines, MN: American Guidance Services.

Durrell, D. D., & Catterson, J. H. (1937, 1988). *Durrell analysis of reading difficulties.* San Antonio, TX: Psychological Corporation.

Dyal, J. A. (1971). Transfer of behavioral bias: Reality and specificity. In E. J. Fjardingsted (Ed.), *Chemical transfer of learned information* (pp. 219–263). Amsterdam: North-Holland.

Dykman, R. A., Ackerman, P. T., Clements, S. D., & Peters, J. E. (1971). Specific learning disabilities: An attentional deficit syndrome. In H. R. Myklebust (Ed.), *Progress in learning disabilities,* Vol. 2 (pp. 56–93). New York: Grune & Stratton.

Dykman, R. A., Peters, J. E., & Ackerman, P. T. (1973). Experimental approaches to the study of minimal brain dysfunction: A follow-up study. *Annals of the New York Academy of Sciences, 205,* 93–108.

Dykstra, R. (1968). Summary of the second grade phase of the cooperative research program in primary reading instruction. *Reading Research Quarterly, 2,* 49–70.

Eaves, L. C., Kendall, D. C., & Crichton, J. U. (1972). The early detection of minimal brain dysfunction. *Journal of Learning Disabilities, 5,* 454–462.

Ebaugh, F. G. (1923). Neuropsychiatric sequelae of acute epidemic encephalitis in children. *American Journal of Diseases of Children, 25,* 89–97.

Edelbrock, D., & Costello, A. J. (1984a). *A review of structured psychiatric interviews for children.* Center for Studies of Child and Adolescent Psychopathology, Clinical Research Branch, NIMH (MIMEO).

Edelbrock, C., & Costello, A. J. (1984b). Empirical corroboration of attention deficit disorder. *Journal of the American Academy of Child Psychiatry, 23,* 285–290.

Edmunds, C. W., & Gunn, J. A. (1937). *Cushney's pharmacology and therapeutics.* Philadelphia: Lea & Febiger.

Eidelberg, D., & Galaburda, A. M. (1982). Symmetry and asymmetry in the human thalamus. Cytoarchitectonic analysis in normal persons. *Archives of Neurology, 39,* 325–332.

Eidelberg, D., & Galaburda, A. M. (1984). Inferior parietal lobule: Divergent architectonic asymmetries in the human brain. *Archives of Neurology, 41,* 843–852.

Eisenberg, L. (1957). Psychiatric implications of brain damage in children. *Psychiatric Quarterly, 31,* 72–92.

Eisenberg, L. (1964). Behavioral manifestations of cerebral damage in childhood. In H. G. Birch (Ed.), *Brain damage in children* (pp. 61–76). Baltimore: Williams & Wilkins.

Eisenberg, L., (1966). Reading retardation: I. Psychiatric and sociologic aspects. *Pediatrics, 37,* 352–365.

Eisenberg, L. (1972). The clinical use of stimulant drugs in children. *Pediatrics, 49,* 709–715.

Eisenberg, L. (1978). Definitions of dyslexia: Their consequences for research and policy. In A. Benton & D. Pearl (Eds.), *Dyslexia: An appraisal of current knowledge* (pp. 29–42). New York: Oxford.

Eisenberg, L., & Earls, F. J. (1975). Poverty, social deprivation and child development. In D. A. Hamburg & H. K. M. Brodie (Eds.), *American handbook of psychiatry*, Vol. VI (pp. 275–291). New York: Basic Books.

Eling, P. (1981). On the theory and measurement of laterality. *Neuropsychologia, 19,* 767–774.

Elkins, R., Rapoport, J., Zahn, T., Buchsbaum, M., Weingartner, H., Kopin, I., Langer, D., & Johnson, C. (1981). Acute effects of caffeine in normal and prepubertal boys. *American Journal of Psychiatry, 52,* 447–457.

Elkonin, D. B. (1973). U.S.S.R. In J. Downing (Ed.), *Comparative reading.* New York: Macmillan.

Elliot, F. (1977). Propranolol for the control of the belligerent behavior following acute brain damage. *Annals of Neurology, 1,* 489–491.

Elliott, D., & Voss, H. (1974). *Delinquency and dropout.* Lexington ME: Heath & Company.

Ellis, E. S., Deshler, D. D., & Schumaker, J. B. (1989). Teaching adolescents with learning disabilities to generate and use task-specific strategies. *Journal of Learning Disabilities. 22,* 108–119.

Elthorne, A., Percy, M. F., & Crosskey, M. A. (1952). Some mechanisms of tactile localization revealed by study of leucotomized patients. *Journal of Neurology, Neurosurgery and Psychiatry, 15,* 272–282.

Emmett, M., Jeffrey, H., Chandler, D., & Dugdale, A. (1980). Sequalae of *Hemophilus influenzae* meningitis. *Australia Pediatric Journal, 16,* 90–93.

Enfield, M. L. (1988). The quest for literacy. *Annals of Dyslexia, 38,* 8–21.

Entus, A. K. (1977). Hemisphere asymmetry in processing dichotically presented speech and non-speech stimuli by infants. In S. Segalowitz & F. A. Gruber (Eds.), *Language development and neurological theory* (pp. 63–73). New York: Academic Press.

Epps, S., Ysseldyke, J., & McQue, M. (1984). I know one when I see one: Differentiating learning disorder and non-learning disorder students. *Learning Disability Quarterly, 7,* 89–101.

Erenberg, G., Cruse, R. R., Rothner, D. O., & Rothner, A. D. (1987). The natural history of Tourette syndrome: A follow-up study. *Annals of Neurology, 22,* 383–385.

Erikson, E. H. (1968). *Identity: Youth and crisis.* New York: W. W. Norton.

Escalona, S. (1974). Intervention programs for children at psychiatric risk: The contribution of child psychology and developmental theory. In E. J. Anthony & C. Koupernik (Eds.), *The child in his family,* Vol. 3 (pp. 33–46). New York: Wiley.

Essman, W., & Nakajima, S. (Eds.) (1973). *Current biochemical approaches to learning and memory.* New York: Spectrum Publications.

Exner, J. E., & Weiner, I. B. (1982). *The Rorschach: A comprehensive system. Assessment of children and adolescents,* Vol. 3. New York: Wiley.

Extein, I., & Dackis, C. A. (1987). Brain mechanisms in cocaine dependency. In A. M. Washton & M. S. Gold (Eds.), *Cocaine* (pp. 73–84). New York: Guilford.

Falkner, B., Koffler, S., & Lowenthal, D. T. (1984). Effects of anti-hypertensive drugs on cognitive function in adolescents. *Pediatric Pharmacology, 4,* 239–244.

Farley, J., & Auerbach, S. (1986). Protein kinase C activation induces conductance change in *Hermissenda* photoreceptors like those seen in associative learning. *Nature, 319,* 220.

Farr, R. (1969). Reading, what can be measured? *ERIC/CRIER Reading Review Series.* Newark, DE: International Reading Association.

Fayen, M., Goldman, M. B., Moulthrop, M. A., & Luchins, D. J. (1988). Differential memory function with dopaminergic versus anticholinergic treatment of drug induced extrapyramidal symptoms. *American Journal of Psychiatry, 145,* 483–486.

Federal Register. (1976). The Education for All Handicapped Children Act, (Public Law 94-142), *42,* 42496–42497.

Feeser, H., & Raskin, L. (1987). Effects of neonatal dopamine depletion on spatial ability during ontogony, *Behavioral Neuroscience, 101,* 812–818.

Fein, D., Pennington, B., Markowitz, P., Braverman, M., & Waterhouse, L. (1986). Toward a neuropsychological model of infantile autism. *Journal American Academy of Child and Adolescent Psychiatry, 25,* 198–212.

Fein, G., Merrin, E. L., Davenport, L., & Buffreon, L. C. (1987). Memory deficits associated with clonidine. *General Hospital Psychiatry, 9,* 154–155.

Feingold, B. F. (1974). *Why your child is hyperactive.* New York: Random House.

Feldman, H., & Michaels, R. (1988). Academic achievement in children ten to twelve years after *Hemophilus influenzae* meningitis. *Pediatrics, 81,* 339–343.

Fenichel, O. (1945).*The psychoanalytic theory of neurosis.* New York: Norton.

Fennel, E. B., Bowers, D., & Satz, P. (1977). Within modal and cross-modal reliabilities of two laterality tests. *Brain and Language, 4,* 63–69.

Ferenzi, S. (1950). *Further contributions to the theory and techniques of psychoanalysis.* London: Hogarth.

Fernald, G. M. (1943, revised 1988). *Remedial techniques in the basic school subjects.* Austin, TX: PRO-ED.

Feuerstein, R. (1979). *The dynamic assessment of retarded performers.* Baltimore: University Park Press.

Field, T. M., & Sostek, A. M. (Eds.) (1983). *Infants born at risk: Physiological, perceptual and cognitive processes.* New York: Grune & Stratton.

Field, T. M. (Ed.), Sostek, A. M., Goldberg, S., & Shuman, H. (1979). *Infants born at risk: Behavior and development.* New York: Spectrum.

Fine, M. J. (1977). *Principles and techniques of intervention with hyperactive children.* Springfield, IL: Charles C Thomas.

Finlayson, M. A., & Reitan, R. M. (1976). Tactile-perceptual functioning in relation to intellectual, cognitive, and reading skills in younger and older normal children. *Developmental Medicine and Child Neurology, 18,* 442–446.

Finucci, J. M., Guthrie, J. T. Childs, A. L., Abbey, H., & Childs B. (1976). The genetics of specific reading disability. *Annals of Human Genetics, 40,* 1–23.

Finucci, J. M., Whitehouse, C. C., Isaacs, S. D., & Childs, B. (1984). Derivation and validation of a quantitative definition of SRD for adults. *Developmental Medicine and Child Neurology, 26,* 143–153.

Fischer, W., Wictorin, K., Bjorklund, A., Williams, L. R., Varon, S., & Gage, F. H. (1987). Amelioration of cholinergic neuron atrophy and spatial memory impairment in aged rats by nerve growth factor. *Nature, 329,* 65–68.

Fish, B. (1977). Neurobiological antecedents of schizophrenia in childhood. *Archives of General Psychiatry, 34,* 1297–1313.

Fish, B., Campbell, M., & Shapiro, T. (1970). Comparison of trifluperazine and chlorpromazine in pre-school schizophrenic children: the value of less sedative antipsychotic agents. *Current Therapy Research, 11,* 589–595.

Fisher, G. L., Jenkins, S. J., Bancroft, M. J., & Kraft, L. M. (1988). The effects of KABC-based remedial strategies on word recognition skills. *Journal of Learning Disabilities, 21,* 307–312.

Fisk, J. L., & Rourke, B. P. (1979). Identification of subtypes of learning disabled children at three age levels: A neuropsychological approach. *Journal of Clinical Neuropsychology, 1,* 289–310.

Fisk, J. L., Finnell, R., & Rourke, B. P. (1985). Major findings and future directions for learning disability subtype analysis. In B. P. Rourke (Ed.), *Neuropsychology of Learning Disability* (pp. 331–341). New York: Guilford.

Fitzgerald, J. (1951). *A basic life spelling vocabulary.* Milwaukee, WI: Bruce.

Fjerdingstad, E. J. (1971). *Chemical transfer of learned information.* New York: Elsevier.

Flapan, D., & Neubauer, P. (1975). *Assessment of early child development.* New York: Jason Aronson.

Flavel, J. (1977). *Cognitive development.* NJ: Prentice Hall.

Flesch, R. (1981). *Why Johnny still can't read.* New York: Harper and Row.

Fletcher, J. M., & Satz, P., (1984). Preschool prediction of reading failure. In M. D. Levine & P. Satz (Eds.), *Middle childhood: Developmental and dysfunction* (pp. 153–182). Baltimore: University Park Press.

Fletcher, J. M. & Satz, P. (1985). Cluster analysis and search for learning disability subtypes. In B. P. Rourke (Ed.), *Neuropsychology of learning disabilities* (pp. 40–64). New York: Guilford.

Fletcher, J. M., Smidt, R. K., & Satz, P. (1979). Discriminant function strategies for the kingergarten prediction of reading achievement. *Journal of Clinical Neuropsychology, 1,* 151–166.

Flexner, J. B., Flexner, L. B., & Stellar, E. (1963). Memory in mice as affected by intracerebral puromycin, *Science, 141,* 57–59.

Flexner, L. B., Flexner, J. B., & Stellar E. (1965). Memory and cerebral protein synthesis in mice as affected by graded amounts of puromycin. *Experimental Neurology, 13,* 264–272.

Flood, J., & Jarvik, M. E. (1976). Drug influences in learning and memory. In M. R. Rosensweig & E. L. Bennett (Eds.), *Neural mechanism of learning and memory* (pp. 483–507). Cambridge, MA: MIT Press.

Flood, J. F., Bennett, E. L., Orme, A. E., & Rosensweig, M. R. (1975). Relation of memory formation to controlled amounts of brain protein synthesis. *Physiology and Behavior, 15,* 97–102.

Folstein, S., & Rutter, M. (1977). Infantile autism: A genetic study of 21 twin pairs. *Journal of Child Psychology and Psychiatry, 18,* 297–321.

Food and Drug Administration. (1988). *FDA Drug Bulletin, 18,* No. 3, 32–33.

Ford, F. R. (1937). *Diseases of the nervous system in infancy, childhood and adolescence.* Springfield, IL: Charles C Thomas.

Fox, B., & Routh, D. K. Analyzing spoken language into words, syllables, and phonemes: A developmental study. *Journal of Psycholinguistic Research, 4,* 331–342.

Frank, J., & Levinson, H. (1973). Dysmetric dyslexia and dyspraxia. Hypothesis and study. *Journal of the American Academy of Child Psychiatry, 12,* 690–701.

Frankenberger, W., & Harper, J. (1987). States' criteria for identifying learning disabled children: A comparison of 1981/82 and 1985/86 guidelines. *Journal of Learning Disabilities, 20,* 118–121.

Frankenburg, W. K., & Dodds, J. B. (1968, 1981). *Denver developmental screening test.* Denver, CO: LADOCA Publishing Foundation.

Freeman, R. J. (1978). The effects of methylphenidate on avoidance learning and risk taking by hyperkinetic children. Doctoral dissertation, McGill University, quoted by V. Douglas *Attentional and cognitive problems* (1983) in M. Rutter, (Ed.) *Developmental neuropsychiatry.* New York: Guilford.

Freides, D. (1974). Human information processing and sensory modality. *Psychological Bulletin, 81,* 284–310.

Freud, A. (1977). Theory of developmental assessment. In R. S. Eissler, A. Freud, M. Kris, & A. J. Solnit (Eds.), *Psychoanalytic assessment: The diagnostic profile. Anthology of the psychoanalytic study of the child* (pp. 1–56). New Haven: Yale University Press.

Freud, S. (1891). *On aphasia*. New York: International Universities Press, 1983.

Freud, S. (1940). *An outline of psycho-analysis*. Translated by James Strachey. New York: W. W. Norton & Co., Inc.

Freud, S. (1920). (1955). Beyond the pleasure principle. In J. Strachey (Ed.), *Standard edition*, Vol. 18 (pp. 1–61). London: Hogarth Press.

Friedhoff, A. J., & Chase, T. N. (Eds.) (1982). *Gilles de la Tourette syndrome. Advances in Neurology*, *35*. New York: Raven Press.

Friedman, D. L., Cancelli, A. A., & Yoshida, R. (1988). Academic engagement of elementary school children with learning disabilities. *Journal of School Psychology*, *26*, 327–340.

Friedman, M., Guyer-Christie, B., La Rue, A., & Tymchuk, A. (1976). Cognitive style and specialized hemispheric processing in learning disability. In R. M. Knights & D. J. Bakker (Eds.), *Neuropsychology of learning disorders: Therapeutic approaches* (pp. 257–263). Baltimore: University Park Press.

Fries, M. D. (1944). Psychosomatic relations between mother and infant. *Psychosomatic Medicine*, *6*, 159–162.

Frith, U. (1972). Cognitive mechanism in autism: Experiments with color and tone sequence production. *Journal of Autism and Childhood Schizophrenia*, *2*, 160–173.

Frith, U., & Baron-Cohen, S. (1987). Perception in autistic children. In D. Cohen & A. Donnellan (Eds.), *Handbook of autism and pervasive developmental disorders* (pp. 85–102). New York: Wiley.

Frosch, J. (1983). *The psychotic process*. New York: International Universities Press.

Fuller, P. W. (1978). Attention and the EEG alpha rhythm in learning disabled children. *Journal of Learning Disabilities*, *11*, 44–53.

Fuller, P. W., Guthrie, R. D., & Alvord, E. C., Jr. (1983). A proposed neuropathological basis for learning disabilities in children born prematurely. *Developmental Medicine and Children Neurology*, *25*, 214–231.

Fundala, J. B. (1978). *Prescriptive reading performance test*. Los Angeles, CA: Western Psychological Services.

Fulton, A. I., & Yates, W. R. (1988). Family abuse of methylphenidate. *AFP*, *38*, 143–145.

Gaddes, W. (1976). Learning disabilities: Prevalence estimates and the need for definition. In R. M. Knights & D. J. Bakker (Eds.), *Neuropsychology of learning disorders: Theoretical approaches* (pp. 3–24). Baltimore: University Park Press.

Gaddes, W. (1980). *Learning disabilities and brain function: A neuropsychological approach*. New York: Springer-Verlag.

Gaffney, G. R., & Tsai, L. Y. (1987). Brief report: Magnetic resonance imaging of high level autism. *Journal of Autism and Developmental Disorders*, *17*, 433–438.

Galaburda, A. M. (1983). Developmental dyslexia: Current anatomical research. *Annals of Dyslexia*, *33*, 41–55.

Galaburda, A. M. (1985). Developmental dyslexia: A review of biological interactions. *Annals of Dyslexia*, *35*, 21–33.

Galaburda, A. M. (1989). Ordinary and extraordinary brain development: Anatomical variation in developmental dyslexia. *Annals of Dyslexia*, *39*, 67–80.

Galaburda, A. M., & Kemper, T. L. (1979). Cytoarchitectonic abnormalities in developmental dyslexia: A case study. *Annals of Neurology*, *6*, 94–100.

Galaburda, A. M., Sanides, F., & Geschwind, N. (1978). Human brain. Cytoarchitectonic left-right asymmetries in the temporal speech region. *Archives of Neurology*, *35*, 812–817.

Gallagher, J. J. (1986). Learning disabilities and special education: A critique. *Journal of Learning Disabilities, 19,* 595–601.

Gallagher, M. (1984). Current perspectives on memory systems and their modulation. In G. Lynch, J. L. McGaugh, & N. M. Weinberger (Eds.), *Neurobiology of learning and memory* (pp. 368–373). New York: Guilford.

Galton, F. (1907). *Inquiries into human faculty and its development.* London, U.K.: Macmillan.

Galvin, G. (1981). Uses and abuses of WISC-R with the learning disabled. *Journal of Learning Disabilities, 14,* 326–329.

Garber, H. J., Ritvo, E., Chu, L., Giswold, V., Kashanian, B., Freeman, B., & Oldendorf, W. (1989). A magnetic resonance imaging study of autism: Normal fourth ventricle size and absence of pathology. *American Journal of Psychiatry, 146,* 532–534.

Gardiner, R. A. (1968). Psychogenic problems of brain-injured children and their parents. *Journal of the American Academy of Child Psychiatry, 7,* 471–491.

Gardiner, R. A. (1979). Psychogenic difficulties secondary to MBD. In J. Nospitch (Ed.), *Basic handbook of child psychiatry* (pp. 614–628). New York: Basic Books.

Gardner, H. (1983). *Frames of mind: Theories of multiple intelligence.* New York: Basic Books.

Gastfriend, D., Biederman, J., & Jellinek, M. S. (1984). Desipramine in the treatment of adolescents with attention deficit disorder. *American Journal of Psychiatry, 141,* 906–908.

Gastfriend, D. R., Biederman, J., & Jellinek, M. S. (1985). Desipramine in the treatment of attention deficit disorder in adolescents. *Psychopharmacology Bulletin, 21,* 144–145.

Gates, A. I., & MacGinitie, W. (1968). *Gates-MacGinitie reading readiness tests.* New York: Teachers College Press.

Gates, A. I., McKillop, G. S., & Horowitz, E. C. (1962, 1981). *Gates-McKillop-Horowitz reading diagnostic test.* New York: Teachers College Press.

Gazzaniga, M. S., Bogen, J. E., & Sperry, R. W. (1962). Some functional aspects of sectioning the cerebral commissures in men. *Proceedings National Academy of Science, 48,* 1765–1769.

Geller, E., Ritvo, E., Freeman, B., Yuwiler, A. (1982). Preliminary observations on the effect of fenfluramine on blood serotonin and symptoms in three autistic boys. *New England Journal of Medicine, 307,* 165–169.

Gelzheiser, L., Solar, R., Shepherd, M. J., & Wozniak, R. H. (1983). Teaching learning disabled children to memorize: A rationale for plans and practice. *Journal of Learning Disabilities, 16,* 421–425.

Gerstmann, J. (1924). Fingeragnosie: Eine Unschriebene Storung der Orienterung am Eigenen Koerper. *Weiner Klinische Wochenschrift, 37,* 1010–1012.

Gerstmann, J. (1927). Fingeragnosie und isolierte Agraphia. *Zeitschrift f.d. ges. Neurol, 108,* 152.

Gerstmann, J. (1930). Zur Symptomatologie der Hirnlasionen im Uberganggebiet der Centaren Parietal und Mitteren Occipitalwindung (das syndrom: Fingeragnosie, Rechts-Links Storung, Agraphia, Akalkulie). *Nervenartzt, 3,* 691–695.

Geschwind, N. (1968). Neurological foundations of language. In H. R. Myklebust (Ed.), *Progress in learning disabilities,* Vol. 1 (pp. 182–198). New York: Grune & Stratton.

Geschwind, N. (1983). Biological associations of left handedness. *Annals of Dyslexia, 33,* 29–40.

Geschwind, N., & Behan, P. (1982). Left handedness: Association with immune disease, migraine and developmental learning disorder. *Proceedings of the National Academy of Science, 79,* 5097–5100.

Geschwind, N., & Levitsky, W. (1968). Human brain: Left-right asymmetries in temporal speech region. *Science, 161,* 168–188.

Gesell, A. L. (1938). The tonic-neck reflex in the human infant: Its morphological and clinical significance. *Journal of Pediatrics, 13,* 455–464.

Gesell, A. L. (1945). *The embryology of behavior.* Reissued in 1969 by University Microfilms, Ann Arbor, MI.

Gesell, A. L., & Amatruda, C. S. (1947). *Developmental diagnosis.* New York: Hoeber.

Gesell, A. L., & Ames, L. B. (1945). The development of handedness. *Journal of Genetic Psychology, 70,* 155–175.

Gesell, A. L., & Thompson, H., (1934). *Infant behavior, its genesis and growth.* New York: McGraw-Hill.

Gibson, E. J. (1969). *Principles of perceptual learning and development.* New York: Appleton-Century Crofts.

Gibson, E. J., & Levin, H. (1969). *The psychology of reading.* Cambridge, MA: MIT Press.

Gillberg, C., Suennerholm, L., & Hamilton-Hallberg, C. (1983). Childhood psychosis and monoamine metabolites in spinal fluid. *Journal of Autism and Developmental Disorders, 13,* 383–396.

Gillingham, A., Stillman, B. (1956). *Remedial training for children with specific disability in reading, spelling and penmanship.* Cambridge, MA: Educators Publishing Service.

Gilman, A. G., Goodman, L. S., Rall, T. W., & Murad, F. (1985). *The pharmacological basis of therapeutics,* (7th ed.). New York: Macmillan.

Gittelman, R., Klein, D. F., & Feingold, I. (1983). Children with reading disorders—II. Effects of methylphenidate in combination with reading remediation. *Journal of Child Psychology and Psychiatry, 21,* 193–212.

Gittelman-Klein, R., & Klein, D. F. (1976). Methylphenidate effects in learning disabilities. *Archives of General Psychiatry, 33,* 655–664.

Giurgea, C. (1972). Vers une pharmacologie de l'activite integrative du cerveau. Tentative du concept nootrope en pharmacologie. *Actualites Pharmacologiques, 25,* 115–156.

Giurgea, C. (1978). Pharmacology of nootropic drugs. In P. Deniker, C. Radouco-Thomas, A. Villaneuva, D. Baronet-LaCroix, & F. Gersin (Eds.), *Neuro-psychopharmacology* (pp. 67–72). New York: Pergamon.

Glasky, A. J., & Simon, L. N. (1966). Magnesium pemoline: Enhancement of brain RNA polymerase. *Science, 151,* 702–703.

Glavin, J. P., & Anneslen, F. R. (1971). Reading and arithmetic correlates of conduct problem and withdrawn children. *Journal of Special Education, 5,* 213–219.

Glavin, J. P., & DeGirolamo, G. (1970). Spelling errors of withdrawn and conduct problem children. *Journal of Special Education, 4,* 199–204.

Goddard, G. V., Bliss, T.V.P., Robertson A., & Sutherland, R. S. (1980). Noradrenaline levels affect long-term potentiation in the hippocampus. *Society for Neuroscience Abstracts, 6,* 89.

Goetz, C. G., & Klawans, H. L. (1982). Gilles de la Tourette on Tourette syndrome. In A. Friedhoff & T. Chase (Eds.), *Advances in neurology,* Vol. 35 (pp. 1–16). New York: Raven Press.

Goetz, C. G., Tanner, C. M., & Klawans, H. L. (1989). Fluphenazine and multifocal tic disorders. *Archives of Neurology, 41,* 271–272.

Goetz, C. G., Tanner, C. M., Wilson, R. S., Carroll, V. S. Como, P. G., & Shannon, K. M. (1987). Clonidine and Gilles de la Tourette syndrome: Double-blind study using objective rating methods. *Annals of Neurology, 21,* 307–310.

Gold, P. E. (1979). Suspected neurological impairment and cognitive abilities: A longitudinal study of selected skills and predictive accuracy. *Journal of Clinical Child Psychology, 8,* 35–38.

Gold, P. E. (1984). Memory modulation: Neurobiological contexts. In G. Lynch, J. L. McGaugh, & N. M. Weinberger (Eds.), *Neurobiology of learning and memory* (pp. 374–384). New York: Guilford.

Golden, G. S. (1984). Psychologic and neuropsychologic aspects of Tourette's syndrome. *Neurology Clinics, 2,* 91–102.

Golden, G. S. (1988). The use of stimulants in the treatment of Tourette's syndrome. In J. D. Cohen, R. Bruun, & J. Leckman (Eds.), *Tourette's syndrome and tic disorder* (pp. 317–325). New York: Wiley.

Goldfine, P., McPherson, P., Heath, A., Hardesty, V., Beauregard, L., & Gordon, B. (1985). Association of Fragile X Syndrome with Autism. *American Journal of Psychiatry, 142,* 108.

Goldstein, A. (1984). Nifedipine treatment of Tourette's syndrome. *Journal of Clinical Psychiatry, 45,* 360.

Goldstein, K. (1938). A further comparison of the Moro reflex and the Startle pattern. *Journal of Psychology, 6,* 33–42.

Goldstein, K. (1954). The brain-injured child. In H. Michael-Smith (Ed.), *Pediatric problems in clinical practice* (pp. 97–120). New York: Grune & Stratton.

Goldstein, M. N., & Joynt, R. J. (1969). Long term follow-up of a collosal-sectioned patient. *Archives of Neurology, 70,* 96–102.

Gonce, M., & Barbeau, A. (1977). Seven cases of Gilles de la Tourette's syndrome: Partial relief with clonazepam, a pilot study. *Canadian Journal of Neurological Sciences, 4,* 279–283.

Goodman, K. S. (1967). Reading: A psycholinguistic guessing game. *Journal of the Reading Specialist, 6,* 126–135.

Gordon, M., & Mettelman, B. B. (1987). *Technical guide to the Gordon diagnostic system.* DeWitt, NY: Gordon Systems.

Gordon, M. N. (1979). The assessment of impulsivity and mediating behaviors in hyperactive and non-hyperactive boys. *Journal of Abnormal Child Psychology, 7,* 317–326.

Gordon, M. N., McClure, F. D., & Post, E. M. (1986). *Interpretive guide to the Gordon diagnostic system.* DeWitt, NY: Gordon Systems.

Gorenstein, E., & Newman, J. P. (1980). Disinhibitory psychopathology: A new perspective and a model for research. *Psychological Review, 87,* 301–315.

Gottesman, R. L., Belmont, I., & Kaminer, R. (1975). Admission and follow-up status of reading disabled children referred to a medical clinic. *Journal of Learning Disabilities, 8,* 642–650.

Goyer, P., Davis, G., & Rapoport, J. (1979). Abuse of prescribed stimulant medication by a 13 year old hyperactive boy. *Journal of the American Academy of Child Psychiatry, 18,* 170–175.

Goyette, C., Conners, C., & Petti. (1978). Effects of artificial colors on hyperactive children: A double-blind challenge study. *Psychopharmacology Bulletin, 14,* 39–40.

Graham, F. K., Ernhart, C. B., Thurston, C. B., & Kraft, M. (1962). Development three years after perinatal anoxia and other potentially damaging newborn experinces. *Psychological Monographs, 76,* 1–58.

Gray, D. B., & Kavanaugh, J. F. (1985). *Behavioral measures of dyslexia.* Parton, MD: York Press.

Gray, S. W. (1983). Cognitive development in relation to otitis media. In C. Bluestone, J. Klein, J. Paradise, H. Eichonweld, F. Bess, M. Downs, M. Green, J. Berko-Gleason, I. Ventry, S. Gray, B. McWilliams, & G. Gates. Workshop in the effects of otitis media on the child. *Pediatrics, 71,* 645–646.

Gray, S. W., Ramsey, B. K., & Klaus, R. A. (1982). *From 3 to 20: The early education project.* Baltimore: University Park Press.

Green, W., Campbell, M., Hardesty, A., Grega, D., Padron-Gayol, M., Shell, J., & Erlenmeyer-Kimling, L. (1984). A comparison of schizophrenia and autistic children. *Journal of the American Academy of Child and Adolescent Psychiatry, 23,* 399–409.

Greenacre, P. (1941). The predisposition to anxiety. *Psychoanalytic Quarterly, 10,* 66–94, and 610–638.

Greenacre, P. (1952). *Trauma, growth and personality.* New York: W. W. Norton.

Greendyke, R. M., & Kanter, D. R. (1986). Therapeutic effects of pindolol on behavioral disturbances associated with organic brain disorder: A double blind study. *Journal of Clinical Psychiatry, 47,* 423–426.

Greendyke, R. M., Schuster, D. B., & Wooten, J. A. (1984). Propranolol on the treatment of assaultive patients with organic brain disease. *Journal of Clinical Psychopharmacology, 4,* 282–285.

Greenhill, L. (1981). Stimulant-related growth inhibition in children: A review. In M. G. Hilman (Ed.), *Strategic interventions for hyperactive children* (pp. 39–63). Armonk, NY: M. E. Sharpe.

Greenhill, L., Chambers, W., Rubinstein, B., Helpern, F., & Sacher, E. (1981). Growth hormone, prolactin and growth responses in hyperkinetic males treated with d-amphetamine. *Journal of American Academy of Child Psychiatry, 20,* 71–84.

Greenhill, L., Puig-Antich, J., Novacenko, H., Solomon, M., Angher, C., Florea, J., Goetz, R., Fiscina, B., & Sachar, E. J. (1984). Prolactin, growth hormone, and growth responses in boys with attention deficit disorder. *Journal of American Academy of Child Psychiatry, 23,* 58–67.

Greenough, W. T. (1984). Structural corrolates of information storage in the mammalian brain: A review and hypothesis. *Trends in Neuroscience, 7,* 229–233.

Greenspan, S. I. (1981). *The clinical interview of the child.* New York: McGraw-Hill.

Gregory, A. H., Efron, R., Divenyi, P. L., & Yund, E. W. (1983). Central auditory processing. I. Ear dominance—a perceptual or attentional asymmetry? *Brain and Language, 19,* 225–296.

Gresham, F. M., & Elliott, S. (1989). Social skills deficits as a primary learning disability. *Journal of Learning Disabilities, 22,* 120–124.

Groh, C. (1978). The psychotropic effect of Tegretol in non-epileptic children with particular reference to the drug's indication. In W. Birxmayer (Ed.), *Epileptic seizures, behavior, pain.* Berne: Hans & Huber.

Gross, K., Rothenberg, S., Schottenfeld, S., & Drake, C. (1978). Duration threshold for letter identification in left and right visual fields for normal and reading disabled children. *Neuropsychologia, 16,* 709–716.

Gross, M. B., & Wilson, W. C. (1974). *Minimal brain dysfunction.* New York: Brunner/Mazel.

Group for the Advancement of Psychiatry. (1957). *Diagnostic process in child psychiatry,* Vol. 3, No. 38.

Gualtieri, T., Kanoy, R., Hawk, B., Koriath, U., Schroeder, S., Youngblood, W., Breese, G., & Pranga, A. (1981). Growth hormone and prolactin secretion in adults and hyperactive children: Relation to methylphenidate serum level. *Psychoendocrinology, 6,* 331–339.

Gualtieri, T., Wafgin, W., Kanoy, R., Patrick, K., Shen, O., Youngblood, W., Mueller, R., & Breese, G. (1982). Clinical studies of methylphenidate serum levels in children and adults. *Journal of the American Academy of Child Psychiatry, 21,* 19–26.

Gubbay, S. S. (1975). *The clumsy child: A study of developmental apraxia and agnostic ataxia.* Philadelphia: Saunders.

Gubbay, S. S., Ellis, E., Walton, J. N., & Court, S. D. M. (1965). Clumsy children: A study of apraxic and agnosic defects in 21 children. *Brain, 88,* 295–312.

Guilford, J. P. (1967). *The nature of human intelligence.* New York: McGraw-Hill.

Guthrie, J. T. (1973). Models of reading and reading disability. *Journal of Educational Psychology, 15,* 663–687.

Haaf, R. G., & Spreen, O. (1986). Empirically derived learning disability subtypes: A replication attempt and longitudinal patterns over 15 years. *Journal of Learning Disabilities, 15,* 285–304.

Haber, S. N., Kowall, N. W., Vonsattel, J. P., Bird, E. D., & Richardson, E. P. (1986). Gilles de la Tourette's syndrome. A post mortem neuropathological and immunochemical study. *Journal of Neurological Science, 75,* 225–241.

Hagin, R. A. (1954). *Reading retardation and the language arts: A comparative study of retarded and non-retarded readers in a group of behavior problems.* (Unpublished doctoral dissertation, New York University).

Hagin, R. A. (1983). Write right or left: A practical approach to handwriting. *Journal of Learning Disabilities, 16,* 266–271.

Hagin, R. A. (1984). Effects of first grade promotion practices of a program for the prevention of learning disabilities. *Psychology in the Schools, 21,* 471–476.

Hagin, R. A., Beecher, R., Pagano, G., & Kreeger, H. (1980). *Final report to the Gatepost Foundation,* mimeo, unpublished.

Hagin, R. A., Beecher, R., Pagano, G., & Kreeger, H. (1982). Effects of Tourette syndrome on learning. In A. Friedhoff & T. Chase (Eds.), *Gilles de la Tourette syndrome. Advances in neurology,* Vol. 35 (pp. 323–333). New York: Raven.

Hagin, R. A., Beecher, R., & Silver, A. A. (1982). Definition of learning disabilities: A clinical approach. In J. P. Das, R. F. Mulcahy, & A. E. Wall (Eds.), *Theory and research in learning disabilities* (pp. 45–57). New York: Plenum.

Hagin, R. A., & Kugler, J., (1988). School problems associated with Tourette syndrome. In D. Cohen, R. Brunn, & J. Leckman (Eds.), *Tourette's syndrome and tic disorders* (pp. 223–236). New York: Wiley.

Hagin, R. A., Silver, A. A., & Corwin, C. G. (1972). Clinical-diagnostic use of the WPPSI in predicting learning disabilities in grade 1. *Journal of Special Education, 5,* 221–232.

Hagin, R. A., Silver, A. A., & Kreeger, H. (1976). *Teach.* New York: Walker Educational Books.

Haines, J., Ames, L. B., & Gillespie, C. (1980). *Gesell preschool test.* Flemington, NJ: Programs for Education.

Hainsworth, P. K., & Hainsworth, M. L. (1980). *Preschool screening system.* Pawtucket, RI: ERISYS.

Hainsworth, P. K., & Siqueland, M. L. (1969). *Meeting street school screening test.* Providence, RI: Crippled Children and Adults of Rhode Island.

Hall, E. T. (1976). Small group instruction for language skills improvement. *Bulletin of the Orton Society, 26,* 63–78.

Hall, M. B. (1947). *Psychiatric examination of the school child.* London: Arnold.

Hallahan, D. L., Keller, C. E., McKinney, J. D., Lloyd, J. W., & Bryan, T. (1988). Examining the research base of the regular education initiative: Efficacy studies and the adaptive learning model. *Journal of Learning Disabilities, 21,* 29–35.

Hallgren, B. (1950). Specific dyslexia ("congenital word blindness"). A clinical and genetic study. *Acta Psychiatrica et Neurologica Scandinavia, Supplement 65.*

Halperin, J. M., Gittelman, R., Klein, D. F., & Rudel, R. G. (1984). Reading-disabled hyperactive children: A distinct subgroup of attention deficit disorder with hyperactivity. *Journal of Abnormal Child Psychology, 12,* 1–14.

Hammill, D. D., & Larsen, S. C. (1974a). The effectiveness of psycholinguistic training. *Exceptional Children, 41,* 5–14.

Hammill, D. D., & Larsen, S. C. (1974b). Relationship of selected auditory perceptual skills and reading ability. *Journal of Learning Disability, 7,* 429–435.

Hammill, D. D., Leigh, E., McNutt, G., & Larsen, S. (1981). A new definition of learning disabilities. *Learning Disability Quarterly, 4,* 336–342, and reprinted in *Learning Disability Quarterly, 11,* 217–223.

Hammill, D. D., Leigh, J., McNutt, G., & Larsen, S. (1987). A new definition of learning disabilities. *Journal of Learning Disabilities, 21,* 109–113.

Hanley, J., & Sklar, B. (1976). Electroencephalographic correlates of developmental reading dyslexics: Computer analysis of recordings from normal and dyslexic children. In G. Leisman (Ed.), *Basic visual process and learning disability*. Springfield, IL: Charles C Thomas.

Hanna, P., Hodges, R., & Hanna, J. (1971). *Spelling structure and strategies*. Boston: Houghton Mifflin.

Harcherlik, D. F., Carronara, C. M., Shaywitz, S. E., Shaywitz, B. A., & Cohen, D. J. (1982). Attentional and perceptual disturbances in children with Tourette's syndrome, attention deficit and epilepsy. *Schizophrenia Bulletin, 8*, 356–359.

Hargreaves, W. A., Atkisson, C. C., Siegel, L. M., McIntyre, M. H., & Sorensen, J. E. (Eds.) (1975). *Resource materials for community mental health program evaluation*. Part IV. *Evaluating the effectiveness of service*, DHEW Publication No. (ADM) 75-222. Rockville, MA: National Institute of Mental Health.

Harlem Youth Opportunities Unlimited. (1964). *Youth in the ghetto*. Haryou Act.

Harley, J., Matthews, C. & Eichman, P. (1978). Hyperkinesis and food additives: Testing the Feingold hypothesis. *Pediatrics, 61*, 818–828.

Harris, A. J. (1970). *How to improve reading ability*. (5th ed.) New York: David McKay.

Hartlage, L. C. (1970). Differential diagnosis of dyslexia, minimal brain damage, and emotional disturbances in children. *Psychology in the Schools, 7*, 402–406.

Hartlage, L. C. (1973). Diagnostic profiles of four types of learning disabled children. *Journal of Clinical Psychology, 29*, 158–463.

Hartlage, L. C., & Lucas, D. G. (1973). *Prereading expectancy screening scales*. Jacksonville, IL: Psychologists and Educators.

Hartlage, L. C., & Telzrow, C. F. (1983). The neuropsychological basis of educational intervention. *Journal of Learning Disabilities, 16*, 521–528.

Hartmann, H. (1964). *Essays on ego psychology. Selected problems in psychoanalytic theory*. New York: International Universities Press.

Haslam, R. A., Dalby, J. T., Johns, R. D., & Rademaker, A. W. (1981). Cerebral asymmetry in developmental dyslexia. *Archives of Neurology, 38*, 679–682.

Hastings, J. L., & Barkley, R. A. (1978). A review of research with hyperkinetic children. *Journal of Abnormal Child Psychology, 6*, 413–447.

Hauser, S. L., De Long, R. G., & Rosman, N. P. (1975). Pneumographic findings in infantile autism syndrome. *Brain, 98*, 667–688.

Hauser, W., & Kurland, L. (1975). The epidemiology of epilepsy in Rochester, Minnesota, 1935 through 1967. *Epilepsia, 16*, 1–66.

Hawkins, R. D., & Kandel, E. (1984). Steps toward a cell-biological alphabet for elementary forms of learning. In G. Lynch, J. L. McGaugh, & N. Weinberger (Eds.), *Neurobiology of learning and memory* (pp. 385–404). New York: Guilford.

Hayes, A., & Silver, A. A. (1970). *Report of the interdisciplinary committee on reading problems*. New York: Ford Foundation.

Haynes, J. R., & Sells, S. B. (1963). Assessment of organic brain damage by psychological tests. *Psychological Bulletin, 60*, 316–325.

Head, H. (1926). *Aphasia and kindred disorders of speech*, Vol. I and II. London: Cambridge University Press. Republished by Hafner Publishing Co., New York, 1963.

Hearne, J. D., Poplin, M. S., Schoenman, C., & O'Shaughnessy, E. (1988). Computer aptitude: An investigation of differences among junior high students with learning disabilities and their non-learning-disabled peers. *Journal of Learning Disabilities, 21*, 489–493.

Hebb, D. O. (1949). *The organization of behavior*. New York: Wiley.

Hecaen, H., De Agostini, M., & Monzon-Montes, A. (1981). Cerebral organization in left handers. *Brain and Language, 12*, 261–284.

Hecaen, H., de Ajuriaguerra, J., & Angelergues, R. (1963). Apraxia and its various aspects. In L. Halpern (Ed.), *Problems in dynamic neurology* (pp. 217–230). Jerusalem, Israel: Department of Nervous Diseases of the Rothschild Hadassah University Hospital at the Hebrew University Hadassah Medical School.

Hechtman, L. (1985) Adolescent outcome of hyperactive children treated with stimulants in childhood: A review. *Psychopharmacology Bulletin, 21,* 178–191.

Hechtman, L., Weiss, G., & Perlman, T. (1984). Young adult outcome of hyperactive children who received long-term stimulant treatment. *Journal of the American Academy of Child Psychiatry, 23,* 261–269.

Hechtman, L., Weiss, G., Perlman, T., & Amsel, R. (1984). Hyperactives as young adults: Initial predictors of adult outcome. *Journal of the American Academy of Child Psychiatry, 23,* 250–260.

Heckelman, R. (1969). A neurological impress method of reading instruction. *Academic Therapy, 4,* 277–282.

Heffron, W., Martin, C., & Welsh, R. (1984). Attention deficit disorder in three pairs of monozygotic twins: A case report. *Journal of the American Academy of Child Psychiatry, 23,* 399–301.

Heh, C. W., Smith, R., Wu, J., Hazlett, B., Russell, A., Asarnow, R., Tanguay, P., & Buchsbaum, M., (1989). Positron emission tomography of the cerebellum in autism. *American Journal of Psychiatry, 146,* 242–245.

Heil, J., Barclay, A., & Endres, J. M. (1978). A factor analytic study of WPPSI scores of educationally deprived and normal children. *Psychological Reports, 42,* 727–730.

Helfgott, E., Rudel, R. G., Koplewicz, H., & Krieger, J. (1987). Effect of piracetam on reading test performances of dyslexic children. In D. Bakker, C. Wilsher, H. Debruyner, & N. Bertin (Eds.), *Developmental dyslexia and learning disorders* (pp. 110–122). Basel: Karger.

Hellman, I. (1954). Some observations on mothers and children with intellectual inhibitions. *The Psychoanalytic Study of the Child, 9,* 259–273. New York: International Universities Press.

Helper, M. (1980). Follow-up studies of children with minimal brain dysfunctions: Outcomes and predictors. In H. E. Rie & E. D. Rie (Eds.), *Handbook of minimal brain dysfunctions: A critical view* (pp. 75–114). New York: Wiley.

Henker, B., & Whalen, C. K. (1980). The changing faces of hyperactivity. Retrospect and prospect. In C. K. Whalen & B. Henker (Eds.), *Hyperactive children: The social ecology of identification and treatment* (pp. 321–363). New York: Academic Press.

Henry, S., & Wittman, R. D. (1981). Diagnostic implications of Bannatyne's recategorized WISC-R scores for identifying learning disabled children. *Journal of Learning Disabilities, 14,* 517–520.

Herjanic, B., & Campbell, W. (1977). Differentiating psychiatrically disturbed children on the basis of a structured interview. *Journal of Abnromal Child Psychology, 5,* 127–134.

Herjanic, B., & Reich, W. (1982). Development of a structured psychiatric interview for children: Agreement between child and parent on individual symptoms. *Journal of Abnormal Child Psychiatry, 10,* 307–324.

Herman, B., Hammock, M., Arthur-Smith, A., Egan, J., Chatour, R., Werner, A., & Zelnik, N. (1987). Naltrexone decreases self-injurious behavior. *Annals of Neurology, 22,* 550–552.

Hermann, K., (1959). *Reading disability: A medical study of word-blindness and related handicaps.* Copenhagen: Munksgaard.

Hermann, K., & Norrie, E. (1958). Is congenital word-blindness a hereditary type of Gerstmann's syndrome? *Psychiatria et Neurologia, 136,* 59.

Hermelin, B. (1978). Images and language. In M. Rutter & E. Schopler (Eds.), *Autism: A reappraisal of concept and treatment* (pp. 141–154). New York: Plenum.

Hermelin, B., & O'Connor, N. (1970). *Psychological experiments with autistic children.* Oxford: Pergamon.

Hermelin, B., & O'Connor, N. (1985). The logico-effective disorder in autism. In E. Schopler & G. B. Mesibov (Eds.), *Communication problems in autism*. New York: Plenum.

Hertzig, M. E. (1982). Stability and change in non-focal and neurological signs. *Journal of the American Academy of Child Psychiatry, 21*, 231–236.

Hess, E. H. (1970). Ethology and developmental psychology. In P. H. Mussen (Ed.) *Carmichael's manual of child psychology, 2*, 3rd ed. (pp. 1–38). New York: Wiley.

Hess, R. D. (1970). Social class and ethnic influences on socialization. In P. Mussen (Ed.), *Carmichael's Manual of Child Psychology, 2*, 3rd ed. (pp. 457–558). New York: Wiley.

Hess, R. D., & Shipman, V. C. (1968). Maternal attitudes toward the school and the role of the pupil: Some social class comparisons. In A. H. Passow (Ed.), *Developing programs for the educationally disadvantaged*. New York: Teachers College Press.

Hier, D. B., LeMay, M., Rosenberger, P., & Perio, V. P. (1978). Developmental dyslexia. *Archives of Neurology, 35*, 90–92.

Hildreth, G., Griffiths, N., & McGauvran, N. (1965). *Metropolitan readiness tests*. New York: Harcourt, Brace & World.

Hildreth, G., Nurss, J. R., & McGauvran, N. (1965). *Metropolitan readiness tests*. San Antonio, TX: Psychological Corporation.

Hillyard, S. A., & Kutas, M. (1983). Electrophysiology of cognitive processing. *Annual Review of Psychology, 34*, 33–61.

Hinshelwood, J. (1895). Word blindness and visual memory. *Lancet, 2*, 1564–1570.

Hinshelwood, J. (1896). A case of dyslexia: A peculiar form of word blindness, *Lancet, 2*, 1451–1454.

Hinshelwood, J. (1900). *Letter, word, and mind-blindness*. London: Lewis.

Hinshelwood, J. (1907). Four cases of congenital word-blindness occurring in the same family. *British Medical Journal, 2*, 1229–1232.

Hinshelwood, J. (1917). *Congenital word-blindness*. London: Lewis.

Hiscock, M., and Kinsbourne, M. (1982). Laterality and dyslexia: A critical view. *Annals of Dyslexia, 32*, 177–228.

Hobbs, S. (1980). Cognitive behavior therapy with children. Has clinical utility been demonstrated? *Psychological Bulletin, 87*, 147–165.

Hodges, K., Kline, J., Fitch, P., McKnew, D., & Cytryn, L. (1981). The child assessment schedule: A diagnostic interview for research and clinical use. *Catalog of Selected Documents in Psychology, 11*, 56.

Hodges, K., McKnew, D., Cytryn, L., Stern, L., & Kline, J. (1982). The child assessment schedule (CAS) diagnostic interview: A report on reliability and validity. *Journal of the American Academy of Child Psychiatry, 21*, 468–473.

Hodges, K., Stern, K., Cytryn, L., & McKnew, D. (1982). The development of a child assessment schedule for research and clinical use. *Journal of Abnormal Child Psychology, 10*, 173–189.

Hoff, H., & Schilder, P. (1927). *Die Lagereflexe des Menschen*. Vienna: Springer.

Hohman, L. B. (1922). Post-encephalitic behavior disorders in children. *Johns Hopkins Hospital Bulletin, 33*, 372–375.

Hohman, M., Banet, B., & Weikart, D. P. (1979). *Young children in action: A manual for preschool education*. Ypsilanti, MI: High Scope Press.

Holcomb, P. J., Ackerman, P. T., & Dykman, R. A. (1985). Cognitive event-related brain potentials in children with attention and reading deficits. *Psychophysiology, 22*, 656–667.

Hollenback, G., & Kaufman, A. (1973). Factor analysis of the WPPSI. *Journal of Clinical Psychology, 29*, 41–45.

Howard, J. (1989). Cocaine and its effects on the newborn. *Developmental Medicine and Child Neurology, 31,* 255–257.

Howard, J., Parmlee, A., Koop, C., & Littman, B. (1976). A neurological comparison of pre-term and full-term infants at term conceptional age. *Journal of Pediatrics, 88,* 995–1002.

Hoy, E., Weiss, G., Minde, K., & Cohn, N. (1978). The hyperactive child at adolescence: Cognitive, emotional and social functioning. *Journal of Abnormal Child Psychology, 67,* 311–324.

Hubel, D. H., & Wiesel, T. N. (1979). Brain mechanisms of vision. *Scientific American, 241,* 150–162.

Huessy, H. R., & Cohen, A. H. (1976). Hyperkinetic behaviors and learning disabilities followed over seven years. *Pediatrics, 57,* 4–10.

Huessy, H. R., Metoyer, M., & Townsend, M. (1974). 8–10 year follow-up of 84 children treated for behavioral disorder in rural Vermont. *Acta Paedopsychiatrica, 40,* 230–235.

Hughes, J. N. (1986). Methods of skill selection in social skills training: A review. *Professional School Psychology, 1,* 235–248.

Hughes, J. R. (1971). Electroencephalography and learning. In H. R. Myklebust (Ed.), *Progress in learning disabilities,* Vol. 2 (pp. 18–55). New York: Grune & Stratton.

Hughes, J. R. (1978). Electroencephalographic and neurophysiologic studies in dyslexia. In A. Benton & D. Pearl (Eds.), *Dyslexia: An appraisal of current knowledge* (pp. 205–240). New York: Oxford University Press.

Hughes, J. R. (1985). Evaluation of electrophysiological studies on dyslexia. In D. B. Gray & J. F. Kavenaugh (Eds.), *Behavioral measures of dyslexia* (pp. 71–86). Parton, MA: York Press.

Hughes, J. R. & Park, G. E. (1968). The EEG in dyslexia. In P. Kellaway & I. Petersen (Eds.), *Clinical electroencephalography of children* (pp. 307–327). Stockholm: Almquist and Wiksell.

Hunt, J. M. (1961). *Intelligence and experience.* New York: Ronald Press

Hunt, R. D. (1988). Clonidine and treatment of ADHD. *The psychiatric times,* September, 1988.

Hutchings, D. E. (Ed.) (1989). Prenatal abuse of licit and illicit drugs. *Annals of the New York Academy of Sciences, 562.*

Hyden, H., & Egyhazi, E. (1962). Nuclear RNA changes of nerve cells during a learning experiment in rats. *Proceedings of the National Academy of Sciences, 48,* 1366–1373.

Hyden, H., & Egyhazi, E. (1963). Glial RNA changes during a learning experiment in rats. *Proceedings of the National Academy of Sciences, 49,* 618–624.

Ilg, F. L., & Ames, L. B. (1965). *School readiness: Behavior tests used at the Gesell Institute.* New York: Harper & Row.

Incagnoli, T., & Kane, R. (1982). Neuropsychological functioning in Tourette syndrome. In A. Friedhoff & T. N. Chase (Eds.), *Advances in Neurology,* Vol. 35 (pp. 305–309). New York: Raven Press.

Ingram, T. T. (1970). The nature of dyslexia. In F. A. Young & D. B. Lindsley (Eds.), *Early experience and visual information processing in perceptual and reading disorders* (pp. 405–444). Washington, DC: National Academy of Sciences.

Ingram, T. T., Mann, A. W., & Blackburn, I. A. (1970). A retrospective study of 82 children with reading disability. *Developmental Medicine and Child Neurology, 12,* 271–281.

Interagency Committee on Learning Disabilities. (1987). *Report to Congress Health Research Extension.* October 1985 (Public Law 99-158).

Irwin, M., Belendink, K., McCloskay, K., & Freedman, D. X. (1981). Tryptophan metabolism in children with attention deficit disorder. *American Journal of Psychiatry, 138,* 1082–1085.

Isaacson, R. L. (1976). *Recovery (?) from early brain damage.* In T. Tjossen (Ed.), *Intervention strategies for high risk infants and young children* (pp. 33–62). Baltimore: University Park Press.

Izquierdo, I. (1984). Endogenous state dependency: Memory depends on the relation between the neurohumoral and hormonal states present after training and at the time of testing. In G. Lynch, J. L. McGaugh, & N. M. Weinberger (Eds.), *Neurobiology of learning and memory* (pp. 333–352). New York: Guilford.

Izquierdo, I., & Graudenz, M. (1980). Memory facilitation by naloxone is due to release of dopaminergic and β-adrenergic systems from tonic inhibition. *Psychopharmacology, 67,* 265–268.

Jagger, J., Prusoff, B. A., Cohen, D. J., Kidd, K. K., Carbonari, C. M., & John, K. (1982). The epidemiology of Tourette's syndrome: A pilot study. *Schizophrenia Bulletin, 8,* 269–278.

James, A., & Barry, R. (1983). Developmental effects in the cerebral lateralization of autistic, retarded and normal children. *Journal of Autism and Developmental Disorders, 13,* 43–45.

James, W. (1890–1950). *Principles of psychology,* (Vol. 2). Authorized unabridged edition by special arrangement with Henry Holt & Company by Dover Publications, 1950.

Jansky, J., & de Hirsch, K. (1972). *Preventing reading failure—prediction, diagnosis, intervention.* New York: Harper & Row.

Jasper, H. (1958). Reticular-cortical systems and theories of the integrative action of the brain. In H. F. Harlow & C. N. Woolsey, *Biological and biochemical basis of behavior* (pp. 37–63). Madison, WI: University Wisconsin Press.

Jastak, J., & Jastak, S. (1940, 1978, 1984). *Wide range achievement test.* Wilmington, DE: Jastak Associates.

Jenkins, R. L. (1966). Psychiatric syndromes in children and their relation to family background. *American Journal of Orthopsychiatry, 36,* 450–457.

John, E. R., Ahn, H., Prichep, L., Trepetin, M., Brown, D., & Kege, H. (1980). Developmental equations for the electroencephalogram. *Science, 210,* 1255–1258.

John, E. R., Prichep, L. S., Fridman, J., & Easton, P. (1988). Neurometrics: Computer-assisted differential diagnosis of brain dysfunctions. *Science, 239,* 162–169.

Johnson, D. J., & Myklebust, H. (1967). *Learning disabilities: Educational principles and practices* (2nd ed.). New York: Grune & Stratton.

Johnson, R. J., Johnson, K. L., & Kerfort, J. F. (1972). A massive oral decoding technique. *The Reading Teacher, 25,* 421–423.

Joint Committee on Testing Practices. (1988). *Code of fair testing practices in education.* Washington, DC: American Psychological Association.

Jones, K. M., Torgesen, J. K., Sexton, M. A. (1987). Using computer guided practice to increase decoding fluency in learning disabled children: A study using the hint and hunt I program. *Journal of Learning Disabilities, 20,* 122–128.

Jorm, A. F. (1979). The cognitive and neurological basis of developmental dyslexia: A theoretical framework and review. *Cognition, 7,* 19–33.

Jorm, A. F. (1986). Effects of cholinergic enhancement therapies on memory function in Alzheimer's disease: A meta-analysis of the literature. *Australian and New Zealand Journal of Psychiatry, 20,* 237–240.

Joschko, M., & Rourke, B. P. (1982). Neuropsychological dimensions of Tourette syndrome: Test-retest stability and implications for intervention. *Advances in Neurology, 35,* 297.

Joschko, M., & Rourke B. P. (1985). Neuropsychological subtypes of learning-disabled children who exhibit the ACID pattern in the WISC. In B. Rourke (Ed.), *Neuropsychology of learning disabilities: Essentials of sub-type analysis* (pp. 65–88). New York: Guilford.

Juhrs, P. D., Brown, S. I., Ingram, M. I. (1987). *Manual III: Finding and keeping job placements in supported employment program for the severely disabled.* CSAAC supported employment model project.

Kagan, J., Rosman, B. L., Day, B., Albert, J., & Phillips, W. (1964). Information processing in the child. Significance of analytic and reflective attitudes. *Psychological Monographs, 78* (1, whole No. 578).

Kahn, A. U., & De Kirmenjian, H. (1981). Urinary excretion of catacholamine metabolites in hyperkinetic child syndrome. *American Journal of Psychiatry, 138,* 108–112.

Kahn, E., & Cohen, L. H. (1934). Organic drivenness: A brain-stem syndrome and an experience. *New England Journal of Medicine, 210,* 748–756.

Kamons, J., Kowalski, R. L., MacGinitie, R. K., & Mackay, T. (1926–1978). *Gates-MacGinitie reading tests.* Riverside Publishing.

Kandel, E. R. (1985). Cellular mechanisms of learning and the biological basis of individuality. In E. R. Kandel, & J. H. Schwartz (Eds.), *Principles of neural science* 2nd ed., (pp. 816–834). New York: Elsevier.

Kandel, E. R., & Schwartz, J. H. (1982). Molecular biology of learning: Modulation of transmitter release. *Science, 218,* 433–443.

Kandel, E. R., & Schwartz, J. H. (Eds.) (1985). *Principles of neural science.* New York: Elsevier.

Kandel, E. R., Abrams, T., Bernier, L., Carew, T. S., Hawkins, R. D., & Schwartz, J. H. (1983). Classical conditioning and sensitization show aspects of the same molecular cascade in Aplysia. *Cold Spring Harbor Symposium in Quantitative Biology,* Vol. 48 (pp. 821–830).

Kanner, L. (1935). *Child psychiatry.* Springfield, IL: Charles C Thomas.

Kanner, L. (1943). Autistic disturbances of affective contact. *Nervous Child, 21,* 217–250.

Kanner, L. (1944). Early infantile autism. *Journal of Pediatrics, 25,* 211–217.

Kanner, L. (1946). Irrelevant and metaphorical language in early childhood autism. *American Journal of Psychiatry, 103,* 242–246.

Kanner, L., & Eisenberg, L. (1955). Notes on the follow-up studies of autistic children. In P. Hoch and F. Zuhin (Eds.), *Psychopathology of childhood* (pp. 227–239). New York: Grune & Stratton.

Kanner, L., Rodriguez, A., & Ashenden, B. (1972). How far can autistic children go in matters of social adaptation?, *Journal of Autism and Childhood Schizophrenia, 2,* 9–33.

Karnes, M. B., Hodkins, A. S., Testa, J. A. (1969). Research and development program on preschool disadvantaged children, Vol. 1. Washington, DC: US Office of Education.

Karrer, R., Cohen, J., & Tueting, P. (Eds.) (1984). *Brain and information: Event related potentials: Annals of the New York Academy of Sciences, 425.* New York: New York Academy of Sciences.

Kaufman, A. S. (1979a). Cerebral specialization and intelligence testing. *Journal of Research and Development in Education, 12,* 96–107.

Kaufman, A. S. (1979b). *Intelligent testing with the WISC-R.* New York: Wiley.

Kaufman, A. S. (1981). The WISC-R and learning disabilities assessment: State of the art. *Journal of Learning Disabilities, 14,* 520–526.

Kaufman, A. S., & Hollenbeck, G. (1974). Comparative structure of the WPPSI for blacks and whites. *Journal of Clinical Psychology, 30,* 316–319.

Kaufman, A. S., & Kaufman, N. L. (1977). *Clinical evaluation of young children with the McCarthy.* New York: Grune & Stratton.

Kaufman, A. S., & Kaufman, N. L. (1983a). *The Kaufman assessment battery for children.* Circle Pines, MN: American Guidance Service.

Kaufman, A. S., & Kaufman, N. L. (1983b). *Kaufman assessment battery for children: An interpretive manual.* Circle Pines, MN: American Guidance Service.

Kavale, K. A. (1981). The relationship between auditory perceptual skills and reading ability: A meta-analysis. *Journal of Learning Disabilities, 14,* 539–549.

Kavale, K. A. (1982). Meta-analysis of the relationship between visual perceptual skills and reading achievement. *Journal of Learning Disabilities, 15*, 42–51.

Kavale, K. A., & Forness, S. R. (1984). A meta-analysis of the validity of Wechsler-Scale profiles and recategorizations, patterns or parodies. *Learning Disabilities Quarterly, 7*, 136–156.

Kavale, K. A., & Forness, S. R. (1985). *The science of learning disabilities.* San Diego, CA: College-Hill Press.

Kavale, K. A., & Forness, S. R. (1987). The far side of heterogeneity: Analysis of empirical subtyping in learning disabilities. *Journal of Learning Disabilities, 20*, 374–382.

Kavanaugh, J. (1988). *New federal biological definition of learning and attentional disorders.* Speech given at the 15th Annual Conference, New York Branch Orton Society.

Kawi, A. A., & Pasamanick, B. (1959). Prenatal and paranatal factors in the development of childhood reading disorders. *Monographs of the society for research in child development,* Vol. 24 (4, Serial No. 73).

Kazdin, A., & Bootzin, R. (1972). The token economy: An evaluative review. *Journal of Applied Behavioral Analysis, 5*, 343–372.

Keating, L. E. (1961). Epilepsy behavior disorders in school children. *Journal of Mental Science, 107*, 161–180.

Keefe, B., & Swinney, D. (1979). On the relationship of hemispheric specialization and developmental dyslexia. *Cortex, 12*, 471–481.

Keeney, A. H., & Keeney, V. T. (1968). *Dyslexia: Diagnosis and treatment of reading disorders.* St. Louis: C. V. Mosby.

Keith, T. Z. (1987). Assessment research: An assessment and recommended interventions. *School Psychology Review, 3*, 276–279.

Kennard, M. A. (1960). Value of equivocal signs in neurological diagnosis. *Neurology, 10*, 753–764.

Keogh, B. K. (1971). Hyperactivity and learning disorders: Review and speculation. *Exceptional Children, 38*, 101–109.

Keogh, B. K. (1980). *Marker variables in reading disability research.* Presented at the 1980 National Conference ACLD, Milwaukee, WI.

Keogh, B. K. (1986). Future of the LD Field: Research and practice. *Journal of Learning Disabilities, 19*, 455–460. Reprinted in S. Chess, A. Thomas, & M. Hertzig (Eds.), *Annual Progress in Child Psychiatry and Child Development* (pp. 207–219). New York: Brunner/Mazel (1988).

Kephart, N. C. (1971). *The slow learner in the classroom.* Columbus, OH: Merrill.

Kerr, J. R. (1897). School hygiene in its mental, moral and physical aspects. Howard Medal Prize Essay. *Journal of Royal Statistical Society, 60*, 613–680.

Kershner, J. R. (1979). Rotation of mental images and asymmetries in word recognition in disabled readers. *Canadian Journal of Psychology, 33*, 39–50.

Kershner, J. R. (1988). Dual processing models of learning disability. In D. L. Molfese & S. J. Sagalowitz (Eds.), *Brain lateralization in children* (pp. 527–546). New York: Guilford.

Kershner, J. R., Cummings, R., Clarke, K., Hadfield, A., & Kershner, B. (1986). Evaluation of the Tomatis Listening Training Program with learning disabled children. *Canadian Journal of Special Education, 2*, 1–32.

Kestenbaum, C. J., & Bird, H. R. (1978). A reliability study of the mental health assessment form of school age children. *Journal of the American Academy of Child Psychiatry, 17*, 338–347.

Kestenbaum, C. J., & Williams, D. T. (1988). *Handbook of clinical assessment of children and adolescents.* New York: New York University Press.

Kety, S. S. (1976). Biological concomitants of affective states and their possible roles in memory processes. In M. R. Rosenzweig & E. L. Bennett (Eds.), *Neural mechanisms of learning and memory* (pp. 321–326). Cambridge, MA: MIT Press.

Keyser, D. J., & Sweetland, R. C. (1983). *Test critiques.* Kansas City, MO: Test Corporation of America.

Kilby, G. A. (1983). An ex post facto evaluation of the junior first grade in Sioux Fall, South Dakota. *Dissertation abstracts international,* Vol. 43 (p. 3271A).

Kimberling, W. J., Fain, P. R., Ing, P. S., Smith, S. D., & Pennington, B. (1985). *Genetic linkage studies of reading disability with chromosome 15 markers.* Paper presented at meeting of the Behavioral Genetics Association, June 1985.

Kimura, D. (1961). Cerebral dominance and the perception of verbal stimuli. *Canadian Journal of Psychology, 15,* 166–171.

Kimura, D. (1963). Speech lateralization in young children as determined by an auditory test. *Journal of Comparative and Physiological Psychology, 56,* 899–902.

Kimura, D. (1969). Spatial localization in left and right visual fields. *Canadian Journal of Psychology, 23,* 445–448.

Kimura, D. (1973). The asymmetry of the human brain. *Scientific American, 228,* 70–80.

Kinsbourne, M. (1973). Minimal brain dysfunction as a neurodevelopmental lag. In F. dela Cruz, B. H. Fox, & R. H. Roberts (Eds.), *Annals of the New York Academy of Sciences,* Vol. 205 (pp. 268–273).

Kinsbourne, M. (1977). The mechanism of hyperactivity. In M. E. Blow, A. Rapin, & M. Kinsbourne (Eds.), *Topics in child neurology* (pp. 289–306). New York: Spectrum.

Kinsbourne, M. (1984). Hyperactivity management: The impact of special diets. In M. Levine & P. Satz (Eds.), *Middle childhood: Development and dysfunction* (pp. 487–500). Baltimore: University Park Press.

Kinsbourne, M., & Caplan, P. J. (1979). *Children's learning and attention problems.* Boston: Little, Brown.

Kinsbourne, M., & Warrington, E. K. (1962). A study of finger agnosia. *Brain, 85,* 47–66.

Kinsbourne, M., & Warrington, E. K. (1963). The development of finger differentiation. *Quarterly Journal of Experimental Psychology, 15,* 132–137.

Kinsbourne, M., & Warrington, E. K. (1966). Developmental factors in reading and writing backwardness. In J. Money (Ed.), *The disabled reader: Education of the dyslexic child* (pp. 59–72). Baltimore: Johns Hopkins Press.

Kirby, J. R., & Das, J. P. (1977). Reading achievement, IQ, and simultaneous-successive processing. *Journal of Educational Psychology, 69,* 564–570.

Kirby, J. R., & Robinson, G. (1987). Simultaneous and successive processing in reading disabled children. *Journal of Learning Disabilities, 20,* 243–252.

Kirk, S. A. (1962). *Educating exceptional children.* Boston: Houghton Mifflin.

Kirk, S. A. (1963). Behavior diagnosis and remediation of learning disabilities. In *Proceedings of the Conference on the Exploration into the Problems of the Perceptually Handicapped Child.* Evanston, IL: Fund for the Perceptually Handicapped Child. (Reprinted in Kirk, S. A., & McCarthy, J. J. (1975). *Learning disabilities: Selected papers.* Boston: Houghton Mifflin.)

Kirk, S.A., & Felkins, J. (1975). Characteristics of children enrolled in child service demonstration centers. *Journal of Learning Disabilities, 8,* 630–637.

Kirk, S. A., & Kirk, W. D. (1963). On defining learning disabilities. *Journal of Learning Disabilities, 16,* 20–21.

Kirk, S. A., & Kirk, W. D. (1971). *Psycholinguistic learning disabilities: Diagnosis and remediation.* Urbana, IL: University of Illinois Press.

Kirk, S. A., McCarthy, J., & Kirk, W. D. (1968). *Illinois test of psycholinguistic abilities* (Rev. ed.). Urbana, IL: University of Illinois Press.

Klaus, R. A., & Gray, S. W. (1968). The Early Training Project for disadvantaged: A report after 5 years. *Monographs of the society for research in child development,* Vol. 120.

Klein, D. F., Gittelman, R., Quitkin, F., & Rifkin, A. (1980). *Diagnosis and drug treatment of psychiatric disorders: Adults and children.* Baltimore: Williams & Wilkins.

Klein, E. (1949). Psychoanalytic aspects of school problems. *The Psychoanalytic Study of the Child, 3/4,* 369–390. New York: International Universities Press.

Kleinpeter, U., & Goellnitz, G. (1976). Achievement and adaptation disorders in brain-damaged children. *International Journal of Mental Health, 4,* 19–35.

Kleist, K. (1934). *Gehirnpathologie.* Leipzig: Barth.

Klesius, J. P., & Homan, S. P. (1985). A validity and reliability update on the informal reading inventory with suggestions for improvement. *Journal of Learning Disabilities, 18,* 71–76.

Kline, C. L. (1977). Orton-Gillingham methodology: Where have all the researchers gone? *Bulletin of the Orton Society, 27,* 82–87.

Kline, C. L., & Kline, C. L. (1975). Follow-up study of 211 dyslexic children. *Bulletin of the Orton Society, 25,* 127–144.

Knights, R. M., & Bakker, D. J. (Eds.) (1976). *Neuropsychology of learning disorders: Therapeutic approaches.* Baltimore: University Park Press.

Knights, R. M., & Bakker, D. J. (Eds.) (1980). *Treatment of hyperactive and learning disordered children.* Baltimore, University Park Press.

Knights, R. M., & Stoddart, C. (1981). Profile approaches to neuropsychological diagnosis in children. In G. W. Hynd & J. E. Obrzut (Eds.), *Neuropsychological assessment and the school-age child* (pp. 335–351). New York: Grune & Stratton.

Knobloch, H., & Pasamanick, B. (1966). Prospective studies on the epidemiology of reproductive casualty: Methods, findings and some implications. *Merrill-Palmer Quarterly, 12,* 27–43.

Knobloch, H., & Pasamanick, B. (Eds.) (1974). *Gesell and Amatruda's developmental diagnosis.* New York: Harper & Row.

Koegel, R. L., Russo, D. C., & Rincover, A. (1977). Assessing and training teachers in the generalized use of behavior modification with autistic children. *Journal of Applied Behavioral Analysis, 10,* 197–205.

Kolvin, I. (1971). Studies in the childhood psychosis: I. Diagnostic criteria and classification. *British Journal of Psychiatry, 118,* 381–384.

Kondracke, M. M. (1989). Two Black Americas. *New Republic, 200,* 17–20.

Konkol, R., Chapman, L., Breese, G., Coller, A., Kits, C., Finley, C., Vogel, R., Mailman, R., & Bendrich, E. (1987). *Hemophilus* meningitis in the rat: Behavioral, electrophysiological and biochemical consequences. *Annals of Neurology, 21,* 253–260.

Koorland, M. A. (1986). Applied behavior analysis and the correction of learning disabilities. In J. K. Torgeson & B.Y.L. Wong (Eds.), *Psychological and educational perspectives on learning disabilities.* New York: Academic Press.

Koppitz, E. M. (1975). *The Bender-Gestalt test for young children: Research and application 1963–1973.* New York: Grune & Stratton.

Kornhuber, H., Bechinger, D., Jung, H., & Sauer, E. (1985). A quantitative relationship between extent of localized cerebral lesions and the intellectual and behavioral deficiency in children. *European Archives of Psychiatric and Neurological Science, 235,* 129–133.

Kovacs, M. (1980–81). Rating scales to assess depression in school aged children. *Acta Paedopsychiatrica, 46,* 305–315.

Kovac, M. (1983). *The interview schedule for children (ICS) interrater and parent-child agreement.* (Unpublished).

Krech, D., Rosenzweig, M. R., & Bennett, E. L. (1960). Effects of environmental complexity and training on brain chemistry. *Journal of Comparative Physiology and Psychology, 52,* 509–519.

Krech, D., Rosenzweig, M. R., & Krueckel, B. (1954). Enzyme concentrations in the brain and adjustive behavior patterns. *Science, 120,* 994–996.

Kuperman, S., Beegitly, J., Burns, T., & Tsai, L. (1985). Serotonin relationships of autistic probands and their first degree relatives. *Journal of the American Academy of Child Psychiatry, 24,* 186–190.

Kussmaul, A. (1877). Die Storungen der Sprache. *Ziemssen's Handbuch d. Speciellen Pathologie u. Therapie, 12,* 1–300.

Kutas, M., & Hillyard, S. A. (1980). Reading senseless sentences: Brain potentials reflect semantic incongruity. *Science, 207,* 203–205.

LaBerge, D., & Samuels, S. J. (1974). Toward a theory of automatic information processing in reading. *Cognitive Psychology, 6,* 293–323.

Labov, W. (1969). Some sources of reading problems for negro speakers of non-standard English. In J. C. Baratz & R. W. Shuy (Eds.), *Teaching black children to read* (pp. 29–67). Washington, DC: Center for Applied Linguistics.

Lahey, B. B., Schaughency, E. A., Strauss, C. C., & Frame, C. L. (1984). Are attention deficit disorders with and without hyperactivity similar or dissimilar disorders? *Journal of the American Academy of Child Psychiatry, 23,* 302–309.

Lahey, B. B., Stempniak, M., Robinson, E. J., & Tyroler, M. J. (1978). Hyperactivity and learning disabilities as independent dimensions of child behavior problems. *Journal of Abnormal Psychology, 87,* 333–340.

Lambert, N., & Sandoval, J. (1980). The prevalence of learning disabilities in a sample of children considered hyperactive. *Journal of Abnormal Child Psychology, 8,* 33–50.

Lambert, N. M., Sandoval, J., & Sassone, D. (1978). Prevalence of hyperactivity in elementary school children as a function of social system definers. *American Journal of Orthopsychiatry, 46,* 446–463.

Langhorne, J. E., Loney, J., Paternite, C. E., & Bechtoldt, H. P. (1976). Childhood hyperkinesis—a return to the source. *Journal of Abnormal Psychology, 85,* 201–209.

Larsen, S. C. (1976). The learning disabilities specialist: Role and responsibilities. *Journal of Learning Disabilities, 9,* 37–47.

Larry vs. Riles—No. C-71-2270 RFP (1989) and No. 80-4027 DC No. CV 71-2270 in the United States Court of Appeals for the Ninth Circuit (1984).

Lashley, K. S., (1951) The problem of serial order in behavior. In L. A. Jeffries (Ed.), *Cerebral mechanisms in behavior,* (pp. 112–135). New York: Wiley.

Laufer, M. W., & Denhoff, E. (1957). Hyperkinetic behavior syndrome in children. *Journal of Pediatrics, 50,* 463–474.

Leboyer, M., Bouvard, M., & Dugas, M. (1988). Effects of naltrexone on infantile autism. *Lancet,* 715.

Leckman, J. F., Cohen, D. J., Detlor, J., Young, J. G., Harcherick, D., & Shaywitz, B. A. (1982). Clonidine in the treatment of Tourette syndrome. In A. Friedhoff & T. Chase (Eds.), *Gilles de la Tourette syndrome. Advances in neurology,* Vol. 35 (pp. 391–401).

Leckman, J. F., Detlor, J., Harcherick, D. F. Young, J. G., Anderson, G. M., Shaywitz, B. A. & Cohen, D. S. (1983). Acute and chronic clonidine treatment of Tourette's syndrome: A preliminary report on clinical response and effect on plasma and urinary catacholamine metabolites growth hormone and blood pressure. *Journal of the American Academy of Child Psychiatry, 22,* 433–440.

Leckman, J. F., Riddle, M. A., & Cohen, D. J. (1988). Pathobiology of Tourette's syndrome. In D. J. Cohen, R. D. Bruun, & S. F. Leckman (Eds.), *Tourette's syndrome and tic disorder* (pp. 104–116). New York: Wiley.

Leckman, J. F., Walkup, J. T., & Cohen, D. J. (1988). Clonidine treatment of Tourette syndrome. In D. J. Cohen, B. D. Bruun, & J. F. Leckman (Eds.), *Tourette's syndrome and tic disorder* (pp. 292–301). New York: Wiley.

Lee, W. W. (1987). Microcomputer courseware production and evaluation guidelines for students with learning disabilities. *Journal of Learning Disabilities, 20,* 430–438.

Lenneberg, E. H. (1967). *Biological foundations of language.* New York: Wiley.

Lerer, R. J. (1987). Motor tics, Tourette syndrome and learning disabilities. *Journal of Learning Disabilities, 20,* 266–267.

Lerner, J. (1988). *Learning disabilities.* Boston, MA: Houghton Mifflin.

Lesser, G. S., Fifer, G., & Clark, D. H., (1965) Mental abilities of children in different social class and cultural groups. *Monographs of the society for research in child development, 20,* (Serial No. 102).

Levine, M., & Satz, P. (Eds.) (1984). *Middle childhood: Development and dysfunction.* Baltimore: University Park Press.

Levy, J. (1974). Psychobiological implications of bilateral asymmetry. In S. J. Diamond & G. Beaumont (Eds.), *Hemisphere function in the human brain* (pp. 121–183). London: Elek Scientific Books.

Levy, J., & Nagylaki, T. (1972). A model for the genetics of the hand. *Genetics, 72,* 117–128.

Lewis, D., Pincus, J. Q., Shanok, S. S., & Glaser, G. H. (1982). Psychomotor epilepsy and violence in a group of incarcerated adolescent boys. *American Journal of Psychiatry, 138,* 882–887.

Lewis, D., Shanok, S., & Bella, A. (1980). Psychiatric correlates of severe reading disabilities in an incarcerated delinquent population. *Journal of the American Academy of Child Psychiatry, 19,* 611–622.

Lewis, D., Shanok, S., Pincus, J., & Glaser, G. H. (1979). Violent juvenile delinquents. *Journal of the American Academy of Child Psychiatry, 18,* 307–319.

Liberman, I. Y. (1973). Segmentation of the spoken word and reading acquisition. *Bulletin of the Orton Society, 23,* 65–77.

Liberman, I. Y., Cooper, F. S., Shankweiler, D., & Studdert-Kennedy, M. (1967). Perception of the speech code. *Psychological Review, 74,* 431–461.

Liberman, I. Y., Rubin, H., Duques, S., & Carlisle, J. (1985). Linguistic abilities and spelling proficiency in kindergartners and adult poor spellers. In D. Gray & J. F. Kavanaugh (Eds.), *Behavioral measures of dyslexia* (pp. 163–176). Parton, MA: York Press.

Lichtenstein, R., & Ireton, H. (1984). *Preschool screening.* New York: Grune & Stratton.

Liepmann, H. (1920). Apraxie. *Ergebness der Medicine* (von Brugsch), *1,* 516.

Lilienfeld, A. M., & Parkhurst, E. (1951). A study of the association of factors of pregnancy and parturition with the development of cerebral palsy—a preliminary report. *American Journal of Hygiene, 53,* 262–282.

Liljequist, R., Linnoila, M., & Mattila, M. J. (1974). Effect of two weeks treatment with chlorimipramine and nortriptyline alone or in combination with alcohol on learning and memory. *Psychopharmacology, 37,* 181–186.

Lindsay, G. A., & Wedell, K. (1982), The early identification of educationally"at risk" children revisited. *Journal of Learning Disabilities, 15,* 338–341.

Lindsay, J., Ounstead, C., & Richard, P. (1979). Long-term outcome in children with temporal lobe seizure. III. Psychiatric aspects in childhood and adult life. *Developmental Medicine and Child Neurology, 21,* 630–636.

Liss, E. (1955). Motivations in learning. *The psychoanalytic study of the child,* Vol. 10 (pp. 100–116). New York: International Universities Press.

Little, W. (1861). On the influence of abnormal parturition, difficult labors, premature birth and asphyxia neonatorum, on the mental and physical condition of the child, especially in relation to deformities. *Transactions of the Obstetrical Society of London, 3,* 293.

Littman, B. (1979). The relationship of medical events to infant development. In T. Fields (Ed.), *Infants born at risk: Behavior and development* (pp. 53–65). New York: Spectrum.

Lobovits, A. (1982). Vision screening. In L. Barness (Ed.), *Advances in Pediatrics,* Vol. 29 (pp. 425–433).

Loney, J. (1983). Research diagnostic criteria for childhood hyperactivity. In S. B. Guze, F. J. Earls, & J. E. Barrett (Eds.), *Childhood psychopathology and development* (pp. 109–137). New York: Raven Press.

Loney, J., Langhorne, J. E., Jr., & Paternite, C. E. (1978). An empirical basis for subgrouping the minimal brain hyperkinetic/dysfunction syndrome. *Journal of Abnormal Psychology, 87,* 431–441.

Looker, A., & Conners, C. K. (1970). Diphenylhydantoin in children with severe temper tantrums. *Archives of General Psychiatry, 23,* 80–89.

Lopez, R. C. (1965). Hyperactivity in twins. *Canadian Psychiatric Association Journal, 10,* 421–426.

Lorente De No, R. (1947). Action potentials of the motoneurons of the hypoglossal nuclus. *Journal of Cellular and Comparative Physiology, 29,* 207–287.

Lorion, R. P., Work, W. C., & Hightower, A. D., (1984) A school-based multilevel preventive intervention: Issues in program development. *Personnel and Guidance Journal, 62,* 479–484.

Lovaas, O. I., Koegel, R., Simmons, J., & Stevens-Long, J. (1973). Some generalization and follow-up measures on autistic children in behavior therapy. *Journal of Applied Behavioral Analysis, 6,* 131–166.

Lovaas, O. I., Schaeffer, B., & Simmons, J. Q. (1965). Experimental studies in childhood schizophrenia: Building social behavior in autistic children by the use of electric shock. *Journal of Experimental Research in Personality, 1,* 99–109.

Lovaas, O. I., Schreibman, L., Koegel, R., & Rehm, R. (1971). Selective responding by autistic children to multiple sensory input. *Journal of Abnormal Psychology, 77,* 211–222.

Lowe, T. L., Cohen, D. J., Detlor, J., Kremenitzer, M. W., & Shaywitz, B. A. (1982). Stimulant medications precipitate Tourette's syndrome. *Journal of the American Medical Association, 247,* 1729–1731, No. 12.

Lucas, A. R. (1970). Gilles de la Tourette's syndrome: An overview. *New York State Journal of Medicine, 70,* 2197–2200.

Lucas, A. R., Kauffman, P. E., & Morris, E. M. (1967). Gilles de la Tourette's disease, a clinical study of 15 cases. *Journal of the American Academy of Child Psychiatry, 6,* 700.

Luk, Siu-Luen. (1985). Direct observation studies of hyperactive behaviors. *Journal American Academy of Child Psychiatry, 24,* 338–344.

Lund, K. A., Foster, G. E., & McCall-Perez, F. C. (1978). The effectiveness of psycholinguistic training: A reevaluation. *Exceptional Children, 44,* 310–319.

Luria, R. A. (1966). *Higher cortical functions in man.* New York: Basic Books.

Lykken, D. (1957). A study of anxiety in the sociopathic personality. *Journal of Abnormal and Social Psychology, 55,* 6–10.

Lyle, J. G., & Goyen, J. D. (1969). Performance of retarded readers on the WISC and educational tests. *Journal of Abnormal Psychology, 74,* 105–112.

Lynch, G., McGaugh, J. L., & Weinberger, N. (Eds.). (1988). *Neurobiology of learning and memory.* New York: Guilford.

Lyon, R. G. (1978). *The neuropsychological characteristics of subgroups of learning disabled readers.* Unpublished doctoral dissertation. University of New Mexico.

Lyon, R. G., & Watson, B. (1981). Empirically derived subgroups of learning disabled readers: Diagnostic characteristics. *Journal of Learning Disabilities, 14,* 256–261.

Lyon, R. G., Moats, L. C. (1988). Critical issues in the instruction of the learning disabled. *Journal of Consulting and Clinical Psychology, 56,* 830–835.

Lyon, R. G., Reitta, S., Watson, B., & Porch, R. (1981). Selected linguistic and perceptual abilities of empirically derived subgroups of learning disabled readers. *The Journal of School Psychology, 19,* 152–166.

Lyon, R. G., Stewart, N., & Freedman, D. (1982). Neuropsychological characteristics of empirically derived subgroups of learning disabled readers. *Journal of Clinical Neuropsychology, 4,* 343–466.

Mach, E. (1959). *The analysis of sensation.* New York: Dover.

MacKeith, R. (1963). Defining the concept of "Minimal Brain Damage." In M. Bax & R. McKeith (Eds.), *Minimal cerebral dysfunction, little club clinics in developmental medicine,* No. 10 (pp. 1–9). London: Spastics Society.

MacKeith, R. (1968). Maximum clarity on neurodevelopmental disorders. *Developmental Medicine and Child Neurology, 10,* 143–144.

Mahler, M. S. (1949). A psychoanalytic evaluation of tic in psychopathology of children. In A. Freud, H. Hartmann, & E. Kris (Eds.), *Psychoanalytic study of the child,* Vol. 3 & 4 (pp. 279–310). New York: International Universities Press.

Mahler, M. S. (1952). On child psychosis and schizophrenia: Autistic and symbiotic infantile psychoses. In A. Freud, E. Hartmann, & E. Kris (Eds.), *Psychoanalytic study of the child,* Vol. 7 (pp. 286–305). New York: International Universities Press.

Mahler, M. S., & Gosliner, B. S. (1955). On symbiotic child psychosis: Genetic, dynamic and restitutive aspects. In R. Eissler, A. Freud, E. Hartmann, & E. Kris (Eds.), *Psychoanalytic study of the child,* Vol. 10 (pp. 195–212). New York: International Universities Press.

Mahler, M. S., Pine, F., & Bergman, A. (1975). *The psychological birth of the human infant.* New York: Basic Books.

Maitland, S., Nadeau, J.B.E., & Nadeau, G. (1974). Early school screening practices. *Journal of Learning Disability, 7,* 55–59.

Malatesha, R., & Aaron, P. (1982). *Reading disorders: Varieties and treatment.* New York: Academic Press.

Mann, V. A., & Liberman, I. Y. (1984). Phonological awareness and verbal short-term memory. *Journal of Learning Disabilities, 17,* 592–599.

Marcel, T., & Rajan, P. (1975). Lateral specialization for recognition of words and faces in good and poor readers. *Neuropsychologia, 13,* 489–497.

Mardell, C. D., & Goldenberg, D. S. (1972, 1975). *Developmental indicators for the assessment of learning.* Edison, N.J.: Childcraft Education.

Mardell-Czudnowski, C. D., & Goldenberg, D. S. (1983). *Developmental indicators for the assessment of learning-revised.* Edison, NJ: Childcraft Education.

Marjoribanks, K., (1972a). Environment, social class and mental abilities. *Journal of Educational Psychology, 43,* 103–09.

Marjoribanks, K. (1972b). Ethnic and environmental influences on mental abilities. *American Journal of Sociology, 78,* 323–337.

Matousek, M., & Petersen, I. (1973). Frequency analysis of the EEG in normal children and adolescents. In P. Kellaway & I. Petersen (Eds.), *Automation of clinical electroencephalography* (pp. 75–102). New York: Raven Press.

Mattes, J. A., & Gittelman, R. (1983). Growth of hyperactive children on maintenance regimen of methylphenidate. *Archives of General Psychiatry, 40,* 317–321, 1983.

Mattila, M. J., Liljequist, R. S., & Seppela T. (1978). Effects of amitryptyline and mianserin on psychomotor skills and memory in men. *British Journal of Clinical Pharmacology, 5,* 538–558.

Mattis, S. (1978). Dyslexia syndromes: A working hypothesis that works. In A. L. Benton & D. Pearl (Eds.), *Dyslexia: An appraisal of current knowledge* (pp. 43–58). New York: Oxford University Press.

Mattis, S. (1981). Dyslexia syndromes in children: Toward the development of syndrome specific treatment programs. In F. J. Pirozzolo & M. C. Wittrock (Eds.), *Neuropsychological and cognitive processes in reading* (pp. 93–108). New York: Academic Press.

Mattis, S., French, J. H., & Rapin, I. (1975). Dyslexia in children and young adults: Three independent neuropsychological syndromes. *Developmental Medicine and Child Neurology, 17,* 150–163.

Maurer, R. G., & Damasio, A. R. (1982). Childhood autism from the point of view of behavioral neurology. *Journal of Autism and Developmental Disorders, 12,* 195–205.

May, D. C., & Welch, E., (1984). Developmental placement: Does it prevent learning problems? *Journal of Learning Disabilities, 17,* 338–341.

McCall, R. B. (1977). Childhood IQ as a predictor of adult educational and occupational status. *Science, 197,* 482–483.

McCarthy, D. (1972). *Manual for the McCarthy Scales of Children's Abilities.* San Antonio, TX: The Psychological Corporation.

McCarthy, J. J. (1978). *McCarthy Screening Test.* San Antonio, TX: The Psychological Corporation.

McCarthy, J. J., & Olson, J. L. (1963). *Validity studies on the Illinois test of psycholinguistic abilities.* Madison, WI: Photo Press.

McClearn, G. E. (1978). Review of "Dyslexia-Genetic aspects." In A. Benton & D. Pearl (Eds.), *Dyslexia: An appraisal of current knowledge* (pp. 285–298). New York: Oxford University Press.

McClure, D. E., & Gordon, M. (1984). The performance of disturbed hyperactive and non-hyperactive children in an objective measure of hyperactivity. *Journal of Abnormal Child Psychology, 12,* 561–572.

McConnell, J. V. (1966). Learning in invertebrates. *Annual Review of Physiology, 28,* 107–136.

McEntee, W. F., & Nair, R. G. (1980). Memory enhancement in Korsakoff's psychosis by clonidine: Further evidence for a noradrenergic deficit. *Annals of Neurology, 7,* 466–470.

McGaugh, J. L., Introini-Collison, I., & Nagahara, A. H. (1988). Memory-enhancing effects of post-training naloxone: Involvement of β-noradrenergic influences in the amygdaloid complex. *Brain Research, 446,* 37–49.

McIntosh, W. J. (1974). The use of a Wechsler subtest ratio as an index of brain damage in children. *Journal of Learning Disabilities, 7,* 161–163.

McKeever, W. F. (1974). Does post-exposure directional scanning offer a sufficient explanation for lateral differences in tachistoscopic recognition? *Perceptual and Motor Skills, 38,* 43–50.

McKeever, W. F., & Huling, M. D. (1970). Lateral dominance in tachistoscopic recognition of children at two levels of ability. *Quarterly Journal of Experimental Psychology, 22,* 600–604.

McKinney, J. D., & Feagans, L. (1984). Academic and behavioral characteristics: Longitudinal studies of learning disabled children and average achievers. *Learning Disability Quarterly, 7,* 251–265.

McLeod, J. (1965). A comparison of WISC subtest scores of pre-adolescent successful and unsuccessful readers. *Australian Journal of Psychology, 17,* 220–228.

McLeod, P. H. (1965). *Lippincott reading readiness tests.* Philadelphia: J. B. Lippincott.

McWilliams, B. (1983). Effect of otitis media on articulation development in children. *Pediatrics, 71*, 646–647.

Meadows, A. T., & Silber, J. (1985). Delayed consequences of therapy for childhood cancer. *CA—A Cancer Journal for Clinicians, 35*, 271–286.

Meadows, A. T., Gordon, J., Massari, D. J., Littman, P., Fergusson, J., & Moss, K. (1981). Declines in IQ scores and cognitive dysfunctions in children with acute lymphocytic leukemia treated with cranial irradiation. *Lancet, 2*, 1015–1018.

Meehl, P. E. (1978). Theoretical risks and tabular asterisks: Sir Karl, Sir Ronald, and the slow progress of soft psychology. *Journal of Consulting and Clinical Psychology, 46*, 806–834.

Meehl, P. E., & Rosen, A. (1955). Antecedent probability and the efficiency of psychometric signs, patterns or cutting scores. *Psychological Bulletin, 52*, 194–216.

Meichenbaum, D. (1977). *Cognitive behavior modification: An integrated approach.* New York: Plenum Press.

Meichenbaum, D., & Goodman, J. (1971). Training impulsive children to talk to themselves: A means of developing self-control. *Journal of Abnormal Psychology, 77*, 115–126.

Meier, J. H. (1987). Screening and Assessments of Young Children at Developmental Risk. Washington, DC: Dept. of HEW, Pub. #(OS) 73–90.

Meige, H., & Feindel, F. (1907). *Tics and their treatment.* London: Sidney Appleton.

Meisels, S. J., & Wiske, M. S. (1983). *Early screening inventory.* New York: Teachers College Press.

Menkes, M. M., Rowe, J. S., & Menkes, J. H. (1967). A twenty-five year follow-up study on the hyperkinetic child with minimal brain dysfunction. *Pediatrics, 39*, 393–399.

Merritt, H., & Putnam, T. (1938). Sodium diphenylhydantoinate in the treatment of convulsive disorders. *Journal of the American Medical Association, 111*, 1068–1073.

Mesibov, G., Schopler, E., & Sloan, J. (1983). Service development for adolescent adults in North Carolina's *Teach* program. In E. Schopler & G. B. Mesibov (Eds.), *Autism in adolescents and adults* (pp. 441–432). New York: Plenum Press.

Miller, M., & Walker, K. P. (1981). The myth of the L. D. WISC-R profile. *Exceptional Child, 28*, 83–88.

Miller, R. G., Jr., Palkes, N. S., & Stewart, M. A. (1973). Hyperactive children in suburban elementary schools. *Child Psychiatry and Human Development, 4*, 121–127.

Milner, B. (1972). Disorders of learning and memory after temporal lobe lesions in man. *Clinical Neurosurgery, 19*, 421–446.

Minde, K., Weiss, G., & Mendelson, N. (1972). "A five-year follow-up study of 91 hyperactive school children." *Journal of the American Academy of Child Psychiatry, 11*, 595–610.

Minderaa, R., Anderson, G., Volkmer, F., Akkernuis, G., Cohen, D. J. (1989). Neurochemical study of dopamine functioning in autistic and normal subjects. *Journal of the American Academy of Child and Adolescent Psychiatry, 28*, 190–194.

Minskoff, E. (1975). Research on psycholinguistic training: Critique and guidelines. *Exceptional Children, 42*, 136–144.

Minskoff, J. G. (1973). Differential approaches to prevalence estimates of learning disabilities. In F. F. de la Cruz, B. Fox, & R. H. Roberts (Eds.), *Minimal brain dysfunction, annals of the New York Academy of Sciences*, Vol. 205 (pp. 139–145).

Minuchin, S., Rosman, B. L., & Baker, L. (1978). *Psychosomatic families.* Cambridge, MA: Harvard University Press.

Mirenda, P., & Donnellan, A. M. (1987). Issues in curriculum development. In D. J. Cohen & A. M. Donnellan (Eds.), *Handbook of autism and pervasive developmental disorders* (pp. 211–226). New York: Wiley.

Mischel, W. (1973). Toward a cognitive social learning reconceptualization of personality. *Psychological Review, 80*, 252–283.

Mishkin, M. (1982). A memory system in the monkey. *Philosophical Royal Society London: (Biology), 298*, 326–334.

Mishkin, M., & Aggleton, J. (1981). Multiple functional contribution of the amygdaloid in the monkey. In Y. Ben-Ari (Ed.), *The amygdaloid complex* (pp. 409–420). Amsterdam: Elsevier.

Mitchell, E., & Matthews, K. L. (1980). Gilles de la Tourette's disorder associated with pemoline. *American Journal of Psychiatry, 137*, 1618–1619.

Mitchell, J. V. (Ed.). (1985). The Buros Institute of Mental Measurements. *The ninth mental measurements yearbook.* Lincoln, NE: University of Nebraska Press.

Moldofsky, H., & Sandor, P. (1988). Pimozide in the treatment of Tourette's syndrome. In J. D. Cohen, R. Bruun, & J. Leckman (Eds.), *Tourette's syndrome and tic disorder* (pp. 282–289). New York: Wiley.

Molfese, D. L. (1983). Event related potentials and language processes. In A.W.K. Gaillard & W. Ritter (Eds.), *Tutorials in ERP Research: Endogenous components* (pp. 345–365). Amsterdam: North Holland.

Molfese, D. L., & Molfese, V. J. (1980). Cortical responses of pre-term infants to phonetic and non-phonetic speech stimuli. *Developmental Psychology, 16*, 574–581.

Molfese, D. L., & Sagalowitz, S. J. (Eds.). (1988). *Brain lateralization in children.* New York: Guilford.

Molfese, D. L., Freeman, R. B., & Palermo, D. S. (1975). The ontogeny of brain lateralization for speech and non-speech stimuli. *Brain and Language, 2*, 356–368.

Mondrup, K., Dupont, E., & Braindgaard, H. (1985). Progabide in the treatment of hyperkinetic extrapyramidal movement disorders. *Acta Neurologica Scandinavia, 72*, 341–343.

Money, J. (Ed.). (1966). *The disabled reader.* Baltimore: John Hopkins University Press.

Monroe, M. (1932). *Children who cannot read.* Chicago: University of Chicago Press.

Monroe, M. (1935). *Monroe's reading aptitude tests.* New York: Houghton Mifflin.

Morgan, W. P. (1896). A case of congenital word blindness. *British Medical Journal, 2*, 1378.

Moyer, S. B. (1982). Repeated reading. *Journal of Learning Disabilities, 15*, 619–623.

Mueller, H. H., Matheson, D. W., & Short, R. H. (1983). Bannatyne-recategorized WISC-R patterns of mentally retarded, learning disabled, normal, and intellectually superior children: A meta-analysis. *Mental Retardation and Learning Disability Bulletin, 11*, 60–78.

Mukherjee, B. N. (1975). The factorial structure of the WPPSI at successive age levels. *British Journal of Educational Psychology, 45*, 214–226.

Murphy, L. B., & Moriarty, A. E. (1976). *Vulnerability, coping and growth.* New Haven: Yale University Press.

Myklebust, H. R. (1965). Picture story language test. *Development and disorders of written language,* Vol. 1. New York: Grune & Stratton.

Myklebust, H. R. (1967). Learning disturbance in psychoneurologically disturbed children: Behavioral correlates of brain dysfunction. In P. Hoch & G. A. Jarvis (Eds.), *Psychopathology of mental development* (pp. 298–320). New York: Grune & Stratton.

Myklebust, H. R. (1968). Learning disabilities: Definition and overview. In H. R. Myklebust, (Eds.), *Progress in learning disabilities,* Vol. 1 (pp. 1–15). New York: Grune & Stratton.

Myklebust, H. R., & Boshes, B. (1960). Psychoneurological learning disorders in children. *Archives of Pediatrics, 77*, 247–256.

Myklebust, H. R. & Boshes, B. (1969). *Final report: Minimal brain damage in children.* Washington, DC: Department of Health, Education, and Welfare.

Myklebust, H. R. Boshes, B., Olson, D. A., & Cole, C. H. (1969). *Minimal brain damage in children.* Final report of USPHS Contract 108-65-142. DHEW, June 1969. Evanston, IL: Northwestern University Publications.

Naidoo, S. (1972). *Specific dyslexia.* New York: Pitman.

Nakajima, S., & Essman, W. B. (1973). Biochemical studies of learning and memory: An historical overview. In W. B. Essman & S. Nakajima (Eds.), *Current biochemical approaches to learning and memory* (pp. 1–28). New York: Spectrum.

National Advisory Committee on Handicapped Children (1968). *Special education for handicapped children*. First annual report, US Department of Health, Education and Welfare, January 31, 1968.

National Center for Educational Statistics. (1987). *The condition of education,* US Department of Special Education and Rehabilitative Services, Ninth Annual Report to Congress on Implementation of Public Law 94–142.

National Council for Teachers of Mathematics (1980). *Priorities in school mathematics.* Reston, VA: National Council for Teachers of Mathematics.

National Diffusion Network. (1980). *Educational programs that work.* San Francisco, CA: Far West Regional Laboratory.

National Institute of Mental Health. (1978). *Bibliography on the hyperkinetic behavior syndrome.* DHEW Publication No. (ADM) pp. 77–449). Washington, DC: U.S. Government Printing Office.

National Joint Committee for Learning Disabilities. (1981). *Learning disabilities: Issues on definition.* Unpublished manuscript. (Available from Drake Duane, Chairperson, NJCLD, c/o The Orton Dyslexia Society, 724 York Road, Baltimore, MD, 21204).

National Joint Committee on Learning Disabilities, (1985) *Learning disability and the preschool child.* ERIC Document 206544.

Neal, J. (1942). *Encephalitis, a clinical study.* New York: Grune & Stratton.

Needleman, H. (1977). Effects of hearing loss from early recurrent otitis media on speech and language development. In B. F. Jaffe (Ed.), *Hearing loss in children* (pp. 640–649). Baltimore: University Park Press.

Nelson, H. E., & Warrington, E. K. (1976). Developmental spelling retardation. In R. M. Knights & D. J. Bakker (Eds.), *Neuropsychology of learning disorders: Therapeutic approaches* (pp. 325–332). Baltimore: University Park Press.

Nelson, K. B. (1968). The "continuum of reproductive casualty." In R. MacKeith & M. Bax (Eds.), *Studies in infancy. Clinics in developmental medicine,* No. 27. London: William Heinemann.

Newborg, J., Stock, J. R., Wnek, L., Guidubaldi, J., & Svinicki, J. (1984). *Battelle developmental inventory.* DLM Teaching Resources.

Nichols, P. L., & Chen, Ta-Chuan. (1981). *Minimal brain dysfunction: A prospective study.* N.J.: Lawrence Erlbaum Associates.

Niemark, F. D., & Lewis, N. (1967). The development of logical problem solving strategies. *Child Development, 38,* 107–117.

Noffsinger, D. (1985). Dichotic-listening techniques in the study of hemisphere asymmetries. In D. Benson & E. Zaidel (Eds.), *The dual brain* (pp. 127–141). New York: Guilford.

Nomura, Y., & Segawa, M. (1979). Gilles del la Tourette's syndrome in oriental children. *Brain and Development, 1,* 103–111.

Nosphitz, J. D. (Ed. in Chief). (1979). *Basic handbook of child psychiatry,* Vol. 1. New York: Basic Books.

Nurss, J. R., & McGauvran, M. E. (1976). *Metropolitan readiness tests.* New York: The Psychological Corporation.

Obrzut, J. E. (1979). Dichotic listening and bisensory memory skills in qualitatively diverse dyslexic readers. *Journal of Learning Disabilities, 12,* 24–34.

Obrzut, J. E. (1981a). Neuropsychological assessment and the schools. *School Psychology Review, 10,* 331–342.

Obrzut, J. E. (1981b). Neuropsychological procedures with school-age children. In G. W. Hynd & J. E. Obrzut (Eds.), *Neuropsychological assessment and the school-age child*. New York: Grune & Stratton.

Obrzut, J. E. (1988). Deficient lateralization in learning disabled children: Developmental lag or abnormal cerebral organization. In D. L. Molfese & S. J. Segelowitz (Eds.), *Brain lateralization in children* (pp. 567–590). New York: Guilford.

Ochroch, R. (1981). *The diagnosis and treatment of minimal brain dysfunction in children*. New York: Human Sciences Press.

O'Connor, N., & Hermelin, B. (1978). *Seeing and hearing and space and time*. London: Academic Press.

O'Donnell, D. J. (1985). Conduct disorders. In J. M. Wiener (Ed.), *Diagnosis and psychopharmacology of childhood and adolescent disorders* (pp. 250–287). New York: Wiley.

O'Dougherty, M., Nuechterlein, K. H., & Drew, B. (1984). Hyperactive and hypoxic children: Signal detection, sustained attention and behavior. *Journal of Abnormal Psychology, 93*, 178–191.

Offord, D. R. (1982). Primary prevention: Aspects of program design and evaluation. *Journal of the American Academy of Child Psychiatry, 21*, 225–230.

O'Leary, K. D., Rosenbaum, A., & Hughes, P. C. (1978). Fluorescent lighting: A purported source of hyperactive behavior. *Journal of Abnormal Child Psychology, 6*, 285–289.

Ollo, C., & Squires, N. (1986). Event-related potentials in learning disabilities. In R. Q. Cracco, & I. Bodis-Wollner (Eds.), *Evoked potentials: Frontiers of neuroscience*, Vol. 3 (pp. 497–512). New York: Alan R. Liss.

Oppenheimer, J. M. (1977). Studies of brain asymmetry: Historical perspectives. In S. J. Diamond & D. A. Blizard (Eds.), *Evolution and lateralization of the brain*, (pp. 4–17). *Annals of the New York Academy of Sciences*, Vol. 299. New York: New York Academy of Sciences.

Ornitz, E. M. (1974). The modulation of sensory input in autistic children. *Journal of Autism and Childhood Schizophrenia, 4*, 197–215.

Ornitz, E. M. (1985). Neurophysiology of infantile autism. *Journal of the American Academy of Child Psychiatry, 24*, 251–262.

Ornitz, E. M., & Ritvo, E. R. (1968). Perceptual inconstancy in early infantile autism. *Archives of General Psychiatry, 18*, 76–98.

Ornitz, E. M., & Ritvo, E. R. (1976). The syndrome of autism: A critical review. *American Journal of Psychiatry, 133*, 609–621.

Orton, S. T. (1928). Specific reading disability—Strephosymbolia. *Journal of the American Medical Association, 90*, 1095–1099.

Orton, S. T. (1937, reissued, 1989). *Reading, writing and speech problems in children*. Austin, TX: PRO-ED.

Orvaschel, H. (1985). Psychiatric interviews suitable for use in research with children and adolescents. *Psychopharmacology Bulletin, 21*, 737–746.

Orvaschel, H. (1988). Structured and semistructured psychiatric interviews for children. In C. Kestenbaum & D. Williams (Eds.), *Handbook of clinical assessment of children and adolescents* (pp. 31–42). New York: New York University Press.

Orvaschel, H., & Walsh, G. (1984). *The assessment of adaptive functioning in children: A review of existing measures suitable for epidemiological and clinical services research*. Monograph for NIMH series No. 3, DHHS publication No. (ADM) 84-1343. Washington, DC: U.S. Government Printing Office.

Orvaschel, H., Sholomska, D., & Weissman, M. (1980). *The assessment of psychopathology and behavior problems in children*. Mental health Service System Reports. Rockville, MD: U.S. Department of Health & Human Services, NIMH, Division of Biometry & Epidemiology.

Ostrom, N. N., & Jenson, W. R. (1988). Assessment of attention deficits in children. *Professional School Psychology, 3,* 254–269.

Ounstead, C. (1955). The hyperkinetic syndrome in epileptic children. *Lancet, 2,* 303–311.

Owen, F. W. (1978). Dyslexia—genetic aspects. In A. L. Benton & D. Pearl (Eds.), *Dyslexia: An appraisal of current knowledge* (pp. 265–285). New York: New York University Press.

Owen, F. W., Adams, P. A., Forrest, T., Stolz, L. M., & Fisher, S. (1971). Learning disorders in children: Sibling studies. *Monographs of the society for research in child development,* Vol. 36 (No. 4, Serial No. 144).

Page, E. (1985). Review of the Kaufman Assessment Battery for Children. In J. V. Mitchell (Ed.), *The ninth mental measurements yearbook* (pp. 773–777). Lincoln: University of Nebraska Press.

Paget, K. D., & Bracken, B. A. (1983). *The psychoeducational assessment of young children.* New York: Grune & Stratton.

Paine, R. S. (1964). Evolution of infantile postural reflexes in the presence of chronic brain syndrome. *Developmental Medicine and Child Neurology, 6,* 345–361.

Paine, R. S. (1965). The contribution of developmental neurology to child psychiatry. *Journal of the American Academy of Child Psychiatry, 4,* 353–386.

Paine, R. S., Werry, J. S., & Quay, H. C. (1968). A study of "minimal cerebral dysfunction." *Developmental Medicine and Child Neurology, 10,* 505–520.

Palfrey, J. S., Singer, J. D., Walker, D. K., & Butler, J. A. (1986). Health and special education: A study of new developments in five metropolitan communities. *Public Health Reports, 101,* 379–388.

Palinscar, A. S., & Brown, D. A. (1987). Enhancing instructional time through attention to meta-cognition. *Journal of Learning Disabilities, 20,* 66–75.

Palkes, H., Stewart, M., & Kahama, B. (1968). Porteous maze performance of hyperactive boys after training in self-directed verbal commands. *Child Development, 39,* 817–826.

Panksepp, J. (1979). A neurochemical theory of autism. *Trends in Neuroscience, 2,* 174–177.

Paradise, J. (1983). Long term effects of short term hearing loss—menace or myth? *Pediatrics, 71,* 647–648.

Parents in Action on Special Education v. Joseph P. Hannon, No. 74C 3586 (Northern District, IL, 1980).

Parloff, M. (1979). Can psychotherapy research guide the policymaker? *American Psychologist, 34,* 296–306.

Parloff, R., Parloff, E., & Sussno, E. (1976). Program evaluation. *Annual Review of Psychology, 27,* 569–594.

Parry, P. (1973). *The effect of reward on the performance of hyperactive children.* Doctoral dissertation, McGill University.

Pasamanick, B., Rogers, M. E., & Lilienfeld, A. M. (1956). Pregnancy experience and the development of behavior disorder in children. *American Journal of Psychiatry, 112,* 613–618.

Pate, J. E., & Webb, W. W. (1969). *First grade screening test.* Circle Pines, MN: American Guidance Service.

Patrick, A. M., Kimball, G. H., & Crawford, J. (1984) *Evaluation of the early prevention of school failure program for kindergarten students.* ERIC Document 244981.

Patterson, K. E. (1981). Neuropsychological approaches to the study of reading. *British Journal of Psychology, 72,* 151–174.

Paul, R. (1987). Communication. In D. Cohen & A. Donnallen (Eds.), *Handbook of autism and pervasive developmental disorders* (pp. 61–84). New York: Wiley.

Paul, R., & Cohen, D. (1985). Comprehension of indirect requests in adults with mental retardation and pervasive developmental disorders. *Journal of Speech and Hearing Research, 28,* 475–479.

Pauls, D. L., & Leckman, J. F. (1986a). The inheritance of Gilles de la Tourette syndrome and associated behaviors. *New England Journal of Medicine, 315,* 993–997.

Pauls, D. L., & Leckman, J. F. (1986b). The inheritance of Gilles de la Tourette's syndrome and chronic multiple tics among relatives of Tourette syndrome patients obtained by direct interview. *Journal of the American Academy of Child Psychiatry, 23,* 134–137.

Pauls, D. L., Kruger, S. D., Leckman, J. F., Cohen D. J., & Kidd, K. K. (1984). The risk of Tourette syndrome and chronic multiple tics among relatives of Tourette's syndrome patients obtained by direct interview. *Journal of the American Academy of Child Psychiatry, 23,* 134–137.

Pavy, R., & Metcalfe, J. (1965). The abnormal EEG in childhood communication and behavior abnormalities. *Electroencephalography and Clinical Neurophysiology, 19,* 414.

Peake, N. (1940). Relationships between spelling ability and reading ability. *Journal of Experimental Education, 9,* 192–193.

Pearson, G. H. (1952). A survey of learning difficulties in children. *The Psychoanalytic Study of the Child, 7,* 322–386. New York: International Universities Press.

Peck, H. P., Harrower, M., & Beck, M. (1950). *A new pattern for mental health services in a children's court.* Springfield, IL: Charles C Thomas.

Pelham, W. E. (1985). Effect of psychostimulant drugs on learning and academic achievement of children with attention deficit disorders and learning disorders. In J. K. Torgesen & B. Wong (Eds.), *Psychological and educational perspectives on learning disorders.* Orlando, FL: Academic Press.

Pelham, W. E., & Murphy, A. A. (1985). Behavioral and pharmacological Rx of attention deficit disorders and conduct disorders. In M. Hersen (Ed.), *Pharmacological and behavioral Rx: An integrative approach.* New York: Wiley.

Pelham, W. E., Bender, M. E., Coddell, J., Booth, S., & Moorer, S. H. (1985). Methylphenidate and children with attention deficit disorders: Dose effects on classroom, academic and social behavior. *Archives of General Psychiatry, 42,* 948–952.

Penfield, W., & Roberts, L. (1959). *Speech and brain mechanisms.* Princeton, NJ: Princeton University Press.

Pennington, B. F., & Smith, S. D. (1983). Genetic influence on learning disabilities and speech and language disorders. *Child Development, 54,* 369–387.

Pennington, B. F., Smith, S. D., Kimberling, W. J., Green, P. A., & Haith, M. M. (1987). Left-handedness and immune disorder in familial dyslexics. *Archives of Neurology, 44,* 634–639.

Perfetti, C. A., & Hogaboam, T. (1975). Relationship between single word decoding and reading comprehension skill. *Journal of Educational Psychology, 69,* 461–469.

Perry, R., Campbell, M., Adams, P., Lynch, N., Spencer, E., Curran, E., & Overall, J. (1989). Long term efficacy of haloperidol in autistic children: Continuous versus discontinuous drug administration. *Journal of the American Academy of Child and Adolescent Psychiatry, 28,* 87–92.

Petrauskas, R., & Rourke, B. P. (1979). Identification of subgroups of retarded readers: A neuropsychological multivariate approach. *Journal of Clinical Neuropsychology, 1,* 17–37.

Pfferbaum-Levine, P., Copeland, D. R., Fletcher, J. M., Ried, H. L., Jaffe, N., & McKinnon, W., Jr. (1984). Neuropsychologic assessment of long term survivors of childhood leukemia. *American Journal of Pediatric Hematology/Oncology, 6,* 123–128.

Pfeiffer, S. I., & Naglieri, J. A. (1983). An investigation of multi-disciplinary team decision-making. *Journal of Learning Disabilities, 16,* 588–590.

Piaget, J. (1954). *The construction of reality in the child.* New York: Basic Books.

Piaget, J., & Inhelder, B. (1958). *The growth of logical thinking from childhood to adolescence.* New York: Basic Books.

Pick, A. (1908). Uber Storungen der Orientierung am eigenen Korper. *Arbeiten aus der Deutschen Psychiatrischen Klinik,* Berlin: Prager.

Pierson, D. E., Walker, D. K., & Tivnan, T. (1984). A school-based program from infancy to kindergarten for children and their parents. *Personal & Guidance Journal, 62,* 448–455.

Pinnell, G. S. (1985). Helping teachers help children at risk: Insights from the reading recovery program. *Peabody Journal of Education, 62,* 70–85.

Pirozzolo, F. J., & Rayner, K. (1979). Cerebral organization and reading disability. *Neuropsychologia, 17,* 485–491.

Pirozzolo, F. J., & Wittrock, M. C. (Eds.) (1981). *Neuropsychological and cognitive processes in reading.* New York: Academic Press.

Polakoff, S. A., Sorgi, P. S., & Ratey, J. J. (1986). The treatment of impulsive, aggressive behavior with nadolol. *Journal of Clinical Psychopharmacology, 6,* 125–126.

Pollack, M. A., Cohen, N. L., & Friedhoff, A. S. (1977). Gilles de la Tourette syndrome—familial occurrence and precipitation by methylphenidate therapy. *Archives of Neurology, 34,* 630–632.

Pontius, A. A. (1983). Finger misrepresentation and dyscalculia in an ecological context: Toward an ecological (cultural) evolutionary neuro-psychiatry. *Perceptual Motor Skills, 57,* 1191–208.

Poremba, C. D. (1975). Learning disabilities, youth and delinquency: Programs for intervention. In H. Myklebust (Ed.), *Progress in learning disabilities, 3,* 123–149. New York: Grune & Stratton.

Porges, S. W., & Smith, K. M. (1980). Defining hyperactivity: physiological and behavioral strategies. In C. K. Whalen & B. Henker (Eds.), *Hyperactive children: The social ecology of identification and treatment* (pp. 75–104). New York: Academic Press.

Prechtl, H.F.R., & Beintema, D. (1964). *The neurological examination of the full-term newborn infant.* London: The Spastics Society Medical Education and Information Center. William Heinemann Medical Books.

Prechtl, H.F.R., & Stemmer, C. J. (1962). The choreiform syndrome in children. *Developmental Medicine and Child Neurology, 4,* 119–127.

Preschool Screening Instrument. (1973). Fort Worth, TX: Forth Worth Public Schools.

Preston, M., Guthrie, J. T., & Childs, B. (1974). Visual evoked response in normal and disabled readers. *Psychophysiology, 11,* 452–457.

Price, R. A., Kidd, K. K., Cohen, D. J., Pauls, D. L., & Leckman, J. F. (1985). A twin study of Tourette syndrome. *Archives of General Psychiatry, 42,* 815–820.

Price, R. A., Leckman, J. F., Pauls, D. L., Cohen, D. J., & Kidd, K. K. (1986). Gilles de la Tourette syndrome: Tics and central nervous stimulants in twins and non-twins, *Neurology, 36,* 232–237.

Prior, M., Sanson, A., Freethy, C., & Geffen, G. (1985). Auditory attentional abilities in hyperactive children. *Journal of Child Psychology and Psychiatry, 26,* 289–304.

Prior, M., Trees, B., Hoffman, W., & Boldt, D. (1984). Computer tomographic study of children with classic autism. *Archives of Neurology, 41,* 482–484.

Prizant, B. (1983). Language acquisition and communicative behavior in autism: Toward an understanding of the "whole" of it. *Journal of Speech and Hearing Disorders, 48,* 196–307.

Psychological Corporation. (1983). *Basic achievement skills individual screener* (BASIS). San Antonio, TX: Harcourt Brace Jovanovich.

Public Law 94–142, Education for All Handicapped Children Act. (1977) *Federal Register,* December 29, 1977, 65083.

Puig-Antich, J., Bleu, S., Mark, N., Greenhill, L., & Chambers, W. (1978). Prepubertal major depressive disorder: A pilot study. *Journal of the American Academy of Child Psychiatry, 17,* 695–707.

Puig-Antich, J., Chambers, W. J., & Tambrizi, M. A. (1983). The clinical assessment of current depressive episodes in children and adolescents: Interviews with parents and children. In D. Cantwell & G. A. Carlson (Eds.), *Affective disorders in childhood and adolescence: An update* (pp. 157–179). New York: SP Medical and Scientific Books.

Quadfasel, F. A., & Goodglass, H. (1968). Specific reading disability and other specific disabilities. *Journal of Learning Disabilities, 1,* 590–600.

Quay, H. C. (1977). Measuring dimensions of deviant behavior: The behavior problems checklist. *Journal of Abnormal Child Psychology, 5,* 277–287.

Quay, H. C., & Peterson, D. R. (1983). *Manual for the revised behavior problem checklist.* Miami: University of Miami.

Quinn, P., & Rapoport, J. L. (1975). One year follow-up of hyperactive boys treated with imipramine or methylphenidate. *American Journal of Psychiatry, 132,* 241–245.

Quiros, J. B. de (1964). Dysphasia and dyslexia in school children. *Folia Phoniatrica, 16,* 201. As cited in P. Satz & R. Morris. (1981). Learning disability subtypes: A review. In F. J. Pirozzolo & M. C. Wittrock (Eds.), *Neuropsychological and cognitive processes in reading* (pp. 109–141). New York: Academic Press.

Quitkin, R., Rifkin, A., & Klein, D. F. (1976). Neurological soft signs in schizophrenia and character disorder. *Archives of General Psychiatry, 33,* 845–853.

Rabinovitch, R. D. (1968). Reading problems in children: Definitions and classification. In A. Keeney & V. Kenney (Eds.), *Dyslexia: Diagnosis and treatment of reading disorders* (pp. 1–10). St. Louis: C. V. Mosby.

Rabinovitch, R. D., Drew, A. L., DeJong, R. N., Ingram, W., & Withey, L. (1954). A research approach to reading retardation. *Research Publications Association for Research in Nervous and Mental Disease, 34,* 363–396.

Rachelefsky, G. S., Wo, J., Adelson, J., Mickey, M. R., Spector, S. L., Katz, R. M., Siegel, S. C., & Rohe, A. S. (1986). Behavior abnormalities and poor school performance due to oral theophylline use. *Pediatrics, 78,* 1133–1138.

Ramey, C., & Campbell, F. A. (1984). Preventive education for high risk children: Cognitive consequences of the Abecedarian project. *American Journal of Mental Deficiency, 88,* 515–523.

Rapaport, L., Coffman, H., Guare, R., Fenton T., Degraw, C., & Twarog, F. (1989). Effects of theophylline on behavior and learning in children with asthma. *American Journal of Disease of Children, 143,* 368–372.

Rapoport, J. (1965). Childhood behavior and learning problems treated with imipramine. *International Journal of Neuropsychiatry, 1,* 635–642.

Rapoport, J. (1983). The use of drugs in the hyperkinetic syndrome: Trends in recent research. In M. Rutter (Ed.), *Developmental neuropsychiatry* (pp. 385–403). New York: Guilford.

Rapoport, J., Buchsbaum, M., Weingartner, H., Zahn, T., Ludlow, C., Bartko, J., Mikkelson, E., Langer, D., & Banney, W. (1980). Dextroamphetamine: Cognitive and behavioral effects in normal and hyperactive boys and normal adult males. *Archives of General Psychiatry, 37,* 933–946.

Rapoport, J., Buchsbaum, M., Weingartner, H., Zahn, T., Ludlow, C., & Mikkelson, E. (1978). Dextroamphetamine: Behavioral and cognitive effects in normal prepubertal boys. *Science, 199,* 560–563.

Rapoport, J., Mikkelsen, E. J., Ebert, M. H., Brown, G. L., Weise, V. L., & Kapin, I. J. (1978). Urinary catacholamine and amphetamine excretion in hyperactive and normal boys. *Journal of Nervous and Mental Disease, 66,* 731–732.

Rapoport, J., Quinn, P. O., & Lamprecht, F. (1974). Minor physical anomalies and plasma dopamine-beta-hydroxylase activity in hyperactive boys. *American Journal of Psychiatry, 131,* 386–390.

Rapoport, J. L., Zametkin, A., Donnelly, M., Ismond, D. (1985). New drug trials on attention deficit disorder. *Psychopharmacology Bulletin, 21,* 232–236.

Rappaport, S. R. (1961). Behavior disorder and ego development in a brain-injured child. *Psychoanalytic Study of the Child, 6,* 423–450. New York: International Universities Press.

Raven, J. C. (1960). *Coloured progressive matrices.* New York: Psychological Corporation.

Rawson, M. B. (1968). *Developmental language disability.* Baltimore: Johns Hopkins University Press.

Rawson, M. B. (1986). The many faces of dyslexia. *Annals of Dyslexia, 36,* 179–191.

Reading and Writing Connection. (1986). Demondale, MI: Hartley Courseware.

Reed, H. B., & Fitzhugh, K. B. (1966). Patterns of deficits in relation to severity of cerebral dysfunction in children and adults. *Journal of Consulting and Clinical Psychology, 30,* 98–102.

Reed, H. B., Reitan, R. M., & Klove, H. (1965). Influence of cerebral lesions on psychological test performance of older children. *Journal of Consulting Psychology, 29,* 247–251.

Regli, F., Filippa, G., & Wiesendanger, M. (1967). Hereditary mirror movements. *Archives of Neurology, 16,* 620–623.

Regular Lives. (1988). Produced by Tom Goodwin, & Geraldine Wurzburg. State of the Art Production, Washington, DC. Syracuse University.

Reid, A., Naylor, G., & Kay, D. (1981). A double-blind, placebo controlled crossover trial of carbamazepine in overactive, severely mentally handicapped patients. *Psychological Medicine, 11,* 109–113.

Reinis, S. (1965). The formation of conditioned reflexes in rats after the parenteral administration of brain homogeneate. *Activitas Nervosa Superior (Praha), 7,* 167–168.

Reitan, R. M. (1974). Psychological effects of cerebral lesions in children of early school age. In R. M. Reitan & L. A. Davison (Eds.), *Clinical neuropsychology: Current status and applications* (pp. 53–89). Washington, DC: Winston.

Remschmidt, H. (1975). The psychotropic effect of carbamazepine in non-epileptic patients with particular reference to problems posed by clinical studies in children with behavior disorders. In W. Birkmayer (Ed.), *Epileptic seizures, behavior, pain* (pp. 253–258). Bern: Huber.

Rett, A. (1975). The so-called psychotropic effect of Tegretol in the treatment of convulsions of cerebral origin in children. In W. Birkmayer (Ed.), *Epileptic seizures, behavior, pain* (pp. 194–204). Bern: Huber.

Reuben, R., & Bakwin, H. (1968). Developmental clumsiness. *Pediatric Clinics of North America, 15,* 601–610.

Reynolds, C. R. (1983). *Critical measurement issues in learning disabilities.* Report of the U.S. Department of Education, Special Education Programs Work Group on Measurement Issues in the Assessment of Learning Disabilities. (Unpublished manuscript).

Reynolds, E. (1982). Pharmacological management of epilepsy associated with psychological disorders. *British Journal of Psychiatry, 141,* 549–557.

Reynolds, E., & Trimble, M. (Eds.) (1981). *Epilepsy and psychiatry,* Edinburgh: Churchill Livingstone.

Reynolds, M. C. (1988). A reaction to the JLD special series on the Regular Education Initiative. *Journal of Learning Disabilities, 21,* 352–356.

Riccardi, R., Brouwers, P., Dichiro, G., & Poplack, D. G. (1985). Abnormal computed tomography brain scans in children with acute lymphoblastic leukemia: Serial long term follow-up. *Journal of Clinical Oncology, 3,* 12–18.

Richardson, E. P. (1982). Neuropathological studies of Tourette syndrome. In A. Friedhoff & T. N. Chase (Eds.), *Gilles de la Tourette syndrome. Advances in neurology,* Vol. 35 (pp. 83–88).

Rickler, K. C. (1982). Episodic dyscontrol. In D. F. Benson & D. Blumer (Eds.), *Psychiatric aspects of neurological disease* (pp. 49–73). New York: Grune & Stratton.

Riddle, K. D., & Rapoport, J. L. (1976). A 2 year follow-up of 72 hyperactive boys. *Journal of Neurology and Mental Disorders, 762,* 126–134.

Rie, H. E. (1975). Hyperactivity in children. *American Journal of Diseases of Children, 129,* 783–789.

Rie, H. E., & Rie, E. D. (Eds.) (1980). *Handbook of minimal brain dysfunctions: A critical view.* New York: Wiley.

Rie, H. E., Rie, E. D., Stewart, S., & Ambuel, J. (1976a). Effects of methylphenidate on underachieving children. *Journal of Counsulting and Clinical Psychology, 44,* 250–260.

Rie, H. E., Rie, E. D., Stewart, S., & Ambuel, J. (1976b). Effects of methylphenidate on underachieving children. A replication. *American Journal of Orthopsychiatry, 46,* 313–322.

Riesen, A. H. (1970). Effects of visual environment on the retina. In D. B. Lindsley & F. A. Young (Eds.) *Early experience and visual information processing in perceptual and reading disorders* (pp. 249–260). Washington, DC: National Academy of Sciences.

Rimland, B. (1964). *Infantile autism.* New York: Appleton-Century-Crofts.

Rincover, A., Cook, R., Peoples, A., & Packard, D. (1979). Using sensory extinction and sensory reinforcement principles for programming multiple adaptive behavior change. *Journal of Applied Behavioral Analysis, 12,* 221–233.

Rinsland, H. (1945). *A basic vocabulary of elementary school children.* New York: Macmillan.

Risser, A. H., & Spreen, O. (1985). The Western Aphasia Battery. *Journal of Clinical and Experimental Neuropsychology, 1,* 463–470.

Ritvo, E. R., Freeman, B. J., Mason-Brother, A., Mo, A., & Ritvo, A. M. (1985). Concordance for the syndrome of autism in 40 pairs of affected twins. *American Journal of Psychiatry, 142,* 74–77.

Ritvo, E. R., Freeman, B. J., Pingree, C., Mason-Brothers, A., Jorde, L., Jenson, W. R., McMahon, W. M., Petersen, P. B., Mo, A., & Ritvo, A. (1989). The UCLA-University of Utah Epidemiological Survey of Autism: Prevalence. *American Journal of Psychiatry, 146,* 194–199.

Ritvo, E. R., Freeman, B. J., Scheibel, A. B., Duong, T., Robins, H., Guthrie, D., & Ritvo, A. (1986). Lower Purkinje cell counts in the cerebella of four autistic subjects. *American Journal of Psychiatry, 143,* 862–866.

Ritvo, E. R., Spence, M. A., Freeman, B. S., Mason-Brothers, A., Mo, A., & Marazita, M. L. (1985). Evidence for autosomal recessive inheritance in 46 families with multiple incidences of autism. *American Journal of Psychiatry, 142,* 187–192.

Robert Wood Johnson Foundation. (1988). *Serving handicapped children: A special report.*

Roberts, J., Burchinal, M., Collier, A., Ramey, C. T., Koch, M. A., & Henderson, F. W. (1989). Otitis media in early childhood and cognitive, academic and classroom performance of the school-aged child. *Pediatrics, 83,* 477–485.

Roberts, J., Burchinal, M., Koch, M., Footo, M., & Henderson, F. W. (1988). Otitis media in early childhood and its relationship to later phonological development. *Journal of Speech and Hearing Disorders, 53,* 424–432.

Roberts, J., Sanyal, M., Burchinal, M., Collier, A. M., Ramey, C. T., & Henderson, F. W. (1986). Otitis media in early childhood and its relationship to later verbal and academic performance. *Pediatrics, 78,* 423–430.

Robins, L., Helzer, J. E., Croughan, J., & Ratcliff, K. S. (1981). NIMH diagnostic interview schedule: Its history, characteristics and validity. *Archives of General Psychiatry, 38,* 381–389.

Robinson, H. M. (1946). *Why pupils fail in reading.* Chicago: University of Chicago Press.

Robinson, L. L., Nesbit, M. E., Jr., Sather, H. N., Meadows, A. T., Ortega, J., & Hammond, G. D. (1984). Factors associated with IQ scores in long term survivors of childhood acute lymphoblastic leukemia. *American Journal Pediatric Hematology Oncology, 6,* 115–121.

Roche, A., Lipman, R., Overall, J., & Hung, W. (1979). The effects of stimulant medication on the growth of hyperkinetic children. *Pediatrics, 63,* 647–650.

Rogawski, M. A., & Aghajanian, C. K. (1980). Modulation of lateral geniculate neuron excitability by noradrenaline microiontophoresis or locus coeruleus stimulation. *Nature, 287,* 731–734.

Rogers, M. E., Lilienfeld, A. M., & Pasamanick, B. (1955). Prenatal and paranatal factors in the development of childhood behavior disorders. *Acta Psychiatrica et Neurologica Scandinavica,* Supplement 102.

Rosenzweig, M. R., & Bennett, E. L. (Eds.) (1976). *Neural mechanisms of learning and memory.* Cambridge, MA: MIT Press.

Rosenzweig, M. R., & Bennett, E. L. (1978). Experiential influences on brain anatomy and brain chemistry in rodents. In G. Gottlieb (Ed.), *Studies on the development of behavior and the nervous system,* Vol. 4 (pp. 289–327). New York: Academic Press.

Rosenzweig, M. R., & Bennett, E. L. (1984). Basic processes and modulating influences in the stages of memory formation. In G. Lynch, J. L. McGaugh, & N. M. Weinberger (Eds.), *Neurobiology of learning and memory* (pp. 263–288). New York: Guilford.

Rosenzweig, M. R., Krech, D., & Bennett, E. L. (1960). A search for relations between brain chemistry and behavior. *Psychology Bulletin, 57,* 476–492.

Rosner, J., & Simon, D. P. (1971). The auditory analysis test: An initial report. *Journal of Learning Disabilities, 4,* 384–392.

Ross, M. S., & Moldofsky, H. (1978). A comparison of pimozide and haloperidol in the treatment of Gilles de la Tourette's syndrome. *American Journal of Psychiatry, 135,* 585–587.

Rosvold, H. E., Mirsky, A. F., Sarason, I., Bransome, Ed., & Beck, L. H. (1956). A continuous performance test of brain damage. *Journal of Consulting Psychology, 20,* 243–350.

Roswell, F. G., & Chall, J. S. (1956, 1978). *Roswell-Chall diagnostic test of word analysis skills.* La Jolla, CA: Essay Press.

Rourke, B. P. (1978). Neuropsychological research in reading retardation: A review. In A. Benton & D. Pearl (Eds.), *Dyslexia: An appraisal of current knowledge* (pp. 139–172). New York: Oxford University Press.

Rourke, B. P. (Ed.) (1985) *Neuropsychology of Learning Disabilities: Essentials of Subtype Analysis.* New York: Guilford.

Rourke, B. P., & Finlayson, M.A.J. (1978). Neuropsychological significance of variations in patterns of academic performance. *Journal of Abnormal Child Psychology, 6,* 121–133.

Rourke, B. P., & Orr, R. R. (1977). Prediction of the reading and spelling performances of normal and retarded readers: A four year follow-up. *Journal of Abnormal Child Psychology, 5,* 9–20.

Rourke, B. P., & Strang, J. D. (1978). Neuropsychological significance of variations in patterns of academic performance: Motor, psycho-motor, and tactile- perceptual abilities. *Journal of Pediatric Psychology, 3,* 62–66.

Rourke, B. P., & Strang, J. D. (1983) Subtypes of reading and arithmetic disabilities: A neuropsychological analysis. In M. Rutter (Ed.), *Developmental neuropsychology* (pp. 473–488). New York: Guilford.

Rourke, B. P., Young, G. C., & Flewelling, R. W. (1971). The relationship between WISC verbal-performance discrepancies and selected verbal, auditory-perceptual, visual-perceptual and problem-solving abilities in children with learning disabilities. *Journal of Clinical Psychology, 27,* 475–479.

Routh, D. K. (1980). Developmental and social aspects of hyperactivity. In C. K. Whalen & B. Henker (Eds.), *Hyperactive children: The social ecology of identification and treatment* (pp. 55–74). New York: Academic Press.

Rowland, J. H., Glidwell, O. J., Sibley, R. F., Holland, J. C., Trull, R., Berman, A., *et al.* (1984). Effect of different forms of central nervous system prophylaxis on neuropsychological function in childhood leukemia. *Journal of Clinical Oncology, 2,* 1327–1335.

Rozin, P. (1976). The psychobiological approach to human memory. In M. R. Rosenzweig & E. R. Bennett (Eds.), *Neural mechanism of learning memory* (pp. 3–48). Cambridge, MA: MIT Press.

Rubin, R. A., & Balow, B. (1977). Perinatal influences on the behavior and learning problems of children. In B. B. Lahey & A. E. Kazdin (Eds.), *Advances in clinical child psychology* (pp. 119–160). New York: Plenum.

Rumsey, J. M., Berman, K. F., Denckla, M. B., Hamberger, S. D., Kruesi, M. J., & Weinberger, D. D. (1987). Regional cerebral blood blow in severe developmental dyslexia. *Archives of Neurology, 44,* 1144–1150.

Rutter, M. (1972). Childhood schizophrenia reconsidered. *Journal of Autism and Childhood Schizophrenia, 2,* 315–337.

Rutter, M. (1974). Epidemiological and conceptual considerations in risk research. In E. J. Anthony & C. Koupernick (Eds.), *The child in his family: Children at psychiatric risk,* Vol. 1 (pp. 67–180). New York: Wiley.

Rutter, M. (1977). Brain damage syndromes in childhood: Concepts and findings. *Journal of Child Psychology and Psychiatry, 18,* 1–21.

Rutter, M. (1978a). Diagnosis and definition. In M. Rutter & E. Shopler (Eds.), *Autism: A reappraisal of concepts and treatment* (pp. 1–25). New York: Plenum.

Rutter, M. (1978b). Prevalence and types of dyslexia. In A. L. Benton & D. Pearl (Eds.), *Dyslexia: An appraisal of current knowledge* (pp. 3–28). New York: Oxford University Press.

Rutter, M. (1981). Psychological sequalae of brain damage in children. *American Journal of Psychiatry, 138,* 1533–1544.

Rutter, M. (Ed.) (1983). *Developmental neuropsychiatry.* New York: Guilford.

Rutter, M. (1984). The family, the child and the school. In M. Levine & P. Satz (Eds.), *Middle childhood: Development and dysfunction* (pp. 293–344). Baltimore: University Park Press.

Rutter, M., & Bartak, L. (1971). Causes of infantile autism: Some considerations from recent research. *Journal of Autism and Childhood Schizophrenia, 1,* 20–32.

Rutter, M., & Bartak, L. (1973). Special education treatment for autistic children, study II. Follow-up findings and implications for services. *Journal of Child Psychology and Psychiatry, 14,* 241–270.

Rutter, M., & Graham, P. (1968). The reliability and validity of the psychiatric assessment of the child: Interview with the child. *British Journal of Psychiatry, 114,* 563–579.

Rutter, M., & Hersov, L. (Eds.) (1977). *Child psychiatry: Modern approaches.* Oxford, England: Blackwell Scientific Publications.

Rutter, M., & Madge, N. (1977). *Cycles of disadvantage: A review of research.* London: Heinemann.

Rutter, M., & Shopler, E. (Eds.) (1978). *Autism: A reappraisal of concepts and treatment.* New York: Plenum.

Rutter, M., & Yule, W. (1975). The concept of specific reading retardation. *Journal of Child Psychiatry, 16,* 181–197.

Rutter, M., Chadwick, O., & Shaffer, D. (1983). Head injury. In M. Rutter (Ed.), *Developmental neuropsychiatry* (pp. 83–111). New York: Guilford.

Rutter, M., Graham, P., & Yule, W. (1970). *A neuropsychiatric study in childhood.* London: Spastics International Medical Publications.

Rutter, M., Tizard, J., & Whitmore, K. (1970). *Education, health and behavior.* London: Longman.

Rutter, M., Yule, B., Quinton, D., Rowlands, O., Yule, W., & Berger, M., (1975). Attainment and adjustment in two geographical areas, III. Some factors accounting for area differences. *British Journal of Psychiatry, 126,* 520–533.

Ryan, E. B., Short, E. J., Weed, K. A. (1986). The role of cognitive strategy training in improving the academic performance of learning disabled children. *Journal of Learning Disabilities, 19,* 521–529.

Safer, D., & Allen, R. (1973). Single daily dose methylphenidate in hyperactive children. *Diseases of the Nervous System, 34,* 325–328.

Safer, D., & Allen, R. (1976). *Hyperactive children. Diagnosis and management.* Baltimore: University Park Press.

Safer, D., & Krager, J. M. (1988). A survey of medication treatment for hyperactive/inattentive students. *Journal of the American Medical Association, 260,* 2256–2258.

Safer, D., Allen, R., & Barr, E. (1972). Depression of growth in hyperative children on stimulant drugs. *New England Journal of Medicine, 257,* 217–221.

Sameroff, A. J., & Chandler, M. J. (1975). Reproductive risk and the continuum of caretaker casualty. In F. D. Horowitz (Ed.), *Review of child development research,* Vol. 4 (pp. 187–245). Chicago: University of Chicago Press.

Sameroff, A. J., & Seifer, R. (1983). Familial risk and child competence. *Child Development, 54,* 1254–1268.

Sandberg, S. T., Rutter, M., & Taylor, E. (1978). Hyperkinetic disorder in psychiatric clinic attenders. *Developmental Medicine and Child Neurology, 20,* 279–299.

Sandoval, J. (1981). Format effects in two teacher rating scales of hyperactivity. *Journal of Abnormal Child Psychology, 9,* 203–218.

Sandoval, J., & Haapenen, R. M. (1981). A critical commentary on neuropsychology in the schools: Are we ready? *School Psychology Review, 10,* 381–388.

Sandoval, J., Lambert, N. M., & Sassone, D. M. (1981). The comprehensive treatment of hyperactive children: A continuing problem. *Journal of Learning Disabilities, 14,* 117–118.

Santostefano, S. (1978). *A biodevelopmental approach to clinical child psychology: Cognitive controls and cognitive control therapy.* New York: Wiley.

Sarazin, F. F., & Spreen, O. (1986). Fifteen year stability of some neuropsychological tests in learning disabled subjects with and without neurological impairment. *Journal of Clinical and Experimental Neuropsychology, 8,* 190–200.

Sarnoff, A., Mednick, B., Baert, A. (Eds.) (1981). *Prospective longitudinal research: An empirical basis for the primary prevention of psychosocial disorders.* WHO. Geneva: Oxford University Press.

Satin, M. S., Winsberg, B. G., Monetti, C. H., Sverd, J., & Foss, D. A. (1985). A general population screen for attention deficit disorder with hyperactivity. *Journal of the American Academy of Child Psychiatry, 24,* 756–764.

Sattler, J. (1988). *Assessment of children* (3rd ed.) San Diego, CA: Sattler.

Satz, P. (1966). A block rotation task. The application of multivariate and decision theory analysis for the prediction of organic brain disorder. *Psychological monographs, 80,* (No. 21, Whole No. 629).

Satz, P. (1976). Cerebral dominance and reading disability: An old problem revisited. In D. S. Bakker & R. M. Knights, (Eds.), *Neuropsychology of learning disorders: Therapeutic approaches* (pp. 273–294). Baltimore: University Park Press.

Satz, P. (1977). Laterality tests: An inferential problem. *Cortex, 13,* 208–212.

Satz, P. (1979). A test of some models of hemisphere speech organization in the left and right handed. *Science, 203,* 1131–1133.

Satz, P., & Fletcher, J. M. (1982). *The Florida kindergarten screening battery.* Odessa, FL: Psychological Assessment Resources.

Satz, P., & Fletcher, J. M. (1987). Left-handedness and dyslexia: An old myth revisited. *Journal of Pediatric Psychology, 12,* 291–298.

Satz, P., & Friel, J., (1973) Some predictive antecedents of specific reading disability: A preliminary one-year follow-up, 1977–78. In P. Satz & J. J. Ross (Eds.), *The disabled learner: Early detection and intervention* (pp. 79–98). Rotterdam: Rotterdam University Press.

Satz, P., & Morris, R. (1981). Learning disability subtypes: A review. In F. J. Pirozzolo & M. C. Wittrock (Eds.), *Neuropsychological and cognitive processes in reading* (pp. 109–141). New York: Academic Press.

Satz, P., & Ross, J. J. (Eds.) (1973). *The disabled learner: Early detection and articulation.* Rotterdam: Rotterdam University Press.

Satz, P., & Soper, H. V. (1986). Left-handedness, dyslexia, and autoimmune disorder: A critique. *Journal of Clinical and Experimental Neuropsychology, 8,* 453–458.

Satz, P., & Sparrow, S. (1970). Specific developmental dyslexia: A theoretical formulation. In D. J. Bakker & P. Satz (Eds.), *Specific reading disability: Advances in theory and methods* (pp. 17–39). Amsterdam: Rotterdam University Press.

Satz, P., & Van Nostrand, G. K. (1973). Developmental dyslexia: An evaluation of a theory. In P. Satz & J. J. Ross (Eds.), *The disabled learner: Early detection and intervention* (pp. 121–147). Rotterdam: Rotterdam University Press.

Satz, P., Morris, R., & Fletcher, J. (1985). Hypotheses, subtypes and individual differences in dyslexia. In D. Gray & J. Kavanagh (Eds.), *Behavorial measures of dyslexia* (pp. 25–40). Parton, MA: York Press.

Satz, P., Rerdin, D., & Ross, J. (1971). An evaluation of a theory of specific development dyslexia. *Child Development, 42,* 2009–2021.

Satz, P., Taylor, H. G., Friel, J., & Fletcher, J. M. (1978) Some developmental precussors of reading disabilities: A 6 year follow-up. In A. E. Benton & D. Pearl (Eds.), *Dyslexia: An appraisal of current knowledge* (pp. 315–347). New York: Oxford University Press.

Saunders, R. E. (1973). *Lincs to writing, reading and spelling.* Cambridge, MA: Educators Publishing Service.

Saunders, T. R. (1977). A critical analysis of the minimal brain dysfunction syndrome. *Professional Psychology, 9,* 293–306.

Sawaguchi, T., Matsumura, M., & Kuboto, K. (1988). Dopamine enhances the neuronal activity of spatial short-term memory task in the primate pre-frontal cortex. *Neuroscience Research, 5,* 465–473.

Schaeffer, E., Aaronson, M., & Edgerton, M. (1977). *Classroom behavior inventory.* Chapel Hill, NC: Frank Porter Graham Development Center.

Schain, R. J. (1977). *Neurology of childhood learning disorders* (2nd ed.). Baltimore: Williams & Wilkins.

Schain, R. J., & Freedman, D. (1961). Studies on 5-hydroxyindole metabolism in autistic and other mentally retarded children. *Journal of Pediatrics, 58,* 315–320.

Schilder, P. (1931). Finger agnosia, finger apraxia, finger aphasia. *Nervenarzt, 4,* 625–629.

Schilder, P. (1935). *Image and appearance of the human body.* London: Kegan Paul, Trench, Trubner.

Schilder, P. (1938a). Organic background of obsessions and compulsions. *American Journal of Psychiatry, 94,* 1397–1413.

Schilder, P. (1938b). Psychological implications of motor development in children. *Proc. Fourth, Institute on the Exceptional Child, Child Research Clinic, Woods School, 4,* 38–59.

Schilder, P. (1964). *Contributions to developmental neuropsychiatry.* New York: International Universities Press.

Schlieper, A., Kisilevsky, H., Mattingly, S., & York, L. (1985). Mild conductive hearing loss and language development: A one year follow-up study. *Journal of Developmental and Behavioral Pediatrics, 6,* 65–68.

Schmitt, B. D. (1975). The minimal brain dysfunction myth. *American Journal of Diseases of Children, 129,* 1313–1318.

Schneider, J. W., Griffith, D. R., & Chasnoff, I. J. (1989). Infants exposed to cocaine in utero: Implications for developmental assessment and intervention. *Infants and Young Children, 2,* 25–36.

Schonhaut, S., & Satz, P. (1983). Prognosis for children with learning disabilities. In M. Rutter (Ed.), *Developmental neuropsychiatry* (pp. 542–563). New York: Guilford.

Schopler, E., & Reichler, R. J. (1971). Parents as therapists in the treatment of psychotic children. *Journal of Autism and Childhood Schizophrenia, 1,* 87–102.

Schrag, P., & Divoky, D. (1975). *The myth of the hyperactive child.* New York: Pantheon.

Schreier, H. (1979). Use of propranolol in the treatment of post encephalitic psychosis. *American Journal of Psychiatry, 136,* 840–841.

Scoville, W. B., & Milner, B. (1957). Loss of memory after bilateral hippocampal lesions. *Journal of Neurology, Neurosurgery and Psychiatry, 20,* 11–21.

Seignot, M.J.N. (1961). Un case de maladie des tics de Gilles de la Tourette gueri par le R-1625. *Annals Medicine Psychologie, 119,* 578–579.

Seligman, M., & Groves, D. (1970). Non-transient learned helplessness. *Psychonomic Science, 19,* 191–192.

Seligman, M., & Meier, S. (1967). Failure to escape traumatic shock. *Journal of Experimental Psychology, 74,* 1–9.

Sell, S., Merrill, R., Doyne E., & Zimsky, E. Jr. (1972). Long term sequelae of *Hemophilus influenzae* meningitis. *Pediatrics, 49,* 206–211.

Selye, H. (1956). *The stress of life.* New York: McGraw-Hill.

Selz, M., & Reitan, R. M. (1979). Rules for neuropsychological diagnosis: Classification of brain function in older children. *Journal of Consulting and Clinical Psychology, 47,* 258–264.

Semmes, J., Weinstein, S., Ghent, L., & Teuber, H. L. (1963). Correlates of impaired orientation in personal and extra-personal space. *Brain, 86,* 747–772.

Senf, G. M. (1973). Learning disabilities. *Pediatric Clinics of North America, 20,* 607–640.

Senf, G. M. (1979). Can neuropsychology really change the face of special education? *Journal of Special Education, 13,* 51–56.

Serwer, B. (1971). Experimental model school program for children with specific learning disabilities. ERIC Document ED087149.

Shafer, S. Q., Shaffer, D., O'Connor, P., & Stokman, C. (1983). Hard thoughts on soft neurological signs. In M. Rutter (Ed.), *Developmental neuropsychiatry* (pp. 133–143). New York: Guilford.

Shaffer, D. (1973). Psychiatric aspects of brain injury in childhood: A review. *Developmental Medicine and Child Neurology, 15,* 211–220.

Shaffer, D. (1977a). Brain injury. In M. Rutter & L. Hersov (Eds.), *Child psychiatry: Modern approaches* (pp. 185–215). Oxford, England: Blackwell Scientific Publications.

Shaffer, D. (1977b). Drug therapy. In M. Rutter & L. Hersov (Eds.), *Child psychiatry: Modern approaches* (pp. 901–992). Oxford, England: Blackwell Scientific Publications.

Shaffer, D., & Greenhill, L. (1979). A critical note on the predictive validity of the hyperkinetic syndrome. *Journal of Child Psychology and Psychiatry, 20,* 61–72.

Shaffer, D., O'Connor, P. A., Shafer, S. Q., & Prupis, S. (1983). Neurological "soft signs": Their origins and significance for behavior. In M. Rutter (Ed.), *Developmental neuropsychiatry* (pp. 144–164). New York: Guilford.

Shaffer, D., Philips, I., & Enzer, N. B. (Eds.) (1989). *Prevention of mental disorders. alcohol and other drug use in children and adolescents.* U.S. Department of Health and Human Services, Office for Substance Abuse Prevention. Prevention Monograph 2. Rockville, MD.

Shaffer, D., Schonfeld, I., O'Connor, P., Stokman, C., Trautman, P., Shafer, S., & Ng, S. (1985). Neurological soft signs and their relationship to psychiatric disorder and intelligence in childhood and adolescence. *Archives of General Psychiatry, 42,* 342–351.

Shaffer, M. (1979). Primal terror: A perspective of vestibular dysfunction. *Journal Learning Disabilities, 12,* 89–92.

Shagass, C., Ornitz, E. M., Sutton, S., & Tueting, P. (1978). Event related potentials and psychopathology. In E. Callaway, P. Teuring, & S. H. Koslow (Eds.), *Event related potentials in man* (pp. 443–496). New York: Academic Press.

Shapiro, A. (1985). Presentation at First National Clinical Symposium on Tourette Syndrome, New York City.

Shapiro, A., & Shapiro, E. (1984). Controlled study of pimozide vs. placebo in Tourette's syndrome. *Journal of the American Academy of Child Psychiatry, 23,* 161–173.

Shapiro, A., & Shapiro, E. (1988). Treatment of tic disorders with haloperidol. In D. J. Cohen, R. Bruun, & J. Leckman, *Tourette's syndrome and tic disorder* (pp. 268–280). New York: Wiley.

Shapiro, A., Shapiro, E., Bruun, R., & Sweet, R. (1978). *Gilles de la Tourette syndrome.* New York: Raven.

Shapiro, A., Shapiro, E., Young, J. G., & Feinberg, T. E. (1987). *Gilles de la Tourette Syndrome* (2nd ed.). New York: Raven.

Shapiro, E. R. (1978). The psychodynamics and developmental psychology of the borderline patient: A review of the literature. *American Journal of Psychiatry, 135,* 1305–1315.

Shapiro, T. (1977). The quest for a linguistic model to study the speech of autistic children: Studies of echoing. *Journal of the American Academy of Child Psychiatry, 16,* 608–619.

Shapiro, T., Burkes, L., Petti, T. A., & Ranz, J. (1978). Consistency of nonfocal neurological signs. *Journal of the American Academy of Child Psychiatry, 17,* 70–79.

Shashoua, V. E. (1968). RNA changes in goldfish brain during learning. *Nature, 217,* 238–240.

Shaywitz, B. A., Cohen, D., & Bowens, M. (1977). CSF monoamine metabolites in children with minimal brain dysfunction: Evidence for alteration of brain dopamine. *Journal of Pediatrics, 90,* 67–71.

Shaywitz, S. E., & Shaywitz, B. A. (1988). Increased medication use in attention-deficit hyperactivity disorder: Regressive or appropriate? *Journal of the American Medical Association, 260,* 2270–2272.

Shaywitz, S. E., Shaywitz, B. A., Cohen, D., & Young, J. G. (1983). Monoaminergic mechanisms in hyperactivity. In M. Rutter (Ed.), *Developmental neuropsychiatry* (pp. 330–347). New York: Guilford.

Sheard, M., Marini, J., Bridges, C., & Wagner, E. (1976). The effect of lithium on impulsive, aggressive behavior in man. *American Journal of Psychiatry, 133,* 1409–1413.

Shekim, W. O., Davis, L. G., Bylund, D. B., Brunngraber, E., Fikes, L., & Lanham J. (1982). Platelet MAO in children with attention deficit disorder and hyperactivity: A pilot study. *American Journal of Psychiatry, 139,* 936–938.

Shekim, W. O., DeKirmenjian, H., & Chapel, J. L. (1977). Urinary catecholamine metabolism in hyperkinetic boys treated with d-amphetamine. *American Journal of Psychiatry, 134,* 1276–1279.

Shekim, W. O., DeKirmenjian, H., Chapel, J., Javid, J., & Davis, J. (1979). Norepinephrine metabolism and clinical response to dextroamphetamine in hyperactive boys. *Journal of Pediatrics, 95,* 389–394.

Shekim, W. O., Javid, J., Dans, J. M., & Bylund, D. B. (1983). Urinary MHPG and HVA excretion in boys with attention deficit disorder and hyperactivity treated with d-amphetamine. *Biological Psychiatry, 18,* 707–714.

Sheldon, W. (1970). Prevalence, report of a task force. In A. Hayes & A. Silver (Eds.), *Report of the interdisciplinary committee on reading problems,* Task Force 4 (pp. 1–10). New York: Ford Foundation.

Shirley, M. (1939). A behavior syndrome characterizing prematurely born children. *Child Development, 10,* 115–128.

Shucard, D. W., Cummins, K., Gay, E., Lairsmith, J., & Welanka, P. (1985). Electrophysiological studies of reading-disabled children: In search of subtypes. In D. B. Gray & J. F. Kavanaugh (Eds.), *Behavioral measures of dyslexia* (pp. 87–106). Parton, MA: York Press.

Siassi, I. (1982). Lithium treatment of impulsive behavior in children. *Journal of Clinical Psychiatry, 43,* 482–484.

Siegel, L. S. (1982). Reproductive, perinatal and environmental factors as predictors of the cognitive and language development of preterm and full term infants. *Child Development, 53,* 963–973.

Siegel, L. S. (1983). The prediction of possible learning disabilities in pre term and full term children. In T. Field & A. Sostek (Eds.), *Infants born at risk: Physiological perceptual and cognitive processes* (pp. 295–315). New York: Grune & Stratton.

Siegel, L. S. (1982). Reproductive, perinatal and environmental factors and predictors of the cognitive and language development of pre-term and full term infants. *Child Development, 53,* 963–973.

Siegel, L. S., Saigel, S., Rosenbaum, P., Morton, R. A., Young, A., Berenbaum, S., & Stoskopf, B. (1982). Predictors of development in preterm and full term infants: A model for detecting the at-risk child. *Journal of Pediatric Psychiatry, 7,* 135–148.

Sigman, M., & Ungerer, J. (1981). Sensori-motor skills and language comprehension in autistic children. *Journal of Abnormal Child Psychology, 9,* 149–165.

Sigman, M., Ungerer, J., Mundy, P., & Sherman, T. (1987). Cognition in autistic children. In D. Cohen & A. Donnellan (Eds.), *Handbook of autism and pervasive developmental disorders* (pp. 103–120). New York: Wiley.

Silver, A. A. (1952). Postural and righting responses in children. *Journal of Pediatrics, 41,* 493–498.

Silver, A. A. (1958). Behavioral syndrome associated with brain damage in children. In H. Bakwin (Ed.), *Pediatric clinics of North America* (pp. 687–699). Philadelphia: Saunders.

Silver, A. A. (1978). *Prevention.* In A. L. Benton & D. Pearl (Eds.), *Dyslexia: An appraisal of current knowledge* (pp. 349–376). New York: Oxford University Press.

Silver, A. A. (1981). Special problems in therapy with children with central nervous system dysfunction. In R. Ochroch (Ed.), *The diagnosis and treatment of minimal brain dysfunction in children* (pp. 217–224). New York: Human Sciences Press.

Silver, A. A. (1984a). *Anxiety and the development of the stimulus barrier.* Tampa: University of South Florida, Department of Psychiatry.

Silver, A. A. (1984b). Children in classes for the severely emotionally handicapped. *Journal of Developmental and Behavioral Pediatrics, 5,* 49–54.

Silver, A. A. (1986). Children with autistic behavior in a self-contained unit in the public schools. *Journal of Developmental and Behavioral Pediatrics, 7,* 84–92.

Silver, A. A. (1988). Intrapsychic processes and adjustment in Tourette syndrome. In D. Cohen, R. Bruun, & J. Leckman (Eds.), *Tourette's syndrome and tic disorder* (pp. 197–206). New York: Wiley.

Silver, A. A. (1989). Electroencephalogram in 33 consecutive admissions to a child psychiatry clinic. (In preparation).

Silver, A. A., & Hagin, R. A. (1960). Specific reading disability: Delineation of the syndrome and relationship to cerebral dominance. *Comprehensive Psychiatry 1,* 126–136.

Silver, A. A., & Hagin, R. A. (1964). Specific reading disability: Follow-up studies. *American Journal of Orthopsychiatry, 34,* 95–102.

Silver, A. A., & Hagin, R. A. (1966). Maturation of perceptual functions in children with specific reading disability. *The Reading Teacher, 19,* 253–269.

Silver, A. A. & Hagin, R. A. (1972a). Effects of perceptual stimulation on perception, on reading disability and on the establishment of cerebral dominance for language. *Report to the Carnegie Corporation.* New York.

Silver, A. A., & Hagin, R. A. (1972b). Profile of a first grade: A basis for preventive psychiatry. *Journal of the American Academy of Child Psychiatry, 11,* 645–674.

Silver, A. A., & Hagin, R. A. (1981). *Search: A scanning instrument for the prevention of learning disability.* (2nd ed.). New York: Walker Educational Books.

Silver, A. A., & Hagin, R. A. (1980). An interdisciplinary model for the prevention of learning disability. In R. Knights & D. J. Bakker (Eds.), *Treatment of hyperactive and learning disordered children* (pp. 3–12). Baltimore, MD: University Park Press.

Silver, A. A., & Hagin, R. A. (1985). Outcomes of learning disabilities in adolescence. In S. Feinstein (Ed.), *Adolescent psychiatry* (pp. 197–213). Chicago: University of Chicago Press.

Silver, A. A., & Hagin, R. A. (1989). Prevention of learning disorders. In D. Shaffer, I. Philips, & N. B. Enzer (Eds.), *Prevention of mental disorders, alcohol and other drug use in children and adolescents* (pp. 413–442). U.S. Department of Health and Human Services, Office for Substance Abuse Prevention. Prevention Monograph 2. Rockville, MD.

Silver, A. A., Hagin, R. A., & Beecher, R. (1978). Scanning diagnosis, and intervention in the prevention of reading disabilities. *Journal of Learning Disabilities, 11,* 437–449.

Silver, A. A., Hagin, R. A., & Beecher, R. (1981). A program for secondary prevention of learning disabilities: Results in academic achievement and in emotional adjustment. *Journal of Preventive Psychiatry, 1,* 77–87.

Silver, A. A., Hagin, R. A., DeVito, E., Kreeger, H., & Scully, E. (1976). A search battery for scanning children for potential learning disability. *Journal of the American Academy of Child Psychiatry, 15,* 224–239.

Silver, L. B. (1981). The relationship between learning disabilities, hyperactivity, distractibility and behavioral problems. *Journal of the American Academy of Child Psychiatry, 20,* 385–397.

Silver, L. B. (1987). The "magic cure": A review of the current controversial approaches to treatment of learning disabilities. *Journal of Learning Disabilities, 20,* 498–504.

Silver, L. B. (1989). Psychological and family problems associated with learning disabilities: Assessment and intervention. *Journal of the American Academy of Child Psychiatry, 28,* 319–325.

Silverman, L. A., & Metz, A. (1973). Numbers of pupils with specific learning disabilities in local public schools in the United States. In E. F. de la Cruz, B. Fox, & R. H. Roberts (Eds.), *Annals of the New York Academy of Sciences,* Vol. 205 (pp. 146–157).

Silverman, S. (1983). The "innate given": A reconsideration in relation to some specific psychic phenomena, transference and treatment considerations. In J. Frosch, *The psychotic process* (p. 297). New York: International Universities Press.

Silverstein, F., Smith, C. B., & Johnston, M. V. (1984). Effect of clonidine on platelet alpha adrenoreceptors and plasma norepinephrine of children with Tourette syndrome. *Developmental Medicine and Child Neurology, 27,* 793–799.

Silverstone, R. A., & Deichman, J. W. (1975). Sense modality research and the acquisition of reading skills. *Review of Educational Research, 45,* 149–172.

Simon, H., Taghzouti, K., & LeMoal, M. (1986). Deficits in spatial-memory tasks following lesions of septal dopaminergic terminals in the rat. *Behavioral Brain Research, 19*, 7–16.

Simmons, J. E. (1987). *Psychiatric examination of children* (4th ed.). Philadelphia: Lea and Febiger.

Singer, H. S., Trifiletti, R., & Gammon, K. (1988). The role of "other" neuroleptic drugs in the treatment of Tourette syndrome. In J. D. Cohen, R. Bruun, & J. Leckman (Eds.), *Tourette's syndrome and tic disorder* (pp. 303–316). New York: Wiley.

Skarda, D. (1974). Preacademic program for children delayed in oral communication skills. ERIC Document 096776.

Skov, H., Lou, H., & Pederson, H. (1984). Perinatal brain ischemina: Impact at 4 years of age. *Developmental Medicine and Child Neurology, 26*, 353–357.

Slavin, R., Madden, N., & Leavy, M. (1984). Effects of cooperative learning and individualized instruction on mainstreamed students. *Exceptional Children, 50*, 434–443.

Slingerland, B. H. (1969, 1977). *Pre-reading screening procedures.* Cambridge, MA: Educators Publishing Services.

Slingerland, B. H. (1971). *Multisensory approach to language arts for specific learning disability children.* Cambridge, MA: Educators Publishing Services.

Small, J. (1975). EEG and neurophysiological studies of early infantile autism. *Biological Psychiatry, 10*, 385–398.

Small, L. (1980). *Neuropsychodiagnosis in psychotherapy.* New York: Brunner/Mazel.

Smalley, S., Asarnow, R., & Spence, A. (1988). Autism and genetics: A decade of research. *Archives of General Psychiatry, 45*, 953–961.

Smith, J. B. (1971). Eye testing in children. *Pediatric Clinics of North American, 18*, 333–342.

Smith, M. M. (1970). *Patterns of intellectual abilities in educationally handicapped children.* Doctoral dissertation, Claremont College, CA.

Smith, M. S., & Bissell, J. (1970). Report analysis: The impact of Head Start. *Harvard Educational Review, 40*, 51–104.

Smith, N. B. (1928). Matching ability as a factor in first grade reading. *Journal of Educational Sociology, 19*, 560–571.

Smith, S. D., Kimberling, W. S., Pennington, B. F., & Lubs, M. A. (1983). Specific reading disability: Identification of an inherited form through linkage analysis. *Science, 219*, 1345–1347.

Smith, W. L., Philippus, M. J., & Guard, H. L. (1968). Psychometric study of children with learning problems and 14-6 positive spike EEG patterns treated with ethosuxamide (Zarontin) and placebo. *Archives of Diseases of Children, 43*, 616–619.

Sobotka, K. R., & May, J. G. (1977). Visual evoked potentials in normal and dyslexic children. *Psychophysiology, 14*, 18–24.

Solomon, S., Hotchkiss, E., Saravay, S. M., Bayer, C., Ramsey, P., & Blum, R. S. (1983). Impairment of memory function by antihypertensive medication. *Archives of General Psychiatry, 40*, 1109–1112.

Somers, A. B., Levin, H. A., & Hannay, H. J. (1976). A neuropsychological study of a family with hereditary mirror movements. *Developmental Medicine and Child Neurology, 18*, 791–798.

Sparling, J., & Lewis, I. (1981). *Learning games for the first three years.* New York: Walker Educational Books.

Sparrow, S. S. (1969). Reading disability and laterality. *Proceedings of the 77th annual convention of the American Psychological Association* (pp. 673–679).

Sparrow, S. S., & Satz, P. (1970). Dyslexia, laterality and neuropsychological development. In D. Bakker & P. Satz (Eds.), *Specific reading disabilities: Advances in theory and method* (pp. 41–60). Amsterdam: Rotterdam University Press.

Spellacy, F. S., & Peter, B. (1978). Dysclaculia and elements of the developmental Gerstmann syndrome in school children. *Cortex, 2*, 197–206.

Spellacy, F. S., & Spreen, O. (1969). A short form of the Token test. *Cortex, 5*, 390–397.

Spence, M. A., Ritvo, E. R., Marazita, M. L., Funderburk, S. J., Sparks, R. S., & Freeman, B. J. (1985). Gene mapping studies with the syndrome of autism. *Behavioral Genetics, 15*, 1–13.

Sperry, R. W. (1961). Cerebral organization and behavior. *Science, 133*, 1749–1757.

Sperry, R. W. (1964). The great cerebral commissure. *Scientific American, 210*, 42–52.

Spillane, J. D. (1942). The disturbance of the body scheme: Anosagnosia and finger gnosia. *Lancet, 242*, 42–44.

Spivack, G., Swift, M., & Prewitt, J. (1971). Syndromes of disturbed classroom behavior: A behavioral diagnostic system for elementary schools. *Journal of Special Education, 5*, 269–292.

Sprague, R. L. (1978). Principles of clinical trials and social ethical and legal issues of drug use in children. In J. S. Werry (Ed.), *Pediatric Psychopharmacology* (pp. 109–135). New York: Brunner/Mazel.

Sprague, R. L., & Berger, B. D. (1980). Drug effects on learning performance: Relevance of animal research to pediatric psychopharmacology. In R. M. Knights & D. J. Bakker (Eds.), *Treatment of hyperactive and learning disordered children* (pp. 167–184). Baltimore, M.D.: University Park Press.

Sprague, R. L., & Sleator, E. K. (1973). Effect of psychopharmacologic agents on learning disorders. *Pediatric Clinics of North America, 20*, 719–735.

Sprague, R. L., & Sleator, E. K. (1977). Methylphenidate in hyperactive children: Differences in dose effects on learning and social behavior. *Science, 198*, 1274–1276.

Spreen, O. (1976). Neuropsychology of learning disorders: Post conference review. In R. Knights & D. J. Bakker (Eds.), *Neuropsychology of learning disorders: Therapeutic approaches* (pp. 445–467). Baltimore: University Park Press.

Spreen, O. (1978a). The dyslexias: A discussion of neurobehavioral research. In A. Benton & D. Pearl (Eds.), *Dyslexia: An appraisal of current knowledge* (pp. 175–194). New York: Oxford University Press.

Spreen, O. (1978b). *Learning-disabled children growing up.* (Final report to Health and Welfare Canada, Health Programs Branch). Ottawa: Health and Welfare Canada.

Spreen, O. (1978c). *Prediction of school achievement from kindergarten to grade five: Review and report of a follow-up study.* Research Monograph No. 33. Victoria B.C., Canada: Department of Psychology, University of Victoria.

Spreen, O. (1988). Prognosis of learning disability. *Journal of Consulting and Clinical Psychology, 56*, 836–841.

Spreen, O., & Benton, A. L. (1969). *Spreen-Benton language examination profile.* Iowa City: University of Iowa.

Spreen, O., & Haaf, R. G. (1986). Empirically derived learning disability subtypes: A replication attempt and longitudinal patterns over 15 years. *Journal of Learning Disabilities, 19*, 170–180.

Sprinthall, N. A. (1984) Primary prevention: A road paved with a plethora of promises and procrastinations. *Personnel and Guidance Journal, 62*, 491–495.

Sproles, E., Azerrad, J., Williamson, C., & Merrill, R. (1969). Meningitis due to *Hemophilus influenzae:* Long term sequelae. *Journal of Pediatrics, 75*, 782–798.

Squire, L. R. (1987). *Memory and brain.* New York: Oxford University Press.

Squire, L. R., & Barondes, S. H. (1973). Memory impairment during prolonged training in mice given inhibitors of cerebral protein synthesis. *Brain Research, 56*, 215–225.

Squire, L. R., & Becker, C. K. (1975). Inhibitors of cerebral protein synthesis impairs long term habituation. *Brain Research, 57*, 367–372.

Stahl, S. M., & Berger, P. A. (1982). Cholinergic and dopaminergic mechanisms in Tourette syndrome. In A. J. Friedhoff & T. N. Chase (Eds.), *Gilles de la Tourette syndrome. Advances in neurology,* Vol. 35 (pp. 141–150). New York: Raven Press.

Standards for educational and psychological testing. (1985). Washington, DC: American Psychological Association.

Stanovich, K. E. (1982). Individual differences in the cognitive processes of reading: I word decoding. *Journal of Learning Disabilities, 15,* 485–493.

Stanovich, K. E. (1986). Cognitive processes and the reading problems of learning disabled children: Evaluating the assumption of specificity. In J. Torgeson & B. Wong (Eds.), *Psychological and educational perspectives on learning disabilities* (pp. 87–132). New York: Academic Press.

Stein, H. H., & Yellin, T. O. (1967). Pemoline and magnesium hydroxide: Lack of effect on RNA and protein synthesis. *Science, 157,* 96–97.

Stelmack, R. M., Saxe, B. J., Noldy-Cullum, N., Campbell, K. B., & Armitage, R. (1988). Recognition of memory for words and event-related potentials: A comparison of normal and disabled readers. *Journal of Clinical and Experimental Neuropsychology, 10,* 185–200.

Stewart, M. A. (1980). Genetic, perinatal and constitutional factors in minimal brain dysfunctions. In H. E. Rie & E. D. Rie (Eds.), *Handbook of minimal brain dysfunctions: A critical view* (pp. 155–168). New York: Wiley.

Stewart, M. A. (1983). Severe perinatal hazards. In M. Rutter (Ed.), *Developmental neuropsychiatry* (pp. 15–31). New York: Guilford.

Stewart, M. A., Pitts, F. N., Craig, A. G., & Dieruf, W. (1966). The hyperactive child syndrome. *American Journal of Orthopsychiatry, 36,* 861–867.

Stewart, W. A. (1969). On the use of negro dialect in the teaching of reading. In J. C. Baratz & R. Shuy (Eds.), *Teaching black children to read* (pp. 156–219). Washington, DC: Center for Applied Linguistics.

Stodolsky, S. S., & Lesser, G. (1967). Learning patterns in the disadvantaged. *Harvard Education Review, 37,* 546–593.

Stokes, J. (1987). *Statistically derived subgroups of children for whom learning disorder is predicted.* Ph.D. thesis, Fordham University, Graduate School of Education.

Stott, D. H. (1974). A preventive program for the primary grades. *Elementary School Journal, 74,* 299–308.

Strauss, A. A., & Kephart, N. C. (1955). *The psychopathology and education of the brain-injured child. Progress in theory and clinic,* Vol. 2. New York: Grune & Stratton.

Strauss, A. A., & Lehtinen, L. E. (1947). *The psychopathology and education of the brain-injured child,* Vol 1. New York: Grune & Stratton.

Strauss, A. A., & Werner, H. (1943). Impairment in thought processes of brain-injured children. *American Journal of Mental Development, 47,* 291–295.

Strecker, E. A., & Ebaugh, F. G. (1924). Neuropsychiatric sequelae of cerebral trauma in children. *Archives of Neurology and Psychiatry, 12,* 443–453.

Striffler, N., & Willig, S. (1981). *The communication screen: A pre-school speech-language screening tool.* Tucson, AZ: Communication Skill Builders.

Stryker, S. (1925). Encephalitis lethargica—the behavioral residuals. *Training School Bulletin, 22,* 152–157.

Stunkard, H. W. (1932). *Lectures in biology.* New York University College of Arts and Science. Unpublished.

Suchard, D. W., Cummins, K. R., Gay, E., Lairsmith, J., & Welanko, P. (1985). Electrophysiological studies of reading disabled children: In search of subtypes. In D. B. Gray & J. F. Kavanaugh (Eds.), *Biobehavioral measures of dyslexia* (pp. 87–106). Parton, MD: York Press.

Summers, W. K., Majovski, L. V., Marsh, G. M., Tachiki, K., & Kling, A. (1986). Oral tetrahy-droaminoacridine in long term treatment of senile dementia, Alzheimer type. *New England Journal of Medicine, 315,* 1241–1245.

Sverd, J., Cohen, S., Camp, J. A. (1983). Brief report: Effects of propranolol on Tourette syndrome. *Journal of Autism and Developmental Disorder, 13,* 207–213.

Swanson, J. M., & Kinsbourne, M. (1976). Stimulant related state-dependent learning in hyperactive children. *Science, 192,* 1354–1357.

Swanson, J. M., & Kinsbourne, M. (1980). Food dyes impair performance of hyperactive children on a laboratory learning test. *Science, 207,* 1485–1487.

Swanson, J. M., Kinsbourne, M., Roberts, W., & Zucker, K. (1978). Time response analysis of the effect of stimulant medication on learning ability of children referred for hyperactivity. *Pediatrics, 61,* 21–29.

Swedo, S., Rapoport, J., Cheslow, D., Leonard, H. L., Ayoub, E. M., Hoiser, D. M., & Wald, E. R. (1989). High prevalence of obsessive-compulsive symptoms in patients with Sydenham's chorea. *American Journal of Psychiatry, 146,* 246–249.

Sweeney, J., & Rourke, B. P. (1978). Neuropsychological significance of phonetically accurate and phonetically inaccurate spelling errors in younger and older retarded spellers. *Brain and Language, 6,* 212–225.

Szurek, S., & Berlin, I. (Eds.) (1973). *Clinical studies in childhood psychosis.* New York: Brunner/Mazel.

Tableman, B., & Hess, R. (Eds.) (1985). *Prevention: The Michigan experience. Prevention in Human Services, 3,* No. 4. New York: Haworth Press.

Tableman, B., & Katzenmeyer, M. (1985). Infant mental health services: A newborn screener. In B. Tableman & R. Hess (Eds.), *Prevention: The Michigan experience,* Vol. 3, No. 4 (pp. 21–33). New York: Haworth Press.

Tableman, B., Marciniak, D., & Bissell, S. (1985). A community model for preventive services. In B. Tableman & R. Hess (Eds.), *Prevention: The Michigan experience* (pp. 87–89). New York: Haworth Press.

Tager-Flusberg, H. (1981). Sentence comprehension in autistic children. *Applied Psycholinguistics, 2,* 5–24. (Reviewed by Paul, 1987).

Tanguay, P., & Edwards, R. (1982). Electrophysiological studies of autism: The whisper of the bang. *Journal of Autism and Developmental Disorders, 12,* 177–183.

Tanner, C. M., Goetz, G. G., & Klawans, H. L. (1982). Cholinergic mechanisms in Tourette syndrome. *Neurology 32,* 1315–1317.

Tant, J., & Douglas, V. (1982). Problem solving in hyperactive, normal and reading disabled boys. *Journal of Abnormal Child Psychology, 10,* 285–306.

Tarnowski, K. J., Prinz, R. J., & Nay, S. M. (1986). Sustained attention in hyperactive children. *Journal of Child Psychology and Psychiatry and Allied Disciplines, 22,* 213–220.

Tarver, S. G., & Dawson, M. M. (1978). Modality preferences and the teaching of reading: A review. *Journal of Learning Disabilities, 11,* 5–17.

Taylor, E. (1983). Drug response and diagnostic validation. In M. Rutter, *Developmental neuropsychiatry* (pp. 348–368). New York: Guilford.

Taylor, E. (1984). Medications and their effects. In M. Levine & P. Satz (Eds.) *Middle childhood: Developmental and dysfunction* (pp. 447–466). Baltimore: University Park Press.

Taylor, H. G. (1987). Childhood sequelae of early neurological disorders: A contemporary perspective. *Developmental Neuropsychology, 3,* 153–164.

Taylor, H. G., Michaels, R., Mazur, P., Baver, R., & Linden, C. (1984). Intellectual, neuropsychological and achievement outcomes six to eight years after recovery from *Hemophilus influenzae* meningitis. *Pediatrics, 74,* 198–205.

Taylor, H. G., Satz, P., & Friel, J. (1979). Developmental dyslexia in relation to other childhood reading disorders: Significance and utility. *Reading Research Quarterly, 15,* 84–101.

Tejani, A., Dobias, B., Samburskey, J. (1982). Long term prognosis after *Hemophilus influenzae* meningitis: Prospective evaluation. *Developmental Medicine and Child Neurology, 24,* 338–343.

Telzrow, C. F., & Speer, B. (1986). Learning disabled children: General suggestions for maximizing instruction. *Techniques, 2,* 341–352.

Terman, L. M. (1916). *The measurement of intelligence.* Boston: Houghton Mifflin.

Terman, L. M. (1921). A symposium. Intelligence and its measurement. *Journal of Educational Psychology, 12,* 127–133.

Teuber, H. L., & Rudel, R. G. (1962). Behavior after cerebral lesions in children and adults. *Developmental Medicine and Child Neurology, 4,* 3–28.

Thomas, A., & Chess, S. (1980). *The dynamics of psychological development.* New York: Brunner/Mazel.

Thomas, A., Chess, S., & Birch, H. G. (1968). *Temperament and behavior disorders in children.* New York: New York University Press.

Thomas, A., Chess, S., Birch, H. G., Hertzig, M. E., & Korn, S. (1963). *Behavioral individuality in early childhood.* New York: New York University Press.

Thomas, C. J. (1905). Congenital "word-blindness" and its treatment. *Ophthalmoscope, 3,* 380–385.

Thorndike, E. L. (1927). *The measurement of intelligence.* New York: Bureau of Publications, Teachers College, Columbia University.

Thorndike, R. L., Hagen, E. P., & Sattler, J. M. (1986) *Guide for administering and scoring the Stanford Binet intelligence scale* (4th ed.). Chicago: Riverside Publishing.

Thurstone, L. L. (1938). Primary mental abilities. *Psychometric Monographs, 1,* Chicago: University of Chicago Press.

Tizard, B., Hughes, M., Carmichael, H., & Pinkerton, G. (1983). Language and social class: Is verbal deprivation a myth? *Journal of Child Psychology and Psychiatry, 24,* 533–542.

Tjossem, T. D. (Ed.) (1976). *Intervention strategies for high risk infants and young children.* Baltimore: University Park Press.

Todd, R. D., & Ciaranello, R. (1985). Demonstration of inter- and intraspecies binding sites by antibodies from an autistic child. *Proceedings of the National Academy of Sciences* (USA), *82,* 612–616.

Torgesen, J. K., & Houck, G. (1980). Processing deficiencies in learning disabled children who perform poorly on the digit span task. *Journal of Educational Psychology, 72,* 141–160.

Torres, F., & Ayers, F. W. (1968). Evaluation of the electroencephalogram of dyslexic children. *Electroencephalography and Clinical Neurophysiology, 24,* 281–294.

Tourette, G., de la (1885). Etude sur une affection nerveuse caracterizee par de l'incoordination motrice accompagnie d'echolalia et coprolalia (jumping, latah, myriachit). *Archives of Neurology* (Paris), *9,* 19–42 and 158–200.

Touwen, B.C.L., & Sporrel, T. (1979). Soft signs and MBD. *Developmental Medicine and Child Neurology, 21,* 528–530.

Towbin, A. (1980). Neuropathological factors in minimal brain dysfunction. In H. E. Rei & E. D. Rie (Eds.), *Handbook of minimal brain dysfunctions: A critical view* (pp. 185–209). New York: Wiley.

Towbin, K. E., Riddle, M. A., Leckman, J. F., Bruun, R. D., & Cohen, D. J. (1988). The clinical care of individuals with Tourette's syndrome. In D. J. Cohen, R. D. Bruun, & J. F. Leckman (Eds.), *Tourette's syndrome and tic disorder* (pp. 329–352). New York: Wiley.

Traub, N. (1972). *Recipe for reading.* Cambridge, MA: Educators Publishing Service.

Treffert, D. A. (1970). Epidemiology of infantile autism. *Archives of General Psychiatry, 22,* 431–438.

Trites, R. L., & Fiedorowicz, C. (1976). Follow-up study of children with specific reading disability. In R. M. Knights & D. J. Bakker (Eds.), *Neuropsychology of learning disorders: Therapeutic approaches* (pp. 41–50). Baltimore: University Park Press.

Trotman, E. K. (1977). Race, IQ and the middle class. *Journal of Educational Psychology, 69,* 266, 273.

Trusdell, M. L. (1985). An analysis of service delivery models for learning disability programs in the U.S., 1984–85 school year. *Annals of Dyslexia, 19,* 175–186.

Tupper, D. F. (Ed.). (1987). *Soft neurological signs.* New York: Grune & Stratton.

Turner, A. M., & Greenough, W. T. (1985). Differential rearing effects on rat visual cortex synapses. I. Synaptic and neuronal density and synapses per neuron. *Brain Research, 329,* 195–203.

Uhr, S. B., Berger, P. A., Pruitt, B., & Stahl, S. M. (1985). Treatment of Tourette's syndrome with RO22-1319, a D2 receptor antagonist. *New England Journal of Medicine, 311,* 989.

Ullman, D. G., Barkley, R. A., and Brown, H. W. (1978). The behavioral symptoms of hyperkinetic children who successfully responded to stimulant drug treatment. *American Journal of Orthopsychiatry, 48,* 425–437.

Ungar, G. (1970). Molecular mechanisms in information processing. *International Review of Neurobiology, 13,* 223–250.

Ungar, G. (1971). Bioessays for the chemical correlates of acquired information. In E. S. Fjerdingsted (Ed.), *Chemical transfer of learned information* (pp. 31–49). New York: Elsevier.

Ungar, G., Desiderio, D. M., & Parr, W. (1972). Isolation, identification and synthesis of a specific-behavior-inducing brain peptide. *Nature, 238,* 198–202.

U.S. Department of Education, Office of Special Education and Rehabilitative Services. (1987). *Ninth annual report to Congress on the implementation of the education of the handicapped act.*

U.S. Department of Health, Education and Welfare. (1969). *Reading disorder in the United States: Report of the secretary's national advisory committee on dyslexia and related disorders.* Washington, DC: U.S. Government Printing Office.

Valett, R. E. (1968). *A psychoeducational inventory of basic learning abilities.* Palo Alto, CA: Fearson Publishers.

Valverde, F., & Ruiz-Marcos, A. (1970). Effect of sensory deprivation in dendritic spines in the visual cortex of the mouse: A mathematical model of spine distribution. In F. A. Young & D. B. Lindsley (Eds.), *Early experience and visual information processing in perceptual and reading disorders* (pp. 261–290). Washington, DC: National Academy of Sciences.

Van Doornick, W. J. (1978). Prediction of school performance from infant and preschool developmental screening. In *Proceedings of the 2nd International Conference on Developmental Screening.* Santa Fe, NM.

Vellutino, F. R. (1978). Toward an understanding of dyslexia: Psychological factors in specific reading disability. In A. L. Benton & D. Pearl (Eds.), *Dyslexia: An appraisal of current knowledge* (pp. 61–111). New York: Oxford University Press.

Vellutino, F. R. (1987). Dyslexia. *Scientific American, 256,* 34–41.

Vellutino, F. R., & Scanlon, D. (1985). Verbal memory in poor and normal readers: Developmental differences in use of linguistic codes. In D. Gray & J. Kavanagh (Eds.), *Behavioral measures of dyslexia* (pp. 177–214). Parton, MD: York Press.

Ventry, D. (1983). Research design issues in studies of effects of middle ear effusion. *Pediatrics, 71,* 644.

Vernon, P. E. (1969). *Intelligence and cultural environment.* London: Methuen.

Vernon, P. E. (1979). *Intelligence: Heredity and environment.* San Francisco: W. H. Freeman.

Vigotsky, L. S. (1960). Development of the higher mental functions, *Izd. Akad. Pedagog.* Nauk RSFR, Moscow as cited by A. L. Luria. (1973). *The working brain: An introduction to neuropsychology.* New York: Basic Books.

Vigotsky, L. S. (1962). *Thought and language.* Cambridge, MA: MIT Press.

Vogler, G., DeFries, J. C., & Decker, N. (1984). Family history as an indicator of risk for reading disability. *Journal of Learning Disabilities, 17,* 616–619.

Volkmar, F., Cohen, D., Bregman, J., Hooks, M., & Stevenson, J. (1989). An examination of social typologies in autism. *Journal of the American Academy of Child and Adolescent Psychiatry, 28,* 82–86.

Wada, J., & Rasmussen, T. (1960). Intracarotid injection of sodium amytal for the lateralization of cerebral speech dominance. *Journal of Neurosurgery, 17,* 262–282.

Waddington, J. L. (1989). CT and MRI abnormalities in schizophrenia: The new developmental biology of psychosis? *Irish Journal of Psychological Medicine, 6,* 19–21.

Wagner, R. K. (1986). Phonological processing abilities and reading implications for disabled readers. *Journal of Learning Disabilities, 19,* 623–630.

Waizer, J., Hoffman, S. P., Polizos, P., & Englehardt, D. M. (1974). Outpatient treatment of hyperactive children with imipramine. *American Journal of Psychiatry, 131,* 587–591.

Walker, D. K., Singer, J. D., Palfrey, J. S., Orza, M. (1988). Who leaves and who stays in special education: A 2-year follow-up study. *Exceptional Children, 54,* 393–402.

Wallace, I., Gravel, J., McCarton, R., Stapells, D., Bernstein, R., & Ruben, R. (1988). Otitis media, auditory sensitivity and language outcomes at one year. *Largyngoscope, 98,* 64–70.

Wallbrown, F. H., Blaha, J., & Wherry, R. J. (1973). The hierarchical factor structure of the WPPSI. *Journal of Consulting and Clinical Psychology, 41,* 356–362.

Wallbrown, F. H., Huelsman, C., Blaha, J., & Wallbrown, J. (1975). A further test of Myklebust's cognitive structure for reading disabled children. *Psychology in the Schools, 12,* 176–182.

Walsh, T. L., Lavenstein, B., Lincamele, W. L., Bronheim, S., & O'Leary, J. (1986). Calcium antagonists in the treatment of Tourette's disorder. *American Journal of Psychiatry, 143,* 1467–1468.

Wang, M. C., & Baker, E. T. (1985). Mainstreaming programs: Design features and effects. *Journal of Special Education, 19,* 503–521.

Wang, M. C., & Birch, J. (1984). Comparison of a fulltime mainstreaming program and a resource room approach. *Exceptional Children, 51,* 33–40.

Wang, M. C., & Walberg, H. J. (1983). Adaptive instruction and classroom time. *American Educational Research Journal, 20,* 601–626.

Wang, M. C., Peverly, S., & Randolph, R. (1984). An investigation of the implementation and effects of a fulltime mainstream program. *Remedial and Special Education, 5,* 21–32.

Waterhouse, B. D., Moises, H. C., & Woodward, D. J. (1980). Noradrenergic modulation of somato-sensory cortical neuronal responses to iontophoretically applied putative neurotransmitters. *Experimental Neurology, 69,* 30–49.

Watson, M. S., Leckman, J. F., Annex, B., Breg, W. R. Boles, D., Volkmar, F. R., Cohen, D. J., & Carter, C. (1984). Fragile X in a survey of 75 autistic males. *New England Journal of Medicine, 310,* 1462.

Wechsler, D. (1944). *The measurement of adult intelligence.* Baltimore: Williams & Wilkins.

Wechsler, D. (1967). *Manual for the Wechsler Preschool and Primary Scale of Intelligence.* New York: Psychological Corporation.

Wechsler, D. (1974). *Wechsler Intelligence Scale for Children-Revised.* New York: The Psychological Corporation.

Wechsler, D. (1975). Intelligence defined and undefined: A relativistic appraisal. *American Psychologist, 30,* 135–151.

Wechsler, D., & Hagin, R. (1964). Problem of axial rotation. *Perceptual Motor Skills, 19,* 319–326.

Wedell, K., (1980) Early identification and compensatory interaction. In R. Knights & D. J. Bakker (Eds.), *Treatment of hyperactive and learning disordered children* (pp. 13–22). Baltimore, MD: University Park Press.

Weener, P., Barritt, L. S., & Semmel, M. I. (1967). Forum: A critical evaluation of the Illinois Test of Psycholinguistic Abilities. *Exceptional Children, 33,* 373–380.

Weikart, D. P. (Ed.) (1967). *Preschool intervention: A preliminary report of the Perry preschool project.* Ann Arbor, MI: Campus Publishers.

Weikart, D. P. (Ed.) (1972). Relationship of curriculum, teaching and learning in preschool education. In J. Stanely (Ed.), *Preschool programs for the disadvantaged.* Baltimore: Johns Hopkins.

Weil-Malharbe, H. (1936). Carbohydrate metabolism. *Nature* (London), *138,* 581.

Weinberg, R. A. (1989). Intelligence and IQ: Landmark issues and great debates. *American Psychologist, 44,* 98–104.

Weiss, B., Williams, J., Mayer, S., Abrams, B., Citron, L. S., Cox, C., McKibben, J., Ogar, D., & Schultz, S. (1980). Behavioral responses to artificial food colors. *Science, 207,* 1487–1489.

Weiss, G. (1980). Critical diagnostic issues. In H. E. Rie & E. D. Rie (Eds.), *Handbook of minimal brain dysfunctions: A critical view* (pp. 347–361). New York: Wiley.

Weiss, G. (1983). Long-term outcomes: Findings, concepts and practical implications. In M. Rutter (Ed.), *Developmental neuropsychiatry* (pp. 422–436). New York: Guilford.

Weiss, G., & Hechtman, L. (1986). *Hyperactive children grown-up.* New York: Guilford.

Weiss, G., Kruger, E., Danielson, W., & Elman, M. (1975). Effect of long term treatment of hyperactive children with methylphenidate. *Canadian Medical Association Journal, 112,* 159–165.

Weiss, G., Minde, K., Werry, J. S., Douglas, V., & Nemeth, E. (1971). Studies on the hyperactive child. VIII. Five year follow-up. *Archives of General Psychiatry, 24,* 409–414.

Weiss, R. S., (1980). Efficacy of INREAL intervention for preschool and kindergarten language handicapped and bilingual (Spanish) children. ERIC Document ED 204071.

Weissman, C. S. (1985) The impact of early intervention, PL 94–142, and other factors on mainstreaming. ERIC Document 245911.

Weizman, A., Weitz, R., Szekely, G., Tyano, S., & Belmaker, R. (1984). Combination of neuroleptic and stimulant treatment in attention deficit disorder with hyperactivity. *Journal of the American Academy of Child Psychiatry, 23,* 295–298.

Weizman, A., Weizman, R., Szekely, G. A., Wijsenbeck, H., Liuni, E. (1982). Abnormal immune response to brain tissue antigen in the syndrome of autism. *American Journal of Psychiatry, 139,* 1462–1465.

Weizman, R., Weizman, A., Tyano, S., Szekely, B., Weissman, B., & Sanner, G. (1984). Humoral-endorphin blood levels in autistic, schizophrenic and healthy subjects. *Psychopharmacology (Berlin), 82,* 368–370.

Wender, P. H. (1971). *Minimal brain dysfunction in children.* New York: Wiley-Interscience.

Wender, P. H. (1973). Some speculation concerning a possible chemical basis of minimal brain dysfunction. In F. de la Cruz, B. Fox, & R. Roberts (Eds.), *Annals of the New York Academy of Sciences,* Vol. 205 (pp. 18–29).

Wepman, J. M. (1958). *The auditory discrimination test.* Chicago: Language Research Associates.

Werner, E. E. (1980). Environmental interaction in minimal brain dysfunctions. In H. E. Rie & E. D. Rie (Eds.), *Handbook of minimal brain dysfunctions: A critical view* (pp. 210–231). New York: Wiley.

Werner, E. E., Bierman, J., & French, F., (1971) *The children of Kauai: A longitudinal study from the prenatal period to age ten.* Honolulu: University of Hawaii Press.

Werner, E. E., Bierman, J. M., French, F. E., Simonian, K., Conner, A., Smith, R. S., & Campbell, M. (1968). Reproductive and environmental casualties: A report on the 10 year follow-up of the children of the Kauai pregnancy study. *Pediatrics, 42,* 112–127.

Werner, E. E., & Smith, R. S. (1977). *Kauai's children come of age.* Honolulu: University of Hawaii Press.

Werner, E. E., & Smith, R. S. (1982). *Vulnerable but invincible.* New York: McGraw-Hill.

Werry, J. S. (1968). Developmental hyperactivity. *Pediatric Clinics of North America, 15,* 581–599.

Werry, J. S. (1972). Organic factors in childhood psychopathology. In H. C. Quay & J. S. Werry (Eds.). *Psychopathological disorders of childhood* (pp. 83–121). New York: Wiley.

Werry, J. S. (Ed.) (1978). *Pediatric psychopharmacology: The use of behavior modifying drugs in children.* New York: Brunner/Mazel.

Werry, J. S., Aman, M. G., & Diamond, E. (1980). Imipramine and methylphenidate in hyperactive children. *Journal of Child Psychology and Psychiatry, 21,* 27–35.

Werry, J. S., & Sprague, R. (1974). Methylphenidate in children: Effect of dosage. *Australian and New Zealand Journal of Psychiatry, 8,* 9–19.

Werry, J. S., Aman, M. G., & Lampen, E. (1975). Haloperidol and methylphenidate in hyperactive children. *Acta Paedopsychiatrica, 42,* 26–40.

Werry J. S., Minde, K., Guzman, A., Weiss, G., Dogan, K., & Hoy, E. (1974). Studies on the hyperactive child—VII: Neurological status compared with neurotic and normal children. *American Journal of Orthopsychiatry, 43,* 441–451.

Werry, J. S., Weiss, G., Douglas, V., & Martin, J. (1966). Studies on the hyperactive child. III. The effect of chlorpromazine upon behavior and learning ability. *Journal of the American Academy of Child Psychiatry, 5,* 292–312.

Wertheim, J. (1982). *Coping with Tourette syndrome in the classroom.* Bayside, New York: Tourette Syndrome Association.

Wertheimer, M. (1923). Studies in the theory of Gestalt psychology. *Psychologische Forschung, 4,* 1–300.

West, J. F., & Cannon, G. S. (1988). Essential collaborative consultation competencies for regular and special educators. *Journal of Learning Disabilities, 21,* 56–63.

Westinghouse Learning Corporation. (1969). *The impact of Head Start: An evaluation of the effects of Head Start on children's cognitive and affective development. Executive Summary.* Washington, D.C.: Clearing House for Federal Scientific and Technical Information.

Wexler, B. E. (1980). Cerebral laterality and psychiatry: A review of the literature. *American Journal of Psychiatry, 137,* 279–291.

Whalen, C., & Henker, B. (Eds.) (1980a). *Hyperactive children: The social ecology of identification and treatment.* New York: Academic Press.

Whalen, C., & Henker, B. (1980b). The social ecology of psychostimulant treatment: A model for conceptual and empirical analysis. In C. K. Whalen & B. Henker (Eds.), *Hyperactive children: The social ecology of identification and treatment* (pp. 3–51). New York: Academic Press.

Whitehouse, P. J., Price, D. L., Struble, L. G., Clark, A. W., Coyle, J. T., & DeLong, M. R. (1982). Alzheimer's disease and senile dementia: Loss of neurons in the basal forebrain. *Science, 215,* 1237–1239.

Wiener, G. (1970). Varying psychological sequelae of lead ingestion in children. *Public Health Reports, 85,* 19–24.

Wiener, J. M. (Ed.) (1977). *Psychopharmacology in childhood and adolescence.* New York: Basic Books.

Wiener, J. M. (Ed.) (1985). *Diagnosis and psychopharmacology of childhood and adolescent disorders.* New York: Wiley.

Wiener, M., & Comer, W. (1967). Reading and reading difficulty: A conceptual analysis. *Harvard Educational Review, 37,* 627–643.

Wiig, E. H. (1985). Review of Slingerland screening tests for identifying children with specific language disability. In J. V. Mitchell (Ed.), *Ninth mental measurement yearbook* (pp. 1399–1400). Lincoln, NE: University of Nebraska Press.

Will, M. C. (1986). Educating children with learning problems: A shared responsibility. *Exceptional Children, 52,* 411–415.

Williams, D. T., Mehl, K., Yudofsky, S., Adams, D., & Roseman, B. (1982). The effect of propranolol on uncontrolled rage outbursts in children and adolescents with organic brain dysfunction. *Journal of the American Academy of Child Psychiatry, 21,* 129–135.

Williams, J. P. (1980). Teaching decoding with an emphasis on phoneme analysis and phoneme blending. *Journal of Educational Psychology, 72,* 1–15.

Williams, J. P. (1984). Phonemic analysis and how it relates to reading. *Journal of Learning Disabilities, 17,* 240–245.

Williams, R. S., Hauser, S. L., Purpura, D. P., DeLong, G. R., & Swisher, C. N. (1980). Autism and mental retardation: Neuropathological studies performed in four retarded persons with autistic behavior. *Archives of Neurology, 37,* 749–753.

Wilsher, C. R. (1987). Treatment of specific reading difficulties (Dyslexia). In D. Bakker, C. Wilsher, H. Debruyne, & N. Bertin (Eds.), *Developmental dyslexia and learning disorders* (pp. 95–109). Basel: Karger.

Winchell, C. A. (1975). *The hyperkinetic child: A bibliography of medical educational and behavioral studies.* Westport, CT: Greenwood.

Wing, L., & Atwood, A. (1987). Syndromes of autism and atypical development. In D. Cohen & A. Donnellan, *Handbook of autism and pervasive developmental disorders* (pp. 3–20). New York: Wiley.

Wing, L., & Gould, J. (1979). Severe impairments of social interaction and associated abnormalities in children: Epidemiology and classification. *Journal of Autism and Developmental Disorders, 9,* 11–29.

Wing, L., Yeates, S. R., Brierley, L. M., & Gould, J. (1976). The prevalence of early childhood autism: Comparison of administrative and epidemiological studies. *Psychological Medicine, 6,* 89–100.

Witelson, S. F. (1976). Abnormal right hemisphere specialization in developmental dyslexia. In R. M. Knights & D. S. Bakker (Eds.), *Neuropsychology of learning disorders: Therapeutic approaches* (pp. 233–255). Baltimore: University Park Press.

Witelson, S. F. (1985). The brain connection: The corpus callosum is larger in left-handers. *Science, 229,* 665–668.

Witelson, S. F., & Kigar, D. L. (1988). Anatomical development of the corpus callosum in humans: A review with reference to sex and cognition. In D. L. Molfese & S. J. Sagalowitz (Eds.), *Brain lateralization in children* (pp. 35–57). New York: Guilford.

Witelson, S. F., & Pallie, W. (1973). Left hemisphere specialization for language in the newborn: Neuroanatomical evidence of asymmetry. *Brain, 96,* 641–646.

Witelson, S. F., & Rabinovitch M. S. (1972). Hemisphere speech lateralization in children with auditory linguistic deficits. *Cortex, 8,* 412–426.

Witt, J. C., & Cavell, R. A. (1986). Psychological assessment. In D. L. Wodrich & J. E. Joy (Eds.), *Multidisciplinary assessment of children with learning disabilities and mental retardation* (pp. 101–130). Baltimore: P. H. Brookes.

Wolff, P. H. (1959). Observations in newborn infants. *Psychosomatic Medicine, 21,* 110–118.

Wolfensberger, W. A. (1980). A brief overview of the principle of normalization. In R. J. Flynn & K. E. Nitsch (Eds.), *Normalization, social integration and community services*. Baltimore: University Park Press Integration and Community Services.

Wolff, P. H., & Hurwitz, I. (1966). The choreoform syndrome. *Developmental Medicine and Child Neurology, 8,* 160–165.

Wong, G. H., & Cook, R. J. (1971). Long term effects of haloperidol on severely emotionally disturbed children. *Australian and New Zealand Journal of Psychiatry, 5,* 296–300.

Wood, C., Powell, S., & Knight, R. C. (1984). Predicting school readiness: The validity of the developmental age. *Journal of Learning Disabilities, 17,* 8–11.

Woodcock, R. B. (1987). *Woodcock Reading Mastery Test-Revised*. Circle Pines, MN: American Guidance Service.

Woodcock, R. B., & Johnson, M. B. (1977–1978). *Woodcock-Johnson Psychoeducational Battery*. Allen, TX: Developmental Learning Materials.

Worcester-Drought, C., & Allen, I. M. (1929). Congenital auditory imperception (congenital word-deafness): With report of a case. *Journal of Neurology and Psychopathology, 9,* 193–208.

Yarrow, L., Rubenstein, J., Peterson, F., & Jankowski, J. (1973). Dimensions of early stimulation and their differential effects on infant development. *Merrill Palmer Quarterly, 19,* 205–219.

Yeni-Komshian, G. H., Isenberg, D., & Goldberg, H. (1975). Cerebral dominance and reading disability. Left visual field deficit in poor readers. *Neuropsychologia, 13,* 83–94.

Yerkes, R. M. (1917). The Binet versus the point scale method of measuring intelligence. *Journal of Applied Psychology, 1,* 111–122.

Yingling, C. D., Galin, D., Fein, G., Peltzman, D., & Davenport, L. (1986). Neurometrics does not detect dyslexics. *Electroencephalography, Clinical Neurophysiology, 63,* 426–430.

Youdin, M. Collins, G., Snadler, M., Jones, A. B., Pare, C.M.B., & Nicholson, W. J. (1972). Human brain monoamine oxidese: Multiple forms and selective inhibitors. *Nature, 236,* 225–228.

Young, G. C., & Rourke, B. P. (1975). *A comparison of visual and auditory sequencing in good and poor readers in grades two and six*. Paper read at meeting of the Canadian Psychological Association, Quebec, June 1975.

Young, J., Cohen, D., Caparulo, B., Brown, S. L., & Mass, J. (1979). Decreased 24 hour urinary MHPH in childhood autism. *American Journal of Psychiatry, 136,* 1055–1057.

Young, J. G., Leven, L. I., Newcorn, J. H., & Knott, P. J. (1987). Genetic and neurological approaches to the pathophysiology of autism and the pervasive developmental disorders. In H. Meltzer (Ed.), *Psychopharmacoloty, the third generation of progress* (pp. 825–836). New York: Raven Press.

Young, W. E. (1936). The relation of reading comprehension to hearing comprehension and retention. *Journal of Experimental Education, 5,* 30–39.

Ysseldyke, J. E. (1983). Current practices in making psychoeducational decisions about learning disabled students. *Journal of Learning Disabilities, 16,* 226–233.

Yudofsky, S., Williams, D., & Gorman, S. (1981). Propranolol in the treatment of rage and violent behavior in patients with chronic brain syndrome. *American Journal of Psychiatry, 138,* 218–220.

Yule, W., & Rutter, M. (1976). The epidemiology and social implications of specific reading retardation. In R. M. Knights & D. J. Bakker (Eds.), *Neuropsychology of learning disorders: Therapeutic approaches* (pp. 25–39). Baltimore: University Park Press.

Zahner, G., & Pauls, D. L. (1987). Epidemiological surveys of infantile autism. In D. Cohen & A. M. Donnellan (Eds.), *Handbook of autism and pervasive developmental disorders* (pp. 199–210). New York: Wiley.

Zaidel, D. W. (1985). Hemifield tachistoscopic presentations and hemispheric specialization in normal subjects. In D. F. Benson & E. Zaidel (Eds.), *The dual brain* (pp. 143–155). New York: Guilford.

Zaidel, E. (1985). Introduction. In D. F. Benson & E. Zaidel (Eds.), *The dual brain* (pp. 47–63). New York: Guilford.

Zametkin, A. J., & Rapoport, J. L. (1986). The pathophysiology of ADDH: A review. In B. B. Lahey & A. E. Kazdin (Eds.), *Advances in Clinical Child Psychology, 9,* 177–216. New York: Plenum.

Zametkin, A. J., & Rapoport, J. L. (1987). Neurobiology of attention deficit disorder with hyperactivity: Where have we come in 50 years? *Journal of the American Academy of Child and Adolescent Psychiatry, 26,* 676–686.

Zametkin, A. J., Karoum, F., Rapoport, J. L., Brown, G. L., Wyatt, R. J. (1984). Phenylethylamine excretion in attention deficit disorder. *Journal of the American Academy of Child Psychiatry, 23,* 310–314.

Zangwill, O. L. (1960). *Cerebral dominance and its relation to psychological function.* Edinburgh: Oliver & Boyd.

Zemp, J. W., Wilson, J. E., Schlesinger, K., Boggan, W. O., & Glassman, E. (1966). Brain function and macromolecules, I. Incorporation of uridine into RNA of mouse brain during short-term training experience. *Proceedings of the National Academy of Sciences, 55,* 1423–1431.

Zenski, J. P. (1983). A study of the effects of a prefirst grade transition class as compared with first grade retention on reading achievement. ERIC Document 248459.

Zentall, S. S. (1977). Environmental stimulation model. *Exceptional Children, 43,* 502–510.

Zentall, S. S. (1980). Behavioral comparions of hyperactive and normally active children in natural settings. *Journal of Abnormal Child Psychology, 8,* 93–109.

Zentall, S. S. (1985). A context for hyperactivity. In K. D. Gadow (Ed.), *Advances in learning and behavioral disabilities, 4,* 273–343. Greenwich, CT: JAI Press.

Zentall, S. S., & Zentall, T. R. (1983). Optimal stimulation: A model of disordered activity and performance in normal and deviant children. *Psychological Bulletin, 94,* 446–471.

Zhurova, L. E. (1963). The development of analysis of words into their sounds by preschool children. *Soviet Psychology and Psychiatry, 2,* 17–27.

Zimmerman, F. T., & Ross, S. (1944). Effect of glutamic acid and other amino acids on maze learning in the white rat. *Archives of Neurology and Psychiatry, 51,* 446–451.

Zimmerman, F. T., Burgemeister, B. B., & Putman, T. S. (1947). A group study of the effect of glutamic acid upon mental functioning in children and adolescents. *Psychosomatic Medicine, 9,* 175–183.

Zurif, E. B., & Carson, G. (1970). Dyslexia in relation to cerebral dominance and temporal analysis. *Neuropsychologia, 8,* 351–361.

AUTHOR INDEX

SUBJECT INDEX